lonely planet

Trekking in
East Africa

David Else

IID684236

MARTIN COUNTY LIBRARY SYSTEM
701 East Ocean Blvd.
Stuart, Florida 34994-2374

Trekking in East Africa

2nd edition

Published by

Lonely Planet Publications

Head Office: PO Box 617, Hawthorn, Vic 3122, Australia

Branches: 155 Filbert St, Suite 251, Oakland, CA 94607, USA

10 Barley Mow Passage, Chiswick, London W4 4PH, UK

71 bis rue du Cardinal Lemoine, 75005 Paris, France

Printed by

Colorcraft Ltd, Hong Kong

Photographs by

Dawn Delaney   David Else

Corinne Else   Peter Robinson

Front cover: View of Kilimanjaro from Kenya, Lisl Dennis (The Image Bank)

First Published

1993

This Edition

January 1998

Although the authors and publisher have tried to make the information as accurate as possible, they accept no responsibility for any loss, injury or inconvenience sustained by any person using this book.

National Library of Australia Cataloguing in Publication Data

Else, David
Trekking in East Africa

2nd ed.
Includes index.
ISBN 0 86442 541 4.

1. Hiking - Africa, East - Guidebooks. 2. Africa, East -
Guidebooks. I. Title.

916.7604

text © David Else 1998
maps & climate charts © Lonely Planet 1998
photos © photographers as indicated 1998

All rights reserved. No part of this publication may be reproduced, stored in a retrieval system or transmitted in any form by any means, electronic, mechanical, photocopying, recording or otherwise, except brief extracts for the purpose of review, without the written permission of the publisher and copyright owner.

David Else

After hitchhiking through Europe for a couple of years, David Else kept heading south and finally reached Africa in 1983. Since then, he has travelled and trekked all over the continent, reaching most of the major mountain ranges and several of the more obscure ones as well. David is now a travel writer concentrating on Africa, and also works as a consultant tour leader for specialist trekking companies. His other books for Lonely Planet include *Malawi, Mozambique & Zambia*, *West Africa* and *Africa – the South*. He has contributed to *Africa on a shoestring*, the *Kenya* and *East Africa* travel guides, and has also written a guide to Zanzibar. When not in Nairobi, or halfway up Kilimanjaro, David lives in the north of England, where he walks to the shops, polishes his mountain bike and occasionally talks about rock climbing.

From the Author

Several words of thanks must go to all the people who helped me research and write this book. Firstly, a special thank you to my wife Corinne, who was with me a lot of the way – on the road, up the mountains, and looking over my shoulder as I tried to get the words in the right order. In her professional capacity as Dr Corinne Else MB BCh DA, she made major contributions to the Health, Safety & First Aid chapter in this book.

Thanks also to the other people who checked route descriptions, contributed large sections of information about places I have not been, or provided details on recent changes. Robin Saxby and Helen Long (UK) valiantly trekked across Mt Elgon and Mt Kenya on some of the more unusual routes, contending with rain, mud, bamboo and charging buffalo. Claude Jakob (Switzerland) provided healthy efficient trekking tips for Mt Kenya and Kilimanjaro. Mike Deady (New Zealand) covered Mt Meru and some treks in Malawi, after initially being roped in for Lonely Planet research when I was laid up with malaria in Mozambique. James Grey and Richard Bendy of Natural Action (UK) wrote much of the section on the Simien Mountains, with extra input from Jon Rigby (UK), Peter Bennett (UK) of Wind, Sand and

Stars and Miles Roddis – co-author of *Africa on a shoestring*. James Grey also provided large amounts of recent information on the Rwenzoris, while Peter Bennett provided information on online services. UK fast boys Rick Mayon-White and Steve Hiorns assisted with Moshi research and kept morale high on Kili. Lonely Planet readers Hugh Dowling and David Wise both wrote long, detailed and fascinating letters about their treks in Malawi, Kenya and Tanzania. Guy Yeoman (High Altitude Africa) helped with proofreading and provided constructive criticism on matters historical, cultural, animal and vegetable.

Special thanks should also go to our various local guides, who showed us the way and were good company on the mountains: Julius Inyas Minja, Salvator Inyas Mtui, Lazaro Aloisi Mtui, Joachim Petri Mtuy (Kilimanjaro), Sammy Kariuki, Edwin Mwalim and Moses Waruteri (Mt Kenya); Idi Lewarani (Loroghi Hills); Manfred Kmwenda (Nyika); Austin Pindan, Raphael Maglas, Thomas Walusa (Mulanje).

For ground support, advice, information and help in many other ways, thanks also to the following people. In the UK: Henry Osmaston, Chris Morris, Jill Leheup and Robert Greenshields. In Tanzania: Gratian

Luhikula (Tanzanian Tourist Corporation), Benjamin Kanza (Tanzania National Parks), Seamus Brice-Bennett, Mike Brydon, Robert M'mari, Eric Christin, Harshit Shah, Frank & Chrissy Atherton. In Kenya: Connie Maina (Kenya Wildlife Services), Paul Clarke and Graeme Watson (Mountain Club of Kenya), Bongo Woodley (Mt Kenya National Park), Patrick Wanjohi, Edwin Sadd, Alan Dixson, James Mbugua, Clive Ward, Iain Allan, Joyce Chianda and Halewijn Scheuerman, John & Jane Bisley, Malcolm Gascoigne, Aussie Walker. In Uganda: Alfred Labongo (Rwenzori Mountains National Park), Paul Vere (Mt Elgon Project), Francis Masola and Reuben Nadanga (Mt Elgon National Park). In Malawi: Mark Kippax (Mountain Club of Malawi), Carl Bruessow (Wildlife Society of Malawi), Hector Banda (Nyika National Park), Pam & Chris Badger.

From the Publisher

This book was edited at the Lonely Planet office in Melbourne by Lindsay Brown. Tim Fitzgerald coordinated the mapping, illustration, design and layout with help from Mark Germanchis, Rachael Scott and Chris Klep. Thanks to Isabelle Young and Nick Tapp for proofreading and to Adam McCrow for designing the cover.

Warning & Request

Things change. Prices go up, schedules change, good places go bad and bad places go bankrupt – nothing stays the same. So, if you find things better or worse, recently opened or long since closed, please tell us and help make the next edition even more accurate and useful.

We value all of the feedback we receive from travellers. Julie Young coordinates a small team who read and acknowledge every letter, postcard and email, and ensure that every morsel of information finds its way to the appropriate authors, editors and publishers. We enjoy hearing from everyone who writes, but legible letters are especially appreciated.

Everyone who writes to us will find their name in the next edition of the appropriate guide and will also receive a free subscription to our quarterly newsletter, *Planet Talk*. The very best contributions will be rewarded with a free Lonely Planet guide.

Excerpts from your correspondence may appear in new editions of this guide; in our newsletter, *Planet Talk*; or in updates on our Web site – so please let us know if you don't want your letter published or your name acknowledged.

Thanks

Many thanks to the following travellers who used the last edition and wrote to us with helpful hints, useful advice and interesting anecdotes: Julie Jeffcott, Robert Greenshields, Claude Jakob, Andrea Niedermann, Rudi Potlitz, Ian Smith, Tracey Wilson.

Contents

Trekking Routes in this Book

Route Name	Days	Standard	Highest Point	Altitude Gain	Access
Tanzania					
Kilimanjaro					
Marangu Route	5-6	medium-hard	Uhuru Peak (5896m)	3916m	OT
Umbwe Route	5-6	hard	as above	4496m	OT
Machame-Mweka Route	6	medium-hard	as above	4096m	OT
Mt Meru					
Momella Route	3-4	medium	Meru Summit (4566m) (Socialist Peak)	3066m	B OT
Crater Highlands					
Ngorongoro to Lengai	3-5	easy-medium	NA	NA	OT
Kenya					
Mt Kenya					
Naro Moru Route	3-4	medium	Point Lenana (4985m)	2985m	BW OT
Burguret Route	3 (A)	medium-hard	(joins other routes)		BW OT
Sirimon-Chogoria Traverse	5-6	medium	Point Lenana (4985m)	2335m	BW OT
Chogoria-Sirimon Traverse	5-6	medium	as above	3485m	BW OT
Timau Route	3 (A)	medium-hard	(joins other routes)		BW OT
Loroghi Hills					
A Loroghi Hills Circuit	3-5	easy-medium	Poror Peak (2580m)	NA	B
Suguta Valley					
Suguta Valley	8	hard	The Barrier (approx 1000m)	NA	B OT
Uganda					
Rwenzori Mountains					
Bujuku-Mubuku Circuit	7	medium-hard	Elana Hut (4540m)	2900m	BW OT
Mt Elgon					
Sasa Route	3-5	medium	Wagagai Summit (4321m)	3270m	B
Malawi					
Mt Mulanje					
A Mulanje Traverse	4-5	easy-medium	Sapitwa Summit (3001m)	NA	B
Chambe-Lichenya Loop	3	easy-medium	Chambe Peak (2557m)	NA	B
Nyika Plateau					
Nyika Highlights Route	4	easy-medium	Nganda Peak (2607m)	NA	B
Livingstonia Route	3-4	easy-medium	NA	NA	B
Ethiopia					
Simien Mountains					
Simien Traverse	8	medium	Ras Deshen Summit (4543m)	1650m	B

A – ascent only; **B** – bus or car access; **BW** – bus and walk/hitch; **OT** – organised trek;

Accommodation	Other Information	Page
b c	Most popular route on 'Kili', and technically the easiest.	124
c	Steep and very direct, suitable for experienced trekkers. Not to be rushed.	128
c	Varied gradual ascent, providing good acclimatisation.	134
b	Spectacular trek combining grassland, lush forest, and a section along the knife edge crater rim. Ideal acclimatisation for Kilimanjaro.	145
c	Top quality trekking in a remote and rugged area. Also wildlife viewing and a chance to meet the Maasai people in their own environment.	154
b c	Most popular and direct route on Mt Kenya; easy access and good bunkhouses.	195
c	Very rarely used route; paths indistinct. Local guide essential.	198
b c	Excellent trekking with easy access, plus good camp sites and bunkhouses.	201
b c	Sirimon-Chogoria in reverse. At least one night's camping essential.	209
c	Rarely used route. Can be combined with other routes to ascend to Pt Lenana.	211
c	Non-strenuous route in a rarely visited area. Homeland of Samburu people.	219
c	Long, hard and very strenuous trek through a harsh and inhospitable region. Stunning scenery. Homelands of Samburu and Turkana people.	226
h c	Tough trekking through highland wilderness; frequent mists, boggy and demanding conditions; slow and tiring.	262
c	Frequently overlooked mountain with excellent trekking opportunities and straightforward access.	275
h	Fine route through the heart of the massif; plantation, natural forest and open	298
h	grassland. Accessible trek, with great views and two impressive peaks to bag.	305
c	An excellent trek. Relatively flat but long trek across open grassland.	315
c	Mostly downhill route across grassland, and then dropping through wooded escarpments towards Lake Malawi.	317
c	The mountains are high, the scenery is stunning and the views go on forever. Gradients are not too severe but some stages are quite long.	338

NA – not applicable; **b** – bunkhouses; **c** – camping; **h** – huts

Map Legend

BOUNDARIES

——————————	International Boundary
—— —— —— ——	Regional Boundary

ROUTES

	Freeway
	Primary Road
	Secondary Road
	City Road
	City Street
	Track
	Walking Path
	Described Walk
	Ferry Route
⊢⊢⊢⊢⊢⊢⊷⊢⊢⊢⊢	Train Route, with Station
⊪⊪⊪⊪⊪⊪⊪⊪	Cable Car

AREA FEATURES

	Park (Country/Regional Maps)
	Park (Walk Maps)
	Built-Up Area
	Glacier
	Rocks
	Reef
	Beach

HYDROGRAPHIC FEATURES

	River, Creek
	Intermittent River or Creek
≫ ⫤	Rapids, Waterfalls
	Lake, Intermittent Lake
	Canal
⚓ ⚓ ⚓ ⚓ ⚓	Swamp

SYMBOLS

✪ CAPITAL	National Capital	✈	Airfield	▲ Mountain, Hill
◉ Capital	Regional Capital	⚲	Beach	⌂ Museum
● City	City	⌢	Cave/Rock Shelter	)(Pass
● Town	Town	‿‿	Cliff, Escarpment	★ Police Station
● Village	Village	500	Contour	✉ Post Office
		⋈	Gate	A25 Route Number
⛺	Camp (Offical)	✛	Hospital	◎ Spring
⋏	Camp (Wild)	⊞	Lookout/Viewpoint	☎ Telephone
⌂	Hut or Bunkhouse	☾	Mosque	⊖ Transport
⛉	Shelter			

Note: not all symbols displayed above appear in this book

Preface

Eastern Africa is largely a flat, dry, bush-covered plain, but often in the distance rises a blue mountain, or perhaps a modest range of snow and ice. These visions stir the minds of imaginative travellers and make them wonder what it must be like to leave behind the hot and dusty lowland world and make their way to the ethereal heights above the clouds.

To walk upon these East African mountains can be a delight, leading to something like an earthly paradise. With every upward step the traveller experiences a thrilling transition, from the tropics, through temperate climes, to sub-alpine conditions, and even alpine conditions in the case of the three great snow-covered peaks. The high mountains are the last secret places of the continent, forever blessed with rain. A wonderful succession of nature is revealed: the flowers and birds are ever new, the streamlets fresh, and the air cool, pure and intoxicating. These experiences, though hard-won, are truly uplifting and provide the motivation for trekking in East Africa.

But before you set out, as an individual or as a member of a group, reflect on two things. First, these upland environments, whether forest, moorland or alpine, are amongst the most delicate in the world. Alas, some routes already call to mind the line that '... every prospect pleases, and only man is vile'. Treat the environment with respect – do nothing to damage it, leave behind no trace of your visit, and have the moral courage to call to task those who transgress. Second, these hills and mountains are the age-old domain of indigenous people who are poor beyond the imagination of even the most impecunious western visitor. You do not have to come, but if you do, grant these people their dignity, behave generously with heart and hand, and let good manners, patience and integrity be your guides.

Guy Yeoman

Guy Yeoman is a mountaineer who has worked and travelled in East Africa for over 50 years, and has made many expeditions into the high mountain areas, always in close companionship with local Africans. He is active in calling world attention to the continuing destruction of these unique ecosystems. In 1984 he undertook the case for the protection of the Rwenzori range by the creation of a national park. This was successfully brought about in 1991, and the park became a World Heritage Site in 1994. Guy Yeoman's book *Africa's Mountains of the Moon* was written as part of that campaign.

Introduction

Trekking on the high mountains of East Africa is like going from the tropics to the tundra and back again, often in less than a week. Here you can walk through grassy hills, dense bush, rainforest, Afro-alpine moors and wide areas of bare rock and ice. It's all completely different to the flat savanna grasslands usually seen by visitors.

East Africa is most famous for its wildlife safaris but, in contrast to the sometimes crowded 'game parks', the mountain wilderness areas are rarely visited. Of course, it takes some physical effort but trekking here means you can leave the vehicles and the hotels behind and experience the wilderness of Africa at first hand.

This book describes a selection of treks in Tanzania, Kenya, Uganda and Malawi, with a brief section on Ethiopia. Some are long-time classics, others are personal favourites

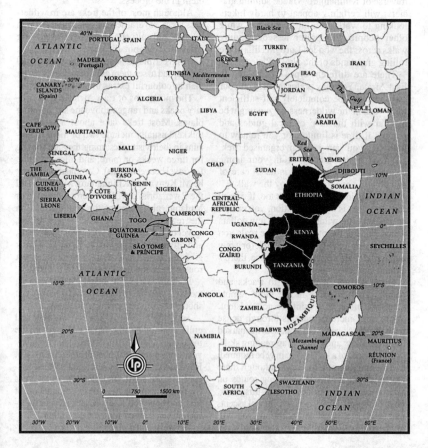

based on my experience of trekking in the region. All the main peaks and ranges are covered, and several smaller mountains and lesser-known trekking areas are also included. Opportunities for wandering away from the more usual routes are also described.

Many visitors to the area will not have a car, but this is not a problem as nearly all the trekking areas covered by this book can be reached by public transport.

Most of the treks are between four and 10 days duration. Some shorter options are outlined, and some routes can be extended. There's a wide range to choose from: a tough traverse of Kilimanjaro, via the summit glaciers, will certainly appeal to hardy hikers looking to work up a bit of a sweat, while other people will prefer less demanding walks across the wooded Loroghi Hills or the rolling grasslands of the Nyika Plateau.

There are different types of trekking in East Africa. You may prefer to carry all your own gear and be completely self-sufficient for a week in the wilderness, or you might be happier with the help of local guides and porters. If time is limited, or you're new to trekking, you can join an organised trek, arranged either locally or in your home country, where everything is taken care of and all you have to do is enjoy the walk.

The costs involved can differ too. If money (or lack of it) is a consideration, you can be at one with the wilderness for a few dollars a day, while at the other end of the scale you can join a top-quality organised trek for a few hundred dollars a day. And, of course, there's a range of choices in between.

Generally, the treks keep to tracks and paths, although paths in the more remote areas are often very faint, or non-existent. Some treks include sections through dense bush or across open moorland, with no marked route to follow and where map-reading skills or the services of a local guide may be required.

Trekking is not climbing. Although there are rock and ice mountaineering routes on several of the peaks covered in this book, none of the treks involve any technical ascents and (with one possible exception) you will not need ropes, crampons or other hardware.

Some treks include optional sections of scrambling, or some fairly exposed sections of walking, but generally it's 'hands in pockets' all the way.

Even though there's no technical climbing, it is still possible to reach the summit of many of the mountains. As well as the pleasures of unspoilt wilderness walking, there's the added satisfaction of getting all the way to the top – an extra attraction for 'peak-baggers'.

Most of the treks described are through national parks. By visiting these mountain wilderness areas we can help to increase their chances of survival, provided we do not destroy them in the process.

Although most of the treks are in wilderness areas, several sections also pass through villages and cultivated land, or cross grazing areas used by nomadic people. On foot, you will have time to stop and meet the local people, and to see them as human beings rather than as colourful extras in the landscape.

The mountains of East Africa rise as solitary peaks and ranges above the surrounding plains. Most treks take about a week, so trekkers usually include two or more mountains in their visit (presuming they are staying for three weeks or more, and allowing time for travel between areas). Combinations might be Mt Kenya and Kilimanjaro, Mt Elgon and the Rwenzoris, or Kilimanjaro and Nyika or Mulanje, plus some of the shorter treks on the region's smaller peaks. This involves travel by local transport between mountains, and often across national borders. This book gives enough information to cover the direct routes from one trekking area to the next.

For further travel in the region (eg the coast, the lakes and the lowland national parks) you should use a more general guidebook.

Trekking in East Africa is rewarding and enlightening. I have been addicted to the mountains and wilderness areas here for many years, and I am sure you will enjoy them also. Beyond the mountains described here, experienced trekkers will find plenty of other areas for further exploration. I wish you the best of luck and hope you'll report back so your information can be used for the next edition.

Go well, and *safiri salama*.

Facts about the Region

HISTORY

The Beginning

In his book *On the Origin of Species ...*, Charles Darwin stated that humans and apes probably had a common ancestor. Because these apes were found in East Africa, he concluded that humankind originated there. This was based on a fair bit of guesswork, but Darwin's theory was later supported by the discovery of ancient hominoid (human-like) skulls at Olduvai Gorge in Tanzania, on the shores of Lake Turkana in Kenya, and along the Kagera River in Uganda. Some of these skulls have been dated at 2½ million years old, and it seems there were at least three different species of hominid wandering around on the plains of Africa at that time. Archaeologists believe that two of these early human species declined and vanished, while the third evolved into *Homo sapiens*, giving East Africa a strong claim to the title 'Cradle of Humanity'.

The Stone Ages

Around 50,000 BC archaeological evidence indicates that *Homo sapiens* first began to experiment with stone tools, but it wasn't until after 10,000 BC that stone-making techniques and the use of fire were mastered. At around the same time early humans also developed a basic language and began to form communities based on the hunting and gathering of food. This period is called the New Stone Age.

The Migrations

During the New Stone Age, while some groups continued as hunter-gatherers, others began to learn about agriculture. Evidence of food production and the tending of cattle, dating from about 1000 BC, has been found in the highland and Rift Valley regions of southern Kenya and northern Tanzania. These were apparently introduced by people from what is now Ethiopia.

This was the first of the 'great migrations' that are an important feature of East Africa's history. In the last 3000 years, waves of peoples have crossed and re-crossed the region, some groups searching for new territory as their populations grew, others forced to move by climatic changes. The movements inevitably had a knock-on effect too, as groups being invaded from one side expanded in the other direction. Most migrations took place over hundreds of years, and were made up of many short moves (from valley to valley or from one cultivation area to the next), with dominant peoples slowly absorbing and assimilating other groups in the process.

The most significant migration was that of the Bantu people. Armed with iron tools to clear forest and cultivate more effectively, the Bantu migrated from the area that is now Cameroon, through the Congo (Zaïre) basin and onto the East African plateau, arriving in the region around 100 BC. Over the next thousand years they spread across present-day Uganda, Kenya, Tanzania and Malawi, as well as several other areas.

Across East Africa the various Bantu peoples generally lived in small farming communities, but around 1300 AD a large kingdom called Chwezi was established in the west of the region. In the 16th century, Nilotic people (originally from the southern Nile Valley) migrated into the area and intermixed with the Bantu. At this time, the Chwezi kingdom split and the Buganda kingdom was founded, which remained in place until the arrival of the British at the end of the 19th century.

Meanwhile, in northern Kenya, it is thought that another Bantu kingdom called Shungwaya existed until an invasion of Cushitic people from the north around 1600 forced the Bantu (including the Kikuyu and Kamba groups) south to their present territories to the west and east of Mt Kenya. (For more details on the terms Bantu, Nilotic and Cushitic, see the People section later in this chapter.)

At around the same period, in Malawi, the Tumbuka and Phoka people (also Bantu) migrated into the north of the country (their traditions do not agree on where from) between the 14th and 16th centuries AD. Meanwhile, in the south, the Maravi people (of whom the Chewa became the dominant group) came in from present-day Congo (Zaïre) and established a large and powerful kingdom that spread all over southern Malawi and parts of present-day Mozambique and Zambia.

In the 18th century another wave of Nilotic people, the Maasai, spread into northern Kenya and then down the Rift Valley into Tanzania. Smaller Bantu groups, such as the Chagga in the Kilimanjaro area, retreated to high ground for safety, while the Kikuyu remained in the forested highlands on Mt Kenya and the Aberdare Range.

In the early 19th century, the Ngoni people, who were related to the Zulu and just as warlike, migrated to Malawi from the south and settled in the middle of the country, conquering the Chewa, while another group of Ngoni pushed further north into Tanzania. It is thought that their northern expansion was stopped by the Maasai who were heading south through the same area. Around the same time, the Yao arrived from northern Mozambique, settling around the Shire Highlands and the southern end of Lake Malawi. The Yao forced the Maravi inhabitants into slavery, selling them to slave traders from the coast.

The Coast

In the early part of the first millennium AD, Arabs from the area now called Yemen sailed around the Horn of Africa and began exploring the east coast. They traded with the local inhabitants, buying mainly ivory, gold and slaves to take back to Arabia.

Trade was brisk. The merchants brought glass and metal spearheads from Arabia and, later, spices from India and porcelain from China. They also introduced new crops such as bananas and yams. By 700 AD the Arabs had founded several trading settlements on the coast from Mogadishu (in present-day Somalia) down to Kilwa (in southern Tanzania). By this time, the Bantu people had arrived on the coast from the interior, and the

Arabs intermarried with them, gradually creating a mixed language and culture, called Swahili.

Islam had been founded by the prophet Mohammed in Arabia around 600 AD and the Arab traders brought the new faith with them to East Africa. By 1100 AD Islam was practised widely all along the coast.

The Swahili civilisation continued to flourish and the towns became wealthy independent city-states ruled by sultans, although they maintained a close link with Arabia. Their wealth was based on the trade of goods from the African hinterland, but no attempt was made to conquer land or create settlements in the interior. The coast and the interior existed as separate worlds.

Arabs, Europeans & Slavery

Things started to change when the first Europeans arrived on the scene. Since the early 1400s, Portuguese navigators had been pushing further round the West African coast, searching for a route to India and China. The breakthrough came in 1498 when a ship under the command of Vasco da Gama rounded the Cape of Good Hope and sailed up the East African coast from the south.

Da Gama was not welcomed by the sultan at Mombasa, although the sultan of Malindi (a great rival of Mombasa) was friendly towards the new arrivals. But diplomacy was not a Portuguese strong point – over the next few years they bombarded and looted several Swahili cities.

The Portuguese remained on the East African coast for 200 years, trading gold from the interior and exporting slaves to work on the plantations in the Americas and East Indies.

But the Arabs did not forget their East African outposts – throughout the 17th century, Omani ships continually threatened the Portuguese trading stations. By the early 1700s the Portuguese had been routed completely and the East African coast was back in the hands of the Arabs.

Throughout the 18th century the Omani Arabs rebuilt their trade links and their cities, and in 1832 the Sultan of Oman, Seyyid

DAVID ELSE

DAVID ELSE

DAVID ELSE

DAVID ELSE

DAVID ELSE

Faces of East Africa: The Maasai (top) and Samburu (middle, bottom left) people live in different regions of East Africa and have different cultures, but share the same language and ancestry. A shepherd boy (bottom right); one of the Amhara people who practice subsistence farming in the Simien Mountains, Ethiopia.

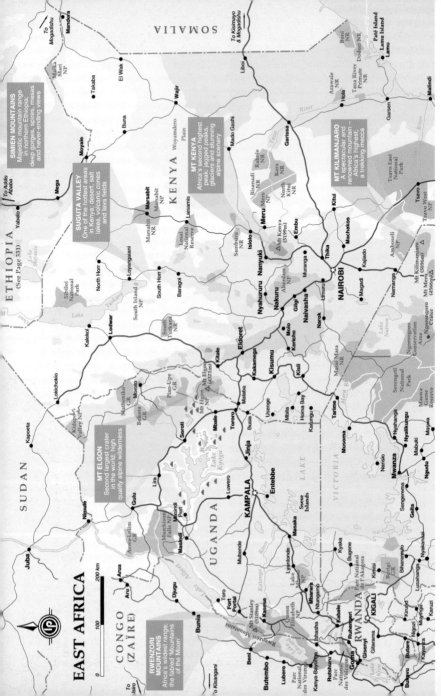

EAST AFRICA

0   100   200 km

SUDAN

CONGO (ZAÏRE)

ETHIOPIA
(See Page 331)

SOMALIA

KENYA

UGANDA

RWANDA

RWENZORI MOUNTAINS
Africa's wildest range; the fabled 'Mountains of the Moon'

MT ELGON
Second largest crater in the world; high quality alpine wilderness

SUGUTA VALLEY
One of the hottest areas in Kenya; desert, salt lakes, volcanic cones and lava fields

SIMIEN MOUNTAINS
Majestic mountain range in northern Ethiopia; deep gorges, spires, mesas and never-ending views

MT KENYA
Africa's second highest peak; jagged peaks, glaciers and stunning alpine scenery

MT KILIMANJARO
A spectacular and renowned mountain. Africa's highest; a trekking mecca

To Mogadishu

To Addis Ababa

To Kisimayo & Mogadishu

To Kisangani

Mandera
Takaba
El Wak
Buna
Moyale
Mega
Yabelo
Marsabit
Marsabit NP
Marsabit NR
Loyangalani
North Horr
Laisamis
Loiyangalani
Baragoi
South Horr
South Island NP
Sibiloi National Park
Kalokol
Lodwar
Lokichokio
Kapoeta
Juba
Nimule
Arua
Aru
Djugu
Bunia
Beni
Butembo
Lubero
Kanya-Bayonga
Rutshuru
Goma
Gisenyi
KIGALI
Kibuye
Kayanza
Butare
Nyanza
Gitarama
Gikongoro
Cyangugu
Bukavu
Kasese
Fort Portal
Toro
Mbarara
Kabale
Rubengera
Ntungamo
Kanungu
Bagene
Kyaka
Kyenjojo
Mubende
Luwero
KAMPALA
Entebbe
Masaka
Jinja
Tororo
Mbale
Soroti
Lira
Gulu
Masindi
Port Bell
Nyahanga
Nyalikungu
Mabuki
Magwa
Mwanza
Musoma
Tarime
Homa Bay
Kadungu
Mbita
Usenge
Busia
Malaba
Kisumu
Kakamega
Kisii
Kericho
Molo
Narok
Naivasha
Nakuru
Nyahururu
Nyeri
Muranga
Thika
NAIROBI
Kajiado
Magadi
Namanga
Arusha
Moshi
Tsavo
Kitui
Embu
Meru
Isiolo
Nanyuki
Maralal
Garissa
Modo Gashi
Hola
Garsen
Malindi
Lamu
Paté Island
Boni NR
Dodori NR
Tana River Primate NR
Arawale NR
Kora NR
Bisanadi NR
North Kitui NR
Meru NP
Tsavo East National Park
Tsavo West NP
Amboseli NP
Lake Natron
Ngorongoro Conservation Area
Serengeti National Park
Maswa Game Reserve
Masai Mara NR
Mawi Game Reserve
Sengerema
Geita
Ngudu
Nansio
Biharamulo
Bukoba
Nyakanazi
Nyakahura
Burigi GR
Parc National de l'Akagera
Lake Victoria
Lake Kyoga
Lake Albert
Lake Edward
Lake Kivu
Lake Mburo NP
Queen Elizabeth NP
Parc National des Virunga
Parc National des Volcans
Rwenzori Mountains
Mt Stanley (5109m)
Mt Elgon (4321m)
Mt Elgon NP
Mt Kenya (5199m)
Aberdare NP
Mt Kilimanjaro (5896m)
Mt Meru (4566m)
Lake Turkana
Lake Stefanie
Omo River
Juba River
Tana River
Kerio River
Athi River
Kagera River
Katonga River
Woyamdero Plain
Losai National Reserve
Kora NR
Rahole NR
Samburu NR
Kidepo Valley NP
Matheniko GR
Bokora GR
Pian-Upe GR
Murchison Falls NP
Aswa-Lolim GR
Kalokol
Seese Islands
Bunagana
Bushenyi
Ishasha
Nyamgasani
Lake Kwania
SOMALIA

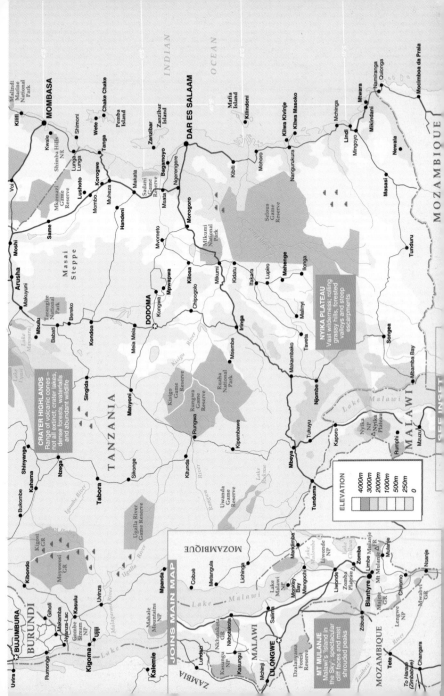

DAVID ELSE

The active volcanic cone of Ol Doinyo Lengai (2878m) rises from the surrounding plains in the Crater Highlands region of Tanzania. Lengai's last major eruption was in 1966, but evidence of the volcano's activity can still be seen in the crater at the summit, where there are steaming fissures and ash cones.

Said, moved his capital and entire court to Zanzibar, an island about halfway down the East African coast and part of present-day Tanzania.

During the first half of the 19th century, Arab slavers pushed into the interior and established several trading centres, including Tabora, in present-day Tanzania, and Karonga on Lake Malawi. The Arabs exploited rivalries between local tribes, encouraging powerful groups to conquer their neighbours and sell them into slavery. The slaves were then forced to the coast, from where they were taken to Zanzibar, which was fast becoming the centre of a very lucrative trade in slaves and ivory from the interior, and spices (particularly cloves) from the island itself.

Exploration & Empire

By the mid-19th century the interest of the powerful countries in northern Europe, particularly Britain, focussed on two things: the abolition of the slave trade and the quest to discover the source of the Nile. The period from around 1840 to 1880 is often called (by Europeans) the Golden Age of Exploration when great explorers such as Livingstone, Stanley, Burton and Speke, confident, brave and certain of their racial superiority, mapped and recorded the interior of Africa.

For the first time Europeans saw the great lakes of Tanganyika, Victoria and Malawi, the sources of the Nile, the Rift Valley and the snowcapped peaks of Mt Kenya, Kilimanjaro and the Rwenzoris. (See the following section on Exploration in East Africa.)

The explorers returned home with the reports of their discoveries, but at first the governments of Britain and the other European powers saw the interior of Africa as hostile and unproductive. At this stage there was no incentive to occupy these lands.

This attitude changed towards the end of the 19th century. Germany, the rising power in Europe, had seen French activity in West Africa, and watched Britain's interests begin to grow in East Africa. Bismarck, the German leader, also wanted 'a place in the sun'. The reaction was sudden: in a very short period, the European powers all laid claim to terri-

tories, mainly to keep the opposing nations out rather than for any other reason. This period became known as the 'Scramble for Africa'.

The various claims of the European powers were settled at the Berlin Conference of 1884-85, when most of the continent of Africa was split neatly into colonies. France got most of West Africa, Germany got some territory in the east (now Tanzania), King Leopold of Belgium got Congo (Zaïre), Portugal kept Mozambique and Angola, and Britain got more or less everything else. The European powers were happy with the results of the conference. What the Africans thought of it remains unrecorded – they weren't invited to attend.

The histories of the individual countries of East Africa, following the Berlin Conference, are covered in more detail in the relevant country chapters.

EXPLORATION IN EAST AFRICA

The history of exploration in East Africa is of special interest to trekkers, as much of the early speculation and 'discovery' involved the region's great snow-covered mountains. And, of course, the early explorers trekked everywhere themselves, across the great plains and up into the highlands around the mountains. When you're on the train from Mombasa to Nairobi, or strolling through the beautiful forest on the slopes of Mt Kenya, or even getting near the summit of Kilimanjaro, remember those early pioneers and their heavily laden porters, who foot slogged and trail-blazed the whole way.

The Source of the Nile

Exploration in East Africa has always been linked to the search for the source of the River Nile. As long ago as 400 BC the Greek geographer Herodotus travelled from Cairo south beyond Aswan, hoping to reach the source of the great river that had maintained the empires of Egypt for thousands of years.

A few hundred years later the Roman emperor Nero sent a military expedition on the same mission. His soldiers got as far as

The Sudd, a massive swamp in present-day Sudan. On their way south they probably passed the junction of the Blue and White Niles, near present-day Khartoum.

It was also realised by the early geographers that the source of the Nile could be reached from the coast of East Africa. Legend has it that a merchant-traveller from Greece called Diogenes went inland from a point somewhere on the north coast of present-day Tanzania, reached two great lakes and saw a snow-covered range of mountains which, he said, were the source of the Nile. The legend was recorded by the Greek scholar Marinus of Tyre, who wrote a guide for shipping on the Indian Ocean in the second half of the 1st century AD.

From that description, in the 2nd century the geographer Ptolemy produced a map of Africa showing the River 'Nilus', the two lakes, called 'Nili Paludes', and the range of mountains which he called 'Lune Montes' – the Mountains of the Moon. The name is evocative, but it is not known where the term 'moon' comes from. Maybe it implied 'beyond the world'; on his map Ptolemy annotated the region south of the range as *'Terra Incognita'* (unknown territory).

It has also been proposed that Ptolemy was referring to the mountains of Ethiopia and Lake Tana, the source of the Blue Nile. This is unlikely, and not suggested by the map, although much of Ptolemy's work was based on conjecture and ancient, second-hand storytelling.

The Explorers

The legendary Mountains of the Moon and the source of the White Nile inspired and intrigued European storytellers and geographers for centuries afterwards, but no new information was received about the mysterious snow-covered mountains of Africa until the mid-19th century, when the first British and German missionary-explorers arrived on the east coast and started to push inland. Often their travels lasted for several months, or even years, and the explorers, along with their followers, suffered considerable deprivation and hardship.

Rebmann & Krapf Kilimanjaro was the first of the great East African mountains to be seen by a European. It was sighted in 1848 by a Swiss missionary called Johannes Rebmann, a member of the London-based Church Missionary Society. With his colleague Ludwig Krapf, he travelled inland from Mombasa following a route similar to the one probably taken by Diogenes and at that time used by Arab slave traders. Krapf recorded that the local Chagga people called the mountain 'Kibo', which he understood to mean 'snow', but the Swahili people of the coast called it 'Kilima Njaro', meaning either 'Mountain of Greatness' or 'Mountain of Caravans' (for more details see the Kilimanjaro section of the Tanzania chapter).

Rebmann and Krapf also travelled south from Mombasa and reached the Usambara Mountains. This was a fertile area, with a cool climate, much more pleasant than the coast. They found the local people agreeable, too, and recommended that a mission be built in the area. Krapf also went north-west, to the region around Kitui. From here, in late 1849, he became the first European to see Mt Kenya. He called it 'Kimaji Kegnia', which he said meant 'Mountain of Whiteness' in the local language, and described the snow on the higher peaks and the 'two large horns' of the twin summits.

Rebmann and Krapf's descriptions of the huge snow-covered peak of Kilimanjaro were published in London in 1849, but they were refuted by WD Cooley, the most influential geographer of the time, and several other members of the Royal Geographical Society (RGS). This was not because they thought snow couldn't exist on the equator, as is often supposed (snow was already known on the equatorial Andes), but because the sighting lent weight to the theory that Kilimanjaro's snows were the source of the Nile. At the time, geographers were divided into two camps, some holding that the source of the Nile was in East Africa, others believing that it arose in Central Africa. Cooley and his followers were in the latter camp. It took until 1861, when the sightings were confirmed by Baron Karl von der Decken, an

aristocratic German explorer, for Rebmann and Krapf's account to be accepted.

Burton & Speke After the snowcapped peaks, the source of the Nile still obsessed most geographers. In 1857 the British explorers Richard Burton and John Hanning Speke were sent by the RGS to East Africa, to find the source of the Nile and settle the disputes. From Zanzibar, they followed the old slave routes inland for six months to reach the settlement of Ujiji on the east shore of Lake Tanganyika. On their return journey Burton became ill and Speke travelled northwards alone. He reached Lake Victoria, near present day Mwanza, in August 1858, the first European to see this huge inland sea. He believed it to be the source of the Nile.

Speke & Grant In 1862 Speke returned to East Africa with another British explorer, James Grant. They retraced Speke and Burton's original route, then travelled to the north side of Lake Victoria, eventually reaching a large river that flowed northwards out of the lake. To prove that it was the Nile, they followed the river downstream to reach Gondokoro, near Juba in southern Sudan, which then was the limit of exploration from the north. This filled the gap, and finally solved the riddle of the source of the Nile.

Livingstone Meanwhile, further south, another British explorer was also busy. Between 1842 and 1856, David Livingstone explored the Kalahari Desert and the Upper Zambezi and crossed the continent from the east to the west coast. On his return to Britain, he spoke at several public meetings about the 'undiscovered' interior of Africa and the horrors of the slave trade. A speech in 1857 led to the founding of the Universities Mission in Central Africa (UMCA), whose aim was to combat the slave trade by encouraging alternative commerce, and to establish missions for promoting the spread of Christianity.

Livingstone returned to Africa in 1858 to explore the Zambezi region. On a small steamboat, Livingstone and his party travelled up the Zambezi River and then the Shire River to reached Lake Malawi in September 1859.

Livingstone's final great expedition started in 1866. This time his aim was to find the true source of the Nile (ie the river which fed Lake Victoria). He returned to the region around Lake Malawi, then travelled north to reach the southern end of Lake Tanganyika. He knew of Ujiji from Speke and Burton's accounts, and reached there in early 1869. In July of that year he pushed even further north, intending to be gone for a few months (a short jaunt by his standards) but he was not seen or heard of for over two years. Livingstone was found by Henry Stanley (a Welsh-American journalist) on the banks of Lake Tanganyika in late 1871, when Stanley uttered the immortal words: 'Dr Livingstone, I presume'.

Stanley In 1874 Stanley returned to Africa and the following year he became probably the first European to see the Rwenzori Mountains, although at the time he didn't realise it. Somewhere to the west of Lake Victoria he recorded a faint sighting of a distant mountain range, but made no attempt at that time to find out more.

Stanley returned to Africa again in 1887. This time his aim was to rescue Emin Pasha, a German who had settled in Africa, taken an Islamic name and become governor of the Anglo-Egyptian province of Equatoria. Emin Pasha had been trapped by the forces of the Mahdi, who two years before had defeated the army of General Gordon. Stanley sailed round Africa to the mouth of the Congo (Zaïre) River, and headed inland from there.

Of all the early European pioneering journeys through Africa, this one was the worst. Conditions were appalling: heat, rain, disease, hunger, and attacks from local people, through 3000km of near-impenetrable forest. Stanley was ruthless. He solved most problems by beating or shooting his hapless load-bearers. After a few months of slow progress he became impatient, named half his company the 'rear column' and simply abandoned them in the middle of the forest. It took him another

John Gregory – Forgotten Explorer?

John Gregory was a Scottish geologist who explored parts of Kenya during the 1890s. Although his works and travels did not capture the public imagination of the time in the same way as those of, say, Livingstone and Stanley, he made several important discoveries in East Africa.

From his studies of the huge escarpments near Mt Longonot and Lake Bogoria in Kenya he deduced that the Rift Valley was created by sinking between parallel fault lines, rather than by more usual erosion by water and ice. He actually coined the term 'Rift Valley' and the eastern section of the valley is sometimes called the Gregory Rift after him.

Gregory was also busy away from the Rift Valley; he was the first explorer to study the geology of Mt Kenya in great detail. Of particular interest to today's trekkers, he also became one of the first explorers in Africa to notice (and record with great attention to detail) the effects of altitude sickness. ■

14 months to reach Lake Albert, where Emin Pasha had a camp.

Stanley was annoyed to find Emin and his troops in good condition, with plenty of supplies. In fact, Emin gave a lot of his stuff to Stanley's party. As one of his men later wrote, 'the rescuers were rescued'.

In his accounts of this expedition, Stanley recorded a sighting of a vast mountain covered with snow but he did not seem to connect this with the range he had seen on his second expedition in 1875. He refers to the range as 'Ruwenzori', a corruption of the local name meaning 'Hill of Rain', and presumed them to be the Mountains of the Moon described by the early geographers. But even here, although Stanley claimed discovery of the range, some of his officers had already spotted it at least a month earlier – Stanley had ignored their reports, and subsequently got the glory.

The First Ascents

By the end of the 19th century, the explorers were not just looking at the mountains from far off but actually going up them. In 1871, a British missionary called Charles New walked for several days up Kilimanjaro to reach the snow line at an altitude above 4000m. He started his expedition in the small settlement of Moshi, today the base for trekking on Kilimanjaro, and was helped by the local chief called Mandara, after whom one of today's huts on the mountain is named.

Mandara was still around in 1883, when the Scottish explorer Joseph Thomson passed through the foothills of Kilimanjaro on his way to explore northern Kenya. Thomson also skirted the edge of the Nyandarua Mountains, renaming them the Aberdare Range, and got to the forest on the western slopes of Mt Kenya. He then crossed the Rift Valley and continued east to reach Lake Victoria, catching an unexpected glimpse of Mt Elgon on the way.

The next explorer to get high on Kilimanjaro was Count Samuel Teleki, an Austro-Hungarian aristocrat who mounted a large private expedition across East Africa in 1887. But Teleki was not just a rich man playing games. With his colleague Ludwig von Hohnel, Teleki travelled to the far north of present-day Kenya, through the Suguta Valley, one of the hottest parts of Africa, to reach Lake Turkana, the legendary Jade Sea. On their route from the coast, Teleki and Von Hohnel reached The Saddle of Kilimanjaro between the main peaks of Kibo and Mawenzi. They also passed the Aberdare (Nyandarua) Range, which they called the Sattima Range, and reached an altitude of around 4000m on Mt Kenya, as far as the base of the main peaks.

The Rwenzori Range was the last of the major mountains to be climbed to any significant height by European explorers. In 1889, after their earlier sightings, Stanley and Emin Pasha explored the area, and a member of their team, Lieutenant Stairs, reached a point at about 3000m on the north-west side of the range.

After more than 2000 years of legend and conjecture, and 50 years of frantic exploration, by the end of the 19th century the major mountains of East Africa had been seen and documented by Europeans. By the first years of the 20th century, all the summits had also been conquered: Hans Meyer reached the summit of Kilimanjaro in 1889; Halford

Mackinder finally climbed Batian, the highest point on Mt Kenya, 10 years later; and in 1906, the Duke of Abruzzi polished off the period of achievement by climbing most of the major peaks in the Rwenzoris.

GEOGRAPHY

Africa is the largest continent in the world but, geographically, it is not a land of great contrasts. It can be divided into two main geographical regions, called simply High Africa and Low Africa, on either side of the line that runs diagonally across the continent from the mouth of the Congo (Zaïre) River to the Red Sea coast in northern Ethiopia.

High Africa consists of the eastern and southern areas of the continent, which are made up mainly of plateaus between 1000m and 2000m above sea level. Low Africa consists of the western and northern areas of the continent, which lie mainly between 200m and 1000m. The region covered by this book is in High Africa.

The high plateau of East Africa is dissected by one of the world's largest geological features: the Afro-Arab Rift System, more commonly known as the Great Rift Valley, a 6500km fissure in the earth's crust that stretches from Turkey to Mozambique. In the region north of Lake Turkana, the valley splits in two. The eastern branch, where it cuts a deep gash through Kenya and Tanzania, is often called the Great Rift Valley; features include sheer escarpments, a chain of lakes (including some of the largest in Africa), hot springs, steaming fissures and volcanic cones.

The western branch of the Rift is on the other side of Lake Victoria, stretching from the Uganda-Congo (Zaïre) border, down Lake Tanganyika and into southern Tanzania. This branch of the Rift is not so well known but some commentators rate it as even more impressive than the eastern Rift. Many of the escarpments are higher, and the lakes even larger; Lake Tanganyika is the deepest in Africa. The two branches meet in northern Malawi. The Rift Valley continues down Lake Malawi and into Mozambique to finally fizzle out near the mouth of the Zambezi River.

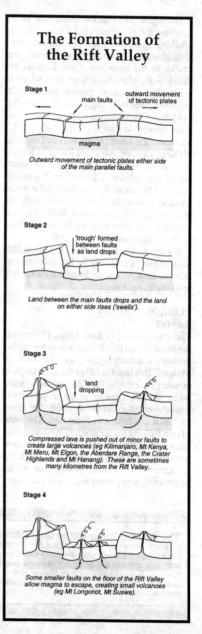

The Formation of the Rift Valley

Stage 1

main faults — outward movement of tectonic plates

magma

Outward movement of tectonic plates either side of the main parallel faults.

Stage 2

'trough' formed between faults as land drops

Land between the main faults drops and the land on either side rises ('swells').

Stage 3

land dropping

Compressed lava is pushed out of minor faults to create large volcanoes (eg Kilimanjaro, Mt Kenya, Mt Meru, Mt Elgon, the Aberdare Range, the Crater Highlands and Mt Hanang). These are sometimes many kilometres from the Rift Valley.

Stage 4

Some smaller faults on the floor of the Rift Valley allow magma to escape, creating small volcanoes (eg Mt Longonot, Mt Suswa).

Geologists say that the Great Rift Valley is where the continent of Africa is literally breaking apart. In the last few million years, huge chunks of land have sunk between giant cracks in the earth's surface. Beyond the valley wall, mountains were formed when gargantuan amounts of magma (molten rock) erupted upwards through these huge cracks.

Most of East Africa's major mountains were created in this way. Kilimanjaro, Mt Meru and the Crater Highlands in Tanzania, Mt Kenya and the Aberdare Range in Kenya, and Mt Elgon on the Kenya-Uganda border are all old volcanoes formed by the movements of the Great Rift Valley. Of the major mountains described in this book, only the Rwenzori and the plateaus of Malawi are not volcanic, but even they are the result of the uplifting associated with the Rift.

It's fair to say that without the Great Rift Valley there'd certainly be far fewer mountains in East Africa, and certainly a lot less trekking to be done.

CLIMATE
Rainfall
The main feature of East Africa's climate is the band of rain that moves across the region between northern Uganda and the south of Malawi. This band is called the inter-tropical convergence zone (ITCZ) and is created when warm air rising in the tropics cools over the equator. As the air cools, the moisture in it condenses to form rain. The band of rain follows the apparent movement of the sun as the earth tilts on its axis. It is at its most northerly point in July and its most southerly in January. Because it crosses East Africa twice each year, most areas get two rainy seasons and two dry seasons. At the northern and southern limits of the rain band there is only one wet and one dry season each year.

In Kenya and Uganda the dry seasons are generally from December to February and from June to September. In northern Tanzania the dry seasons are at more or less the same time as Kenya's, although they tend to start and end slightly later. In southern Tanzania and Malawi there is only one dry season, from April to September or October. (More details about each country's climate are given in the individual country chapters.)

During the rainy season, most mornings are clear, getting hotter towards midday, and then rain falls as a shower or a deluge in the afternoon.

Away from the highlands of the interior, weather patterns on the low coastal strip are hot and humid, and are influenced by ocean currents and monsoonal winds. Here it can rain at any time, but the heaviest falls come between March and May/June.

Temperatures
East Africa is cooler than other equatorial regions of the world – its climate is more temperate than equatorial – because of the strong influence of altitude. Put simply – the higher you go, the cooler it gets. And this applies most obviously on the mountains themselves. Even though they lie virtually on the equator, the large isolated massifs of East Africa, such as Mt Kenya and Kilimanjaro, have a complete range of climatic conditions, which have in turn created a range of vegetation types. A trek on one of these mountains is like going from the tropics to the tundra and back again, usually in less

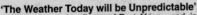

'The Weather Today will be Unpredictable'
In recent years, the climate of East Africa – and, indeed, the whole world – has become harder to predict. Rainfall levels since the early 1980s have continued to decrease; the rainy seasons seem to start later and end earlier. Droughts in marginal areas all over East Africa have become increasingly common. Even in areas such as Malawi, where once the seasons were as reliable as clockwork, the rains either come late, if at all, or fall in a condensed period with sudden heavy storms verging on monsoon conditions. ■

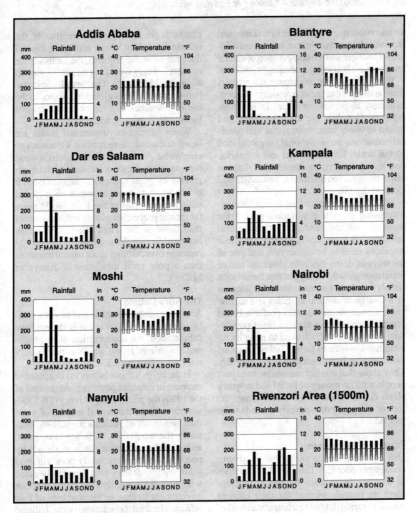

Addis Ababa

Blantyre

Dar es Salaam

Kampala

Moshi

Nairobi

Nanyuki

Rwenzori Area (1500m)

than a week! Starting from dry savanna plains, you pass through lush rainforest and woodland, then zones of heath and grassy moor, before reaching the bare rock and ice of the high peak areas. (More details on each country's climate are given in the individual country chapters. More details on the vegetation are given in the separate Flora & Fauna section.)

ECOLOGY & ENVIRONMENT

The terms 'ecology' and 'environment' are bandied around a lot these days, and used in such a variety of contexts that actual meanings often become vague. Generally speaking, however, the factors relevant to East Africa are similar to those elsewhere in the world. Ecological and environmental issues such as air and water degradation, deforestation, soil erosion, urban encroachment, habitat and wildlife destruction, and the conservation of natural resources are becoming increasingly pertinent.

When discussing environmental matters there is often a danger of oversimplification. It is easy to regard the issues in isolation, when in fact they are all interrelated and linked to wider economic, social and political situations on a national, regional and global scale. Environmental and conservation issues are never straightforward. Experts often disagree on methods, solutions, and even on definitions.

For example, all over East Africa, an ever-increasing human population puts great demands on the land and other natural resources. It is generally agreed that these resources need to be conserved, and one of the ways of doing this is to lower the rate of population growth. To suggest that the solution simply involves contraception, sterilisation or a change in cultural attitudes is a narrow view. Conservationists who prefer a broad perspective point out that the rapid population growth is closely linked to poor living conditions, which in turn is linked to social issues such as lack of education and ill health. They argue that it is not reasonable to expect people with no money or little food to worry about conservation in its widest sense; the root of the problem – poverty – needs to be tackled.

Poverty & Resources

One argument for the alleviation of poverty encourages poor (or 'Third World') countries to increase large-scale economic development, to provide income for their citizens which in turn will lead to a better standard of living and thus, by extension, an interest in environmental conservation in its widest form. Opponents of this argument hold that economic development can cause its own environmental damage: heavy industry leads to air and water pollution, and inevitably requires the use of natural resources, while large scale farming can also cause pollution and soil erosion.

Moreover, even if Third World population growth stabilised and people had higher living standards (ie the high consumption of the industrialised 'First World' countries), this still does not solve the problem; the earth's finite resources simply would not be able to support all the world's people. The 'broad' conservationists hold that this global imbalance in the use of resources is a major environmental factor which must be addressed.

When African environmental issues are being discussed, there is often a tendency to emphasise 'indigenous' situations (wood burning stoves create deforestation, and over-grazing by goats causes soil erosion), but it is important to recognise that on a global scale the countries of the First World use a far greater proportion of the earth's resources than those in the Third World. An urban citizen of Britain, Australia or the USA might consume over 50 times more natural resources than a poor rural inhabitant of Kenya or Malawi.

The Ivory Debate

Another example to show that environmental issues are never clear cut is the emotive debate about the conservation of elephants and the sale of ivory, which is particularly relevant in East Africa.

In the 1970s various factors led to a massive increase in elephant poaching. At the end of the 1980s the price of 1kg of ivory (US$300) was three times the annual income of more than two-thirds of Africa's population. Naturally the temptation to poach was great, although the real money was made not by poachers – often desperately poor villagers – but by the dealers who frequently acted with the full knowledge (and help) of senior government figures. In the countries of East Africa, elephant populations were reduced by 80% to 90% in about 15 years.

In 1990, following a massive world-wide campaign from various conservation organisations, a world body called the Convention on International Trade in Endangered Species (CITES) banned the trade in ivory, and the global demand collapsed. At the same time there was an increase in funds for the protection of elephants. The improved law enforcement and closure of the trade were both important

steps in elephant protection, but after a few years it seemed that poaching was once again on the increase, mainly due to a lack of funds and government commitment. For example, in Tanzania, a report issued in 1995 by the IUCN African Elephant Specialist Group noted that in 1990 the country's anti-poaching budget was almost US$700,000, but in 1993 it had dropped to US$12,000. It also noted insufficient facilities and poor morale among field staff, plus an inefficient and inconsistent judicial process. The report also recorded over 50 tonnes of ivory (collected legally from dead animals or confiscated from poachers) in government stockpiles.

In some parts of Africa, there are increasingly strong arguments for the trade to be legalised again, and strictly controlled, so that funds raised from sales of ivory (from government stockpiles, replenished from commercially hunted or culled elephants) could go to conservation projects that would benefit both animals and people. In this way the elephants would become a resource with a tangible value, giving governments and local people an incentive to ensure their survival.

As this book was in production, CITES altered the protection status of the elephant, allowing some southern African countries with relatively healthy elephant populations to start controlled sales of ivory in early 1999 – although they have to first convince CITES that adequate safeguards are in place to prevent laundering of poached ivory. Elephant populations in East Africa are still low, compared to those in southern Africa, but the trade here may also be re-started, much to the dismay of some conservationists who argue that controls will never be strict enough, and a resumption of the ivory trade will inevitably mean a resumption of poaching.

Community-Based Conservation

The 'pay to stay' arguments used when discussing the elephant and the ivory trade are frequently applied in a general manner to wildlife and protected areas throughout Africa. Established thinking for many years has regarded human populations as a negative factor, and local people have been excluded from protected wildlife areas. However, many conservationists now argue that national parks and reserves are unlikely to succeed in the long-term unless local people can obtain real benefits from them. Until recently, the importance of including local communities in conservation planning and management has not been fully recognised. Put very simply, the argument goes like this: if local people protect the areas and the animals, foreigners pay to come and visit, and some of the money goes back to the local people. If there is no benefit, there is no incentive to conserve. (For more thoughts on community benefits see the National Park Benefits boxed text in the Regional Facts for the Trekker chapter.)

In East Africa, many thousands of local people (mainly nomadic pastoralists such as the Maasai) were forcibly removed from traditional grazing lands when national parks such as Kenya's Amboseli and Shaba or Tanzania's Tarangire and Mkomazi were created in the 1970s and 1980s. This caused great poverty and hardship for the displaced people, and frequent incidents of 'revenge' against the wildlife were reported. Local Maasai assisted poachers or laid poisoned carcasses to kill animals such as lion and leopard. In one park, several rhino were speared to death. Campaigners for the rights of the Maasai argue that allowing them to graze cattle once more within national parks would actually be of more benefit to people and animals.

In an attempt to prevent conflicts between humans and animals arising, community-based conservation schemes have been established in certain areas. These include Tarangire Wildlife Conservation Area (TWCA), to the north-east of Tanzania's Tarangire National Park, where visitors come for wildlife viewing and walking safaris. The landscape is very similar to that inside the park, and as there is no fence the animals roam freely between both areas. Local people benefit directly from tourist revenue and thus have a tangible incentive in environmental conservation. In Kenya the Magadi, Shaba and Northern Mara Conservation areas run along similar lines. Other schemes have been established in Uganda

and Malawi. While this allows local people to continue living in their traditional manner, there is also an option to receive income from the jobs that wildlife tourism creates, such as game rangers, tour guides and various posts in the hotels, lodges and camps. Further spin-offs include the sale of crafts and curios – another way for local people to earn money direct from the tourists.

Tourism & the Environment

Although tourism can be a saviour in some instances, it can also have very negative effects. Either way, tourism itself is a major environmental issue (it is one of the largest global industries), and is impossible to ignore. A problem arises when destinations cannot cope with the number of tourists they attract, so that natural and social environments quickly become damaged.

This can be seen in Kenya's Masai Mara Reserve, where uncontrolled safari vehicles in the more accessible parts destroy sections of grassland and lodges burn firewood at an unsustainable rate to provide hot showers for their guests. Another example is Tanzania's Serengeti and Ngorongoro areas, where local Maasai were allowed to graze cattle but prevented from burning the grass (which they do to encourage nutritious new shoots) because tourists found it 'unsightly'.

More relevant for trekkers is Kilimanjaro, where the sheer number of people on the Marangu Route has created serious path erosion. The park authorities have established short alternative routes to give the eroded areas time to re-establish, but while trekkers may heed the signs, porters (about 75% of the people on the mountain) simply ignore them, and hammer along the old routes as they've always done. Footpath erosion is also a problem in the Rwenzoris: as trekkers attempt to avoid the mud, the routes get wider and delicate vegetation is destroyed. Another problem on Kili and Mt Kenya is the uncontrolled use of firewood, especially on the upper slopes where giant heather and even old groundsels are being cut for firewood. (Since 1994 Kilimanjaro National Park's management plan has paid lip service to the prevention of firewood collection, but away from the Marangu Route, guides and porters are rarely provided with tents and blankets so are forced to make fires to survive outside in the sub-zero temperatures.)

Eco-Tourism

Another environmental issue, particularly relevant for visitors in Africa, is the growth of so-called 'eco-tourism'. This is one of the most over-used and meaningless terms around. Don't be fooled by travel companies blithely claiming to be 'eco-friendly' just because they do things outdoors. Activities such as trekking, camping, white-water rafting or game viewing (by car, foot or balloon), or sightseeing trips to remote and fragile areas can be more environmentally or culturally harmful than a conventional hotel holiday in a specifically developed resort.

Environmentalists point out that tourism relies on natural resources, such as healthy wildlife populations, clean rivers and rich cultural traditions, but quite often does little to maintain, sustain or restore them.

If you want to support tour companies with a good environmental record, you have to look beyond the glossy brochures and vague 'eco-friendly' claims and ask what they are really doing to protect or support the environment (and remember that includes local people as well as animals and plants).

Visitors to East Africa (or to any other part of the world) are often asked by environmental organisations to consider the amount of money they pay during their holiday, and to ensure that as much as possible stays within the 'host' country for the benefit of local people. With this in mind, opponents of the 'high-cost low-density' tourism policies adopted by some countries elsewhere on the continent, point out that overland truck passengers, independent backpackers and other low-budget travellers on a long trip contribute just as much to local economies as high-rolling tourists who come to a country on a short all-inclusive trip paid for overseas. Other observers point out that all visitors can be beneficial by supporting local business whenever possible.

The effect that tourists have on the environ-

ment is not just financial. It is important for visitors to East Africa (and anywhere else) to behave in a manner which limits their impact on the natural environment and the local inhabitants – animal and human. Some ideas are listed below. To be a responsible tourist you have to question some of your own actions and those of tour companies providing the services and facilities you use. You also have to look pretty closely at the actions of governments, both local and around the world. Being a responsible tourist doesn't mean you have to get depressed and spoil your holiday. In fact, by asking a few questions and getting a deeper insight, it can make your trip even more rewarding.

Guidelines for Responsible Tourism

Some specific guidelines for trekkers and campers are given in the boxed text on Responsible Trekking in the Regional Facts for the Trekker chapter. Some thoughts on cultural responsibility are given in the section on the Kipengere Range, towards the end of the Tanzania chapter. Further to this, a British organisation called Tourism Concern has come up with several guidelines for travellers who wish to minimise negative impacts on the countries they visit. These include:

- Save precious natural resources. Try not to waste water. Switch off lights and air-conditioning when you go out. Avoid establishments which clearly consume limited resources such as water and electricity at the expense of local residents.
- Support local enterprise. Use locally owned hotels and restaurants and support trade and craft workers by buying locally made souvenirs. But do help safeguard the environment by avoiding souvenirs made from local wildlife – ivory, fur, skins etc – particularly endangered species.
- Recognise land rights. Indigenous people's ownership of land they use and occupy is recognised by international law. This should be acknowledged irrespective of whether the national government applies the law or not. (Governments are among the principal violators of tribal rights.) When in tribal lands tourists should behave as they would on private lands at home.
- Ask before taking close-up photographs of people. Don't worry if you don't speak the language. A smile and gesture will be understood and appreciated.
- Please don't give money, sweets, pens etc to children. It encourages begging and demeans the child.

A donation to a recognised project – a health centre or school – is a more constructive and meaningful way to help.
- Respect for local etiquette earns you respect. Politeness is a virtue in most parts of the world, but remember that different people have different ideas about what's polite. In many places, tight fitting clothes, revealing shorts or skimpy tops are insensitive to local feelings. Loose lightweight clothing is preferable. Similarly, public displays of affection are often culturally inappropriate.
- Learning something about the history and current affairs of a country helps you understand the idiosyncrasies of its people, and helps prevent misunderstandings and frustrations.
- Be patient, friendly and sensitive. Remember that you are a guest.

Tourism Concern (☎ (0171) 753 3330; fax 753 3331; email tourconcern@gn.apc.org), Stapleton House, 277-281 Holloway Rd, London N7 8HN, is a membership organisation. If you want to support its work, it costs UK£18 per year to join. In the USA, the Centre for Responsible Tourism (☎ (415) 258 6594; fax 454 2493), Box 827 San Anselmo CA 94979, is similar.

PEOPLE

The modern states of East Africa are all less than a century old and the concept of 'nation' is still fairly new. For many African people, it is easier to identify with other members of the same tribe than with people of the same nationality. (For more comments on the term 'tribe' see the boxed text below.)

You might notice that tribes or groups of people have different names. The Kikuyu and Shambala, for example, may be referred to as Wakikuyu and Washambala. The 'Wa' prefix implies 'people' in some African languages. Similarly, the prefix for language is 'Ki', hence Kiswahili, the language of the Swahili people. When writing in English, these prefixes are usually dropped and, generally, they have not been used in this book.

The peoples of Africa are usually classified according to their main language group, of which there are four in East Africa. These are Bantu, Nilotic, Cushitic and Khoisan. (You'll also find terms like Semitic, Hamitic or even Nilo-hamitic, although these aren't

---

Tribes in East Africa

The word 'tribe' opens a real can of worms. It is commonly used when discussing different groups of people in Africa but it is vague and some Europeans are embarrassed to use it, especially as, for them, it can have slightly negative implications: 'tribalism', for example, is always regarded as a bad thing. Anthropologists favour the term 'ethnic group', but this is equally vague, and is used by different writers to categorise people in confusingly broad or narrow bands. Other words that are sometimes used are 'race', 'clan' and even 'caste', all correct in some contexts but all adding to the general confusion. The word 'people', used in its singular context, for example 'the Maasai people', is 'safe' but sometimes clumsy. It is interesting to note that most Africans use the word 'tribe' without any embarrassment. The best thing is to use whatever term seems suitable, but just be aware of the differences and implications. ■

---

used much these days.) In Kenya there are people of all four groups; most are Bantu, but there are large groups of Nilotic and Cushitic origin. In Tanzania, Uganda and Malawi, Bantu groups are even more predominant.

More information about specific groups, their cultures and traditions, are given in the individual country chapters.

SOCIETY & CONDUCT

As in any part of the world, the best way to learn about a society's conduct is to watch or listen to the locals. The first thing to remember is not to worry: Africans are generally very easy-going towards foreigners, and any social errors that you might make are unlikely to cause offence (although they may cause confusion or merriment). Having said that, there are a few things that are frowned upon pretty much wherever you go in East Africa. These include: public nudity, open displays of anger, open displays of affection (among people of the same or opposite sex), and criticism of the government or country.

On top of these basics, a few straightforward courtesies may greatly improve your chances of acceptance by the local community, especially in rural areas. Pleasantries are taken quite seriously, and it's essential to greet someone entering or leaving a room. Learn a few local words, such as 'hello', 'how are things?', 'fine' and 'goodbye' and use them unsparingly. (Try and get beyond *Jambo*, which Africans themselves rarely use.) For those out of earshot, offer a smile and a

pleasant wave, even if you're just passing in a vehicle.

Great emphasis is also placed on handshakes. There are various local variations, involving linked thumbs or fingers, or the left hand touching the right elbow, which you'll pick up by observation, but these are reserved for informal occasions (not greeting officials). A 'normal' western handshake will do fine in most situations. Sometimes, people who know each other continue to hold hands right through their conversation, or at least for a few minutes.

As in most traditional societies, older people are treated with deference. Teachers, doctors and other professionals (usually men) often receive similar treatment. Likewise, people holding positions of authority – police, immigration officers and so on – should be dealt with pragmatically. In most of the countries in this book officials are normally courteous and fairly efficient, sometimes even friendly. On your side, manners, patience and cooperation will get you through most situations. Even if you meet somebody awkward, the same rules apply. It is one thing to stand up for your rights but undermining an official's authority may only serve to waste time, tie you up in red tape and inspire closer scrutiny of future travellers.

At the other end of the spectrum, children rate very low on the social scale. They are expected to do as they're told without complaint and defer to adults in all situations. Unfortunately for half the region's population, the status of women is only slightly

higher. For example an African man on a bus might give his seat to an older man, but not normally to a woman, never mind that she is carrying a baby and luggage and minding two toddlers. In most areas, women are expected to dress and behave modestly, especially in the presence of chiefs or other esteemed persons. Visitors should act in the same way.

If you're trekking through rural inhabited areas, it is a good idea to request the chief's permission before setting up camp or wandering around a village. You will rarely be refused. In such situations, local guides are particularly useful, as they can advise on necessary protocol. Visitors should also ask permission before drawing water from a community well. Avoid letting water spill on the ground, especially in desert areas. If you want to wash your body or your clothing, fill a container with water and carry it elsewhere.

Most travellers will have the opportunity to share an African meal sometime during their stay. Although concessions are sometimes made for foreigners, table manners are probably different from what you're accustomed to. Before eating, a member of the family may pass round a bowl of water, or jug and bowl, for washing hands. If it comes to you first as honoured guest and you're not sure of the routine, indicate that the bowl should be taken to the head of the family, then do what they do when it comes to you.

The African staple, *ugali* (maize meal), is the centre of nearly every meal. It is normally taken with the right hand from a communal pot, rolled into balls, dipped in some sort of sauce – meat gravy or vegetables – and eaten. As in most societies, it is considered impolite to scoff food; if you do, your hosts may feel that they haven't provided enough. In fact, for the same reason, it may be polite *not* to be the one who takes the last handful from the communal bowl. If your food is served on separate plates, and you can't finish your food, don't worry; again this shows your hosts that you have been satisfied. Often, containers of water or home-brew beer may be passed around from person to person. However, it is not customary to share coffee, tea or bottled soft drinks.

If you do visit a remote community, please 'tread lightly' and leave as little lasting evidence of your visit as possible. In some African societies, it isn't considered impolite for people to ask others for items they may desire; but likewise it isn't rude to refuse. So if a local asks for your watch or camera, say 'no' politely, explaining it's the only one you've got, and all will be fine. If you start feeling guilty about your relative wealth and hand out all your belongings, you may be regarded as strange. Reciprocation of kindness is OK but indiscriminate distribution of gifts from outside, however well intentioned, tends to create a taste for items not locally available, erodes well-established values, robs people of their pride and, in extreme cases, creates villages of dependent beggars.

On the other hand, when you're offered a gift, don't feel guilty about accepting it; to refuse it would bring shame on the giver. To politely receive a gift, local people may accept it with both hands and perhaps bow slightly, or they may receive it with the right hand while touching the left hand to your right elbow; this is the equivalent of saying 'thanks'. You can try this if you think it's appropriate. Spoken thanks aren't common and local people tend to think westerners say 'thank you' too often and too casually, so don't be upset if you aren't verbally thanked for a gift.

Dress Codes

None of the countries in the region included in this book have any specific regulations regarding clothing or behaviour. Malawi used to be a celebrated exception, because women visitors were required by law to wear skirts that covered the knees, while men were required to have short hair and tidy beards. The reason for this was partly because many women travellers used to tour Malawi wearing shorts, which offended the locals (men and women), particularly in the mainly Muslim north, but also in the centre and south where people are pretty conservative. The law was dropped in 1994 and you are now allowed to wear what you like, although it's still pretty insensitive to wander around with most of your legs

showing (although this is no problem on the lake beaches or for trekking).

For women, the same applies in most other countries in the region. Apart from the disrespect you are showing to local sensibilities, you also make things harder for yourself – don't be surprised if kids laugh, adults (men and women) treat you disdainfully, and some young guns see you as easy prey. From a practical point of view, keeping reasonably covered with loose-fitting clothes also helps prevent sunstroke.

What you wear is also important for men. Look around you: the only people wearing shorts or tatty clothes are kids, labourers or the poor. Then ask yourself why some officials and other locals treat bare-legged travellers with contempt.

Photographs

Before you take someone's photo, ask them for permission. It's a simple matter of manners. Think how you would feel if complete strangers constantly invaded your personal privacy in this way. Some people may ask you for money before posing. This is fair enough – most people, particularly in poor areas, must take any chance they get of earning a buck. If you don't like the idea, don't pay and don't take the photo.

Meeting the People

Most of the treks described in this book are through wilderness areas, which are either uninhabited or sparsely populated, but several routes pass villages and farmland on the mountains' lower slopes and others go through populated areas for the whole trek.

One of the rewards of trekking in East Africa is having the chance to meet the locals face to face, having time to stop and talk (or nod and smile across the language barrier), and to see them as real people rather than as colourful extras in a movie-set backdrop.

If you're trekking with a local guide through a populated area, you will often feel less of a stranger. Your guide can also help with introductions and translations, and this is a much more interesting way to learn about other peoples' culture and way of life than ploughing through a stodgy textbook.

Have respect for the people you meet. In some areas, very short trousers, particularly on women, will create embarrassment. It's like walking down your own main street in your underwear. There's no need for full body cover, but just be aware of local sensitivities. In this way, local people will find it much easier to accept and talk to you. Open displays of affection are also frowned upon, although you're unlikely to start necking with your partner halfway up a mountain path! ■

DAWN DELANEY

LANGUAGE

Within East Africa there are several hundred distinct languages or dialects. The common language used throughout the region is Swahili (or *Kiswahili* when you're speaking the language), originally developed by traders on the coast. Over the centuries, especially in the coastal region, it developed into a rich language, lending itself particularly to poetry. Zanzibar is today regarded as the home of Swahili, where the language is purest. Although it is derived from Arabic and various Bantu languages, Swahili also has many words of Indian, Portuguese and English origin.

Swahili is widely spoken in Kenya and Tanzania. As you get further away from the coast the language becomes more basic, with a lot more English words. (While stuck on a broken-down bus once, I heard the driver describe the problem as 'Breaki pipi faili'.) In Uganda, Swahili is not used as much and in Malawi it is hardly used at all; English is the common language. The national papers of both these countries are printed in English, and very little published work is available in local languages.

English is also widely spoken throughout Kenya and Tanzania, especially in towns and tourist areas, and by educated people. English is taught in all schools in Uganda, Tanzania, Kenya and Malawi. In Kenya there are more books and newspapers available in English than there are in Swahili.

Swahili for Trekkers

A small grasp of Swahili is particularly useful when you're trekking in fairly remote areas, or if you want to do more than just nod at your porters on Kilimanjaro and the other high mountains. The best way to learn more is to start talking. Most people will always be happy to teach you more words or explain their proper uses.

Generally, Swahili is a straightforward language with regular rules and pronunciation. It can be slightly confusing for beginners as most words have prefixes, as well as suffixes, which change according to context. Fortunately, you can often ignore these rules and still be understood, especially in 'up-country' areas where the local people use Swahili as a second or third language and probably speak it almost as badly as you. The most common word suffixes are included in this section.

The words listed here will help you survive in the hills. If you want to do more than just get by, there are several phrasebooks available. Lonely Planet's *Swahili Phrasebook* is probably the most accessible and the easiest to carry in your rucksack.

Greetings & Civilities

Hello.	*Jambo.*
Hello (Can I come in)?	*Hodi?*
Welcome (come inside).	*Karibu.*
Thankyou.	*Asante (sana).*
Thank you very much.	*Asante sana.*
How are things?	*Habari?*
Fine.	*Mzuri.*
Very fine.	*Mzuri sana.*
Completely fine.	*Mzuri kabisa.*
OK.	*Sawa sawa.*
Not bad.	*Si mbaya.*
Greetings.	*Salama salama.*
Good night.	*Lala salama.*
Yes.	*Ndiyo.*
No.	*Hapana.*
Sorry.	*Pole.*
No problem.	*Hakuna matata.*
Please..	*Tefadhali.* (not used much)
Goodbye.	*Kwaheri.*
Have a good journey.	*Safiri salama.*

Features

mountain	*mlima*
hill	*kilima/mlima kidogo*
col/pass/ small valley	*bonde*
summit/top	*kilele*
lake	*nyanza/ziwa*
pond/tarn	*nyanza/ziwa kidogo*
river	*mto*

stream	*kijito*
stone/rock	*jiwe*
road/street	*barabara*
dirt road	*barabara ya mchanga*
path/track	*njia*
track for cars	*njia ya ghari*
track for walking	*njia ya miguu*
short-cut	*njia ya mkato/ shortikuti*
village	*kijiji* (or 'centre')
field/farm	*shamba*
hut	*chuba*
house	*nyumba*
compound	*boma* (*manyatta* in Samburu and Maasai areas)
shop	*duka*
lodging	*nyumba ya kulala*
toilet	*choo*
water	*maji*
food	*chakula*
donkey	*punda*
firewood	*kuni*
white person/white people	*mzungu/wazungu*
journey	*safari*
traveller/s	*msafiri/wasafiri*
guest/s, visitors/s	*mgeni/wageni*

Directions

Let's go.	*Twende.*
now	*sasa*
early	*mapema*
late	*chelewa*
stop	*simama*
wait	*ngoja*
wait a bit	*ngoja kidogo*
quickly	*haraka*
slowly	*pole pole*
straight on	*moja kwa moja*
here	*hapa*
there	*hapo*
there isn't	*hakuna*
left	*kushoto*
right	*kulia*
middle	*kati*
between	*kati kati*
up/high	*juu*
down/low	*chini*

more/again/another	*ingine*
north	*kaskazini/si kasini*
south	*kusini*
west	*magaribi*
east	*mashariki*

(The last four terms can cause confusion, so use as a general direction, not for precise compass bearings.)

Weather

rain	*mvua*
snow	*theruji*
hail/ice	*barafu*
cloud	*mawingu*
mist/fog	*ukunga*
wind	*upepo*
storm	*dhoruba*
hot sun/outdoors	*jua kali*

Adjectives

cold	*baridi*
warm	*moto*
hot	*moto sana*
good	*mzuri*
bad	*mbaya*
big	*kubwa*
small	*kidogo*
easy	*rahisi*
hard	*ngumu*
strong	*dhabiti*
tired	*choka*
heavy	*nzito*
happy	*furaha*
unhappy	*kihoro/huzuni*
expensive	*ghali*
cheap	*rahisi*
hungry	*njaa*
thirsty	*kiu*
many	*mingi*

Pronouns

me	*mimi*
you	*wewe*
him/her	*yeye*
us	*sisi*
you	*nyinyi*
them	*wao*

Questions

How much/many?	*Ngapi?*
Where?	*Wapi?*
Is there?	*Iko?*
What?	*Nini?*
When?	*Lini?*
Why?	*Kwa-nini?*

Dangers & Difficulties

Help!	*Saidia!*
help	*usaidizi*
danger	*hatari*
ill/sick	*mgonjwa*
very ill/sick	*mgonjwa sana*
medicine	*dawa*
chemist	*duka ya dawa*
doctor	*daktari*
problem	*matata*
police	*polisi*
buffalo	*nyati*
lion	*simba*
crocodile	*mamba*
snake	*nyoka*
insect	*dudu*

Numbers

0.5	*nusu*
1	*moja*
2	*mbili*
3	*tatu*
4	*nne*
5	*tano*
6	*sita*
7	*saba*
8	*nane*
9	*tisa*
10	*kumi*
11	*kumi na moja*
12	*kumi na mbili*
20	*ishirini*
30	*thelathini*
40	*arobaini*
50	*hamsini*
60	*sitini*
70	*sabini*
80	*themanini*
90	*tisini*
100	*mia moja*
200	*mia mbili*
1000	*elfu moja*

Time

Swahili time, sensibly, starts at dawn (6 am), so 7 am is *saa moja* (literally hour one), even though it's usually written 7 am, but it can lead to all sorts of confusion when finding out what time buses leave, or arranging to meet porters. Double check everything.

one o'clock (hour seven)	*saa saba*
two o'clock (hour eight)	*saa nane*
six o'clock (hour twelve)	*saa kumi na mbili*
daytime	*mchana*
night-time	*usiku*
dawn	*alfajiri*
morning	*asubuhi*
afternoon	*alasiri*
evening	*jioni*
today	*leo*
tomorrow	*kesho*
yesterday	*jana*
this/last/next week	*hii/lililopita/lijayo*
	juma/wiki

Monday	*Jumatatu*
Tuesday	*Jumanne*
Wednesday	*Jumatano*
Thursday	*Alhamisi*
Friday	*Ijumaa*
Saturday	*Jumamosi*
Sunday	*Jumapili*

Useful Phrases

Where are you going?	*Unakwenda wapi?*
I am going to Namanga.	*Ninakwenda/Nenda Namanga.*
I came from Nairobi today.	*Nina toka Nairobi leo.*
Where are you from?	*Unatoka wapi?*
I come from (England/America).	*Nina toka (England/America).* (countries have proper Swahili forms but this will be understood)

What is your name?	*Jina lako nani?*
My name is ...	*Jina langu ni .../ Mimi ninaitwa ...*
I don't speak/ understand Swahili.	*Sijui Kiswahili.*
I only speak a little Swahili.	*Nazungumza Kiswahili kidogo tu.*
I am lost.	*Nimepotea.*
Please help me.	*Tafadhali nisaidie.*
Can I find/hire a guide?	*Naweza kupata msaidizi?*
Can you show me the way to ... ?	*Unaweza kunionyesha njia ya kenda ...?*
I will pay you.	*Nita kulipa.*
How much?	*Pesa ngapi bei gani/ Shilling ngapi bei gani?*
What time is it?	*Saa ngapi?*
How many hours to ...?	*Masaa mangapi ...?*
Can I pass this way?	*Naweza kupita njia hii?*
Can I sleep here?	*Naweza kulala hapa?*
Is the water good to drink?	*Maji haya nisafi ya kunywa?*
Is there a shop in the village?	*Kuna duka hapa kijijini?*
Can I buy food?	*Naweza kununua chakula?*
Is there food here/there?	*Iko chakula hapa/ hapo?*
I want to walk to ...	*Nataka kutembea hadi ...*
Where does this path go to?	*Njia hii inaenda wapi/Njia nenda wapi?*
I will come back tomorrow/on Friday/next year.	*Nitarudi kesho/ ijumaa/mwaka ujao.*

In Kenya and Tanzania, the following Swahili/ African words are commonly used and generally not translated:

askari	security guard
banda	cabin/bungalow
boma	compound
drift	dry river bed
duka	small shop
fundi	expert/repairer/ mechanic
lugga	dry river bed (northern Kenya)
manyatta	compound (Samburu/Maasai)
matatu	minibus
moran	warrior (Samburu/ Maasai)
mzee	old man
panga	machete
shamba	field/small farm
soda	any bottled fizzy drink
hoteli	small teashop

(a small hotel is usually called a lodging *'nyumba ya kulala'*, or boarding & lodging, or simply B & L)

The following Alpine/English mountain terms are also commonly used:

cairn	pile of stones for waymarking
col	pass/low point between hills
gendarme	pinnacle
tarn	small mountain lake/pool
scree	loose stones
snout	lower end of a glacier
crevasse	deep fissure in a glacier
kop/inselberg	isolated rocky hill rising from a plain

You will also hear the term 'game' being used for large wildlife, even though in the walking areas animals are not hunted for sport. The term 'soda', as in soda lake, means saline. A murram road is a graded dirt road.

Flora & Fauna of East African Mountains

FLORA

As altitude influences the climate of the East African mountains, so it also has a great effect on the vegetation. The vegetation in turn determines which birds and other animals are found in these areas, and these are discussed in the Fauna section following.

Vegetation Zones

The major mountains of East Africa generally stand as isolated peaks or ranges above the plains, and the various types of vegetation occur very broadly as concentric zones, separated one from the other according to altitude. Generally, the lower slopes are wet and warm, with luxurious growth and many different species. Higher up the mountain, the climate becomes colder and drier (except in the Rwenzoris where it becomes colder and wetter), with increasingly extreme variations between day and night temperatures, and the vegetation becomes less diverse and more specialised.

These zones of vegetation occur in a similar pattern on all the major mountains of East Africa, although their width and density, and the range of species they contain, varies considerably between mountains and even between areas on the same mountain. For example, species more normally found on the lower slopes can grow higher up the mountain in sheltered valleys, while highland plants may be found on exposed ridges further down.

The flora of the East African mountains is very rich, and many species are unique to the region. In this section, only the common species, which you're more likely to see and easily recognise, are described. The common English names have been used for the plants, with their genus name in italics (sometimes this is the same).

The vegetation of Mt Kenya contains characteristics of all the major mountains, so its patterns are described in detail here by way of example. Some other mountains of East Africa are then described more briefly, noting the similarities and differences between them and Mt Kenya. (Throughout this section, altitudes are approximate.)

Mt Kenya

Lower Montane Forest Much of the land around the lower slopes of the mountains has been cleared and farmed, but where the natural vegetation remains, above 2000m, it is usually dense montane forest, containing many large trees including the **East African camphor** *(Octea)*, a tall species, often buttressed and with a dark-red, fluted trunk. Lower montane forest grows particularly on the wet southern and eastern slopes of Mt Kenya, where it forms a dense barrier, so there are no regularly used trekking routes on this side of the mountain.

DAVID ELSE

Plants growing in the high-altitude zones of Mt Kenya and the other high peaks of East Africa must cope with exposure to extreme climatic conditions on a daily basis.

Upper Montane Forest On the drier northern slopes the trees are still large, although their canopy is less dense. This zone is called upper montane forest. The main trees here are the **East African yellowwood** or 'podo' *(Podocarpus)*, and the juniper or **African pencil cedar** *(Juniperus)*. Both these trees are very tall, with straight trunks, although the bark on the juniper is pale brown and the branches grow much lower down the main trunk. The bark on the podo is pale grey and very rough. To further help identification, juniper leaves are triangular, whereas podo leaves are long and narrow.

Also in this zone you may see shorter trees, such as the **East African olive** *(Olea)*, with smooth pale-grey bark and a dense canopy of olive-green leaves, and **pillar wood** *(Cassipourea)*, about the same size as the olive, but with a straighter trunk, lined bark and darker leaves.

In high or low montane forests, you may also see the **Nuxia** tree, with stumpy trunk, crooked branches and a bushy canopy of green leaves and white flowers, or the many-tentacled **strangler fig** *(Ficus)* growing round one of the other trees.

Another feature of the upper montane forest is the great range of lichens, mosses and ferns that grow on the trees. The most obvious is *Usnea*, known more appropriately as **'old man's beard'**.

Bamboo At around 2500m the forest gives way to the bamboo zone. This is much denser on the wet southern slopes, and almost non-existent on the drier north side. Some bamboo trunks are very thick; the plants can grow

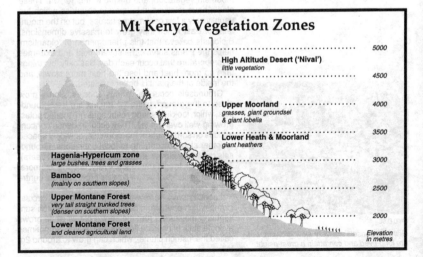

Mt Kenya Vegetation Zones

High Altitude Desert ('Nival')
little vegetation — 5000 / 4500

Upper Moorland
grasses, giant groundsel & giant lobelia — 4000

Lower Heath & Moorland
giant heathers — 3500

Hagenia-Hypericum zone
large bushes, trees and grasses — 3000

Bamboo
(mainly on southern slopes) — 2500

Upper Montane Forest
very tall straight trunked trees (denser on southern slopes)

Lower Montane Forest
and cleared agricultural land — 2000

Elevation in metres

PETER ROBINSON

Several species of 'everlasting' flower (Helichrysum) are found on East African mountains.

to heights of over 15m. Bamboo grows very quickly and can colonise areas where the original vegetation has been destroyed. It is also very hard (or impossible) to walk through, unless you're on a cut path.

Hagenia-Hypericum Beyond the bamboo, at about 2900m, is a small zone of **East African rosewood** *(Hagenia)*, trees about 12m high with red bark, crooked branches and huge clusters of leaves, and **Giant St John's Wort** *(Hypericum)*, a large bush around 10m high, with long, thin stalks and leaves, and bright orange flowers. These plants are usually well spaced, with grass in between, creating open 'glades'.

Heath & Moorland Above 3200m, trees can no longer grow, and the main plants are the **giant heathers** *(Erica* and *Philippia)*, which are similar in appearance to the heather in temperate countries, except that some species grow over 10m high. In the lower part of this zone, you'll also see **protea** bushes, about 2m high with large red flowers. Also occurring in this zone is the red **Mackinder's lily**.

In the upper moorland, grass is the dominant vegetation, growing in humps or tussocks about half a metre high, which can make moorland walking very tiring! Also in this zone are the dry, delicate **'everlasting' flowers** *(Helichrysum)*, of which there are several species, varying in size and colour.

The plants that dominate the upper moorland zone are the **giant groundsel** *(Senecio)* and the **giant lobelia** *(Lobelia)*, growing between the tussock grass above 3500m. These are the classic symbols of African mountain vegetation, and unique to this region. These plants have relatives in temperate countries which are usually only a few centimetres across, but on the mountains of East Africa they grow to massive dimensions. Biologists believe that this phenomenon of 'gigantism' helps the plants survive the severe cold and extremes of temperature that occur each day. Basically, big things take up more heat and lose the heat more slowly, and the inside of the plant is better insulated.

Groundsels occur as various species. Some grow close to the ground, while the largest are tree-groundsels, which look like shaggy cabbages on gnarled poles, growing well over 5m tall. They occur in dense concentrations on some parts of the mountain, or widely spaced on other slopes according to local conditions. Groundsels grow very slowly and up to a great age (120 years). They flower irregularly, once every decade or more, when large stalks of yellow flowers grow from the centre of the 'cabbage'.

Lobelias have narrower, firmer leaves, in a circular clump which opens and closes every day to catch sunlight and moisture. From the centre of this circle grows a single stalk of delicate flowers and leaves, sometimes called the 'ostrich plume', which can grow to around 2m tall.

DAVID ELSE

Giant groundsels are very slow growing, but are long-lived and can attain a great height.

Also in this zone you may find **lady's mantle** (*Alchemila*), a low plant with narrow stems and small pale green leaves, growing between the groundsels.

High Altitude Desert As you gain height, the grass becomes thinner, and the groundsels become smaller, until about 4300m, where you get above most of the vegetation and reach the zone called high altitude desert, or 'nival'. The only thing that grows here is bright orange lichen, or maybe a 'lost' groundsel or everlasting in the more sheltered spots between the rocks.

Kilimanjaro

The distinction between the vegetation bands is clearer on Kilimanjaro than on Mt Kenya, as there are fewer valleys on the upper slopes of the mountain, so intermixing is limited. There are also fewer bands, as Kili has no significant bamboo forest, and no *Hagenia-Hypericum* zone.

Kilimanjaro receives less rain than Mt Kenya and the ground is also drier, as the lava rock is very porous. Consequently, the montane forest contains many of the trees found on the dry slopes on Mt Kenya, and the treeline is lower, with the forest giving way abruptly to heath at about 3000m.

The very extensive zone of giant heathers and moorland spreads up to about 3800m. Giant groundsels and lobelias occur in this zone, although not in such large numbers as on Mt Kenya.

The vegetation thins out almost completely above 4000m, apart from a few deep valleys. Above this level is Kilimanjaro's high altitude desert zone, which is similar to Mt Kenya's but much larger.

Rwenzori Range

The major feature of the Rwenzoris is the very wet climate. Even when it's not raining, the mountains are continually covered in mist and cloud. But this cloud acts like a blanket and the temperature variations between day and night are less pronounced on the Rwenzoris than on Mt Kenya or on Kilimanjaro.

Also, the range's many deep valleys provide shelter. Consequently, growth is very luxuriant and the vegetation zones generally extend to higher altitudes, although the valleys create a lot of intermixing.

The montane forest and bamboo extend up to 3500m. There is no distinct *Hagenia-Hypericum* zone, although both species occur. Beyond the forest, the heath and moorland zone extends to about 4200m, and the giant heather, giant groundsels and giant lobelias here are even bigger than on other mountains. There are small nival zones above 4200m on the range's several peaks.

Flora on Other Mountains

The other large mountains of East Africa generally share the characteristic zonal vegetation pattern of the major

DAVID ELSE

The distinctive giant lobelia flowers only once in its life, developing a spectacular floral plume.

Black & white colobus monkeys are usually found in troops of up to 12 animals. They are black, with a white face, tail, and a 'cape' around the back which flows out behind when the monkey swings through the trees.

Hyrax are extremely sociable animals, living in colonies of up to 60 individuals. They feed mostly in the morning and evening on grass, bulbs and roots, and on insects such as grasshoppers and locusts. Surprisingly, hyrax are more closely related to the elephant than any other living creature.

mountains. On Mt Elgon and the Aberdare Range, the montane forest and bamboo extend to about 3000m, with small areas of *Hagenia*, and zones of heath and moorland continue to the summits. These mountains are too wet and low to have nival zones.

Several unique plant species occur on these mountains: Mt Elgon has particularly tall podo and olive trees in the forest zone, and its own species of lobelia in the moorland. The Aberdare Range has a subspecies of lobelia *(L. deckenii satimae)*, which is even more localised, being found only on the slopes below Satima, the summit peak.

Mt Meru is similar in height to Mt Elgon and the Aberdares, but much drier. The montane forest contains similar species to those of Kilimanjaro and the northern slopes of Mt Kenya up to about 2800m, plus areas of giant St John's wort and *Hagenia* up to 3000m. The heath zone extends to 3500m and there are a few groundsels in the very small moorland, but beyond 3600m, the mountain consists of bare rock.

FAUNA

Mammals

The broad range of vegetation types on the East African mountains creates a similarly broad range of wildlife habitats. Most mammal species occur in the forests, as animals depend on plants for food. As the vegetation decreases with altitude, and conditions become increasingly harsh, so animals become more scarce. Even though East Africa is famous for its wildlife, generally you won't see much while trekking on the mountains. Most mammals will run away long before you even know they were there.

The forested lower slopes of most of the major mountains are inhabited by **elephant** and **buffalo**, but these are unlikely to be seen. (Mt Meru is an exception, as you will almost certainly see **buffalo**, **giraffe** and **zebra** here.) There may still be a few **rhino** hiding deep in the forests, but sightings are extremely rare. You're more likely to see **waterbuck**, **bushbuck**, **duiker** (all types of antelope), **giant forest hog**, **bush pig**, or **forest warthog**, but you'll still have to be lucky. Most forests also have **squirrel** populations, but even these animals are quite shy.

The large mammals you've got most chance of seeing are monkeys. The distinctive **black & white colobus monkey**, with shaggy coat and brush-like tail, occurs in many of the mountains. You may also see **vervet monkey** (mainly grey, with a black face and distinctive blue genitalia), in the forest and bamboo of Mt Kenya, or **blue monkey** (mainly dark, with short fur and a long thin tail) on Kilimanjaro. On Mt Meru and Kilimanjaro groups of **baboon** are often seen, and the Rwenzoris also have small populations of **chimpanzee**, although these are very rarely sighted.

Higher up, on the moorland zones of most of the

major mountains, and particularly on the Aberdare (Nyandarua) Range, there are **leopard** and **hyena**, and even **lion**, but these are very rarely seen, although you might notice footprints and droppings. On rocky outcrops you're more likely to see the small **klipspringer**, with its distinctive 'tip-toe' hooves.

One moorland area where you have a very good chance of seeing several types of large mammal is the Nyika Plateau in Malawi. Animals occurring here include **roan antelope**, **reedbuck**, **warthog** and **zebra**. There's also a good possibility of seeing **jackal** and even **leopard**. This is an excellent area for walking safely among wildlife.

The most common animal on the upper forests and moorland of most East African mountains is the **hyrax**, a rodent-like animal about the size of a rabbit, a close relative of the **rock hyrax** (dassie) found at lower altitudes. There are also several different kinds of **rat** and **shrew** in this zone.

Standing about 50cm at the shoulder, klip-springer are easily recognised by their 'tip-toe' stance (the hooves are designed for balance and grip on rocky surfaces) and the greenish tinge of their speckled coarse hair.

Above the vegetation line, mammals of any kind are very rarely encountered. However, Kilimanjaro has at least one herd of **eland** (large, spiral-horned antelope), sometimes seen on the sandy plateau of The Saddle (although more often on the Shira Plateau), and Leopard Point on Kibo is named after a leopard that was found frozen in a block of ice here. A pack of **wild dogs** (also called African hunting dogs) were also once recorded crossing the glacier at about the same altitude.

On Mt Meru there's a pile of rhino bones above the moorland, which may indicate one of these great beasts had wandered far from its normal habitat, and there used to be the skeleton of an elephant, nicknamed Icy Mike, just below the peaks of Terere and Sendeo on Mt Kenya. More recently, in 1996, a trekking group found the dried skin and bones of a buffalo high on the north side of Kilimanjaro, once again far beyond its normal habitat; it had probably wandered up from the forest and got stuck in a cave searching for natural salts to lick. During your trek, guides and porters may tell you other stories about legendary non-human mountain ascents.

Birds

You are much more likely to see birds than other animals during your trek. Almost 1500 bird species occur in the East African region (for birding purposes this includes Ethiopia but not Malawi, and the number increases further when Malawi's species are added). Over 1000 bird species have been recorded in Kenya alone, and about the same in Uganda (which is half Kenya's size), but once you get beyond the forest zones the high mountains are not noted for their abundant avifauna. However, there are several common, easily recognised species, which will enhance a trek for beginners and 'twitchers' alike.

The eastern mountains (Kilimanjaro, Mt Kenya, Mt Meru and the Aberdare Range) share many common species and there is considerable overlap with the birds

Eland are the biggest of the East African antelope being about 170cm high at the shoulder. They are usually found in groups of around six to 12, but there may be as many as 50 in a herd.

The common bulbul is one of the most abundant of African birds. It inhabits open forest, woodland and areas of human habitation, feeding on fruits and insects.

The malachite sunbird with its distinctive emerald green colouring can be seen throughout the highlands of East Africa, feeding from proteas, lobelias and other flowering plants.

of Mt Elgon and the Rwenzoris, although these have several western African species not found elsewhere. Similarly, on the mountains of Malawi there are several southern African species particular to that region. (These are covered in the Malawi chapter.)

Each mountain has its own local species, and keen birdwatchers should invest in a good field guide which covers all the areas in detail. There are various types of lightweight binoculars which can be easily carried and which further help with species identification.

Birds regularly seen in the eastern mountain forests include the **common bulbul** (mainly brown with a broad tail and yellow rump), the **white-browed robin-chat** (grey upper body, orange chest, and black and white head) and the **speckled mousebird** (short bill, tuft on head and a long tail giving it a mouse-like appearance).

Higher up, you may also see the **silvery-cheeked hornbill** (a large black bird with a ridge across the top of its bill) and possibly a **Hartlaub's turaco** (mainly green with red underwings and a cry very similar to the colobus monkey's). Different species of turaco are seen on various mountains. **Olive doves** (small pigeons) are very common.

In the moorland you might see the **hill chat** (short, brown with white stripes on the tail) or the **scaly francolin** (a brown, grouse-like bird). A beautiful bird often seen on the high moorland is the **malachite sunbird** (vivid green, small and slender with a fairly long tail and long curving bill) often seen feeding on lobelias. Lower down you'll see the **regal sunbird**, similar in shape with a shorter tail and red and yellow chest.

Around huts and camp sites you'll see the **white-necked raven** (like a large crow) usually scavenging in the rubbish pit. On the bare rocky areas of the high mountains, birds of prey are seen. The most common is the **augur buzzard** (usually grey, with a fairly short reddish tail) and the **Verreaux's eagle** (larger and mainly black, with a white back and rump).

WILDLIFE & WALKING SAFARIS

Because the mountain areas are not noted for their wildlife populations, many visitors to East Africa combine a trek with a safari to a lower savanna area, where the 'classic' African animals (lion, leopard, elephant, wildebeest etc) are more readily seen. This is most often done in a vehicle (overland truck, minibus or Land Rover) but walking safaris are becoming increasingly popular. Options for this type of safari are outlined in the individual country chapters.

FIELD GUIDES

Birds

To help recognise the birds you see while trekking a field guide is almost essential. The long-standing *Birds of East Africa* by Williams & Arlott (published by Collins) has over 650 species illustrated in colour, covering Kenya, Uganda, Tanzania, Malawi, Ethiopia and several other countries. The style of the book is noticeably dated (it was last revised in 1980) and the further you get from Kenya the less likely the birds you see will be illustrated.

Also Kenya-biased (but at least this is clear by the title) is the recently published (1996) and already highly respected *Birds of Kenya & Northern Tanzania* by Zimmerman, Turner & Pearson, with exquisite illustrations and comprehensive descriptions of over 1100 birds; but this US$60 hardback is no featherweight and not really suitable as a field guide for trekkers.

By far the most useful book for trekkers requiring light but complete coverage is the *Illustrated Checklist of the Birds of Eastern Africa* by Ber van Perlo (Collins). The title says it all; a colour picture of every bird in the region (that's almost 1500), with brief notes on call, size, habitat, distribution, density and distinguishing features, plus non-technical and informative introductory sections. If you prefer less comprehensive coverage, the *Common Birds of East Africa* by Withers & Hosking has photos and brief descriptions of 360 readily seen and identified species.

Mammals

If you're combining trekking on the high mountains with a safari by foot or car in the wildlife areas, then a mammal guide will also help you get much more out of your visit. Once again, Collins has published the classic volume, *A Field Guide to the Mammals of Africa* by Haltenorth & Diller, but once again it now looks a little dated. For keen animal watchers, the recently published (1997) *Kingdon Field Guide to African Mammals* by Jonathan Kingdon is highly regarded by naturalists. The author is a leading authority, and the book covers over 1000 species, discussing ecology, evolutionary relationships and conservation status as well as the more usual notes on identification and distribution, with colour pictures and maps throughout. Also good for a deeper insight is *The Safari Companion* by Richard Estes: a marvellous book for understanding animals – why they behave as they do, their courtship rituals, territorial displays and so on.

If your interest is of a more casual nature, the Collins Safari Guide *Larger Animals of East Africa* by Hosking & Withers is ideal: slim and portable, with large colour photos and non-technical information on over 70 of the more common species; handy for quick-reference and enough to inform and enlighten keen amateurs.

Flowers

If you need more detail on local plant life, *A Field Guide to the Wild Flowers of East Africa* by Blundell is recommended by local natural history enthusiasts, although the sheer variety of species takes some getting used to when presented on the printed page.

The silvery-cheeked hornbill, which grows to a length of about 70cm, is found throughout the forests of East Africa. Its loud call is a series of throaty calls and grunts.

Regional Facts for the Trekker

This chapter covers information you need about travel and trekking in East Africa. Some sections cover general information which applies to all visitors (eg Visas and Money); other sections cover information of specific relevance to trekkers (eg Equipment and Specialised Guidebooks & Manuals). Information which refers to only one country is given under Facts for the Trekker in the individual country chapters.

PLANNING
When to Trek

The main feature of East Africa's weather is the pattern of wet and dry seasons. Over much of the region there are two of each per year (see the Climate section in the Facts about the Region chapter). Walking in the rain can be a bit of a downer after a while, so the best time for trekking is during the dry seasons. In Uganda, Kenya and northern Tanzania, broadly speaking, these are from December to February, when it's dry and warm, and from May to September, when it's dry and cool. In Malawi the dry season is April to September – cool in the early months, getting hotter in August and September.

However, the climate of East Africa is becoming increasingly unpredictable – it seems that the amount of rain falling during the wet seasons is decreasing, making trekking at this time more attractive. Usually, the rain falls in the afternoon, which means you can walk in the morning and get to your hut or put your tent up not long after midday and avoid the worst of the weather. On the high mountains, like Mt Kenya, Kilimanjaro and the Rwenzoris, snow usually falls in the rainy season and routes can be more difficult or blocked completely. But even in the dry seasons, rain on the mountains is never unlikely. You should be prepared for bad weather at *all* times.

A country's public holidays won't stop you trekking, but they might sometimes make travelling or buying supplies difficult, and

could involve a small alteration to your plans. They could also mean some trekking areas having more visitors than usual. Public holidays are listed in the individual country chapters.

The Nature of Trekking in East Africa

The trekking routes of East Africa are generally through mountains or wilderness areas. Most of the treks described in this book keep to paths or tracks, but they are not always clear. There are few, if any, signposts. Most of the areas are uninhabited or have only a sparse, scattered population, so often there'll be nobody around to show you the way.

This means you normally need to hire a local guide (see the Guides & Porters section in this chapter) or should be reasonably competent with a map and compass (see the boxed text, 'Map Reading', under Maps later in this chapter).

The lack of population in the wilderness areas also means that supplies will not be available on most of the treks described in this book, so you will need to be self-sufficient in food, usually for several days.

Generally, you will also need to be self-contained, with a tent and a full set of camping gear, although some routes have huts and bunkhouses where you can sleep. In nearly all areas, at each hut or camp site there will be a supply of water (either tap, borehole or stream) but you should carry everything else.

The beauty of trekking in East Africa is that all the major mountains can be easily reached by car, bus or hitching. This is an extra bonus for trekkers relying on public transport, who are so often excluded from wilderness areas. In this book, approach routes to the mountain area, and access routes to the start of each trek, are all fully described. Only two of the trekking areas described are difficult to reach without a vehicle. To get to these areas, you can hire a car (if your budget allows) or join an organised trek.

Types of Trek

There are various types of trekking in East Africa. The three main ones are independent trekking, supported trekking and organised trekking. There are some 'sub-types' and overlaps, but the following outlines will give you a general idea.

Independent Trekking In this book, 'independent' means completely self-contained with a tent and a full set of camping gear. The lack of population (and therefore shops) in wilderness areas means you need to be self-sufficient in food for the duration of the trek, usually for several days.

Independent trekking allows you to be completely flexible. The end of your day's walking is determined only by where you can find water and a space to pitch your tent. With enough food for an extra couple of days (which you should always carry anyway, in case of emergency) you can extend your trek, or sidetrack off the main route, as the fancy takes you.

Where huts and bunkhouses exist on the routes, independent trekkers can use these, or combine camping and 'hutting'. In nearly all areas, there will be a supply of water at each hut or camp site, but you should carry everything else.

Independent, in this sense, does not necessarily mean a single person trekking alone, although this is possible in several of the areas (albeit not always recommended).

Supported Trekking A supported trek means you are self-contained and self-sufficient in equipment and supplies, but you use the services of local porters to carry all or some of your gear. On a few of the treks described in this book, you may be supported by donkeys or a vehicle instead of human porters.

You might also employ a local guide to organise the porters and to take the worry out of route-finding, especially if you're inexperienced or trekking alone. It is also possible to hire only a guide if you prefer to carry your own gear or want to keep the size of your party to a minimum.

With porters carrying your gear, you can

usually go further each day or keep going for longer (if you want to). It also makes your trek much easier on the legs and back, and generally adds to the overall enjoyment. Using porters can give you more freedom (diverting off the main route to 'bag' an extra peak or explore an interesting valley is a lot more inviting if you haven't got a week's worth of food on your back!). But porters can also restrict you, as they generally do not have their own tents, and you must plan to stay each night near a hut or cave so that they have somewhere to sleep.

It's also possible to hire porters just for the first half of your trek, or even for the first day, until you've limbered up or your rucksack becomes a bit lighter. At the halfway point, or first night's camp, you can pay the porter his wages and he'll go back down, leaving you to carry on.

Guides and porters can be arranged through local trekking companies and agencies in the main towns and at local porter/ guide cooperatives near the mountains. Employing people in this way obviously costs more than doing a trek independently, but wages are not expensive and it's a good way to put some of your money directly into the local economy.

Some guides will also cook, and you can arrange to hire tents and equipment from the trekking companies, but if you get this far, you might as well do an organised trek.

For more information, see the Guides & Porters section in this chapter.

Organised Trekking You can have your whole trek organised by a trekking company in East Africa. For straightforward routes this can be done on the spot, in Nairobi, Arusha, Moshi or wherever. If you don't want to take a chance, you can arrange things in advance by contacting a company based in East Africa from your own country. Using faxes and email, this can be very easy.

A third alternative is to arrange a trek, or even a series of treks, plus other items such as hotels, transport and airport pick-ups with a trekking company or specialist tour agent in your own country. Many trekking companies in Europe, North America and Australasia

Organised Treks – A Sample Itinerary

If you arrange an all-inclusive trek with a company, it will probably follow an itinerary that has become well established over the years, originally based on the Himalayan style of trekking.

The trek begins when the company's vehicle drops you off at the roadhead or a national park entrance gate. Here you meet your porters and guide (unless he's travelled with you). If it hasn't already been done, some time might be spent sorting out porter loads, although normally the guide will oversee this. Park fees may need to be paid.

Then you start trekking. Your guide will stay with your group, which may spread out as people walk at different speeds. (This is why it's better to go with a company that also provides assistant guides.) Stronger porters will go ahead, while others lag behind. Even with organised treks, it's important to give the right bags to the right porters, otherwise you might arrive at your camp site to find a week's worth of food already there, while dry clothes and the tents are still three hours back down the mountain. Explain to your guide what you need and he will arrange the porters.

You carry a packed lunch for the midday break. While you're resting, more porters will come by. Loads seem to become particularly heavy at this stage!

You continue walking to reach your bunkhouse or camp site for the night. You might have to help put up the tents, depending on whether you're on a fully serviced trek or one where you're expected to lend a hand. Tea and biscuits will be provided while you rest for a while and change into dry clothes, then relax while the evening meal is prepared. Again, depending on your trek, you may be expected to lend a hand with cooking or washing up.

Next day, any small problems will have been ironed out and you can get into the rhythm of the trek proper. Sunrise is between 6 and 6.30 am, and sunset is always 12 hours later. You normally get up at first light, to make the most of the clear weather, as afternoon mist sometimes occurs. Breakfast will be served in your hut or mess tent, or outside on the grass of your camp site. You pack your main rucksack ready for the porters to carry, and leave the cook to pack up the group food and equipment. You may help with taking tents down before starting the day's trek at around 8 am.

You walk until noon for lunch, and arrive at the next hut or camp site in the middle of the afternoon. Tea and biscuits are served while you rest. If the weather is good, there's often time for a short walk in the area around the camp, or you may prefer just to relax while the cook prepares the evening meal. After the meal, and the effects of a hard day's trekking, most trekkers hit the sack pretty soon after sunset. ∎

can also arrange a complete deal including international flights, local transport and accommodation, as well as the trek itself, and many also provide a trek leader to oversee the running of the whole trip and to act as intermediary between the trekkers and the local guides and porters (see the Organised Treks & Tours section in the main Getting There & Away chapter).

On an organised trek, you either join a group and fit in with a pre-set schedule and itinerary, or you can request that the company arrange something to suit your own specifications. For an idea of how an organised trek works on a day-to-day basis see the boxed text, 'Organised Treks – A Sample Itinerary'.

Whether your trek is organised locally or in advance from your home country, the main advantage is that all the pre-trek preparation is taken care of, including transport to the start of the trek, buying food, arranging supplies and hiring equipment and porters. If your holiday time is limited, an organised trek can save you several precious days.

On the other hand, an organised trek means you have to follow a fixed itinerary, with less opportunity for alterations and diversions, although good companies will always build in a bit of flexibility. Also, you'll probably be trekking with people you have not met before, which may add extra interest to your trip, or may not ...

Costs of an organised trek vary considerably and depend on many factors. These include the number of days included in the trip as a whole, the number of days spent actually trekking, the standard of accommodation before and after the trek, the quality of bunkhouses or tents in the mountains, and the knowledge and experience of the guide or trek leader. When making comparisons, note that companies which camp when on trek tend to use the more unusual routes or visit remote areas; these extra logistics mean they may be more expensive than companies using bunkhouses on the more well-used routes.

The number of porters and guides used is also important. Check that the company employs enough staff to carry everything. Most outfits also provide a cook. The better companies will often provide an assistant guide (or even two) to back up the main guide in case the group splits into slower and faster factions, or in case anybody has to return due to illness or altitude sickness.

Many of the treks are in national parks where entrance fees have to be paid. When comparing costs it's very important to check whether the price includes park entrance fees, or whether these are extra. Also check the number of days on offer: a five-day trek usually means four nights accommodation, a six-day trek means five nights, and so on.

Wherever you arrange your trek, it's usually better to deal with the companies that actually organise the treks (the 'operators'), rather than the agents who simply sell them. Operators can usually give you much more practical help and advice, and the treks are often cheaper too.

Organised treks arranged locally in East Africa start at about US$50 per day (all inclusive), and the better companies charge considerably more than this. Around US$100 per day is not unusual, and US$200 per day may be charged by upmarket companies operating walking safaris in lowland areas as well as mountain treks. If you organise a complete deal in your own country, the price will of course be much higher, as it will also include international air fares, local transport, trek-leader costs, accommodation, administration and so on.

Obviously, you can do things much more cheaply than on an organised trek if you arrange your own supported trek or go independently. But if you wanted to cover the same route in the same time, and with the same provisions and facilities, normally it would be very difficult to do it more cheaply yourself.

Confusion can be caused by travel companies offering 'walking safaris'. Check these very carefully. Some walking safaris are fully organised mountain or wilderness treks, but others are more conventional vehicle-based trips with some sections of walking (long or short) included. This may not be what hardened mountain trekkers are looking for, but vehicle-based walking safaris are ideal if you want to see wildlife or savanna landscapes without being cooped up in a car all day. (See the separate Walking Safari sections at the end of the Kenya and Tanzania country chapters.)

You may also see the terms 'climbing safari' or 'mountain climbing expedition' which almost certainly mean a trek, rather than technical rock climbing or mountaineering (see the boxed text, 'Trekking is not Climbing', later in this chapter).

Note Of all the treks described in this book, only on Kilimanjaro is it obligatory to use the services of a trekking company (see the Kilimanjaro section in the Tanzania chapter). In a few other areas (eg the Crater Highlands) going with an organised trek is virtually essential (and certainly a lot easier than trying to do it on your own). By their very nature, walking safaris in lowland national parks have to be organised through a tour company.

Maps
Regional Maps General maps of the East African region include Bartholomews' *Africa, Central & Southern* at a scale of 1:5,000,000 and *Africa, East* at 1:2,500,000. Both cover the countries included in this book. The maps have altitude tinting, so the mountains and highland areas are easy to find. These maps look very nice when you're planning your trip or if you want a souvenir to hang on the wall afterwards, but the information on roads and settlements is not so good.

The Michelin map *Africa, Central & South* at 1:4,000,000 (sheet 955) does not indicate high ground as clearly as the Bartholomews, but the practical details (especially roads) are

Map Reading

The trekking routes of East Africa are generally through mountains or wilderness areas. Most of the treks described in this book keep to paths or tracks, but they are not always clear. Apart from on the main routes up major peaks (such as Mt Kenya and Kilimanjaro) there are few, if any, signposts. Most of the areas are uninhabited or have only a sparse, scattered population, so usually there'll be nobody around to show you the way. This means you should be reasonably competent with a map and compass – particularly important if you want to follow a seldom-used route. As on any mountain, mist or fog can completely block your view and make good navigation essential. If you are not sure about your ability, you should not even consider trekking without somebody more competent. Much of this advice is not so important if you use a local guide, but it still helps to have a basic knowledge – at least enough to know whether you're going in the right direction. ■

detailed and this is a much easier map to use for general travel.

Locally produced maps showing Kenya, Tanzania and Uganda are available from bookshops in Nairobi. Details of maps covering single countries in more detail are given in the individual country chapters.

Detailed Maps For detail, government survey maps mostly at scales of 1:50,000 and 1:250,000 are produced in each country. These are usually based on surveys made during colonial times, and the British Directorate of Overseas Surveys (DOS) continues to assist with the production of maps. However, some maps are reprinted but not corrected, and so the information on roads and villages becomes considerably out of date, although most of the topographical information is reasonably correct. You can buy DOS/government survey maps at the Government Map Office in each country's capital city. Maps of popular areas are often out of stock, and you might not be able to buy maps which are considered 'strategic' (eg those of border areas).

For some of the most popular mountain areas, commercially produced maps are also available. These are often more readily available than government survey maps and more useful for trekkers. More details about specific maps and where to buy them are given in the individual country and mountain sections.

What to Bring

If you are doing an independent or supported trek (see Types of Trek earlier in this chapter) you'll need all your own equipment including tent, sleeping bag and cooking kit. On an organised trek you normally just need a sleeping bag. On any kind of trek you're also going to need a rucksack to carry your gear (a kit-bag is OK if you're using porters), and a set of appropriate clothes.

Although you're in Africa and near the equator, don't be fooled into thinking it's always going to be dry and warm. You'll probably get some days of blistering heat, but rain can fall at any time of year, and many treks go above 4000m, where night temperatures often drop below freezing. The higher you go, the colder it gets. At dawn on the summit of Kilimanjaro, wind-chill can force the apparent temperature down to -30°C. That's cold enough for you to lose all feeling in your fingers if you take your gloves off for more than a couple of seconds.

So the most important thing about trekking in East Africa is the huge range of temperatures and weather conditions you will encounter, even on a fairly short trek. Your clothing and equipment must be versatile. And if you're carrying it yourself, it also needs to be light.

Good lightweight clothing and equipment for camping and trekking is difficult to buy in East Africa. Most trekkers bring everything they need with them. If you are already a regular walker or backpacker, you'll probably have most of the gear required, so you may want to skip some parts of this section. But make sure all your gear is in good condition before you leave. It's no good finding out you've got a split fly sheet or worn boots halfway up the Rwenzoris. If you are fairly new to trekking, and kitting yourself out from scratch, you should also read a few outdoor magazines or equipment manuals, and discuss your trek with a good outdoor gear shop where the staff have trekked themselves and can offer suggestions.

Choosing suitable equipment is either complicated or very simple, depending on who you talk to. There's a lot of specialised, highly technical gear around these days. The effectiveness of some of it is exaggerated, but other stuff is very good and worth having if you can afford it. Some trekkers make do with very simple equipment. This is fine if there's no other choice. Not having high-tech gear shouldn't stop you going, but whatever you have must provide adequate levels of safety and comfort. If it doesn't, there's no point going on a trek.

The following list is based on the presumption that you'll be trekking on at least one of the high mountains of East Africa, where the weather conditions are more severe (Kilimanjaro, Mt Kenya, the Rwenzoris). If you're only going to the lower mountain areas you won't need quite so much. (See the individual mountain sections for details on weather and climate.)

Clothing To give you more flexibility, it's better to take several thin layers of clothing, rather than a few thick layers. The range of fabrics and styles available is mind-boggling, but important buzz words when you're looking round the gear shops are 'wicking' and 'breathability'. Basically, clothes which wick moisture away from your skin keep you dry and warm on the inside, and clothes which breathe allow the moisture to escape.

Jacket This includes anoraks, cagoules, parkas, coats and so on. This is the outside layer of clothing you wear most of the time for trekking when temperatures are cool. A jacket should be reasonably wind-proof and shower-proof. There are many different fabric types, including close-weave nylon or cotton and acrylic pile, but the most usual is fleece, usually available in a range of thicknesses, and sometimes with a wind-proof or shower-proof membrane attached.

On the high mountains, carrying another jacket is highly recommended for when you

Equipment Checklist

This list will help you with planning and act as a check-list. More details on each item are given in the body of the What to Bring section.

Clothing
- [ ] jacket/s
- [ ] outer shell\waterproof jacket
- [ ] outer shell\waterproof pants
- [ ] shirts
- [ ] trousers
- [ ] skirt
- [ ] shorts
- [ ] underwear
- [ ] sun hat
- [ ] woollen hat
- [ ] gloves

Footwear
- [ ] walking boots
- [ ] training shoes
- [ ] sandals
- [ ] socks
- [ ] gaiters

Trekking Equipment
- [ ] rucksack
- [ ] tent
- [ ] sleeping bag
- [ ] sleeping mat
- [ ] cooking & eating kit

Personal Equipment
- [ ] sunglasses
- [ ] snow goggles
- [ ] walking pole
- [ ] water bottle/s
- [ ] water purification kit
- [ ] torch/flashlight
- [ ] emergency foil blanket
- [ ] toiletries
- [ ] toilet paper

Miscellaneous Items
- [ ] sun cream/block & lip salve
- [ ] washing kit
- [ ] sewing kit
- [ ] first-aid kit
- [ ] compass
- [ ] map case
- [ ] whistle
- [ ] penknife
- [ ] towel
- [ ] camera & film

need an extra layer of warmth around camp in the evening, for pre-dawn summit approaches, or for wearing inside your sleeping bag on very cold nights. This can be any sort, but many trekkers favour a padded sleeveless 'body warmer' or 'duvet jacket', as these are light and pack down fairly small, which is important as you'll probably be carrying it more than wearing it.

An 'outer shell' jacket is required when conditions get more serious. It should be capable of coping with heavy rain and high winds. A hood and elasticised cuffs and waistband are also essential. Several types of jacket are available, some lined or padded for extra warmth, but remember that when it rains on African mountains, it doesn't always get colder, so putting on a waterproof jacket warms you up, which just makes you sweat more and get wet anyway.

To get round this problem some jackets are made in waterproof breathable fabrics such as Gore-Tex. Alternatively, clothes made from a combination of pile fabric and close-weave nylon such as Pertex are ideal for trekking in African mountains: one layer is fine for the warm, wet conditions on the lower slopes, and two or three layers can cope with the snow and high winds on the summits. The main manufacturer of this type of clothing is called Buffalo (an appropriate name for trekking in Africa!).

Shirt This is another catch-all term for the middle layer between your jacket and your underwear. You can choose from all sorts of technical synthetic fabrics or use a traditional wool sweater, or you may just use another thin jacket of fleece, pile or whatever. Cotton sweatshirts are not really suitable; they get wet when you perspire and take ages to dry. Fleece sweatshirts are available, which are basically a thin fleece jacket without a zip.

Trousers & Skirts Shorts are ideal for warm conditions. Many women trekkers find skirts comfortable. For when it gets cooler, lightweight, breeze-proof trousers are available. These are usually called 'trekking trousers', and you pay extra for pockets with zips and

a nice badge, but nevertheless they're ideal. For more freedom of movement, you may prefer stretch-nylon tracksuit trousers (not cotton sweat-pants). As conditions get colder you can build up the layers by using these under your trekking trousers or over long underwear. (Almost as much heat is lost through your legs as through your upper body.)

You may also find a pair of padded trousers useful for evenings in camp and for sleeping in, in the same way as the 'duvet jacket' already mentioned. This is a real luxury, but well worth it on the high mountains.

Underwear Cotton T-shirts and undies are OK for warm conditions, but for higher, colder areas an insulating, wicking fabric (usually called 'thermal') that keeps moisture away from your skin is much better. The best method is to carry two sets of thermal undies. Use one set for walking every day and change into a dry set as soon as you reach camp in the evening. Thermal T-shirts and undershorts are good for walking, while long-sleeved vests and long johns are better for cold evenings. The walking set can be dried overnight inside your sleeping bag; your body warmth will get rid of most of the dampness.

Hats & Gloves The sun is strong at high altitudes, so a sun hat that also covers the back of your neck is essential. A scarf can also be used. For the cold days, you need a warm hat. Balaclavas that can be rolled up are ideal. Again, wool takes a long time to dry, so synthetic materials are better. With a balaclava and the hood on your jacket you should be able to withstand that chill wind screaming across the summit of Kili!

Even with gloves a layer system is best: use light silk or thermal gloves for cool days, with overmitts to cope with strong winds and rain.

Footwear Boots or shoes are probably the most important piece of kit required by trekkers. They have to be right. Badly fitting boots will ruin your trip, and possibly even cause you to 'retire' early. If you buy new boots and socks for a trip, check that they're completely comfortable before leaving home. A useful tip we've heard is always to buy your boots in warm conditions, preferably in the afternoon; your feet swell slightly at these times, and you can avoid buying boots which may pinch later.

Boots & Shoes For lower treks, walking shoes or training shoes with good support are suitable. For the higher mountains, medium-weight boots – leather or synthetic – are required. Kilimanjaro, and possibly Mt Kenya and the Rwenzoris, are the only mountains where you'll be on snow for a short period, but even here you won't need stiff plastic mountaineering boots. Unless you're really keeping the weight down, a pair of light training shoes for the evenings in camp are a very good idea. Sandals let your feet breathe on warm evenings and reduce the chance of blisters or other skin problems.

Socks Good socks are as important as good boots. Wool dries slowly, but there are several synthetic fabrics available which are more suitable. Some people prefer to wear two pairs, but there's no reason for this if your boots are good. Extra layers can chafe as much as cushion; it's a personal choice. Take several pairs, so you always have a dry set to put on. Wet socks in the morning can ruin a trek!

Gaiters These are very useful, as you'll almost certainly be crossing snow, scree or swamp (or all three!) during a trek. Unless you're doing a Rwenzoris trek, gaiters do not need to be the heavy-duty 'Yeti' type. (See the special note on footwear in the Rwenzoris section of the Uganda chapter.)

Trekking & Personal Equipment A lot of trekking equipment is optional and a matter of personal taste. However, the items listed here are pretty much essential. For more ideas on the practicalities of outdoor life in East Africa see the section on Responsible Trekking later in this chapter.

Rucksack If you're trekking independently, your rucksack obviously needs to be large enough to carry all your gear and food. Many trekkers in East Africa visit more than one mountain, which means travelling between different areas on public transport, when this large rucksack can be half-full and unwieldy.

To overcome this, some makes of 'alpine' rucksacks have zips or straps to change the size of the sack, which is very useful for this kind of situation. Most alpine sacks do not have side pockets, which also makes things easier on public transport, although less handy for trekking. Some rucksacks come with detachable pockets, or you can buy separate pockets to fit on.

If you're going on a completely supported or organised trek, a porter will carry your main bag while you carry only a day-pack with your camera, spare clothing, lunch and so on. Several rucksacks are available which have a small day-pack attached by zips or straps, and these are ideal for this purpose.

Some manufacturers produce rucksacks that convert into travel bags, which are good if you're combining trekking with some general travelling, or if you want to appear respectable when you spend a night in a smart hotel to celebrate a successful trek. Another advantage is that the harness can be protected by a zippered flap to avoid the sort of airline damage mentioned below. Note,

---

Trekking is not Climbing
On several of the treks in this book you may reach peaks and passes at heights between 4000m and 5000m, and the summit of Kilimanjaro tops the lot, at almost 6000m. Although you can go very high, this book describes trekking (ie walking) routes only, and does not cover technical climbing or mountaineering. Therefore no specialised equipment, such as ropes, crampons and ice axe, is required. ■

however, that these convertible bags are OK if you're on a supported trek, but they should not be overloaded for long independent treks, as they tend to sag and be uncomfortable.

No matter what rucksack makers claim about waterproofing, your spare clothing and sleeping bag should be wrapped inside tough plastic bags to keep them dry – heavy-duty garbage bags are ideal. This also helps to keep out dust when you're travelling.

On any flight, tie all your rucksack straps so none can get snagged by trolleys and conveyer belts. I've seen several rucksacks come down the carousel at Nairobi airport with half the harness torn off. (If this does happen, rucksacks can be repaired by the shoe and bag *fundis* (menders) usually found near the market in any large town, but it's best to avoid it happening in the first place.)

Tent Some trekking routes described in this book have huts and bunkhouses, so a tent is not always required. If you want to be independent or explore more unusual areas a tent is essential.

There's an amazing range of designs and fabrics available, but there are a few pointers to look for. If you're carrying everything yourself, your tent needs to be small and light, but even on supported treks you need to keep the weight fairly low. For trekking and travelling in East Africa one of the most important features is mosquito netting across all openings. Free-standing tents are also useful, as many camp sites are on areas of very thin soil, and even on bare rock in the higher mountains.

Weather conditions do not usually reach Himalayan storm standards, so your tent will not need to have several hoops or poles and a whole web of guy-ropes. Heavy falls of snow are also very unlikely during the trekking seasons, so a steep-sided 'four-season' tent is not necessary.

A good example of a tent for tropical trekking is the Tadpole made by The North Face. It was designed for Californian campers who are up in the mountains one weekend and on the beach a few days later, but it's also ideal for the range of conditions in East Africa.

The inner has large panels of netting and can be used alone in warm conditions. I've even used it in hotel bedrooms to keep the bugs out!

Some light tents must be erected with care. If you're on a supported trek, it's usually a good idea not to let porters put them up, as zips or poles could be damaged.

Sleeping Bag There are endless variations and, as with clothes, flexibility and layering are important features when choosing a bag for treks in East Africa, so that you can cope with the range of temperatures and conditions. The two main types of bag are those filled with natural down or feathers and those with synthetic filling. Basically, the difference is this: down bags are lighter, smaller when compacted and last longer; synthetic bags are cheaper and lose less of their warmth if they get wet.

For the high camps on the major mountains you need a good 'four-season' bag. So that you can also use it in lower, warmer conditions a long zip allows ventilation. Alternatively, as with the clothing, you can build up a series of layers from two or more lighter sleeping bags used together. Sleeping bag liners made from Pertex (a close-weave nylon) or silk can add a lot of warmth to your system for very little extra weight. For high camps on Kili and Mt Kenya experienced trekkers find an ideal combination to be two sleeping bags, plus one liner inside the bags and a big one outside which envelops the whole lot. As the trek gets lower down the mountain, fewer layers are required. You can put together your own layers, or buy a complete set.

If you don't want to carry an extra sleeping bag just for a few nights, you could hire one. Details on equipment hire are given in the various trekking sections.

Sleeping Mat A sleeping mat is very important to insulate your body from the cold ground at night. The traditional closed-cell foam Karrimat is robust and light, but beware of cheap copies which compress easily and soon become useless. Therm-a-Rests are a more recent innovation; they are very comfortable and only slightly heavier, and they provide more insulation, which means if you're really counting the grams, you can save weight by using a lighter sleeping bag.

Cooking & Eating Kit Relying on open fires is not recommended and is ecologically unsound, so if you're going to be cooking for yourself (ie not on a supported trek) a stove is essential.

Camping stoves can be classified according to fuel type and are really a matter of personal preference. Many trekkers use multi-fuel stoves (eg those made by MSR) while others prefer stoves which run on methylated sprits (eg Trangia) as they have no moving parts and nothing to break. Meths can be bought in hardware shops and chemists in large towns all over East Africa. For petrol stoves, the low-grade petrol in Kenya, Tanzania and Uganda is OK, but tends to be very dirty, which can cause stoves to block. In Malawi, petrol is blended with ethanol, which is ideal for stoves. Note that cartridges for butane gas stoves (eg Gaz) cannot be carried on aeroplanes. The most popular disposable canisters (size C206) are available in Nairobi but in very few other places.

To go with your stove, you need a windshield, fuel bottle, cooking pots (those with a non-stick coating make washing up easier and require less soap), a pan grip, wooden spoon for cooking, plastic mug and bowls, plus lightweight (eg aluminium or polycarbonate) knife, fork and spoon. You also need a lighter, a spare lighter and a box of waterproof matches for emergencies, plus a foam pad for washing up and some detergent (preferably biodegradable). A foldable bowl is useful and helps avoid polluting streams with dirty water (see the Responsible Trekking section later in this chapter), although a large plastic bag in a ring of stones will do the job.

Sunglasses & Snow Goggles Sunglasses are recommended to cut the intense glare you often get on the high mountains. Snow goggles with side flaps are only essential for the summit stage on Kili, but are also useful on the lower slopes below the glaciers, and on Mt Kenya.

Walking Poles For years walkers have found sticks or poles useful for taking some of the stress off the knees going up or down hills, particularly on the steep approaches to the summits of the major mountains. They're also good for providing extra balance on scree, snow and tussock grass. You can use a wooden pole or section of bamboo cut from the lower slopes of a mountain, but most trekkers use telescopic walking poles made for the job. One pole is fine, but using two spreads the load more evenly and, anecdotal evidence suggests, may help you avoid backache.

Water Bottle You should carry at least a 1L bottle while on trek. Flexible water bags, holding between 4L and 10L, are ideal for extra water on long or hot days, and very good for camping as they help avoid pollution and will save several trips between your tent and the nearest river.

Water Purification Kit This consists of a water filter and/or a supply of purification tablets or solution (see the Health, Safety & First Aid chapter).

Torch/Flashlight A head-torch (ie mounted on your head using a wide elastic strap) is more useful than hand-held models, as it leaves your hands free for eating and cooking or for putting in your pockets when it's cold. Bring spare bulbs and plenty of batteries, as they fade quickly in cold conditions. Locally made batteries do not last long.

Miscellaneous Items A silver foil emergency 'blanket' is small and light to carry in the bottom of your day-pack, but can be useful if you get unexpectedly delayed in cold, wet conditions. Note, however, that they do not breathe, and if they are in use for a long period condensation can build up on the inside.

The sun can be strong at high altitude, so protect arms and legs with sun cream. For nose and ears use a complete sun block. Also vital is lip salve.

Your washing kit should be small. Take only the essentials. (I've seen people up Mt Kenya with giant beach towels!)

Physical Preparation

It's no good having loads of fancy kit if your body isn't up to trekking. Although some routes described in this book will not be hard for anyone already used to even a bit of walking, others are unrelentingly strenuous and demanding. Some major treks involve days where you might be walking for more than 10 hours, or covering distances of more than 30km, although many are much shorter. The spectacular landscape can often make things harder too, whether you're walking through bamboo forest, tussock grass or desert sand. And you may be surprised to learn that some of these mountains have steep sides; going up or down can put considerable strain on your lungs and legs. Add to that the effects of lack of oxygen when you're at high altitude – trekking is not to be taken lightly.

Although none of the treks in this book involves technical mountaineering, some do include very airy sections on narrow ridges, exposed peaks or fairly steep snow slopes. There are also a few optional sidetracks which may involve a bit of easy scrambling (using your hands).

Of course, if you're a regular walker in your own country, or have trekked in other parts of the world, you will be used to (and relish) these situations. But you should not think of doing a serious trek in East Africa as a way of getting in shape. If you're not properly prepared, 'doing' Kilimanjaro or Mt Kenya, just as you'd tick off Serengeti or the Masai Mara, is not advised. ■

Likewise for the sewing kit and first-aid kit (see the Health, Safety & First Aid chapter). Medicated hand-wipes are useful for cuts and grazes, and for a final clean just before eating.

A compass is essential if you're going off the main routes. Make sure you know how to use it. Note also that good compasses are calibrated differently for various parts of the world. For the treks in this book, you need one for equatorial regions. If your compass is set for another region you'll need to keep changing the angle of the base plate to make it work. Silva make a range of compasses for all regions.

A transparent map case, or a strong clear plastic bag, will protect maps (or this book) from rain.

A whistle can be very useful if you get lost or separated from companions in mist or darkness (although it's better not to get into this situation), and for scaring off animals in bush areas. A penknife is also useful but it doesn't need 97 blades and gadgets. The essentials are sharp knife, bottle opener and tin opener. Nail scissors are useful for mid-trek pedicures.

Toilet paper can be bought in even quite small shops all over East Africa, although it tends to be a bit on the coarse side. Keep it dry. Wet loo roll is even worse than wet socks! (Bring matches to burn it after use, or a plastic bag – see the Responsible Trekking section.) Tampons and sanitary towels are available from chemists in Nairobi, Dar, Lilongwe, Blantyre and some other large towns.

Buying & Hiring Locally There is nothing you need for trekking in East Africa which cannot be brought from home, but if you forget or lose something, or need a few extra items of trekking gear, it can be bought or hired in Nairobi (details in the Equipment Hire & Supply section in the Kenya chapter) and from various trekking companies at the base of Mt Kenya, Kilimanjaro and the Rwenzoris (details in the mountain sections).

Basic items, such as aluminium cooking pots, plastic plates, kerosene stoves and blankets, even pullovers, hats and gloves, can be bought cheaply in the shops or market of any large town.

SUGGESTED ITINERARIES

This book covers a selection of trekking routes in all the major mountains of East Africa, plus several other routes across plains, plateaus or rolling hill country in lesser-known areas. Generally, the treks are through wilderness areas, although some sections may pass through farms and villages on the foot-hills of mountains, and some routes pass through lightly populated areas.

The emphasis of this book is firmly on treks, meaning long walks of several days duration, so areas where shorter walks are possible have been covered only briefly. Because this book is written mainly for visitors who may have limited time, treks which involve difficult or time-consuming access or complex logistics have not been included.

Most of the mountains in East Africa are isolated peaks or massifs surrounded by plains. They are not extended ranges like the Alps or Himalaya. Therefore, most treks are between four and seven days, although on the major mountains this can be extended by splitting some days in two and adding rest days and long sidetracks.

For each major mountain, between one and four trekking routes are described in detail. Some of the routes are established classics while others are more unusual. Further possibilities for more adventurous or experienced trekkers are also outlined.

In some mountain areas there are no properly defined trekking routes, so we have 'created' them by joining a series of existing paths and tracks, or made suggestions on where you can do this yourself.

It is common for trekkers visiting East Africa to include two or more mountains, which usually means travelling overland (or by air) between the trekking areas. Consequently, this book also contains enough travel information to help you get between the different mountains.

Part of the joy of travel and trekking anywhere in the world is planning your own itinerary, but here are a few suggestions to get you started.

Two Weeks If this is your first visit to East Africa, you'll almost certainly want to include a major trek on one of the region's main attractions, Kilimanjaro and Mt Kenya, where there's a choice of several different trekking routes of varying lengths and standards. Two weeks will give you plenty of time to arrive, sort out an organised trek (if required), and get acclimatised and limbered up with perhaps a short visit to a smaller mountain (eg the Cheranganis before Mt Kenya, or Mt Meru before Kilimanjaro). The main trek itself will take between four and seven days, which might still leave a few days spare for a wildlife safari or trip to the coast. If you're on a fully organised trek, both peaks *can* be done in just over two weeks, but this may be pushing your luck when it comes to acclimatisation.

Three Weeks to One Month With three weeks you could do treks on Mt Kenya and Kili, or Mt Kenya and the Rwenzoris, still allowing time for proper acclimatisation. With a month, you could include another area (Elgon, Meru or the Cheranganis), which will help you acclimatise for the major trek, and also show you a wider selection of East African mountains. You might also want to tie in some trekking in a more unusual area, such as Kenya's Loroghi Hills or Tanzania's Usambara Mountains. Another option might be to combine treks in Tanzania and Malawi, or Kenya and Ethiopia, using regional flights to cut journey times. If you only visited one or two areas this would still leave time for a wildlife safari (eg in the Masai Mara or Selous) or some beach relaxation at Mombasa or Zanzibar.

Three Months With three months to spare, a keen trekker could visit a very good selection of mountains and wilderness areas. The extra time required for travel by public transport would not be a problem here. A dream itinerary might be as follows. Fly into Nairobi, do some short walks in the Rift Valley areas such as Longonot and Hell's Gate, and maybe take a walking safari in the Masai Mara area. Then head north to the Loroghi Hills, to do some bush walking with Samburu guides, and possibly camels, then continue to the Cherangani Hills and Mt Elgon (either the Kenya or Uganda side, or both). Already with some good acclimatisation under your belt, you could do a trek in the Rwenzoris or Mt Kenya (or both) before returning to Nairobi to restock, change money, send mail and so on.

From Nairobi, you might get a regional flight to Addis Ababa, and then get to Gonder for a trek in the Simien Mountains. Intrepid travellers may even go overland between Addis and Nairobi, at least in one direction. (Once you've done it one way overland, you'll be happy to fly back!)

If Ethiopia isn't in your plans, from Kenya you can head south, to Arusha in Tanzania (which might be a better place than Nairobi for sorting out supplies, money and mail) and there arrange treks on Kilimanjaro and Meru, tours of the Serengeti, or walking safaris in the Crater Highlands or Tarangire Conservation Area. But if your sights are set firmly on Kili, then aim straight for Moshi, where you can normally set up a trek on the spot within a day or two.

After a hard trek on Kili, keep going south for relaxing hikes and a change of scene in the Usambara Mountains, and possibly a real rest on the beaches of Zanzibar. Next stop – southern Tanzania, where intrepid trekkers might want to explore the Kipengere Range before crossing into Malawi. Trekking highlights here include the Nyika Plateau and the Mulanje Massif, and once again wildlife safaris or beach activities are also available.

At the end of this trip you could fly home from Lilongwe, or return to Nairobi (overland or by regional flight) and get home from there. Of course, by this stage the trekking bug may have bitten badly, and you might just head on south where the mountains of Zimbabwe and South Africa beckon ...

The table on pages 8 & 9 at the front of the book shows all the trekking routes that are described in detail in this book.

TOURIST OFFICES

Of all the countries covered by this book, only Kenya maintains dedicated tourist offices in other countries around the world. These are listed below. The Tanzania Tourist Board is represented in the UK by the Tanzania Trade Centre (☎ (0171) 407 0566), and in other countries around the world by Tanzania embassies and high commissions (these are listed in the Tanzania chapter later in this book). Visitors to Tanzania from the UK may also get tourist information from Tanganyika Wildlife Safaris (☎ (01708) 372899; fax 373181). It is an upmarket safari company, but the friendly staff are happy to help anyone with general enquiries about travel in Tanzania.

Uganda and Malawi do not have separate offices but have tourist information desks attached to some of their embassies (also listed in the individual country chapters). Most Ethiopian embassies have tourist information desks (although in some countries tourist information is handled by the local Ethiopian Airlines office).

The tourist offices and desks may be able to post you some very general information on the country, usually in the form of glossy (and sometimes hopelessly optimistic) brochures, but don't expect much in the way of technical trekking details. They might also be able to provide you with names of specialist trekking companies, but mostly they only have details of mainstream travel agents and tour operators. Local tourist information centres in East Africa are listed in the individual country chapters.

Kenya Tourist Offices Abroad

France
    5 Rue Volney, Paris 75002 (☎ 01 42 60 66 88; fax 01 42 61 18 84)
Germany
    Neue Mainzer Strasse 22, 60311 Frankfurt (☎ (069) 232017; fax 239239)
Sweden
    Birger Jarsgaten 37 2TR, 11145 Stockholm (☎ 24 04 45; fax 20 92 61)
Switzerland
    Bleicherweg 30, CH8039 Zürich (☎ (01) 202 2244; fax 202 2256)
UK
    25 Brook's Mews (off Davies St), Mayfair, London W1Y 1LF (☎ (0171) 355 3144; fax 495 8656)
USA
    9150 Wilshire Blvd, Beverly Hills, CA 90212 (☎ (213) 274 6635; fax 859 7010)
    424 Madison Ave, New York, NY 10017 (☎ (212) 486 1300; fax 688 0911)

VISAS & DOCUMENTS
Passport

A full passport is essential for entering Tanzania, Kenya, Uganda and Malawi. Some officials prefer passports which expire at least a few months after your trip ends. Change your passport if it has stamps from anywhere that might be considered suspect (Libya, for example).

Visas

A visa is a stamp in your passport giving you permission to enter a country – usually for a month. They are available from embassies of the country you wish to enter, and usually a fee is payable. For nearly every visa application you need two or three passport photos.

Not everyone needs a visa to enter every country – the rules change according to your nationality. For example, British citizens may not need visas to enter some Commonwealth countries. A particular anomaly in many countries is that Commonwealth citizens of Asian origin sometimes need visas that are not required by their black or white compatriots. More specific details about who needs what for where are given in the individual country chapters. Information on visa extensions is also given there.

You can get all your visas before you go, or in neighbouring countries as you travel. This will probably be determined by the length of your trip. Some visas are only valid for a certain period from when they are issued – in other words, you may have to enter the country pretty soon after getting the visa, so don't get them all in advance if your plans are likely to change. On other visas you have to say when you plan to enter the country and get there within a month of that date.

When you actually arrive, you may find yourself subject to further entry requirements. These may include a return ticket, to prove you will leave the country and not settle down to build a hut somewhere. You may also need 'sufficient funds' to support yourself during your stay, especially if you don't have a return ticket. In reality, this tends to be flexibly applied, and is mainly so that immigration officials can prevent 'undesirables' from entering, but a few hundred US dollars for a short visit (or a credit card) is usually enough. It also helps if you don't look like an undesirable.

It is important to note that regulations are always under review and likely to be altered, so it's best to check at the relevant embassy in your own country before you leave (or in a neighbouring country as you're travelling), so as not to be caught out at a border or airport.

Walking Permits

For countries that are often bogged down by their own bureaucracies, the paperwork involved for trekking in East Africa is remarkably straightforward. For treks in national parks, you have to pay park fees, but these can be settled at each entrance gate (see National Parks & Entrance Fees below for more details). For areas outside the national parks, there are generally no formalities, apart from maybe 'checking in' at a police post in some remote areas (details are given in the individual trek sections).

Bunkhouses and huts can be reserved in advance, but this is not always essential, and booking procedures are sometimes a bit slack, so you often end up taking your chances anyway.

Advance planning might be necessary for Kilimanjaro, where the number of trekkers on some routes could be restricted in the future. If this does happen, space will be allocated by the national park authorities, but as all Kili treks have to be organised this will be taken care of by your trekking company anyway.

If you want to take an organised trek on any other area during the 'high' season (see each mountain section for details), you might need to contact the various trekking companies well in advance to be sure of a place. Having said that, whatever the season, it seems you can always find something.

National Parks & Entrance Fees Most of the mountain wilderness areas described in this book are national parks, and this normally means you have to pay to trek there. Fees vary between parks and between countries. In some areas the fees are very low, but in other parks they can bump up costs considerably. (See the individual mountain sections for details.) Wherever you go in East Africa it is essential to realise that park fees must usually be paid for in cash (either in local currency or 'hard' currency – see Money later in this chapter). In some parks, travellers cheques are accepted. If you buy an organised trek with includes park fees using a credit card your tour company will take care of fee payments at the gate.

National Park Benefits

It is generally agreed that the conservation of natural habitats (forests, grasslands or whatever) has many benefits, on local and global levels, and many of the mountain national parks and reserves in East Africa protect such areas. It is important to remember, however, that national parks are a luxury in Africa, where populations continue to expand and the demand for cultivable land is high. When local people are prevented from clearing the forests and cultivating the land, this naturally leads to resentment. Even if the forest on the mountain protects the land lower down and ensures water supplies, and may have several other benefits, this is not always understood or appreciated. (Put more simply, for a family with 10 hungry kids, the long-term benefits of national parks are less important than the immediate task of finding somewhere to grow food for next year.)

It may be possible to overcome this clash of interests if some of the money earned by the national parks goes to local people in the surrounding areas. In this way the land is seen to have a tangible value, and the park itself (and everything it contains) is more likely to survive intact.

The local people could benefit in many ways. In the most direct (although rather unproductive) way, the park revenue could be passed on in the form of cash hand-outs, or go towards providing food to replace the crops that couldn't be grown. More far-sighted uses for the revenue could include putting it into schemes to improve farming techniques or the development of clean water supplies. Other uses might be the provision of health centres or family planning clinics, or education schemes where the benefits of the national parks, and the forests they contain, are clearly explained.

In this way, eventually, the demand for more land might be reduced and the revenue earned by the park would have gone towards ensuring its own survival, as well as benefiting the local people in the process. (These arguments are necessarily simplified but they are still very important.)

Park management and conservation schemes employing some of these proposals already exist in several parks in East Africa, but they are noticeably lacking in others. But generally things are changing, and as they do the local people will benefit and the parks themselves will become increasingly secure. Trekkers should bear all this in mind before complaining about entrance fees. ■

Many trekkers complain about the high prices charged by many East African national parks, but there is no reason why rich visitors from the west should come to a developing country and expect everything to be cheap. If national parks can produce revenue, rather than be a drain on limited financial resources, this should be welcomed. It's only fair that part of your money should contribute to this process. This issue is discussed more fully in the Ecology & Environment section of the Facts about the Region chapter.

In some parks, the money you pay is channelled back into management or conservation, or directed to local people who live in the surrounding areas (see the boxed text on this page for more thoughts on this). Unfortunately, in many places the revenue goes to government treasuries, where it gets swallowed up by other schemes or simply 'disappears'. And that's the real issue: paying to enter a national park is fine, but making sure the money goes to the right place is a major problem.

Travel Insurance

An insurance policy that covers you for medical expenses, and an emergency flight home, is very highly recommended. Hospitals in East Africa are not free, and the good ones are not cheap. Air ambulances and emergency international flights are frighteningly expensive. Most travel insurance also covers your baggage in case of loss, and several other items such as cancellation or hijack. (Although it's important to read the small print, some aspects it covers are enough to put you off flying!)

Some insurance companies are jumpy about the word 'trekking'. They seem to equate a hike up Kilimanjaro with storming the south face of Everest, and quote an extra premium to match. Others are much more sensible and only raise the premium if you trek above a certain altitude, or get into technical mountaineering with ropes, crampons, ice axes and all the rest.

If your travel agent can't help you with a good policy, try a student travel service or your national walking/climbing organisation for advice.

Other Documents

Other essential documents you may need include a vaccination certificate to show you've been jabbed for yellow fever, and possibly some other diseases (more details are given in the Health, Safety & First Aid chapter). Also useful will be your driving licence and an International Driving Permit (if you intend hiring a car), a membership card for a national youth hostelling association (which gets you cheap accommodation in similarly affiliated hostels), and a student or young persons identity card (good for various discounts). Also take a set of passport photos for visa application forms, if you're getting them along the way.

Photocopies of all your important documents, plus airline tickets and credit cards, will help speed up replacement if they are lost or stolen. Keep these and a list of travellers cheque numbers separate from other valuables, or leave copies with someone at home so they can be faxed to you in dire emergency.

EMBASSIES
East African Embassies Abroad

Most of the East African countries covered in this book have embassies in neighbouring countries. So if you're on a long or flexible itinerary you can get your visas when you need them while travelling. If you know pretty much where you're going, and when, you can get visas in your home country before you leave. Whichever way you do things, a list of embassies is included in each country chapter. Readers from countries not listed should use the phone directory of their own capital city, to check which East African countries are represented. (The term 'embassy' here includes consulates and high commissions.)

Embassies in East Africa

Assuming you are a visitor from Europe, Australasia or North America, most capital cities in East Africa have an embassy of your

---

Your Own Embassy

As a tourist, it's important to realise what your own embassy (the embassy of the country of which you are a citizen) can and can't do. Generally speaking, they won't help much in emergencies if the trouble you're in is even remotely your own fault. Remember that you are bound by the laws of the country you're in; embassies will not be sympathetic if you end up in jail after committing a crime locally, even if such actions are legal in your own country. In genuine emergencies you might get some assistance, but only if other channels have been exhausted. For example, if you need to get home urgently, a free air ticket is exceedingly unlikely; the embassy would expect you to have insurance. If you have all your money and documents stolen they might assist with getting a new passport, but a loan for onward travel is out of the question. Embassies used to keep letters for travellers or have a small reading room with home newspapers, but these days the mail holding service has been stopped, and even their newspapers tend to be out of date.

On the more positive side, some embassies post useful warning notices about local dangers or potential problems. The US embassies are particularly good for providing this information, and it's worth scanning their notice boards for 'travel advisories' about security, local epidemics, dangers to lone travellers etc. ∎

'home' country. The details are listed in the individual country chapters.

If you intend trekking in a very remote or potentially unstable area, it might be worth registering with your embassy, although in this situation the embassy staff may strongly advise you not to go to that area. It's your choice. If you do register, make sure you tell the embassy when you've returned, otherwise search parties or mountain rescue teams may get sent to rescue you. When such services are not required, it can be very embarrassing and very expensive.

MONEY

All the countries in East Africa have their own currencies, but exchange rates are unpredictable, so throughout this book we have quoted most prices in US dollars. Even though local prices (in Kenyan shillings, Malawian kwacha or whatever) may increase dramatically, the prices in US dollars are likely to remain more stable, and will at least still be recognisable by the time you arrive.

Costs

Trekking For trekking in East Africa it is not possible to give a single daily rate of expenditure. Trekking itself costs nothing more than food and boot leather. It's all the other things that add up – park charges, hut and camping fees, guide and porter wages, and so on. Much depends on where and how you trek; a long organised trek on a large popular mountain such as Kilimanjaro will cost much more than a simple do-it-yourself trip through quiet areas such as Kenya's Loroghi Hills or Malawi's Mt Mulanje. The descriptions in the individual country chapters cover all these things, and will give you a better idea.

Travelling When you're not trekking, how you travel between the mountains also affects costs. Generally, costs in all the countries covered in this book are pretty much on a par; no one country is noticeably cheaper or more expensive than the others. If you're on a tight budget, you could allow about US$10 per day for food, accommodation and local transport, although we often hear from hardened travellers who hitch, camp everywhere, buy local food from markets, and only get through a few dollars a day. If you want to travel in a less spartan manner, for example using more comfortable hotels and forms of transport, you should allow US$20 to US$30 per day. Of course, if you've got plenty of money you can go in real style, staying in good hotels and eating in fine restaurants (where they exist), easily getting through US$40 to US$80 per day. Full details about all these aspects of trekking and travelling are given in the relevant country and mountain sections.

If time is short and you want to move in a hurry, your costs may include regional flights and rental cars; these are discussed in the Getting There & Away and Getting Around chapters. As well as your trek on the high ground, you may also want to go on an organised wildlife safari (by vehicle or by foot). Once again the price range is enormous, from US$30 per day for low budget trips, up to US$300 or more per day for luxurious exclusivity.

Carrying Money

Before You Go The money you take to East Africa should be in a mixture of cash and travellers cheques, which you can buy from banks or specialist travel agencies such as American Express in your home country before leaving. The currency should be freely convertible ('hard'). In East Africa the hard currency easiest to deal with is US dollars. In main banks, UK pounds, French francs, Swiss or German marks, South African rands and Japanese yen are also recognised. Australian, New Zealand and Canadian dollars are difficult to deal with anywhere.

When the banks are closed or far away, cash can be exchanged more easily in other places (hotels, shops or travel companies), but it cannot be replaced if lost. Travellers cheques (TCs) can be replaced if lost or stolen (although this can sometimes take a long time), but can only be exchanged in banks or change bureaux.

While Travelling If you're travelling for a long time, or don't want to carry too much money around, you can use credit, debit or charge cards to draw local cash or travellers cheques in hard currency. This normally has to be done in a bank, usually in the capital or a large town. The process can be painfully slow. In Kenyan banks you may wait a couple of hours for your cash, although recently introduced cash machines (ATMs) connected to the worldwide Visa system can reduce this time to a few minutes. In Tanzania and Malawi it can take all day (or even longer if the phone lines are cut – which is quite often).

Another option is to use a 'telegraphic transfer' to move money from your home bank account to the branch of a bank in Nairobi, Arusha or wherever, where you can pick it up in local currency. Your own bank or card company will be able to advise on this process. You can also have money sent from your home country to Kenya (although not yet to other countries in East Africa) by the Western Union International Money Transfer system. This company has offices and reps all over the world; contact them direct for more details (in the UK ☎ (0800) 833833; elsewhere check the phone book).

Additional details about regulations, currency rates and places to change money are given in the individual country chapters.

Safety Once you've decided on the best combination of cash, cards and cheques, turn your thoughts to the practical aspects of carrying your money safely. To confound pickpockets and bag-snatchers, keep day-to-day cash in zipped pockets, and the bulk of your money in a pouch round your neck or elsewhere under your clothing. Keep it tied with at least two cords in case one gets broken in an attempted attack (more details in Dangers & Annoyances later in this chapter). Some travellers go for 'invisible pockets', money belts and other imaginative devices.

The Black Market

In some countries, there may be an unofficial ('black') market for hard currency. In East Africa, however, the draconian currency laws which created the black market have all been repealed, and you can change money at floating rates without difficulty. You might get up to 10% more for your money if you change on the black market but you'll also be breaking the law and stand a high chance of getting robbed or conned. You're on pretty dodgy moral ground as well.

Tipping

In small local bars and eating houses tips are not usual. In smarter places frequented by tourists tips may be expected – around 10% is usual, if the service warrants it – but check that a service charge hasn't already been added to your bill. On trek and on safari, it's usual to tip drivers, guides, porters and so on, but only if the service has been good. It's not automatic. As a rough guideline, a tip might be an extra day's pay for every five days worked. Further details on tipping are given in each country chapter.

Bargaining

In most parts of East Africa, bargaining over prices – often for market goods – is a way of life. Visitors from the west often have difficulty with this idea, especially when it comes to buying crafts and curios from roadside stalls. You may be used to things having a fixed value, whereas in Africa commodities are considered worth whatever their seller can get for them. It really is no different to the concept of an auction and should be treated as one more aspect of travel in the region. (See the boxed text 'The Fine Art of Bargaining' on the next page.)

Another aspect of bargaining is the negotiation sometimes possible when arranging an organised tour or trek, especially (but not always) amongst on-the-spot budget operators. Competition is high in Nairobi and Moshi, so a tour company may drop its price a little to stop you going to a rival. Additionally, if you can get a group of four of five people together you are in a much stronger position when it comes to 'rate shaving'.

POST & COMMUNICATIONS
Sending Mail

It is generally cheap to send letters and postcards out of all the countries covered in this book. The service is also generally reliable. All cities and large towns have a post office. Mail from any East African capital usually takes about a week to reach Europe, and slightly longer to reach North America or Australasia. Details of rates are given in the individual country chapters.

Receiving Mail

While travelling, you can have letters sent to you by using the poste restante service. Letters should be addressed in this form:

Your NAME
Poste Restante
General Post Office
Nairobi
Kenya

To collect your mail, go to the main post office in that town and show your passport.

The Fine Art of Bargaining

At craft and curio stalls, or in markets which are frequented by foreigners, sellers will invariably put their asking price high, but bargaining is very much expected, and should always be conducted in a friendly and spirited manner. If you pay the first price asked – whether out of ignorance or from guilt about how much you have compared with locals – you may be considered foolish. You'll also be doing fellow travellers a disservice by creating the impression that all foreigners are willing to pay any price named! You may also harm the local economy: by paying high prices you put some items out of reach of locals. You can't blame the sellers – why sell to locals when foreigners will pay twice as much?

The vendor's aim is to identify the highest price you're willing to pay. Your aim is to find the price below which the vendor will not sell. People have all sorts of formulae for working out what this should be, but there are no hard and fast rules. Some vendors may initially ask a price four (or more) times higher than what they're prepared to accept. Decide what you want to pay or what others have told you they've paid; your first offer should be about half this. The vendor may laugh or feign outrage, but the price will quickly drop from the original quote to a more realistic level. When it does, you can begin making better offers until you arrive at a mutually agreeable price.

And that's the crux – *mutually agreeable*. You hear travellers all the time moaning about how they got 'overcharged' by souvenir sellers. When things have no fixed price, nobody really gets overcharged. If you don't like the price, it's simple – don't pay it.

There's no reason to lose your temper when bargaining. If you become fed up with intransigence or the effort seems a waste of time, politely take your leave. Sometimes sellers will call you back if they think their stubbornness has been counterproductive. Very few will pass up the chance of making a sale, however thin the profit.

If sellers won't come down to a price you feel is fair (or one you can afford), it either means that they aren't making a profit, or that too many high-rolling foreigners have passed through already. Remember the sellers are under no more obligation to sell to you than you are to buy from them. You can go elsewhere, or (if you really want the item) accept the price. This is the raw edge of capitalism! ■

Letters sometimes take a few weeks to work through the system, so have them sent to a place where you're going to be for a while, or will be passing through more than once. Most poste restantes are reliable, although Nairobi's is a bit chaotic as so many letters are sent to it. American Express customers can have mail sent to Amex offices.

Mail is filed alphabetically by family name – that's why it's important to write this clearly and in capital letters. If you can't find mail you're expecting, see if it's been filed under one of your other names. When mail gets lost it's usually due to bad writing or an unclear address. Ask people writing to you to use just your family name and initials. If your family name is common, it should be underlined and your given name written in lower case.

Telephone & Fax

Most cities and large towns have public telephone offices where you can make international calls, or send messages by fax. You can also make calls from large hotels but these tend to charge a high commission. Cost and reliability varies. Calls from Nairobi and Lilongwe are fairly cheap and easy, from Kampala it takes time, and calls from anywhere in Tanzania are very expensive.

Email

An increasing number of tour companies in East Africa have email addresses. If you book a tour or trek, the company will probably allow you to use their line for a nominal sum. Otherwise, service providers offering short-term access for sending and receiving email are few. The only ones we know of are:

Kenya
> Thorn-Tree E-Mail, Omega Microsystems, Embassy House, corner of Harambee Ave and Parliament Rd, Nairobi (☎ 229650), charging around US$0.50 per message.

Malawi
> Epsilon & Omega, ADL House, City Centre, Lilongwe (☎ 784444; fax 781231; email E&O@eo.wn.apc.org). Access to a terminal provided for an hourly charge.

BOOKS

This section lists publications covering the whole (or most) of East Africa. Books on separate countries or individual mountains are listed in the relevant chapters and sections. Note that bookshops and libraries search by title or author so we have not included details of publishers unless particularly relevant. Some natural history field guides are listed in the Flora & Fauna section.

Lonely Planet

If you're looking for more in-depth coverage on any of the countries covered by this book, Lonely Planet has specific travel guides on *East Africa* (which includes coverage of Tanzania, Kenya and Uganda) and *Malawi, Mozambique & Zambia*. For onward travels, *Africa – The South* takes you from Malawi to South Africa via Zambia, Zimbabwe and several other countries. For pan-continental jaunts, and advice on overland routes *to* East Africa from the north, west or south, *Africa on a shoestring* has all you need to know.

For coverage of Kenya and northern Tanzania you can't go past Lonely Planet's *Kenya travel atlas*. And Lonely Planet's *Swahili phrasebook* will help you solve most of your basic language problems in East Africa.

Travel Manuals

For general advice, a very good choice is the large and comprehensive *Travellers Handbook*, published by Wexas, which covers all aspects of international travel, from buying a backpack, shipping a vehicle or catching a camel to selling your photos, meeting companions and surviving a shipwreck. The more concise *A to Z Guide for Lightweight Travellers* by Clive Tully contains good information and advice for independent travellers and trekkers. If you want to know more about travelling and trekking without destroying the country and the mountains you've come to enjoy, have a look at *Holidays that Don't Cost the Earth* by John Elkington & Julia Hailes.

Specialised Guidebooks & Manuals

Among the specialised guidebooks, the *East Africa International Mountain Guide* by Andrew Wielochowski is mainly for technical mountaineers, covering rock and ice routes on Mt Kenya, Kilimanjaro and the Rwenzoris plus several more obscure crags in the region, although it does contain some information on trekking.

A useful manual to read before you go is *Backpacking & Camping in the Developing World* by Scott Graham; the title is self-explanatory and the book contains useful information which will help you plan your trip.

Mountains & Landscapes

The books listed here are large-format hardbacks of particular interest to trekkers in East Africa, combining full-colour pictures with descriptions and travelogues. They provide excellent background information and inspiration before you go, or make good souvenirs after your trek.

Snowcaps on the Equator by Iain Allan & Gordon Boy, with photos by Clive Ward, beautifully portrays many of East Africa's mountains, including all the major snowcapped peaks, plus some of the smaller ranges in Tanzania, Kenya and Uganda. *The Great Rift: Africa's Changing Valley* by Anthony Smith is illuminating and entertaining; it covers history, geology and anthropology. *Africa's Mountains of the Moon* by Guy Yeoman mostly covers the Rwenzoris, with stories of the author's epic journeys through this range and other mountains in the region, plus good photos and exquisite hand-drawn pictures, as well as thoughts and positive suggestions on the future of Africa's people and wilderness areas.

Pan-continental mountain-lovers may also like to check *Trekking in Africa* by Stefan Ardito. This large-format paperback covers 16 wilderness hikes and trek areas from the Atlas of Morocco to South Africa's Otter Trail, via Algeria, Mali, the Virungas, Mt Kenya, Kili, Drakensberg and Fish River Canyon. The translation from the original Italian has produced a few odd blips, but overall it's a good combination of coffee-table adulation and precise route descriptions, lavishly illustrated with maps and photos.

Specialist Subjects

If you're looking for something which covers your own special interest, such as history, geology, politics, women's issues, African literature, art or natural history, contact your library or a good quality bookshop. Alternatively, you can find almost everything that has been written about the region (including most of the titles listed here) in Nairobi, which has some very good bookshops. To point you further in the right direction, you could refer to *The Sub-Saharan African Travel Resource Guide* (published by Bowker Saur), which critically annotates some 1500 books and maps on the region, and covers other aspects such as travel bookshops, magazines and publishers.

ONLINE SERVICES

If you have access to the Internet, you can get hold of all sorts of information about East Africa. Some of this is not particularly useful, but there are some real nuggets available which can add considerably to your travel or trekking experience. Of course, the Internet is most useful for travel information which may be just days or even hours old, and you should take advantage of this.

Your first stop should be Lonely Planet's own web site at http://www.lonelyplanet .com. Click on *SUBWWWAY* to access a complete range of travel-related links, including web pages dedicated to the countries of East Africa.

An extremely useful site is Africanet at http://www.africanet.com/, with facts on 50 countries, details on visas, health and many other subjects plus a bulletin board at http:// www.africanet.com/wwwboard/wwwboard .html and adverts for hotels, airlines and tour operators. CNN has breaking news stories relating to Africa at http://www.cnn .com/WORLD/africa/index.html. The most useful newsgroup for travel locations and logistics is rec.travel.africa. You can get advice on the use of newsgroups from http://

www.solutions.net/rec-travel/rtw/html/faq-rtw-51.html.

CINEMA

Movies about East Africa filmed on location really hit the big time in the early 1980s when *Out of Africa* was released. Meryl Streep and Robert Redford, plus of course the Masai Mara landscapes, did more for Kenya's tourism figures than any million dollar ad campaign, although the benefits of this great influx have proved to be questionable. Other well-known films based in East Africa include Disney's recent *The Lion King*, which brought 'Hakuna Matata' to every street from London to LA; the influential *Born Free* trilogy about Joy Adamson and lioness Elsa; and *The Snows of Kilimanjaro*, based on Hemingway's book, in which the eponymous mountain plays little more than a backdrop role. There are many more.

Movies of specific interest to trekkers include *Gorillas in the Mist*, based on Diane Fossey's work in the mountains of Zaïre (not far from the Rwenzoris) although actually filmed in Kenya's Aberdare Range; and the entertaining though strangely titled *Mountains of the Moon*, which ignores the Rwenzoris and covers the journey to the source of the Nile by John Speke and Richard Burton (the explorer, not the actor).

A new film to look out for is *The Ascent*, based on the classic mountaineering book *No Picnic on Mt Kenya* about Italian prisoners of war who escaped from their camp to climb Lenana and Batian.

PHOTOGRAPHY
Equipment & Film

Before You Go If you're buying a new camera for your trekking trip, go to a good photographic shop and tell them what you're doing; they can advise you on the suitable equipment and film.

For trekking you don't necessarily need anything with a long lens, as most of your shots will be of landscapes. Many people get excellent results with a good 30mm to 40mm lens compact camera. However, if you're also visiting a wildlife area, a zoom lens is almost essential for good shots. The best combination for a trekking and wildlife trip is a camera with a long zoom for close-ups, say 70mm to 210mm (if you go up to 300mm or 400mm you'll need a tripod, and that's a whole different ball game), and a short zoom which can go down to a wide angle for landscapes, say 35mm to 70mm. Some models are available with one lens covering the whole range.

If you're not fully conversant with your camera, buy a book (there are several which specialise in mountain and landscape photography) and practise techniques by shooting a few rolls of film before you go. It's worth getting it right – there are no second chances if your shots on the summit don't come out!

In East Africa The only places with a good selection of quality film are Nairobi, Blantyre and Lilongwe. Elsewhere it is possible to find film (for example, in Kampala, Dar es Salaam and Arusha, where it's imported from Nairobi) but supplies are not always reliable.

You can get prints developed in several large towns, but slides can only be done in Nairobi. There's a choice of places doing developing, some better than others. Camera spares and repairs are also a problem. Batteries for sale are often of poor quality, and camera *fundis* may attack your precious Nikon with nothing more than a blunt knife. Bring batteries and have your camera serviced before you leave home.

If your camera does develop problems, or you just need some more film, the place where everybody goes is the Expo Camera Centre in Nairobi (on Mama Ngina St, a block up from the Hilton). Mo, the bloke who runs the shop, is a genius and will do his best to fix any problem for you. He sells film, does overnight print processing, and also does specialist developing. Some of the best wildlife photographers bring their stuff to him from all over East Africa, so he must be good.

Security Use your camera sensitively when outside the national parks and wilderness areas. Do not take photos of anything that may be considered 'strategic', such as army camps, police stations, bridges, railways etc. You may get arrested as a spy. At best you

---

Photography Hints

Timing The best times to take photographs on sunny days are the first two hours after sunrise and the last two before sunset. This takes advantage of the colour-enhancing rays cast by a low sun. To further reduce the bad effects of glare, filters (eg ultraviolet, polarising or 'skylight') can help; ask for advice in a good camera shop.

Exposure When photographing animals or people, take light readings on the subject and not the brilliant African background or your shots will turn out underexposed.

Camera Care Factors that can spoil you camera or film include heat, humidity, very fine sand, salt water and sunlight. Take appropriate precautions.

Animals When photographing animals try to be patient. If your subject is nothing but a speck in the distance, don't waste expensive film, but keep the camera ready in case it (or something else) comes closer.

People If you can't get a candid shot, ask permission; don't just snap away. Like people everywhere, some Africans may enjoy being photographed, others do not. They may be superstitious about your camera, suspicious of your motives, or simply interested in making a dollar from your desire to photograph them. Even though this may not be 'authentic', it's an aspect of tourism you'll just have to accept. Put yourself in their position and try to think what you'd do.

People may agree to be photographed if you give them a picture for themselves. If you don't carry a Polaroid camera, take their address and make it clear that you'll send the photo by post. Never say you'll send a photo, and then don't. Alternatively, just be honest and say that so many people ask you for photos that it's impossible to send to everyone. ∎

could have your film confiscated. At worst you could be imprisoned.

TIME
Time in Kenya, Uganda and Tanzania is GMT/UTC plus three hours. In Malawi it's GMT/UTC plus two hours. There is no daylight saving in East Africa.

ELECTRICITY
The countries of the region use 240V AC. The power supply varies – from mostly reliable in Kenya to wildly fluctuating in Malawi. Plugs and sockets also vary, but are usually of the British style three-square-pin or two-round-pin variety.

LAUNDRY
Weight restrictions on a long trek may mean wearing the same set of clothes for many days, so one of your first concerns once you're down off the mountain is likely to be getting your gear clean. Most hotels don't allow you to do laundry in your room, although they probably wouldn't mind a few socks and undies being hand-washed. Small packets of washing power ('Omo') can be bought in shops and markets. All but the most basic hotels usually have a laundry service, where you can drop off dirty stuff first thing in the morning and get it back clean next day, or even that evening. Generally this service is relatively cheap; an average set of clothes costs only a few dollars. If you have clothes made from technical fabrics (ie 'thermal' underwear or a fleece jacket) be sure to tell the hotel staff not to use scrubbing brushes or irons, which can do permanent damage.

TOILETS
There are two main types of toilet in Africa: the 'western' style, with a toilet bowl and seat; and the 'eastern' or African style, which is a hole in the floor, over which you squat. As with anywhere else, the standard of toilets can vary tremendously, from pristine to unusable. Some travellers complain that African toilets are difficult to use, or that you have to remove half your clothing to use them. This is not so, and it only takes a small degree of

practice to master a comfortable squatting technique.

In some places (particularly rural areas, or in national parks, including the main mountains) the squat toilets are built over a deep hole in the ground. These are called 'long-drops', and the crap in the hole just fades away naturally over time, as long as the hole isn't filled with too much other rubbish (such as paper or synthetic materials, including tampons – these should be burnt separately).

In remote trekking areas, there may be no toilets at all, and you have to find a quiet bush or rock to relieve yourself behind. For more useful thoughts on this subject, see the Responsible Trekking section later in this chapter.

Some 'western' toilets are not plumbed in, but just balanced over a long-drop, and sometimes seats of one sort or another are constructed. The lack of running water usually makes such cross-cultural mechanisms a disaster. A non-contact squat loo is better than a filthy box to hover over any day.

WOMEN TREKKERS
For women trekking in the national parks, there are no major aspects worth noting, except perhaps the frequent lack of toilet facilities or any other privacy in some areas. Some women have reported that high altitudes or hard conditions play hell with menstrual cycles, so be prepared for unexpected periods, or none at all.

In remote populated areas, western trekkers of either gender may be greeted by local people with some surprise or suspicion. A woman walking alone, with no apparent motive and *no husband* is likely to be met with sheer disbelief. A local guide (see Guides & Porters later in this chapter) is especially useful in these situations – not so much to show the way, but to make explanations.

When travelling around East Africa between mountain areas, generally speaking, women travellers (alone or with other women) will not encounter specifically female problems, such as harassment from men, any more than they might in other parts of the world. In fact, many women travellers report that, compared with North Africa (including Morocco and Egypt), South America, and not a few western countries, the region is relatively unthreatening from this point of view.

Of course, in the 'rough' parts of some East African cities mugging is a possibility and, as in any place worldwide, women (particularly lone women) are generally seen as easy targets, so it pays to keep away from these areas, especially at night.

East Africa is very much a conservative male-dominated society, and because of these prevailing attitudes it can be hard to meet and talk with local women in the countries you're travelling through. It may require being invited into a home, although several women travellers have reported that buses and markets are a good place to try striking up conversation. Because many women have received little or no education, sometimes language barriers can be a problem, but this is changing to some extent because more recently girls have stayed at school while the boys are sent away to work. Thus in some countries, many staff in tourist offices, government departments and so on are educated young women, and this can be as good a place as any to try striking up a conversation. In rural areas, a starting point might be women teachers at a local school or staff at a health centre.

TREKKING WITH CHILDREN

It is not advisable to take young children above 3000m, as the altitude can have serious effects. On Kilimanjaro it is specifically forbidden for children under 10 to go over 3000m, although they are allowed up to Mandara Hut (from where Maundi Crater can be reached before descending the next day) for a taste of the high peaks. Groups of teenagers often trek on Kili and Mt Kenya, and seem to suffer from cold and altitude no more or less than adults, although mud and scree can ruin trendy sports clothing.

Over many years of trekking in East Africa, we've met several parents who have taken offspring walking on the lower mountains (eg Nyika and Mulanje in Malawi, Cherangani and Loroghi hills in Kenya, the Usambaras

in Tanzania) and thoroughly enjoyed their trip. Naturally, distances covered are shorter, but children are a great common denominator and an ideal way to strike up conversation with local people. Of course, the kids have to like a bit of walking too, but most seem to enjoy the outdoor life and the constantly varying situations.

A major concern for parents may be the scarcity of decent medical facilities (as with most parts of the developing world). There's no easy way around this. In many parts of East Africa, however, you can be in the wilderness but still be within a couple of days of a major city, where good medical facilities exist.

On a more practical note, when travelling long distances between mountain areas, especially on public transport, parents of younger kids will need to have a good supply of distractions to hand. ('Let's count how many black goats we can see ...') In hotels, specific family rooms are generally not available, but triple rooms are often only slightly more than the price of a double. Alternatively, arranging an extra mattress or two so that children can share a standard adult double is generally not a problem.

Lonely Planet's book *Travel With Children* by Maureen Wheeler provides more sound advice on clothing, hotels, health and food, plus several ideas for games on the bus.

USEFUL ORGANISATIONS

Each country covered in this book has a national mountain club for local walkers and climbers. These clubs are mainly for citizens and expatriate residents and they do not usually cater for visitors. Generally they are not able to reply to individual requests for advice and information unless you are a member of a mountain club in your own country which has reciprocal arrangements with the club overseas. Some mountain clubs in East Africa produce guidebooks to local mountains and climbing areas which are for sale to the general public. (Details of mountain clubs and other useful organisations are given in each country chapter.)

DANGERS & ANNOYANCES
Animals

Most of the treks described in this book are in highland areas, where you are unlikely to meet large unfriendly animals. On mountains where potentially dangerous wildlife does occur (Mt Meru, the Aberdare Range and the Nyika Plateau), national park rangers usually accompany trekkers, although close encounters are very unlikely. You might also see elephant droppings on the forested slopes of Mt Kenya, and even leopard prints on Mulanje, but you'll be very lucky (or unlucky) to even catch a glimpse of the animals themselves.

If you are walking in an area where there might be dangerous wildlife about, the best thing to do is make a noise as you walk. Most animals will move out of your way long before you even know they were there. One trekker we know ties a couple of bells to his rucksack when walking through the bush, which seems to have worked well to date.

Unfortunately, some old buffalo are deaf! In the very unlikely situation of you suddenly coming face to face with a buffalo, it will probably be as surprised as you and will almost certainly run off. If it doesn't move, you should back away slowly to show no sign of threat. If you're in forest, drop your pack and climb a tree. Fast. If there are no trees, lie down or 'run like a rat', crawling through the bush so the buffalo's horns can't reach you.

In reality, the biggest problem you're likely to have with animals is mice in the mountain huts, or hyrax wandering around the camp site, nibbling your food. Mosquitoes can be problematic too (see the Health, Safety & First Aid chapter).

Humans

In rural areas there is very little chance of robbery or theft. On mountains and in wilderness areas there is even less chance, as these places are usually uninhabited. Porters, guides and bunkhouse caretakers are generally trustworthy. Even on the most popular routes on Mt Kenya and Kilimanjaro, where the porters and guides have a reputation for

being somewhat mercenary, actual theft is uncommon.

Even so, if you do use porters, you should carry valuables in your day-pack, and it's better not to leave money or items like cameras and penknives lying around unattended at huts or camp sites. This is not necessarily because they will be stolen, although it's certainly going to tempt some people (including other trekkers), but because such action might be seen as a casual display of wealth and only go to increase the perception of the already large financial gap between visitors and locals.

In small towns and villages, security is rarely a problem. You are usually quite safe walking around, and your hotel room is very unlikely to be broken into. In the larger towns and cities, such as Nairobi, Mombasa, Kampala, Dar, Moshi and Arusha, pickpockets operate in the bus stations and markets, but hotels are generally safe. Unfortunately, violent robberies do occur in Nairobi and Dar, and western tourists are often the victims (because they've got more money), but such cases still happen far less often than they do in, say, London or New York.

When wandering around any large town try not to look too lost. Pretend you know where you are going, even if you don't. Avoid standing on busy street corners with the guidebook open at the city map page. It's best to keep your camera out of sight, and hang on tightly to your day-pack. Use your common sense and be careful, but there's no need to be paranoid. Nairobi (sometimes called 'Nai-robbery') is particularly bad, and a bit of paranoia doesn't hurt in this town. Indeed, some travellers say it's the only way to survive! Bag-snatching is not uncommon, and you should be on your guard for groups of thieves operating on crowded buses.

TREKKING ROUTES

Some suggested itineraries have been described earlier in this chapter, and an outline of each country's trekking highlights is given in each country chapter. This section looks at various aspects of the routes in more detail.

Route Standard

Classification can be tricky but each route description in this book outlines condition (eg clear or hard to follow, boggy or easy underfoot) and difficulty (eg long or short days, generally flat or several steep gradients).

Obviously, some people will find the routes easier than others. The classifications are based on the assumption that you're a fairly regular walker who would have no trouble covering 15 to 20km per day on reasonable paths.

Days Required

The trekking routes in this book have all been divided into stages, each corresponding to a day's walk. Some stages are short, while others are very long. It's sometimes possible to divide a long stage in half or combine two shorter stages. For many stages, alternatives are suggested which are either harder or easier.

The end of each stage is either a bunkhouse, hut or place for camping. Most of these overnight sites have water, but there are a few dry sites where water has to be carried in. It's not always possible to stop for the night just anywhere. Even if you're not using mountain huts (where they exist) you'll still be restricted to places that can provide a good camp site.

Most treks also include 'sidetracks', which branch off the main route for a few hours, or even for an extra couple of days.

Distance, Time & Altitude

Each stage heading includes details on the number of kilometres, hours required, and metres of ascent (where these figures are useful or relevant).

Distances are approximate, and cannot take account of winding paths, steep gradients, or conditions such as snow, scree or thick mud. Distance alone is virtually meaningless. It is essential to note the time required to cover the stage. The hours given are based on average minimum and maximum walking times, and are intended as a guideline only. They do not include long stops. You should allow extra for photo and lunch breaks, especially if you're a keen photographer (or have

a hearty appetite). On higher stages, times presume you're reasonably well acclimatised.

The kilometres-to-hours ratio gives you an indication of the difficulty of the stage. For example, heading for the summit of Kilimanjaro, it takes at least six hours to cover 3km (that's 500 *metres* per hour). By this you know the going is very steep and very hard!

Where metres of ascent are given, this is the overall altitude gain between one night's camp and the next, and is most useful for calculating your rate of ascent, important when trying to avoid mountain sickness (see the Health, Safety & First Aid chapter). It is not the total ascent you actually have to cover on that stage, although on major mountains most stages are either mainly up (or mainly down) anyway. Crossing several large ridges and valleys in Himalayan style, although it does occur, is not common.

Note that when referring to heights, distances and altitudes, metres are abbreviated to m (eg Lenana is 5199m). Altitudes are rounded to the nearest 10m (except for major features). Some figures are also given in feet, abbreviated to ft (for all you imperialists out there). There's a conversion table at the back of the book.

Asking for Directions

When asking local guides or porters how far it is to the next camp or wherever, you should always ask in terms of hours, as most have a fairly hazy idea about distance and, as already indicated, this is often meaningless anyway. In practice, many guides have a fairly hazy idea about time too, so never take things too literally.

Outside the wilderness areas, asking local people for information can also be tricky. 'Short', 'long', 'near' and 'far' take on completely different meanings. Most people in Africa don't have our obsession with time. It may not matter to them whether a town is two or eight hours away. They just know they'll get there some time that day, and can't see why you should want it any more precise than that.

Asking directions can also be problematic. At a fork in the path, never say 'Is this the way to ...?', as you'll almost certainly be told 'Yes', whichever way you point. Asking 'Where is ...?' gives you a much better chance of success.

Terminology in This Book
Paths & Tracks The treks in this book generally keep to a 'path', which is normally clear to follow, and for walkers only. A path is shown on the maps in this book by a line of small dashes (see the Map Legend near the front of the book).

Some routes may also follow 'tracks' – shown on the maps in this book by larger dashes. It is important to note that a 'track' in East Africa is drivable even though most of the tracks followed by treks in this book are unsurfaced and very rarely used by vehicles. Most are in national parks or wilderness areas. Some may be completely disused by cars and make ideal walking routes, especially through bush or forest.

Unsurfaced roads ('dirt roads') may also be followed in sections of treks described in this book. All minor roads (whether dirt or tar) are shown on the maps by thin solid lines. Major roads are shown by thicker solid lines.

Throughout this book, some treks follow routes where paths are very faint or non-existent; here you make your own way through bush or open moorland. This is shown on the maps in this book by the stippled 'route' strip, with no other dots or dashes.

Trails The term 'trail' has generally not been used in this book. A trek generally would not follow a trail, because in East Africa these are created by animals (either wild or domestic – eg buffalo trails in the forests of Elgon, or cattle trails in the Maasai areas). The exception is in Malawi, where in some national parks the term 'trail' is used to mean a walking route, ie 'hiking trail' or 'wilderness trail'.

Bunkhouses, Huts & Camp Sites We have distinguished between 'bunkhouses' (usually with facilities and a caretaker) and 'huts' (usually without) in the accommodation sections. We have also distinguished between

official 'camp sites', which may have facilities for which a fee is usually charged, and 'camping places' which are unofficial and have no facilities (you just put up your tent).

Place Names
During your trek, you are likely to find books and maps using various spellings for place names. Variations are usually slight and shouldn't cause too much confusion. Some are due to 'old' colonial spellings being Africanised, others are due to error and inconsistency. The emphasis some writers put on the 'correct' spelling of places, where traditionally names were never written down, is sometimes just a tad too obsessive. In this book, where mountains or features have been completely renamed we include old and new names, and, if the change is slight, generally the latest version is used. But if you come across inconsistencies between this book and the real world don't worry about it too much.

Similarly, you may also come across slight inconsistencies where various maps give different heights for mountains and other features. Usually, the differences are slight and unlikely to cause any problems.

Maps in This Book
The maps in this book provide enough information if you keep to the routes described, although they are not enough in themselves for accurate navigation. It is impossible to show every single topographical feature. Small streams, for example, have been omitted unless they are an important reference point. Minor paths and tracks have also been omitted, unless they form part of the route. On some treks there is no path at all and you must make your own way – this is shown on the map as a stippled 'route' strip, with no other dots or dashes.

Trek Profiles
The trek profile diagrams indicate daily altitude gains and losses for major treks. The stage numbers shown on the horizontal line relate to the stages in the text.

Route Changes

Most of the treks in this book are in mountain wilderness areas which are unlikely to be affected by major projects such as road-building schemes or logging concessions. Natural features are unlikely to change, although fragile soil and vegetation covers are slowly disappearing on some routes, and glaciers are receding at an alarming rate on the major peaks.

In some managed areas, the authorities make alterations to trekking routes. This can involve opening up new paths to take the pressure off existing routes, or closing old ones to allow the damaged land to recover.

On some mountains, the routes are being 'improved' by the addition of facilities such as bridges and signposts. In some areas, huts are being constructed, while in other places old huts are being removed and new camp sites established.

New regulations concerning fires, rubbish disposal, camp sites and so on are frequently introduced. The most likely changes are outlined in the individual route descriptions. In Africa an old saying states that 'a plan is a predetermined alternative to what actually happens', but by trekking through this region you will normally have more than the usual amount of control over your own destiny. If you are ready and prepared for the changes you can usually take them (often quite literally) in your stride.

GUIDES & PORTERS

For treks in East Africa, local guides and porters (nearly always men) are sometimes available. Using their services is generally optional, and depends on the trekking you want to do (see Types of Trek earlier in this chapter). More specific information about guides and porters in each area is provided in the individual mountain sections.

Guides

Guides are highly recommended in some areas, especially if you're inexperienced or trekking alone, or where routes do not follow clear paths and maps do not show enough detail for accurate navigation.

Guides are either freelancers or work directly for the trekking companies. Generally, you shouldn't expect too much. Guides will usually be able to show you the way, and that's it. Only a very few have qualifications or formal training. Even on the popular mountains, many guides only know the common routes, and are not much use if you want to do something unusual. For the less-frequented routes, even if you take a guide, it is very important to familiarise yourself with route conditions, water points, the likelihood of wild animals and so on. How you perceive factors such as 'near', 'far', 'easy', 'good to drink' and so on may be very different from how your guide sees them. Of course, there are exceptions: some companies employ experienced professional guides with knowledge of local vegetation and wildlife, first aid, map and compass work, rescue techniques and so on.

Several of the trekking areas described in this book are also wildlife reserves inhabited by animals such as buffalo, elephant and lion. An armed park ranger is obligatory here to protect you in case of close encounters. If required, these rangers will also act as guides. They are normally very knowledgeable and reliable.

Porters

Porters are nearly always freelancers, carrying loads for tourists when they're not working on their farms in the foothills. In the major mountain areas, they have formed 'clubs' or unions to standardise wages and improve conditions. If you want to do a supported trek, you can go to the club headquarters at the foot of the mountain and make arrangements there. The porters will usually be ready within a few hours, or the following day at the latest.

Porters rarely have any equipment of their own, so you have to provide rucksacks for them. The usual way of doing things is for a porter to carry your main bag while you walk with just a day-pack containing camera, waterproofs, lunch and so on. There's normally a weight limit of 14 to 18kg, so if you're on a long trek, with camping gear and food for a week, you'll probably need two or even three porters per trekker. If you haven't got a spare rucksack, these can sometimes be hired, or you can make something up out of sacks and ropes from a market.

If you're hiring more than one porter, it's usual to appoint a 'chief porter' who will arrange the others. If you have hired a guide as well, he will often organise porters for you.

Anything in your rucksack that's likely to be damaged should be well packed, as bags are not always handled with reverence. Make sure the porter carrying the tomatoes or bottle of oil knows what he's got in his bag, and ask him to take care.

RESPONSIBLE TREKKING

Most of the treks in this book pass through mountain wilderness areas where the natural environment is protected. It's usually protected because it's in danger, and the danger comes from many sources, including the presence of trekkers.

To trek in the mountains of East Africa is a privilege, but with this privilege comes responsibility. There are several things you can do to lessen your own impact upon this fragile environment.

Routes

Stay on established paths and tracks where they exist. When hiking in a group through open country, spread out to avoid doing irreparable damage to vegetation and creating new paths.

Camping

In areas of heavy use, camp only at established camp sites. In seldom-visited areas try to minimise your impact as much as possible by camping on durable surfaces, not fragile vegetation.

Fires

Fires are not allowed in many areas. Even where they are permitted, wood is usually scarce so try to avoid using fires or keep them as small as possible. This is especially relevant in the high moorlands above the forests on the main mountains. Encourage porters to

do the same. Even burning dead heather and groundsels is harmful, as this rotting vegetation supports various insects which are a vital link in the food chain; it also protects the thin covering of soil which is otherwise washed away by rain.

Wood can be saved if you treat your drinking water with purification solutions instead of boiling it (this is usually more effective anyway). If possible, you should support trekking companies who use stoves rather than wood fires for cooking.

A complete ban on wood fires may soon be introduced on several of the major mountains in East Africa. As the number of trekkers continues to increase, this is to be welcomed and encouraged.

Water

Do not pollute water supplies. For washing, take water from streams or tarns in a bowl or mug; do not wash or rinse cooking pans in the stream itself. Encourage porters to do the same. Wherever possible, use biodegradable soap and detergent (although even these take a long time to break down). Again, support trekking companies who follow these methods.

Toilets

Wherever a toilet is provided at a hut or camp site, always use it, even if it's close to overflowing. If your hut or camp site does not have a toilet, you have to go outside in the open. The Mt Kenya authorities recommend that at lower altitudes all crap and toilet paper should be buried (well away from paths and water supplies) as they will be decomposed by natural organisms in the soil. Some trekking companies provide groups with toilet tents, or a small spade. However, at high altitudes these organisms are not abundant, so the advice is not to bury your crap but to leave it in the open where UV light from the sun will break it down. In this situation toilet paper should not be buried, but it should not be left in the open either; you can burn it (if you've stopped using a fire, use matches, although this is very hard on wet windy days) or keep it in a strong plastic bag until you can dispose of it properly.

Rubbish

Some huts and camp sites have rubbish pits, but these are ugly and can injure scavenging wildlife. Burying rubbish on high mountains is not good as stuff takes a very long time to decay and may be washed up by rain or dug up by animals. Burning rubbish is fine, in areas where fires are allowed, as long as it burns completely. The best solution is to bring down everything you take up. It's got to be lighter than when it came up. This is especially the case with silver foil, plastics and tins. (I've seen trekkers, who *appeared* completely rational, dispose of tins and foil packets by throwing them on the fire. They seem to believe metal can burn.) Take strong plastic bags for carrying rubbish down and instruct your porters to do the same. A promise of a slightly larger tip for their trouble will make the matter easier. Once again, you can support trekking companies who instruct their porters to carry rubbish down.

Cultural Responsibility

Some thoughts on cultural responsibility are given in the section on the Kipengere Range, towards the end of the Tanzania chapter.

ACCOMMODATION
Cities & Towns

When travelling in East Africa, getting to and from the mountain areas, you'll inevitably need accommodation in some of the cities and towns you pass through. Each country chapter mentions a few hotels in the towns nearest the trekking areas, and in the capital city (as you'll probably arrive there first, or pass through between mountains).

In all the countries covered in this book, you can find a wide range of places to stay, from international-class Hiltons and Sheratons in the cities, through reasonably priced, comfortable, mid-range hotels, down to the most basic lodging houses out in the sticks or at the rough end of town. Some towns in Kenya and Tanzania have youth hostels and YMCAs, with dormitories or private rooms. In Malawi, most towns have a Council Resthouse providing cheap accommodation. Many hotels have separate bungalow sleeping rooms in a courtyard or garden; these are called *bandas* or *rondavels*.

Standards vary between countries, but quality generally reflects price. Hotels at the top end of the range have clean, air-conditioned, rooms with hot showers and toilets en suite that work all the time. In the middle of the range, rooms have bathrooms en suite, but there may not always be hot water, and there will probably be fans instead of air-con. Near the bottom end, hotel rooms are not always clean (they are sometimes downright filthy), bathrooms are usually shared and often in an appalling state, and a hole in the window may provide fresh air.

Some hotels charge for a bed only, with all meals extra. If breakfast is included it's usually on a par with the standard of accommodation: a full buffet in more expensive places; tea and bread further down the scale.

On Trek

Most treks described in this book are through wilderness areas; there are no settlements with accommodation, and nothing in the way of Alpine hotels or Himalayan tea shops. On some of the more popular routes there are bunkhouses or huts, but in many areas you have to camp.

Bunkhouses are generally well maintained, with separate sleeping and dining rooms, and a permanent caretaker. The bunkhouses on Kilimanjaro's Marangu Route even have electric lights. Huts are usually smaller and more basic, with little more than a roof and four walls (if you're lucky), such as the tin sheds found on some parts on Mt Kenya and the Rwenzoris. The word 'hut' is often used to describe any kind of building on a mountain, so if you're planning to rely on them, make sure you know what facilities are available. Wherever you stay, you nearly always need a sleeping bag. If you're not on an organised trek, you often need cooking gear too.

To trek in the more remote areas you need a tent and a full set of camping gear. (Even on the routes where basic accommodation is available, many trekkers camp anyway.) This means you can be completely self-contained and self-sufficient, allowing you to trek on unusual routes and through more remote mountain areas, with freedom and independence. Although some routes on the main mountains have huts, a tent is either essential or highly recommended for most of the treks described in this book. If you are using local guides and porters, they usually sleep in the huts or in their own section of the bunkhouses, even if you are camping (see the Guides & Porters section earlier in this chapter).

Bunkhouses, huts and camp sites, and the facilities available at each, are described in detail in the individual mountain sections. For more advice on the practicalities of outdoor life in East Africa see the section on Responsible Trekking earlier in this chapter.

FOOD
Buying Food
Wherever you go in East Africa you can always find enough food in the cities and towns to provide for a trek. Freeze-dried lightweight meals used by mountaineers are not available in East Africa, so you'll have to bring them from home if you want them, but such food isn't usually necessary.

For treks in Kenya, the best place to buy food and supplies is Nairobi. Here you can get just about anything in the many large shops and supermarkets. Some items are imported and expensive, but you can usually find a locally made, cheaper version. Available food suitable for trekking includes: rice, several sorts of pasta, lentils, packet soups, bread, porridge oats, corn flakes, sweet biscuits, crackers, margarine and jam (in tins), peanut butter, honey, cheese, eggs, fresh meat, packets of bacon, sausage and cooked meats, tins of cooked mince and steak, corned beef, luncheon meat and sardines, tins of beans, tomatoes and other vegetables, dried fruit, nuts, chocolate, coffee, tea, drinking chocolate, and dried or UHT milk in cartons. There are sometimes shortages of flour and loose sugar, although you can usually find sugar cubes. You can also buy vegetable or meat stock cubes, curry powder and all sorts of herbs and spices to liven up your meals.

Most of the stuff listed above can also be found in other large towns in Kenya, so you won't need to go back to Nairobi in between treks. A lot of food from Kenya is shipped to Tanzania and Uganda, so you also can find most of the things on this list in Arusha, Moshi and Kampala (although not always with the same range or choice).

In the cities and large towns of Malawi, there's even more choice than in Nairobi. Most of it is imported from South Africa and the choice in the supermarkets is the same as in any developed country, although prices are about the same too. If you've been in the bush for a while, it's fairly mind-blowing to come into the hypermarket in Lilongwe and see a whole aisle of different breakfast cereals, and at least six sorts of mustard.

Fruit and vegetables can be bought in markets all over East Africa. Depending on the seasons, you can usually find potatoes, carrots, cabbage, onions, tomatoes, zucchinis (courgettes), aubergines (eggplants), avocados, green beans, spinach, peas and all sorts

Cooking Tips
When you're on trek, it's always worth trying to carry as much fresh food (fruit and vegetables) as you can, to cut down on tins and packets. This saves weight and also reduces the amount of rubbish you need to bring down. Many vegetables are also cheap, easy to find, nutritious, quick-cooking (if you chop them up small), long-lasting and almost unbreakable. Soft fruit and veg (tomatoes, bananas, avocados) have a much shorter life-span on trek and should be packed and carried carefully.

Remember that water boils at a lower temperature as you get higher in the mountains, so food takes longer to cook. When you're above 4000m, lentils and rice are bad news for the fuel supply and the digestion. Pasta is better at this height. Dried beans always take a long time to cook and are not really suitable as trekking food. If you're a bean fiend, you can buy them in tins, or wait until you get off the mountain and then go to a restaurant. ■

of dried beans. In the fruit line there are bananas, pineapples, oranges and mangoes.

Places to Eat

In the cities and large towns there's usually a good choice of places to eat, ranging from quality restaurants serving international or speciality foods, through a broad spectrum of mid-range cafes, down to basic snack-bars with only three things on the menu, two of them 'finished'.

In villages and rural areas the choice is also limited. The eating houses cater for the locals and serve straightforward, cheap, filling meals, usually a meat stew with some stodge – rice, plantain bananas or the ubiquitous maize meal (*ugali* in Kenya, Uganda and Tanzania, *nsima* in Malawi).

Vegetarians don't have an easy time. The smarter places usually have fish; otherwise it's egg and chips in the mid-range places and bean stew in the cheapies. Many large towns have at least one Indian restaurant, and some of these do good vegetarian meals.

Snacks are available everywhere, at roadside stalls or in snack-bars with a cup of tea. These include *mandazis/ndazi*, a deep-fried dough ball, not unlike a doughnut when fresh, plus chapattis, samosas (usually called *sambusas*) and cake.

If your tongue craves a break, Nairobi has an amazing selection of junk-food joints, which are great to come back to after a few weeks of trekking in the wilds. You can also get pizzas in Blantyre, Ethiopian food in Kampala, and Chinese takeaway in Arusha.

Health, Safety & First Aid

Keeping healthy during your treks and travels depends on your predeparture preparations, your daily health care and how you handle any medical problem that does develop. While the potential dangers can seem quite frightening, in reality few travellers experience anything more than upset stomachs.

Predeparture Planning

Make sure that you have adequate health insurance. (See Travel Insurance under Visas & Documents in the Regional Facts for the Trekker chapter.)

GENERAL HEALTH & FITNESS

Before leaving for a trek in East Africa consider carefully your physical health. Trekking in Africa can be very strenuous, so it is sensible to be reasonably fit before you start. Strange as it may seem, the best training for walking is walking. Many fit footballers and squash players come to grief on the high mountains when they realise their own sport is not the best preparation for a long walk. For many of the treks in this book, you should at least have done some regular walking in the preceding months. Don't leave 'training' until the last minute!

FIRST AID TRAINING

In the unlikely event of a medical emergency, a good understanding of resuscitation techniques (CPR) and control of bleeding could save a life. If your first aid skills and knowledge are not up to date, it would be a good idea to do an appropriate course before you leave home.

IMMUNISATIONS

To protect yourself against various diseases while in Africa, several immunisations (also called vaccinations) are required. Once again,

don't leave everything until the last minute. Some vaccinations require more than one injection, while others cannot be given together. It is recommended you seek medical advice at least six weeks before travel. Be aware that there is often a greater risk of disease with children and in pregnancy.

You may have been already immunised during childhood to diseases such as polio, typhoid and tuberculosis, in which case you may only need booster injections. If you're not sure, ask your doctor to check your medical records. Your doctor or government health department will also supply an International Health Certificate; all your vaccinations can be clearly recorded here, as proof to immigration officials that you have the necessary protection.

Discuss your requirements with your doctor, but before a visit to East Africa you should consider vaccinations for the following diseases:

Hepatitis A This is the most common travel-acquired illness after diarrhoea and can put you out of action for weeks. Havrix 1440 is a vaccination which provides long-term immunity (possibly more than 10 years) after an initial injection and a booster at six to 12 months.

Gamma globulin is not a vaccination but is ready-made antibody collected from blood donations. It should be given close to departure because, depending on the dose, it only protects for two to six months.

Typhoid This disease is always a possibility where hygiene is a problem, so for trekking in Africa a vaccination (available either as an injection or oral capsules) is very important.

Tetanus & Diphtheria Tetanus can be introduced into the body through injury – dirty puncture wounds, burns or even relatively minor wounds. Diphtheria can be a fatal throat infection. Vaccination is essential. After an initial course of three injections, boosters are necessary every 10 years.

Meninogococcal Meningitis Healthy people carry this disease; it is transmitted like a cold and you can die from it within a few hours. There are many carriers, and vaccination is recommended for travellers to Africa. A single injection will give good protection for three years. The vaccine is

76

not recommended for children under two years because they do not develop satisfactory immunity.

Hepatitis B This disease is spread by blood or by sexual activity. Travellers who should consider a hepatitis B vaccination include those visiting countries where there are known to be many carriers, where blood transfusions may not be adequately screened or where sexual contact is a possibility. It involves three injections, the quickest course being over three weeks with a booster at 12 months.

Polio This is a serious, easily transmitted disease, still prevalent in many developing countries. Everyone should keep up to date with this vaccination. A booster every 10 years maintains immunity.

Yellow Fever This serious disease is endemic in Africa and the vaccine is a legal requirement for entry into many countries, although *usually* only enforced when coming from an infected area. Protection lasts 10 years. You usually have to go to a special yellow fever vaccination centre. Vaccination poses some risk during pregnancy but if you must travel to a high-risk area it is advisable. People allergic to eggs may not be able to have this vaccine. Discuss with your doctor.

Rabies This virus exists in Africa and is transmitted by infected animals. It cannot be transmitted through intact skin. Vaccination is not routinely recommended, as visitors are quite unlikely to be bitten by animals. It should be considered if you are spending a long time in remote areas, handling animals, caving or cycling (as mad dogs just love chasing bikes). It may also be recommended for children (who may not report a bite). Discuss with your doctor. Pre-travel rabies vaccination involves having three injections over 21 to 28 days. If someone who has been vaccinated is bitten or scratched by an animal they will require two booster injections of vaccine; those not vaccinated require more.

Cholera It is now widely recognised that vaccinations give poor protection against this disease, but very occasionally travellers in Africa are asked by immigration officials to present a certificate, even though all countries and the WHO have dropped a cholera immunisation as a health requirement. You might be able to get a certificate without having the injection from a doctor or health centre sympathetic to the vagaries of travel in Africa.

Tuberculosis The risk to travellers of contracting this disease is usually very low, although for those who will be living with or closely associated with local people in Africa there may be some risk. As most healthy adults do not develop symptoms, a skin test before and after travel to determine whether exposure has occurred may be considered. A vaccination is recommended for children living in these areas for three months or more.

MALARIA MEDICATION

There is no vaccination against malaria, so antimalarial drugs have to be taken. These do not prevent you from being infected but kill the malaria parasites during a stage in their development and significantly reduce the risk of becoming very ill or dying.

Expert advice on medication should be sought, as there are many factors to consider including the area to be visited, the risk of exposure to malaria-carrying mosquitoes, the side effects of medication, your medical history and whether you are a child or an adult or pregnant. Travellers to isolated areas in high-risk countries may like to carry a treatment dose of medication for use if symptoms occur.

TRAVEL HEALTH GUIDES

If you are planning to be away or travelling in remote areas for a long period of time, you might consider taking a more detailed health guide.

Staying Healthy in Asia, Africa & Latin America, Dirk Schroeder, Moon Publications, 1994. Probably the best all-round guide to carry; it's compact, detailed and well organised.

Travellers' Health, Dr Richard Dawood, Oxford University Press, 1995. Comprehensive, easy to read, authoritative and highly recommended, although it's rather large to lug around.

Where There is No Doctor, David Werner, Macmillan, 1994. A very detailed guide intended for someone, such as a Peace Corps worker, going to work in an underdeveloped country.

Travel with Children, Maureen Wheeler, Lonely Planet Publications, 1995. Includes advice on travel health for younger children.

Mountaineering Medicine by Fred Darvill is a technical guide specifically for trekkers and mountaineers.

ONLINE INFORMATION

There are also a number of excellent travel health sites on the Internet. From the Lonely Planet home page there are links at (http://www.lonelyplanet.com/health/health.htm/h-links.htm) to the World Health Organisation and the US Centers for Disease Control & Prevention.

OTHER PREPARATIONS

If you have any known medical problems or are concerned about your health, have a full

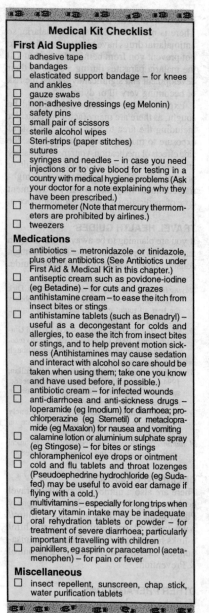

Medical Kit Checklist

First Aid Supplies

☐ adhesive tape
☐ bandages
☐ elasticated support bandage – for knees and ankles
☐ gauze swabs
☐ non-adhesive dressings (eg Melonin)
☐ safety pins
☐ small pair of scissors
☐ sterile alcohol wipes
☐ Steri-strips (paper stitches)
☐ sutures
☐ syringes and needles – in case you need injections or to give blood for testing in a country with medical hygiene problems (Ask your doctor for a note explaining why they have been prescribed.)
☐ thermometer (Note that mercury thermometers are prohibited by airlines.)
☐ tweezers

Medications

☐ antibiotics – metronidazole or tinidazole, plus other antibiotics (See Antibiotics under First Aid & Medical Kit in this chapter.)
☐ antiseptic cream such as povidone-iodine (eg Betadine) – for cuts and grazes
☐ antihistamine cream – to ease the itch from insect bites or stings
☐ antihistamine tablets (such as Benadryl) – useful as a decongestant for colds and allergies, to ease the itch from insect bites or stings, and to help prevent motion sickness (Antihistamines may cause sedation and interact with alcohol so care should be taken when using them; take one you know and have used before, if possible.)
☐ antibiotic cream – for infected wounds
☐ anti-diarrhoea and anti-sickness drugs – loperamide (eg Imodium) for diarrhoea; prochlorperazine (eg Stemetil) or metaclopramide (eg Maxalon) for nausea and vomiting
☐ calamine lotion or aluminium sulphate spray (eg Stingose) – for bites or stings
☐ chloramphenicol eye drops or ointment
☐ cold and flu tablets and throat lozenges (Pseudoephedrine hydrochloride (eg Sudafed) may be useful to avoid ear damage if flying with a cold.)
☐ multivitamins – especially for long trips when dietary vitamin intake may be inadequate
☐ oral rehydration tablets or powder – for treatment of severe diarrhoea; particularly important if travelling with children
☐ painkillers, eg aspirin or paracetamol (acetamenophen) – for pain or fever

Miscellaneous

☐ insect repellent, sunscreen, chap stick, water purification tablets

checkup. It is far better to have any problems recognised and treated at home than to find out about them halfway up a mountain. Get your teeth checked as well; dental fillings are more likely to come loose at high altitude. If you wear glasses take a spare pair and your prescription.

If you require a particular medication take an adequate supply, as it may not be available locally. Take part of the packaging showing the generic name, rather than the brand, which will make getting replacements easier. It's a good idea to have a legible prescription or letter from your doctor to show that you legally use the medication to avoid any problems.

FIRST AID & MEDICAL KIT

You cannot possibly cover every eventuality while trekking and travelling in Africa, but you should equip yourself with enough to cope with minor accidents and illnesses. The type and extent of medication that you carry with you will probably depend on how many days from help you are likely to be. You can obtain practically any type of medicine in Nairobi, and most large towns throughout East Africa have a pharmacy or local hospital where you can buy some of the frequently used medicines, including a variety of antibiotics. Cities and most large towns also have private doctors' surgeries, where you can obtain advice or have tests done. As at home, you may well be required to obtain a doctor's prescription before buying any medicines. If you are on regular medication at home, take enough supplies for your trip if there is any doubt of its availability abroad.

Your first aid kit should include most of the items in the list on this page.

Antibiotics

The use of metronidazole or tinidazole is discussed in the section on giardiasis and amoebiasis. Which other antibiotics (if any) are worth carrying is debatable. No single antibiotic works for all types of infection, and there is frequent resistance of bacteria to antibiotics because of their widespread use. The treks described in this book are not as remote as in some other parts of the world (eg the Himalaya), and you will rarely be more than a few days from medical help. It could be argued that if you are ill enough to require antibiotic treatment you ought to be seeking medical advice rather than self-administering these drugs.

Having said that, it is probably worth carrying a course of antibiotics such as co-trimoxazole to treat a persistent bacterial diarrhoea. In addition, if you know that you are prone to certain infections – for example, of the ear or the urinary tract – then it is worth carrying one or two courses of the appropriate antibiotic to treat the symptoms.

If you do take antibiotics, take only the recommended dose at the prescribed intervals and use the whole course, even if the illness seems to be cured earlier. Stop immediately if there are any serious reactions and don't use the antibiotic at all if you are unsure that you have the correct one. Some people are allergic to commonly prescribed antibiotics such as penicillin or sulphur drugs; carry this information when travelling, eg on a bracelet.

In summary, try to keep things simple, and discuss with your doctor all the medication you intend to take with you.

Staying Healthy

HYGIENE

To reduce the chances of contracting any illness, you should wash your hands frequently, particularly before handling or eating food. If you are on an organised trek, make sure your cooks, and any other people handling your food or utensils, also wash their hands. (Take an extra bar of soap to give to the cook.)

FOOD

Whether on trek or travelling between mountains, be careful about eating fresh fruit or uncooked vegetables, as these may have been contaminated through handling or soaked in contaminated water. Salads are notorious for harbouring all sorts of disease organisms. Fruit such as bananas, or anything that you

peel or prepare yourself (presuming your own hands are clean) should be safe. Try to avoid food which has not been freshly cooked or has been not been fully reheated. Avoid raw meat and raw seafood.

WATER

Many diseases are carried in water in the form of insect eggs, worms, protozoa, bacteria, viruses and so on. You can avoid these illnesses if your drinking water is purified.

This can be done by boiling, but this is a waste of fuel, and not always effective when you're on trek, as water boils at a lower temperature at altitude. For example, at the high camps on Mt Kenya, which are around 4200m, water boils at 86°C. (This is also the reason why your tea is never really hot!)

Instead of boiling, you can use a chemical agent to purify water. Chlorine and iodine are normally used, as tablets, powder or liquid, which you can buy from outdoor equipment suppliers and pharmacies. Both are effective if you keep to the recommended dosages and allow the water to stand for the correct length of time. They are particularly effective if you use a filter to clear out the larger substances (such as silt or vegetation) before adding the chemicals. Silver-based tablets are also available, but these may not be effective against some protozoa when they are in their 'cyst' stage, in which case a filter is essential.

Silver-based tablets are tasteless, whereas chlorine and iodine leave a taste which some people find unpleasant. Iodine can also have side effects if used on a very long-term basis, although it should be fine for a few weeks (or even a few months) on trek.

Water filters range from a simple canvas bag to high-tech pumps with ceramic inserts which are 100% effective. A cheap filter bag is fine if you're also using a chemical agent. Some filter systems also contain chemical agents, so you don't need to treat the water afterwards. When buying a water filter, make sure you find out exactly what the it does and what it doesn't. A good supplier should be able to advise you. In the UK, a handy booklet on water treatment is produced by SafariQuip (☎ (01433) 620320, fax 620061),

The Stones, Castleton, Derbyshire S30 2WX. They also supply water filters and chemical agents, and other equipment for treks and safaris in Africa.

NUTRITION

If your food is poor or limited in availability, if you're travelling hard and fast and therefore missing meals, or if you simply lose your appetite, you can soon start to lose weight and place your health at risk.

Make sure your diet is well balanced. Cooked eggs, beans, lentils and nuts are all safe ways to get protein. Fruit you can peel (bananas or oranges for example) is usually safe and a good source of vitamins. Try to eat plenty of grains (including rice) and bread. Remember that although food is generally safer if it is cooked well, overcooked food loses much of its nutritional value. If your diet isn't well balanced or if your food intake is insufficient, it's a good idea to take vitamin and iron pills.

Medical Problems & Treatment

This section outlines the symptoms and treatment of some of the illnesses frequently encountered in East Africa. It also touches on certain conditions which are less common but which could have serious implications if left unrecognised. Don't forget: most travellers and trekkers have a healthy trip or suffer nothing more than a few of bouts of diarrhoea.

ENVIRONMENTAL HAZARDS
Altitude Sickness

Several of the treks described in this book are on high mountains, where the altitude can lead to an illness called acute mountain sickness (AMS), more usually known as altitude sickness. The symptoms of AMS can be unpleasant enough to spoil your trek, and in some cases cause you to abandon it. It can also be fatal. However, if you understand something about the causes of AMS there are

> **Warning – Medical Treatment**
> Self-diagnosis and treatment can be risky. You should always seek medical help for correct diagnosis and treatment. An embassy, consulate or good hotel can usually recommend reliable doctors or clinics. Although we do give drug dosages in this section, they are for emergency use only. ■

many steps you can take to minimise its effects, or even avoid it completely.

Altitude Atmospheric pressure and the oxygen content of the air decrease in an approximately exponential manner as altitude increases. This means that as you trek higher, the breaths you take contain less oxygen. Above a certain altitude this can have a detrimental effect on your body's function and performance. For most trekkers, the effects of reduced oxygen become apparent at around 3000m.

However, some 15 million people in the world live above 3000m, and there are permanent residents in some mountain areas living above 4000m. These people are acclimatised to the altitude – their bodies have adapted to cope with the lower oxygen content of the air.

Acclimatisation is the resetting of physiological mechanisms which allow the body to return oxygen levels in the tissues to normal or near-normal. In this way, climbers and trekkers can continue to perform reasonably well at altitudes that would otherwise make them incapable of any strenuous exercise, or even render them unconscious.

This process is not instantaneous, and when your rate of ascent is faster than the body's ability to adjust to the gain in altitude, AMS occurs. The symptoms of AMS can be unpleasant, serious or even fatal. It is therefore essential that your own rate of ascent should allow for this adjustment.

There is wide variation between people in their ability to acclimatise. Obviously, it is helpful to be reasonably fit when walking up a mountain, although fitness seems to bear no direct correlation to the speed of acclimatisation. Indeed, a very fit person may be tempted to ascend faster than normal, so bringing upon themselves more severe symptoms of AMS. In general, although there is a lot of variation between individuals, each person's response to altitude is fairly constant on different occasions, given similar conditions and speed of ascent.

Symptoms & Treatment Acute mountain sickness usually develops in the first eight to 24 hours at high altitude. It occurs infrequently at altitudes below 3000m. Mild symptoms include headache, poor appetite, nausea, fatigue and poor sleep quality. At this stage you should stop your ascent. Rest, frequent small meals and mild painkillers may be all that is required to relieve the symptoms. Avoid alcohol. After the symptoms have fully abated, you may be able to continue your ascent.

If the symptoms worsen to severe headache and vomiting, you must not ascend any further, and should descend to an altitude where the symptoms abate. Altitude sickness in its most severe form can progress to either pulmonary oedema (fluid on the lungs) or cerebral oedema (swelling of the brain). Symptoms of fluid on the lungs include shortness of breath and frothy spit, sometimes pinkstained. Symptoms of cerebral oedema include severe headache (which may be worse when lying down), vomiting, dizziness and loss of balance, blurred or double vision, and drowsiness progressing to coma. These conditions can be fatal, and the only treatment is immediate descent.

Prevention The surest way to acclimatise properly and prevent the development of AMS is by gradual ascent. Recommendations from the international mountain rescue organisations vary, and include ascending at a rate of not more than 500m per day over an altitude of 3000m. Some recommendations follow this method and also advise a rest day every third day. Of course, sometimes it's not possible to do this, because of the position of huts or campsites, in which case you should

follow the recommendations as closely as you can.

Another recommended method is that of 'staging', where you remain at an intermediate altitude between 3000m and 4000m for an extra day before ascending further. This seems to be more appropriate to the high mountains of East Africa. On Mt Kenya, most of the roadhead or low moorland camps (eg Met Station, Judmaier Camp, the Chogoria roadhead, the new Timau roadhead) are between 3000m and 3200m; you should try to stay two nights here. On Kilimanjaro the mid-way huts or camps (eg Horombo, Shira Cave, Barranco Hut) are all between 3700m and 4000m; two nights here is even more strongly recommended.

Whatever your method of ascent, another way to assist acclimatisation is to sleep at a lower altitude than the highest point reached that day. Once again, this may not always be possible because of the position of huts or camp sites.

In the Rwenzoris, the ascent is more gradual, and on the other mountains above 3000m the trekking altitudes are not so high, so AMS is less likely to be a problem. Although a rest day is not essential here, it always helps.

Other ways to help avoid AMS include drinking extra fluids, eating high-carbohydrate meals and avoiding alcohol and sedatives.

Diamox Many trekkers on the high mountains now use a drug called acetazolamide (generally known as Diamox), but its use is controversial and Lonely Planet cannot recommend it for trekkers. There are plenty of trekkers who reach high altitudes successfully without the use of Diamox, and without suffering from AMS.

Diamox works by imitating the acclimatised state of the body, and has been shown to substantially reduce the frequency of AMS. It also reduces the incidence of pulmonary and cerebral oedema. It may also help in the treatment of AMS, although this is debatable. In any case, it should never be used as substitute for descent to a lower altitude. It must also never be used to allow further ascent by a person with AMS.

Diamox is generally a safe drug when taken in the correct dosage. Side effects are usually mild, and include tingling of the hands, feet and face, and mild gastrointestinal upset. Some trekkers report an increase in urination rate. If you notice this, make sure you increase your liquid intake accordingly. Dizziness, vomiting, confusion and rashes can occur, but these are unusual. People who are allergic to sulphonamide antibiotics may also be allergic to Diamox.

If you should decide to use Diamox, a trial dose of 250mg twice daily for two days at your normal altitude, several weeks before your trek starts, is recommended. If you suffer no distressing side effects, on the ascent take a dose of 250mg twice a day for three days before reaching an altitude of 3000m, and then continue it for two or three days afterwards. Some trekkers find that they get a good response using half the dose, whereas others may need to increase the dose to 250mg three times a day.

Climatic Extremes

Trekking in East Africa may expose you to some of the most extreme conditions you are ever likely to encounter, from blistering heat in the low parts of the Rift Valley to temperatures way below freezing on the summits of the high peaks. Having said that, much of the trekking in this book falls comfortably between the extremes, and any potential problems can be easily avoided.

Heat Exhaustion Very hot conditions can cause dehydration (see later in this section) and salt deficiency, which lead to heat exhaustion. To avoid dehydration, drink sufficient liquids and do not do anything too physically demanding until you are acclimatised. Salt deficiency is characterised by fatigue, lethargy, headaches, giddiness and muscle cramps; salt tablets may help, but adding extra salt to your food is better.

Heat Stroke This serious, occasionally fatal, condition can occur if the body's heat-regulating mechanism breaks down and the body temperature rises to dangerous levels. Long,

continuous periods of exposure to high temperatures and insufficient fluids can leave you vulnerable to heat stroke.

The symptoms are feeling unwell, not sweating very much (or at all) and a high body temperature (39 to 41°C or 102 to 106°F). Where sweating has ceased, the skin becomes flushed and red. Severe, throbbing headaches and lack of coordination will also occur, and the sufferer may be confused or aggressive. Eventually the victim will become delirious or convulse. Hospitalisation is essential, but in the interim get victims out of the sun, remove their clothing, cover them with a wet sheet or towel and then fan continually. If they are conscious, give them fluids.

Hypothermia Too much cold can be just as dangerous as too much heat. Hypothermia occurs when the body loses heat faster than it can produce it and the core temperature of the body falls. It is surprisingly easy to progress from very cold to dangerously cold due to a combination of wind, wet clothing, fatigue and hunger, even if the air temperature is above freezing. Appropriate clothing and equipment is discussed in the What to Bring section in the Regional Facts for the Trekker chapter. Carry basic supplies, including food containing simple sugars to generate heat quickly and fluid to drink.

Symptoms of hypothermia are exhaustion, numb skin (particularly toes and fingers), shivering, slurred speech, irrational or violent behaviour, lethargy, stumbling, dizzy spells, muscle cramps and violent bursts of energy. Irrationality may take the form of sufferers claiming they are warm and trying to take off their clothes.

To treat mild hypothermia, first get the person out of the wind and/or rain, remove their clothing if it's wet and replace it with dry, warm clothing. Give them hot liquids – not alcohol – and some high-energy, easily digestible food. Do not rub victims, instead allow them to slowly warm themselves. This should be enough to treat the early stages of hypothermia. The early recognition and treatment of mild hypothermia is the only way to prevent severe hypothermia, which is a critical condition.

Dehydration

This is a potentially dangerous and generally preventable condition. It is caused by excessive fluid loss through sweating, diarrhoea, vomiting or high fever, or inadequate fluid intake. The first obvious symptoms of dehydration are weakness, thirst, and passing small amounts of very concentrated urine. In extreme cases this may progress to drowsiness, inability to stand upright without fainting, and, finally, coma.

It is easy to forget how much fluid you are losing via perspiration whilst you are trekking, particularly if a strong breeze is drying your skin quickly. A good fluid intake should be maintained. A minimum of 3L a day is recommended, although up to 5L is better.

It is particularly important to maintain a reasonable fluid intake if you are suffering from diarrhoea or vomiting. Drink as much clear fluid as possible to replace what you are losing. If fluid loss is severe, use an oral rehydration solution as well. In the unlikely event that you cannot keep down any fluids and the vomiting and diarrhoea continue, you should not be trekking at all, and should seek medical attention.

Fungal Infections

Fungal infections occur more commonly in hot weather and are usually found on the scalp, between the toes or fingers, in the groin and on the body (ringworm). You get ringworm (which is a fungal infection, not a worm) from infected animals or other people. Moisture encourages these infections.

To prevent fungal infections wear loose, comfortable clothes, avoid artificial fibres, wash frequently and dry carefully. If you do get an infection, wash the infected area at least daily with a disinfectant or medicated soap and water, and rinse and dry well. Apply an antifungal cream or powder like tolnaftate (Tinaderm). Try to expose the infected area to air or sunlight as much as possible and wash all towels and underwear in hot water, change them often and let them dry in the sun.

Prickly Heat

Prickly heat is an itchy rash caused by excessive perspiration trapped under the skin. It usually strikes people who have just arrived in a hot climate. Keeping cool, bathing often, drying the skin and using a mild talcum or prickly heat powder or resorting to air-conditioning may help.

Sunburn

In the tropics, the desert or at high altitude you can get sunburnt surprisingly quickly, even through cloud. Use a sunscreen, wear a hat, and apply barrier cream to your nose and lips. Calamine lotion or Stingose are good for mild sunburn. Protect your eyes with good quality sunglasses, particularly if you will be near water, sand or snow.

INFECTIOUS DISEASES

Diarrhoea

Simple things like a change of food or climate can all cause a mild diarrhoea, but a few rushed toilet trips with no other symptoms are not indicative of a major problem. More serious diarrhoea (bacterial diarrhoea) is caused by infectious agents which are transmitted by faecal contamination of food or water, by contaminated utensils, or directly from one person's hands to another. When trekking it can usually be avoided by maintaining good personal hygiene, by ensuring your water is safe to drink, and by taking care with what you eat, as discussed earlier in this chapter.

Dehydration is the main danger with any diarrhoea, particularly in children or the elderly as dehydration can occur quite quickly. Under all circumstances fluid replacement is the most important thing to remember. Weak black tea with a little sugar, soda water, or soft drinks allowed to go flat and diluted 50% with clean water are all good. With severe diarrhoea a rehydrating solution is preferable to replace minerals and salts lost. Commercially available oral rehydration salts (ORS) are very useful; add them to boiled or bottled water. In an emergency you can make up a solution of six teaspoons of sugar and a half-teaspoon of salt to a litre of boiled or bottled water. You need to drink at least the same volume of fluid that you are losing in bowel movements and vomiting. Urine is the best guide to the adequacy of replacement – if you have small amounts of concentrated urine, you need to drink more. Keep drinking small amounts often. Stick to a bland diet as you recover.

Lomotil or Imodium can be used to bring relief from the symptoms of diarrhoea, although they do not actually cure the problem. Only use these drugs if you do not have access to toilets (eg if you *must* travel). For children under 12 years Lomotil and Imodium are not recommended. Do not use these drugs if you have a high fever or are severely dehydrated.

Occasionally things may get more serious: diarrhoea with blood or mucus (dysentery), watery diarrhoea with fever and lethargy, persistent diarrhoea not improving after 48 hours, or severe diarrhoea. In this situation, antibiotics may be required, and gut-paralysing drugs like Imodium or Lomotil should be avoided.

A stool test is necessary to diagnose which kind of dysentery you have, so you should seek medical help urgently. Where this is not possible the recommended drugs for dysentery are norfloxacin 400mg twice daily for three days or ciprofloxacin 500mg twice daily for five days. These are not recommended for children or pregnant women. Co-trimoxazole (Septrin or Bactrim) or amoxicillin may also be prescribed. The drug of choice for children is co-trimoxazole with dosage dependent on weight. A five-day course is given. Ampicillin or amoxicillin may be given in pregnancy, but medical care is necessary.

Bacillic dysentery is a severe form of bacterial diarrhoea, most commonly caused by a bacterium called shigella. The symptoms are rapid onset of high fever, feeling unwell, and profuse, watery, bloody diarrhoea a few days later. Vomiting and severe abdominal cramps are common. Again, the fundamental treatment is rest and adequate hydration, preferably using oral rehydration solutions. Take small amounts of fluid at frequent intervals – about two to four times

an hour. You may well need at least 5L of fluid per day, if not more. The symptoms will abate after about five days to a week, usually without antibiotic treatment, and will not recur.

Amoebic dysentery is more gradual in the onset of symptoms, with cramping abdominal pain and vomiting less likely; fever may not be present. It will persist until treated and can recur and cause other health problems. Treat as per giardiasis.

Giardiasis is another type of diarrhoea. The parasite causing this intestinal disorder is present in contaminated water. The symptoms are stomach cramps, nausea, a bloated stomach, watery, foul-smelling diarrhoea and frequent gas. Giardiasis can appear several weeks after you have been exposed to the parasite. The symptoms may disappear for a few days and then return; this can go on for several weeks. Tinidazole, known as Fasigyn, or metronidazole (Flagyl) are the recommended drugs. Treatment is a 2gm single dose of Fasigyn or 250mg of Flagyl three times daily for five to 10 days.

Hepatitis

Hepatitis is a general term for inflammation of the liver. It is a common disease worldwide. The symptoms are fever, chills, headache, fatigue, feelings of weakness and aches and pains, followed by loss of appetite, nausea, vomiting, abdominal pain, dark urine, light-coloured faeces and jaundiced (yellow) skin. The whites of the eyes may also turn yellow.

Hepatitis A is transmitted by contaminated food and drinking water. The disease poses a real threat to the western traveller. You should seek medical advice, but there is not much you can do apart from resting, drinking lots of fluids, eating lightly and avoiding fatty foods. People who have had hepatitis should avoid alcohol for some time after the illness, as the liver needs time to recover.

Hepatitis E is transmitted in the same way. It can be very serious in pregnant women.

There are almost 300 million chronic carriers of **hepatitis B** in the world. It is spread through contact with infected blood, blood products or body fluids, for example through sexual contact, unsterilised needles and blood transfusions, or contact with blood via small breaks in the skin. Other risk situations include having a shave, a tattoo, or having your body pierced with contaminated equipment. The symptoms of type B may be more severe and may lead to long-term problems. **Hepatitis D** is spread in the same way, but the risk is mainly in shared needles.

Hepatitis C can lead to chronic liver disease. The virus is spread by contact with blood, usually via contaminated transfusions or shared needles. Avoiding these is the only means of prevention.

HIV & AIDS

The human immunodeficiency virus (HIV) develops into acquired immune deficiency syndrome (AIDS), which is a fatal disease. HIV is a major problem in many countries. Any exposure to blood, blood products or body fluids may put the individual at risk. The disease is often transmitted through sexual contact or dirty needles – vaccinations, acupuncture, tattooing and body piercing can be potentially as dangerous as intravenous drug use. HIV/AIDS can also be spread through infected blood transfusions; some developing countries cannot afford to screen blood used for transfusions.

If you do need an injection, ask to see the syringe unwrapped in front of you, or take a needle and syringe pack with you.

Fear of HIV infection should never preclude treatment for serious medical conditions.

Intestinal Worms

These parasites are most common in rural, tropical areas. The different worms have different ways of infecting people. Some may be ingested on food, including undercooked meat, and some enter through your skin. Infestations may not show up for some time, and although they are generally not serious, if left untreated some can cause severe health problems later. Considering having a stool test when you return home to check for these and determine the appropriate treatment.

Meningococcal Meningitis

There are recurring epidemics in sub-Saharan Africa of this very serious disease, which attacks the brain and can be fatal. It is spread by close contact with people who carry it in their throats and noses, spread it through coughs and sneezes and may not be aware that they are carriers. Initial symptoms are fever, severe headache, sensitivity to light and neck stiffness which prevents forward bending of the head. There may also be purple patches on the skin. Death can occur within a few hours, so urgent medical treatment is required. Treatment is large doses of penicillin given intravenously, or chloramphenicol injections.

Schistosomiasis

Also known as bilharzia, this disease is carried in water by minute worms. It is prevalent throughout Africa. The worms infect certain varieties of freshwater snails found in rivers, streams, lakes and particularly behind dams. They multiply and are eventually discharged into the water.

The worm enters through the skin and attaches itself to your intestines or bladder. The first symptom may be a tingling and sometimes a light rash around the area where it entered. Weeks later a high fever may develop. A general feeling of being unwell may be the first symptom, or there may be no symptoms. Once the disease is established abdominal pain and blood in the urine are other signs. The infection often causes no symptoms until the disease is well established (several months to years after exposure) and damage to internal organs is irreversible.

Avoiding swimming or bathing in fresh water where bilharzia is present is the main method of preventing the disease. Even deep water can be infected. If you do get wet, dry off quickly and dry your clothes as well.

A blood test is the most reliable test, but the test will not show positive in results until a number of weeks after exposure.

Sexually Transmitted Diseases

Gonorrhoea, herpes and syphilis are among these diseases. Common symptoms are sores, blisters or rashes around the genitals, and discharges or pain when urinating. In some STDs, such as wart virus or chlamydia, symptoms may be less marked or not observed at all, especially in women. Syphilis symptoms eventually disappear completely but the disease continues and can cause severe problems in later years. While abstinence from sexual contact is the only 100% effective prevention, using condoms is also effective. The different sexually transmitted diseases each require specific antibiotics. There is no cure for herpes or AIDS.

Typhoid

Typhoid fever is a dangerous gut infection caused by contaminated water and food. In its early stages sufferers may feel they have a bad cold or flu on the way, as early symptoms are a headache, body aches and a fever which rises a little each day until it is around 40°C (104°F) or more. The victim's pulse is often slow relative to the degree of fever present – unlike a normal fever where the pulse increases. There may also be vomiting, abdominal pain, diarrhoea or constipation.

In the second week the high fever and slow pulse continue and a few pink spots may appear on the body; trembling, delirium, weakness, weight loss and dehydration may occur. Complications such as pneumonia, perforated bowel or meningitis may occur.

Medical help must be sought. If this is not possible, the fever should be treated by keeping the victim cool and giving them fluids as dehydration is also possible. Ciprofloxacin 750mg twice a day for 10 days is good for adults. Chloramphenicol is recommended in many countries. The adult dosage is two 250mg capsules, four times a day. Children aged between eight and 12 years should have half the adult dose, and younger children one-third the adult dose.

INSECT-BORNE DISEASES

Typhus and yellow fever are insect-borne diseases, but they do not pose a great risk to travellers, and are described briefly under Immunisations earlier in this Health section.

Malaria

This disease is widespread in East Africa. The malarial parasite is transmitted by the *Anopheles* mosquito. The infective parasites are stored in the salivary glands of the female mosquito and are injected via the insect bite into the bloodstream. From there they travel to the liver, where they develop and multiply. Then follows the cyclical release of parasites from the liver, which establishes serial infections of the red blood cells. It is this release of parasites and invasion of the red cells that causes periodic sweats and fever, which are characteristic of malaria.

Although mosquitoes may be found at high altitudes, the malarial parasite cannot survive in cold temperatures. However, evidence suggests that the parasites are becoming increasingly resistant to cold conditions. Trekkers should continue taking antimalarial pills at all times, to remain protected for lowland travel and to allow for the organism's incubation period.

Prevention Don't underestimate malaria. Take your antimalarial tablets, starting a week before you reach East Africa, and finishing four weeks after you leave. Antimalarial recommendations vary, depending on where you live, but generally the current options are: proguanil (Paludrine) two tablets every day and chloroquine (several trade names) two tablets once a week; or mefloquine (Larium) once a week, where it is licensed for such use. There are obvious advantages to only having to take a tablet once a week, but on anecdotal evidence at least, mefloquine seems to have side effects which are more frequent and more noticeable than chloroquine and proguanil. Neither drug regime guarantees 100% protection but they may lessen the severity of symptoms if you are unlucky enough to contract malaria while taking the tablets.

The surest protection is avoiding mosquito bites in the first place. Mosquitoes are most active around dusk, so at this time (or others if necessary) the main messages are:

- wear light-coloured clothing
- wear long trousers, socks and long-sleeved shirts

- avoid highly scented perfumes or aftershave
- use mosquito repellents on exposed areas of skin (those containing the compound DEET are recommended, but its prolonged use may be harmful, especially to children, although this is preferable to being bitten by disease-transmitting mosquitoes; several effective natural repellents are also available)
- use a mosquito net – those impregnated with mosquito repellent (permethrin) are most effective – it may be worth taking your own
- consider impregnating clothes with permethrin – several sprays are available

Symptoms The incubation period from bite to development of symptoms can vary from about six to 30 days. The onset may be sudden, with violent chills and sweats, and a high temperature. The fever may be constant at first, becoming intermittent. Alternatively, the onset may be more gradual, with symptoms such as diarrhoea, headache, abdominal pain, breathlessness or muscle pain. The fever may not start until later. If malaria is left untreated, serious complications can follow rapidly, including cerebral malaria, which is frequently fatal.

Treatment If you think you have malaria, get a blood test and seek medical advice. A positive blood test result will give you the diagnosis, but a negative result does not necessarily exclude malaria. If you cannot get to a doctor you may have to start treatment yourself. Malaria tablets can be used for treatment, but you need to use a malaria tablet which is different to the one you were taking when you contracted malaria.

The treatment that used to be recommended was 600mg chloroquine (four 150mg tablets) followed by 300mg six hours later and 300mg the next day. But because there is now so much chloroquine-resistant malaria in East Africa, it is now recommended to use mefloquine (two 250mg tablets and a further two six hours later) although this treatment may make you feel worse than you did before, with dizziness, abdominal pain, diarrhoea and vomiting being common side effects. Mefloquine should normally be avoided in pregnancy. Alternative treatments are Fansidar (single dose of three tablets), halofantrine

(three doses of two 250mg tablets every six hours) or quinine sulphate (600mg every six hours). There is a greater risk of side effects with these dosages than in normal use.

After Travel A final word of warning – continue your antimalarial tablets for the recommended period when you get home. If you become ill within about a month of arriving home, tell your doctor where you've been. It could save a lot of people, including yourself, a great deal of trouble trying to work out what's wrong.

Trypanosomiasis
This disease, which is also known as sleeping sickness, is caused by a parasite transmitted by the tsetse fly. This only occurs in low areas, so trekkers on the mountains will not be effected. However, you may be exposed if you join a walking safari in a lowland area.

The main characteristic of trypanosomiasis is a red, painful nodule appearing on the skin about three to four days after being bitten. The glands in the same area may also become inflamed. After about two weeks the lesion disappears and the sufferer develops a generalised illness of fever, chills, headache and widespread inflammation of the glands. Three to six weeks after the bite, the parasites may invade the nervous system, causing weakness, recurrent fever and a constant headache. A patchy rash may appear and the person may become irritable and develop mood changes. If it is not treated it can be fatal.

You would probably notice if you were bitten by a tsetse fly. It is large (about 12mm long), with scissor-like wings and a painful bite. The risk of infection is low, but if you think you are developing sleeping sickness seek medical help immediately.

BITES, STINGS & CUTS
Insect Bites
Bedbugs Bedbugs live in various places, but particularly in dirty mattresses and bedding, evidenced by spots of blood on bedclothes. Trekkers are unlikely to be affected, but if you're travelling between the mountains on a low budget you might suffer – the neat rows

of itchy bites are diagnostic. The best prevention if staying in basic lodgings is to use your own sleeping bag. Once bitten, calamine lotion or antihistamine cream may help.

Lice Lice may also be picked up in low-budget lodgings or simply during a bout of communal living in mountain bunkhouses. All lice cause itching and discomfort. You catch lice through direct contact with infected people or by sharing combs, clothing and the like. They make themselves at home in your hair (head lice), your clothing (body lice) or your pubic hair ('crabs'). Powder or shampoo treatment will kill the lice and infected clothing should then be washed in very hot, soapy water and left in the sun to dry.

Ticks Ticks are about half the size of a match-head, and occur in lowland areas, often associated with long grass, cattle or wild animals, so you are more likely to get bitten when on a walking safari than a mountain trek. Ticks attach themselves to your skin or clothes, so you should always check all over your body if you have been walking through a potentially tick-infested area. Their bites can cause skin infections and other more serious diseases. If a tick is found attached, press down around the tick's head with tweezers, grab the head and gently pull upwards. Avoid pulling the rear of the body as this may squeeze the tick's gut contents through the attached mouth parts into the skin, increasing the risk of infection and disease. Smearing chemicals on the tick will not make it let go and is not recommended.

Insect Stings Bee and wasp stings are usually painful rather than dangerous, but in people who are allergic to them severe breathing difficulties may occur and require urgent medical care. Calamine lotion or antihistamine cream will give relief and ice packs will reduce the pain and swelling.

Snake Bites

While trekking on the high mountains of East Africa, your chances of encountering snakes are almost nil. They can't survive in

the cold conditions. If you are in lower, warmer areas, you may see a snake or two, but this is still very unlikely. Most snakes hear your footsteps and will slither far out of reach before you even knew they were there. The main exception to this is the puff adder, which seems to be either deaf or extremely lethargic, and may very occasionally be stepped on by hikers in the bush.

To minimise your chances of being bitten always wear boots, socks and long trousers when walking through undergrowth where snakes may be present. Don't put your hands into holes and crevices, and be careful when collecting firewood.

Snake bites do not cause instantaneous death. If someone in your group is bitten, immediately wrap the bitten limb as you would for a sprained ankle, keeping the pressure firm and even along the length of the limb (but make sure you don't completely cut off the blood supply) and then attach a splint to immobilise it. Keep the victim still and seek medical help, if possible with the dead snake for identification. Don't attempt to catch the snake if there is a possibility of being bitten again. Tourniquets and sucking out the poison are now comprehensively discredited and not recommended.

Cuts & Scratches

Even small cuts and grazes should be washed well and treated with an antiseptic. Dry wounds heal more quickly, so where possible avoid bandages and Band-aids, which can keep wounds wet. Infection in the wound is indicated by the skin margins becoming red, painful and swollen. More serious infection can cause swelling of the involved limb and of the neighbouring lymph glands. The sufferer may develop a fever, and will need medical attention.

If cuts or bites become infected, tropical ulcers may develop as a small red blister which bursts to form a painful spreading ulcer. The ulcer tends to stop growing after a few weeks, but by this time may be as big as 10cm in diameter. Treat by cleaning the ulcer with antiseptic and then covering it with a sterile, preferably non-adherent, dressing. Keeping the ulcer clean is of fundamental importance, as is removing dressings very carefully so as to avoid destroying all the healing that has taken place. A course of antibiotics will probably be needed.

WOMEN'S HEALTH
Gynaecological Problems

Poor diet, lowered resistance due to the use of antibiotics for stomach upsets, and even contraceptive pills, can lead to vaginal infections when travelling in hot climates. Maintaining good personal hygiene, and wearing skirts or loose-fitting trousers and cotton underwear, will help to prevent infections.

Yeast infections, characterised by a rash, itch and discharge, can be treated with a vinegar or even lemon-juice douche or with yoghurt. Nystatin suppositories are the usual medical prescription. Trichomonas is a more serious infection; symptoms are a discharge and a burning sensation when urinating. Male sexual partners must also be treated and, if a vinegar-water douche is not effective, medical attention should be sought. Flagyl is the prescribed drug.

Sexually transmitted diseases are discussed elsewhere in this Health section.

Pregnancy

It is not advisable to travel to some places while pregnant as some vaccinations normally used to prevent serious diseases, eg yellow fever, are not advisable in pregnancy. In addition, some diseases are much more serious for the mother (and may increase the risk of a stillborn child) in pregnancy; malaria is an example.

Most miscarriages occur during the first three months of pregnancy. Miscarriage is not uncommon, and can occasionally lead to severe bleeding. The last three months should also be spent within reasonable distance of good medical care, although during this time you're unlikely to feel up to trekking across Mt Kenya or Kilimanjaro anyway. A baby born as early as 24 weeks stands a chance of survival, but only in a good modern hospital. Pregnant women should avoid all unnecessary medication, so additional care should be taken to prevent illness and particular attention should be paid to diet and nutrition. Alcohol and nicotine should be avoided.

If you do travel during pregnancy, discuss it with your doctor first and sort out the most appropriate vaccinations and antimalarial medication you will need.

Emergency & Rescue

On the main mountains, it is very important to realise that if you have a serious accident it may be several days before you reach a hospital. In the more remote ranges it may take even longer. That's why trekking alone is never recommended.

Because you'll be trekking rather than climbing, an incapacitating accident is quite unlikely. In mountain national parks, rangers at the park entrance gates are usually in radio contact with their headquarters, so if you are involved in an emergency situation, help can be arranged. On the high mountains there are ranger posts on the mountain itself, at the bunkhouses on the main routes (the Marangu Route on Kilimanjaro and the Naro Moru Route on Mt Kenya). On these mountains, the park rangers have stretchers and operate a mountain rescue service.

Obviously, you should try to avoid leaving an injured person alone, but if there is no other option you should put them in a tent and sleeping bag and leave them plenty of food and water. If you send a local porter or guide to get help, it is better to write down all the details of the accident, in order to avoid confusion. A promise of a large bonus payment for speedy work is usually appropriate.

Getting There & Away

This chapter gives you the basics on how to get to East Africa from Europe, North America or Australasia. For more details, refer to a general guidebook such as Lonely Planet's *East Africa*. General information on travel in East Africa is given in the main Getting Around chapter and in the Getting There & Away and Getting Around sections in the relevant country chapters. Approach routes to the mountain areas and access routes to the start of each trek are fully described in the individual mountain sections of this book.

AIR

Most visitors reach East Africa by air because it's the easiest way of getting there, and many go to Nairobi because there's a greater choice of flights and they tend to be cheaper. If you're planning to trek in more than one country, or to combine trekking with some general travel in this region, Nairobi is a good place to start and finish. As well as regular flights to/from Europe and the rest of the world, there are also good air links with other countries in the region.

Buying an air ticket can be a confusing business. There's often a bewildering choice of routes, fares and airlines. Some flights have restrictions on the maximum or minimum

---

Warning

The air travel information in this section is particularly vulnerable to change: prices are volatile, routes are introduced and cancelled, schedules change, special deals come and go, and rules and visa requirements are amended. Airlines and governments seem to take a perverse pleasure in making price structures and regulations as complicated as possible.

The upshot of this is that you should get opinions, quotes and advice from as many airlines and travel agents as possible before you part with your hard-earned cash. The details given here should be regarded as pointers and are not a substitute for your own careful, up-to-date research. ∎

---

number of days you can be away. Prices depend on the quality and reliability of the airline, the number and length of stopovers, and many other factors. Don't automatically go for the cheapest fare. Sometimes, for very little extra, you can get a flight with a superior airline, with fewer stopovers and better service.

Generally speaking, buying a ticket direct from an airline is expensive; you're much better off going to a travel agent or specialist flight agency, who can offer a wide choice and explain all the options. Offers come and go, so it's well worth contacting several agencies to see what's available. It's usually best to deal with agencies who are 'bonded' (eg members of ABTA in the UK, AFTA in Australia and AATA in the USA) so that your money remains safe should the airline go bust after you've bought your ticket. Flight agencies normally advertise in travel magazines or in the travel sections of newspapers such as the *Observer* in Britain; the *Los Angeles Times*, *San Francisco Examiner* and *New York Times* in the USA; or the *Sydney Morning Herald* and Melbourne the *Age* in Australia.

On some airlines you can buy an 'open jaw' ticket, which lets you fly into one place and out of another (eg London to Nairobi, return from Lilongwe to London). This is useful if you want to trek in two or more areas and travel overland between them. Another option if you're coming from the USA or Australasia is a round-the-world (RTW) ticket, via one or more places in East Africa. Specialist agencies can also arrange regional flights around East Africa, for example Nairobi to Kampala.

The UK & Ireland

London is one of the cheapest places in Europe to buy flights to East Africa although these days specialist travel agents outside the capital are often just as competitive and can be easier deal with. There are many agencies, but some stand out as Africa specialists. Many of the following can arrange additional items such accommodation, tours, safaris or car hire.

Africa Travel Centre
21 Leigh St, London WC1H 9QX (☎ (0171) 387 1211)
African Travel Specialists
Glen House, Stag Place, Victoria, London SW1E 5AG (☎ (0171) 630 5434)
Bridge the World
52 Chalk Farm Rd, Camden Town, London NW1 8AN (☎ (0171) 911 0900)
Campus Travel
52 Grosvenor Gardens, London SW1W 0AG (☎ (0171) 730 8111); also has offices in large YHA Adventure Shops and universities/colleges around the country. Telephone bookings: ☎ (0171) 730 2101, ☎ (0161) 273 1721 or ☎ (0131) 668 3303.
Council Travel
28A Poland St, London W1V 3DB (☎ (0171) 437 7767)
STA Travel
86 Old Brompton Rd, London SW7 3LQ (☎ (0171) 581 4132) and 117 Euston Rd, London NW1 2SX (☎ (0171) 465 0486); also branches in Manchester, Bristol and large university towns.
Trailfinders
42-50 Earls Court Rd, London W8 6FT (☎ (0171) 938 3939) and 194 Kensington High St, London W8 7RG (☎ (0171) 938 3366); also in Manchester, Bristol and several other towns.

Outside London, others to try include the following. Again this is just a list to get you started on price comparisons.

Footloose Adventure Travel
105 Leeds Rd, Ilkley, West Yorkshire LS29 8EG (☎ (01943) 604030)
Quest Worldwide
29 Castle St, Kingston, Surrey KT1 1ST (☎ (0181) 547 3322)
Travel Bug
597 Cheetham Hill Rd, Manchester M8 5EJ (☎ (0161) 721 4000)
Trips Worldwide
9 Byron Place, Bristol BS8 1JT (☎ (0117) 987 2626)
USIT Travel
19 Aston Quay, Dublin, Ireland (☎ (01) 679 8833)

Airlines serving East Africa from London include British Airways, KLM (in conjunction with Kenya Airways), Lufthansa and SwissAir. Ethiopian Airlines offer a very good value international service all over East Africa. Also worth looking out for are flights on Alliance Air (a joint venture between Air Uganda, Air Tanzania and South African Airways).

To Kenya The main airport in Kenya is Nairobi. Return London-Nairobi fares start at UK£350, although they are often more expensive in the high season, starting at about UK£500. You can sometimes get amazing charter flight bargains to Mombasa (around UK£200 return), although these are usually only available for two weeks. However, there are good transport links between Mombasa and Nairobi, and most of the trekking areas described in the Kenya chapter are within a day's travel of Nairobi, so visiting trekkers may still be able to take advantage of the charter flights.

To Tanzania Tanzania has two main airports: Dar es Salaam and Kilimanjaro International (KIA) which, as the name implies, is nearer the main trekking areas. If you're only trekking in Tanzania it's easier to fly to KIA than to Dar. Return London-KIA fares start at UK£400, or UK£550 in the high season.

To Uganda The main airport is Entebbe, on the outskirts of Kampala. Return flights to Kampala from London start at around UK£400. If you're visiting the Uganda side of Mt Elgon only, it's easier to approach from Nairobi.

To Malawi Return flights from London to Malawi start at about UK£500 in the low season, and UK£600 in the high season. International flights arrive at Lilongwe, the administrative capital in the centre of the country. If you're heading for Mulanje, it's easier to fly on to Blantyre, the commercial capital in the south, which costs an extra UK£35 each way.

To Ethiopia Flights to Addis Ababa start at UK£350 return from London, although a domestic flight to Gonder (base for Simien trekking) will add about another UK£50 each way onto your bill.

Australia & New Zealand

There are no direct flights from Australia or New Zealand to East Africa. The nearest you get are Qantas and South African Airways flights to Harare (Zimbabwe) or Johannesburg (South Africa) for around A$2000 return (although there are sometimes cheaper 'specials' available). From Harare you can get a regional flight to Lilongwe or Nairobi. Other options are flights via Mauritius (on Air Mauritius) or Cairo (on EgyptAir) at prices comparable to those via southern Africa, or via Asia where prices are slightly lower. Australasians should also look at RTW tickets, via one or more places in Asia and East Africa.

African flight specialists include:

Africa Travel Centre
Level 11, 456 Kent St, Sydney, NSW 2000, Australia (☎ (02) 267 3048)

Africa Travel Shop
21 Remuera Rd, Newmarket, Auckland, New Zealand (☎ (09) 520 2000)

The USA & Canada

Bargain deals from the USA or Canada straight to East Africa are hard to find. Most flights go to Nairobi via Europe (eg on British Airways or Air France). Return fares from New York start at US$2600 (low season) and US$3000 (high). From Toronto, you're looking at similar prices. Some agencies in New York advertise special deals to Nairobi starting at around US$550 one way, although in reality you'll probably end up paying more like US$1200 one way and US$1700 return.

Many trekkers from North America save money by flying to the UK on a cheap transAtlantic deal, then buying the second leg of their flight to Africa in London. This takes time and a bit more organisation.

LAND

If you've got plenty of time, and a fair bit of cash to spare, it's possible to get to East Africa overland from Europe or from other parts of Africa. You can do it by public transport or in your own vehicle, but a detailed description of overland routes to East Africa is beyond the scope of this book. The boxed

---

Overland Routes Across Africa

Whatever your means of travel (bus, train, own vehicle or borrowed camel), before even leaving Europe you should decide which of the two main routes through Africa you want to take: the Sahara Route or the Nile Route. Each also has several variations.

If you go for the Sahara, your options are currently limited to the route through Morocco and Mauritania into Senegal and the rest of West Africa, as, at the time of writing, the routes through Algeria into Mali and Niger are blocked due to local political unrest. Whichever way you go through West Africa your onward route across Congo (Zaïre), then into Uganda either directly or via Rwanda, is likely to be blocked due to local unrest. See the boxed text on Congo (Zaïre) for more details. This will mean you will probably have to fly from Accra or Lagos to Kampala or Nairobi.

If you go for the Nile Route, this starts in Egypt, and goes into Sudan (either via Lake Nasser or via the Red Sea from Suez to Port Sudan). Southern Sudan is blocked to overland travellers due to civil war, so most fly from Khartoum to Kampala or Nairobi, or go from northern Sudan through Eritrea and Ethiopia to Nairobi.

Once in Nairobi, there are several options for reaching other parts of East Africa. The most popular route seems to be via Mombasa or Arusha and Moshi to Dar es Salaam. From here drivers follow the Great North Road, and those without wheels take the Tazara Railway; both lead to Kapiri Mposhi in Zambia, from where Victoria Falls (a travellers' hub for the whole of southern Africa) is easily reached. If you're heading for Malawi, you can leave the road/train at Mbeya (in southern Tanzania) from where Karonga, in northern Malawi, is usually only a day's travel away.

Another option from Dar takes you across the country to Kigoma on Lake Tanganyika, then by steamer to Mpulungu in Zambia, from where you can continue overland to Lusaka or strike out eastwards on minor roads to reach northern Malawi at Chitipa. Once in Zambia or Malawi, the rest of southern Africa and even Cape Town, if you want to go all the way, is easy to reach. ■

Congo (Zaïre)

It is important for visitors travelling around East Africa to know something about the country formerly known as Zaïre, which borders Uganda and Tanzania and is a major feature of the politics of the region.

The former colony of Belgian Congo became independent in 1960. Five years later, the former army chief, Joseph Mobutu, became president and changed the name of the country to Zaïre. Propped up by western nations for his anti-Communist stance, President Mobutu remained in power for the next 32 years, despite various separatist uprisings, deeply entrenched corruption and a decaying infrastructure, not to mention widespread poverty suffered by most of the population.

He became one of Africa's most notorious dictators and one of the world's richest men. Things changed dramatically in May 1997, when Mobutu and the Zaïre army were toppled from power by a rebel force led by Laurent Kabila. One of Kabila's first moves (after proclaiming himself president) was to rename the country the Democratic Republic of Congo. However, several commentators have noted that Kabila and the new government are no less dictatorial than the ousted Mobutu regime, and that their long-term hold on power is far from guaranteed. Threats of counter-revolution and partition of this huge, ethnically complex country into smaller states are commonplace, and the Democratic Republic of Congo may turn out to be a short-lived entity.

In this book we have used the term 'Congo (Zaïre)' to reflect the recent political changes and to distinguish this country from the Congo (formerly French Congo, and often called Congo-Brazzaville after the name of its capital) just over the north-west border of Congo (Zaïre). Names aside, as we went to press nearly all parts of Congo (Zaïre) are closed to outside visitors, and travel here is likely to be dangerous even if you do manage to get entry permission. Do not enter Congo (Zaïre) or travel near its borders with Uganda and Tanzania without checking the local security situation first. ■

text on Overland Routes gives a brief insight. For more ideas refer to one of the travel guides listed under Books in the Regional Facts for the Trekker chapter.

Overland Trucks

If you don't have your own wheels, or don't fancy public transport, another option is to join an organised trip in a specially converted overland truck, where you travel with about 18 other people, a couple of drivers/leaders, and tents and other equipment. Some overland trips through Africa start in Europe (particularly London) and finish in Nairobi (travelling via the Sahara and West Africa, or through Ethiopia, depending on local conditions), but a more popular route goes from Nairobi to Zimbabwe or South Africa, via Tanzania and Malawi.

Of course, the trucks also go in the opposite direction, so an overland trip might be a good way of getting from Southern Africa up to East Africa. Prices vary and depend very much on itinerary and duration. Most of the travel agents listed in the previous Air travel section also represent overland truck companies and can help arrange a trip.

Truck Transfers It's worth noting that overland companies tend to run more Nairobi to Harare trips in a north-south direction than the other way around. Therefore empty trucks are often running south to north, and some offer lifts for around US$15 per day, plus food. Just visit a camp site where the overland trucks park in a place like Harare or Victoria Falls and ask the drivers if there's anything going. This is a particularly useful way to transfer quickly between Vic Falls and Lilongwe, or to go all the way to Nairobi. But don't expect sightseeing stops on the way.

ORGANISED TREKS

If time is short, or you haven't got the inclination to make all the arrangements yourself, you can arrange a trek in East Africa through a specialist company based in your own country. You can have arrangements made just for you or a group of friends and choose your own itinerary ('tailor-made'), or you can join an existing group on a set route and departure date ('scheduled'). These companies will either arrange just the trek, leaving you to buy your own flight and make other arrangements, or they can arrange the whole thing, including all your flights, transport, accommodation and so on. If you go for the whole lot, they usually provide a trek leader to organise porters and guides, and to take care of things along the way. The idea is that you pay one price, then have nothing more to worry about.

Because these companies are set up specifically to run treks and tours, and already have their own contacts on the ground, they can usually arrange to do a lot more in the holiday time available (normally two to four weeks) than you could yourself, thus avoiding a lot of the hassle experienced by independent trekkers.

Length, difficulty, standard, quality and (of course) price of organised trekking trips varies enormously between companies. Some companies are East Africa and Ethiopia specialists, while others cover all parts of the world. Some offer a fairly straightforward range of treks on the main mountains such as Mt Kenya and Kilimanjaro, while others are more imaginative, with treks on the high profile peaks and to more unusual areas, such as Kenya's Chyulu Hills or Tanzania's Monduli Mountains. Some outfits run general tours with a bias towards wildlife or local cultures, where trekking or walking is part of a broader experience. Others are total trekking specialists, and may also offer technical mountaineering or 'treknical tours', ie mainly trekking with a small amount of crampon work and on-the-spot instruction.

Some companies act as agents, selling treks organised by local companies, while others operate the whole thing themselves. Agents tend to be cheaper, although operators usually have more knowledge about the area and trek conditions.

The best way to find something to suit your taste and budget is to phone the companies, tell them what you're interested in, ask for brochures and price-lists, read them all – then decide!

After getting a brochure, don't be afraid to phone them again if you want to know more. Some companies are run by people who are trekkers and walkers themselves, so they'll know how to answer your questions.

The following is not a complete list of companies organising treks and tours in East Africa, but it will give you somewhere to start.

Companies Organising Treks

The UK Companies operating treks include:

Exodus Expeditions
   9 Weir Rd, London SW12 0LT (☎ (0181) 673 0859; fax 673 0779)
Explore Worldwide
   1 Frederick St, Aldershot GU11 1LQ (☎ (01252) 319448; fax 343170; email info@explore.co.uk)
EWP
   Haulfryn, Cilycwm, Llandovery SA20 0SP (☎ (01550) 721319; fax 720053)
Footloose Adventure Travel
   105 Leeds Rd, Ilkley, West Yorkshire LS26 8EG (☎ (01943) 604030; fax 604070)
Gane & Marshal International
   226 East Barnet Rd, East Barnet EN4 8TD (☎ (0181) 441 9592; fax 441 7376; email 101630 .533@compuserve.com)
High Places
   Globe Works, Penistone Rd, Sheffield S6 3AE (☎ (0114) 275 7500; fax 275 3870)
Hoopoe Adventure Tours
   Kebbell House, Carpenders Park, Watford WD1 5BE (☎ (0181) 428 8221; fax 0181 421 1396)
Natural Action
   163 Latchmere Rd, London SW11 2JZ (☎/fax (0171) 350 2069)
Peak International
   15 Moor Park, Wendover, Aylesbury HP22 6AX (☎/fax (01296) 624225)
Sherpa Expeditions
   131a Heston Rd, Hounslow TW5 0RD (☎ (0181) 577 2717; fax 572 9788; email sherpa.sales @dial.pipex.com)
Travelbag Adventures
   15 Turk St, Alton GU34 1AG (☎ (01420) 541007; fax 541022; email mail@travelbag adventures.co.uk)
Travel Friends International
   The Old Shop, The Street, Pakenham, Bury St Edmunds, Suffolk IP31 2JU (☎/fax (01359) 232385)
Savage Wilderness Safaris
   22 Wilson Ave, Henley, Oxon RG9 1ET (☎ (01491) 574752)
Wind Sand & Stars
   2 Arkwright Rd, Hampstead, London NW3 6AD (☎ (0171) 433 3684; fax 431 3247)

Australia & New Zealand Companies operating treks include:

Adventure World
　　73 Walker St, North Sydney, NSW 2060 (☎ (02) 956 7766);
　　101 Great South Rd, Remuera, Auckland (☎ (09) 524 5118)
African Wildlife Safaris
　　Level 1, 259 Coventry St, South Melbourne, Victoria 3205 (☎ (03) 9696 2899; fax 9696 4937)
Exodus Expeditions
　　8th floor, 350 Kent St, Sydney, NSW 2000 (☎ (02) 9251 5430; fax 9299 8841)
Outdoor Travel
　　382 Little Bourke St, Melbourne, Vic 3000 (☎ (03) 670 7252)
Venture Treks
　　PO Box 37610, 164 Parnell Rd, Auckland (☎ (09) 799 855)

The USA & Canada Companies operating treks include:

Adventure Center
　　1311 63rd St, STE 200, Emeryville, CA 94608 (☎ (800) 227 8747 toll free, (510) 654 1879)
Himalayan Travel
　　110 Prospect St, Stamford, CT 06901 (☎ (800) 225 2380 toll free, (203) 359 3711)
International Expeditions
　　1 Environs Park, Helena, Alabama 35080 (☎ (800) 633 4734 toll free, (205) 428 1700)
Mountain Madness
　　Suite 203, 4218 SW Alaska St, Seattle, WA 98136 (☎ (800) 328 5925 toll free, (206) 937 8389)
Mountain Travel-Sobek
　　6420 Fairmount Ave, El Cerrito, CA 94530 (☎ (888) 687 6235 toll free, (510) 548 0420)

Savage Wilderness Safaris
　　Agent: Wild and Scenic River Tours, PO Box 22606, Seattle WA 98122, (☎ (800) 413 6840 toll free, (206) 323 1220)
Scan East West Travel
　　Suite 420, 500 Union, Seattle, WA 98101 (☎ (206) 623 2157; fax 623 2970)
Trek Holidays
　　8412, 109 St, Edmonton, Alberta T6G 1E2 (☎ (800) 661 7265 toll free, (403) 439 9118)
Wilderness Travel
　　801 Alston Way, Berkeley, CA 94710 (☎ (800) 368 2794 toll free, (510) 548 0420)

LEAVING EAST AFRICA
Air
If you came in overland or on a single ticket, Nairobi is one of the best places in Africa to buy a ticket home after your trek. There are plenty of travel agents who can arrange flights (some are listed in the Organised Treks & Tours section in the Kenya chapter) and some real bargains are sometimes available. Flights home can also be bought in Kampala, Dar es Salaam or Lilongwe. Agents in these cities are listed in the individual country chapters.

Departure Taxes If you fly out of Nairobi, Mombasa, KIA, Dar es Salaam, Kampala, Lilongwe or Blantyre to another country (even the one next door) you have to pay a departure tax of US$20. Only hard currency is acceptable, but even using UK pounds or German marks you tend to lose out. These guys want US dollars!

Getting Around

This chapter provides general information about travelling around East Africa. For more specific details see the Getting Around sections in the individual country chapters. Approach routes to the mountain areas and access routes to the start of each trek are fully described in the individual mountain sections of this book.

The beauty of trekking in East Africa is that nearly all the major mountains can be easily reached by public transport, which is ideal for visitors without their own wheels. Relatively few people in Africa own private cars, so buses and trains are reasonably priced and frequent on the main routes. Consequently, most trekkers use public road and rail transport to get around East Africa, although planes and rental cars are other options to consider.

On a few of the routes described in this book there is no public transport access, in which case you must hire a car (if your budget allows) or join an organised trek.

AIR

There are domestic and regional flights between all the capital cities and main towns in East Africa. For long distances, regional flights can be quick but can take a large chunk out of your budget. They also have a habit of being cancelled. In the last few years, though, the countries of eastern and southern Africa have started sharing planes and co-operating on routes, which means there are now fewer delays.

Even if you're short of time, don't automatically assume that flights are the best way to get around. For example, if you're planning to trek on Mt Kenya and Kilimanjaro, it's usually not worth flying between Kenya and northern Tanzania, as road travel is just as quick.

However, if time is limited, and you want to combine Mt Kenya or Kilimanjaro with the Rwenzoris or Mulanje then you'll certainly find it helpful to use regional flights between Nairobi and Kampala or Lilongwe.

ROAD

Roads in East Africa vary in quality: some main roads have been tarred recently and are in excellent condition. In other places, tarred roads have become badly potholed, and their conditions range from bad to worse. Sometimes, as a local bus driver once said to me, they're 'more than worse'.

In most African countries, the main roads are tarred usually as part of an aid project, often paid for by a western country, but there never seems to be a long-term maintenance plan tied in with the deal, so after a few years (or even less) of use by heavy trucks and no repairs, the roads often become full of holes again.

Secondary roads are usually untarred. The surface may be graded dirt, making driving a lot better than on a potholed tar-sealed road, or ungraded, making it about the same.

The standard of driving in East Africa is generally bad. Breakdowns are very common and accidents frighteningly frequent. Despite this happy thought, most of your travelling will probably be by road.

Traffic keeps to the left (or is supposed to) in all the countries covered by this book. If you're driving, watch out for cattle, children and cyclists, especially at night.

Bus, Matatu & Shared Taxi

The type of public transport available is determined by the quality of the road, which in turn is based on the size or importance of the towns it connects.

On the main routes there are usually local buses (which are slow and crowded) and luxury buses (which are fast and comfortable), and often a wide range to choose from in between. Away from the main routes, there's usually no choice – buses are local, slow and uncomfortable, and that's it.

On the main routes, buses usually keep to a vague timetable or at least leave on time. You can often reserve a seat in advance, and sometimes this is essential.

In rural areas, there's often one bus per day between the main town and each surrounding village. You'll hear the term 'the bus sleeps at ...', which means it goes to that village in the afternoon, stays there, and comes back to the main town early next morning.

There are also minibuses (called *matatus* in Kenya and northern Tanzania) which fill in the gaps in the bus schedules around towns and in the country. Another option is to go by one of the shared taxis (usually Peugeot 504 seven-seaters, also called 'taxi-matatus' or 'Peugeot-taxis') which ply between the main towns in Kenya, Uganda and northern Tanzania. Although more expensive, these are the fastest and most comfortable way to travel, and the drivers are usually safer than matatu drivers. All matatus and shared taxis leave when they're full.

Local Truck & Hitching

In many countries, as you venture into rural areas, the frequency of buses drops dramatically – sometimes to nothing. Then the only way to get around is to ride on trucks and pick-ups, in the same way as the locals. Usually a fee is payable to the driver, often on a par with local bus fares for a similar distance. Ask the price before getting in; it may be cheaper on top than in the cab. In cases like this the line between hitching and public transport is blurred – but if it's the only way to get around you've got no choice anyway.

Hitching lifts in the western sense (ie for free) is also possible in all of the countries covered in this book, and can be a cheap and very interesting way to get around the region. As few local people own cars, you're quite likely to get lifts in vans and trucks, and drivers usually expect payment. However, on the main routes, you might get picked up by a well-off local or expatriate worker, who won't charge. If the journey is long you should still offer to pay your way by buying lunch for the driver.

Note, however, that as in any other part of the world, hitching is never entirely safe, and we therefore don't recommend it. Travellers who decide to hitch should understand that they are taking a small but potentially serious risk. However, many people do hitch around East Africa, using common sense and the occasional bus to avoid potential hot spots, and have no difficulties. If you're planning to hitch, take advice from other hitchers (locals or travellers) first. Hitching in pairs is obviously safer, and hitching through less salubrious suburbs, especially at night, is asking for trouble.

Car

Car hire is available in some countries. Driving can sometimes save you time and make access to a few of the trekking areas easier. On the down side, for budget travellers car rental can be expensive, although costs can be reduced when three or four people share.

Bicycle

More and more people are travelling around by bike these days, and you can easily cycle between the mountain areas covered in this book. A lot of trekkers seem to be mountain bikers too, and some of the routes in this book can even be done by bike.

Traditional touring machines will cope with most tar-sealed and dirt roads without too much trouble, although very narrow tyres and rims are not recommended. But unless you plan to cover long distances on mainly tarred roads, a mountain bike is more suitable.

Cyclists are regarded as second-class citizens in Africa even more than they are in western countries, and motorists are more cause for alarm than any road surface. Make sure you know what's coming up behind you and be prepared to take evasive action onto the edge of the road, as local cyclists are often forced to do.

If you get tired, or want to cut out the boring bits, bikes can easily be carried on buses and matatus. Intrepid cyclists may want to check the US-based International Bicycle Fund's 'Bicycle Africa' website at www. halcyon.com/fkroger/bike/bikeafr.htm which includes announcements on cycling tours in Uganda, Tanzania, Malawi and several other African countries.

TRAIN

Trains in Kenya and Tanzania are mostly good, in both comfort and reliability. In Uganda and Malawi trains are very slow, in bad condition and not worth using, although Ugandan railways are undergoing renovation and services may improve in the future.

In Kenya and Tanzania, 1st class is a twin cabin, sometimes with wood panelling, where you can travel in faded colonial style. Second class is either comfortable seating or sleeping cars divided into men-only and women-only four-berth or six-berth compartments. Third class is usually very crowded, with wooden seats, tons of baggage, and a few goats and chickens stuffed in for good measure.

LOCAL TRANSPORT

Around towns and cities, you can use local buses or minibuses/matatus. Fares are always cheap, and transport is always crowded.

If you prefer a bit more breathing room, taxis are available in most towns and cities and can be useful for travel at night, or for going to/from the airport. Fares are reasonable compared with those in western cities, but tend to be flexible: meters are rare – always establish the fare before you get in the cab.

Tanzania

For most visitors, Tanzania is famous for the huge wildlife reserves of Serengeti, Lake Manyara and Ngorongoro Crater, and for the island of Zanzibar that lies off the Indian Ocean coast. Tanzania was also once famous for its shortages, restrictions and suffocating bureaucracy. But since the early 1990s things have been changing: public transport now runs fairly smoothly, the hotels have electricity, there's food in the shops and it no longer takes all day to change a travellers cheque.

For trekkers, the biggest attraction is, of course, the massif of Kilimanjaro, the highest mountain in Tanzania and indeed the whole of Africa, with several spectacular trekking routes from the forested foothills to the top of the snowcapped summit dome. Tanzania's other mountains include Mt Meru, the country's second-highest peak, where the trekking is dramatic and exhilarating. Further to the south-west is Mt Hanang – a mysterious, solitary giant, rarely reached by visitors.

Away from the high peaks, other trekking areas include the rolling hills and volcanic cones of the Crater Highlands, rising above the floor of the Great Rift Valley. For a complete change of scenery, trekkers can explore the Usambara Mountains in the east or the Kipengere Range in the south; areas of villages and farmlands contrast sharply with the uninhabited wilderness further north.

DAVID ELSE

Tanzania – Trekking Highlights
Africa's highest mountain, **Kilimanjaro**, tops the wish-list for most trekkers – and, when approached in the right manner, rarely disappoints. In Kili's shadow lies **Mt Meru** – compact and often overlooked, but pristine, dramatic and immensely satisfying. The **Crater Highlands** offer excellent trekking through Maasai lands dominated by **Ol Doinyo Lengai** – a classic Great Rift Valley volcano.

Facts about the Country

HISTORY
The early history of Tanzania is closely linked with that of the other East African countries and is described in the Facts about the Region chapter.

The Colonial Period
After the Berlin Conference of 1884-5 the two largest European powers, Germany and Britain, divided East Africa between them by drawing a line from Lake Victoria to the Indian Ocean coast. North of the border was British territory, to become Kenya and Uganda. South of the border was German East Africa, declared a protectorate in 1891.

For the next 20 years the protectorate was developed by the German colonial government. The sleepy fishing port of Dar es Salaam was declared the new capital. Sisal and rubber plantations were established, and a railway was built across the country, from the coast to Lake Tanganyika. In many parts of the territory this development was resisted by local African people, who resented the German

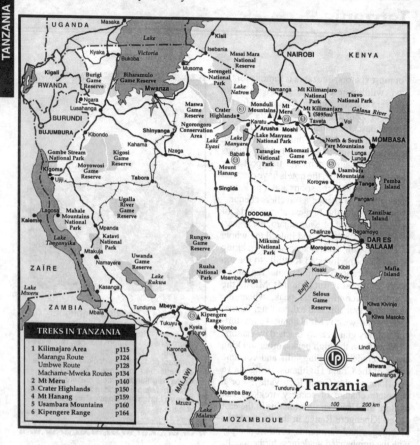

TREKS IN TANZANIA

1 Kilimajaro Area	p115
Marangu Route	p124
Umbwe Route	p128
Machame-Mweka Routes	p134
2 Mt Meru	p140
3 Crater Highlands	p150
4 Mt Hanang	p159
5 Usambara Mountains	p160
6 Kipengere Range	p164

methods of land control. One of the largest revolts, between 1905 and 1907, became known as the Maji Maji uprising.

During WWI German and British forces, both made up of European and African soldiers, were engaged in a long campaign in East Africa. After the war, most of the region was mandated by the League of Nations to Britain, who renamed the territory Tanganyika and continued to administer it for the next 40 years. (The extreme western province of Ruanda-Burundi was similarly mandated to Belgium.)

A new series of land laws and a system of local government were established and the railway line was extended to Lake Victoria. But Tanzania was always seen as the least attractive of the East African territories and was never settled by Europeans in a big way. The only areas which attracted any significant numbers of European settlers were the areas around Kilimanjaro and the southern highlands.

Transition & Independence

After WWII African people were given more opportunities to take part in the politics of the territory. Through the 1950s several nationalist organisations were founded, including the Tanganyika African National Union (TANU) led by Julius Nyerere.

In 1961 Tanganyika gained independence from Britain, and became a republic a year later. Nyerere was the first president, a post he held for over 20 years. In 1964 he combined Tanganyika with the then independent state of Zanzibar to form the United Republic of Tanzania. Nyerere's most significant move came in 1967, when he introduced his own *Ujamaa* system of government, combining aspects of Marxist socialism and African tradition, and emphasising the importance of collectivism and self-reliance. Banks and most privately owned businesses were nationalised and state-managed collective farms were established. During this period Tanzania received aid from China and East Germany, but the schemes were beset by problems and never succeeded.

Tanzania's problems were compounded in 1977, when the East African Economic Community of Tanzania, Kenya and Uganda collapsed, badly affecting Tanzania's economy. The border with Kenya was closed, leading to a reduction in the number of tourists and a further loss of revenue.

The situation became even more serious in late 1978 when the army of Uganda, under orders from Idi Amin, invaded northern Tanzania. The Ugandans were ousted by a Tanzanian 'people's army', but the financial cost of this war (quite apart from the cost in human life and suffering) was something Tanzania could ill afford.

Modern Times

Tanzania continued to be one of the poorest and least developed countries in Africa until the mid 1980s, when Nyerere resigned, and Ali Hassan Mwinyi became president. Tanzania struck a deal with the International Monetary Fund, and the new government made several significant policy changes. Private ownership was once again encouraged and businesses were allowed to trade in hard currency. As support from the rapidly disintegrating eastern bloc decreased, invest-

ment and aid money from western countries was attracted.

Nyerere remained chairman of the Chama Cha Mapinduzi (CCM) – the Party of the Revolution – until 1990, when he stepped down and President Mwinyi took over this post. In mid-1992 Mwinyi, under pressure from several major western donor countries, declared that Tanzania would cease to be a single party state. The CCM structure within the civil service and armed forces was disbanded and, in the excitement, more than 20 groups announced plans to become opposition parties.

Most people seemed happy with a slow and peaceful changeover to pluralism. Elections were held in 1995 and easily won by CCM throughout the country (except on Zanzibar, where the result was much closer). The new CCM leader, Benjamin Mkapa, became president. Generally speaking, Tanzania remains politically stable. The next elections are due in 2000.

GEOGRAPHY

Tanzania consists largely of highland plain, covered mainly by light woodland and grassy savanna. Settlement on the plains is light; crop and cattle farming are not possible due to the unsuitable climate and the presence of tsetse flies. The population is concentrated on the hills and low mountains that rise out of the plain, forming two large arcs across the north-eastern and southern parts of the country.

Despite the general flatness, there are also some great extremes of altitude in Tanzania. The summit of Kilimanjaro is the highest point in Africa, and Lake Tanganyika, in the western arm of the Great Rift Valley, is the deepest lake.

CLIMATE

The climate of Tanzania is technically 'equatorial' but it is actually more tropical – largely influenced by the high altitude of the plateau. Seasons are wet and dry, rather than hot and cold. The long dry season, when conditions are cool, is from June to early October, and the short dry season, when it's warmer, is from mid-December until March. In the south there is one rainy season, from December to April.

Temperatures vary considerably in different parts of the country, and are generally influenced by altitude. On the plains, maximum daytime temperatures can rise to 28°C, although nights are cool. On the mountains, temperatures rise and fall only slightly throughout the year, but vary considerably between night and day. On the lower slopes, maximum daytime temperatures are normally around 15 to 20°C, falling to a chilly 5°C at night. At higher altitudes, daytime temperatures range between 10°C and 15°C, and night-time temperatures can drop to around freezing point. On the high mountains, above 4000m, maximum daytime temperatures are usually around 5°C. It's always below freezing at night, sometimes dropping to -10°C, with strong icy winds that make it even colder.

ECONOMY

Tanzania's economy is based predominantly on agriculture. Crops grown on plantations for export include coffee, tea and sisal (used in string manufacture, although this is declining). The large communal farms introduced by Nyerere were in general not successful, most people preferring to cultivate small plots of land, called *shambas*, at a subsistence or local trading level. Tourism is also a major foreign currency earner. After decades of neglect, Tanzania's manufacturing and processing industries are being revitalised, mainly in Dar es Salaam, Tanga and Arusha, with investment from various countries, most notably South Africa.

POPULATION & PEOPLE

In 1996 Tanzania's population was estimated at 29 million, expanding at around 2.5% to 3% annually. There are more than 100 different tribes, mostly of Bantu origin. (For more information on tribes see People in the Facts about the Region chapter.) Other distinct groups are the Maasai, semi-nomadic people of Nilotic origin inhabiting the Rift Valley plains and highlands in the north, and the Swahili people, descendants of intermixed Africans and Arabs on the coast.

RELIGION

Christians, Muslims and people who practice traditional beliefs each make up about a third of the population. There are various Christian groups, including Catholics, Protestants and several local African faiths. Islam is particularly widespread on the coast and in the large towns.

LANGUAGE

The official languages are English and Swahili (called Kiswahili locally), although there are many indigenous languages. English is spoken widely in areas used to tourists (eg the towns of Moshi and Arusha), but far less so in rural areas or places off the beaten track. Many of the porters on Kilimanjaro and Mt Meru, for example, speak very little English, although guides and rangers are usually conversant in English. Swahili is a common language spoken by most people as a second tongue, except on the coast where it is the first language. For useful phrases in Swahili see the Language section in the Facts about the Region chapter.

Facts for the Trekker

PLANNING
When to Trek

The best time for trekking in Tanzania is during the dry seasons, which are from mid-December to March, when the weather is generally dry and warm, and from June to early October, when it's dry and cool (see the Climate section earlier in this chapter).

Over the last few years the weather patterns in East Africa (and all over the world) have become less predictable and the rainy seasons have become less rainy. Trekkers going up Kilimanjaro and Meru in November can often get several days of good weather while still paying cheaper rates. However, paths through the forest are very slippery at this time and the final sections of routes up to the summit are more likely to be blocked by snow.

Remember that dry seasons are dry only when compared with the wet season! Although rain and snow are less likely during the dry months, you should be prepared for them (they can sometimes be very heavy) at any time of the year.

Maps

Regional maps are discussed in the Regional Facts for the Trekker chapter. For travel around Tanzania between trekking areas, the BP/Shell *Map of Tanzania* is pretty good, although it's available only in Tanzania. Others include the *Tanzania* road map produced by the Tanzania Tourist Board, available free from the tourist office in Dar es Salaam and from some hotels and tour companies elsewhere in the country. If you're also trekking in Kenya, most Kenya maps also cover northern Tanzania, including Kilimanjaro and Meru, and sometimes the Usambara Mountains and the Crater Highlands.

Tanzania is covered by DOS/government survey maps at scales of 1:50,000, 1:100,000 and 1:250,000. These are available in Dar es Salaam from the Public Map Sales Office in Ardhi House, next to the Ministry of Foreign Affairs, which is three blocks along from the Kilimanjaro Hotel, Kivukoni Front. Maps cost around US$4 and there are no formalities, although the maps of popular areas are often out of stock.

Maps of individual mountain areas are covered in the relevant sections.

TOURIST OFFICE

Despite the fact that most of Tanzania's tourism industry is based in Arusha, the country's only tourist office is in Dar es Salaam, on Samora Ave. The staff are friendly and quite helpful but not too sure about job function. Asking about walking safaris, we were proudly handed *Selling Tanzania* a resource booklet for overseas travel agents.

VISAS

Visas are required by citizens of most countries, including the USA, Japan and most of Europe (although citizens of Ireland and the Scandinavian countries do not require visas). Citizens of most Commonwealth countries do not require visas, but citizens of Canada

and the UK do. Visas are usually valid for three months. The cost depends on your nationality: US$55 for Britons, US$45 for Americans, US$26 for Japanese, US$16 for Germans, and US$10 for others. If you're travelling overland, visas must be obtained in advance, as they are not available at land borders. If you're flying into Tanzania you can get a visa at the airport on arrival. However, having a visa in advance still saves hassle and time.

Be warned that there is no Tanzanian high commission in Malawi so if you need a visa it must be obtained elsewhere. If you're coming from the south, Lusaka and Harare are the closest places. (If you do need a visa and you're flying in, you can get it at your airport of arrival.)

Note that entry regulations are constantly changing. It's likely that citizens of several other non-African Commonwealth countries will need visas in the future. For up-to-date information, contact your nearest Tanzanian embassy, high commission or tourist office.

EMBASSIES
Tanzanian Embassies Abroad

Tanzanian high commissions abroad include:

Kenya
    Continental House, corner of Uhuru Highway and Harambee Ave, Nairobi (☎ (02) 331056; fax 218269).
Uganda
    6 Kagera Rd, Kampala (☎ (041) 256272)

There are also Tanzanian embassies or consulates in Belgium (Brussels), Canada (Ottawa), Ethiopia (Addis Ababa), France (Paris), Germany (Bonn), Italy (Rome), Japan (Tokyo), the Netherlands (The Hague), South Africa (Pretoria), Sweden (Stockholm), Switzerland (Geneva), UK (London) and USA (New York and Washington DC).

Foreign Embassies in Tanzania

Countries which maintain diplomatic missions in Tanzania include the following (all in Dar es Salaam). Some are open in the afternoon,

TANZANIA

but the best time to visit is between 9 am and noon. The telephone code for Dar is ☎ 051.

Belgium
    NIC building, Samora Ave (☎ 46968)
Canada
    38 Mirambo St, Garden Ave (☎ 46000)
Denmark
    Ghana Ave (☎ 46319)
France
    Corner of Bagamoyo and Kulimani Rds (☎ 66021)
Germany
    10th Floor, NIC building, Samora Ave (☎ 46334)
Italy
    316 Lugalo Rd (☎ 46352)
Japan
    Plot 1018, Ali Mwinyi Rd (☎ 46356)
Kenya
    NIC building, Samora Ave (☎ 46362; fax 46519)
Malawi
    NIC building, Samora Ave (☎ 46673)
Netherlands
    New ATC building, corner of Garden Ave and Ohio St (☎ 46391)
South Africa
    c/o Oysterbay Hotel, Touré Drive, Oyster Bay (☎ 68062)
Uganda
    Extelecoms building, Samora Ave (☎ 31004; fax 46256)
UK
    Hifiadhi House, Samora Ave (☎ 29601)
USA
    36 Laibon Rd (☎ 66010)

The nearest Australian and New Zealand high commissions are in Nairobi.

MONEY

This section covers money in Tanzania. Outlines of costs and other general money aspects are given in the Regional Facts for the Trekker chapter.

Currency Exchange

The unit of currency is the Tanzanian shilling (TSh). Since the relaxation of currency laws the black market has virtually disappeared and inflation has steadied but is still unpredictable. Therefore we have quoted the prices of most things in US dollars (US$) throughout this chapter. Although the actual exchange rate may have changed by the time you reach Tanzania, the cost of things in US$ (or any

other hard currency) will not have altered much. The approximate exchange rates in 1997 were:

US$1	=	TSh 500
UK£1	=	TSh 900

Changing Money

You can change money at a bank or bureau de change. A few banks still change money at official (pegged) rates, which are low, and 'free' (floating) rates, which are better. Make sure you go to the right desk!

Before changing all your money, note that you won't need too many shillings. Entrance fees for national parks (including Mt Meru and Kilimanjaro), organised treks and safaris, and all but the very cheapest hotels are quoted and can be paid for in hard currency. However, if you're short of dollars, TSh can be widely used without any problem, and most places convert at the current rate of exchange so you don't lose out. If you're sticking with hard currency, most kinds are officially acceptable, but US dollars are the most convenient way to pay, and often work out cheaper than paying with, say, UK pounds.

The only catch is that at national parks and some other official places, even though you pay in dollars, change may be given in TSh, converted at the official (ie low) rate. The best way to avoid this is to carry your money in a mix of high and low-denomination US dollar bills and travellers cheques.

If you are travelling between Tanzania and Kenya, there are no foreign currency restrictions, but you are not allowed to import or export more than KSh 200 or TSh 2000,

---

Warning
Beware of con-artists in Arusha and Dar who offer high rates for money changed on the street. One ploy is to give you a stack of small TSh notes, which are difficult to count and inevitably amount to less than they should. Another scam once they've got your money is to say they're police informers (which they might be) and only a high 'fine' (paid on the spot, naturally) will let you off the hook. Sometimes they save time by pulling a knife or knocking you to the ground and simply running off with your dollars. ■

although if you are coming back and want to keep some money a search is unlikely. If you have cash you no longer need, there are moneychangers on both sides of the border who will take surplus money off you, but check the rates. There are also several shops where you can spend your remainder on supplies, or you can haggle with the Maasai women selling souvenirs.

BOOKS

Books covering all or part of East Africa are listed in the Regional Facts for the Trekker chapter. Guidebooks on individual mountain areas are covered in the relevant sections.

Guidebooks

There are not many general guidebooks on Tanzania, but the country is well covered in Lonely Planet's *East Africa* – companion volume to this guide. The *Guide to Tanzania* by regional specialist Philip Briggs covers the whole country, including many overlooked corners, with an emphasis on natural history. Of special relevance to trekkers (and despite its title) *Mountains of Kenya* also covers northern Tanzania (see Guidebooks in the Kenya chapter).

General

General books of interest to trekkers include *Journey Through Tanzania*, a lavishly illustrated coffee-table book, produced by celebrated photographer Mohamed Amin, with purple prose by Brian Tetley, covering all aspects of the country, including the mountains. More specific is *Kilimanjaro* by John Reader; an entertaining account of the trek to the top of Africa's highest peak, with plenty of historical asides and excellent colour pictures. Another fine coffee-table book is *Kilimanjaro: Legendary Summits* with photos by Jean-Denis Joubert and words by Eric Christin (a respected Arusha-based guide).

Smaller, more portable, books include *The Tree Where Man Was Born* by Peter Matthiessen; part travelogue, part anthropology and part idle musings, it is based on the author's travels through Tanzania's Crater Highlands, and on his fascination with the last remnants of the original 'Old People' of East Africa. Also highly recommended is *No Man's Land* by George Monbiot (for more details see the boxed text on Maasai Land Issues in the Crater Highlands section).

USEFUL ORGANISATIONS

The Kilimanjaro Mountain Club is made up mainly of expatriates in Tanzania, and does not usually cater for tourists. There are no regular meetings, but activities are listed in the members' newsletter, which is printed a few times per year. The club also produces a journal called *Ice Cap*, but this is rarely seen (there have been eight issues since 1932). The club's address is PO Box 66, Moshi.

The Wildlife Conservation Society of Tanzania is a small but growing organisation campaigning to protect wildlife and areas of wilderness in Tanzania. You can support this cause by joining the society (PO Box 70919, Dar es Salaam). If you join, you'll receive a free magazine which often contains information on the mountain national parks.

PUBLIC HOLIDAYS

Public holidays include the following, but others may be added:

12 January	Zanzibar Revolution Day
26 April	Union Day
1 May	International Workers' Day
7 July	Peasants' Day *(Saba Saba)*
9 December	Tanzania Independence & Republic Day

Other public holidays are Christmas Day, the Friday and Monday before Easter Sunday, and the Muslim feast of Eid-ul-Fitr (the end of Ramadan). The dates of Muslim feasts are not fixed because they are based on the Islamic lunar calendar; in general, they fall eleven or twelve days earlier each year. In 1997 Ramadan was from mid-January to late February.

PLACES TO STAY IN DAR ES SALAAM

You might arrive in Dar es Salaam if you're flying in from Europe or elsewhere, or you might pass through on your way between the trekking areas of northern Tanzania and southern Tanzania or Malawi. This is not an exhaustive list of places to stay in Dar, but it will give you an idea of what's available. For information on accommodation in Moshi, Arusha and other places nearer the trekking areas, see the individual mountain sections.

Unless stated otherwise, all prices quoted below include breakfast. Dar's phones are being renovated; six figure numbers are on the new exchange, five figure numbers are on the old exchange and often out of order.

Places to Stay – bottom end

Cheap rooms always seem to be hard to find in Dar. You've got more chance of finding something if you arrive in the morning. One of the best-value cheapies, and a long-time shoestringers' favourite, is the *Jambo Inn* (☎ 114293) on Libya St, with en suite singles/doubles for US$10/16. A block away is the equally popular *Safari Inn* (☎ 38101) with similar rooms and rates.

Slightly further away from the centre is the friendly *New Happy Hotel* (☎ 180505), at the junction of Lumumba St and Morogoro Rd, with singles/doubles at US$8/10 (or US$10/12 en suite). Nearby, just off Lumumba St, on the junction of Kariakoo and Ukami Sts, is the *Harare Inn* (☎ 189 595); a real gem – clean and safe, with good en suite singles/doubles at US$14/20 including breakfast. Also on Lumumba St is the *Hotel Esmail* (☎ 180129) with fair doubles at US$12 (US$20 with air-con); it's gloomy, but worth a try if others in this range are full. Nearby, the *Kiboyda Annex* on the junction of Lumumba and Uhuru Sts also has simple doubles for US$12.

Places to Stay – middle

Cheapest in this range is the rather faded *Continental Hotel* on Nkrumah St, with acceptable en suite rooms for US$30/40, bed only. Much better value is the friendly *Peacock Hotel* (☎ 114071, 115568; fax 117 962) on Bibi Titi Mohamed St (formerly UWT St), between Morogoro Rd and Uhuru St, on the edge of the city centre. Clean en suite, air-con rooms cost US$55/60 (with TV

and phone), and there's a comfortable bar and reasonable restaurant. If this place is full, the nearby *Starlight Hotel* (☎ 37182) comes a poor second but has rooms for US$40/50.

Places to Stay – top end

Long-established and in a central location, the *Motel Agip* (☎ 23511), near the junction of Samora Ave and Maktaba St has singles/doubles at US$90/95. Nearby, the vast *Hotel Embassy* (☎ 111181; fax 112634) has rooms from US$70/80 to US$100/115.

Top of the range is the shiny new *Sheraton* on Ohio St, with all the features you'd expect of an international standard hotel; rack rates start at US$260/275, plus US$10 for breakfast, but booking though an agent may get you discounts. Also worth trying is the *Kilimanjaro Hotel* (☎ 110881; fax 113304) on the sea front with rooms at US$90/100, still staggering under state management in 1997 but due for takeover by an international chain in the near future; expect vast improvements and prices to match.

Getting There & Away

Getting to Tanzania from Europe or further afield is covered in the Getting There & Away chapter earlier in this book. This section assumes you're already in Tanzania and need to go elsewhere; it covers travel *from* Tanzania *to* the neighbouring East African countries of Kenya, Malawi and Uganda using air, road or rail transport. For going the other way (eg from Kenya to Tanzania) see the relevant country chapters.

How you travel depends on how much time you've got and the amount of travelling (as opposed to trekking) you want to do. In this section it's presumed you want to take fairly direct routes between the trekking areas in the various countries.

KENYA

Air

There are international scheduled flights between Dar es Salaam and Nairobi every day for around US$110 one way. Tanzania's other major airport is Kilimanjaro international airport (KIA) which is nearer the main trekking areas, but generally it's not worth flying between KIA and Nairobi as road connections are good. If time is very short, Precision Air (see the following Getting Around section) have regular flights between KIA and Nairobi with road connections from Arusha.

Road

By far the busiest route from Tanzania to Kenya is the mostly good tar road between Arusha and Nairobi. (This is the route most trekkers take for the journey between Kili and Mt Kenya.) The border is at Namanga, roughly halfway between the two. You need to complete arrival/departure forms and get your passport stamped, but otherwise formalities are straightforward.

Another possible border crossing is at Taveta, east of Moshi, from where you can reach Mombasa. (More details in the Kenya chapter.)

Bus The journey between Arusha and Nairobi can be done by direct public bus, without changing at the border. There are several bus companies covering this route, with at least one service every day in each direction. In Arusha, all the companies have booking offices at the bus station. Arusha to Nairobi costs about US$10. The journey time varies; some buses take hours to cross the border, as all passengers have to be individually stamped through and the customs officials like to check each item among the tons of luggage on the roof.

Shuttle Bus By far the most comfortable way of going between Arusha and Nairobi is by shuttle bus. These are comfortable 20-seater buses, with good drivers, which cover the route in about five hours, including about half an hour to cross the border. There's normally two or three non-stop services every day, leaving in the morning or around midday. The one-way fare on all the buses is about US$25. The fare from Moshi to Nairobi is US$35.

Shuttle bus companies include:

Davanu Shuttle
  Buses depart at 8 am and 2 pm daily each way from the Novotel in Arusha and the Norfolk Hotel in Nairobi, with connections to/from Moshi. For information and reservations contact Let's Go Travel (listed in the Organised Treks & Tours sections of the Tanzania and Kenya chapters) or go direct to the company at Windsor House, University Way, Nairobi (☎ 217178/ 222002); in Moshi the agent is the Keys Hotel (see Kilimanjaro – Places to Stay).
Riverside
  Buses depart at 8 am and 2 pm from the service road on Kenyatta Ave near the New Stanley Hotel in Nairobi and from Riverside Car Hire (☎ 2639) in Arusha. The Nairobi office is at Style Travel, Koinange St (☎ 219020). There are connections to/from Moshi, and pick-ups at Nairobi airport.

Shared Taxi & Minibus Falling between the bus and the shuttle bus in terms of speed and comfort, but lower than both in terms of safety, are the seven-seater shared taxis. These do not cross the border, so you have to do the trip in two stages. You have to walk between the two customs posts and pick up another vehicle on the other side. It's only a few hundred metres but if you've got a lot of gear, young boys with barrows will help you for a small fee.

Taxis and minibuses leave Arusha bus station for Namanga on a fill up and go basis regularly throughout the day. From Namanga to Nairobi it's the same deal. Fares are: Arusha to Namanga US$3; Namanga to Nairobi US$6. In Nairobi, shared taxis for Namanga leave from the junction of Accra and River Rds. (Minibuses also cover the route; they're slower and charge about 25% less than shared taxis.) Drivers will accept Kenyan shillings, Tanzanian shillings or US dollars for either stage of the journey, usually at a fair rate (but make sure you know what it should be).

Train

Some maps show a railway line from Moshi to Mombasa. There is no international passenger service, but one is rumoured to be starting in late 1997.

MALAWI

Air

International direct flights from Dar to Lilongwe go twice a week and cost around US$200 one way. If you're in northern Tanzania, you could fly from Kilimanjaro international airport to Dar and change there for an onward flight, although you may have a long wait (possibly a day or longer).

Road

The only land crossing between Tanzania and Malawi is at the Songwe River Bridge, near Kyela, south-east of Mbeya.

On the Tanzanian side, from Mbeya there are about three buses each day to Kyela (if you come to Mbeya on the Tazara train, a bus to Kyela waits for it to arrive). About 5km before Kyela, get off at the junction where the road goes to the border (ask the driver to drop you, although he'll have probably guessed already). From the junction to the Tanzanian border post is 7km; you have to walk, or get a lift on the back of a bicycle taxi. You then walk across the bridge over the Songwe River to the Malawi border post, from where public transport runs to Karonga and Mzuzu (for more details see the Malawi chapter).

We've received reports of a new bus service running directly between Dar and the Songwe River Bridge border, via Mbeya and Kyela. It leaves Dar very early in the morning and arrives at the border around 4 pm. The fare is around US$15.

UGANDA

Air

International direct flights between Dar es Salaam and Kampala go about three times a week, and cost about US$200 one way, or you can fly via Nairobi. There are daily flights from KIA, which is nearer Tanzania's main trekking areas, to Dar but it's much easier to travel between Arusha or Moshi and Nairobi by road (as described in the Kenya section earlier) then fly from Nairobi to Kampala.

Road

The easiest way to get between the trekking areas of Tanzania and Uganda is by road

through Kenya, via Nairobi (see Getting There & Away in the Kenya chapter).

Getting Around

The normal way of getting around Tanzania, when travelling between the trekking areas, is by road. Other options include the train between Moshi and Dar or between Dar and southern Tanzania (or Malawi). There are also domestic flights.

AIR

Domestic flights within Tanzania are operated by the state airline Air Tanzania. This company has recently merged with Uganda Airways to form an airline called Alliance (with support from South African Airways) to cover international routes. Alliance may cover domestic routes in the future.

The domestic flight most trekkers are likely to use is between Dar es Salaam and Kilimanjaro international airport (KIA). Scheduled one-way fares start at around US$80. Many travellers also use the regular service operated by a charter airline called Precision (Arusha ☎ (057) 6903; fax 8204; or Dar es Salaam ☎ (051) 30800), with flights between Dar and KIA, with road connections to/from Arusha, costing about US$100 one way.

If you need to reach any of the southern parks and reserves (such as Selous or Ruaha), another charter line called Coastal Travels (☎ Dar 117 959) serves these areas daily from Dar. A one-way fare between Dar and Selous is US$80.

Domestic flights can be arranged direct with the airlines, but it's usually easier to use a reliable travel agent as they can advise you on all the choices. In Arusha, use Let's Go Travel; in Dar use Rickshaw Travel (both are listed in Organised Treks & Tours later in this section).

The Airport

If you arrive by air at KIA (about midway between Arusha and Moshi), a taxi to Moshi will cost around US$50. Going from town to the airport, competition means this fare is around US$30. The nearest public transport is on the main Arusha-Moshi road, 7km from the airport. You can walk, try hitching or take a taxi to the junction and catch a bus to Moshi or Arusha from there.

ROAD
Bus & Minibus

For getting around on the main routes, especially between Namanga, Arusha and Moshi, there are regular buses, minibuses and shared taxis. Once you get south of Moshi (ie on the road to Dar) road transport is pretty much limited to buses and minibuses. Basically there are two types of bus: fast or slow. On the main routes you get both sorts: the express buses are often called 'luxury', although the seats may not be any more comfortable than those on a slow bus, but they stop less often and are less crowded, so it makes your journey more enjoyable. As an example, an express bus between Arusha and Dar costs around US$13; Moshi to/from Dar is US$11. An express minibus between Moshi and Arusha is US$2. Off the main routes there is usually no choice: the buses are slow and basic.

Seats on long-distance express buses usually need to be reserved in advance. In the main towns, each bus has its own office at the bus station. For shorter distances, and destinations off the main routes, buses and minibuses leave when full. Routes around towns, or between towns and their surrounding villages, are served by local minibuses. In Dar es Salaam, and most of southern Tanzania, minibuses are called *dala dala*.

Sometimes express buses go terrifyingly fast, especially on the recently completed super smooth highways between Moshi and Dar or Dar and Mbeya. Given the choice, most travellers go by train rather than by bus on this route.

Bus Stations Most towns have one bus station where all buses arrive and leave. Unfortunately, this is not the case in Dar, where there are several bus stations, each for different destinations. The station for buses to Moshi and Arusha is on the corner of Libya St and Morogoro Rd, just outside the city centre.

Car Rental

If you want to get to the more remote mountains in Tanzania (such as Lengai or Hanang) using a rental car might make things easier, but generally speaking costs are very high, and if you leave the car for a few days while you're actually trekking this makes spending the money even more painful. Added to this, most of Tanzania's conventional car rental agencies (Hertz, Avis etc) are based in Dar, a long way from the main trekking areas. In Moshi and Arusha, if you get a group of around five or six people together, you can hire a Land Rover with driver from a tour company for what is essentially a private safari. Expect to pay between US$100 and US$200 per day for the vehicle (depending on its quality), plus fuel (at around US$0.50/L). Naturally, all other costs such as park fees, hotels and food are your responsibility. It is very important to check before leaving who is responsible for repairs should the vehicle break down.

TRAIN

If you're travelling between the trekking areas of northern Tanzania and southern Tanzania, or going to/from Malawi, you can use the railway between Moshi and Dar or between Dar and Mbeya (this latter line is called the Tanzania-Zambia Railway, or Tazara, and continues south towards Lusaka). Trains are usually slower than buses on the same route, but they are cheaper, generally more comfortable and safer than road transport. On the Dar-Moshi train, 1st class is a compartment for two; 2nd class is compartments of six, or comfortable seating; 3rd class is crowded and very basic, with wooden seats and no glass in the windows. On the Tazara train, 1st class is a compartment for four; 2nd class is compartments of six; and 3rd class is comfortable seating. All trains have dining cars.

There is one train a week in each direction between Dar and Moshi, and there are two express trains and three ordinary trains each way per week between Dar and Mbeya.

Moshi to Dar costs US$30/26 in 1st/2nd class (sleeper) or US$19/12 in 2nd/3rd class (seat). Dar to Mbeya costs US$40/26/15 for 1st/2nd/3rd class on the express train, slightly less on ordinary trains.

You should book seats three days to a week in advance, although you might be lucky and be able to do it nearer the day you want to go. Sometimes booking clerks will tell you that the train is full, just to get a bribe out of you, so a certain degree of tact and diplomacy, and (if it comes to it) a small fee, may be required.

Railway Stations

In Dar, the main station for the Moshi line is in the city centre, but the Tazara station is in a southern suburb on the main road towards the airport. In Mbeya, the Tazara station is also on the outskirts of town; there are taxis and minibuses from the station to the city centre.

ORGANISED TREKS & TOURS

Once in Tanzania, many visitors use the services of a tour company to arrange their trekking and possibly other items such as a wildlife safari, hotel accommodation, airport transfers, train reservations and so on. Using a tour company generally makes things easier, and is well worth considering if your time is limited. However, if you've got plenty of time and not much money to spare, you can usually (but not always) do things yourself at a cheaper rate.

Some tour companies in Tanzania specialise in trekking and walking, while others have a wider portfolio and set up any kind of trip. Some outfits are merely agents and just pass you on to a specialist company. Using an agent may cost you more, but they may get their commission from the actual operators, in which case the price you pay is the same wherever you go. Sometimes, however, if you deal directly with the operating company, you can get a better deal.

It is very important to realise that on Kilimanjaro all treks must be arranged through a licensed tour company. Independent trekking is *not* permitted (see the Kilimanjaro section for more details). Consequently, much

of the information provided in the list of companies below is biased towards Kilimanjaro. In and around Moshi and Arusha (the two towns nearest Kili) there are many companies which arrange treks to suit all budgets and standards. Some companies also organise treks on Mt Meru (although independent trekking is allowed here) and in the Crater Highlands (which is hard to do on your own unless you have a vehicle), as well as wildlife safaris to the lowland national parks or other parts of Tanzania.

The trekking company you use can make or break your trek, so it's important to choose carefully. On Kilimanjaro, the minimum you'll be able to get away with is an obligatory guide and a few porters, while you provide your own tent, gear and food, pay your own park fees, and make your own way by public bus to the start of the trek. At the other end of the scale, a trek can include everything: hotel accommodation before and after the trek, transport, park fees, guide, assistant guides, porters, cook, food, utensils, sleeping tent, mess tent, camping equipment, and even portable showers and toilets. Most trekkers take something in between these two extremes.

Costs

Prices and standards of trekking companies vary. Obviously, the price you pay depends on what's included (see Organised Treks, in the Regional Facts for the Trekker chapter). At the bottom end, competition is stiff and, if cheapness is your main criterion, you can find some outfits doing all-inclusive treks on Kilimanjaro for around US$350, and on Mt Meru for around US$200, although for trekkers on a tight budget, this still takes a sizeable chunk out of the funds. In the low season, or if you can get a group of eight to 10 people together, the cost can be reduced even further. But, as with anything else, you get what you pay for, and the service offered by some of the cheaper outfits leaves a lot to be desired. If you base your choice on cheapness, it will be harder to justify complaints afterwards if anything goes wrong.

If the price of your trek is not such a problem, there are several companies offering

Kilimanjaro treks between US$500 and US$1000 which are generally of a much higher quality. Usually, the price of the trek falls as the size of the group increases (on Kili, the difference between going alone or in a group of around six to eight can be several hundred dollars). The prices given here are per person, based on a group of four, and include park fees, guides, porters, food and accommodation on the mountain, unless stated otherwise. On Kilimanjaro's Marangu Route, going alone or as a pair will add around 10% to 20% to the price. On other routes (eg the Machame and Umbwe routes) it can add 25% to 50%. All prices will inevitably increase over the next few years, but these figures are useful for comparisons.

If the cost of a trek on Kilimanjaro or Mt Meru does not include transport, you can usually arrange to hire the company's own vehicle for a drop-off and pick-up for an extra US$50 to US$100 (divided between the group), or take public transport (details are given in individual trek descriptions).

Trekking Companies

The companies listed here specialise in trekking, or include trekking and walking as part of their services. Nearly all offer treks on Kilimanjaro. If you want something specialised, you can contact the more upmarket companies from your home country to set things up before you arrive. Upmarket companies tend to run treks on demand, specifically for groups and individuals. If you are already in Tanzania, most middle and bottom-end companies can organise treks almost immediately, or within a couple of days. Budget outfits often put together groups, so you may not always know the people you'll be trekking with.

Choosing a Trekking Company

If you are arranging things on the spot, choosing the right company to organise your trek on Kilimanjaro (or anywhere else) is very important. This is especially true for budget travellers, as a lack of money and an eagerness to save every last dollar often seems to cloud the judgement. At Lonely Planet we get endless letters from backpackers who have arrived in Arusha or Moshi, arranged a trek with the first company they come across, and ended up having a bad time. Touts patrol the budget hotels promising great things for ridiculously low sums, and it's amazing how many people fall for it. What sounds like a dream bargain turns into a nightmare as food runs out, huts are not booked and porters go on strike.

We frequently hear from travellers who end up camping in substandard tents even though their company assures them they have hut bookings. The park runs a wait-list system and huts are frequently overbooked. Ask to see proof of your company's *confirmed* hut booking (unless of course you're happy to camp). We also hear from people who pay for five nights on the Marangu Route, so as to have an extra night's acclimatisation at Horombo, but only the usual four nights actually get paid for at the gate, so they find themselves being forced on up to Kibo instead of having a nice rest day.

Another common trick is for the company to 'run out' of money at the gate and travellers having to pay a contribution to the entrance fees. Promises of refunds when the group gets back from the trek are of course forgotten or flatly denied back in Arusha. We've even heard of travellers having to pay park fees virtually at gunpoint, after their tour company has told them these fees were already included in the price.

One of the worst scams of all involves travellers being promised a bargain deal by a tout, but to seal it payment must be made on the spot for which, of course sir, a receipt will be issued. Next day, the promised transport to Kilimanjaro doesn't show at their hotel, the receipt turns out to be for a bogus company, and the tout (now renamed 'thief') is never seen again. What's even worse is sometimes the tout *is* seen again, casually strolling the streets, but naturally he denies everything and there's nothing anyone can do.

So if you're fresh off the plane or the bus in Moshi or Arusha, don't rush into any deals however good they sound. Take the time to shop around the reliable outfits and see what's on offer. Never give money to anyone who doesn't work out of an office. By far the best way to get a low-down is by talking to travellers who have returned from a trek. Personal recommendations of companies and guides can generally be relied upon. Anybody who's had a raw deal will be more than happy to stop the company conning anyone else! ■

However, for lone travellers wanting to save costs, teaming up with others can save quite a bit of money. The treks and safaris mentioned are examples only. Most companies offer a wide range of trips and can also organise things to suit your own requirements.

Kilimanjaro trek prices quoted here are per person and include transport to and from the start of the trek, all park fees, guides, porters, food, hut fees (Marangu Route) or tents (other routes), unless otherwise stated. If you're a bargain hunter you might get discounts with low-budget outfits by providing your own tent, making your own way to the start of the trek, and possibly even bringing and cooking your own food.

For any trek, you always need to bring your own trekking clothes, plus personal items such as water bottle, walking poles and sunglasses. Most trekkers also supply their own sleeping bag and mat. The better companies and hotels rent out clothing and equipment which can supplement your own gear, although quality is not always good. Prices are pretty much on a par wherever you go. Cost for five days are: US$5 to US$10 for sleeping bag, rucksack and boots; US$4 to US$8 for jacket, gloves, socks, leggings, overtrousers or coat, and goggles.

All prices quoted here are for guidance only. Variable and unpredictable factors, such as national park fees and the vagaries of the Tanzanian tax system may alter things considerably in the future.

If writing for more information, use the PO Box number in the relevant city/town unless otherwise stated. If phoning from anywhere within Tanzania, Kenya and Uganda, the code for Arusha is ☎ 057, Moshi ☎ 055 and Dar ☎ 051. If phoning or faxing from any other country, use the international code for Tanzania ☎ +255 and omit the 0 in the city codes.

Arusha Trekking companies operating out of Arusha include the following:

African Environments
    PO Box 2125 (☎ 7285; fax 8256). This is one of the most experienced trekking companies in Tan-

zania. Its speciality is a seven-day Kilimanjaro traverse on the little-used western side of the mountain, with one night camping inside the crater. It also does treks on Mt Meru and wildlife safaris which fit in with the Kilimanjaro trek. This outfit operates mainly for upmarket tour groups, so you have to book treks in advance, either direct or through specialist agents overseas (see Organised Treks in the Getting There & Away chapter).

Dik Dik Hotel
    PO Box 1499 (☎ 8110). This smart Swiss-run hotel on the outskirts of Arusha runs a range of very swish and expensive treks, tailored to individual clients' wishes.

Equatorial Safaris
    4th floor, Serengeti Wing, Arusha International Conference Centre, PO Box 2156, Arusha (☎ 7006, 3302; fax 2617; email equatorial @form-net.com). This long-established company does a good value five-day Marangu Route trek for US$675, which covers everything, including transport both ways between Arusha and the park gate. This is ideal if you're based in Arusha and short of time. A seven-day luxury version of the same trip, including two full-board hotel nights, costs US$850. Equatorial also do treks in the Crater Highlands and walking safaris in the Selous for US$130 per person per day, as well as tours of north-eastern Tanzania which include the Usambaras for US$170 per day, plus wildlife safaris in other parks fitting in with the treks.

Euro-Tan
    PO Box 1028 (☎ 8777/3896). Office in AICC (see above). It offers various safaris and treks, including Kilimanjaro. Its Mt Meru trip is recommended: US$280 for three days.

Gametrackers
    Uchumi House, Sokoine Rd, PO Box 2735, Arusha (☎/fax 7314; email game@users .africa online.co.ke). This is a popular and reliable budget safari outfit with links to the company of the same name in Nairobi. It offers a good range of treks and safaris including standard Kilimanjaro Marangu treks starting at US$850 which includes transport from Nairobi, so if you're on the spot it might be cheaper.

Hoopoe Adventure Tours
    PO Box 2047 (☎ 7011, 7541; fax 8226). This high quality outfit with an office on India St mainly organises wildlife safaris, but also arranges treks on Kilimanjaro. A five-day trek on the Marangu Route plus accommodation at the Marangu Hotel before and after the trek is US$790 per person. Hoopoe also arranges treks on Kili's Machame Route, Mt Meru and through the Crater Highlands, with prices starting at

US$1200 for six days. The UK office is listed in the Getting There & Away chapter.

Kahembe's Enterprises
PO Box 366, Babati (Babati ☎ 88; fax (057) 8801). A small local-style outfit, based in the area west of Arusha, with treks on Mt Hanang and walking safaris in the surrounding area at US$60 per person per day.

Let's Go Travel
PO Box 12799 (☎ 7111, 2814; fax 8997, 4199; website http//:www.kenya-direct.com/letsgo). This company is a safari operator and Arusha's first dedicated travel agent, with an office at The Adventure Centre, on Goliondoi Rd, in the city centre. Let's Go have close links with the company of the same name in Nairobi, and also work in conjunction with the respected East African Safari & Touring Company. They arrange scheduled or tailor-made safaris to the national parks, treks on Mt Meru and Kilimanjaro, plus walking and mountain bike safaris from US$100 per day all inclusive in Tarangire Wildlife Conservation Area, east of Tarangire park. They also make hotel, train, shuttle bus and plane bookings.

Moon Adventure Tours
PO Box 12023 (☎ 2275). A recommended budget company, with all-in five-day Marangu route treks on Kili for US$400 and three-day Meru trips for US$320. Six-day wildlife safaris to the lowland national parks start at US$400.

Roy Safaris
PO Box 50 (☎ 2115, 8010, 2800; fax 8892). This company's office is just off Sokoine Rd (Arusha's main street), about 250m down from the clock tower. A straightforward, reliable outfit, doing standard wildlife safaris, and five-day Marangu Route treks on Kili from US$520.

Tropical Tours
Adventure Centre, Goliondoi Rd, PO Box 727, Arusha (☎ 8353). A specialist and highly respected company offering a good range of treks and safaris by foot or vehicle, including various routes on Kili, Mt Meru, the Crater Highlands and a recommended three-day trek in the Monduli Hills for US$220.

Tropical Trails
PO Box 6130 (☎/fax 8299). Based at Masai Camp, on the edge of Arusha (see Places to Stay, Arusha, Mt Meru section), this company specialises in treks and walking safaris in all parts of Tanzania, with an emphasis on introducing visitors to the culture and art of local peoples. They arrange treks on Mt Meru, Kilimanjaro and the Crater Highlands, with a range of prices to suit your own budget. They also specialise in the Monduli Mountains, where they have good relations with the local Maasai people.

Sengo Safaris
PO Box 207, Arusha (☎ 3935, 8424; fax 8272; email sengo@habari.co.tz). This long-standing company has an office at 26 Themi Industrial Estate and does good mid-range wildlife and hiking safaris using its permanent bush camps near Manyara and Serengeti, and at Lake Natron in the Crater Highlands. Safari rates are from US$100 per person per day (plus park fees); a two-day Crater Highlands trek is $75.

Moshi The town of Moshi is near Kilimanjaro and the traditional starting-off point for trekkers heading up the mountain. There is a good choice of companies here, once again catering for a wide range of budgets. The telephone code for Moshi is ☎ 055.

Keys Hotel
PO Box 933 (☎ 52250; fax 50073; email keys @form-net.com). This friendly hotel (see Kilimanjaro, Places to Stay) runs good trips on Kili: five days on Marangu costs US$540 (per person for a group of four) plus US$125 per extra day. Six days on Machame costs US$720.

Kilimanjaro Crown Birds Tours & Safaris
PO Box 9519 (☎ 51162; fax 52038). Office in Kindoroko Hotel. Five days on the Marangu Route costs US$530 per person for groups over three, plus US$80 per extra day. Six days on any other route costs US$750 per person for two or more, plus US$80 per extra day.

Kilimanjaro Guide Tours & Safaris
PO Box 210 (☎ 50120; fax 51220). Office opposite the Moshi Hotel. It quotes five-day Marangu Route treks at US$550 per person for two or three people, or US$520 for groups of four to six, but we've heard from travellers who have got this trip for US$400. An extra day costs US$100. Six-day treks on the Machame cost US$700 each for two to three people, US$670 for groups of four to six, and an extra day costs US$120.

Samjoe Tours
PO Box 1467 (☎ 52136). Office under Coffee Tree Hotel. A cheap and cheerful outfit, with standard five-day Marangu treks for US$420 per person for two people or US$380 each for six.

Shah Tours & Travel
PO Box 1821 (☎ 52370; fax 51449). Office on Mawenzi Rd between the clock tower and the bus station. The company specialises in quality treks on Kilimanjaro's Marangu, Machame and Umbwe routes and mainly deals with groups arranged by agents overseas, but will happily handle bookings from individuals and small parties, in advance or on the spot. Treks are not the cheapest, but they are well run and good value. For walk-in clients,

five-day treks up the Marangu Route cost US$450 starting from Marangu (you can get there by bus, or arrange transport at US$35 for four people). Six-day Machame treks cost US$750, including transport to/from Moshi. During quiet periods, groups of more than four may be able to negotiate discounts. Shah Tours also organise treks on Mt Meru and wildlife safaris.

Trans-Kibo Travels
PO Box 1320 (☎/fax 52017). Office at the YMCA. Five-day treks on the Marangu Route start at US$500 for groups of four, up to US$570 for two or three people, although prices seem to be negotiable. Treks on Meru start at US$570 for four days.

Zara Tours
PO Box 210 (☎/fax 50120). Office behind Moshi Hotel. No-frills outfit, starting at a bargain-basement US$350 for five-day Marangu treks for groups of five or more.

Marangu North-east of Moshi, on the road up to the park headquarters and main entrance to Kilimanjaro National Park are several hotels which also operate treks. They all concentrate on Kili, but some can also arrange treks on Meru, or safaris to the lowland national parks. For accommodation details and more information for finding the hotels, see Places to Stay in the Kilimanjaro section.

If phoning, note that Marangu is switching from a local exchange (one, two or three digit numbers) where you must go through an operator, to the Moshi exchange (five digit numbers) which can be dialled direct using the Moshi code (☎ 055). Some hotels have a representative in Arusha (code ☎ 057).

Alpine Tours
PO Box 835 (Marangu ☎ 163; Moshi fax (055) 50096). This company has its office in the shop at Marangu Gate. You can turn up and arrange budget five-day trips up the Marangu Route on the spot, to leave next day. Groups of three or more pay US$510 per person. Other routes cost from US$700.

Ashanti Lodge
PO Box 6004, Arusha (☎ (057) 2745). Budget operator with standard five-day Marangu Route treks from around US$400 to US$450.

Babylon Lodge
PO Box 227 (☎ 5; or Arusha ☎ (057) 2253; fax (057) 8220). Standard five-day treks on the Marangu Route go for US$ 400 to US$450 per person. Prices are all-inclusive and negotiable.

Kibo Hotel
PO Box 102 (☎ 4, ☎/fax (055) 51308). Five-day treks on the Marangu Route cost US$300, plus US$60 per extra day. A six-day trek on the Machame Route costs US$580, plus US$100 per extra day. These charges do *not* include park fees, which you pay direct to the national park (see Park Fees & Regulations, in the Kilimanjaro section). Transfer between the hotel and KIA airport is US$80 for up to eight people.

Natural Action
Based at the Hotel Capricorn, PO Box 938 (☎/fax (055) 51309). A mid-range good quality outfit, using well-trained guides, and linked to companies of the same name in Kenya and UK. It offers standard five-day Marangu Route treks for US$770, or six-day treks on other routes for US$1000 (plus US$150 if you want to go to/from Nairobi).

Marangu Hotel
PO Box 40, Moshi (☎ (055) 50639; fax 51307; email marangu@users.africaonline.co.ke). This is a quality and very well established operation, currently in its sixth decade of arranging treks on Kili. Five-day treks on the Marangu Route cost US$350, plus US$70 per extra day, including transport to and from the park gate, food, guides and porters, but excluding park fees (see Park Fees & Regulations, in the Kilimanjaro section). If you're strapped for cash, the hotel can help you do the Marangu Route 'the hard way', by reserving huts and providing the mandatory guide and his porter, while you provide your own food and equipment, do your own cooking and carry your own rucksack. This costs US$170, plus park fees. Six-day treks on the Machame Route are US$570 per person, plus park fees; extra days are US$100. If you organise your trek here, the hotel discounts its room rates (see Kilimanjaro, Places to Stay).

Dar es Salaam Most tour and safari companies based in Dar act as agents for trekking companies based in Arusha or Moshi, so if you want to trek in northern Tanzania you're better off going direct. Specialist outfits operating wildlife tours, including walking safaris, to the national parks in southern Tanzania are listed here. The code for Dar is ☎ 051.

Foxtreks
This small and highly respected family firm run two lodges in Ruaha National Park, where game-viewing and short walking safaris are available. It also runs safaris in Selous and has another lodge on the coast at Bagamoyo. Inquiries should be made through agents: in Tanzania contact Rickshaw Travel (see below), in the UK contact Africa Connections (☎ (01822) 810135; fax 810230).

Rickshaw Travel
PO Box 1889 (☎ 115620, 112416; fax 113227; email ricksher@twiga.com). A friendly, quality travel agent, with offices on Upanga Rd and in the Sheraton Hotel, which can help you organise things if you're already in Tanzania. It represents many safari and trekking companies, plus several hotels and lodges in remote locations, such as Usambara Mountains and the southern parks. It can also arrange flights, hotels, car hire etc.

Selous Safari Co
PO Box 1192 (☎ 28485; fax 112794). An up-market outfit operating Mbuyuni Luxury Camp in Selous, where short walking safaris can be arranged. Two-day walks, using 'fly camps' in the bush, start at US$350 per day. Most clients book through agents: in Tanzania contact Rickshaw Travel (see above); in the UK contact Tours & Trade International (☎ (01367) 253810).

Southern Tanzania Game Safaris
PO Box 2341 (☎ 38758; fax 24897) This operator runs a range of safaris from three to 14 days, travelling by vehicle, boat and foot, in Selous and Ruaha. It arranges one-day walking safaris or longer trips using overnight 'fly camps' in the bush. Most clients use agents: in Tanzania contact Rickshaw Travel (see above), in Europe contact the UK office (☎ (01524) 262496; fax 261863).

Tent with a View Safaris
PO Box 40425 (☎/fax 113688). A small, ambitious and refreshingly different company, deliberately ignoring the north, and concentrating on the quieter wildlife areas in southern Tanzania, including Selous and Katavi, where walking safaris are possible. Their *pièce de résistance* is a private camp in Saadani, on the Indian Ocean coast opposite Zanzibar – 'where the bush meets the beach'. Safaris start at US$65 per person per day, plus park fees. The nature of these trips means things have to be organised in advance; their agent in Tanzania is Rickshaw Travel (see above) and in the UK it is Footloose Adventure Travel (see Organised Treks in the Getting There & Away chapter.)

Kenya Several of the trek operators listed in the Kenya chapter can also arrange things on Kilimanjaro and elsewhere in Tanzania. Most Kenyan companies have reciprocal arrangements with Tanzanian companies, so you're normally better to go direct to a local company if you're already in Tanzania. A notable exception to this is Kibo Slopes Safaris; although Kenya based they run an excellent series of Kilimanjaro treks. See the Organised Treks & Tours section in the Kenya chapter for more details.

Kilimanjaro

Kilimanjaro's huge snowcapped summit dome, rising high above the surrounding savanna, often with a giraffe conveniently posing in the foreground, is one of Africa's all-time classic images. At 5896m (19,344 ft), Kilimanjaro is the highest mountain in Africa, and one of the highest volcanoes in the world. The lure is irresistible, and a trek up 'Kili' is an essential part of a visit to Tanzania. The trek is even more attractive because, with the right preparation, you can walk all the way to the summit without the need of ropes or technical climbing experience.

HISTORY

For the local Chagga people who farm Kilimanjaro's foothills, the mountain has always been revered. When Johannes Rebmann reached this area in 1848, and became the first European to see Kilimanjaro, he reported that his guide had once tried to bring down the 'silver' from the summit, which mysteriously turned to water on the descent. A later explorer, Charles New, who reached the foothills of Kilimanjaro in 1871, heard stories from the local chief, Mandara, about spirits on the mountain jealously guarding piles of silver and precious stones. It was said that anybody trying to reach the summit would be punished by the spirits with illness and severe cold.

New was later followed by other explorers: Gustav Fischer and Joseph Thomson both reached the lower slopes of Kilimanjaro, and in 1887 Count Samuel Teleki managed to get to a point only 400m below the top of Kibo. The summit was eventually reached in October 1889 by Hans Meyer, a

German professor of geology, accompanied by Ludwig Purtcheller, an experienced Alpinist, and Yohannes Lauwo, a local guide from the village of Marangu. Meyer named the summit Kaiser Wilhelm Spitze, after the German emperor. When mainland Tanzania (then called Tanganyika) gained independence in 1961, the name of the summit was changed to Uhuru (Freedom) Peak.

The derivation of the name Kilimanjaro has never been satisfactorily explained. Johannes Rebmann believed that the name translated as 'Mountain of Greatness' or 'Mountain of Caravans' (on the premise that slaving caravans travelling between the coast and the interior would have used the mountain as a landmark). Other writers have since suggested that the name means 'Shining Mountain', 'White Mountain' or 'Mountain of Water'.

There is certainly a reliable supply of water which, together with the rich volcanic soil in the area, makes the foothills of Kilimanjaro ideal for cultivation. Of course, the Chagga knew this and a group of British settlers, led by Sir Harry Johnston, who arrived here in 1884 also took advantage of these conditions. They cleared and planted an area of land near Taveta to the east of Kilimanjaro's foothills. Johnston had visions of the region becoming a second Ceylon.

In 1886, when the governments of Germany and Britain agreed on a border to officially define their territories, the line they drew – from Lake Victoria to the coast – was perfectly straight, broken only by an untidy curve around Kilimanjaro. This divided the original British territory claimed by Johnston, now in Kenya, from the rest of the area around Kilimanjaro, now in Tanzania.

You may be told that the border curves around Kilimanjaro because Queen Victoria gave the mountain to Kaiser Wilhelm (her grandson) as a birthday present. While such an action would have been no different to the arbitrary partitioning of East Africa by these two monarchs' own governments, there is no evidence that this story is true. But it remains one of many popular myths that add to the mystique and attraction of Kilimanjaro.

GEOGRAPHY

The massif of Kilimanjaro is roughly oval in shape, 40km to 60km in diameter, and rises almost 5000m above the surrounding plains. Kilimanjaro is even more distinctive because it is not part of a chain or extended range. As well as being the highest mountain in Africa, Kili is one of the highest free-standing mountains in the world. The mountain has been declared a World Heritage Site by UNESCO.

The two main peak areas are Kibo, the flat-topped dome at the centre of the massif, and Mawenzi, a group of jagged points and pinnacles on the eastern side. In fact, the top of Kibo is not flat, but dips inwards to form a crater which cannot be seen from below. Kibo and Mawenzi are separated by a broad plain called The Saddle. A third peak area, Shira, lies at the western end of the massif but is lower and less distinctive than Kibo and Mawenzi.

The highest point on Kibo and the whole Kilimanjaro massif is Uhuru Peak at 5896m (19,344 ft), and this is the goal for most trekkers. The highest point on Mawenzi is Hans Meyer Point, at 5149m (16,894 ft) but this cannot be reached by trekkers, and is only rarely visited by mountaineers.

TREKKING INFORMATION

Since 1991 independent trekking has not been allowed on Kilimanjaro. All treks must be organised through a tour company. (More details and a list of companies are given under Organised Treks & Tours in the Getting Around section earlier in this chapter.) When this rule was introduced trekkers and travellers saw it as a major blow, but it has not changed things very much. Even before the new regulation, it was obligatory to take a guide and one porter, and it was virtually impossible to do anything other than the Marangu Route without going through a trekking company anyway.

Arranging a trek on Kili used to be a real hassle, requiring all sorts of wheeling and dealing between guides, porters and park officials, which often spoilt the trek itself. But now procedures are much simpler, without affecting costs much either as there are a lot

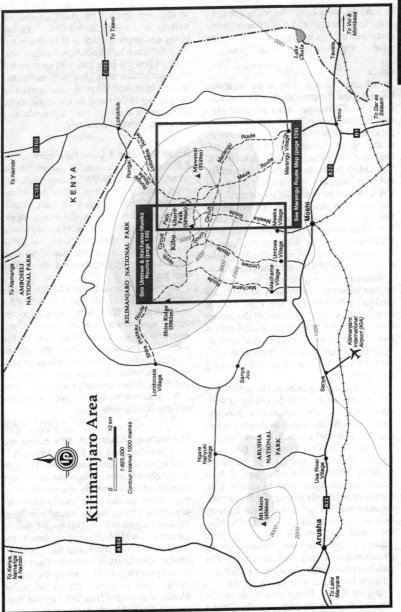

Kilimanjaro Area

0   5   10 km

1:625,000
Contour Interval 1000 metres

To Kenya,
Namanga
& Nairobi

To Namanga
AMBOSELI
NATIONAL PARK

KENYA

To Nairobi

To Tsavo

To Voi & Mombasa

Lake Challa

1000

To Dar es Salaam

Taveta

Himo

B1

Lokitoktok

Rongai Route

Rongai

Loitokitok Route

KILIMANJARO NATIONAL PARK

Mawenzi
(5149m)

Marangu Route

Maua Route

Maua

See Marangu Route Map (page 126)

Marangu Village

Moshi

A23

Shira Plateau Route

Uhuru
Peak
(5896m)

Kibo

North Circuit

South Circuit

6000

Mweka Route

Mweka
Village

Circuit Path

See Umbwe & Machame-Mweka
Routes (page 130)

Shira Ridge
(3962m)

5000

4000

3000

2000

Umbwe Village

Machame Village

Umbwe Route

Machame Route

Londorossi
Village

1000

Sanya
Juu

Sanya

Kilimanjaro
International
Airport (KIA)

Ngare
Nanyuki
Village

ARUSHA
NATIONAL
PARK

Usa River
Village

A23

Mt Meru
(4566m)

3000

2000

Arusha

A104

To Lake
Manyara

To Lake
Maryara

C103

C102

C103

Loitokitok

C102

of trekking companies competing for business. At the bottom end of the market, some companies arrange treks that are only slightly more expensive than the old DIY price.

Costs

As all treks up Kili have to be organised through a tour company, this is your main cost. Prices for Kilimanjaro treks are given with details of companies listed under Organised Treks & Tours in the Getting Around section of this chapter. Standard five-day (four-night) treks up Kili's Marangu Route start at US$350 to US$450, but at the absolute bottom end of this price range don't be surprised if your hut is double booked, meals are on the small side and porters are desperate for tips. For budget treks of six or seven days on the Machame Route you should expect to pay upwards of US$650 to US$750. Better quality trips on the Marangu Route go from US$500, while they start at US$850 on the Machame Route.

Whatever you pay for your trek, remember that between US$300 and US$500 of this goes on park fees (see the Park Fees & Regulations section). The rest of the money covers food, tents (if required), guides, porters and transport to and from the start of the trek. With these figures in mind, we honestly can't see how some of the budget outfits make a legal profit.

Unfortunately, because trekking on Kili is seen as expensive, many people try to walk up and down in the shortest time possible. Do not fall into this trap. You should not feel that it is essential to reach Uhuru Peak, or that you have 'failed' if you don't. If time (or money) is limited, you'd be far better off spending US$350 in another part of East Africa. If you really want to sample Kili, instead of stubbornly pushing for the summit, consider walking up to one of the midway huts and reaching an area like The Saddle, the top of the Barranco Wall or the Shira Plateau to appreciate the splendour of the mountain from there before descending. The park has plans to introduce lower routes specifically for people who want to do this.

If your budget is really tight, do *not* be tempted to enter the park illegally. Guides with other groups will report unaccompanied walkers to the park authorities. Fines are heavy and imprisonment is not unknown. I once met three lads from New Zealand who sneaked past the park gate and went up the mountain on their own. They were spotted and chased by armed rangers, then spent two days hiding in the forest on the lower slopes. Although it was a funny story afterwards, they were pretty worried at the time.

Route Standard & Days Required

Kilimanjaro is surrounded by a zone of dense forest, so to get to the higher moorlands and main peaks, you have to follow one of the established routes. There are at least 10 trekking routes that begin on the lower slopes. Some of these join other routes as they climb, but most routes reach the North and South Circuit Paths that circle the base of the main Kibo dome roughly following the 4000m contour.

Beyond the Circuit Paths only three routes continue to the summit. These are all on the southern side of Kibo, so the trekking routes on the western and southern slopes of the mountain are used more than those on the north side. The South Circuit Path links all these routes so several combinations are possible. This makes the treks more interesting and the extra time also helps acclimatisation.

In this section we describe two direct routes and one combination route:

The Marangu Route This is the easiest and most popular route up Kilimanjaro and is used by most trekking companies. The path is straightforward and there are three large bunkhouses conveniently spaced along the way. A trek on this route usually takes five days (four nights) for the round trip. Most trekkers only go as far as Gillman's Point, on the crater rim at 5685m, as from here to the summit at Uhuru Peak and back requires another four hours of walking. You can increase your chances of reaching the summit by spending an extra night on the ascent, ideally at Horombo Hut. Treks on this route usually descend by the same route.

The Umbwe Route This is a steep route leading straight to Uhuru Peak. It is interesting and very enjoyable if you can resist the temptation to gain height too quickly. Huts are in bad condition or non-existent. For trekkers a tent is essential. A trek on this route usually takes five days (four nights), although an extra night (ideally at Barranco Hut) is recommended to help acclimatisation. Treks on this route usually descend by either the Mweka or the Marangu Route.

The Machame-Mweka Combination Route This is the most scenic route on the mountain, passing through Kili's complete range of landscape and vegetation types. The ascent is longer and more gradual than the Umbwe Route and, because of the extra time (and expense) required, it is usually quieter than the Marangu Route. Trekkers on this route normally reach Uhuru Peak. The huts along the way are in poor condition and are used by porters. Trekkers must use tents. A trek usually takes six days (five nights), although an extra night on the ascent (ideally at Shira Hut) is recommended to help acclimatisation. Treks on this route usually descend by either the Mweka or the Marangu Route. (Note that several companies organise treks on this route, but just refer to it as the Machame Route.)

Guides & Porters

Guides, and at least one porter (for the guide), are obligatory on all routes on Kilimanjaro. You can carry your own gear on the Marangu Route, although porters are generally used, but one or two porters per trekker is essential on all other routes. Most trekking companies allow two to three porters per trekker depending on the length of the trek. Guides and porters on Kilimanjaro are usually freelancers arranged by the company organising your trek.

All guides must be registered with the national park authorities. If in doubt, check that your guide's permit is up to date. On Kili, the guide's job is to show you the way, and even then they're not always totally reliable (see Warning, later in this section). Only the very best guides, working for good trekking companies, will be able to tell you about wildlife, birds, flowers, or any of the other features on the mountain.

Porters will carry bags weighing up to 15kg (not including their own food and clothing, which they strap to the outside of your bag). Heavier bags will be carried for a negotiable extra fee.

The guides and porters provided by some of the cheaper trekking outfits leave a lot to be desired. If you're a hardy traveller you might not worry about basic meals and substandard tents, but you might be more

---

The Importance of Acclimatisation

The number of days quoted for a trek on each of the routes is the usual number most trekkers take. If you can spend an extra night on any of the routes, at about halfway, this will help acclimatisation and will also give you time to see some other parts of the mountain. It will also greatly increase your chances of actually getting to the top.

Although many hundreds of trekkers reach Uhuru Peak every year without any real difficulty, many thousands more don't make it because they suffer terribly from altitude sickness, having ascended too quickly. Part of the fault lies with some trekking companies who run quick up-and-down trips, although they are only responding to demand. The real fault lies with trekkers who overestimate their own ability or who simply don't appreciate the serious nature of trekking at altitude and the importance of proper acclimatisation. There have been too many sad cases of trekkers who went too high too quickly on Kili. At best, they felt ill and went down; at worst, they became so sick that they had to be carried down. Every year, a few unlucky (or unprepared) trekkers die.

Most people seem to forget that Uhuru Peak, at 5896m, is 500m *higher* than Everest Base Camp in the Nepal Himalaya, which trekkers often take at least two weeks to reach from Kathmandu. All trekkers should read and observe the advice on Altitude Sickness in the Health chapter.

If you are not already well acclimatised, trying to cut days just to save time and money is not recommended – in fact, it's just plain stupid. ■

TANZANIA

Tipping Guides & Porters on Kilimanjaro

Most guides and porters are honest and hard working, so you will probably want to give them a tip after your trek. Over the years, some high-rolling trekkers on Kili have tipped very generously, causing the local guys to expect large bonuses at the end of every trek. This situation is understandable. The porters know that you have just paid anything from US$300 to US$1000 for the trek. Even if you think of yourself as a budget traveller, they will regard you as a wealthy tourist, with a lot of spare cash to throw around. So don't plead poverty. If the service has been good, pay a fair tip.

Many travellers have complained that arguing about tips after coming down off Kili has spoilt the trek itself. This may be due to genuine misunderstandings, greed on the part of the guides or a simple reluctance to pay on the part of the trekker.

As a guideline, a tip could be around 10% of the total bill paid for the trek (or the trekking section of the tour, if it also includes other items such as transport or hotels) divided between the guides and porters. Some guides and porters may imply that official 'tipping rates' are set by the park authorities, but this is not true. US dollars or local currency is accepted.

For example, if each member of a group paid US$450 for a short trek, everyone could pay around US$40 into a tips 'kitty', to be divided between the guide and porters. Generally for a trip up the Marangu route guides get about US$30 (more with a large group, especially if they've also done the cooking) and porters around US$10. For longer treks, guides usually get around US$50 and porters around US$15. Of course, you can pay more if you're particularly impressed, and less if you're not. But explain why you're doing this – it will help porters and future trekkers if it's understood that tips are not automatic. Note that any gifts you may leave for guides and porters (old boots, clothing, food etc) will not be regarded as part of (or accepted instead of) a hard cash tip.

Some disreputable characters have been known to use a variety of methods to extract large tips from visitors. Techniques range from pathetic pleading, through aggressive demands, to virtual strikes. To avoid misunderstandings, it may be necessary to agree on all tips *before* the start of the trek. This may seem an odd concept, but writing down the agreed amount will help memory on both sides. But even after a tip has been agreed, you should make it quite clear that it will only be paid – at the end of the trek or when you're back at your hotel – if the service is satisfactory. ■

DAVID ELSE

concerned about incompetent guides or dishonest porters. We've heard stories about guides who leave the last hut deliberately late on the summit day, so as to avoid going all the way to the top. But if you use this book – so that you know about all aspects of the route – and are polite but firm with your guide, you should avoid problems like this.

Park Fees & Regulations

The forest around Kilimanjaro is an official reserve and the area beyond this, mostly above 2700m, is Kilimanjaro National Park, and fees must be paid. Although it is obligatory to organise your trek through a company, you may have to pay your park fees separately at the park gates. Other companies quote a price that includes park fees and make the payments on your behalf. It is therefore very important when arranging your trek to check whether park fees are included in the price.

If you're paying fees yourself, you must do so in hard currency. US dollars (travellers cheques or cash) are recommended as all prices are quoted in this currency. For non-Tanzanians, fees are:

Entrance	US$25	per day
	US$5	for under 16s
Overnight	US$40	per night
Rescue	US$20	per trip

Citizens and residents of Tanzania pay lower park entrance and hut fees. For each adult trekker this comes to a total of US$305 for a standard five-day Marangu trip and US$370 for six days on any other route. Guides and porters also have to pay fees, but this should be handled directly by your trekking company. When calculating park fees most companies work on a total of US$310 for a five-day Marangu trip and US$380 for six days on any route (including Marangu). The extra US$5 or US$10 covers park fees for guides and porters.

Certificates If you reach Uhuru Peak you will be awarded a very nice certificate when you get back to Marangu Gate. If you make it to the rim you can get one saying you reached Gillman's Point.

Maps
Kilimanjaro and its surrounds are covered by 1:50,000 DOS/government survey maps, sheet Nos 56/1, 56/2, 56/3 and 56/4. The main part of the mountain is on sheet 56/2. A special 1:100,000 map (No 522) of the whole area was also produced. Unfortunately, some of these maps are now out of print, but the sheet numbers will be the same if there's a reprint.

Other maps include the Ordnance Survey Worldmap *Kilimanjaro* (1:100,000) which is an updated reprint of the old sheet 522, but even this is out of print now although copies can still be found in good map shops.

One of the easiest maps to get is *Map & Guide to Kilimanjaro* by Andrew Wielochowski, a 1:75,000 topo map with insert maps of the surrounding area and detailed maps of Kibo and Mawenzi peaks.

There's also *Kilimanjaro Map & Guide* by Mark Savage, at a scale of 1:50,000 which should make map-reading easier, but contains less information, and because it covers a smaller area omits the park boundary and the start of each trekking route. The back of both sheets contain brief information on access and equipment, plus lots of other tips.

Where Does all the Money Go?
For a standard five-day trek on the Marangu Route, park fees come to a total of US$305 per trekker. For six days (five nights) on any route (including the Marangu) the fees total US$370. An extra day puts it up by another US$75. These fees certainly bump up the cost of a trek on Kili, but to complain that they are too high is to miss the point. There is no reason why Tanzania shouldn't earn money from tourists (see National Parks in the Regional Facts for the Trekker chapter). The problem is that the revenue earned by Kilimanjaro National Park does not seem to benefit the local people who inhabit the area around the park and does not seem to benefit the park itself.

For example, some of the revenue could go towards cleaning up the huts and camp sites, particularly on the Marangu Route. Horombo Hut is getting more like a shanty town every year. It wouldn't take much to stop cooks emptying bowls of dirty water straight onto the ground outside the huts, turning the whole area into a quagmire. Some money could go towards cleaning the routes up a bit and building proper rubbish pits, although ideally rubbish pits should not be needed, as anything brought up should be taken down again. Guides and porters could be paid a 'trash bonus' for everything they carry down.

Toilets are a different matter. In the first edition of this book we suggested that '... deep, long-drop toilets should be constructed and maintained at every hut and camp site. Some people say that providing facilities of this nature destroys the wilderness aspect of trekking on the mountain. But piles of crap and toilet paper everywhere are unpleasant too ...'. While we at Lonely Planet would never be vain enough to claim any influence, since the last edition toilets have been built at several sites along the Marangu, Machame, Mweka, Umbwe and Shira routes. This is definitely a step in the right direction; however, the holes are simply not deep enough. During my most recent research trek, at some of the camp sites the matter which should be deep in the hole was perilously close to coming back up.

To the park I say 'Congratulations on this improvement, but you've got to dig deeper, guys'. ∎

TANZANIA

These maps are sometimes available from shops or trek operators in Moshi or Arusha for about US$5. In the UK the maps are available from Savage Wilderness Safaris and EWP (see Organised Treks in the Getting There & Away chapter).

Guidebooks

General books on Tanzania's mountains are described in the Books section in this chapter. For specific detail on Kili, the *Guide to Mount Kenya & Kilimanjaro* published by the Mountain Club of Kenya is mainly a technical climber's guide, with detailed descriptions of the rock and ice routes on Kibo and Mawenzi, but it also contains good background information on history, glaciation, geology, wildlife and so on. Beware of old copies of this book; many of the huts (and even a few of the glaciers!) have disappeared since it was printed. The *East Africa International Mountain Guide* (see Books, in the Facts for the Trekker chapter) has a brief section on Kilimanjaro, but is also mainly for technical climbers.

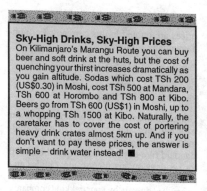

Sky-High Drinks, Sky-High Prices

On Kilimanjaro's Marangu Route you can buy beer and soft drink at the huts, but the cost of quenching your thirst increases dramatically as you gain altitude. Sodas which cost TSh 200 (US$0.30) in Moshi, cost TSh 500 at Mandara, TSh 600 at Horombo and TSh 800 at Kibo. Beers go from TSh 600 (US$1) in Moshi, up to a whopping TSh 1500 at Kibo. Naturally, the caretaker has to cover the cost of portering heavy drink crates almost 5km up. And if you don't want to pay these prices, the answer is simple – drink water instead! ■

Warning

Although guides are obligatory, and provided with every organised trek, you should still familiarise yourself with all aspects of the route, such as distances between huts or camping places, availability of water, and condition of the paths. This is particularly important on the unusual routes (everything except the Marangu Route) as guides are not necessarily as experienced as they claim, or they may suggest itineraries and changes to the route which are completely unsuitable or even dangerous. ■

Supplies

Most organised treks on Kili include food, but you can sometimes save money by providing your own, or you might just prefer to cook for yourself. There are no shops inside the national park, although you can buy beer and sodas (soft drinks) at huts on the Marangu Route (see boxed text). In Marangu village there are some small shops and stalls selling vegetables, and there's a shop at Marangu

---

Gate selling a limited range of dried and tinned food, beers, books, maps and postcards. In Moshi, the nearest town, you'll find everything you need for a trek, and there's even more choice in Arusha.

PLACES TO STAY

Some of the hotels mentioned in this section can arrange treks on Kili. See Organised Treks & Tours in the Getting Around section of this chapter for more details. Rates include breakfast unless otherwise stated.

Moshi

One of the cheapest places in town is the *YMCA*, which has been popular with trekkers and travellers for many years. The bedrooms and bathrooms are clean, the staff friendly and the food excellent value. Singles/doubles cost US$13/15. There's also a swimming pool, small shop and a travel agency specialising in treks up Kilimanjaro.

Other options if the Y is full include the nearby *Green Cottage Hostel*, a private house with a few rooms, which is a bargain at US$10 for doubles; the *Coffee Tree Hotel*, near the clock tower, with clean basic singles for US$5, and en suite doubles for US$11, plus a bar and cheap restaurant; and the friendly *Kindoroko Hotel*, with clean rooms at US$9/10 (US$11/ 12 en suite), plus a bar, restaurant and rooftop terrace with good views of Kili.

Slightly further from the centre is the friendly *Keys Hotel* (☎ (055) 52250; fax 50073;

email keys@form-net.com), run by a local family, with good self-contained rooms and cottages for US$50/80, including breakfast and a five-course evening meal. There's also a bar and small pool.

The *Moshi Hotel* (☎/fax (055) 55211, 54 160), in the centre of town, is a large, plain, state-run hotel with poor value singles/doubles at US$50.

The *Mountain Inn* is a fairly new hotel set in nice gardens 4km from the YMCA on the road towards Himo and Marangu. The self-contained rooms at US$35/45 including breakfast are clean and there's always plenty of hot water. There's a restaurant serving good-value food if you fancy a splurge.

Marangu

The spread-out village of Marangu lies north of Himo (on the main road between Moshi and Taveta). There's a good range of places to stay – especially useful if you're trekking on the Marangu Route.

Coming from Moshi, the first place you reach is the *Marangu Hotel* (☎ (055) 50639; fax 51307; email marangu@users.africaonline .co.ke), PO Box 40, Moshi). This place is steeped in history. Formerly a colonial coffee farm, the octogenarian owner Mrs Lany trekked on the mountain 50 years ago with famous climbers such as Reuche and Gillman, remembered today by features bearing their names. Today's management is friendly, very knowledgeable (the hotel has been running treks on Kili for many decades) and goes a long way to please. Accommodation in rooms and cottages set among trees and manicured gardens is US$50 per person with dinner and breakfast. Credit cards are accepted. Camping costs US$10 per night. Room and camping prices are discounted if you join one of the hotel's treks (see Organised Treks & Tours in the Getting Around section) – a room and meals for one night before the trek and one night after costs a total of US$60 per person. Pickups and drop-offs at KIA airport and transfers to Moshi or Arusha can also be arranged.

A few km up the road from here you reach the 'centre' of the village, where the bus stops, there are a few shops and market stalls, and

two minor roads branch off. A short walk west from the junction is the *Kibo Hotel* (Marangu ☎ 4; Moshi ☎/fax (055) 51308), PO Box 102, an old colonial-style place with a great atmosphere. People climbing Kili have been staying here since the 1930s and the walls are covered with old maps and mementos. Rooms cost US$60/80 including breakfast; other meals are from US$10. The hotel has a lounge with a large open fire in the centre of the room. Camping in the grounds costs US$7.

If you go right (east) at the junction, 1km down the dirt road towards Rombo is the *Babylon Lodge*, owned and run by the affable Mr Stephen. Clean, en suite doubles cost US$25/40 including breakfast, with other meals from US$5. Budget treks can be arranged. Another 2km down the same road is *Ashanti Lodge*. Rooms in the main hotel or in the bandas in the garden cost US$20 per person including breakfast. Camping is free if you arrange your trek here.

If you continue (north) up the road to Marangu Gate, about 3km from the junction *Coffee Tree Campsite* is well signposted down a dirt track on the right. Camping here costs US$10 but may be negotiable. For supplies, Top Kibo Grocery & Bar is just half a km up the road from where the dirt track turns off. A little further up the hill is the smart new *Hotel Capricorn* with bed and breakfast for US$90 per person (single or double), lunches and dinners for US$10 to US$12, and a good in-house trekking company.

Next to the Marangu Gate, *Kilimanjaro Mountain Lodge* (formerly the Youth Hostel) charges US$25 per person in double rooms (including breakfast) or US$5 for camping, and seems to have some connection to the Coffee Tree Campsite and Alpine Tours, where treks can be arranged. There's a restaurant and bar attached.

Arusha

Arusha has a much wider choice of hotels; particularly useful if you're coming from Nairobi or doing a trek on Mt Meru as well as Kilimanjaro. For details see Places to Stay in the Mt Meru section of this chapter.

On Kilimanjaro

Accommodation on Kilimanjaro is limited to the Marangu Route, which has three large, well-built bunkhouses spaced at convenient intervals, about six to eight hours (or a day's) walk apart. The huts are administered by the national park and you pay hut fees with your entrance fees. You can also camp on this route but, amazingly, you still have to pay hut fees. (School Hut, at the top of the Rongai/Loitokitok Route, is privately owned and for the sole use of groups on that route only.)

All the other routes have small metal huts called 'uniports', usually dirty and in very bad condition, and only used by local guides and porters. Consequently, on routes other than the Marangu Route, trekkers must camp. It is usual to camp near the huts so that the guides and porters have somewhere to sleep, as very few trekking companies provide tents for their staff. Also, the only reliable water sources are those near huts.

It's possible that in the future all the small metal huts on Kili may be removed by the park authorities, as they are unsightly and rarely used by tourists. This means all trekking companies using these routes will have to provide tents and equipment for their staff. If the huts are removed, the camp sites will remain in the same places, or nearby, as these are generally flat spots at a suitable position between daily stages.

Bunkhouses, huts and camp sites on the mountain are covered more fully in the route descriptions.

GETTING THERE & AWAY

The Kilimanjaro massif lies in north-eastern Tanzania about 500km from Dar es Salaam, just below the border with Kenya. The nearest large town is Moshi.

Air

Kilimanjaro international airport (KIA) is 40km from Moshi, 7km south of the main road between Moshi and Arusha. There are daily flights between KIA and Dar. (More details in the Tanzania Getting There & Away and Getting Around sections.)

Bus, Minibus & Taxi

Moshi is linked to Dar by good tar roads and to Nairobi (Kenya), via Arusha and Namanga (the border). Public buses, shuttle buses, minibuses and shared taxis run regularly between these main points. Some sample bus fares to/from Moshi are: Arusha US$2, Dar US$11, Nairobi US$12, Mombasa US$9. (More details in the Tanzania Getting There & Away and Getting Around sections.)

Train

The train between Moshi and Dar goes three times per week in each direction, overnight. It takes longer than the bus, but is comfortable (in 1st and 2nd class), safe and reasonably priced. From Dar it's usually necessary to reserve seats at least three days in advance, but from Moshi you can sometimes find a seat on the day. (More details in the Tanzania Getting There & Away and Getting Around sections.)

The Marangu Route

> **Area** Kilimanjaro National Park
> **Distance** 64km
> **Duration** 5 days minimum
> **Start/Finish** Marangu Gate
> **Highest Point** Uhuru Peak (5896m)
> **Overall Altitude Gain** 3916m
> **Nearest Large Town** Moshi
> **Accommodation** Bunkhouses or camping
> **Access** Organised trek
> **Summary** Most popular route on 'Kili', and technically the easiest, although fewer trekkers on this route reach the summit than on other routes.
> Note: no independent trekking allowed; all treks must be arranged through a lisensed tour operator. Altitude sickness is a common problem; trekkers should consider spending an extra day on ascent.

The Marangu Route is the oldest and most popular route on Kilimanjaro. It's also the easiest, with a series of bunkhouses, so more than 80% of trekkers go this way. The route goes up the south-east side of the mountain and approaches the summit of Kibo via the crater rim at Gillman's Point.

Because most people do the whole trek in five days (four nights), only about 10% actually get to Uhuru Peak. About half get to Gillman's Point, and the rest bail out somewhere between there and Kibo Hut. To increase your chances of reaching Uhuru, or even getting to Gillman's in a reasonable state, an extra day can be spent on the ascent, ideally at Horombo Hut, to help acclimatisation.

Treks on this route usually descend the same way.

Access

The Marangu Route starts at Marangu Gate, near Marangu village, on the south-eastern side of Kilimanjaro, about 40km by road from Moshi. Most trekking companies provide transport to the gate.

If you're making your own way there by car, from Moshi take the tar road towards Dar. After about 20km, in the small town of Himo, turn left (north) and follow this road for a further 13km to reach Marangu village. Marangu Gate is a further 5km up the hill. The road is tar all the way. Vehicles can be left at the park gate, but the car park is *inside* the park and if your car has non-Tanzanian registration you'll be charged US$30 per day. Even if you park in the car park for a few minutes (for example to make some enquiries at the office for a trek starting the next day), the horribly officious staff will still charge you the full day rate.

If you're taking public transport, the bus between Moshi and Marangu runs several times each day and costs about US$0.60. The bus goes only as far as the village, as the road up to the gate is too steep. You might be lucky and hitch a ride up to the gate. Otherwise you'll have to walk – look on it as a good warm up!

Stage 1: Marangu Gate to Mandara Hut
7km, 4-5 hours, 700m ascent
From Marangu Gate (1980m) the track is wide and clear, passing through forest. A short distance from the gate the track divides:

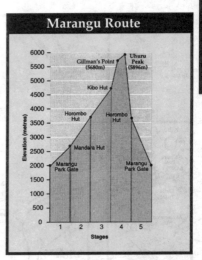

the right fork is the 'main' track and the usual way to Mandara Hut; the left fork is a slightly longer alternative route designed to give you more opportunity to observe the wildlife and enjoy the forest. After an hour or so, the main track becomes a path but is still very clear. The forest path is not as wide as the main path because fewer people use it. The paths rejoin after 1½ to two hours, and again after two to 2½ hours. From this final junction it's another one to 1½ hours to Mandara Hut.

Mandara Hut (2700m) is a group of bunkhouses, in good condition, with beds for 80 people, toilets and a clean water supply.

Sidetrack: Maundi Crater
2 hours return
From Mandara Hut you can visit nearby Maundi Crater, a small mound rising out of the trees to the north. Views from the top, over the forest up to the main peaks of Kibo and Mawenzi, provide plenty of inspiration for the trek to come. The path is clearly signposted.

Stage 2: Mandara Hut to Horombo Hut
11km, 5-7 hours, 1000m ascent
From Mandara Hut there are two paths

TANZANIA

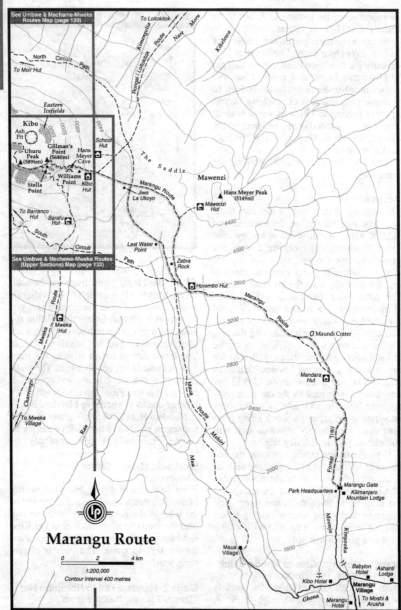

See Umbwe & Machame-Mweka Routes Map (page 130)

North Circuit Path

To Moir Hut

Eastern Icefields

Kibo

Ash Pit

Uhuru Peak (5896m)

Gillman's Point (5680m)

Hans Meyer Cave

Stella Point

Williams Point

Kibo Hut

To Barranco Hut

Barafu Hut

South Circuit

See Umbwe & Machame Routes (Upper Sections) Map (page 133)

To Loitokitok

Kimberosho

Rongai / Loitokitok Route

Nare Moru

Kikelewa

The Saddle

Mawenzi

Hans Meyer Peak (5149m)

School Hut

Marangu Route

Jiwe La Ukoyo

Mawenzi Hut

4400

Last Water Point

Zebra Rock

4000

Horombo Hut

3600

Marangu Route

3200

Maundi Crater

Mweka Route

Mweka Hut

Charrongo

Rau

To Mweka Village

Maua Route

Makiri

2800

Mandara Hut

2400

Forest Trail

2000

Park Headquarters

Marangu Gate

Kilimanjaro Mountain Lodge

Moonja

Kingooka

1600

Maua Village

Marangu Route

0   2   4 km

1:200,000
Contour Interval 400 metres

Kibo Hotel

Ghona

Marangu Hotel

Babylon Hotel

Ashanti Lodge

Marangu Village

To Moshi & Arusha

running roughly parallel through the forest and then a narrow band of heather before meeting near the start of the moorland. The eastern path is slightly longer but more pleasant. As you leave the forest you'll get your first clear view of the top of the Kibo dome. To the right are the jagged peaks of Mawenzi, looking higher than Kibo from this angle. The path, although undulating and steep in places, is easy to follow all the way up to Horombo Hut.

Horombo Hut (3700m) is a large group of bunkhouses, similar to those at Mandara, with space for about 120 people.

Most trekkers spend their second night here and push on to Kibo Hut on the following day. If you've got more time to spare you may prefer to spend two nights at Horombo to help acclimatisation. A good rest-day walk is up to The Saddle by the eastern path, where you can explore the area around the lower slopes of Mawenzi for some of the day.

Stage 3: Horombo Hut to Kibo Hut
10km, 5-7 hours, 1000m ascent

After Horombo Hut the path divides. Take the western path (ie the left fork) and continue, gradually gaining height, past the Last Water point (signposted), which is the highest running water on this route. Your porters will fill up containers here. Continue across The Saddle – the flat plain between Kibo and Mawenzi – until you join the eastern path at a point called Jiwe La Ukoyo (meaning 'pointed rocks'), at 4394m. From here to Kibo Hut takes one to 1½ hours.

The eastern path (reached by forking right after Horombo) is steep and rough, passing the black-and-white striped Zebra Rock and a Last Water point (marked by a signpost). It is not used much but is worth considering if you want to escape the crowds plodding along the western path.

Kibo Hut (4700m) is more basic than Horombo and Mandara, with space for about 60 people. During the busy season the huts are very full, often at double capacity, with people sleeping two to a bunk and all over the floor. There is no reliable water supply. All water

must be carried from Horombo or one of the Last Water points. The hut caretaker sells bottled drinks at high prices, allowing for portering costs.

Stage 4: Kibo Hut to Uhuru Peak, plus descent to Horombo Hut
4km, 7-8½ hours, 1200m ascent;
plus 14km, 4½-7 hours, 2200m descent

Most trekkers spend their third night at Kibo Hut and walk up towards the summit on the fourth day. This stage of the trek can involve up to 16 hours of walking, which is very strenuous, but it's easy to bail out on this route at any point and return the way you've come.

It's usual to start this day's walking very early in the morning, to see the sunrise from the crater rim, and to give you more chance of avoiding the mist. Also, the scree slope up to Gillman's Point, and the snow on the path to Uhuru Peak, will still be frozen, which will make the walking safer and less strenuous. Sunrise is around 6 am, and you should allow five to six hours to get from Kibo Hut to Gillman's Point (5680m), plus another two hours to reach Uhuru Peak (5896m). This normally means leaving Kibo Hut between midnight and 1 am.

It is important not to arrive at Gillman's Peak too early, as this will mean waiting, sometimes in extremely cold conditions, for sunrise. Experienced guides will have assessed the abilities of their clients and pace the walk up the scree to arrive on the rim at exactly the right time.

Ascent Route From Kibo Hut, the path is easy to follow as it zigzags up the scree. You pass Williams Point (5000m) and Hans Meyer Cave (5182m) which are useful markers, helping you to pace the walk. After the cave the gradient gets steeper and the walk becomes, without doubt, a slog. It seems endless but, some five or six hours later, when you finally get to the rim at Gillman's Point, it's all worth it. From here you can see down into the snow-filled crater, across to the spectacular stepped cliffs of the Eastern Icefields, back down to The Saddle with the dark bulk of

Mawenzi behind, and along the edge of the crater rim to Uhuru Peak.

Most people are happy with reaching Gillman's Point, especially when they see how much further it is to Uhuru Peak, but if you're feeling good and there's still time, it's well worth carrying on to the summit. The walk around the crater rim, with the steep drop into the crater on one side and the smooth snow-covered outer slopes of the dome on the other, is one of the most spectacular in Africa. From Gillman's to Uhuru takes another two to 2½ hours.

At Uhuru Peak (5896m) there's a flag pole, a plaque inscribed with a quote of President Nyerere, and a book (in a wooden box) where you can sign your name, but in 1997 this was very tatty and in danger of blowing away through holes in the box. If the weather's good you might want to hang around up here to revel in your success and take in the views. If the weather is bad, you'll probably be content with a quick photo and hightailing it down again.

Descent Route From Uhuru Peak or Gillman's Point it's usual for trekkers on the Marangu Route to descend by the same route. The return from Uhuru Peak to Gillman's Point takes about one to 1½ hours. You should aim to be back at Gillman's about three hours after sunrise, as after this time the top layer of snow becomes wet, slippery and much harder for walking.

From Gillman's back down to Kibo Hut the scree is blissfully easy going compared with the slog up. An easy walk takes 1½ to 2½ hours. If you've got strong knees and nerves of steel you can run down the scree and be back at Kibo Hut in less than an hour.

From Kibo, retrace the path to Horombo Hut – this will take two to three hours.

Stage 5: Horombo Hut to Marangu Gate
18km, 5-7 hours, 1900m descent
On the last day, retrace the route, following the clearly marked path down to the park gate at Marangu. Mandara Hut is about halfway down – a good place for a break.

The Umbwe Route

Area Kilimanjaro National Park
Distance 48km or 56km
Duration 5 days minimum
Start Umbwe Gate
Finish Marangu Gate or Mweka Gate
Highest Point Uhuru Peak (5896m)
Overall Altitude Gain 4496m
Nearest Large Town Moshi
Accommodation Camping
Access Organised trek
Summary Steep and very direct route, suitable for more experienced trekkers. Should not be rushed. Combines pleasant forest walking with exhilarating approach to summit. Descent on either Marangu Route or Mweka Route.
Note: no independent trekking allowed; all treks must be arranged through a lisensed tour operator. Altitude sickness is a common problem; trekkers should consider spending an extra day on ascent.

This is a very direct route to Uhuru Peak, suitable for more experienced trekkers. It has only become popular in the last few years as other routes have become crowded. If followed sensibly, it offers a pleasant walk through the lower slopes and an exhilarating final approach to the summit via the Western Breach.

Although the paths are steep, the distances walked on most days are short, except on Stage 4, the summit section, which involves up to 15 hours of walking, and is made even more strenuous by the effects of altitude and extreme cold. If you're unfit, inexperienced, or unlikely to acclimatise well, you should not attempt this top section of the route.

From Uhuru Peak, you can descend on the Mweka Route or the Marangu Route. The Mweka has fewer trekkers on it and is shorter but much steeper; the Marangu is longer but with an easier gradient. Park regulations may be introduced making it obligatory to use the Mweka in high season, but the Marangu is very crowded at this time and well worth avoiding anyway. Both options are described in this section.

The whole trek can be completed in five days (four nights), although an extra day spent on the ascent, ideally at Barranco Hut, is strongly recommended to help acclimatisation.

Access

The route starts at Umbwe Gate, near Umbwe Mission on the southern side of the mountain, about 15km from Moshi. All organised treks include transport to the village or gate.

Stage 1: Umbwe Gate to Forest Caves
13km, 4-5 hours, 1450m ascent

From the gate (1400m) follow the track up through the forest. The track becomes a path and continues through the forest on a ridge between two valleys. In some places you may have to scramble up steep sections of the path using tree roots for support. Continue following the path, and the occasional red paint marks on the trees, to reach Forest Caves (2850m).

The 'caves' are little more than overhanging rocks and, although dry, provide only limited shelter; a tent is recommended. Next to the caves is a small flat area suitable for camping. Guides and porters usually sleep in the caves. Water is available from a small pool 20m back down the path.

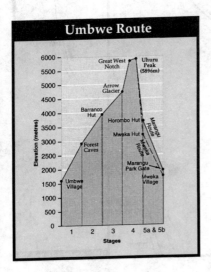

Stage 2: Forest Caves to Barranco Hut
5km, 3-4 hours, 1100m ascent

From the caves, continue following the path up the ridge. The path leaves the forest and passes through heather, and then open moorland, where the main peaks first come into clear view. After about an hour you'll reach the Upper Caves – these are slightly overhanging cliffs which don't provide much shelter.

The path keeps to high ground (as the Great Barranco Valley drops steeply down to the right), following cairns to reach a solitary signpost at an indistinct junction. (The left path leads to Arrow Glacier and Lava Tower Hut.) Keep right to reach Barranco Hut (3950m).

Barranco Hut is a single uniport in poor condition with an earth floor. Around the hut are some flat spaces where about eight tents can be pitched. Water is available from a stream (five minutes further along the path). There's more space for camping about 10 minutes further along the path, next to another stream, and 10 minutes beyond that, right at the foot of the Barranco Wall, is a large boulder with a cave underneath (used by guides and porters) and more space for camping nearby.

From Barranco Hut the Umbwe Route continues up to Arrow Glacier and approaches Uhuru Peak via the Western Breach. This route is described here. Alternatively, from Barranco Hut you can follow the South Circuit Path to Barafu Hut and approach Uhuru Peak from there. (For details of the latter option see the Machame-Mweka Combination Route description.)

Sidetrack: Barranco Wall
5-6 hours return

From the camp sites near Barranco Hut, the Barranco Wall can be clearly seen as a huge dark cliff on the opposite side of the Great Barranco Valley. If you plan to spend two nights at Barranco Hut, the route up the Barranco Wall and then up to the base of the Heim Glacier is a good sidetrack. The route up the wall is steep and exposed, requiring scrambling in places, but marked by cairns. At the top of the wall, the views of the glaciers and lava fields make even the most indifferent trekkers shut up and simply stare. The South Circuit Path continues in an easterly

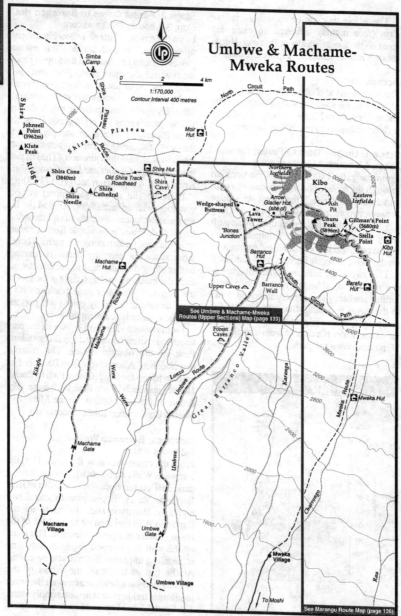

Umbwe & Machame-Mweka Routes

0   2   4 km

1:170,000
Contour Interval 400 metres

North   Circuit   Path

Simba Camp

Shira Plateau Route

Johnsell Point (3962m)

Klute Peak

Shira Ridge

Shira Cone (3840m)

Old Shira Track Roadhead

Shira Needle

Shira Cathedral

Shira Hut

Shira Cave

Moir Hut

Northern Icefields

Kibo

Arrow Glacier Hut (site of)

Ash Pit

Eastern Icefields

Wedge-shaped Buttress

Lava Tower

Uhuru Peak (5896m)

Gillman's Point (5680m)

Stella Point

Kibo Hut

"Bones Junction"

Barranco Hut

Machame Hut

Upper Caves

Barranco Wall

South Circuit

Barafu Hut

See Umbwe & Machame-Mweka Routes (Upper Sections) Map (page 133)

Forest Caves

Kikafu

Machame Route

Weru

Weru

Lonzo

Umbwe Route

Great Barranco Valley

Karanga

Mweka Route

Mweka Hut

Machame Gate

Umbwe

Chemango

Machame Village

Umbwe Gate

Umbwe Village

Mweka Village

To Moshi

Rau

See Marangu Route Map (page 126)

direction towards Barafu Hut; another path, also cairned, leads directly to the foot of the Heim Glacier, an ice mountaineering route aiming directly up to the Kibo rim.

From Barranco Hut to the top of Barranco Wall takes one to 1½ hours, then another two to 2½ hours to get to below the glacier snout. Allow an hour to get back from there to the wall, and the same again down to the valley.

Stage 3: Barranco Hut to Arrow Glacier
5km, 4-5 hours, 850m ascent

From the hut, take the path which climbs steeply up onto the main ridge on the west side of the Great Barranco Valley. The path then leads north-west along the ridge top, aiming directly towards the Western Breach, a section of the main wall of Kibo where a giant chunk has been eroded away, so that the gradient is slightly less steep than the sheer cliffs on either side. The most distinctive feature of the Western Breach is the series of high cliffs that form the Breach Wall on the right (east) side of the Breach itself. This is one of the hardest areas for technical mountaineering on Kilimanjaro, and has been compared in seriousness to the north face of the Eiger.

On the ridge, the vegetation thins out completely and the path crosses bare rock and scree, but is well cairned. About 1½ to two hours from Barranco Hut is a junction marked by signs and some painted animal bones. (Some guides call this 'Bones Junction'.) Shira Hut and the South Circuit Path are signposted left. Keep right (east) and continue up steeply over scree, with the high orange cliffs of the Lava Tower across to your left (west). The path becomes increasingly steep until you reach a flat platform at the base of the Western Breach – the site of Arrow Glacier Hut (4800m).

Arrow Glacier Hut was damaged by a rock fall in the mid-1980s, but porters have constructed a few very basic shelters from the wreckage. For trekkers, there are a few good flat pitches for camping. Water comes from a stream of glacial run-off a few hundred metres to the east of the camp site.

If you feel you might be ascending too quickly, a good place to camp is the site of Lava Tower Hut (4600m), about 15 to 30

minutes down to the west. Once again, the hut itself has been damaged by a rock fall but there's some flat places for camping and a couple of caves and shelters for porters. Staying here adds about an hour on to the next day's walking time, which is already very long, but might be a good pay-off if you're feeling altitude sick at Arrow Glacier.

If you know Arrow Glacier is going to be too high, you can go from Barranco direct to Lava Tower Hut, by keeping left at the junction of animal bones, and forking right up the valley when you reach the large stream flowing south-west from below the Tower. Discuss this with your guide before leaving.

Stage 4: Arrow Glacier to Uhuru Peak, plus descent to Mweka or Horombo Huts
3km, 6-7½ hours, 1100m ascent;
plus 12km, 4½-7 hours, 2800m descent (Mweka Route); or 14km, 4½-7 hours, 2200m descent (Marangu Route)

This stage of the trek involves between 10 and 15 hours of walking, which is made even more strenuous by the effects of altitude and extreme cold. You can descend by either the Mweka Route or the Marangu Route. Unlike the Marangu Route, where you can go as far as the rim at Gillman's or bail out before that, you don't have such a choice here. There are no real shortcuts, so you must go all the way, unless you're planning to come back down the Western Breach after reaching the summit. If you don't feel up to this section, you can go from Arrow Glacier direct to Mweka or Horombo Hut (depending on your descent route), but this is also a very long hard walk.

You need only your guide on this section of the route. Your porters will go straight to the next hut and wait there (in fact they'll probably arrive after you, as the route is long, and you'll have had seven hours start).

After heavy snow (which occurs occasionally in the dry season), this section of the route may be impassable for trekkers. Do not attempt it unless you've got rope and ice-axes for protection, and know how to use them (although this is verging on mountaineering techniques). It's better to go straight to Mweka or Horombo Hut. Even in good conditions, you will have to use your hands and scramble for some sections of this route.

It is usual to start this day's walking very early in the morning, to see the sunrise at the crater rim and to avoid the mist. Also, the scree and snow on the ascent will still be frozen, which will make the journey safer and less strenuous. Sunrise is at about 6 am, and it takes four to five hours to get from Arrow Glacier to the rim at the Great West Notch, plus another two to 2½ hours to reach Uhuru Peak. This normally means leaving Arrow Glacier between 1 and 2 am. Porters usually depart around 7 am. If anyone in your group turns back from the Western Breach, they can walk with the porters to the next hut and rejoin the rest of the group.

This section is the steepest non-technical route on the mountain and should not be taken lightly. Great care should be exercised, as the rock is very loose in places. A torch is essential (preferably a head-torch, leaving your hands free) and walking poles (or even a long-shaft ice-axe) are highly recommended for balance. You may have to cross patches of snow and ice; good trekking companies give their guides ice-axes to cut steps and make the going easier. When conditions are right, some of the scree can be avoided if you have crampons – and know how to use them – by going up the snow-field parallel to the main route.

Note: there is no water supply on this route until Mweka or Horombo huts (although the caretaker at Kibo Hut sells bottled drinks at high prices). Take all you need for this stage.

Ascent Route From the site of Arrow Glacier Hut, the path climbs steeply, over loose scree, marked by cairns (some with fluorescent strips attached), keeping to the left (west) of the Little Breach Glacier. Beyond the top of the glacier, the path continues, with a few short stretches of easy scrambling, to reach the crater rim at a low point, sometimes called the Great West Notch, after about four to five hours.

From this point on the crater rim Uhuru Peak can be seen to the right (south-east). The path, which may be obscured by snow, does not aim directly for the peak but goes round the north side of the Furtwangler Glacier. Keeping the cliffs of the glacier to

your right, head east, then south-east, back towards the edge of the rim to the north-west of Uhuru Peak. Alternatively, if visibility and conditions underfoot are good, you can cut between the western snout of the glacier and the top of the cliffs of the Western Breach, but great care should be taken on this option as a slip could send you plummeting down the cliffs. South of the glacier, you go up a broad easy gully (shallow snowfield after snow) to reach Uhuru Peak (about two to 2½ hours from the Great West Notch).

For details of Uhuru Peak and the views of the crater, see the Marangu Route description.

Mweka Route Descent From the summit, follow the path eastwards around the rim to reach Stella Point, a gap in the crater rim, after one hour. The path then leads steeply down, crossing some snow on the upper section, then scree with occasional cairns. You should reach Barafu Hut after another 1½ to 2½ hours. Aim to be at Stella Point two hours after sunrise, as after this time the top layer of snow becomes wet and slippery, which can be harder for walking and more dangerous on the descent.

From Barafu Hut, continue down the clear path to the junction with the South Circuit Path, and go straight on, steeply downhill through patchy giant heather to reach Mweka Hut (3100m), on the edge of the forest, after another two to three hours. Note: there is no water on the descent between the summit and Mweka Hut.

Mweka Hut is two uniports, in reasonable condition, as this route is rarely used. Nearby are some places for camping, and water is available from a nearby stream.

Marangu Route Descent From the summit, follow the path through the snow eastwards around the rim to reach Stella Point after one hour, then continue round the rim to reach Gillman's Point after another 30 minutes. You should aim to be at Gillman's about three hours after sunrise, as after this time the top layer of snow becomes wet, slippery and much harder for walking.

From Gillman's Point, descend to Kibo Hut and then to Horombo Hut. For full details of this section see the Marangu Route description.

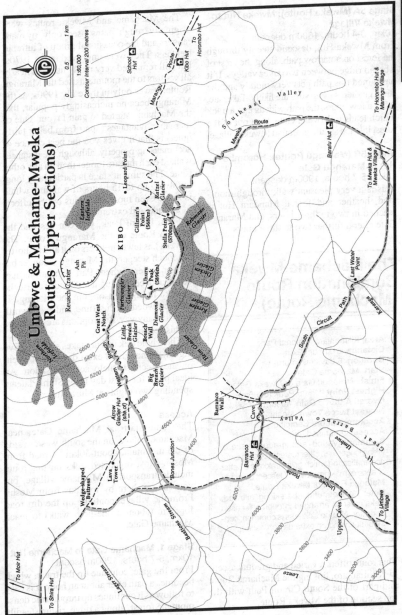

Umbwe & Machame-Mweka Routes (Upper Sections)

1:60,000
Contour interval 200 metres

0   0.5   1 km

Stage 5A (Mweka Route): Mweka Hut to Mweka Village
10km, 3-4 hours, 1600m descent

From Mweka Hut, descend steeply through the forest on a narrow path, along the crest of a broad ridge between two river valleys. If it has rained this path gets very muddy and the steep gradients mean slips are likely. Take care. After a few hours, the path widens into a track which leads to Mweka Gate, then out of the forest into the shambas around Mweka village.

Stage 5B (Marangu Route): Horombo Hut to Marangu Gate
18km, 5-7 hours, 1900m descent

This is a very pleasant walk through moorland, heather and forest. Mandara Hut is reached in two to three hours, and Marangu Gate after a further two to three hours.

The Machame-Mweka Combination Route (Machame Route)

Area Kilimanjaro National Park
Distance 61km or 69km
Duration 6 days minimum
Start Machame Gate
Finish Marangu Gate or Mweka Gate
Highest Point Uhuru Peak (5896m)
Overall Altitude Gain 4096m
Nearest Large Town Moshi
Accommodation Camping
Access Organised trek
Summary Varied and gradual ascent, taking longer than other routes providing extra acclimatisation which gives trekkers a better chance of making summit. Descent on either Marangu Route or Mweka Route.
Note: no independent trekking allowed; treks must be arranged through a lisensed operator. Altitude sickness is common; consider spending an extra day on ascent.

This route offers a varied and gradual ascent of Kilimanjaro, linking the Machame Route and part of the South Circuit Path with the top section of the Mweka Route.

The Machame and Mweka routes were originally rough paths used only by park rangers and the occasional group of intrepid trekkers. They were improved in the 1970s, but still remained very rarely used, as nearly all visitors to the mountain used the Marangu Route. It was only in the early 1990s, as the Marangu became increasingly popular, that the Machame started to gain favour. One of its main advantages (apart from being fairly quiet) is that it gives you the best chance of acclimatising properly, although the distances walked each day are longer than on any other route. The summit stage is particularly long, involving up to 15 hours of walking, which is made even more strenuous by the effects of altitude and extreme cold.

From Uhuru Peak, you can descend the Mweka Route or the Marangu Route. The Mweka has fewer trekkers on it and is shorter but much steeper; the Marangu is longer but with an easier gradient. Park regulations may be introduced making it obligatory to use the Mweka in high season, but the Marangu is very crowded at this time and well worth avoiding anyway. Both options are described in this section.

The whole trek usually takes six days (five nights), although an extra day can be spent on the ascent, to help acclimatisation. An ideal place for a rest day is the Shira Plateau, spending two nights at Shira Hut.

Access
The route starts at Machame Gate, near Machame village, on the south-western side of the mountain, about 30km by road from Moshi. Most organised treks on this route include transport to Machame village, but you can get here by minibus from Moshi. From the village, continue up the dirt road for 3km (about a one-hour walk) to reach Machame Gate.

Stage 1: Machame Gate to Machame Hut
10km, 5-7 hours, 1200m ascent

From the gate, continue up the track, which becomes a path after about an hour. It is easy to follow as it continues up through the dense montane forest, along a ridge, rising steadily

Warning
There have been a few isolated incidents of local people coming up from Machame village during the night and stealing from Machame Hut camp site. Keep your stuff inside while you sleep and make sure someone keeps an eye on the tents during the evening. ■

with some steep sections. On sunny days this section is beautiful, so don't rush it. After 2½ to three hours you reach a small opening in the trees known as 'Halfway Clearing' – a good place for a rest. The gradient relents as the forest merges into giant heather, and the path leads more easily to Machame Hut (3000m). Cloud permitting, the summit of Kibo is visible beyond the foothills.

Machame Hut is two uniports in bad condition. There is space to pitch about four tents next to the huts and several more spaces beside the path back along the ridge. Water is available from a stream 30m down a steep slope to the north-west of the huts. In the dry season this stops flowing, so you must go a further 10 minutes down the stream bed to collect water from pools.

Stage 2: Machame Hut to Shira Hut

6km, 5-7 hours, 840m ascent

From Machame Hut follow the clear path up the steep rocky ridge, crossing and re-crossing the crest a few times. Two hours from the hut you'll reach a small semicircular cliff. It's an easy scramble up this to reach easier ground and a good rest spot known as Picnic Rock. From here there are excellent views of the Shira Plateau and the pinnacles on its southern edge.

The path continues up and then left, across several small stream beds (all empty in the dry season), to reach the flatter ground of the Shira Plateau after another hour. From here the path is almost level, winding through thin bush, clumps of grass and across patches of bare sand and ash. After half an hour you'll reach Shira Cave. Over the last few years it has become more popular to camp here than at Shira Hut; there's more tent space and porters can sleep in the cave. There's also a new long-drop toilet.

Beyond the cave, the path climbs over a small ridge, then drops to cross a stream, before another small rise up to Shira Hut (3840m), on a rocky platform overlooking the flat expanse of Shira Plateau. From the cave to the hut takes less than half an hour.

Shira Hut is a uniport in bad condition, with space to camp nearby and water available from the stream 50m north of the hut. In the dry season, this source is not reliable, so you have to get water from the stream below Shira Cave.

Sidetrack: The Shira Plateau Edge

7 hours minimum return

Shira Cave or Shira Hut are good places to spend two nights to give yourself a rest day. If you're feeling fit, the southern edge of the Shira Plateau is a fascinating area to explore on this day. There are no paths, and very few people (or guides) come this way. You need to be competent with a map and compass here and should not rely on your guide unless he has been here before. If the weather is bad and visibility low, forget it.

From Shira Hut take the Shira Plateau Route downhill in a westerly direction towards the flat floor of the plateau. After half an hour drop down a steep section to meet the old

Machame-Mweka Combination Route

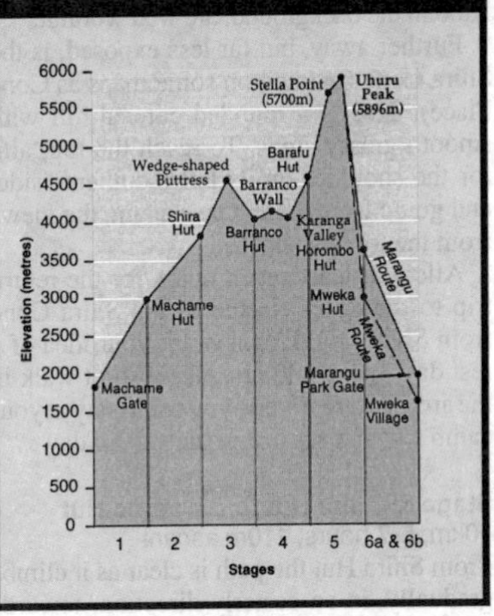
6000
5500
5000
4500
4000
3500
3000
2500
2000
1500
1000
500
0
Elevation (metres)
Stella Point (5700m)
Uhuru Peak (5896m)
Barafu Hut
Wedge-shaped Buttress
Barranco Wall
Shira Hut
Barranco Hut
Karanga Valley
Horombo Hut
Marangu Route
Mweka Hut
Machame Hut
Mweka Route
Marangu Park Gate
Machame Gate
Mweka Village
1
2
3
4
5
6a & 6b
Stages

Shira Track roadhead. (There's a turning circle here and some flat places for camping, but no water.) Follow the track for about 1km and then, as it swings right, aim left (south-west) and uphill slightly towards the top of the ridge. From here follow the crest of the ridge as it leads to a cairn on a small summit. From this small summit, it's possible to follow the ridge crest to the summit of Shira Cathedral, a huge buttress of rock surrounded by steep spires and pinnacles. This is an excellent walk but the crest of the ridge is very steep in places, with sheer drops down several hundred metres on the southern side. Take great care if you decide to follow the crest of the ridge. Some sections require serious scrambling, while others are completely impassable. If in doubt, tend right (north) and down to easier ground and walk through the grassland, keeping parallel to the ridge. Eland are sometimes seen in this area.

Beyond the Shira Cathedral, descent is essential, as the ridge ends at a sheer cliff. But beyond this it's possible to scramble back up again to the summit of the Shira Needle. This ascent requires a few moves of rock climbing and you'll need a head for heights on the top, which is not much bigger than a few tables end to end, but the views from the summit, across the Cathedral and the southern slopes of the mountain, with the main peak of Kibo in the background, are well worth it.

Further away, but far less exposed, is the Shira Cone (marked on some maps as Cone Place). This is a rounded conical hill with smooth grassy sides. To reach the top, aim for the shoulder on its left (southern) side, and go up from there. Once again, the views from the top are superb.

Allow at least seven hours for the return trip to the Shira Needle or the Shira Cone from Shira Hut. If this is not your idea of a rest day, you could just take a short walk in the area. Alternatively, you could stay at your camp site and snooze in the sun all day ...

Stage 3: Shira Hut to Barranco Hut
10km, 5-7 hours, 110m ascent

From Shira Hut the path is clear as it climbs gradually, in an easterly direction, towards

the main peak of Kibo. If you stayed at Shira Cave, another path goes direct from here, meeting the original path further up. After about two hours, a line of cairns leads off to the left (north). An arrow and the words 'Moyr Hut' (sic) are painted on a nearby rock. This is the start of the North Circuit Path. Ignore this and continue uphill directly towards the main peak. If you camped at Shira Cave, most guides know a direct path which leads across the moorland and meets the main route near the Moir Hut Junction.

Beyond Moir Hut junction the gradient eases and the path tends right, dropping into a broad valley, then climbing steeply up the other side to a ridge crest. Fifteen minutes further on, the route divides, with paths going either side of a large, distinctive, black wedge-shaped buttress. (The left path goes up to the Lava Tower.) Keep right, below and to the right of this buttress. Continue following the contour, then drop down a scree slope and cross a stream. (This stream always seems to be running and is a rest place for porters.) Up to the left, the orange cliffs of the Lava Tower can be seen. Behind the Lava Tower is the Western Breach, a section of the main wall of Kibo where a giant chunk has been eroded away so that the gradient is slightly less steep than the sheer cliffs on either side.

From the stream the path climbs back up onto a ridge. About an hour from the wedge-shaped buttress a path (from the Western Breach) comes in from the left at a junction marked by several signposts and painted animal bones (some guides call this 'Bones Junction'). The main path continues down the ridge, with the deep sides of the Great Barranco Valley falling away to the left, for another hour before dropping steeply down the side of the ridge to reach Barranco Hut (3950m).

Barranco Hut is a single uniport with an earth floor. Around the hut are some flat spaces where about eight tents can be pitched. Water is available from a stream (five minutes further along the path). There's more space for camping about 10 minutes further along the path, next to another stream, and 10 minutes beyond that, right at the foot of the

Barranco Wall (the large, dark cliff on the opposite side of the valley) is a large boulder with a cave underneath, which makes a good shelter (often used by guides and porters), and more space for camping nearby.

Stage 4: Barranco Hut to Barafu Hut
8km, 8-9 hours, 650m ascent

From Barranco Hut, follow the path across the floor of the Great Barranco Valley, crossing several streams, up to the huge boulder at the base of the Barranco Wall. The path passes to the right of the boulder and then very steeply up the Barranco Wall, following cairns and red paint marks to the top. It takes about one to 1½ hours to reach the top of the Wall. The path is steep and exposed in sections; great care should be taken.

From the top of the Wall you'll get some truly excellent views of the main bulk of Kibo up to your left. Now you'll really feel you're on a big mountain!

The path aims generally south-east, undulating slightly, crossing several small valleys and streams, but generally keeping level, until dropping steeply down into the Karanga Valley, after a further two hours. If you intend to camp at Barafu Hut, the Karanga River is the last water point; make sure your porters fill up here for all your needs until you get down to Horombo (on the following day). Large containers are essential. Trekking companies who organise treks regularly on this route will have a supply of containers for you to use. Allow around 7L per person for the time at the hut and the following day's walk, and arrange for the porters to carry the extra weight.

Continue on the path as it crosses two shallow valleys, then a flat desolate area of dry heather and moorland, and up towards the crest of a broad ridge, following cairns. About two hours from Karanga you'll reach a junction. Turn left (north) here and follow the path up the broad ridge, and a final steep section over rocky slabs, to reach Barafu Hut (4600m) after another 2½ hours.

Barafu Hut is two small uniports with space to pitch about 15 tents on the rocky ground nearby. There is no water at the hut

or anywhere nearby. It must be carried from the Karanga River. To compensate for the difficulties with water, the views from Barafu Hut are among the most impressive on the whole mountain: up to the main peak of Kibo, across The Saddle to Mawenzi and down to the plains below.

Stage 5: Barafu Hut to Uhuru Peak, plus descent to Mweka or Horombo Huts
5km, 6-7½ hours, 1300m ascent;
plus 12km, 4½-7 hours, 2800m descent (Mweka Route); or plus 14km, 4½-7 hours, 2200m descent (Marangu Route)

This stage of the trek involves between 10 and 15 hours of walking, which is made even more strenuous by the effects of altitude and extreme cold. You can descend on either the Mweka Route or the Marangu Route on this trek, so if you decide not to do the summit stage you can go straight to Mweka Hut or Horombo Hut (depending on your descent route).

You need only your guide on this section of the route. Your porters will go straight to your next hut. Porters should not depart immediately in case anyone in your group turns back on this section. They can then walk with the porters to the next hut and rejoin the rest of the group.

This section of the route may occasionally be impassable after heavy snow, and should not be attempted if this is the case. Instead, you should go straight to Mweka Hut or Horombo Hut.

It is usual to start this day's walking very early in the morning, to see the sunrise at the crater rim and to try to avoid the mist. Also, the scree and snow on the ascent will still be frozen, which will make it safer and less strenuous. Sunrise is about 6 am, and it takes five to six hours to get from Barafu Hut to the rim at Stella Point, plus another one to 1½ hours to reach Uhuru Peak. This normally means leaving Barafu Hut between midnight and 1 am.

This section is steep and should not be taken lightly. A torch is essential (preferably a head-torch, as this leaves the hands free), and walking poles are highly recommended.

Ascent Route From Barafu Hut the path leads up the western ridge of the Southeast Valley. The ridge blends into the main wall of Kibo and the path becomes very steep, zigzagging up across scree and snow. The path is fairly clear and well cairned until you cross a section of steep snow, to the right of the Rebmann Glacier, to reach the crater rim at Stella Point (5700m). At this point on the rim, the route from Barafu Hut joins the route from Gillman's Point, which continues westward (clockwise) round the Kibo rim, gaining height gradually, to reach Uhuru Peak (5896m) after another one to 1½ hours. For information about this section, and the summit itself, see the Marangu Route description.

Mweka Route Descent From the summit, retrace the path eastwards around the rim to get back to Stella Point after one hour, then retrace the top section of the Mweka Route to Barafu Hut, reached after another 1½ to 2½ hours. Aim to be back at Stella Point two hours after sunrise, because after this time the top layer of snow becomes wet and slippery, which can be more difficult for walking and more dangerous on the descent.

From Barafu Hut, continue down the clear path to the junction with the South Circuit Path, and go straight on, steeply downhill through patchy giant heather to reach Mweka Hut (3100m), on the edge of the forest, after another two to three hours.

Mweka Hut is two uniports in reasonable condition, as this route is rarely used. Nearby are some places for camping, and water is available from a stream.

Marangu Route Descent From the summit, follow the path through the snow eastwards around the rim to reach Stella Point after one hour, then continue round the rim to reach Gillman's Point after another 30 minutes. You should aim to be at Gillman's about three hours after sunrise, as after this time the top layer of snow becomes wet, slippery and much harder for walking.

From Gillman's Point, descend to Kibo Hut and then to Horombo Hut. For details see the Marangu Route description.

Stage 6A (Mweka Route): Mweka Hut to Mweka Village
10km, 3-4 hours, 1600m descent
From Mweka Hut, descend steeply through the forest on a narrow path, along the crest of a broad ridge between two river valleys. If it has rained this path gets very muddy and the steep gradients mean slips are likely. Take care. After a few hours, the path widens into a track which leads to Mweka Gate, then out of the forest into the shambas around Mweka village.

Stage 6B (Marangu Route): Horombo Hut to Marangu Gate
18km, 4-6 hours, 1900m descent
A very pleasant walk through moorland, heather and forest. Mandara Hut is reached in two to three hours, and Marangu Gate after a further two to three hours. (For details of this route, and the huts on it, see the Marangu Route description.)

Other Routes on Kilimanjaro

Routes other than those described here are possible but are usually fairly complex to arrange. They normally involve longer and more difficult approach drives, and trekking groups usually need to be completely self-contained, with tents and equipment for local guides and porters. As all treks on the mountain have to be organised through a trekking company, these logistical problems tend to make treks on these routes very expensive, which in turn means they are seldom used. However, if you've got the money to spare trekking the 'quiet way' can be very enjoyable.

MAUA ROUTE
This is on the south-eastern side of the mountain, linking Maua village to Horombo Hut, and is parallel to the Marangu Route. It used to be preferred by some mountain aficionados as an alternative route between Marangu

and Horombo because it avoided the main 'tourist route'. Today, it is very rarely used and is reported to be overgrown in the forest section, although the park authorities could consider opening it again, to relieve some of the pressure on the Marangu Route.

MWEKA ROUTE (Descent)
On the southern side of the mountain, the top section of this route is used in the Machame-Mweka Combination. Park regulations may be introduced stipulating that trekkers ascending the Machame, Umbwe or Shira routes in busy periods must descend the Mweka Route, so this option has been described in the full route descriptions above.

MWEKA ROUTE (Ascent)
The national park may introduce regulations making the Mweka Route usable for descent only for trekkers ascending the Machame, Umbwe or Shira routes in busy periods. However, until these rules are introduced, the Mweka Route can also be used for ascent. However, as one of the most direct ways up to the summit of Kibo, this route is very steep and strenuous and not normally recommended. It starts near Mweka Village, about 12km from Moshi. The first night is spent at Mweka Hut (about 3100m), but there's no water after this point, which means carrying supplies for two days, or arranging for porters to divert into the Karanga Valley to collect enough for the whole group. The second night is at Barafu Hut and the third night is on the descent route. Very fit and well-acclimatised trekkers ascending this route can do the whole trek in four days (three nights).

RONGAI & LOITOKITOK ROUTES
These routes ascend the north side of the mountain, from a village called Rongai just south of the Kenya-Tanzania border, and from the nearby village of Loitokitok, a few km north of the border in Kenya. The Loitokitok Route is also known as or the Outward Bound Route, and many local guides seem to use all three names interchangeably. This is not surprising as the routes join halfway

up the northern slopes (at around 3000m) and continue as one to meet the North Circuit Path.

For many years these routes were hardly used, as the border area was considered 'sensitive'. Since the mid-1990s, however, a couple of specialist operators (see Organised Treks & Tours in the Getting Around section) are running treks here, camping for two or three nights on the ascent and spending a night at School Hut (4770m), also known as Outward Bound Hut, before heading for the summit.

From a historical point of view, this route is very interesting. It was first developed in the 1960s when a local chief called Salakana (whose traditional land included the lower slopes on this part of the mountain) arranged for camp sites, huts and toilets to be built along the path, setting it up as an alternative to the Marangu Route (which at that time was effectively the only other choice). Trekking groups paid to use the facilities and the money went to the village. In this way local people benefited directly from trekkers. Thirty years later 'community involvement' has become a responsible tourism buzzword. The Rongai/Loitokitok Route is also interesting because it's the only route on Kili where both local men and women work as porters.

SHIRA PLATEAU ROUTE
On the far western side of the mountain, this route is rarely used because the approach track is long and in bad condition. However, once on the route, the scenery is fascinating: the flat grasslands of the plateau, ringed by sharp ridges (the remains of the ancient Shira Crater), are unlike any other part of the Kilimanjaro massif. The route starts at Londorossi Gate, on the western side of the mountain, about 80km by road from Moshi, and leads to Lava Tower, via Shira Hut. From Lava Tower the summit can be approached via the Western Breach or the South Circuit Path and the top of the Mweka Route.

From Londorossi Gate a drivable track leads through forest and then across heathland to the old Shira Track roadhead, within a one-hour walk of Shira Hut. This drivable track is in very poor condition; the top section is rarely used and is closed off by a barrier at about 3000m (although some vehicles get permission to open the barrier and drive higher up the mountain). Groups using this route either drive to the barrier (where there's a toilet and space for camping) or occasionally all the way to the old Shira Track roadhead. If you're considering this option, it would be worth spending at least one extra day at Shira Hut to acclimatise before your trek.

A better alternative would be to walk from the barrier to Shira Hut. Even better, to acclimatise properly, you should walk the whole way from Londorossi Gate through the forest to the barrier on the first day, then to Simba Camp (in the heart of the plateau) on the second day, then up to Shira Hut via some of the features on the Shira rim on the third day.

To walk through the forest, which is inhabited by buffalo and elephant, you must be accompanied by an armed ranger, which needs to be arranged in advance. The UK-based company Gane & Marshall (see under Organised Treks in the Getting There & Away chapter) is the only outfit we know of taking this quiet and pleasant route. Given the extra time it allows for acclimatisation most of their clients reach the summit.

At the other end of the scale, I once met a group of German trekkers doing this route who'd flown from Europe one day, driven up to the old Shira Track roadhead and walked to Shira Hut on the next day, then walked to Barranco on the day after that. Needless to say, they were looking (and feeling) pretty close to death.

Mt Meru

At 4566m (14,979 ft), Mt Meru is the second-highest mountain in Tanzania, although it is overshadowed by Kilimanjaro, its famous neighbour, and frequently overlooked by trekkers. But Meru is a spectacular classic volcanic cone, and well worth a visit. A trek to the summit involves hiking through the grassland and lush forest on the mountain's beautiful lower slopes, followed by a dramatic and exhilarating walk along the knife-edge rim of the horseshoe crater.

Like most of the mountains in this region, Meru was formed by volcanic action associated with the creation of the Great Rift Valley. The circular wall of the crater was broken by subsequent explosions to make today's horseshoe shape, and more recent volcanic activity has created the ash cone that stands inside the crater. Small eruptions have been reported in the last 100 years, indicating that Meru is still not quite extinct.

The local Warusha people who live in the area regard the mountain as sacred. Every year a bull or sheep is sacrificed and offered to the mountain to ensure rain in the coming season. While it is likely that local people

have been visiting the forest and even the area on the crater floor for generations, it is not known whether anybody ever reached the summit. The exposed nature of the walk, the unpredictable weather and the effects of altitude would probably have deterred casual curiosity.

HISTORY

The first European to record a sighting of Mt Meru was the German explorer Karl von der Decken who reached this area in 1862. The mountain was later seen by other explorers, including Gustav Fischer in 1882 and Joseph Thomson the following year. In 1887 the Austro-Hungarian Count Samuel Teleki and members of his team penetrated the dense forest on the lower slopes and reached a point where the trees thinned out enough for them to see Kilimanjaro, which they planned to climb later in their expedition. The first ascent to the summit of Meru is credited to either Carl Uhlig in 1901 or Fritz Jaeger in 1904.

By the end of the 1880s the area around Meru had become part of German East Africa. In 1907 the land east of the mountain was cleared and farmed by a settler family. Although used mainly for ranching, part of their land was set aside as a reserve for indigenous wildlife and this area remained the property of the family until 1960, when the Ngurdoto Crater National Park, which included the farm, was established.

In 1967 the boundaries were extended to include Mt Meru, and the park was renamed Arusha National Park. During the early days of Tanzania's independence, the summit of Meru was named Socialist Peak, although this title was never commonly used. In more recent years the Tanzanian government has abandoned many of its left-leaning principles, so it's likely that this name will be forgotten.

GEOGRAPHY

Mt Meru has a circular base some 20km across at 2000m where it rises steeply above the foothills and plains. The mountain is an almost perfect cone with an internal crater, or caldera, surrounded by a steep wall of cliffs. At about 2500m the wall has been broken away so the top half of the mountain is shaped like a giant horseshoe, with the opening on the east side of the cone and the highest point directly opposite. The cliffs of the inner wall below the summit are over 1500m high which makes them among the tallest in Africa. Inside the crater more recent volcanic eruptions have created a subsidiary peak called the Ash Cone.

TREKKING INFORMATION

Despite its attractions Meru remains a relatively obscure mountain completely overshadowed by its more famous neighbour, Kilimanjaro, whose lower slopes are only 40km away to the north-east. For trekkers this obscurity is an advantage: you will probably meet only a few other trekking groups on the mountain and for the rest of the time have the place completely to yourself.

Although Meru appears small compared with Kilimanjaro don't be fooled into thinking that conditions won't be as serious as those on the larger mountain. The effects of altitude can be a problem, so you shouldn't try to rush up Meru if you are not properly acclimatised.

If you've got the time and money for two treks a visit to Meru is a great way to prepare for Kilimanjaro. It helps you build up acclimatisation and the view from Meru, across the plains to Kili's great dome rising above the clouds, provides plenty of inspiration for the major trek to come.

Costs

Your costs for an independent trek on Meru are mostly park entrance and hut fees. Guides, provided by the park, are obligatory and also have to be paid for. Porters are optional. The cost of getting there and your supplies are also important points to consider. All these items are detailed separately below.

Route Standard & Days Required

The Momella Route is currently the only route up Meru. It starts at Momella Gate on the eastern side of the mountain and goes to the summit along the northern arm of the horseshoe crater. The trek route is steep but can be done comfortably in four days (three nights), although trekkers often do it in three days by combining stages 3 and 4. Some fit and very well-acclimatised trekkers even do it in two days.

Walking to and from the start of the trek, between Usa River and Momella Gate (see Access in the Momella Route section), adds another two days to the trek (one day each way).

Guides & Porters

A guide is mandatory. Unlike those on Kilimanjaro, guides here are national park rangers provided to protect you in case you meet some of the park's buffalo or elephant, rather than to show you the way (although they do know the route). The rangers are well trained and professional and will be as informative or unobtrusive as you like. They all speak English, and most trekkers find them friendly and knowledgeable companions. They carry guns and, even though it is unlikely that an animal will have to be shot,

TANZANIA

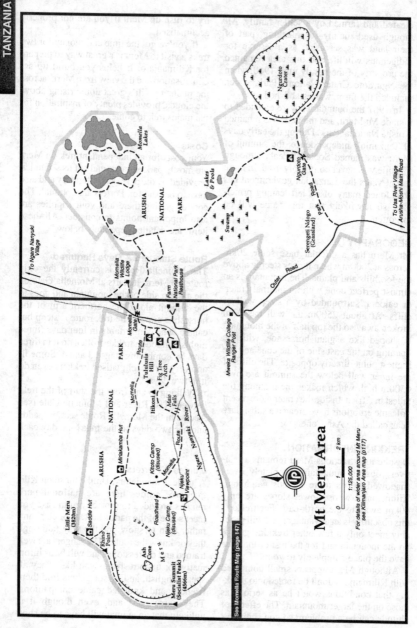

Mt Meru Area

1:125,000

0 1 2 km

For details of wider area around Mt Meru
see Kilimanjaro Area map (p117)

See Momella Route Map (page 147)

To Ngare Nanyuki Village

Momella Lakes

Lakes & Pools

Swamp

Ngurdoto Crater

ARUSHA NATIONAL PARK

Momella Wildlife Lodge

Momella Gate

Farm

National Park Resthouse

Ngurdoto Gate

To Usa River Village
Arusha-Moshi Main Road

Serengeti Ndogo (Grassland)

Outer Road

Mweka Wildlife College Ranger Post

Momella Route

Tululusia Hill

Itikoni

Fig Tree Arch

Maio Falls

Ngare Nanyuki River

Miriakamba Hut

Kitoto Camp (disused)

Momella Route

Njeku Viewpoint

Njeku Camp (disused)

Roadhead

ARUSHA NATIONAL PARK

Little Meru (3820m)

Saddle Hut

Rhino Point

Ash Cone

Meru Crater

Meru Summit (Socialist Peak) (4566m)

you should not underestimate the danger and walk too far away from your guide.

Guides are arranged at Momella Gate. The fee of US$15 per day is paid to the national park (not to the guide himself). Guides receive a fixed monthly salary and apparently get no additional payment from the park for guiding.

Most trekkers go up Mt Meru with only a guide, but if you want porters they are also available at Momella Gate. They come from one of the nearby villages and are not park employees. The charge is US$5 per porter per day. This is paid at the gate and given to the porters after the trip. You may also have to pay park entrance and hut fees for porters (US$1 per day, US$1.50 per night). Porters will carry rucksacks weighing up to 15kg (not including their own food and clothing). Heavier bags will be carried for a negotiable extra fee.

Generally the guides and porters on Mt Meru are hard working and reliable. They do not expect the huge tips sometimes demanded by their counterparts on Kilimanjaro. For a standard length trip reasonable tips might be US$10 to US$15 for the guide (depending on group size) and around US$5 for each porter.

Park Fees & Regulations

Mt Meru is in Arusha National Park and all visitors have to pay national park entrance fees in hard currency. US dollars (travellers cheques or cash) are recommended as all prices are quoted in this currency. For non-Tanzanians, national park fees are:

Entrance	US$20	per day
Hut	US$20	per night
Rescue	US$20	per trek
Services of guide	US$15	per day
Park commission	US$5	per trek

All fees are payable at Momella Gate. If you enter the park at Ngurdoto Gate you must pay your entrance fees there, but your mountain fees at Momella. A 'day' is a 24-hour period. Entry permits are marked with the time of entry. If you enter at noon on Monday morning and leave before noon on Wednesday you should only need to pay two days

fees, although this might be difficult to agree with the rangers at the gate.

Maps

Mt Meru is covered by the DOS/government survey maps (1:50,000) sheet numbers 55/1 (Ol Doinyo Sambu), 55/2 (Ngare Nanyuki), 55/3 (Arusha) and 55/4 (Usa River). These four sheets join right in the centre of Mt Meru crater, but 55/2 is available in an expanded version which shows the whole of Mt Meru on the one sheet. It is not possible to buy these maps in Arusha or at the park gate, but they are sometimes available from the map office in Dar es Salaam.

Guidebooks

The Guide to Arusha National Park is a very good booklet produced by Tanzania National Parks and the African Wildlife Foundation. It has a section on Mt Meru, with information on animals and birds, vegetation, geology, and so on. It is sometimes for sale at the park gate, and also available from bookshops in Arusha.

Supplies

There are no shops inside the park or at the gate. In Arusha, you can buy all the food required for a trek. There's a very good market, plus several shops and supermarkets.

PLACES TO STAY

The town nearest Mt Meru is Arusha. This is the centre of Tanzania's safari industry and so has a very wide range of hotels. Most visitors stay a few nights in Arusha as it's the best place to arrange a safari in the famous wildlife areas of Serengeti and Ngorongoro, as well as treks on Meru. Crater Highlands and Kili treks can also be arranged here. Safari and trekking companies are listed under Organised Treks & Tours in the Getting Around section of this chapter. The telephone area code for Arusha is ☎ 057

Arusha

Camping Masai Camp is a long-time favourite on the outskirts of town along the Old Moshi Road, about 3km past the cross-roads near the Motel Impala. Camping costs US$3 per

TANZANIA

person. There are toilets, hot showers, a bar and restaurant. The site guards are Maasai warriors, armed with spears, so there's no problem with security! A newer place is *Vision Campsite*, in town near the Equator Hotel. The owner is friendly and helpful, camping is US$2, and there are tents for hire. They can also arrange treks on Meru and Kili.

Places to Stay – bottom end There's a batch of cheap lodging houses in the area around the bus station and stadium. Most double as bars and brothels and are not for the faint-hearted. Better is the *YMCA* (which also seems to be the *Youth Hostel*) on India Street behind the New Safari Hotel, but US$10 a double is a bit on the steep side for basic rooms, dirty toilets and a meagre breakfast.

Up the scale slightly, the very popular *Naaz Hotel*, on Sokoine Rd (the main street down from the clock tower), has clean doubles (no singles) for US$20. There's usually hot water, night security staff and a good serve-yourself snack bar. The interestingly titled *Hotel Arusha By Night*, near the central market, also has doubles at US$20 including breakfast, plus a roof garden bar and 'the best disco in town'.

We've heard several good reports of a new place called *Bamakambi Lodge* set in quiet gardens on Sakini St on the outskirts of town; rooms are US$20/30 and the in-house tour company is also recommended.

Places to Stay – middle & top end The *Arusha Resort Centre* (☎ 8033), just down from the clock tower, has clean self-contained rooms, most with a balcony (from where Meru can be seen, clouds permitting), a restaurant and a garden bar. Doubles cost US$40 including breakfast (no singles). If you're in a group, the hotel's self-contained apartments are a good deal at US$80; each has two double rooms, a bathroom and a fully equipped kitchen.

Also near the clock tower is the *Hotel Equator* (☎ 3127); it's a bit of a concrete block but inside the large en suite rooms are fine, and good value at US$45 a double with breakfast. Get a room on the upper floor for better views and to avoid the sound of the band in the bar.

The *Motel Impala* is also good value, with a fine restaurant, efficient staff and clean, en suite rooms for US$40/60 including breakfast. It's about 1.5km out of the centre on the Old Moshi Road.

In the town centre, next to the clock tower, the *New Arusha Hotel* (☎ 8541) has rooms at US$65/70 including breakfast, but it's pretty sleazy and service is slow, although the garden bar is good for a lunch time refresher. Nearby, the similarly tatty *New Safari Hotel* (☎ 3261) has en suite singles/doubles for US$40/60 and a pleasant beer garden. The adjoining New Safari Grill has reasonable food.

On the eastern outskirts, the *Mount Meru Novotel* (☎ 2712) is generally regarded as the best hotel in town, with singles/doubles at US$110/140 including breakfast. Most of the shuttle buses to/from Moshi and Nairobi stop here.

Arusha National Park
Momella Wildlife Lodge is on the edge of Arusha National Park, near Momella Gate and the start of the route up Mt Meru. There's a large main building, with restaurant, bar and conference rooms, surrounded by separate bungalows and chalets. Singles/doubles cost US$56/65 including breakfast. The main building was once the home of John Wayne and Hardy Kruger, who used the house while making the adventure film *Hatari*, and later developed it as a hunting lodge. From the terrace there are excellent views of Meru and Kilimanjaro. Camping is also possible here; rather pricey at US$20 per night although groups may find this rate negotiable (especially if you eat in the restaurant). The lodge is run by Lion's Safari International, PO Box 999, Arusha (☎ 6423).

The *National Park Resthouse* is an old colonial farm cottage near Momella Gate. It has five beds (although there's space for more people on the floor), a kitchen and a bathroom, for US$20 per person. You can also camp outside the resthouse, but it still costs US$20. There are three camp sites near Momella Gate, and another at Ngurdoto Gate (all charging US$20 per night). As the camp sites and resthouse are inside the park you also have to pay the US$15 entrance fee, which makes it expensive unless you're paying park fees for that day anyway. The resthouse can be reserved in advance by writing to the Mount Meru National Park, Tanzania National Parks Office, PO Box 3134, AICC, Arusha.

The Mweka Wildlife College has a small ranger post on the road to Momella Gate, about 5km before the gate. There's a small *resthouse* here which has fallen into disrepair and is officially closed, but the rangers on duty might let you sleep here for a small fee. There is also an area for camping nearby. Park fees are not payable, as this area is outside the park boundary.

On Mt Meru

There are two large, well-maintained *bunkhouses* on the main route up the mountain, conveniently spaced for a three-day or four-day trek, so a tent is not usually necessary. You can also camp near the huts, although this won't save you any money. If a large group of trekkers is on the mountain at the same time as you, the huts may be full and you might have to camp, but this is unlikely. Check at the gate before starting your trek. Each bunkhouse has a cooking and eating area, which you can use if you've got your own stove. There's a separate kitchen shack with a wood fire and a few battered saucepans mostly for the rangers, although trekkers can use them too. There's also a separate dormitory for guides and porters.

GETTING THERE & AWAY

Mt Meru is in north-eastern Tanzania, about 80km south of the border with Kenya, and about 500km north-west of Dar es Salaam. The nearest large town is Arusha, which is linked to Moshi and Nairobi (Kenya) by good tar roads. You can travel between Arusha and Dar by air or road. For more details see the Kilimanjaro Getting There & Away section.

It is much easier to reach Arusha from Nairobi than from Dar. (For details see the Tanzania Getting There & Away and Getting Around sections).

The Momella Route

Area Arusha National Park
Distance 33km
Duration 3 or 4 days
Start & Finish Momella Gate
Highest Point Meru Summit (Socialist Peak) 4566m
Overall Altitude Gain 3066m
Nearest Large Town Arusha
Accommodation Bunkhouses
Access Bus & walk/hitch, organised trek
Summary Wonderful hiking through grass-land and lush forest, plus a dramatic and exhilarating section along the knife-edge crater rim make this a spectacular trek in its own right, and ideal acclimatisation for Kilimanjaro.
Note: Large animals such as buffalo and elephant inhabit the forest; it is obligatory to trek with an armed park ranger.

Access

Arusha National Park consists of two main areas, the Ngurdoto Crater and Momella Lakes on the east side, and Mt Meru in the west, joined by a narrow strip of land. Momella Gate, the start of the trek, is at the centre of this narrow strip.

If you're driving, turn north off the main Moshi-Arusha road 1km east of a village called Usa River, onto a good dirt road. After about 10km this divides: the left fork (the Outer Road) crosses the park, but fees are not required for transit traffic; the right fork (the Park Road) goes through the park proper. The dirt roads rejoin at Momella Gate. If you have a vehicle you can leave it at Momella Gate, although park fees will have to be paid. Vehicles can also be left at Momella Wildlife Lodge, for a more reasonable fee.

For trekkers without a car, take any bus between Arusha and Moshi, and get off at Usa River. The fare is about US$1.50. From Usa River there's a bus and pick-ups (US$3) most days to the village of Ngare Nanyuki, about 10km beyond Momella Gate. Your other options are to hitch or walk. If you get a lift in a vehicle going through the park you'll have to pay park fees. This is no problem if you intend to start your trek up Meru on the same day, as fees have to be paid at Momella Gate anyway.

If you don't find a lift, the 24km walk from Usa River to Momella Gate along the Outer Road takes between six and eight hours. Many local people walk this way. The track rises very gently for the first 10km, passing through farmland and coffee plantations, to reach the fork where the Outer and Park roads divide. Keep left here. Just after the fork, the track passes through an area of grassland called Serengeti Ndogo (Little Serengeti). On the final 8km, the dirt road becomes rougher and steeper as it climbs towards the gate. Carry water, as sources are unreliable until the Mweka Wildlife College Ranger Post, about 5km before the gate.

If you stay at Momella Wildlife Lodge, you can arrange transport from Arusha to the start of the trek at the offices of Lion's Safari International, the owners of the lodge (see Places to Stay for details). Other Arusha tour companies can provide transport to Momella Gate (for around US$100 per vehicle, divided between up to five passengers), or you can arrange a one-day safari to Arusha National Park (for slightly more) which drops you at Momella Gate at the end of the tour.

Paying park fees and arranging guides and porters at Momella Gate can take a couple of hours. You can save time by making arrangements the night before. The park office officially opens at 6 am, but delays may occur.

Stage 1: Momella Gate to Miriakamba Hut
10km, 4-5 hours, 1000m ascent

Two routes are available from Momella Gate. The first is a track that goes through the forest towards the crater floor, and then steeply up to Miriakamba Hut, with a possible diversion onto the crater floor. The second is a path that climbs gradually through the grassland, along the lower section of the northern spur of the crater, direct to the hut. The first option is more interesting and is described here. The second option is shorter and makes a suitable descent route.

Miriakamba Hut could be reached by a

4WD, but this track is rarely used by vehicles, so you are unlikely to be disturbed.

From Momella Gate, cross the Ngare Nanyuki River and follow the track past the camp sites into the forest. The track winds uphill, and there are a couple of narrow paths which cut across the bends (the guide will show you). One hour from the gate is Fig Tree Arch. This is a parasitic wild fig which originally grew around two other trees, eventually strangling them. Now only the fig tree remains, with its distinctive arch big enough to drive a car through.

The track continues to climb, reaching Itikoni Clearing on the left side of the track, after another 15 minutes. From a small hill on the right, you can often see buffalo grazing in the clearing. Half an hour further on, the track crosses a large stream just above the Maio Falls, which are signposted down to the left. Continue for another hour, crossing the Jekukumia River (the last reliable water source until Miriakamba Hut), to reach Kitoto Camp, a wide open space overlooking the forest below, with excellent views over the Momella Lakes and plains beyond to Kilimanjaro in the distance. There is a ruined hut nearby. (From here, a path leads steeply up to Meru Crater floor, but this path is overgrown and difficult to follow. An easier alternative, described in the next section, is available.)

Continue following the track, passing a few faint grassy paths branching off, to reach a junction after half an hour. There's an old wooden signpost leaning on a rock. (The left track leads to the crater floor.) Take the right track, over flat ground, to cross a rocky stream bed (usually dry) and descend slightly through trees, ignoring the path that comes in from the left, to reach Miriakamba Hut (2514m), one hour from Kitoto Camp.

Miriakamba consists of two bunkhouses, large and well built, each with room for about 40 people. They contain bunk beds (most with mattresses) and a separate room to be used as a kitchen, although no cooking equipment is provided. The caretaker will provide a lamp if he has fuel. There are toilets, and a good supply of water.

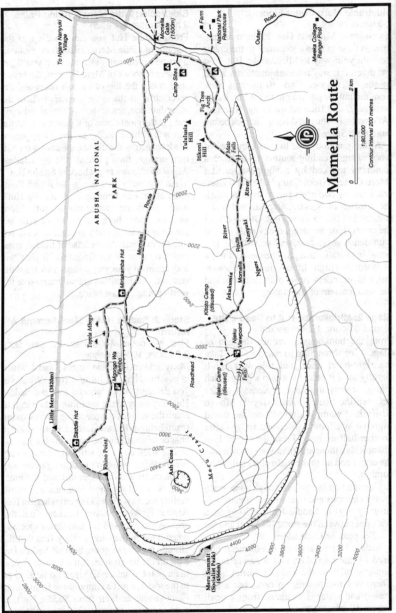

To Ngare Nanyuki
Village

Momella
Gate
(1500m)

Farm

National Park
Resthouse

Outer Road

Mweka College
Ranger Post

Camp Sites

Fig Tree
Arch

Tululusia Hill

Itikoni Hill

Maio Falls

Ngare Nanyuki River

Momella Route

2 km

1:80,000

Contour Interval 200 metres

0   1   2 km

ARUSHA NATIONAL PARK

Momella Route

Miriakamba Hut

Ngare Nanyuki River

Jekukumia River

Kitoto Camp
(disused)

Njeku
Viewpoint

Njeku Falls

Njeku Camp
(disused)

Roadhead

Topela Mbogo

Mgongo Wa
Tembo

Little Meru (3820m)

Saddle Hut

Rhino Point

Ash Cone

Meru Crater

Meru Summit
(Socialist Peak)
(4566m)

Sidetrack: Meru Crater Floor
2-3 hours return

If you leave Momella Gate in the morning, there is time to take a sidetrack to the crater floor on your way to Miriakamba Hut. You can divert this way from the junction marked by the old wooden sign, 30 minutes back from the hut, or go straight to the hut, dump your gear, and then return to the junction. (Alternatively, you can do this sidetrack before beginning Stage 2.)

At the junction, take the track by the old wooden sign heading south-west to reach a roadhead marked by a signpost reading 'Meru Crater, Njeku Camp'. A path continues, crossing two open grassy areas, to reach the remains of Njeku Camp (an old forest station) and Njeku Viewpoint. Other parts of the crater floor are steep, rocky and covered with dense vegetation, and so virtually impossible to walk through. The viewpoint is a platform on a high cliff overlooking a waterfall, with excellent views of the ash cone and the whole extent of the crater.

Stage 2: Miriakamba Hut to Saddle Hut
4km, 2-3 hours, 1050m ascent

From the bunkhouses, retrace the end of Stage 1 for about 50m to reach a fork. Take the right-hand track and follow it uphill slightly until it peters out into a path which climbs steeply up through pleasant glades between the trees, to reach Topela Mbogo (Buffalo Swamp) after 45 minutes and Mgongo Wa Tembo (Elephant Ridge) after another half an hour. From the top of Elephant Ridge there are great views down into the crater and up to the main cliffs below the summit.

Continue up the path, through some open grassy clearings and over several stream beds (usually dry) to Saddle Hut (3570m) on a wide col between the slopes of Meru and the smaller peak of Little Meru.

Saddle Hut consists of an old metal hut, used by the caretaker, and a newer bunkhouse similar to the ones at Miriakamba. There is a toilet (with no door, but a fine view!) and water is available from a small stream 10 minutes away.

Sidetracks: Little Meru & Rhino Point
2 hours return for each

From Saddle Hut you can walk up to the summit of Little Meru (3820m) in about an hour on a clear path. From the top you'll get impressive views of Meru Summit, the horseshoe crater, the top of the ash cone, and the sheer cliffs of the crater's inner wall. In the other direction, across the top of the clouds, you can see the great dome of Kilimanjaro. As the sun sets behind Meru, casting huge jagged shadows across the clouds, the snows on Kili turn orange, then pink, as the light fades. Allow 45 minutes to get back to Saddle Hut.

Alternatively, you can go to Rhino Point (also about one hour up from Saddle Hut), which is on the main route towards Meru summit. From here the views of Kili are similarly stunning and you can also see down into Meru Crater to the base of the ash cone and across the crater floor. You'll pass this way again on your way up and back from the summit, but the views are so impressive it's worth going at least twice.

Stage 3: Saddle Hut to Meru Summit & return
5km, 4-5 hours, 1000m ascent; plus 5km, 2-3 hours, 1000m descent

Many trekkers combine Stages 3 and 4, which is possible, but is a bit of a rush. Whatever you decide to do, it's usual to leave Saddle Hut very early in the morning (2 to 3 am) to reach the summit in time to see the sun rising from behind Kilimanjaro, and to stand a chance of avoiding the late morning mist.

The walk up to the summit, along a very narrow ridge between the sloping outer wall of the crater and the sheer cliffs of the inner wall, is one of the most dramatic and exhilarating sections of trekking anywhere in East Africa. However, some trekkers find this section too exposed for comfort, especially when done in the dark, or they find that the altitude makes the going beyond Saddle Hut a bit on the tough side. If the sunrise is your main point of interest, there's no need to go to the top. It's just as impressive from Rhino Point (about an hour from Saddle Hut), or even more so because you also see the main cliffs of the inner wall of the crater slowly being illuminated by the rising sun.

If you decide to go for the summit, take plenty of water. Even though it can be below freezing just before dawn, as soon as the sun comes up the going becomes hot and hard. During the rainy season, ice and snow can occur on this section of the route, so take care.

The ideal combination is sunrise at Rhino Point, then up to the summit for the views (depending on the mist). If you spend two nights at Saddle Hut you can still see the sunrise at Rhino Point, then trek up to the summit and back in daylight. If you're combining stages 3 and 4, it's just about possible to see the sunrise from Rhino Point, do the summit, and get back to Momella Gate before dark, although this doesn't leave a margin for delays.

To reach Rhino Point, take the path from behind Saddle Hut, across a flat area, tending left then steeply up through bushes. After an hour the vegetation gives way to bare rock and ash. Rhino Point is marked by a cairn and a pile of bones (presumably rhino, but what was it doing up here?).

From Rhino Point the path drops slightly then rises again to climb steeply round the edge of the rim over ash scree and bare rock patches. Continue for three to four hours to reach the summit (4566m). The views are, of course, spectacular. To the west, if it's clear, you can see towards the Rift Valley, and the volcanoes of Kitumbeini and Lengai, while down below you can see the town of Arusha, and the plains of the Maasai Steppe beyond.

To descend from the summit, simply retrace the route round the rim, back to Saddle Hut (two to three hours).

Stage 4: Saddle Hut to Momella Gate
9km, 3-5½ hours, 2000m descent
From Saddle Hut, retrace the Stage 2 route to Miriakamba Hut (1½ to 2½ hours).

From Miriakamba Hut, you can either return through the forest (2½ to three hours), or take a shorter route down the ridge which leads almost directly to Momella Gate (1½ to 2½ hours). This direct route goes through forest for some of the way, then through open grassland, where giraffe and zebra are often seen.

Other Routes on Mt Meru

There used to be two other routes up to the summit of Mt Meru, on the north and west sides of the mountain, but these fell into disuse after the national park was extended to include the entire mountain. The current route from Momella Gate is easier than these two old routes, as it makes a more gradual ascent. The paths that do exist on the north and west sides of the mountain have been cut through the forest by local woodcutters and poachers, and are not permanent.

Even if you could find any of the old routes or poachers' paths, special permission to use them has to be granted by the national park chief warden (because it involves entering the park at a point other than Momella Gate), and this process can take several months.

It's OK to walk on the western slopes, outside the park, but a local guide is recommended. We've heard from travellers who recommended a guide called Japhet Jackson, contactable through a company called Sunny Safaris (☎ (057) 7145; fax 8094) on Middleton Rd, a block north of the stadium, in Arusha.

With a guide, it's possible to go up into the forest, although this is technically illegal. It's also possible to get to the summit, which is definitely illegal, by leaving the edge of the forest at 3 am to get to the top by sunrise. This probably follows the disused route from the site of an old forestry hut at about 3600m, going straight up the steep scree on the western side of the mountain, to come out on the crater rim only a short distance down from the summit.

An illegal attempt on the summit cannot be recommended – this route is very strenuous and if you get into trouble you'll be on your own. Nobody will come and rescue you. In fact, it's likely that any guide who might agree to such an escapade will abandon you for fear of being reported to the police.

The Crater Highlands

The Crater Highlands are a range of volcanoes – not all extinct – rising steeply from the side of the Great Rift Valley in northern Tanzania. West of the Crater Highlands are the great savanna plains of the Serengeti, while to the south and east the land drops to the Rift Valley floor and Lake Manyara. Peter Matthiessen, who wrote about this area in his classic book *The Tree Where Man Was Born* called it 'the strangest and most beautiful of all regions that I have come across in Africa'.

For most people, a visit to the Crater Highlands means a day of wildlife viewing in Ngorongoro Crater – one of the best-known wildlife reserves in Africa. Its fame is undeniably justified, for nowhere else in Africa can you see so many different animals in such a spectacular area. But the Crater Highlands consist of much more than this.

Beyond Ngorongoro are several impressive peaks, with steep escarpments, crater lakes, dense forests and grassy ridges, streams and waterfalls. There's even an active volcano. It's also home to many Maasai people who have grazed cattle on the grasslands here for hundreds of years. This part of the highlands is an excellent walking area, but is very seldom visited.

GEOGRAPHY

The range known as the Crater Highlands is roughly oval in shape, measuring about 80km by 40km, pinched at one end, rising steeply from the surrounding plains at about 1500m to heights of between 2500m and 3500m.

Like many of East Africa's mountains, the Highlands are volcanic in origin although the different peaks were created over many millions of years by a series of eruptions connected with the formation of the Great Rift Valley. The older volcanoes have been eroded and most have collapsed to form the craters (more correctly known as calderas) which give the range its name.

At the southern end of the Crater Highlands are the oldest volcanoes, Oldeani and Lemagrut, with both summits at around 3100m. North-east of these lies Ngorongoro Crater, measuring some 20km across (making it one of the largest calderas in the world) with the rim at about 2200m. Inside the crater are examples of various vegetation and wildlife habitat, including forest, grassland, swamp, salt pans and a freshwater lake, with a wide range of animals to match.

North of Ngorongoro is the main part of the Crater Highlands, where the trek described in this section takes place. Only a few km away from Ngorongoro, the mountain of Olmoti rises to 3100m, which can easily be seen from Ngorongoro. East of Olmoti is Loolmalasin (3648m), the highest peak in the range, with its eastern side dropping steeply down to the plains near Engaruka. North of here is Empakaai (also spelt Embagai), with a steep-sided circular crater, partly filled by a lake. In between the peaks of Olmoti, Loolmalasin and Empakaai the ground dips to form the large Embulbul Depression.

At the northern end of the range is Kerimasi, one of the more recent volcanoes, rising to 2300m. Beyond this lies the Crater Highlands' northernmost mountain, Ol Doinyo Lengai (2878m), a classic volcanic cone with steep sides rising to a small flat-topped peak. Lengai was the last volcano of the Crater Highlands to be formed, and is still active. Its name means 'mountain of God' in the local Maasai language. The last big eruption was in the 1960s, and at the top of the mountain today you can see hot steam vents and growing ash cones.

TREKKING INFORMATION

Most of the Crater Highlands lie within the boundaries of the Ngorongoro Conservation Area (NCA). This is not a national park like Serengeti or Kilimanjaro, as it contains settlements and a permanent human population living alongside the wildlife. Unfortunately, the coexistence is not always completely peaceful (see the boxed text 'Maasai Land Issues').

Maasai Land Issues

Although the Maasai have grazed cattle for many centuries in the Serengeti, the Crater Highlands and surrounding parts of the Great Rift Valley, in the last two or three decades they have been forcibly excluded from much of their traditional homelands. The reason given for this is wildlife conservation – it has long been believed by some conservationists that the Maasai cattle compete with wild animals for grazing and water, while the large herds contribute to soil erosion.

Conservationists who take a broader view hold that the needs of indigenous people must also be included in any plan to conserve wildlife or natural resources, not for simple altruistic reasons but because without the full support of local people any conservation project is ultimately doomed to failure. (The principles of 'broad' conservation are discussed more fully in the Ecology & Environment section in the Facts about the Region chapter.) This subject is discussed in the excellent book *No Man's Land* by George Monbiot, in which the author – a highly respected investigative journalist – points out that in the name of conservation the Maasai have been excluded completely from the Serengeti and Mkomazi national parks because 'tourists did not like to see them there'. The Maasai were forced onto private farmland on the edge of the parks, became 'trespassers' and were unable to return to their traditional grazing areas. Of those Maasai that dared enter the national parks, many were fined and imprisoned. Those who stayed outside the parks, and managed to avoid trespassing on farmland, were safe – but, cut off from essential migration routes and grazing lands, their cattle all died of starvation.

Monbiot also writes about Ngorongoro Crater, another traditionally important grazing area, where the Maasai were excluded by conservationists 'to make it look as natural as possible'. At the same time, the Maasai saw new roads built to bring in tourists and new hotels being constructed on the crater rim. Ironically, most tourists would not find the presence of Maasai and their cattle in the national parks 'unsightly'; seeing traditional tribespeople would be another aspect of a visit to Africa. But a generation of tourists brought up on *Born Free* and TV wildlife documentaries simply don't expect local people to be mixed in with the animals. It shatters their illusions. And that could be bad for the tourist industry. So the Maasai remain excluded from much of their traditional homelands. Naturally, they feel that they are seen as less important than the wildlife or the tourists, and this leads to resentment. Many

Maasai have turned to poaching, some simply for meat because their cattle have died, others for ivory and rhino horn. The Maasai and the wildlife have co-existed for hundreds of years, but Monbiot says conservation has forced them to become enemies of nature: 'Conservation has done as much as anything to destroy the East African environment'.

Of course, there are those who argue against George Monbiot's assertions. But most of the Maasai would probably agree with them. As well as being excluded from their land, the Maasai also complain about being excluded from the revenue that is earned by the NCA. Although they are not at all the only answer to this major, and often overlooked, problem the treks across the Crater Highlands are one small way that the Maasai can benefit from tourism. Reading *No Man's Land* before you visit this area (or any part of East Africa) will increase your awareness of these issues, and add another dimension to a Crater Highlands trek. ■

DAVID ELSE

Due to the rugged terrain, and the presence of some fairly rugged animals, unaccompanied trekking is not allowed, although it is impossible to do things independently anyway. A vehicle and local guide are essential, as are donkeys to carry supplies and water. Nearly all visitors arrange treks through a tour company. Various specialists in Arusha operate treks across the Highlands, allowing several days of excellent walking through this fascinating landscape.

Organised treks in the Crater Highlands usually include a visit by vehicle to Ngorongoro Crater, or the trek can be included in a longer safari taking in the Serengeti and Lake Manyara as well. If you were planning a safari here anyway this is an ideal way to combine top-notch trekking and wildlife viewing, and it provides a chance to meet the local people in their own environment.

Costs

The cost of an organised trek in the Crater Highlands depends on the number of days, the quality of guides, vehicles, tents and equipment you require, and the number of people in your group. For precise information you must contact the companies arranging Crater Highlands treks listed under Organised Treks & Tours in the Tanzania Getting Around section. As an example, we heard from two travellers who arranged a seven-day (six-night) Crater Highlands trek in Arusha, which included an ascent of Lengai and two days of game viewing at Ngorongoro, for US$750 each, all inclusive.

The NCA fees (outlined opposite) comprise a considerable chunk of the cost of any trek in this area. The prices are on a par with a good trek on Kili, but the cost can be prohibitive for some people. To help put the payment of fees into perspective, see the boxed text 'Where Does all the Money Go?' earlier in this chapter.

Route Standard & Days Required

Trekking in the Crater Highlands is a fairly new activity, and there are no established routes. Most treks start just north of Ngorongoro Crater and head north via Olmoti and Empakaai to finish near Ol Doinyo Lengai.

Trekking in the Crater Highlands is not as strenuous as on the mountains of Kilimanjaro and Meru. You generally follow paths, although some sections cross trackless grassland. Some paths can be very dusty, but conditions underfoot are generally good.

Daytime temperatures on the high ground can be high (up to 28°C), although nights are chilly, with mist and rain not uncommon, especially in June, July and August. On the lower areas, around Lengai, it gets very hot, with daytime maximums often above 35°C

during the warm season (see the Tanzania Climate section).

Most of the walking is at about 3000m, so you might feel some slight effects of altitude, such as shortness of breath for the first day or two, but this is unlikely to be a problem.

The route outlined here is a suggestion only, to give an idea of what's available. There are many options, but it usually takes four days from Ngorongoro to Ngare Sero (the village near Ol Doinyo Lengai). This part of the trek can be cut to three days by driving Stage 1 and starting your trek at Nainokanoka. Stage 5, the ascent of Lengai, could also be cut if you were short of time or the required degree of energy. You should allow another day at either end of the trek for travelling by car to and from Arusha.

Fees

All visitors inside the NCA have to pay fees. For non-residents these are:

Entrance	US$25 per 24-hour period
Camping:	
public sites	US$20 per night
'special' private sites	US$40 per night
Vehicle:	
foreign-registered	US$30 to US$100
Tanzanian-registered	US$3

You also have to pay an extra fee to enter the Ngorongoro Crater. This is US$10 and includes the services of a park ranger, who acts as guide. There are plans to introduce an additional crater fee of up to US$50 for vehicles. You'll also have to hire a NCA ranger for the treks at US$20 per day, for every day he is away (including travelling days).

You may pay these fees yourself at the gate, but on organised treks all fees are normally included in the total price you pay the trekking company. When arranging your trek, check all fees are included.

Note that part of the trek covered in this section is outside the NCA, so you only pay for days you are inside. The northern boundary passes about midway between Empakaai and Lengai. The area may be extended in the future to include Lengai and the southern shore of Lake Natron. This will probably have no effect on the trekking itself, but it will mean having to pay a few days' extra fees.

Maps

The trekking area described in this section is covered in detail by the 1:50,000 DOS/government survey sheets 53/1 (Ngorongoro), 53/2 (Kitete), 39/4 (Ol Doinyo Lengai) and 39/2 (Mosonik). Gelai is on sheet 40/1 (Gelai). These are available from the map office in Dar (see Maps under Facts for the Trekker at the beginning of this chapter), but not in Arusha.

The whole Crater Highlands area is also covered by the Survey of Kenya 1:250,000 map sheets SA-36-16 (Oldeani) and SA-36-12 (Loliondo), which may also be available in the map office in Dar.

Probably the easiest map to find, especially in Arusha, is Ngorongoro Conservation Area, a beautifully crafted hand-drawn colour map covering the area from Lake Eyasi to Ol Doinyo Lengai, with two detailed maps of Ngorongoro Crater (one in the wet season, one in the dry). The same artist has also produced maps to the Serengeti and several other national parks.

Guidebooks

The Ngorongoro Conservation Area booklet, produced by David Bygott and the Wildlife Conservation Society of Tanzania, has a lot of good information about the wildlife and vegetation in the different zones within the NCA, plus sections on ecology, geography, history, and many other subjects. This book is usually available in Arusha.

For details on walking and driving routes beyond those given in this book, and further ideas about other mountains in the Crater Highlands area, the Mountains of Kenya guidebook (see the Kenya chapter for details) has a good section on Northern Tanzania.

Supplies

There are small shops at Ngorongoro village, plus a post office and petrol station, but only basics are available. There's a lot more choice in Arusha. On organised treks food is usually arranged and included in the price.

PLACES TO STAY

Arusha is Tanzania's safari capital, with plenty of accommodation (see the Mt Meru Places to Stay section).

On organised treks accommodation inside the NCA will be included. Where you stay depends on the type of trip you arrange. On the southern side of Ngorongoro Crater are (in ascending price order): The Drivers' Hostel, Rhino Lodge, Wildlife Lodge and Crater Lodge. There's also Simba Campsite on the crater rim. Camping is no longer permitted on the crater floor. On the north side of the crater is the top-end Sopa Lodge.

In the trekking area, there is nothing in the way of solid accommodation, so you must camp. There are some NCA 'special' (ie exclusive) camp sites with no facilities, or you can camp near the Maasai villages. To the north of the range, around Lengai and Lake Natron, there's a camp site and a tented camp, where you can stay in large walk-in tents or camp nearby.

GETTING THERE & AWAY

The Crater Highlands are about 200km west of Arusha by road. The main NCA entrance gate is at Lodoare, just south of the Ngorongoro Crater.

If you have a vehicle, you can drive to the NCA headquarters at Ngorongoro village, and make arrangements there. However, it will take at least a day for NCA staff to contact the local Maasai (and their donkeys). You'll also need to bring all your own gear and food for the trek, and arrange for someone to drive the car to the end of the trek to collect you, plus bring the ranger back to Ngorongoro.

If you don't have a vehicle, it's generally not worth hiring one, as it will be parked for several days while you're trekking, which is a complete waste of money.

For most visitors, the easiest way of doing things is to arrange an organised trek in Arusha. This is straightforward, cuts all the hassles about vehicles, guides, accommodation, food and so on, and is probably the cheapest option anyway.

Ngorongoro to Lengai

Area Ngorongoro Conservation Area
Distance 59km or 71km
Duration 3 or 5 days
Start Ngoronogoro Crater northern edge or Nainokanoka village
Finish Ngare Sero village, near Lengai
Nearest Large Town Arusha
Accommodation Camping
Access Organised trek
Summary Top quality trekking in a remote and rugged area, with wildlife viewing and a chance to meet the Maasai people in their own environment.
Note: independent trekking is impossible, and all trekking groups must be accompanied by an armed park ranger, plus donkeys to carry supplies and equipment.

There are no set routes in the Crater Highlands. The route outlined here, from Ngorongoro Crater across the heart of the range to Ol Doinyo Lengai, is one of many options. Your tour company may suggest other routes.

Access

After driving from Arusha, it is usual to stay at Ngorongoro on your first night and go into the crater for wildlife viewing. Late afternoon or early morning is best, when the animals are more active. On the second day, you can visit the Crater again by driving across and leaving by the northern track. In the area north of the crater you'll meet your Maasai guides and donkeys.

Stage 1: Ngorongoro Crater to Nainokanoka
12km, 4-5 hours

From the northern side of the crater, you walk through the forest on a good track to reach the ranger post near the village of Nainokanoka, your first night's camp. (Some treks start at Nainokanoka, in which case you can drive to this point, and the trek described here is done in four days.) Your vehicle returns to Ngorongoro village, and then drives round the eastern side of the Highlands to Ngare Sero to collect you.

Sidetrack: Olmoti
2-3 hours return

From Nainokanoka, you can sidetrack up through open forest to reach the summit of Olmoti Mountain, where there's a small crater and the spectacular Munge Waterfall. Water collected in the Olmoti crater flows down this waterfall and eventually into the lake in Ngorongoro Crater.

Stage 2: Nainokanoka to Empakaai Crater
25km, 7-8 hours

From Olmoti, you follow Maasai cattle trails north-east across the grasslands of the Embulbul Depression, towards Empakaai Crater, to reach the lightly wooded crater rim on its southern edge. A path circles the whole crater and you can follow this anticlockwise (east then north) to reach a low point on the western rim, where camping is possible, although there is no water. (Your guide will have arranged to fill containers at one of the streams crossed earlier.) The view from here down into the crater is stunning. The steep inner walls are densely forested and drop to the flat crater floor, which is partly submerged under a lake, often surrounded by huge flocks of flamingos. The Maasai are not allowed to graze cattle here, and there's a good chance of seeing wildlife.

Some groups descend into the crater itself and camp by the lake, although this means carrying gear as it's too steep for donkeys. It's more usual to go down into the crater in the morning of the next day and then do Stage 3 (which is short and easy) in the afternoon. Other groups camp on the rim for two nights and descend into the crater for a whole day.

Stage 3: Empakaai to Nairobi Village
7km, 2 hours

From the north or north-east side of the crater (depending on your route) you follow tracks which descend gradually to a village called Nairobi (also spelt Naiyobi). The name is derived from a Maasai word for 'spring' or 'bubbling water' (as is the name of Kenya's capital). Some groups camp in the village

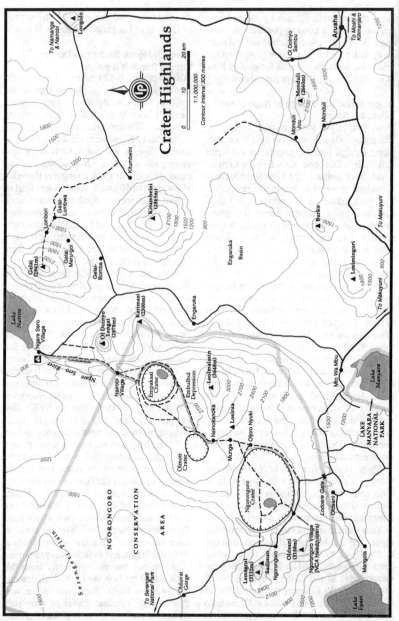

Crater Highlands

1:1,000,000

Contour interval 300 metres

0   10   20 km

itself on the football field by the primary school. This is a good opportunity to meet and talk with the locals, rather than just snap away with your camera. Other groups collect water here and may continue for another hour or so to camp in the bush beyond the village.

Stage 4: Nairobi Village to Ngare Sero
27km, 8-9 hours

From Nairobi, you follow paths through beautiful grassy hills and patches of light woodland, along a ridge running parallel to the main Rift Valley. The cone of Ol Doinyo Lengai, which has dominated the view since leaving Empakaai becomes increasingly impressive. The path passes a distinctive hill called Emowoengoilil (gazelle horn) and drops steeply, lush vegetation soon giving way to scrubby grass and patches of bare rock and lava. At the base of the steep section is a single tree (offering welcome shade) and a few remote Maasai huts.

The route continues north, losing height, with the main escarpment wall to your left. Lengai is on your right shoulder and then behind. The path becomes a sandy track as you pass some more Maasai settlements below the cliffs of the escarpment.

The first sign of civilisation is *Waterfalls Camp* a simple camp site on the banks of the Ngare Sero River, which flows north from the Crater Highlands into Lake Natron. After the long hot walk, a swim in the clear running water is very refreshing, but the water contains too many soapy minerals to be thirst-quenching. Drinkable water comes from a small separate spring.

About 1km further is *Lake Natron Tented Camp* – a smarter affair with large walk-in tents under sun-shades and better facilities. Nearby is the village of Ngare Sero, which boasts four small shops on its dusty high street.

Your vehicle should meet you here on this night, and the Maasai guides and donkeys will go back to Nainokanaka. From Ngare Sero, a rough dirt road leads south, along the eastern edge of the Crater Highlands, back towards Mto Wa Mbu and the main dirt road to Arusha. You can end the trek at Ngare Sero and return to Arusha the next day, or spend two nights camped here and go to the summit of Ol Doinyo Lengai on the day in between.

Stage 5: Ngare Sero to Ol Doinyo Lengai Summit & return
10km (approx), 8-10 hours

From Ngare Sero, Lengai is best approached on its western side. Between Ngare Sero and Lengai's lower slopes is three hours walking each way. It's important that your vehicle comes out to Ngare Sero the day before you do this stage, so you can use it to drive up a large gully on the north-west side, saving those six hours. It's still a long day though – allow eight to 10 hours. A very early start (4 or 5 am) is important in order to gain as much height as possible in the cool of the morning. Alternatively, you could camp the night here, so as to be on the spot for the next day's ascent. It's usual to hire a local guide from Ngare Sero for this stage.

From where the vehicle drops you, you follow a path through grassland at first, but this soon gives way to volcanic dust and ash (from the 1966 eruption), then bare rock. It's very steep and you have to keep to narrow exposed ridges between steep furrows and gullies, which can be difficult. It is also very hot: sun hats and a large water in-take are essential.

When you finally reach the rim, the hard slog is worth it. You can look down into the crater, and see steam outlets and the growing cones of volcanic ash. Obviously, this is a VERY dangerous area, and although people do it, dropping down to the crater floor is not advised.

To reach the summit, turn right (south) and follow a precipitous path which leads up to the highest point on the crater rim and the summit of Lengai (2878m). From here, the view back to the rest of the Crater Highlands (if not obscured by cloud) is splendid and you can see the route you took to get here. To the north you can look over the crater to Lake Natron and the dome of Shompole at its northern end, just over the Kenyan border.

If you can tear yourself away from this view, which really is most beautiful, descend by the same route. Take care on the way down: loose volcanic gravel on bare rock makes for perilous going in places.

Other Routes in The Crater Highlands

Your trekking in the Crater Highlands area can be extended for several more days, and will be restricted only by your own time and money. Some other mountains and areas which could be added to your trek are outlined below. For all, local guides are essential.

OLDEANI & LAKE EYASI

From Ngorongoro village you can reach the summit of Oldeani, the large dome-shaped peak overlooking the village from the south. This is about 1000m of ascent, mainly across open grassland, although there are a few patches of bamboo. ('Oldeani' is the Maasai word for 'bamboo'. It grows nowhere else on the Crater Highlands.)

From the summit you can look north-east across Ngorongoro and the whole Crater Highlands range, with excellent views all the way to Lengai if the weather is clear. To the north-west, the plains of the Serengeti stretch to the horizon, broken only by a few rocky kopjes and inselbergs. Also to the north-west are Oldeani's neighbouring peaks of Lemagrut and Sadiman.

Oldeani is shaped like a semicircle at the top, where a giant chunk has been blasted

---

People of Eyasi

The area around Lake Eyasi is inhabited by the Hadza (also called Watindiga), a very ancient people who are believed to have lived here for over 10,000 years. Their language is vaguely similar to that of the San ('Bushmen') of southern Africa. Also in this area are the Iraqw (also called Wambulu), a people of Cushitic origin, although they are comparative newcomers compared with the Hadza, having arrived in the area only about 2000 years ago. Also in the area are Maasai people, of Nilotic origin, and various Bantu groups. (For more details on peoples and their origins see the History section in the Facts about the Region chapter.) The Lake Eyasi area is possibly unique as it contains peoples belonging to all four main language groups of East Africa. ■

---

away by a volcanic eruption. The remaining rim dips in the middle, forming north and south summits. To the south-west, the land drops steeply to the hot area around Lake Eyasi. Along the northern shore of the lake runs the Eyasi Escarpment, also called Ol Doinyo Ailipi, an ancient fault-line that is part of the Rift Valley system. Eyasi is a soda (saline) lake and the surrounding land is hot and dry, except for a few spots where clear springs, running underground from Oldeani, emerge by the lake shore. In the past, adventurous trekkers have walked from Oldeani through the bush on paths down to Lake Eyasi. Some companies in Arusha may be able to arrange this. One guide who does this route is Japhet Jackson of Sunny Safaris (for more details see the Other Routes on Mt Meru section).

GELAI

Standing apart from the main Crater Highlands range, to the north-east of Lengai, is Gelai. This is a huge dome-shaped mountain about the same height as Lengai, but appearing much larger as the surrounding plains are lower. Using your vehicle, you could extend your trek by another day or two and reach this summit.

Note that dirt roads and tracks are very faint here and you may find yourself driving across bare open country. This is a harsh and remote area and driving here can be a serious enterprise, although this is all part of the attraction. If you add Gelai to your trek, you should ensure your vehicle is well equipped with water, fuel and spares. Very few drivers know this area, and only the specialised trekking and safari companies come here. This is no place for self-drive unless you are very experienced.

Access To reach Gelai from Lengai, follow the rough dirt road back towards Mto Wa Mbu, then branch off left on another track (if you can find it) heading east, then north-east round the base of Gelai, passing through the settlement of Gelai Bomba on the southern side, to finally reach another settlement called Gelai Lumbwa, on the eastern side of the mountain. A guide can usually be arranged here (although you'll probably need some basic Swahili). Leave your vehicle here.

Route From Gelai Lumbwa a path leads west up a small ridge towards a small collection of huts. This area is called Lombori. Continue in the same direction, through a grassy area which becomes more densely vegetated. There are many paths and cattle trails, but keep heading in the same direction. The final section, near the summit, is covered in dense vegetation, so a *panga* (machete) will come in useful. Allow eight to 11 hours to get to the summit and then back to Gelai Lumbwa.

Return Journey From Gelai, the usual way back to Arusha is on the small dirt road past Kitumbeini, to meet the main tar road between Namanga and Arusha opposite the rocky peak of Longido.

LONGIDO

Separate from the main Crater Highlands, Longido is a conical mountain lying just to the east of the main road between Arusha and Namanga (the Tanzania-Kenya border). Despite appearances it is not volcanic in origin, but a remnant of much older rock. The lower slopes are covered in dense bush, but Longido's summit is a peak of bare rock, giving excellent views west of the Rift Valley, north into Kenya south to Mt Meru and east to Kilimanjaro. A hike from the main road to the summit and back takes eight to 10 hours, and an early start is recommended to enjoy the cool morning temperatures.

The local Maasai people have organised themselves into a cooperative (assisted by SNV – the Netherlands aid organisation) and provide guides for walkers who want to reach the summit. They charge US$10 per person, and in 1997 the money raised was going to fund a cattle-dip. There's a small camp site and hut at the base of the mountain. Fit walkers can go up and down in a day.

You can also do easier walks around the base of the mountain, see the cattle, visit a *manyatta* homestead, and simply take the time to meet the people. Thousands of tourists come along this road, but very few ever stop, so a visit here is interesting and quite refreshing. This mountain is easily reached by public transport – take a bus or shared taxi between Arusha and Namanga and ask to be dropped at Longido. For more information visit the SNV office in the AICC in Arusha.

Other Trekking Areas in Tanzania

The mountains and routes covered in detail in this Tanzania chapter have been chosen because they provide interesting and exciting treks, and because most of them can be reached fairly easily by visitors. The following mountains will also be of interest to competent and adventurous trekkers looking for more areas to explore.

Monduli Mountains

The Monduli Mountains lie to the north-west of Arusha. This small range appears low and unimpressive when viewed from the southern side, but on the northern side it has high peaks and some fine open ridges which are ideal for walking. This is a good area to consider if you want do something other than Kili or Meru, but can't afford the time and money required for a trek in the Crater Highlands.

The northern side of the range has some very contrasting landscapes within a fairly small area. The lower slopes, at about 1000m, are covered by dry scrubland. On the middle slopes are Maasai settlements and a few small areas of cultivation, and the higher sections consist of open grassland, bamboo zones and swathes of dense forest. The highest point of the range is the summit of Monduli Mountain (2660m). There are several smaller peaks

forming a long ridge running west-east through the middle of the range. From the high ground, you can get great views down into the Rift Valley, and see the giant dome of Kitumbeini rising above the plains to the north, and sometimes the distant cone of Lengai, faint on the horizon.

Trekking Information

The base for trekking in this area is a private camp site at Monduli Juu, a small village on the north-west side of the range. You have to get permission to use the Monduli Juu camp site from Tropical Trails, a company in Arusha (listed under Organised Treks & Tours in the Getting Around section of this chapter). They operate walking safaris and can also advise on trekking routes and arrange local Maasai guides – essential for any walks in the area. However, it is very unusual for independent trekkers to come here; most people join an organised trek. Some other companies also run trips here including the similar sounding but unrelated Tropical Tours also listed in the Getting Around section.

From Monduli Juu you can walk for as many days as you like in the surrounding area. A popular option is a complete traverse of the main ridge, starting at Monduli Juu and heading eastward to finally meet the main road between Namanga and Arusha near Ol Doinyo Sambu. This trek takes three days, and can also be done in the opposite direction.

Mt Hanang

Some 180km south-west of Arusha is Mt Hanang. At 3417m (11,212 ft) it is the fourth-highest mountain in Tanzania. It is a grand volcanic cone, rising steeply above the surrounding plains, with an excellent trek to the summit, but very few visitors know of its existence.

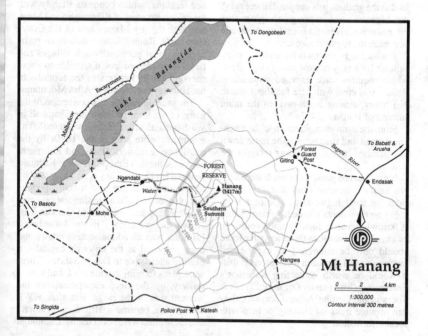

Mt Hanang
0   2   4 km
1:300,000
Contour Interval 300 metres

Getting There & Away

To reach Hanang, first get to Katesh, on the mountain's southern side. The road goes via Makuyuni and Babati, and buses to Singida pass through Katesh. From here, drive or walk to Ngendabi, on the mountain's west side, and ask around for a local guide. There is no accommodation here, so you need to be completely self-sufficient. Ask permission to camp outside the village.

Starting early, you can reach the summit and return in a day. An overnight trip would make the trek less arduous. Water supplies up high are unreliable and local porters not available.

The Route

From Ngendabi the route follows old cattle trails and paths through dense bush then along the crest of a large ridge, leading south-easterly up the mountain. After a few hours the bush thins out and you pass through trees and grassland as the gradient gets steeper. The trees give way to protea bushes as you gain height and the ridge narrows. Five to six hours from Ngendabi you reach the southern summit.

The southern summit is linked to the main summit by a very narrow rocky ridge crest, which requires some exposed scrambling. Follow this crest with care for about one to 1½ hours, aiming north-east, to the main summit of Hanang (3417m).

From the main summit, return to the southern summit and then retrace the route down to Ngendabi (five to six hours total for the descent).

It may also be possible to reach the southern summit directly from Katesh via the ridge up the left (western) side of a large valley on the mountain's south-western flanks. A knowledgeable local guide would be essential, and even then this alternative route should only be attempted by experienced trekkers. If you approach this area via Babati it would be worth contacting Kahembe's Enterprises (listed under Organised Treks & Tours in the Getting Around section); they can arrange treks on Hanang or help with local information.

Usambara Mountains

The Usambara Mountains rise above the coastal plains about 250km north of Dar es Salaam (340km by road). The range is not volcanic in origin but was created by uplift. Rather than the sloping sides found on many volcanoes, the edges of the Usambaras consist mainly of almost sheer escarpments, some up to 1000m high. At the centre of the range the two highest peaks rise to 2220m and 2400m.

Although the surrounding plains are dry and hot, these mountains catch the moist winds blown in from the Indian Ocean and receive a lot of rainfall. The land is fertile and the tops of the mountains are covered in patches of natural forest, while the lower slopes are intensely cultivated. There are many villages and scattered settlements across the range, linked by a network of paths and tracks. It is an interesting area for walking and trekking, which contrasts sharply with the wilderness areas of Kilimanjaro and Meru, and with the dry Maasai area of the Crater Highlands. Routes follow well-worn paths used by local people through villages and fields – conditions not dissimilar to those encountered by trekkers in the foothills of the Himalaya or the lower Atlas Mountains.

The mountains' title is a corruption of the name of the local people – the Shambali or Washambala, which means 'scattered'. The mountains were seen in the 1840s by the missionary explorers Krapf and Rebmann, who were the first Europeans to see Kilimanjaro and Mt Kenya. They were impressed by the fertile conditions and friendly people, and planned to build a mission station here.

When this area was part of German East Africa the main town in the Usambaras, Lushoto, was an administrative centre and once proposed as the colony's capital – a healthy alternative to Dar es Salaam. There were plans to bring a wide road, and even a railway, up the steep escarpments on the western side of the range. But after WWI, Tanganyika became a British protectorate and these plans were never realised, although

DAVID ELSE

DAVID ELSE

DAVID ELSE

Top: The jagged spires of Mawenzi (5149m) as seen from Stella Point, on Kilimanjaro.
Middle: Mt Kilimanjaro (5896m) is an impressive backdrop for East Africa's wild savannah.
Bottom: Picking their way between large boulders, trekkers head towards Barafu Hut, with the imposing snow-covered dome of Kilimanjaro behind.

DAVID ELSE

DAVID ELSE

DAVID ELSE

Top Left: Hard going near the top of Ol Doinyo Lengai, Crater Highlands, Tanzania
Top Right: Overlooking the inner ash cone from the crater rim on Tanzania's Mt Meru
Bottom: Easy walking through open grasslands near Empakaai Crater in the Crater Highlands region of Tanzania

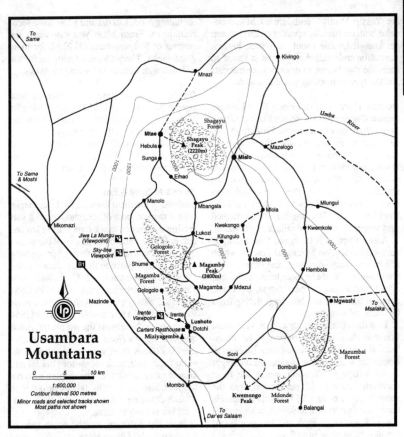

To Same

Kivingo

Mnazi

Umba River

Shagayu Forest

Mtae

Shagayu Peak (2220m)

Hebula

Mazelogo

Sunga

Mlalo

To Same & Moshi

Emao

Manolo

Mbangala

Mlungui

Mkomazi

Kwekongo

Mlola

Jiwe La Mungu (Viewpoint)

Lukozi

Kifungulo

Kwemkole

Sky-line Viewpoint

Gologolo Forest

Magambo Peak (2400m)

Mshalai

Shume

Hembola

Magamba Forest

Magamba

Mdezui

Gologolo

Mazinde

Irente Viewpoint

Irente

Mgwashi

To Msalaka

Carters Resthouse

Lushoto

Miziyagembe

Dotchi

Usambara Mountains

Soni

Mazumbai Forest

0   5   10 km

Bombuli

1:600,000

Contour interval 500 metres

Minor roads and selected tracks shown

Most paths not shown

Mombo

Kwemongo Peak

Mdonde Forest

Balangai

To Dar es Salaam

today Lushoto is the centre of various church and missionary organisations in Tanzania.

Trekking Information

There are no set trekking routes in the Usambaras. Basically, you can go where you like for as many days as you like, along the network of paths and tracks covering the area. A few destinations are suggested below. To reach some places, you can combine trekking with rides on a local bus.

Guides A local guide is highly recomended to show you the way and provide intro-

ductions in remote areas. There have also been a few incidents of tourists walking alone getting hassled by local youths, and even a case of robbery. To help visitors, a group of local young men have organised themselves into a cooperative (with assistance from SNV – the Netherlands aid organisation) and offer guiding services. Some of the funds raised go to support local tree planting and farming improvement projects.

The guides use the Green Valley Restaurant in Lushoto as a base, and can usually be found here every day. Evenings are the best time to catch them. Chief guides and organisers are Yassin Madiwa and Jeromy Mwambo-neke; both are friendly, speak good English and are knowledgeable about the routes, history, vegetation and wildlife of the area. It's usual to meet the day before to discuss your interests and the type of trekking you'd like to do.

Routes Places you can reach from Lushoto include Carter's Resthouse (see Places to Stay), two to three hours walk away. From there you can work your way north along the escarpment (although you have to come away from it in several places to get round deep gullies and ravines) to reach Irente Viewpoint. You can continue northwards to eventually reach Sky-line Viewpoint and Jiwe la Mungu (God's Rock), but these places might be better reached on a separate trip, via the village of Shume.

Another option is Gologolo Forest (and its southerly extension Magamba Forest), which has many indigenous trees and other plants, some unique to these mountains. Trips can also be arranged to local farms, or to see some of the historical buildings dating from German colonial times.

Two-day options include a trip to Mazumbai Forest in the south-eastern part of the mountains. It's usual to take a bus from Lushoto to Soni, start walking from there, and overnight at the village of Bumbuli, where the *local resthouse* costs US$2 per person, and the *mission hostel* costs US$4. Another option is the *Forest Department Resthouse* at Mazumbai Forest. Kwemongo Peak and Mdonde Forest can also be reached from Soni.

North of Lushoto lies Magambo Peak (2400m) the highest point in the Usambaras. It's best to take a bus to Magamba village and follow paths from there.

A good four-day trek goes from Lushoto to Lukozi (via Gologolo Forest), then to Emao (via some local farms), and to Mtae, a large village in the northern part of the mountains. It is noticeably drier on this side of the range; the views from the end of the ridge are spectacular over the South Pare Mountains and north across the plains of Tsavo in neighbouring Kenya. On a clear day, even Kilimanjaro can be seen on the horizon. Emao has a *mission hostel* which costs US$6 per person

including food; Lukozi and Mtae have *local resthouses*. From Mtae you can reach the summit of Shagayo Peak (2220m), for more great views. The walk goes through a section of forest with a chance of seeing monkeys.

Costs For a one-day walk, one to four people pay a fee of US$12 to the guide plus US$3 per person to the projects. For a trip more than one day, the group pays US$20 to the guide, plus US$3 per person per day to the projects. All other costs (transport, food, accommodation) are paid direct.

Places to Stay & Eat
Lushoto is the main town in the Usambaras, with a market, post office, shops, and a surprising number of snack bars selling tea and cakes. If you want to phone any of the places in Lushoto, you have to go through an operator.

The nearest place to the bus station is the *Green Valley Restaurant & Hotel*, with good value meals (including breakfasts) from US$1 to US$2, plus a well-stocked bar, discos (at weekends) and a few double rooms for US$4 out the back. Nearby, is the simple but much quieter *Kimunyu Hotel* where singles/doubles are US$2/3. A short walk away is the *Kilimani Resthouse*, with rooms for US$3/4 and simple meals available. The women who run the resthouse are friendly (although prone to double-charging attempts), and the courtyard bar is busy at night.

Near the Kilimani, on the south side of Lushoto, is the *Lawns Hotel* (☎ 66), a faded colonial-style place with singles/doubles at US$12/16 including breakfast. Meals are US$7, but not especially good value. In a similar price range is the vast and incongruous *Mandarin Grand Hotel* (☎ 14), still under construction when we passed through, although what *is* finished is good. Rooms range from small singles/doubles at US$10/14 up to US$30 for a triple suite, all en suite and with breakfast.

Outside Lushoto, at Miziyagembe, a peak jutting out from the western escarpment, you can stay at *Carter's Resthouse*. Carter, an American hang-glider pilot, and his friend George regularly fly off the escarpment here, and once trained a pair of augur buzzards to fly with them to indicate the best air currents and thermals. Strange but true. It costs US$8 to stay in the resthouse, US$4 to camp, and the money goes to a local tree-planting scheme. You can help with the planting.

On the road from Mombo up to Lushoto, just outside the village of Soni, you can stay at the exceedingly pleasant *New Soni Falls Hotel* (☎ 27), where singles are US$6 and en suite doubles US$15 with breakfast.

Beyond Lushoto are two other places to stay, more suited to visitors with vehicles as they're off the main bus routes. *Muller's Mountain Lodge* is an old colonial farm-house, complete with antiques, library and log fire, about 11km by road north-east of Lushoto, sleeping ten people in four rooms for US$30 per person including breakfast. Lunches and dinners are US$10. Even if you're not staying, passing walkers can call in for tea and coffee. You can get more info on this place at the BP garage in Lushoto, or from Rickshaw Travel (☎ 115620) in Dar. Close to Muller's is *New Grant's Lodge*, well signposted all the way from Mombo, where conditions are slightly better and prices are slightly higher. A taxi to either place from Lushoto will cost US$20. (Getting directions to these places can be confusing, mainly because until 1996 Muller's was called Grant's. Mr Muller replaced Mr Grant and Grant's was changed to Muller's, so Mr Grant set up New Grant's. Got that?)

Getting There & Away

Lushoto can be reached from Mombo, on the main road between Moshi and Dar es Salaam. There are some direct buses to Lushoto from Moshi and Dar (the fare is US$7), but it may be easier (although more expensive – US$10 to US$15) to get any bus running between Arusha/Moshi and Dar es Salaam, and get off at Mombo. Between Mombo and Lushoto minibuses go on a fill-up-and-go basis several times per day; the fare is US$1. The road up is steep and twisting, with some sheer drops off the edge of the road down into the valley below. The road was tarred in 1987. It must have been a nightmare before this.

You can also walk from Mombo to Lushoto up the old dirt road. This is now badly eroded and no longer used by vehicles, but it makes a good path and is used regularly by local people. To reach the start of the path, get to the north side of Mombo, just beyond the junction by the petrol station where the tar road to Lushoto branches off. A dirt track runs alongside the river. Follow this, over a bridge, past a wood yard and the secondary school. After this the path crosses some flat fields then starts climbing up the escarpment. It's clear and wide most of the way, and some narrow paths cut off some of the larger loops. There are many people around to ask the way if you're not sure. Allow five to six hours for the ascent. You meet the main tar road just south of Lushoto at a village called Dotchi. (There are quite a few places with this name in the area; it's a corruption of the word 'Deutsch', from the German colonial period.)

Eastern Usambara Mountains

Lying to the south-east of the main Usambaras, the Eastern Usambara range is a smaller group of mountains enjoying similar weather conditions, which is also well populated. Near the small town of Amani is a fascinating Forest Reserve and Botanical Garden, with several long and short walks possible in the area. The place was founded in 1902 by the 'Deutsch Ost-Afrika Geselschaft' and fell on hard times when the research centre was moved to Nairobi in the mid-1980s. The reserve and gardens have recently been revived by IUCN, the international conservation organisation. It has an extensive collection of tropical spice and fruit trees, and is used to promote the conservation of several endemic and endangered species of tree and shrub, many of which have medical properties.

Amani can be reached by public transport from Muheza, which is on the road between Segera and Tanga. The reserve headquarters has a *resthouse*, charging US$20 per person, and camping is sometimes permitted. One of the old German houses is being converted into a hotel. There are also some cheaper *local guesthouses* in Amani village. For the short walks, you can follow well-marked paths, but guides are necessary (and provided) for longer all-day walks in the forest. The guides at Lushoto can also arrange trips here.

Pare Mountains

The Pare Mountains lie south-east of Kilimanjaro and north-west of the Usambara range. There are two main groups: the North Pare Mountains and the South Pare Mountains. (Pare is pronounced 'Par-ay'.) Together with the Usambaras, they make up a chain of highlands sometimes called the Eastern Arc Mountains. The Pare Mountains stand just east of the main road between Moshi and Dar, so their steep cliffs and forested slopes are often seen by travellers, but they are rarely visited. For intrepid trekkers and hikers, the options are almost endless.

We heard from a traveller called David Wise (UK), who based himself at the village of Mwanga, on the main road about 50km south-west of Moshi, and did several day walks in the area. The mountain sides are heavily cultivated, with small villages linked by paths and tracks. From the high points, views over the plains to the west are superb. On clear days, Kilimanjaro to the north is an obvious feature. Mwanga can be easily reached by bus from Moshi, Himo or Mombo at the base of the Usambaras. The village centre, which has a large well-stocked market, is about 2km east of the main road. For a place to stay, the *Hotel Mamba* charges US$2 for basic rooms, but the food is good and the friendly manager is a good source of information on walks in the area. There is public transport along the road towards Usangi, which takes you further into the heart of the range.

Kipengere Range

The Kipengere Range lies in southern Tanzania, in the area between the towns of Mbeya and Njombe. This is part of a wider chain of hills and highlands stretching from the southern end of Lake Tanganyika to the town of

Cultural Responsibility

The people of the Kipengere Range are very unused to tourists, especially once you get off what might be called the 'main' routes. Naturally, most people are curious when they see foreigners with backpacks, but when we passed through this area we experienced no hostility, although camping near one large village we were visited by the local policeman to check that our motives were honourable.

We were greeted politely by everyone we met, and returned these greetings enthusiastically. After *'Habari?'*, the most common question we heard was *'Gari wapi?'* – 'Where is your car?'. Children were particularly polite, although often very shy. Most said *'Shikamuu'*, the traditional Swahili greeting used for addressing superiors, to which the correct response is *'Marahaba'*. We didn't have *'Muzungu'* called out to us at all. We were only asked for money once, by a very old lady who seemed ill.

Any visitor trekking in this region (or any other like it) carries a large responsibility to behave courteously towards the local community. You should greet all adults and children with respect and friendliness, and answer questions honestly and politely (even though you'll be asked them very often). Photos of people should be avoided, unless they specifically ask to have their picture taken.

If you buy food in small shops and markets, you're very unlikely to be overcharged (anything requiring transport will be expensive here), so avoid haggling or keep it to a minimum. If you camp near a settlement, always ask permission first, either from the village chief or any older man. If you want to show appreciation (eg to someone letting you camp on their land) a small payment is probably OK, but indiscriminate gift-giving of the 'pens to children' variety should be avoided.

The future of this area is in your hands. Remember – remote places only become 'spoilt' by the people who visit them. ■

Morogoro (west of Dar) – sometimes called the Southern Arc Mountains or Southern Highlands. This area is dotted with small villages, where the local people are subsistence farmers, and crossed by paths, tracks and small dirt roads. It offers endless opportunities for independent trekking, but there are no specific facilities for walkers and it is very rarely visited by tourists.

The most interesting and probably the most accessible parts of the Kipengere Range are the Mbeya Mountains and the Poroto Mountains, both reached from the large town of Mbeya. This is on the main road and rail route between Tanzania and Malawi, and might be a good place to stop off for a few days. The smaller town of Tukuyu, also on the Tanzania-Malawi overland route, is a useful base for exploring the region by foot.

Planning

Routes & Supplies The choice of walking routes in this area is almost endless; the following brief outlines will give you some ideas. For any walk involving overnight stops you should be completely self-sufficient with camping gear and carry most of your supplies. There is no accommodation and only limited foodstuffs available from village stores and markets. Few people in this area speak English, so some basic Swahili is also essential.

Maps Detailed maps are not available locally, but DOS maps (1:50,000) can be bought at the map office in Dar. The 1:250, 000 sheet covering the whole range is out of stock but may be reprinted.

Trekking & Hiking Routes

Your routes in this area will follow paths, tracks and small dirt roads. Traffic on the dirt roads is usually limited to one or two vehicles per day, sometimes not even that, but a combination of hitching and walking allows you to cover more ground.

Mbeya Mountains To the north of Mbeya town is the peak of Lolozi (2656m), also called Loleza and Kaluwe, which can be easily reached as a day walk. The lower

slopes are partly covered in forest, while the upper slopes are grassland, offering excellent views of the town and Poroto Mountains beyond, but it's best to avoid walking to the summit as a large telecommunications aerial has been built here, and the soldiers guarding it may think your motives suspicious. From the southern slopes of Lolozi you can follow paths onto the steeply undulating ridge which leads for about 5km west to the summit of Mbeya Peak (2826m), the highest point in this part of the range. West of here the ridge continues to Pungulomo (2273m), the third peak in the Mbeya Mountains.

Mbeya peak can also be reached direct from the village of Mbalizi, about 12km south-west of Mbeya town on the road towards Tunduma (the Tanzania-Zambia border). Many buses pass this way. From Mbalizi it's 8km on small dirt roads through farmland to Lunji Farm (also called Luji Farm), from where paths lead up to Mbeya Peak. The farm owners (a Swiss-Tanzanian couple) can sometimes provide a guide for this section if they have staff available. Fees and tips depend on the number of walkers and should be discussed before leaving. The walk up and down takes four to five hours.

From Mbeya Peak, instead of retracing, another option might be to go east along the ridge towards Lolozi, then drop down into Mbeya town. Allowing for the walk in from Mbalizi, this would be a serious all-day outing. Whichever way you go, you'll need warm waterproof clothing as storms are not uncommon here, plus a large water bottle – there is no water on the ridge.

Poroto Mountains The Poroto Mountains form the highest part of the Kipengere Range. There are four main peaks: Ishinga (2688m), Rungwe (2960m), Chaluhangi (2933m) and Motorwe (2961m), all lying to the east of the road between Mbeya and Tukuyu. A fifth peak, Ngosi (2621m) – most noted for its impressive crater lake – lies to the west of this road. Rungwe and Ngosi can both be reached as day walks from the village of Isongole, north of Tukuyu. A longer option is to go from near Isongole to Kitulo Farm (a former agriculture project headquarters) and from there north across the Kitulo Plateau (also known as the Elton Plateau, after a late 19th century British explorer) to the village of Matamba, then steeply down the range's northern scarp to Chimala, on the main road between Mbeya and Iringa.

If you could find transport from Mbeya or Tukuyu to Kitulo (there are occasional trucks), this walk would take two or three days. If you're walking the whole way from the Tukuyu-Mbeya road, plan on four or five days. A longer option is to continue east from Kitulo, following the old dirt road to Njombe – this would take the best part of a week.

Another alternative is to cross the Kitulo Plateau starting at Chimala and walking to Kitulo. Initial access is more straightforward, and in Kitulo it may be easier to find transport back to Mbeya or Tukuyu, but this direction involves more ascent, especially on the first day going up the scarp from Chimala.

A very interesting trip would be to follow the paths and tracks from Chimala up to Matamba, passing near Kitulo then continuing southwards, either to Tukuyu or all the way to Matema on Lake Malawi (Tanzania calls this section Lake Nyasa). Local people have been walking these routes for centuries.

Places to Stay

Mbeya The main town in this area is Mbeya,

Walking Safaris in Tanzania

The nature of walking safaris in East Africa is discussed fully at the end of the Kenya chapter. In Tanzania walking is not allowed in the main lowland national parks (such as Serengeti, Lake Manyara and Tarangire) but it is permitted in game reserves, conservation areas, and some smaller national parks in the south of the country.

Tanzania's most famous conservation area is the Ngorongoro Conservation Area (NCA), where long treks using donkeys to carry equipment are operated in the Crater Highlands by various Arusha-based safari companies (see Organised Treks & Tours in the Tanzania Getting Around section). To the north-east of Tarangire National Park is Tarangire Wildlife Conservation Area (TWCA), where a unique scheme in wildlife conservation allows local people to benefit directly from tourist revenue. The landscape is very similar to that inside the park, and as there is no fence the animals roam freely between both areas. Walking safaris are operated here by Let's Go Travel (see Organised Treks & Tours in the Tanzania Getting Around section), with rates from US$100 per day.

National reserves where 'normal' game viewing can be combined with walking safaris include Selous National Reserve, in the south-west of Tanzania. It is one of the largest protected wildlife areas in the world (covering around 50,000 sq km), with a very wide range of habitats and associated animals. Other places where short walking safaris are arranged include the national parks of Ruaha and Katavi, also in the south.

The parks and reserves of southern Tanzania were virtually ignored during the 1970s and 1980s as the country concentrated its tourism efforts on the famous northern areas such as Serengeti and Manyara. But since the early 1990s, as the high profile parks have become more crowded, the southern parks have started to receive visitors once again. They are still known for their feel of remote wilderness, which appeals to Africa aficionados. Animals are not habituated to human presence and tend to be more timid than their northern cousins. Lion and elephant may take some searching out, but when you find them your view will not be spoilt by a herd of other vehicles.

In Selous, places to stay include *Mbuyu Camp*, operated by Southern Tanzania Game Safaris; they organise a wide range of safaris from three to 14 days, travelling by vehicle, boat and foot, based in Selous and also visiting Ruaha. They arrange one-day walking safaris or longer trips using overnight 'fly camps' in the bush. Another place is *Mbuyuni Luxury Camp* (Selous Safari Co), also offering one-day walking safaris and fly camps. For more information, both places have offices in Dar es Salaam (listed under Organised Treks & Tours in the Tanzania Getting Around section).

In Ruaha, places to stay include *Mwagusi Safari Camp* and *Ruaha River Lodge*, both operated by Foxtreks (listed in the Tanzania Getting Around section). They offer mostly vehicle trips, with short walking safaris available. The only operator taking vehicle and walking safaris into remote Katavi National Park is Tent with a View (listed in the Tanzania Getting Around section). They also have a lodge and run walking and boat safaris in Sadaani National Reserve.

As in Kenya, rates for remote lodges and walking safaris are not cheap. Most start between US$100 which has a wide choice of places to stay. The *Nkwenzulu Hotel*, opposite the bus station, is a long-time favourite where basic but clean rooms cost from US$3 to US$7. Shoestringers aim for the *Moravian Youth Hostel* on a quiet road to the east of the bus station, with double rooms for US$5, but we've heard from more than one set of people who got mugged walking here, so take great care. Another cheap choice is the *Warsame Guesthouse* on Sisimba St, in the town centre near the market. There's a huge list of rules, but it's clean and friendly with single/double rooms at US$4/6, and several good eating houses nearby.

East of the centre are three more places,

reached by a dusty road between the market and the stadium. The nearest to town is the faded *Mount Livingstone* (☎ 3331) used by tour groups but pricey for individuals at US$40/60 for en suite rooms. Better value is the new *Rift Valley Hotel* (☎ 3756) charging US$20/25 for en suite rooms. Next door, the *Holiday Lodge* has basic double rooms for US$3 (en suite US$5). To reach any of these, if you've come by bus, a taxi from the bus station to the hotel is recommended. If you've come by train, the Tazara station is a few km outside town, so a taxi is almost essential.

Tukuyu Tukuyu is a much smaller place than Mbeya. There are a couple of cheap lodging

and US$150 per person per day full board, and several go up to US$250 or more. This normally includes reserve entrance fees, down from US$25 to US$15 per person per day in 1997 to encourage more visitors to the southern parks and reserves. You also have to add US$10 to US$30 extra for walking safaris, plus the cost of flights to/from Dar es Salaam (US$160 return for Selous). A notable exception is Sadaani, which is more accessible and more reasonably priced. If you're in Tanzania, contact Rickshaw Travel in Dar (listed in the Tanzania Getting Around section) – they often have special all-inclusive flight and lodge deals available which can cut costs considerably. If you do have the money for a walking safari, it's a good way to see wildlife in a pristine environment, and a very good way to unwind after a high mountain trek! ∎

DAVID ELSE

houses along the main street, but most travellers recommend the *Langiboss Hotel*, a couple of blocks east of the main street, where rooms start at US$3. Tukuyu is a major trading centre, and the hotel manager here can help with information on trucks heading from the market up to isolated villages in the Poroto range and beyond.

Getting There & Away

Bus There are several buses each day between Dar and Mbeya. Express fares start at US$10. Many travellers use the Tazara train between Dar and Mbeya, where they switch to a bus for the trip to the Malawi border at Songwe (for details see Malawi in the Getting There & Away section of this chapter).

If you're coming from Arusha or Moshi and don't want to go to Dar, there's a daily bus from Arusha to Mbeya. The fare is US$32. The bus departs at 6 am and arrives at 11 pm. Another option for avoiding Dar, if you're heading straight from Arusha/Moshi/Lushoto to southern Tanzania, is to change at Chalinze, where you can pick up buses from Dar heading south to Mbeya.

Train The Tazara line links Dar and Mbeya (and continues into Zambia). For details on trains and fares, see the Getting There & Away and Getting Around sections of this chapter.

Kenya

Kenya is one of the most popular tourist destinations in sub-Saharan Africa. Some visitors come for the world-famous wildlife reserves of Tsavo and the Masai Mara, while others come for the Indian Ocean coast: package tourists from Europe head for the Mombasa resorts, while travellers head for Lamu, the 'Kathmandu of East Africa'.

For trekkers, the main attraction is Mt Kenya, the highest mountain in the country and the second-highest in Africa, with an excellent selection of long and short treks. But Kenya has more than just one high mountain: other places for high-altitude trekking are the mountain wilderness areas of the Aberdare (Nyandarua) Range, in the Aberdare National Park, and Mt Elgon, straddling the Kenya-Uganda border in the far west of the country.

Away from these high mountains, trekking is also possible on the Rift Valley escarpment and through the forests of the Loroghi Hills, or through the rolling downs and farmland of the Cherangani Hills, where conditions are less strenuous, and visitors can meet traditional Kenyan farmers or nomadic herders in their own territories. Further north, you can trek through the blistering desert of the Suguta Valley, as far removed from the glaciers, mist and hail of the highlands as it's possible to get.

DAVID ELSE

Kenya – Trekking Highlights
Mt Kenya is Africa's second-highest peak and one of the region's main attractions for trekkers, with a wide range of routes for all tastes and abilities. For intrepid visitors, the **Aberdare Range** and **Mt Elgon** also offer excellent high-altitude wilderness trekking. In contrast, the **Cherangani Hills** and the **Loroghi Hills** provide less strenuous and more accessible options.

Facts about the Country

HISTORY
The early history of Kenya up to the end of the 19th century is closely linked with that of other East African countries, and this is covered in the Facts about the Region chapter.

The Colonial Period
By 1886, after the Berlin Conference, the European powers had neatly divided Africa into spheres of influence. The territories claimed by Germany and Britain were divided by a line drawn from the coast to Lake Victoria; south of this line was German East Africa, to become Tanganyika and then Tanzania, while to the north was the protectorate of British East Africa, to become Kenya and Uganda.

But the British government was reluctant to develop the Kenya Protectorate. The fertile land of Uganda was seen as more valuable. To link Uganda to the coast, a railway was built from Mombasa to Lake Victoria. This massive project, called by many the 'Lunatic Line', was completed in 1903. Thousands of labourers from India were brought in for the construction work and many remained in East Africa after the line was finished.

KENYA

To fund the railway Britain tried to exploit the surrounding land and actively encouraged European settlement. By this time Nairobi, originally built as a temporary rail depot, had become the capital. In 1920 the protectorate became the Kenya Colony, but although this changed things for the European settlers (and, to a lesser extent, the Indians) it had little effect on the African population. So during the 1920s and 1930s several African organisations – including the Kikuyu Central Association, led by Jomo Kenyatta – campaigned for land rights and improved working conditions.

Transition & Independence

After WWII opposition finally crystallised into the Mau Mau rebellion, or The Emergency, which lasted from 1952 until 1957. During this time, guerrilla fighters mostly from the Kikuyu territories of the Central Highlands attacked settler farms and plantations, and villages where inhabitants were held to be pro-European. The British retaliated by setting up 'defensive villages', which were intended to protect local Kikuyu who resisted the Mau Mau guerrillas, although some writers have compared them to concentration camps.

At the end of The Emergency, the need to include more Africans in the running of the colony was recognised. By 1960 there were more African than European members in the colony's legislative council, and two African political parties had been formed: the Kenya African Democratic Union and the Kenya African National Union (or KANU), led by Kenyatta. In 1963 Kenya gained full independence and a year later the country became a republic, with Kenyatta as president.

Kenyatta advocated a mixed economy of agriculture and industry with private and state investment. He encouraged personal effort and group co-operation in a doctrine called Harambee, meaning 'all pull together'. Kenyatta died in 1978 and was succeeded by his vice-president, Daniel Arap Moi, who continued to encourage the development of Kenya as a nation, while at the same time strengthening his position and consolidating the power of KANU.

Modern Times

In 1982 Kenya became a one-party state, and by the end of the 1980s Moi was unassailable. All opposition had been outlawed or crushed and independent bodies (such as the judiciary) brought under political control.

But in 1990 things began to change. In the new era of post Cold War global politics, Kenya's 'anti-Communist' stance was no longer valuable to western countries. Moi was encouraged to release political detainees and legalise opposition parties. In Nairobi there were several large demonstrations calling for political reform.

At the end of 1991, Moi gave way to the pressure and multi-party politics were introduced. The pressure group Forum for the Restoration of Democracy (FORD) became a legal party, and the main opposition to KANU.

Kenya's first multi-party elections for 20 years were held in December 1992. The opposition parties were split by in-fighting and KANU retained power by a narrow majority.

The various FORD groups remained divided through the rest of the early 1990s, allowing Moi and KANU to remain secure. In 1995 a new party called Safina was formed by several major opposition figures including Richard Leakey (son of the famous palaeontologists) who'd earlier resigned as head of Kenya Wildlife Services. To counter this new threat KANU played the race card, claiming that 'neo-colonialists' and 'settlers' should stay out of politics, even though Leakey is a Kenyan-born citizen.

Many Kenyans are in favour of Safina, but there's still considerable support for KANU in some parts of the country. The next elections are due in December 1997. Political corruption and embezzlement remain major problems, while at grassroots level Kenya has a high population growth rate. Lack of schools, health care and job opportunities are just some of the social problems which will have to be faced by the next government, whichever party wins.

GEOGRAPHY

Kenya measures about 900km north to south and 750km east to west, covering around

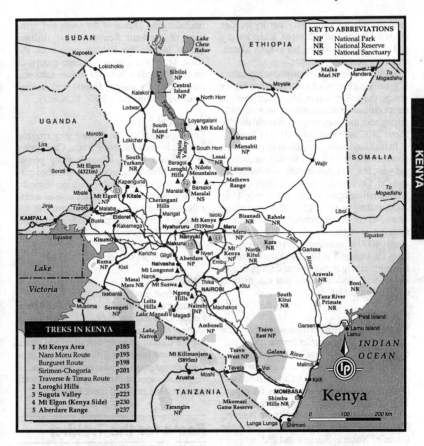

600,000 sq km – about half the size of Tanzania. Kenya has a wide variety of landscapes, ranging from sparsely inhabited desert in the north, through farmland, forest and highlands in the central region and grassy savanna in the south, to a humid coastal plain bordering the Indian Ocean.

The highland areas of the central region (called, not surprisingly, the Central Highlands) are dominated by Mt Kenya – the country's highest mountain. The Central Highlands' other main massif is the Aberdare Range, still widely known by its colonial name, although its local name is Nyandarua.

Kenya's other major mountain area is Mt Elgon, on the border with Uganda.

The Great Rift Valley runs the length of the country. Its lowest point is around Lake Turkana in the north, only 250m above sea level. At its highest point, the valley floor rises to about 1800m, with the top of the Rift escarpment a further 700m above that, as it passes through the Central Highlands.

CLIMATE

Kenya's climate is determined by the band of rain that moves over East Africa, giving two wet seasons and two dry seasons each year. For most of the country, the dry seasons are late May to early October, when it's dry and cool, and late November to early March, when it's generally warmer.

Within these broad seasons, temperature is greatly influenced by altitude: the higher you go the colder it gets. Maximum daytime temperatures on the coast are around 28°C throughout the year, while in Nairobi they're about 24°C in January and 20°C in June.

In highland areas, maximum daytime temperatures rise and fall only slightly throughout the year, but vary considerably between night and day. On the hills and lower slopes, maximum daytime temperatures are around 15 to 20°C, falling to 10 to 15°C in the moorland zones, where the temperature hovers around freezing at night. On the high mountains, above 4000m, maximum daytime temperatures are around 5 to 10°C, and always below freezing at night, sometimes dropping to -10°C, with violent winds that can make it seem much colder.

ECONOMY

Kenya's economy is predominantly based on agriculture. In rural areas people either cultivate a small plot of land *(shamba)*, growing food for their own needs plus a surplus to sell in local markets, or work on larger farms and plantations, often producing crops for export. Industrial development, although high by the standards of the region, is limited to Nairobi, Mombasa and, to a lesser extent, the large towns of Nakuru, Kisumu and Eldoret.

Tea and coffee are Kenya's main exports, but the largest provider of foreign currency is tourism. Over half a million tourists a year were coming to Kenya at the end of the 1980s, but political and civil unrest through the first half of the 1990s led to a sharp drop in this figure, which has had detrimental effects on the economy as a whole.

POPULATION & PEOPLE

Kenya's population was estimated at 28 million in 1996, growing at about 4% a year, which was one of the fastest rates in Africa. Most African people in Kenya are either Bantu (including the Kikuyu of the Central Highlands) or Nilotic

(including the Maasai of the south and Samburu of northern Kenya). Other distinct groups include the Swahili people on the coast. In the cities there are large groups of people originating from the Indian subcontinent (generally called Asians) and several thousand Europeans, mainly in Nairobi.

RELIGION

The population can be divided very roughly into thirds, each following Islam, Christianity or traditional beliefs, although many people combine African tradition with established religions, which makes categorisation difficult. Islam is practised mainly in the coastal areas, although most large up-country towns have a mosque. Christian groups include mainstream Catholics, Protestants and Nonconformists, originally introduced by European missionaries, as well as several local African faiths.

LANGUAGE

All the main groups in Kenya have their own language and Swahili is used as a common tongue. On the coast, Swahili is a language in its own right, but as you get further into the interior it becomes more simplified and basic. In cities and towns English is also used as a common language by educated people, and is very widely spoken. Anybody connected with the tourist business will speak English too.

Facts for the Trekker

PLANNING
When to Trek

The best time for trekking in Kenya is during the dry seasons, from the end of May to early October, when the weather is cool, and from late November to early March, when it's generally warmer (see the Climate section).

Because weather patterns in East Africa are becoming less predictable, you could take a chance on going up Mt Kenya in mid-November and you may get several days of good weather. Alternatively, it could still be raining heavily in December, which might mean snow blocking the route up to Lenana.

Don't forget that even in the dry seasons it can still rain. I've seen thick snow on the summit of Mt Kenya in August, and hail on Mt Elgon at the same time of year. You should be prepared for bad weather at any time.

Maps

For general travel around the country or in between trekking areas, the *Kenya Traveller's Map* published by Macmillan is one of the best. It shows all but the very minor roads and has contour shading. On the back is a Nairobi street map and various bits of tourist information. Macmillan also produce good maps of some high profile national parks and reserves, including Amboseli and the Masai Mara. Other maps of the whole country are published by Nelles, Freytag & Berndt and Survey of Kenya (SK).

For specific coverage of the mountains and trekking areas included in this chapter, more detailed maps are available (these are listed in the individual trekking sections).

The country is covered by SK maps to scales of 1:50,000, 1:100,000 and 1:250,000, but many are not sold to the public for security reasons, unless you go through an elaborate and time-consuming application procedure. And even then success is not guaranteed. This regulation may change, so details on SK maps are given in the individual trekking sections. The SK Public Map Office is on Harambee Ave in Nairobi, near the Kenyatta International Conference Centre.

TOURIST OFFICE

Unbelievably, in a country economically dependent on tourism, there is no public tourist office in Kenya.

VISAS

Visas are required by citizens of most countries, except those from some European countries (including Denmark, Germany, Ireland, Italy, Norway, Spain and Sweden). Citizens from some Commonwealth countries are also exempt (British visitors do not need visas). Citizens of the US, France, Canada, Australia and New Zealand do need visas.

Visas cost around US$20 to US$50 (or the equivalent in local currency), depending on your nationality, and are available from Kenyan embassies (listed below) and at Nairobi airport on arrival (although it's better to get one in advance if you can). Visas remain valid for between one and three months. Your Kenyan visa remains valid if you go to Tanzania or Uganda and return to Kenya.

Entry regulations are always liable to change, so it's worth checking the latest situation at your nearest Kenyan embassy, high commission or tourist office.

EMBASSIES
Kenyan Embassies Abroad

Kenyan embassies, consulates and high commissions abroad include:

Australia
    QBE Building, 33 Ainslie Ave, Canberra, ACT 2601 (☎ (02) 6247 4788; fax 6257 6613)
Belgium
    1-5 Avenue de la Joyeuse, 1040 Brussels (☎ (02) 230 3065; fax 230 8462)
Canada
    415 Laurier Ave, Ottawa, Ontario KIN 6R4 (☎ (613) 563 1773; fax 233 6599)
France
    3 Rue Cimarosa, 75116 Paris (☎ 01 45 53 35 00; fax 01 45 53 95 32)
Germany
    Villichgasse 17, 5300 Bonn-Bad Godesburg 2, Micael Plaza (☎ (0228) 356042; fax 358428)
Italy
    Via Icilio No 14, 00153 Rome (☎ (06) 578 1192; fax 5742 2788)
Japan
    24-3 Yakumo, 3 Chome, Meguru-ku, Tokyo 152 (☎ (03) 723 4006; fax 723 4488)
Netherlands
    Niewe Parklaan 21, 2597 The Hague (☎ (070) 350 4215; 355 3594)
South Africa
    302 Brooke St, Menlo Park, Pretoria (☎ (012) 342 5066)
Sweden
    Birger Jarlsgatan 37, 2tr, 10395 Stockholm (☎ (08) 218300; fax 209261)
Tanzania
    NIC Investment House, Samora Ave, PO Box 5231, Dar es Salaam (☎ (051) 46362; fax 46519)
Uganda
    Plot No 2030, Muyenga Kansanga Rd, PO Box 5220, Kampala (☎ (041) 267386; fax 267369)

UK
>45 Portland Place, London W1N 4AS
>(☎ (0171) 636 2371; fax 323 6717)

USA
>2249 R St NW, Washington DC 20008
>(☎ (202) 387 6101; fax 462 3829)

Foreign Embassies in Kenya

Countries which maintain diplomatic missions in Kenya include the following (all in Nairobi). Some are open in the afternoon, but the best time to visit is between 9 am and noon. The telephone code for Nairobi is ☎ 02.

Australia
>Riverside Drive (☎ 445034; fax 444617)

Canada
>Comcraft House, Haile Selassie Ave (☎ 214804; fax 226987)

Denmark
>HFCK Building, Koinange St (☎ 331088; fax 331492)

Ethiopia
>State House Ave (☎ 723027; fax 723401)

France
>Barclays Plaza, Loita St (☎ 339783; fax 220435)

Germany
>Williamson House, 4th Ngong Ave, (☎ 712527; fax 714886)

Israel
>Bishops Rd (☎ 722182; fax 715966)

Japan
>ICEA Building, Kenyatta Ave (☎ 332955; fax 216530)

Malawi
>Waiyaki Way, Westlands (☎ 440569; fax 440568)

Netherlands
>Uchumi House, Nkrumah Ave (☎ 227111; fax 339155)

New Zealand
>Minet-ICDC House, Mamlaka Rd (☎ 722467; fax 722549)

South Africa
>Lonrho House, Standard St (☎ 228469; fax 223687)

Spain
>Bruce House, Standard St (☎ 335711; fax 332858)

Sweden
>International House, Mama Ngina St (☎ 229042; fax 218908)

Tanzania
>Continental House, corner of Uhuru Highway and Harambee Ave (☎ 331056; fax 218269)

Uganda
>Uganda House, Baring Arcade, Kenyatta Ave (☎ 330801; fax 330970)

UK
>Upper Hill Rd, Nairobi (☎ 716064; fax 712233)

USA
>Moi Ave (☎ 334141; fax 340838)

MONEY

This section covers money in Kenya. Outlines of costs and other general money aspects are given in the Regional Facts for the Trekker chapter.

Currency Exchange

The unit of currency in Kenya is the Kenyan shilling (KSh), divided into 100 cents. Inflation in Kenya is high and unpredictable. Therefore we have quoted prices in US dollars (US$) throughout this chapter. Although the actual exchange rate may have changed by the time you reach Kenya, the cost of things in US$ (or any other hard currency) will not have altered much. The approximate exchange rates in 1997 were:

US$1	=	KSh 60
UK£1	=	KSh 90

Changing Money

You can change money at a bank or bureau de change, but note that you won't need too many shillings as national park entry, organised treks and all but the cheapest hotels can be paid for in hard currency (or KSh at the current rate). Although most hard currencies are officially acceptable, US dollars are the most convenient way to pay.

If you are travelling between Tanzania and Kenya, advice on taking currency over the border is given in the Tanzania chapter.

BOOKS

Books covering all or part of East Africa are listed in the Regional Facts for the Trekker chapter. Guidebooks on individual mountain areas are covered in the relevant sections.

Guidebooks

Among the many general guidebooks that have been written about Kenya, Lonely

Planet's *Kenya* and *East Africa* are natural companions to this book, with detailed information for all styles of independent traveller.

For more specialised guidance, the Mountain Club of Kenya has published *Mountains of Kenya*, a 'blatant peak-baggers' guide' to almost 100 summits in Kenya and northern Tanzania, aimed mainly at residents or visitors with their own vehicles. It costs US$16 and is available in Nairobi bookshops.

Guidebooks on individual mountains and trekking areas are covered in the relevant sections.

General

General books of interest to trekkers include the many large format books produced by Mohamed Amin and his Camerapix crew: *Journey Through Kenya* provides good information and excellent photos; more specific is *On God's Mountain* which covers Mt Kenya. The pictures are what you'd expect from Africa's leading photographers, and the accompanying text covers all aspects of the landscape and history of the mountain.

Smaller, more portable, books include *No Picnic on Mount Kenya* by Felice Benuzzi – a ripping yarn of three Italian prisoners of war who escaped from a camp in Nanyuki during WWII, and climbed halfway up Batian and all the way to Lenana on Mt Kenya, using homemade equipment and a meat tin label for a route map. Also worth looking out for is *The First Ascent of Mt Kenya* by HJ Mackinder, the journal of his 1899 expedition. Both books have been recently reprinted and are available in Nairobi.

Journey to the Jade Sea by John Hillaby is the story of one man's walk through northern Kenya to Lake Turkana. *In Teleki's Footsteps* by Tom Heaton covers similar ground, plus Mt Kenya, Kilimanjaro and the Rift Valley, as the author follows the great explorer's route through Kenya and Tanzania on foot and by bike. If you're walking in northern Kenya, *Nomad* by Mary Anne Fitzgerald provides an immediate and fascinating insight into current aspects of the Samburu and Turkana lifestyle.

Another book on nomads is *No Man's Land* by George Monbiot, an incisive and disturbing account of recent hardships suffered by pastoral people in Kenya and Tanzania (most notably the Maasai), resulting from the attitudes of settled people and the increase of tourism. (See also the boxed text 'Maasai Land Issues' in the Tanzania chapter.)

Bookshops

Several very good bookshops in Nairobi carry huge stocks of maps and books (local and foreign) on Kenya, including most of the ones mentioned above. The Nation Bookshop (next to the New Stanley Hotel in the city centre) and the Text Book Centre (several outlets around the city selling all kinds of books) are recommended.

USEFUL ORGANISATIONS

The Mountain Club of Kenya (PO Box 45741, Nairobi) is a members' club for local climbers. Meetings are held every Tuesday at 8 pm in the clubhouse at Wilson airport. The club may provide information to genuine mountaineering parties and to members of reciprocal mountain and hiking organisations, but cannot help tourists with general queries on aspects of trekking or travel in Kenya.

The East African Wildlife Society is a non-profit organisation whose main aim is to safeguard the environment in all its forms. The membership fee helps them continue this campaign. You can join the society in Nairobi at their office and shop in the Hilton Hotel shopping mall, or write direct to EAWLS, PO Box 20110, Nairobi. Members get a free bimonthly magazine.

PUBLIC HOLIDAYS

As well as Christmas Day, Boxing Day, New Year's Day and Easter Friday and Monday, public holidays include:

1 May	Labour Day
1 June	Madaraka Day
10 October	Moi Day
20 October	Kenyatta Day
12 December	Independence Day

PLACES TO STAY IN NAIROBI

Most trekkers in East Africa start and end their journey in Nairobi, and spend a few days here arranging treks and safaris, sorting out paperwork, or stocking up on supplies.

Nairobi is one of the largest cities in Africa (although the centre is still not big enough to get lost in) and there's a wide range of hotels.

To stay at one of the hotels in the top or mid-range it's sometimes worth booking through a travel agent or trekking company as they can often get good discounts.

More details on places to stay in or near the trekking areas are given in the relevant sections.

Places to Stay – bottom end

City Centre There are several cheap and basic places around River and Latema Rds, on the down-at-heel edge of the city centre: these include the *New Kenya Lodge*, a legendary hippy hangout where you sometimes have to watch your gear; the *Iqbal Hotel*, which has a good restaurant; and the *Sunrise Lodge*, where the security is good and there's usually hot water. All have rooms for about US$3 to US$5 per person. Higher up this range, the popular *Dolat Hotel* on Mfangano St, where basic but clean en suite singles/doubles go for US$10/12. The similar *Hotel Africana* (☎ 20 654,331886) on Dubois St, with singles at US$13, has also been recommended.

Suburbs A legendary stopover for travellers is *Mrs Roche's House*, on 3rd Parklands Ave, about 3km from the city centre. Camping is US$2. There are also cheap rooms (US$4) and a place to park vehicles. In the last few years, however, we've heard from many travellers that security has become a real problem here. Most shoestringers now recommend *Upper Hill Campsite* on Menangai Rd south of Haile Selasse Rd, about 2km south-west of the city centre. It's friendly, secure and popular with backpackers and overlanders; camping is US$3 and dorm beds US$5.

Also west of the city centre is the *Youth Hostel*, on Ralph Bunche Rd off Valley Rd, where a bed in the dorm costs US$7. Security and hygiene lapsed here at one time, but latest reports say the new management have smartened up the place; it's now clean friendly and as safe as communal rooms can be.

Lockers and a long-term storage room are available. A local guide called Mike Mwai works out of the hostel arranging budget Mt Kenya treks.

During the day you can reach Upper Hill and the Youth Hostel by bus and walking. At night, don't even think about walking: between the centre and the western suburbs you have to cross Uhuru Park – a mugger's paradise.

Places to Stay – middle

All the places in this range have en suite rooms and include breakfast.

The *Parkside Hotel* (☎ 214154/6) on Monrovia St, opposite Jevanjee Gardens is good value. Clean, safe, en suite singles/doubles/triples cost US$28/35/52. Just around the corner, on University Way, the *Suncourt Inn* (☎ 221418) has friendly staff and reasonable en suite rooms at US$30/50.

Bang in the centre of town, just off Kenyatta Ave, is the large and impersonal but reasonably priced *Six-Eighty Hotel* (☎ 332680), with singles/doubles at around US$60/80. Also central (opposite the New Stanley Hotel on Kimathi St), and better value, is the small and friendly *Oakwood Hotel* (☎ 220 592), with rooms at US$50/60.

West of the city centre, the slightly bland but not unreasonable *Milimani Hotel* (☎ 720 760), on Milimani Rd, has rooms for US$50/70. Further up the same road, the *Sagret Hotel* (☎ 720934) has rooms for US$40/60 and a pleasant, more local flavour

Places to Stay – top end

Highly recommended in this bracket is the *Fairview Hotel* (☎ 723211; fax 721320), on Bishops Rd; this is a quiet place, well decorated with a personal touch, set in pleasant gardens with straightforward rooms from US$50/70 and more comfortable en suite rooms from US$60/90. To reach the city centre, taxi rides (highly recommended) are about US$6.

Nairobi has a range of high class international hotels, including the *Hilton*, the *InterContinental* and the historic *Norfolk Hotel*, all with doubles from US$200 to US$300 (and singles hardly any cheaper).

EQUIPMENT HIRE & SUPPLY

Atul's Shop (☎ 228064) on Biashara St, Nairobi, has been providing trekking equipment for many years. They have locally made tents and sleeping bags, and a lot of second-hand walking and camping gear, for sale or hire. Gear for hire includes: thin sleeping bags US$1.20, mountain sleeping bags US$4, small tents US$4, large tents US$12 (all rates per day). They also have stoves, pots and pans, lamps, rucksacks, binoculars, clothing and boots. Naro Moru River Lodge and Mountain Rock Hotel, near Mt Kenya, also have gear for hire (see the Mt Kenya Places to Stay section).

Getting There & Away

Getting to Kenya from Europe or further afield is covered in the Getting There & Away chapter earlier in this book. This section assumes you're already in Kenya and need to go elsewhere; it covers travel *from* Kenya, *to* Tanzania, Uganda and Malawi using air, road or rail transport. For going the other way (eg from Tanzania to Kenya), see the relevant country chapters.

How you travel depends on how much time you've got, and the amount of travelling (as opposed to trekking) you want to do. In this section it's presumed you want to take fairly direct routes between the trekking areas in the various countries.

TANZANIA

Air

There are international flights between Nairobi and Dar es Salaam every day, starting at about US$110 one way. From Dar you can fly to Kilimanjaro international airport (KIA) in northern Tanzania near the trekking areas, but this is expensive and a very long way round, so you're better going by road.

Nairobi – Security Advice

You'll often hear Nairobi referred to as 'Nairobbery' by residents, both Kenyan and expatriate, and you'll certainly read about robberies and muggings, some of them violent, in the newspapers almost daily. This is something you should bear seriously in mind and you should act in a manner which will minimise your chances of becoming a victim.

Some of the precautions you should take ought to be common sense but it's amazing how many travellers inadvertently set themselves up for a mugging. The most common error is not to know where you're going, then to stop in the middle of the pavement to consult this book and to start pointing in all directions. This is an advertisement to any thief that you're a newcomer and will probably have your mind on things other than vigilance. If you're lost and need to consult a map, duck into a shop or hotel lobby, decide which direction to take and then put the book away. Another error, almost as common, is the wearing of money belts outside your clothing. Everyone knows that's where all your valuables are and to a thief it's an irresistible invitation. Tuck them under a T-shirt or inside your shirt where the strap (which is what will be cut) is more difficult to locate. Better still, think of an alternative means of carrying your cash and documents, or leave them in a hotel safe.

Other specific precautions you should take are:
• Keep a small amount of money separate from your main stash so that you don't have to pull out the whole lot every time you buy something.
• Beware of confidence tricksters who want to take you down obscure alleys to transact 'business' of whatever nature. You'll lose the lot.
• Do not walk from the city centre to any of the hotels on Milimani Rd or to the Youth Hostel, YMCA or YWCA after dark. Uhuru Park is infamous for its muggers. Take a taxi. That US$5 fare could save you everything you've got.
• Keep your hand(s) on your valuables at all times on buses and in crowded public places. The man in the suit and tie and the shiny shoes may look respectable (and probably is) but it's a great disguise for a thief. Not all thieves are ragamuffins.
• Avoid walking alone at night carrying valuables in any of the streets between Tom Mboya and Kirinyaga (the River Rd area). If that's unavoidable, take with you only as much as you can afford to lose.

Road

There's a good tar road all the way between Nairobi and Arusha, the centre of Tanzania's safari industry. This road continues to Moshi, the base for Kilimanjaro, and eventually to Dar es Salaam. The main Kenya-Tanzania border is at Namanga, roughly halfway between Nairobi and Arusha.

The journey between Nairobi and Arusha or Moshi can be done by direct public bus or luxury shuttle bus, without the need to change at the border. Or you can go by shared taxi and minibus, which means crossing the border on foot. For more details on prices and frequencies see Getting There & Away in the Tanzania chapter.

If you arrive by air in Mombasa, you can go direct to Moshi or Arusha by crossing the border at Taveta. There is a very slow daily bus between Mombasa and Moshi which costs US$10. Alternatively, there are buses between Mombasa and Voi (on the Mombasa-Nairobi road), and shared taxis between Voi, the border and Moshi.

UGANDA
Air

There are regular services between Nairobi and Kampala – usually about five or six flights per week in each direction. The one-way fare is about US$100.

Road

The main border crossing between Kenya and Uganda is at Malaba, which is linked to Nairobi and Kampala by good tar roads. The Akamba Bus Company operates direct buses (day or overnight) between Nairobi and Kampala, which you can book in advance at their Nairobi office on Lagos Rd, just off Latema Rd; the one-way fare is US$18. There's also a luxury service for US$40.

Alternatively, you can do the journey in stages. There are frequent buses and shared taxis between Nairobi and Bungoma, then matatus between Bungoma and the Malaba border. Akamba also has a direct bus between Nairobi and Malaba for US$9. You can easily walk across to the Ugandan side.

Formalities at the Malaba border point are straightforward for both countries. Arrival/departure forms need to be completed, but there are no currency forms to worry about on either side. You are not allowed to import or export more than KSh 200 or USh 5000, but if you're going to be crossing back across the border after a few weeks and want to keep some money, a search is unlikely. There is a bank and foreign exchange bureau on the Ugandan side and plenty of moneychangers on both sides. Know the rates and you'll get a good deal.

On the Uganda side, there are minibuses from the bus park (about 1km from the border) to Tororo, Mbale or Kampala (see the Uganda chapter for more details on these places). The drivers accept Kenyan shillings.

Train

There's a good quality direct train from Nairobi to Kampala every Tuesday (returning on Wednesday). This service may be increased, and departure days may be altered. The one-way fare is US$80/60 in 1st/2nd class, including bedding and meals. Passports and customs formalities are handled on the train. If you're heading for the Ugandan side of Mt Elgon you can take this train as far as Tororo.

MALAWI
Air

Flights between Nairobi and Lilongwe go about four times a week in each direction. One-way fares cost between US$200 and US$300, depending on the airline.

Road

Kenya and Malawi do not share a border, so overland journeys between these two countries must go through Tanzania. See Getting Around and Getting There & Away in the Malawi and Tanzania chapters.

Getting Around

The normal way of getting around Kenya, when travelling between the trekking areas, is by road. Other options include trains or domestic flights. Generally things are fairly efficient, but bad roads and long waits become more common as you get further away from the main routes and centres.

AIR

Using domestic air services can be a good way to get around the country if you're short of time, or if you plan to visit areas such as the Masai Mara which cannot be reached easily by road. Many visitors arrive in Kenya at Mombasa, and a very useful domestic service run by Air Kenya Aviation links Mombasa to Nairobi, with several flights a day and one-way fares from around US$100. Flights between Nairobi and the Masai Mara on Eagle Aviation cost US$158 return. Nairobi to/from Nanyuki (the nearest airport to Mt Kenya) is US$74 one way, US$120 return. It's usual to go through a travel agent to buy domestic flights. In Nairobi, Let's Go Travel (address under Organised Treks & Tours in this chapter) represents all the airlines and can make instant reservations. If by any chance you need to charter your own plane, costs start at around US$2 per km for a five-seater aircraft; once again Let's Go Travel have all the details.

ROAD

Main roads in Kenya are generally good, although some of the busier routes have become increasingly potholed in recent years, because of overloaded trucks and lack of maintenance. The main routes used by trekkers are: south from Nairobi to the Tanzanian border at Namanga; north-west to the Ugandan border at Malaba; and north to Mt Kenya and the Central Highlands. All these main routes are tar, and many secondary roads are also tar or well graded. Minor dirt roads tend to be in bad condition or impassable after rains.

Bus, Shared Taxi & Matatu

The cheapest way to travel is by bus, although this can often be slow, crowded and uncomfortable. Express buses (faster, less crowded and slightly more expensive) run between the main towns, with definite departure (if not arrival) times. On long-distance buses,

seats can be reserved in advance at the bus company's office, which is usually a wooden shed at the bus station. In Nairobi, several bus companies also have offices on the streets in the area around Accra and River Rds. Sample fares include: Nairobi to the towns around Mt Kenya, US$3 to US$5; Nairobi to Kitale or Mombasa, US$6 to US$8.

Shared taxis (usually Peugeot 504 seven-seaters) are generally faster than buses, although some drivers tend to be on the crazy side. Fares are generally between 1½ and two times the cost of a bus. In Nairobi, shared taxis to different towns leave from various streets or junctions, all in the area around Accra and River Rds. In the other towns they generally leave on a fill-up-and-go basis from a corner of the bus station. There's usually one going at least every couple of hours throughout the day.

Away from the main routes, in rural areas, local buses and minibuses (called *matatus*) are often slow and uncomfortable, running to no fixed schedule, and leaving when full.

Taxi

In Nairobi there are several taxi ranks. Rates are slightly negotiable, but always ask before getting in. Across town costs US$5 to US$10, between the city and the airport about US$18 (cheaper if you're coming from the city).

Warning

We've heard reports of travellers on buses (particularly Nairobi to Mombasa) being offered fruit, sweets or soft drinks by fellow passengers. These have been laced with a sleeping drug and while travellers have been unconscious their luggage has been stolen. Don't accept this kind of gift from strangers. Some offers are genuine friendliness, but you can't tell. If you don't want to offend, say you're ill or don't like that flavour.

Several shoestring travellers using the crowded No 34 bus from Nairobi airport to the city have had bags slashed or pockets picked. A taxi here is a good investment, and not too expensive if you get together with other travellers (ask around in baggage reclaim). ∎

Car Rental

For most trekkers the plan is to get away from cars, but a vehicle can be useful for visiting some of the more remote mountain areas, or if you want to combine trekking with a wildlife safari.

Most car hire companies are based in Nairobi. You can arrange things virtually on the spot or book ahead before you leave home. International companies, such as Hertz and Budget, have offices all over the world and you can often make inquiries and reservations at an office in your own country. A small selection of companies is listed here to show the range of options available.

Apollo Tours, Kimathi House, Kimathi St (opposite the New Stanley Hotel), PO Box 42391, Nairobi (☎ 333606; fax 214026). Mid-budget outfit, with saloons and 4WDs and good reputation for reliability and service.

Budget Rent-a-Car, Hilton Hotel, PO Box 49713, Nairobi (☎ 223581; fax 223584; email payless @formnet.com). Part of the international group, this company also has offices in Mombasa and at the airport.

Central Rent-a-Car, Fedha Towers, Standard St, Nairobi (☎ 222888; fax 339666). Reliable mid-range outfit, with good insurance rates.

Glory Car Hire, Diamond Building, Tubman Rd, Nairobi (☎ 250224; fax 331533). A cheap rental outfit, also a driving school. Some reports indicate that the same vehicles may be used for both businesses. Watch out for heavy insurance conditions.

Habib's Car Hire, Agip House, Haile Selassie Ave, PO Box 48095, Nairobi (☎ 220463; fax 220985). Friendly and long-established company, with good value deals, including fully kitted-out 4WDs and camper vans.

Hertz, corner of Muindi Mbingu and Kaunda Sts, PO Box 42196, Nairobi (☎ 331960, 331974, 217 259; fax 216871). International company also with bases in Mombasa and Nairobi airport, so you can pick up and drop off at different locations. Staff are efficient, cars mostly less than a year old, and everything seems to run smoothly. They also have an arrangement with Shell; if you have a breakdown or any emergency out on the road, staff at petrol stations will assist. If you're heading for the wilds, Hertz also have a 'self-drive safari' scheme where a 4WD car comes complete with camping gear, jerry cans, tools and equipment.

Let's Go Travel, Caxton House, Standard Street, PO Box 60342, Nairobi (☎ 340331; fax 336890; email letsgo.travel@commsol.sprint.com.ke). A long-standing and highly efficient company with a small fleet of their own cars, plus good discount deals with other rental firms.

Costs Rates for a small saloon car (sedan) hired from a budget outfit start at about US$20 per day and can go up to almost double that if you get a new car from a smart multi-national. Add to this the daily insurance charge of US$12 to US$30, and a distance charge of between US$0.20 and US$0.40 per km.

Most companies also rent small 4WD cars (mostly Suzukis) and these are likely to be more useful for reaching the trekking areas where roads are unsealed or gradients steep. Bottom-end rates start at US$30 and can double with the smarter companies. Insurance for these vehicles usually is the same as for saloon cars and the distance charge somewhere between US$0.30 and US$0.50 per km.

Most companies also do weekly rates which include insurance and around 1000 'free' km, and these deals can often work out cheaper. For example, weekly saloon car rates start at US$300, and go up to around US$500 for the top-end companies. Weekly 4WD rates star at US$500 and go up to around US$700.

All rental rates are obviously more affordable for budget travellers if shared between a group of four or five. Note also that low-season rates are often cheaper: we heard from four British lads who hired a small 4WD for a week, just at the end of the rains, for only US$250, and used it to reach some good trekking areas on Mt Elgon and the Aberdares. They finished at the foot of Mt Kenya, where they were going to do another trek, while one of them took the car to Nairobi and then hitched back next day to join the others.

To compare prices you need a good idea of your intended route and distance, so you can weigh up the various options and shop around the companies. Don't forget to add petrol costs. A small 4WD does about 10km to the litre, on a mix of tar and dirt roads, and petrol costs about US$0.70/L.

TRAIN

From Nairobi the main railway lines go south to Mombasa and north-west to the Ugandan border at Malaba. These services are generally reliable. Trains compare favourably with buses and matatus on the same route in terms of speed, and probably come out on top for comfort and safety.

Each train usually has double-berth 1st class cabins, four or six-bed 2nd class compartments, and seats only in the 3rd class carriages, which can be very crowded. Cabins and compartments are either men or women only unless you reserve both/all beds.

Between Nairobi and Mombasa, there are two overnight trains in each direction every weekday, and one at weekends. There are three trains a week in each direction between Nairobi and Malaba. Trains have restaurant cars, and fares are reasonable: Nairobi-Malaba (2nd/1st class one way) is US$36/52; Nairobi-Mombasa is US$40/55. Reservations at least three days in advance are recommended, although you can be lucky and get one at shorter notice. If you want to avoid queues at the station, tickets can be arranged by Let's Go Travel in Nairobi.

ORGANISED TREKS & TOURS

You can trek independently in all the areas covered by this Kenya chapter, but many visitors use the services of a tour company to arrange their trekking, as well as other items such as a wildlife safari, hotel accommodation and airport transfers. If your time is limited, this can save a lot of messing about and sometimes it's not a lot more expensive than arranging a trek of the same length and standard yourself (see Organised Trekking, in the Regional Facts for the Trekker chapter).

Nairobi has an infinite number of safari companies but only a few that operate genuine treks. Some companies claim to run treks but in reality just pass you on to specialist operators. This may cost you more, but most companies get their commission from the operators, in which case the price you pay is the same wherever you go. Sometimes, however, if you go straight to the operating company you get a better deal.

The list below also includes a few travel agents. Using an agent to make your arrangements can save time, especially if you'd rather be trekking on the hills rather than walking the streets of Nairobi. As most agents make their commission from the hotels and tour companies they deal with on your behalf, there is usually no additional cost to you.

Around Mt Kenya are various hotels (see the Mt Kenya Places to Stay section for accommodation details) and local tour companies offering various trekking services (eg porters and guides) plus a range of fully supported treks on the mountain. You can contact the hotels in advance to make reservations, or just turn up: treks can usually be arranged with one day's notice, and you may be able to get together with some other people to reduce costs.

The list of companies here is not exhaustive but will give you an idea of the range of options and prices available. Some companies (especially the budget operators) cater specifically for 'walk-in' clients and can organise a trek almost immediately or within a couple of days, while other companies only run treks and safaris with scheduled departures which you can join if the dates suit you. The more upmarket companies tend not to deal with walk-in clients but arrange things in advance; you can join a trek already scheduled or have one designed exclusively to your own specification.

If you want something between an organised trek and an independent trek, the hotels and companies near Mt Kenya can arrange guides and porters only or make reservations in the bunkhouses, while you plan your own route, provide your own gear and food, and make all the other arrangements yourself (see the Mt Kenya section for details).

Costs

The price of any organised trek depends on the number of days, the quality of transport, equipment and food provided (if any), the knowledge and experience of the guides, and many other factors. When comparing prices of the budget outfits, check whether they include park fees, as most of the highland

KENYA

KENYA

Choosing a Trekking Company

Choosing the right company to organise your trek to Mt Kenya or your safari to Masai Mara can be a tricky business. The sheer number of companies and options available can be quite daunting. This is particularly the case at the bottom end of the market. Touts selling bargain deals cruise the low-budget hotels and will promise all kinds of discounts to split you from your hard-earned cash. Here at Lonely Planet, we've received hundreds of horror stories from travellers who have paid for treks or safaris which have been severely sub-standard or simply haven't materialised. Read the 'Choosing a Trekking Company' boxed text in the Tanzania chapter – many of the scams played in Arusha were honed to perfection in Nairobi. The advice is the same wherever you are – always try to get personal recommendations from other travellers before an organised trek or safari. ∎

---

trekking areas are in national parks, and this can make a big difference to the overall cost. The prices quoted here include all park fees, food, accommodation in bunkhouses or tents, guides and porters, unless otherwise stated.

For the companies based in Nairobi the price normally includes transport to the start of the trek and back to Nairobi. For the companies based near Mt Kenya the price includes transport to the start of the trek and back to their base, although transfers to/from Nairobi can be arranged for an extra fee.

You can contact the companies for more information by writing or phoning. If writing, include the PO Box number. If phoning from anywhere inside Kenya, Tanzania or Uganda, the area code for Nairobi is ☎ 02. If phoning from any other country, use the international code for Kenya ☎ 254 and omit the 0 from the area code. Agents overseas are mentioned where relevant.

Bike Treks
PO Box 14237, Nairobi (☎ 446371; fax 442439), Nairobi agent: Let's Go Travel, Caxton House, Standard St, PO Box 60342, Nairobi (☎ 340331, 213033; fax 336890; email letsgo.travel@com msol.sprint.com.ke). The name says it all: mountain bike trips in various parts of Kenya, treks and walking safaris of two to six days through the Masai Mara and Loita Hills area, combined with game viewing in the reserve, plus various treks on Mt Kenya. Mara trips start from US$60 per day. Cycling trips around US$120 per day. A seven-day Mt Kenya trek using the Naro Moru Route is US$300 per person. A seven-day Sirimon-Chogoria traverse is US$720. Bike Treks are also agents for Olperr-Elong Public Campsite, on the west side of the Masai Mara.

Bushbuck Adventures
Gilfillan House, Kenyatta Ave, PO Box 67449, Nairobi (☎ 212975/7; fax 218735, 212977; email bushbuck@arcc.or.ke, website: http://www.kili-manjaro.com/safaris/bushbuck). This high quality mid-market company specialises in wildlife and walking safaris in mountain and wilderness areas all over Kenya, including Mt Kenya, Mt Elgon, the Aberdares and the Masai Mara. Safaris are usually tailor-made to suit your own requirements and need to be organised in advance, but trips arranged at short notice are also possible. For example, safaris based at Bushbuck's own private camp in the Masai Mara are US$300 for the first day, then US$135 for subsequent days. Five-day treks from here, or one of Bushbuck's other private camps, cost from US$750 per person. Five-day safaris including treks in the Masai Mara and Aberdare Range cost US$850 per person. Longer safaris, of a week or more, taking in the Masai Mara, the Aberdares, Mt Elgon, the Cheranganis and Shaba, including walking and game viewing from vehicles, costs about US$195 per person per day. All these prices are for groups of four. Prices come down as numbers go up. Bushbuck also put groups together, so individuals can also be catered for.

Camel Trek
Nairobi agent: Let's Go Travel, Caxton House, Standard Street, PO Box 60342, Nairobi (☎ 340331, 213033; fax 336890; email letsgo .travel@commsol.sprint.com.ke). A smart and long-established operation, running regular safaris in the Lewa Downs area, west of Isiolo. Clients can ride camels or walk beside them. A three-night safari costs US$570 per person, all inclusive. A five-night trip is US$710.

Chogoria Guides & Porters
PO Box 310, Chogoria, Tharaka-Nithi. This is a local 'club' (association), efficiently run by Carr Rufas, based at the Transit Motel (☎ (0166) 22096) in Chogoria village, at the foot of the Chogoria Route on the eastern side of Mt Kenya.

You can book things in advance, but it usually isn't necessary unless you want something 'specialised'. Just turn up and you can usually go next day. You can simply hire porters and guides as required, or go for an all-inclusive trek: five days on Mt Kenya costs US$545 per person for groups of between three and six. Extra days are US$100. The price includes transport to/from Nairobi, so if you don't want this a reduction is usually negotiable. For Batian-bound mountaineers the club also have technical guides available, trained at the American National Outdoor Leadership School (NOLS).

Courtesy Guides & Tours
2nd floor, Trust Mansions House, corner Koinange St and Tubman Rd, PO Box 45093, Nairobi (☎ 227820, 345195; fax 333448). A bottom-end outfit with no care for detail and a weird sense of humour – their brochure advertises Mt Kenya treks 'full of fun and scenic scenarios' on the 'Chongoria' Route with 'friedly mountain animals' at all-inclusive prices from US$45 per day. They also offer a Mt Kenya special with no tent, no guide and no shoes, plus death certificate and mortuary accommodation in the price. Strange.

Desert Rose Camel Safaris
PO Box 44801, Nairobi (☎ 330130; fax 212160). Agent: Let's Go Travel (☎ 340331, 213033; fax 336890; email letsgo.travel@commsol.sprint.com.ke) A very upmarket outfit specialising in camel treks through northern Kenya. Clients can walk or ride the camels. Rates start at about US$250 per person per day for groups of six, plus transfers to/from Nairobi, although this daily rate drops for longer trips.

EWP
PO Box 15014, Nairobi (☎ 891049). This company offers trekking and technical mountaineering on Mt Kenya, Mt Elgon, Kilimanjaro and the Rwenzoris. Treks can be designed to suit your budget, experience and time limit.

This company has a UK office – listed under Organised Treks in the Getting There & Away chapter.

Gametrackers
1st floor, Kenya Cinema Plaza, Moi Ave, PO Box 62042, Nairobi (☎ 338927, 212830/2; fax 330 903). Frequently recommended for their safaris to Lake Turkana, Masai Mara and the other national parks, Gametrackers also do canoe and mountain bike safaris, plus treks on Mt Kenya, the Aberdares and camel-assisted walks in northern Kenya. A combined Turkana truck and camel trek costs US$750 for 13 days; the same trip plus the Rift Valley and Masai Mara is US$1200 for 17 days.

Joseph Muthui Gathu
PO Box 391, Naro Moru or c/o Across Kenya Safaris, 3rd floor, Victoria Court Building, opposite Ambassador Hotel, Tom Mboya St, Nairobi (☎ 243986; fax 241170). Joseph is a private guide who has been highly recommended by independent trekkers on Mt Kenya for his skills, good humour and very reasonable rates. He arranges treks to suit your requirements, and also handles porters, supplies, accommodation and equipment as required. Prices for all-inclusive Mt Kenya treks start at about US$50 to US$60 per day, but are less if, for example, you want to carry your own pack or bring your own food. Joseph was trained by NOLS (the American National Outdoor Leadership School) and is a former member of the mountain rescue team.

Kenya Hiking & Cycling
2nd floor, Arrow House, Koinange St (opposite the City Market), PO Box 39439, Nairobi (☎ 218336/8; fax 224212; email jadesea@africaonline.co.ke). A smart and well-organised company running various safaris combining wildlife and walking, with monthly scheduled departures. Areas include the Rift Valley Lakes, Mt Elgon, Masai Mara, Cherangani Hills and the Suguta Valley. Quality is high so prices are not the cheapest; the 14-day 'Ultimate Kenya Journey' costs US$1488 per person. Hiking & Cycling also organises a quality five-day Mt Kenya trek for US$700 per person, irrespective of group size – a good deal if you're alone. Lake Turkana is their specialist area – they have boats on the lake to take trekkers from the Suguta to Loyangalani and Sibiloi National Park (Koobi Fora). An upmarket section of the company called Jade Sea Journeys uses boats on Lake Turkana to take visitors to the various islands and up the Omo Delta into Ethiopia. An exclusive 17-day trip combining northern Kenya and southern Ethiopia (monthly departures, US$2489 per person) can be arranged direct or through top-end adventure travel operators in Europe.

KG Mountain Expeditions
PO Box 199, Naro Moru (☎ (0176) 62403; fax 62078; email kgexpd@arcc.or.ke) A small specialist outfit run by James Kagambi (known to all as 'KG') an experienced trekker and mountaineer who has worked as an instructor on Mt Kenya with NOLS (the American National Outdoor Leadership School) for over 10 years. He is also the first African to have reached the summits of Aconcagua and McKinley. In short – he knows his stuff! KG organises a five-day traverse of Mt Kenya using the Naro Moru Route for US$400 per person in groups of four. A Sirimon-Chogoria traverse is US$520. Transfers to/from Nairobi are US$150 return. He also arranges technical

mountaineering on Mt Kenya plus treks and climbs on Kilimanjaro (US$750 per person from Nairobi) and the Rwenzoris. His US agent is Great Tours (☎ (307) 332 3123).

Kibo Slopes Safaris
PO Box 218, Loitokitok (☎ (0302) 22091; fax 22427). A good quality outfit running a range of mountain treks and wildlife safaris. On Mt Kenya it offers an unusual Timau-Chogoria traverse for US$900 per person in groups of four, or a standard six-day Sirimon-Chogoria traverse for US$820. It also arranges treks on the Aberdares, and walking safaris in the Chyulu Hills and Kimana Wildlife Sanctuary. The company does not usually cater for walk-in clients, mainly because they are 200km from Nairobi, at the foot of the northern slopes of Kilimanjaro. However, this wonderful position allows them to operate treks on Kili using the remote and rarely travelled northern Rongai/Loitokitok routes. An eight-day all-inclusive trip out of Nairobi costs US$950 per person in groups of four. More elaborate treks, taking in Mawenzi and the Shira Plateau, are also available, starting at around US$1100.

Let's Go Travel
Caxton House, Standard Street, PO Box 60342, Nairobi (☎ 340331, 213033; fax 336890; email letsgo.travel@commsol.sprint.com.ke; website http//:www.kenya-direct.com/letsgo). This long-standing and highly efficient company operates a range of camping and walking safaris, and can tailor-make any kind of tour, either with advance notice or on the spot. Let's Go Travel is also a major travel agent and represents just about every airline, hotel, lodge and tour company in Kenya (plus many more in Tanzania, Uganda and elsewhere in Africa). They arrange car hire, make reservations for trains and flights, and also handle bookings for huts and bunkhouses on Mt Kenya and the Aberdares. As well as the more straightforward stuff, Let's Go are also agents for several specialist outfits of particular interest to trekkers, such as remote lodges and camel or donkey trek operators in northern Kenya.

Lobelia Tours & Safaris
Room 59, Krishna Mansion, corner Moi Ave and Moktar Dadda St (near Jevanjee Gardens), PO Box 12459, Nairobi (☎/fax 211426). A small outfit, running good budget trips – mostly to Mt Kenya (eg four-day Naro Moru Sirimon Traverse at US$370 and five-day Sirimon-Chogoria at US$420, for groups of four), although they also offer the Aberdares and some other mountain areas. They normally handle walk-in clients (trips can be arranged within a day or two), but bookings can also be made in advance.

Mountain Rock Tours
2nd floor, Jubilee Insurance Building, corner of Wabera and Kaunda Sts, PO Box 40270, Nairobi

(☎ 210051, 242133; fax 210051, 242731). This company specialises in Mt Kenya treks and has a huge range of options available: comfortable all-inclusive four-day trips up and down the Sirimon Route cost US$344 per person for groups of four; a five-day Sirimon-Chogoria traverse is US$565. No-frills budget trips on the same routes cost US$295 and US$360 respectively.

This company also runs Mountain Rock Hotel, PO Box 333, Nanyuki (☎ (0176) 62051), originally called Bantu Lodge, on the west side of the mountain, 8km north of Naro Moru, with a range of rooms and a camp site. The hotel has two bunkhouses on the Sirimon Route. You can also arrange treks starting/ending here. All-inclusive four-day trips up and down the Sirimon Route cost US$315; five-day Sirimon-Chogoria traverse is US$480. Budget treks from the hotel are even more of a bargain: US$270 and US$335, respectively. Mountain Rock also arranges walking and trekking safaris to the Aberdares, Masai Mara, Loita Hills and other parts of Kenya.

Naro Moru River Lodge
PO Box 18, Naro Moru (☎ (0176) 62622; fax 62211; or fax Nairobi (02) 219212). The lodge is an old country house near the start of the Naro Moru Route on the western side of Mt Kenya. They have rooms, cottages, a bunkhouse and camp site, plus two bunkhouses on the Naro Moru Route. A four-day trek, going up and down the Naro Moru Route, costs US$535 per person, or US$385 each for a group of four. An extra day to do a circuit of the peaks adds US$90 to the four-person price. Various traverse routes are available from five to seven days; a seven-day trek up the Chogoria and down the Naro Moru costs US$700 per person in groups of four. Seven days on the Timau Route is US$660.

Natural Action
Nairobi (☎ 763927). A quality mid-range outfit, with well-trained guides and links to companies of the same name in Tanzania and UK (see list in Organised Treks section of the Getting There & Away chapter). The Nairobi office is run by Sammy Kariuki, an experienced trekker who trained for a while in Britain and is one of the few African technical climbers. The company mostly operates Mt Kenya, Kilimanjaro and Rwenzoris treks for overseas agents, but also caters for private groups on request. A seven-day traverse on Mt Kenya, up Chogoria down Naro Moru, costs US$900, including a hotel night at the end.

Samburu Trails Trekking Safaris
PO Box 56923, Nairobi (☎ 506139; fax 502739), agent: Let's Go Travel (☎ 340331, 213033; fax 336890; email letsgo.travel@commsol.sprint .com.ke). On offer is a range of treks in remote semi-desert areas of northern Kenya, using donkeys as pack animals. One-day treks operate

from Maralal Safari Lodge. Longer treks go from Maralal to Lesiolo and across the Rift Valley floor, at a rate of US$160 per person per night.

Savage Wilderness Safaris

PO Box 44827, Nairobi, (☎ 521590; fax 501 754). Adventure specialists, with trekking, mountaineering, bush walking, desert hiking and even white-water rafting on offer. Areas include Mt Kenya, Mt Elgon, the Loita Hills and the Chyulu Hills. Six days on Mt Kenya for four people is US$700 each, five days US$620. They also run Kilimanjaro trips including all transport to/from Nairobi (see the Tanzania chapter). All trips (from four to 10 days) are run to order – either contact the company when you're in Nairobi, or arrange things in advance through their offices in the UK and USA (listed in the Getting There & Away chapter).

Travel Concepts

3rd Floor, Town House, Kaunda St, PO Box 52296, Nairobi (☎ 230049, 241499) We've had good reports on this budget operator; they do various treks on Mt Kenya from US$60 per person per day, plus the usual range of wildlife safaris, and can set things up within a day or two.

Tropical Ice

PO Box 57341, Nairobi (☎ 740811; fax 740826; email tropice@users.africaonline.co.ke). This upmarket company, run by respected mountaineer Iain Allan, offers very high quality treks on Mt Kenya and the Loita Hills, lowland walks through wilderness areas along the Tsavo and Galana Rivers in eastern Kenya, plus general wildlife safaris. It can also organise mountaineering. All trips cost around US$300 per person per day, and must be arranged in advance.

Yare Safaris

1st floor, Union Towers, corner Moi Ave and Mama Ngina St, PO Box 63006, Nairobi (☎ 214 099; fax 722338). Part of the Africa Travel Centre chain, which has branches in London and Sydney, this company first entered the safari scene pioneering overland gorilla-viewing trips from Nairobi to Zaïre. Today they specialise in operating safaris by foot, camel and truck from their base at Maralal in northern Kenya. They are also an agent for travel around Kenya, and can advise or make reservations on wildlife safaris all over East Africa. If you arrived on a one-way ticket and aren't in a hurry to get home, Yare can also help you find seats on an overland tour northwards to Europe, or southwards to Harare, Victoria Falls or all the way to Cape Town.

Mt Kenya

Mt Kenya, from where the country takes its name, stands at the centre of the Central Highlands, and is often visible from Nairobi some 130km to the south. Of all East Africa's mountains this is where you get nearest to equatorial icecaps: Mt Kenya's glaciers are only 16km south of the equator, just pipping the Rwenzoris which lie 40km north of the equator, and beating Kilimanjaro by more than 300km.

Like Kilimanjaro, Mt Kenya was formed by volcanic action associated with the creation of the Rift Valley. But Mt Kenya is much older than Kili and geologists believe it once stretched at least 1500m above its current height of 5199m (17,057 ft). Mt Kenya has been trimmed to its present size by glacial erosion. Today the jagged central peaks of Batian and Nelion contrast sharply with the smooth dome of Kibo. But despite being a mere shadow of its former self, Mt Kenya is still the highest mountain in the country, and the second-highest in Africa after Kili.

Mt Kenya has a wide range of top-quality walking and climbing routes attracting trekkers and mountaineers from all over the world. To reach the highest summits – the twin peaks of Batian and Nelion – you need to be a technical mountaineer, armed with ropes and a full harness of climbing gear. The trekkers' summit is Lenana, the third-highest point on the mountain, and most visitors try to reach this peak during their trek.

HISTORY

The Kikuyu people, who settled in the Central Highlands some 200 to 300 years ago, cultivated the foothills and hunted in the forests surrounding the mountain, but it's unlikely that any went above the high moorland. Cold, and respect for Ngai (God) who they believed lived on the top of Mt Kenya,

KENYA

would have prevented any high-altitude hunting forays. The mountain was revered and Kikuyu houses were always built with the door towards the mountain as a sign of respect. Its Kikuyu name is Kirinyaga, meaning 'White (or Bright) Mountain', although its modern title is more likely to come from the language of the neighbouring Kamba people, who called it Kee Nyaa (also spelt in several other ways), meaning 'Place of the Ostrich'. The black and white stripes of bare rock and ice on the high peaks looked like an ostrich's feathers.

The first sighting of the mountain by a European was in 1849, when Ludwig Krapf, a Swiss missionary and colleague of Johannes Rebmann, who had earlier spotted Kilimanjaro, saw the twin peaks and glaciers from the area near the present-day town of Kitui. Forty years later, Count Samuel Teleki, passing through on his way to Lake Turkana, managed to cut through the forest and reach a point above the moorland on the south-west side of the mountain. The geologist JW Gregory in 1893 got as far as the top of the Lewis Glacier just below Point Lenana. The high peaks were first climbed in 1899 by the British mountaineer Halford Mackinder and his two Alpine guides Cesar Ollier and Joseph Brocherel. Several features on the mountain, including the Mackinder Valley and the Cesar and Joseph glaciers, bear the names of these three men.

GEOGRAPHY

The Mt Kenya massif is roughly circular, about 60km across at the 2000m contour, where the steep foothills rise out of the more gradual slopes of the Central Highlands. At the centre of the massif, the main peaks rise sharply from around 4500m to the summits at just under 5200m.

For the record, Batian is 5199m (17,054 ft), Nelion is 5188m (17,025 ft) and Lenana is 4985m (16,355 ft). Other major summits on the mountain include Point Pigott (4957m), Point Dutton (4885m) and Point John (4883m).

From the main peaks, which are the remains of the volcanic plug, a series of large U-shaped valleys descend in a radial pattern towards the lower foothills. The largest of these valleys are the Teleki, the Hohnel, the Hobley, the Gorges, the Mackinder and the Hausberg. In between the valleys are broad ridges that become increasingly steep and narrow where they join the main peaks.

All the routes up the mountain follow a major valley or ridge to reach the main peak area, and the Summit Circuit Path around the peaks goes over several high cols (passes) as it crosses from the head of one valley to the next. High cols which can be reached by trekkers include Simba Col (4620m), Hausberg Col (4591m) and Tooth Col (4720m).

Mt Kenya's unique and valuable landscape and vegetation has been declared an International Biosphere Reserve by UNESCO.

TREKKING INFORMATION

Mt Kenya is completely surrounded by dense forest so you have to follow one of the trekking routes from the lower slopes up to the main peaks area, although those not in regular use have become overgrown and difficult to follow. These ascent routes are all connected by the Summit Circuit Path which circles the main peaks between the 4300m and 4800m contour lines. Beyond the Summit Circuit Path, two routes lead up to the trekkers' summit of Point Lenana, the highest peak on the mountain that can be reached without technical rock climbing.

Costs

Costs for trekking on Mt Kenya fall under two main categories: fees for guides and porters (if required); and park entrance fees (obligatory). Other aspects to consider are food and supplies for the trek, equipment hire, and transport to/from the roadheads. These are covered in detail below.

Route Standard & Days Required

On your Mt Kenya trek you can go up and down the same route, or use the Summit Circuit Path to link different routes and do a traverse of the mountain.

The number of days given for each route is the 'usual' amount, but it's much better to

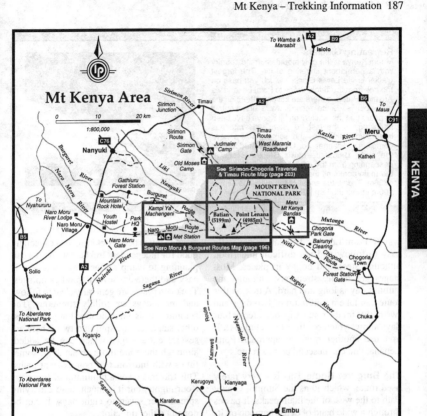

Mt Kenya Area

0   10   20 km

1:800,000

spend an extra day ascending on any of the routes, or stop for two nights at about halfway, as this helps you acclimatise (see the Health, Safety & First Aid chapter).

If you are fit and well acclimatised you can do these routes in a shorter time, although this normally means combining two stages into one, rather than doing an extra bit every day. But if you're not acclimatised, don't even think about cutting a day just to save time or money (see Warning, later in this section). Remember that Point Lenana is just under 5000m; this is higher than a lot of Himalayan passes that trekkers there take

several days to reach. If you rush up Mt Kenya, the chances are you'll get sick, and wish you'd never come, wasting all the money you paid to get here.

This Mt Kenya section describes in detail a short straight-up-and-down route, a longer traverse which is more satisfying, and some other routes which can also be linked into a traverse of the mountain. Other trekking possibilities are outlined later.

The Naro Moru Route This is the most popular route on the mountain, with easy access, good bunkhouses, and the quickest

KENYA

Retreating Glaciers

Mount Kenya is the only mountain in the country with a permanent covering of ice. The largest glacier is the Lewis Glacier, which you pass on the trek from the Teleki Valley to Point Lenana via Austrian Hut, and there are several others on the main peaks. Since records were first kept, it appears that the glaciers on Mt Kenya have been shrinking. In the last 20 years, this rate has increased noticeably, and some glaciers have completely disappeared. On maps produced in the early 1960s the Lewis Glacier is shown descending from the ridge between Lenana and the main peaks all the way to the Lewis Tarn at 4700m. Today, the snout of the glacier is almost 100m above the tarn. ■

DAVID ELSE

way to Point Lenana. The path is generally easy to follow and not difficult underfoot, although steep and boggy in places. Most stages are mildly strenuous, although the summit day is long and hard. A trek on this route can take a minimum of two days and two nights for the round trip, but three or four days allows you more time to acclimatise. If you use another route to approach Point Lenana, you can descend on this route.

The Burguret Route This is a very rarely used route, which joins the Summit Circuit Path to the west of the main peaks. It passes through a wide band of dense bamboo on its lower sections, and paths are indistinct, so a local guide is essential. Porters are not generally used as there are no huts.

This route is hard, very muddy and rough underfoot on the open moorland, with buffalo and elephant in the forest, so this will appeal to real wilderness aficionados.

It normally takes three days to meet the Naro Moru or Sirimon Route, and Point Lenana can be reached on the morning of the fourth day.

This route can also be used as a descent, but a skilled guide is absolutely essential to find the path down through the bamboo.

The Sirimon-Chogoria Traverse This trek combines two routes which are used less frequently than the Naro Moru ascent and

provide much better trekking. It is especially good for independent trekkers without a car, planning to camp all the way, as access is easy and there are several good camp sites. The main routes are generally clear to follow, and most days are mildly strenuous. The summit day is unavoidably long but most other stages can be split into two. There are several extra stages which can be added, although these are more demanding, sometimes with indistinct or non-existent paths. This traverse takes a minimum of five days (four nights) but it is much more satisfying spread over seven to eight days. It can be done in either direction.

The Timau Route This is a very rarely used route, which joins the Chogoria Route east of the main peaks. On its higher sections there is no path at all and you walk through open country, relying totally on your map and compass for navigation. Some stages are long and strenuous, and there are no facilities of any kind, although there are several good places to camp. This is an excellent route for experienced, self-sufficient trekkers.

From the start of the route to its junction with the Chogoria Route usually takes three days. From here, you can reach Point Lenana by various ways (from a few hours to a few days) depending on your route. After Lenana, you can descend on the Sirimon, the Chogoria or the Naro Moru Route, with one or two more nights, to reach the foot of the mountain.

For logistical reasons the Timau Route cannot be done easily in reverse.

Other Route Options Different route sections can be combined to create several other treks on Mt Kenya. For example, if you don't have a tent, it's still possible to do a traverse by going up the Sirimon and coming down the Naro Moru, as there are bunkhouses on both routes. (You'll still need a sleeping bag and cooking gear though.)

Alternatively, you can link the Chogoria and Naro Moru routes, and go in either direction. If you are fully self-contained and looking for something more adventurous, you can tie in either the Timau or the Burguret Route. It is better to use these routes as ascents, and then descend on one of the other more regularly used routes. However, a Burguret-Timau or Timau-Burguret traverse would be the ultimate Mt Kenya wilderness trek.

Guides & Porters

General aspects of hiring assistants are discussed under Guides & Porters in the Regional Facts for the Trekker chapter. For Mt Kenya, guides and porters are not obligatory. Many people backpack here completely independently, and for experienced trekkers this is fine. If you decide to take a guide and/or porters, they can be arranged at several places in and around Naro Moru village on the west side of the mountain, at Nanyuki on the north-west side and in Chogoria town on the east side.

Some guides and porters are employees of the hotels around Mt Kenya, or work as freelancers. Many have formed 'clubs' or associations, in an attempt to standardise rates and improve conditions. If you hire straight from a club, daily rates are about US$5 for porters and US$8 for a guide. If you hire from one of the hotels, rates are higher: US$8 for a porter, US$15 for a guide, although usually guides from the hotels are more skilled, with some basic knowledge of first aid and mountain sickness treatments,

and may also inform you about flora and birdlife on the mountain.

These prices are per stage (ie the distance between two huts/bunkhouses, or a usual day's walking). If you combine two stages in one day, you'll still have to pay for both stages. If you have a rest day, and stay two nights at one hut/bunkhouse, that counts as a stage. The access and exit days of your trek, where you might be using a vehicle, also count as stages, even if your porters get a lift as well. This is fair enough: it may be easy for the porters but it's still a day when they could be carrying bags for somebody else.

If you hire direct from a club you normally have to pay national park entrance fees for guides and porters – around US$2 per day. You may have to be expected to pay an extra fee of US$1 to US$3 per day for food, which guides and porters provide and cook themselves. Make sure your guides and porters know how long your trek is going to be, and that they bring enough to eat. It's not unknown for porters to run out of food after a few days and then expect trekkers to provide for them. The hotel rates generally cover the guides/porters own park entrance fees and their food.

If you hire a guide first, he can arrange porters for you. Porters' loads are limited to 16kg (or 18kg if the trek is less than four days), to which they add their own kit. They do not have their own rucksacks, so usually tie their food and blankets onto the bags you provide.

Guides are normally experienced and knowledgeable but, particularly among the freelancers, there are a few sharks on the loose around Naro Moru and Nanyuki, so beware. We've even heard stories of streetboys in Nairobi approaching tourists getting on the bus for Nanyuki and pretending to be mountain guides.

The national park issues reliable organisations with entry vouchers for porters and guides. This makes it cheaper for them to enter the park and is also a way of keeping out the bad guys. The park recommends that all visitors hire guides and porters who hold entry vouchers. To cut out the sharks even more, the park plans to introduce a proper licensing system. Even so, if you want to do something different (such as the Burguret Route) or even slightly unusual (such as a circuit of the peaks), make absolutely sure your guide knows the way. A few questions to check won't do any harm.

On Mt Kenya, the distinction between porters and guides is normally clear: porters carry loads and that's all; guides show you the way and may require a porter to carry their own gear, even if you're carrying yours. Sometimes, though, the difference is blurred – you can find porters who will also act as guides for an extra fee (but, again, make sure they know their stuff before hiring them).

Tipping After your trek you will probably want to give a tip to the guide and porters who have worked for you. Some get a bit pushy towards the end of a trek when it comes to tipping time, although you can't always blame them (see Guides & Porters, in the Regional Facts for the Trekker chapter). As a guideline, for a five-day trek on Mt Kenya, a tip should be an extra day's wages for each porter and guide, or slightly less for short treks and more for a longer one. Emphasise at the start, however, that tips will only be paid for good service.

Park Fees & Regulations

All of the area above 3200m is Mt Kenya National Park. Below this, down to 2000m on the south of the mountain and 3000m on the north, is forest reserve. Two tongues of park land (called 'salients') descend through the forest to the Naro Moru and Sirimon gates at about 2500m.

To enter the park all visitors have to pay park fees. For non-residents, these are:

entrance	US$15	per day
	US$5	for students under 23
'climbing rate'	US$10	per day
(2 days or more)		
camping	US$8	per night *

*not payable if you've already paid to stay in a bunkhouse and have a voucher as proof.

These fees are paid at the gate where you enter the park, and receipts are checked when you leave. You're supposed to pay in advance for all the days you spend in the park, but if you stay longer than planned, you can pay for the extra days on your way out.

The most important regulation to remember is that trekkers are not allowed to enter the park in groups less than two. This is a sensible rule, with your safety in mind, so all you lone wolves out there will have to find companions or a local guide.

Maps

The *Mt Kenya Map & Guide* produced by Mark Savage, has a scale of 1:50,000 with a more detailed map of the main peaks and a road map of the surrounding area. The back of the map contains some useful information on porters, huts, access and so on. It is available in Nairobi for around US$5, or from Savage Wilderness Safaris (address listed under Organised Treks & Tours in this chapter). A very similar map titled *Map & Guide of Mt Kenya* produced by Andrew Wielochowski also has good information on the back for trekkers and climbers, and is available (for around the same price) from specialist bookshops worldwide or from UK tour company EWP (listed in Getting There & Away chapter).

The Survey of Kenya (SK) 1:50,000 map of Mt Kenya is not usually available, but you may be able to find copies of the SK 1:125,000 *Tourist Map of Mt Kenya* in some bookshops; this map was re-issued by Ordnance Survey (UK) in their Worldmaps series, with some updated information, but the scale of the peaks section is too limiting to be useful, and it seems to be out of print anyway (although it's still seen in Nairobi and UK bookshops).

Guidebooks

The *Guide to Mt Kenya & Kilimanjaro* (published by the Mountain Club of Kenya) is mainly for rock climbers and mountaineers, although it does have some brief sections on trekking routes, and a lot of good background information on the history, geology and wildlife of these two mountains. The book was reprinted in 1992, and altered slightly, mainly to take account of the receding glaciers and disappearing ice routes. A brand new version is planned for 1997 or 1998.

Supplies

There are no shops inside the park. Basics can be bought in Naro Moru village or Chogoria town, and most things can be purchased in the large towns of Embu and Nyeri. In Nairobi, you can buy almost anything (see Buying Food, in the Regional Facts for the Trekker chapter).

PLACES TO STAY
Around Mt Kenya

Naro Moru Village The village of Naro Moru is on the western side of the mountain, and many trekkers pass this way before going up the mountain. For shoestringers, there are a couple of basic lodging houses behind the village 'main street', although they're seldom used by trekkers. Better than most is *Watamu Lodge* charging US$6/8 for reasonable single/doubles, although the bathrooms' proximity to the lively bar would put some people off. They also have en suite doubles for US$11

A much better choice, about 2km outside Naro Moru village, is *Naro Moru River Lodge* (☎ (0176) 62622; fax 62211; Nairobi reservations office ☎ 332825; fax 219212), an old-style country hotel catering for all types of trekkers, with singles/doubles for US$72/94 (including bed, breakfast and evening meal), self-catering cottages from US$20 per person, a bunkhouse for US$6 a bed, and a good camp site for US$4 per person. (Room and cottage prices are almost half these rates in the low seasons – mid-April to June and mid-September to mid-December – and go up by US$20 over Christmas and New Year.) There's a restaurant and bar, and even a swimming pool and tennis court, if trekking isn't already enough exercise.

The lodge arranges all-inclusive treks (see Organised Treks & Tours in this chapter), and can supply guides and porters if you want to organise your own itinerary. The staff can also help with information and advice; they have been arranging treks on the mountain for years and know their stuff.

The lodge also administers the two bunkhouses on the Naro Moru Route, at Met Station and Teleki Lodge (usually called Mackinder's Camp). They also hire out equipment such as jackets, rucksacks and boots (both US$4 per day), gloves (US$3) and sleeping bags (US$5), although the quality is varied: there's some modern gear, while other items are pretty basic.

Naro Moru Area About 8km north of Naro Moru village, on the main road towards Nanyuki, is *Mountain Rock Hotel* (formerly *Bantu Lodge*; ☎ (0176) 62051) PO Box 333, Nanyuki. It is a very friendly place with accommodation for all budgets. Simple en suite rooms sleeping four people cost US$68. Standard en suite single/twin/triple rooms are US$25/39/66 with breakfast. 'Superior' rooms are US$35/49/76. Discounts are available in the low season. Lunches and dinners are available in the restaurant, and the hotel also has a couple of nice bars: one inside near the fire and another on a terrace overlooking the garden. Camping is US$5. The camp site is a good deal: there's a kitchen, plenty of firewood, hot showers and even a bath! You can use the hotel's own tents for US$15 per person per night.

Mountain Rock also arranges treks on the mountain, mainly on the Sirimon Route (see Organised Treks & Tours in this chapter), where they have bunkhouses at Old Moses Camp and Shipton's Camp. They also hire out mountain gear, with tents going at US$12 per day, rucksacks for US$5 and gloves for US$3. The hotel can also arrange trout fishing and horse riding, for any idle moments you may have before or after your trek.

About 7km east of Naro Moru village, up the dirt road towards the Naro Moru park gate, is the *Mount Kenya Youth Hostel*. The original hostel burnt down a few years ago, but this replacement does an excellent job; it's quiet and clean with very friendly staff and a splendid view of the mountain. Camping is US$3, dorm beds are US$4. There are a few double rooms and a kitchen where you can make your own food, plus a couple of local stores selling basics nearby. Meals can be arranged on request. Porters and guides from the local association can also be arranged here at reasonable rates for a straightforward service. A matatu ride from Naro Moru village to near the hostel costs US$0.50. When you get off the bus at Naro Moru village ignore the boys who tell you the hostel is still a fire-wrecked ruin. They even give you a phone number to ring, and whoever is on the other end says 'yes, the hostel has burned down'. It's all an elaborate scam to make you stay in one of the village places.

Nanyuki The old settler town of Nanyuki lies north-west of Mt Kenya, on the main road that circles the mountain. This is the nearest settlement of any size to the Sirimon Route, so independent trekkers heading this way can base themselves here. Places to stay include the *Jambo House Hotel*, basic but friendly, with singles/doubles at US$3/6. Another cheapie is the *Sirimon Guest House*, although the minibuses in the courtyard can be noisy.

Up a grade from these is the popular *Joskaki Hotel* (☎ (0176) 22820) with gloomy en suite rooms for US$7/12 including breakfast. Better value is the friendly *Lion's Court Inn* (☎ 32308), on the southern edge of town, with accommodation in cottages at US$8/15. Smarter is the *Nanyuki River Lodge* with en suite rooms at US$11/ 17 including breakfast, and large dinners for around US$4. Top of the range is the *Sportsman's Arms Hotel* (☎ (0176) 32347; fax 22895), an old colonial watering hole now frequented by British soldiers from the nearby base, where comfortable rustic cottages in pleasant gardens cost US$30/50 with breakfast. There's a good restaurant, bar, tennis court and even a gym, in case you need to tone a few pre-trek muscles.

All the places to stay listed here can arrange fully inclusive treks, or set you up with guides and porters. Various freelance characters tout for work around town, but some give the impression they've never walked further than the nearest bar. Mountain Rock Hotel (see Naro Moru Area above) plans to build a *Mountain Rock Café* on the main street, selling food and drinks, where you'll also be able to hire reliable guides and porters or join one of their treks.

Chogoria On the east side of the mountain, at the start of the Chogoria Route, Chogoria is a small town, with a choice of places to stay. Opposite the hospital, on the main street, are the *Chogoria Guest House* and the *Chogoria Cool Inn*, both with rooms for US$3 per person. The Guest House is in slightly better condition. The Cool Inn also has a restaurant and bar, and can be noisy at night. About 2km away from the main street, is the slightly more upmarket *Chogoria Transit Motel*, with doubles for US$10 and a restaurant with good food (although it has to be ordered several hours in advance). All the Chogoria hotels can arrange porters and guides and transport up to the Chogoria Park Gate (see Access in the Naro Moru Route section).

About 29km from Chogoria town, where the Chogoria Route breaks out of the forest, are the *Meru Mt Kenya Bandas*, administered by Meru County Council. The bandas are good quality wooden cabins, set in a pleasant forest clearing, and cost US$20 per person. (Park entrance fees may also be payable, but this is normally not a problem as you'll have paid for that day's trekking anyway.) Each banda has a bedroom sleeping three or four (the beds have clean sheets and blankets), a bathroom (with hot showers), a sitting room (with log fire) and fully equipped kitchen. There's even a shop selling beer. After a long, tough trek on Mt Kenya the luxury here is almost too much to take! You can just turn up and take a place, if there's room, or make an advance booking through the Bandas' agent, Let's Go Travel, in Nairobi (listed under Organised Treks & Tours). There is also camping here.

DAVID ELSE

DAVID ELSE

DAVID ELSE

Left: Queens Falls flows over the entrance to a large cave, Aberdare Range, Kenya
Right: Simba Col, with the summits of Mt Kenya – Nelion (5188m) and Batian (5199m) behind
Bottom: Giant groundsels endure the harsh conditions on the upper slopes of Mt Kenya
below the mountain's jagged summits, including Pt John (4883m), seen on the right

DAVID ELSE

DAVID ELSE

CORINNE ELSE

The Cherangani Hills (top) provide pleasant walking through inhabited hills in Kenya's west. The escarpment at Lesiolo (middle) in the western Loroghi Hills drops almost 600m to the Rift Valley floor below. One of the lowest areas in the Rift Valley system is the Suguta Valley (bottom), which is also one of the hottest and most inhospitable regions in Kenya.

On Mt Kenya

Places to stay on the mountain itself include four bunkhouses with simple but adequate facilities, and about five basic huts. It's perfectly possible to do a trek on Mt Kenya without a tent if you stay in the bunkhouses, and you can even do it using the huts, but some of these are in unpleasantly bad condition and only provide rudimentary shelter.

It's also possible to camp, either near the bunkhouses or huts, or at several other good sites on the mountain. If you hire a guide or porters, you'll need to camp near a hut or bunkhouse every night so they have somewhere to sleep, unless you provide tents for them.

There are also some huts exclusively for the use of Mountain Club of Kenya members and some basic bivvy shelters for mountaineers on the main peaks, but these are of no use for trekkers.

Bunkhouses The bunkhouses on Mt Kenya each have several large rooms with bunk-beds, an area with tables and benches, toilets outside and water nearby. There are permanent caretakers and separate quarters for porters.

On the Naro Moru Route the bunkhouses are at the Meteorological Station (shortened to Met Station) and Teleki Lodge at Mac-kinder's Camp, both administered by Naro Moru Lodge. It costs US$8 per night at Met Station, and US$9 at Mackinder's. Payments for the bunkhouses have to be made in advance at Naro Moru Lodge, or their agents in Nairobi, Let's Go Travel. You can camp near the bunkhouses and use their facilities for US$1.

On the Sirimon Route the bunkhouses are at Old Moses Camp and Shipton's Camp, both administered by Mountain Rock Hotel. It costs US$8 per night at Old Moses, and US$9 at Shipton's or US$1 to camp nearby and use the facilities. Payments have to be made in advance at Mountain Rock Hotel, or at their Nairobi office (addresses under Organised Treks & Tours).

When you pay in advance for a bunkhouse, vouchers are issued to present to the caretakers and to show at the gate so you don't have to pay the US$8 per night camping fee. If you decide to use a bunkhouse while you're on trek (eg because bad weather puts you off camping) you can pay on the spot but space is not guaranteed and this is a few dollars more expensive than paying in advance, plus you'll have already paid camping fees at the gate.

On the Chogoria Route, there are no bunkhouses, but the Meru Mt Kenya Bandas

---

Warning

An important feature of Mt Kenya, and where it differs from the other major mountains of East Africa, is the speed at which you can reach serious altitudes. It's possible to drive from Nairobi up to one of the roadheads, walk to a high hut, and be on the summit of Lenana the next morning. This may be fine for fit and very well-acclimatised mountain athletes but for most visitors this is just asking for trouble. Many organised treks on offer only spend two nights on the mountain, which is just about OK for some people, but a lot of trekkers still get altitude sickness, which means they miss the summit and generally have a miserable time. It is not by chance that a great proportion of reported cases of pulmonary oedema (a severe, often fatal, form of altitude sickness) occur on Mt Kenya.

The situation is made worse by some tour companies (and some guidebooks) billing the trek to Lenana as an easy hike, something to tick off along with Lamu and the Masai Mara. This has led to many people going up completely unprepared for the conditions, and suffering terribly from the cold or the altitude, or both. It's not difficult for ill-prepared independent trekkers to go off-route and have an accident, or even get hopelessly lost, sometimes fatally. Most years there are reports of independent trekkers simply disappearing on the mountain.

It is important to remember that Mt Kenya is a big mountain, where conditions can be very serious. If you can spend at least three nights on the ascent before going to the summit of Lenana, you stand a much better chance of enjoying yourself. And if you're prepared, with proper clothes and equipment, you stand a much better chance of surviving too! If you're not a regular mountain walker, and don't know how to use a map and compass, going up and down anything other than the Naro Moru Route, or trekking without a competent companion or a local guide, is not recommended. ■

The Mt Kenya Challenge

The Mt Kenya challenge is something to look out for if you happen to be on Mt Kenya in August. It is a fund-raising event in which trekkers are sponsored by companies or individuals on their way to Point Lenana. The event is organised by the Association of Mt Kenya Operators (AMKO), an alliance of hotels, lodges, porters and guides' clubs, with support from the Mountain Club of Kenya, The National Outdoor Leadership School and Kenya Wildlife Services.

Money raised goes towards community-based conservation projects in the area round the mountain, and rubbish clean-up operations along the main tourist routes. You can get more information from the Challenge main coordinator: Mountain Rock Tours (listed under Organised Treks & Tours in the Getting Around section of this chapter). ■

(described previously under Chogoria) provide good accommodation. You can walk from Shipton's on the Sirimon Route to the Mt Kenya Bandas on the Chogoria Route, which means you can still do the Sirimon-Chogoria Traverse without a tent.

Huts The huts on Mt Kenya belong to the Mountain Club of Kenya (MCK) and officially you're supposed to pay a fee (around US$2) to the club to use them. This is payable at Naro Moru River Lodge or Let's Go Travel in Nairobi (not to some of the sharper porters who take the money and 'promise to pass it on'). Many trekkers don't pay at all, but it's only fair to contribute to the maintenance of the huts, even though they don't actually seem to get any.

In reality, the MCK seems to have abandoned most of their huts on Mt Kenya's trekking routes. They are often in very bad condition, with filthy dirt floors, broken windows, smoke-blackened walls and absolutely no facilities. They are used mainly by porters, while most trekkers camp. We've even heard stories from trekkers who have tried to use the huts, only to be evicted by irate porters claiming they were 'their huts'.

The only hut which is still in reasonable

condition (mainly because not many people actually sleep here) is Austrian Hut, just below Point Lenana, but every year it becomes slightly more dilapidated and unless something is done, it will soon be in a similar state of disrepair to the others.

It is possible in the future that some of the MCK huts may be handed over to the national park and possibly leased to private operators to become bunkhouses. Others may be removed. This will have little effect on self-sufficient trekkers, but if you're planning to rely on these old huts for porters, check the latest situation before starting your trek.

GETTING THERE & AWAY

The main towns near Mt Kenya are Nyeri and Nanyuki on the west side, and Embu and Meru on the east. The road north from Nairobi divides near Sagana and completely circles the mountain. It's tar all the way, and there are frequent buses, matatus and shared taxis, making access very easy. If you're in a group, you can arrange to hire a shared taxi. This will cost seven times the one-person fare (however many people there are in your group), but it's an easy way to get to the start of your trek.

There is no single 'base' town for Mt Kenya (like Moshi for Kilimanjaro), so before taking transport to the mountain, first decide what route you're going to do. For routes on the western and northern side of the mountain, from Nairobi take a direct bus or shared taxi towards Nanyuki (dropping there or at Naro Moru). It may be easier to find transport to Nyeri, which is a larger town, and then take a local matatu or bus from there. This journey costs about US$5 by bus or US$8 in a shared taxi. Naro Moru River Lodge (see the Places to Stay section) runs a shuttle bus between Nairobi and the lodge, costing US$50 per person, with discounts for groups of five or more. Contact the Lodge or Let's Go Travel in Nairobi for more details. Mountain Rock Hotel (also in Places to Stay) can provide a four-seater car for US$90 and a nine-seater for US$150.

To reach the Chogoria Route, on the

eastern side of the mountain, take a bus or shared taxi to Meru, via Embu, and get off at the road junction near the small town of Chogoria. It may be easier to find transport to Embu, then take a local matatu to Chogoria town from there. From Nairobi this costs about the same as to Nanyuki.

The Naro Moru Route

Area Mt Kenya National Park
Distance 38km
Duration 3 days minimum
Start Naro Moru Park Gate
Finish Met Station
Highest Point Point Lenana (4985m)
Overall Altitude Gain 2985m
Nearest large towns Neyri, Nanyuki
Accommodation Bunkhouses or camping
Access Bus & walk/hitch, car or organised trek
Summary Most popular route on Mt Kenya, with easy access and good bunkhouses. Most direct route to Point Lenana (the trekkers' summit). Easy to follow, but steep and boggy in places.
Note: easy and quick ascents mean altitude sickness is a very common problem on this route. All trekkers are advised to take at least one extra day on the ascent.

This is the most popular trekking route on the mountain, with easy access to the start of the route and good facilities on the way up. There are two good bunkhouses, one hut and several places to camp.

This route also allows a very quick ascent to Point Lenana, which is fine if you're well-acclimatised. But most people who do this route aren't, and they get altitude sickness because they do it too quickly (see the Health chapter). The usual way of doing a trek on this route is to be dropped off by vehicle at Met Station (the first bunkhouse), then on the following day walk up to Teleki Lodge at Mackinder's Camp (the second bunkhouse), and attempt to reach the summit of Point Lenana the next morning (only the second

day of walking), before returning all the way to Met Station. Thus, a trek on this route can take as little as two days, not enough to give you a good chance of getting to Lenana, and very little chance at all of actually enjoying the trek. You are strongly recommended to walk to Met Station from the park gate, and to spend one extra night at either Met Station or Teleki/Mackinder's on the way up. This makes four days (three nights) for the round trip. Options for making a slower ascent (involving an extra day) are outlined in Stage 3.

Access

The route starts at Naro Moru Park gate, near the village of Naro Moru, on the west side of Mt Kenya, between the larger towns of Nyeri and Nanyuki, about 200km by road from Nairobi.

From Naro Moru village to the park gate is about 18km along a good dirt road through fields and small villages. There are a few junctions, but the park is signposted at each one; in any case, there'll be enough people around to ask for directions. A good option is to walk to the Youth Hostel (about 7km from Naro Moru village) and, with an early start the next day, walk from there to Met Station in a day (a total of 19km).

If you're itching to get on the mountain, lifts can be arranged at Mountain Rock Hotel; prices start at US$80 for a nine-seater vehicle to the park gate, or US$100 to Met Station. Naro Moru River Lodge transport rates are slightly lower.

Local matatus from Naro Moru village go up the dirt road to the village near the Youth Hostel; the fare is US$0.50 per person. If you want to go further, negotiate with the driver. Alternatively, get a small group together and charter the whole matatu from Naro Moru village to the gate; prices range from US$15 to US$25 depending on the vehicle, but can easily be double this if the driver thinks you're a soft touch. A charter rate from Naro Moru village to Met Station is US$30 to US$50. For some reason, a few drivers take great pleasure in over-charging trekkers, or promising lifts to the gate and stopping

KENYA

several km short. The way round this is to pay on arrival.

Stage 1: Naro Moru Park Gate to Met Station
10km, 3-4 hours, 1000m ascent

From the gate, keep to the park track, which follows the crest of a broad ridge between the Northern and Southern Naro Moru valleys. The going is easy, and it's pleasant walking through the forest.

About two thirds of the way up, after the bridge, there are good views to your left (north), down into the Northern Naro Moru Valley. The track ends at the Met Station (3050m), a group of large bunkhouses surrounding a flat patch of grass for camping.

Stage 2: Met Station to Mackinder's Camp
10km, 5-6 hours, 1150m ascent

From Met Station, head uphill on the track to pass the radio mast on your right after about half an hour. The track turns into a path. After another 30 minutes you'll reach the end of the forest belt and enter moorland. This area is called the Vertical Bog; conditions range from the damp to the glutinous

depending on when it last rained. Wade through (or hop across tussocks) until the going gets easier and you reach a fork, overlooking the Teleki Valley, about 3½ hours from the Met Station: the left path drops down into the valley, then runs alongside the North Naro Moru River up towards Mackinder's Camp; the right path stays on the ridge and reaches the river higher up. The right path is easier, so more people go this way. The paths meet about an hour later, from where it's another 45 minutes to the Mackinder's Camp area (4200m). Camping is possible here, or you can sleep in the bunkhouse, which is officially named Teleki Lodge, although it's more generally called Mackinder's Camp.

Stage 3: Mackinder's Camp to Point Lenana, plus descent to Met Station
4km, 3½-5½ hours, 785m ascent;
plus 14km, 5-6 hours, 1935m descent

The usual way of doing this stage involves a start around 3 am to get to the summit of Point Lenana by sunrise, or just after, then a walk all the way back down to Met Station on the same day. This is long and hard, and the speed of ascent is one of the major

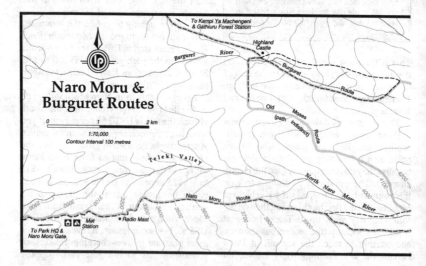

reasons why so many people get sick and don't enjoy their trek on this route. Nevertheless, if you're only interested in bagging the summit in the shortest possible time, this is the way to go.

If you can afford an extra day, it's far better to go up in the daylight as far as Austrian Hut and spend the night of Stage 3 there before going up to Lenana next morning, and descending to Met Station the same day. Alternatively, you can spend a second night at Mackinder's after Lenana, and go down to Met the next day. Even better, spend two nights at Mackinder's before going up to Lenana, to give yourself more time to acclimatise and a much better chance of enjoying the walk to the top.

Ascent To reach Austrian Hut from Mackinder's head north-east up the valley, past the ranger post, then swing right, across the head of the valley, so that the main peaks are up to your left. After half an hour you'll reach the bottom of a large scree slope. The path zigzags up this to reach the crest of a ridge then tends left across easier ground to reach Austrian Hut (4790m). This section takes

between two and four hours depending on how you feel.

Austrian Hut is in a reasonable state, with wooden sleeping platforms, windows and doors, but it has no caretaker, so its condition gets worse every year. There's a toilet, and water is available from the small tarn nearby called the Curling Pond (although this has become quite polluted over the last few years). Next to Austrian Hut is the old Top Hut, closed to the public.

From Austrian Hut you get excellent views: north-east up to the summit of Point Lenana, with the area on the left (west) of the main South-West Ridge usually a snowfield covering the Lewis Glacier; west, across the Lewis Glacier itself, to the steep south-east face of Nelion; and south-east, down into the Hobley Valley, with Gallery Tarn over to the left (north) side of the valley.

To reach Lenana from Austrian Hut, aim north-east, following the clear path up the rocky South-West Ridge, aiming directly towards the summit. You can usually follow footprints, as most days there's a group of trekkers going up this way. If there has been snow, the path up to the summit may be

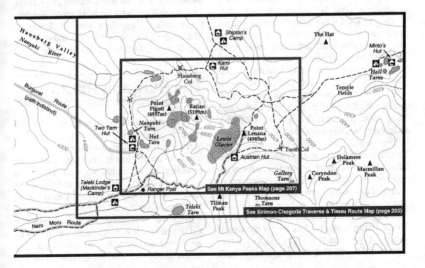

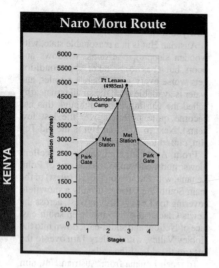

Naro Moru Route

Pt Lenana
(4985m)

Mackinder's
Camp

Met
Station

Met
Station

Park
Gate

Park
Gate

Elevation (metres)

Stages

hidden and extra care must be taken. If bad weather obscures the route or the view up to the summit, this section should not be attempted by inexperienced trekkers without a guide.

About 20 to 30 minutes from Austrian Hut, tend left onto the edge of the snowfield, keeping the crest of the ridge to your right. Do not go too far left, onto the main glacier itself, as there are crevasses. Do not go too far right as you'll get onto steep rock. If the going becomes difficult or unsafe, you're on the wrong route. About 45 minutes to one hour from Austrian Hut, you'll pass below and to the left of the summit, then up to reach a metre-high rock step. Scramble up this and keep right to reach the summit (4985m), marked by a white painted rock. There's also a large metal cross with a Latin inscription (a gift from the Pope in the 1930s), and a star and crescent on a pole, erected more recently.

From the summit of Point Lenana, especially at dawn, the views are spectacular. To the west, across the top of Lewis Glacier, the main south-east face of Nelion glows orange in the rising sunlight. Just below the top of the peak you can make out the tiny silver square of Howell Hut, a climbers' bivvy built

in the 1970s by Iain Howell, one of Mt Kenya's pioneering technical mountaineers.

From Nelion, looking round to the right (north), you can see the head of the Mackinder Valley, with the two subsidiary peaks of Terere and Sendeo on the ridge beyond. Further to the right, you can look down the Gorges Valley and see the sheer cliffs of The Temple, with Hall Tarns on top of the cliffs, appearing to slope sideways.

Beyond them, you can see the huge mound of Ithanguni, with the flat-topped hill called the Giants' Billiards Table down to its right (south). Further round again, to the south of The Temple, you can see the three large peaks of Macmillan, Coryndon and Delamere on top of the ridge between the Gorges and Hobley valleys. To your south you can look back down to Austrian Hut and the steep U-shaped Teleki Valley, with the Mackinder's Camp bunkhouse visible at its head. And to the right of that, at the base of Nelion and the Lewis Glacier, is the leaning tower of Point John. If it's really clear, far to the south you can sometimes see the faint purple dome of Kilimanjaro rising above the clouds, some 300km away.

Descent If you can tear yourself away from Lenana, descent is by the same route. Retrace to Austrian Hut, then steeply down to Mackinder's (about two hours) and on to the Met Station (another four to five hours).

The Burguret Route

This is a very rarely used route on the western side of the mountain, following narrow paths through a wide zone of dense bamboo on its lower sections, and open moorland on the higher slopes. It gives you a taste of what the Naro Moru and Chogoria routes were like before the dirt roads were cut through the forest.

Because the vegetation is so dense you can get hopelessly lost on this route, even with a good map and compass, so a local guide is essential. Guides who are familiar with this route are available from Mountain Rock Hotel, which is also within walking distance of the start of the route.

There are no huts or facilities of any kind on this route, so porters are not normally used as there is nowhere for them to stay (unless you hire tents for them). You will have to provide tent-space for your guide, or hire a tent for him from the hotel.

The route follows a ridge to the north of the Burguret River, and leads to Mackinder's Camp on the Naro Moru Route, or to Hut Tarn, south-west of the main peaks, from where Shipton's Camp on the Sirimon Route can be reached.

It normally takes three days to get to Shipton's, and Point Lenana can be reached on the morning of the fourth day. If you're heading for Mackinder's, stages 2 and 3A can be combined, so you can reach Lenana on the third day. Some of the first stage can be driven, which reduces the ascent by a day, but this is not so good for acclimatisation. This route can also be used as a descent, which takes two or three days, but a guide is absolutely essential, to find the path down through the bamboo.

There is no park gate on this route, so you have to go to Naro Moru Gate or Sirimon Gate to pay your park fees. Mountain Rock Hotel can help you with this. If you descend this route you have to return to one of these gates to sign out. If you come down another way you can sign out at the gate on your descent route. It may be tempting to avoid park fees, but guides will play it by the book. And you shouldn't do it without a guide.

Access
The route proper starts at Gathiuru Forest Station. If you're driving, this is reached by turning off the main road between Nanyuki and Nyeri 12km north of Naro Moru village. The Forest Station is another 11km along tracks. Mountain Rock Hotel can also arrange transport to the Forest Station for US$60 for up to nine people.

It is also possible to walk through the forest direct from Mountain Rock Hotel to the Forest Station, via the caves where Mau Mau fighters were based during The Emergency (see the Kenya History section). There are many tracks in the forest, so a guide is essential. The 13km walk takes four to five hours.

In the Forest Station compound a barrier crosses the track, and the route starts here.

Stage 1: Gathiuru Forest Station to Kampi Ya Machengeni
10km, 4-5 hours, 600m ascent

In the forest station there's a barrier which is closed in wet conditions. Beyond the forest station there are many logging tracks which cause confusion, but keep heading roughly eastwards for about one hour, to leave the plantation area and enter natural forest. Soon after, the path widens slightly. This grassy area is called Elephant Camp. If you walked from Mountain Rock Hotel, you could camp here. Water is available from the nearby stream.

After Elephant Camp you enter the bamboo forest and continue following a faint path along a vague ridge. There are buffalo and elephant in this section of the forest so make a noise as you walk. After three to four hours you reach a clearing in the forest. This is Kampi Ya Machengeni (3000m). Water is available from the nearby stream.

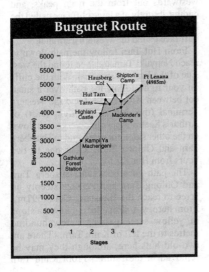

Burguret Route

Stage 2: Kampi Ya Machengeni to Highland Castle
5km, 4-5 hours, 700m ascent

From Kampi Ya Machengeni, the gradient gets steeper. Continue through the bamboo for about one hour, then enter the heathland zone, and after another 30 to 45 minutes you leave the trees behind and reach moorland. There are a few old marker posts around, but no path. Head right and up, across a broad expanse of moorland, until you reach a point overlooking the Burguret River, after another one to two hours. Do not go down to this river but traverse below the crags of Highland Castle which are above you on the left. At the base of one of the crags is a large cave (3700m). This is a good site, with room to pitch your tent inside the cave. Water is available from the Burguret River, about 10 minutes away.

Stage 3A: Highland Castle to Mackinder's Camp
8km, 6-8 hours, 500m ascent

(This stage follows the top section of the Old Moses Route. The lower section of this route is overgrown and no longer used.) From Highland Castle, drop to cross the Burguret River then aim south-west, over the next ridge, or contour around it, descending slightly to reach a small col. The going can be hard over tussock grass and takes one to two hours. Drop down into the next valley, to reach the stream flowing into the North Naro Moru River, and follow this uphill, keeping to its north bank for a further hour until you see another larger col on the ridge to your south with a large rocky outcrop at its western side. Work your way up though mud and tussock grass to reach this col, then aim east along the crest of a broad ridge, passing several small outcrops. There is no clear path. After 1½ to two hours from the larger col, tend right then contour off the ridge crest to reach the North Naro Moru River and the path which runs along its north bank leading to Mackinder's Camp (4200m), reached after another 1½ to two hours.

From Mackinder's Camp you can reach the summit of Point Lenana the following

morning, as detailed in Stage 3 of the Naro Moru Route description.

Stage 3B: Highland Castle to Shipton's Camp
9km, 6½ to 8½ hours, 530m ascent

From the cave below Highland Castle, pass beneath the other crags and then go up to regain the crest of the ridge. Continue heading east, as the ridge becomes broad and featureless. There is a faint path in places and occasional cairns to mark the way. Two to three hours from Highland Castle the ridge levels out for a short section, and you cross some flat stony areas.

Continue gaining height, keeping right (south-east), aiming to the right of the main peaks which are now clearly visible. The path becomes clearer as you swing back eastwards and descend slightly to reach Hut Tarn (4490m) four to five hours from Highland Castle. Camping is possible here, if you want to break this stage. There is also a small hut (Two Tarn Hut), but this may be removed in the future.

You are now on the Summit Circuit Path. Looking north from Hut Tarn, you can see a large ridge called Arthur's Seat extending westwards out from the main peaks, and ending abruptly at a large cliff face called the Eastern Terminal. North of this is another cliff face called the Western Terminal.

From Hut Tarn follow the path down to reach Nanyuki Tarn and then round the west side of the Eastern Terminal. With the cliffs on your right, follow the path over a small col between Arthur's Seat and the Western Terminal (the path to the right (east) of Arthur's Seat is harder and very steep down on the other side), then descend to Hausberg Tarn and Oblong Tarn, about one to two hours from Hut Tarn.

The path goes between Hausberg Tarn and Oblong Tarn and zigzags steeply up scree to reach the Hausberg Col (4591m). From here, you drop steeply down a slope of yellow scree passing a few hundred metres to the left of Kami Tarn. (There are two old huts here, although they may be removed in the future.) From Kami Tarn continue straight down the valley side to reach Shipton's Camp (4230m), about 2½ to 3½ hours from Hut Tarn.

From Shipton's Camp, you can reach the summit of Point Lenana on the morning of the following day, as described in the Sirimon-Chogoria Traverse.

The Sirimon-Chogoria Traverse

Area Mt Kenya National Park
Distance 71km or 77km
Duration 5 days minimum
Start Sirimon Park Gate
Finish Chogoria Town
Highest Point Point Lenana (4985m)
Overall Altitude Gain 2335m
Nearest large towns Nanyuki, Embu
Accommodation Bunkhouses or camping
Access Bus & walk/hitch, car or organised trek
Summary Combines two routes less frequently used than the Naro Moru ascent and provides much better trekking, especially good for independent trekkers without a car, planning to camp all the way, as access is easy and there are several good camp sites. The route can also be done staying at bunkhouses.
Note: a slower ascent than the Naro Moru route means altitude sickness is less of a problem, but still not uncommon. All trekkers are advised to take at least one extra day on the ascent.

This is an ideal route for self-sufficient trekkers, with several alternative stages. The shortest way you can do it requires five days (four nights), and goes via the camp sites at Judmaier, Shipton's, Hall Tarns and the Mt Kenya Bandas. This route passes to the north of the main peaks and goes up the north face of Point Lenana. It's possible (and advisable) to take another day on the ascent by camping at Liki North Hut, or by staying two nights at Shipton's before ascending to Lenana. Another day can also be added by going back to Shipton's after Lenana, completing a circuit of the main peaks. You can also add another day by going south of the main peaks from Shipton's, camping on the way at either Hut Tarn or American Camp, before going up to Lenana via the South-West Ridge. These additions turn the traverse into a very satisfying trek of seven or eight days. If you're not camping, it's possible to go from Shipton's to the Mt Kenya Bandas in one go, without staying at Hall Tarns, but including an ascent of Point Lenana on this day as well would really be pushing it.

We have described this traverse going up the Sirimon and down the Chogoria Route. The traverse can also be done in the other direction, but this involves a very long first stage, which is easier done coming down, although you can arrange transport over most of it in Chogoria.

Access

This route starts at the Sirimon Gate, on the north-west side of the mountain. The park gate is linked to the main tar road between Nanyuki and Isiolo by a dirt road. If you're driving from Nanyuki, look for the junction on your right (signposted) about 15km north-east of Nanyuki. If you're on public transport, ask to be dropped at Sirimon junction.

From the junction to the gate is 9km along the small dirt road, which climbs gently through the forest and is a pleasant walk – useful for limbering up. There are three forks along the way – keep left at each one to reach the gate.

You can also arrange transport to the park gate from Mountain Rock Hotel (about US$50 per vehicle) or Naro Moru River Lodge (US$90 per vehicle). Alternatively, you can charter a matatu in Nanyuki for about US$25.

Camping is permitted at the gate and it's outside the park so no entrance fee is payable, although you might need to pay an overnight fee.

Stage 1: Sirimon Gate to Judmaier Camp
9km, 3-4 hours, 690m ascent
From the gate follow the track as it winds uphill through the forest, which becomes heathland after about three hours. About

3½ hours from the gate, the track veers right and crosses a small stream next to some concrete blocks and an old barrier. Just before the stream, on the left, is Judmaier Camp (3340m), a flat camping area in between large clumps of heather. If you're not camping, 10 minutes further up the hill is the Old Moses Camp bunkhouse.

From Judmaier Camp, the summits of Batian and Nelion are visible to the south, just to the right of two other peaks called Terere and Sendeo, which look larger than the main peaks when viewed from this angle. When the main peaks are obscured by cloud, Terere and Sendeo do a good imitation, and this confuses a lot of people!

Stage 2A: Judmaier Camp to Shipton's Camp (direct)
13km, 6-7 hours, 890m ascent

From Judmaier Camp, follow the track uphill, forking left at the junction after 10 minutes (right goes to the Old Moses Camp bunkhouse). Continue, passing three more forks: keep right at each. One hour from Judmaier the track crosses a stream and reaches a fork (left goes to Liki North Hut). Go right, contouring through moorland on the track. After half an hour take a path that forks left off the track, aiming uphill towards a ridge. You should reach the crest of this ridge 2½ to three hours from Judmaier Camp.

Drop to cross the Liki North River and go up to the top of another large ridge overlooking the Mackinder Valley, reached after another hour. From here you get good views up the valley towards the main peaks.

The path goes up the left (east) side of the Mackinder Valley, gradually gaining height and getting nearer the main Liki River, which is down to your right. After one to 1½ hours the path from Liki North Hut comes in from the left. Continue up the valley for another hour to cross the river and reach a flat grassy area below a cliff of small overhangs called Shipton's Caves. The path goes steeply up the valley side to the right of the caves to reach easier ground and the Shipton's Camp camp site after another 30 minutes. The camp site has a toilet block, and

Judmaier Camp

Judmaier Camp is named after Dr Gert Judmaier, an Austrian mountaineer who suffered a bad fall after reaching Batian, the highest summit, in September 1970. The site of today's Judmaier Camp, at the top of the drivable track, was the base for a team of rescuers who tried to help him. Various attempts failed or were stalled by bad weather. To keep him alive during this time, supplies were dropped by parachute from a small plane. A helicopter trying to drop a rope crashed, killing the pilot.

After a week Dr Judmaier was still trapped on a ledge below the summit. In a final desperate attempt his father arranged for an Austrian Alpine mountain rescue team to come all the way to Kenya from Innsbruck. Just over two days after getting the 'call out' they had flown to Nairobi, got to the mountain, climbed to the summit, reached Dr Judmaier and winched him down to safety. He survived the ordeal with all limbs intact (although his leg was in plaster for a year) and returned to climb the mountain again in 1990.

After the rescue, the Austrian government provided funds and expertise to establish a technical mountain rescue team on Mt Kenya. They also built Austrian Hut, still in fair condition, and passed by most trekkers on their way to Point Lenana. ∎

water is available from the stream. If you're not camping, the Shipton's Camp bunkhouse (4230m) is another five minutes up the path. The camp site has an excellent setting, below the looming north faces of Nelion and Batian.

Stage 2B: Judmaier Camp to Shipton's Camp (via Liki North Hut)
13km, 8-9½ hours, 890m ascent; total 1 or 2 days

This stage is harder than Stage 2A, as it crosses more ridges, and it is less frequently used, but the scenery is better. The path is not clear, so care and good map-reading are required. This stage can be broken into two by overnighting at Liki North Hut. Porters do not like going this way, and usually refuse to sleep at Liki North Hut, but this is no problem if you're trekking independently. (If you have porters, you could send them on to Shipton's Camp and meet them the following day.)

From Judmaier Camp, follow the directions

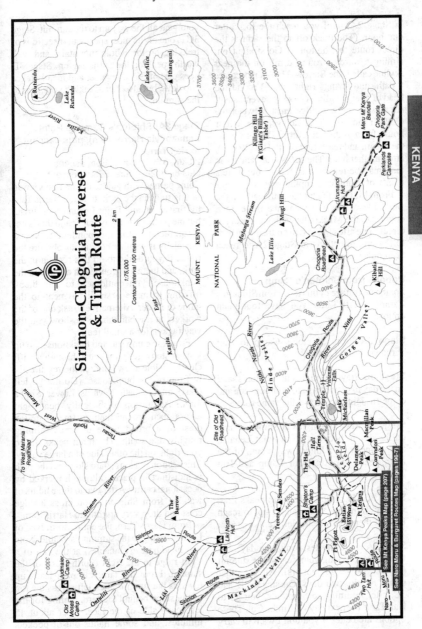

Sirimon-Chogoria Traverse
& Timau Route

1:75,000

Contour Interval 100 metres

0   1   2 km

MOUNT KENYA NATIONAL PARK

KENYA

Rutundu
Lake Rutundu
Kazita River

Lake Alice
Ithanguni

Kilingo Hill
('Giant's Billiards Table')

Mugi Hill
Mutonga Stream

Lake Ellis

Chogoria Roadhead

Meru Mt Kenya Bandas
Chogoria Park Gate

Parklands Campsite

Utamandi Hut

Kibatia Hill

To West Marania Roadhead

West Marania

Timau Route

Site of Old Roadhead

Kazita East River

North River

Hinde Valley

Nithi River

Chogoria Route

Gorges Valley

The Temple
Vivienne Falls
Lake Michaelson

Hall Tarns
The Hat

Temple Fields

Delamere Peak
Macmillan Peak
Corydon Peak

The Barrow
Tereri
Sendeo

Shipton's Camp

Batian (5199m)
Pt Lenana

Pt Pigott

Liki North Hut

Sirimon River

Sirimon Route

Liki North River

Ontulili River

Judmaier Camp
Old Moses Camp

Mackinder Valley

Two Tarn Hut

Naro Moru
Moru Route

See Mt Kenya Peaks Map (page 207)

See Naro Moru & Burguret Routes Map (pages 196-7)

in Stage 2A, until you reach the fork after one hour. (The track off to the right is the direct route to Shipton's.) Go straight on, aiming towards a rounded hill on the near skyline called The Barrow. The track becomes a path, and swings right (south) round the head of a large valley, crossing several small streams to reach a ridge crest between the Ontulili and Liki North valleys, three to four hours from Judmaier Camp. Drop to cross the stream and reach Liki North Hut (3990m), after another hour. The hut is small and basic (and may be removed in future) but there's plenty of room for camping nearby.

From Liki North Hut the path leads up the west side of the valley, over a ridge, then down into the Mackinder Valley to meet the direct route after 1½ to two hours. From here follow the directions in Stage 2A to reach Shipton's Camp.

Options from Shipton's Camp
For the next stage of this trek, from Shipton's Camp to Hall Tarns, you have four main options:

Stage 3A From Shipton's Camp to Hall Tarns via Point Lenana.

Stage 3B Stay two nights at Shipton's, and on the day in between go to Point Lenana and come straight back down the same route.

Stage 3C Stay two nights at Shipton's, and on the day in between go to Point Lenana, then come back a longer way, south of the main peaks via American Camp and Hut Tarn.

Stage 3D Go south of the main peaks first, via Hut Tarn and American Camp, to reach Lenana then continue to Hall Tarns.

Stage 3A is the shortest (only one day), but this means carrying your gear to the summit (unless you've got porters). All the other stages require two days. On stages 3B and 3C, after returning to Shipton's, you go to Hall Tarns the next day via Simba Col. These options are better if you don't want to carry

your gear all the way up to the summit. Stage 3C is one of the most spectacular sections of trekking on the whole mountain, and well worth spending the extra day on. Stage 3D does part of 3C in reverse, and ideally takes two days, but also means taking your gear to the summit.

Stage 3A: Shipton's Camp to Point Lenana (via Harris Tarn), plus descent to Hall Tarns
2.5km, 3½-5 hours, 755m ascent;
plus 6km, 2-3 hours, 685m descent
Some parties with guides do the first section of this stage in the dark, to reach Harris Tarn by first light, and Point Lenana by sunrise, but the path is not always clear and this is not recommended for independent trekkers, especially if weather conditions obscure the route. If you'd like to do this section in the dark, and there's a group with a guide in the bunkhouse, you could ask to join them, offering to make a small payment to the guide or leader. Alternatively, ask one of the workers at the bunkhouse to show you the way (again, for a small fee).

From the camp site and bunkhouse, go up a steep stony gully that cuts through a cliff, clearly visible a few hundred metres directly in front of the bunkhouse. (Do not go left (east) on the path towards Lower Simba Tarn.) At the top of the gully, head right across open ground then go steeply up the crest of a broad ridge of scree, aiming roughly due south. The main peaks are to your right, on the other side of a large valley. This section is a long, hard slog, and the path is indistinct in places, although marked by occasional cairns. After two to three hours of walking from Shipton's you cross a ridge crest and drop very slightly to Harris Tarn.

From Harris Tarn, the entire north face of Lenana, rising to the summit, is visible. Note two *gendarmes* (pinnacles) at the end of a short ridge to the right (north-west) of the summit. From the tarn, the path leads up towards the summit, then left across the top of the slope behind the tarn, aiming for the left (east) side of the face. After about 45 minutes, and some hands-out-of-pockets sections, the path swings back right (west) at the foot of a series of cliffs below the summit, aiming for a point on the ridge in between the summit and the gendarmes. From this point you get a great view down onto the Lewis Glacier. The route swings left, along the ridge for about 50m, to meet the route up from Austrian Hut just below a short rock step. Scramble up this to reach the summit, marked by white rocks, a cross and several marker poles. The ascent of Lenana by the north face is one of the most exhilarating sections of walking on the whole mountain, but it can be serious in bad weather and impassable after snow. Allow 1½ to two hours to get from Harris Tarn to the summit

(If this section of the route is impassable, you can still reach Lenana from Harris Tarn. Drop to Simba Tarn then follow a faint path southwards to Square Tarn and go round to the south side of Lenana via Tooth Col to reach Austrian Hut. From here, approach Lenana by the South-West Ridge, as outlined in the Naro Moru Route description.)

Views from the summit of Lenana are spectacular (see the Naro Moru Route description).

Descent Options from Lenana to Hall Tarns

From the summit of Lenana, there are two ways down to Hall Tarns. If the ascent route up the north face from Harris Tarn was not passable, do not attempt to descend it. If it was clear, you can retrace this back to Harris Tarn and from there go down to (Upper) Simba Tarn and the top of the Gorges Valley. Go down the valley, keeping right to avoid large cliffs just after the tarn, to meet a clear path leading to Hall Tarns (about two hours from Lenana).

Alternatively, you can drop down the South-West Ridge to Austrian Hut, and from there come round the south side of Lenana. If it is misty, the section between Austrian Hut and Tooth Col can be difficult to follow. Several trekkers have become seriously lost here. If you lose the path, it is very important not to drop steeply down into the Hobley Valley. The path contours round the head of the valley, dropping only gradually, before a

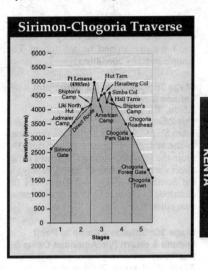

Sirimon-Chogoria Traverse

short steep section up to Tooth Col. Some green marker posts indicate the correct route. From Tooth Col, drop to Square Tarn and then steeply down into the top of the Gorges Valley on the scree slope overlooking a flat grassy area called Temple Fields. Here you'll meet the clear path from Simba Tarn leading to Hall Tarns (about three hours from Lenana).

Hall Tarns Area There are several good places for camping around the picturesque Hall Tarns (4300m). Nearby is Minto's Hut, a tin shack in very bad condition, used mainly by porters, although some hardy trekkers without tents do occasionally sleep there. (This hut may be removed in the future.)

Water used to be available here, but the tarns have been polluted by the washing of greasy billycans by thoughtless trekkers and their porters, so now you have to get it from a stream back up the path, about 20 minutes before you reach the tarns. Do not wash anything in the tarns and they may recover.

As a short sidetrack, you can go to the top of the nearby huge cliff, called The Temple, which overlooks Lake Michaelson and the Gorges Valley. To get to the edge of the cliff from the tarns, aim south, across the bare rock slabs for about five minutes. It's a sheer drop of over 300m to the valley bottom, so don't wander around on the top of The Temple in misty conditions!

Stage 3B: Shipton's Camp to Point Lenana & return (direct)

2.5km, 3½-5 hours, 755m ascent;
plus 2.5km, 2-4 hours, 755m descent
From Shipton's Camp, follow the directions to the summit of Lenana as in Stage 3A. From the summit, return to Shipton's either direct via the north face or the longer way via the South-West Ridge and Tooth Col (as described in Descent Options from Lenana) then either Harris Tarn or Simba Col.

Stage 3C: Shipton's Camp to Point Lenana & return (via American Camp & Hut Tarn)

2.5km, 3½-5 hours, 755m ascent;
plus 8km, 5½-7½ hours, 755m descent
This stage goes to Point Lenana then returns to Shipton's going south of the main peaks along the Summit Circuit Path. It is one of the most spectacular stages on the mountain and should not be missed. With an early start, fit trekkers can do this stage in a day, which means you can leave your tent and gear at Shipton's and travel light. Alternatively, you can do this stage in two days, or in the other direction as described in Stage 3D.

From Shipton's Camp, follow the directions to the summit of Lenana as in Stage 3A. From Lenana, descend the South-West Ridge to Austrian Hut, then follow the clear path south and then south-west, steeply down scree into the head of the Teleki Valley towards Mackinder's Camp. At the bottom of the steep scree slope, head right, away from the path, across an area of groundsels and boulders, then up the other side of the valley to reach American Camp, a small patch of grass on the northern side of the head of the valley (1½ to two hours from Lenana). Above you is the classic view of Mt Kenya's south-west face, with the long, thin Diamond Couloir leading up to the Gates of the Mists between the summits of Batian and Nelion.

From here go steeply up the scree to the north-west of American Camp to reach Hut Tarn (4490m) after less than an hour. (Next to the tarn is Two Tarn Hut, although this may be removed in the future.)

From Hut Tarn, you can see a large ridge extending westwards out from the main peaks. This is called Arthur's Seat, after a rocky hill in Edinburgh which it resembles, and it ends abruptly at a large cliff-face called the Eastern Terminal. North of this is another cliff-face called the Western Terminal.

Keeping Hut Tarn to your left, follow the path down to Nanyuki Tarn and then round the west side of the Eastern Terminal, scrambling over large boulders. With the cliffs on your right, the path climbs over a small col between Arthur's Seat and the Western Terminal, then descends to Hausberg Tarn and Oblong Tarn, about one to two hours from Hut Tarn.

The path goes between Hausberg Tarn and Oblong Tarn and zigzags steeply up a scree slope to reach Hausberg Col (4591m). From here, you drop steeply down a slope of yellow scree passing a few hundred metres to the left of Kami Tarn. Nearby are two huts: one belongs to the MCK and is supposedly for members only, although in recent years the lock has been forced several times and the hut may soon become disused; the other is a 'public' hut, although its tin walls are badly damaged and it provides hardly any shelter. (Both huts may be removed in the future.)

From Kami Tarn continue straight down the valley side to reach Shipton's Camp, about one to 1½ hours from Hausberg Col.

Stage 3D: Shipton's Camp to Point Lenana (via American Camp), plus descent to Hall Tarns

8km, 6-9½ hours, 755m ascent; plus 6km, 2-3 hours, 685m descent; total 1 or 2 days
This route follows most of Stage 3C in reverse, going to the south of the main peaks along a spectacular section of the Summit Circuit Path on the way to Point Lenana, so only brief directions are given here. Though this stage can be done in a day by fit and well-acclimatised trekkers, it means getting to the summit of Lenana in the afternoon,

KENYA

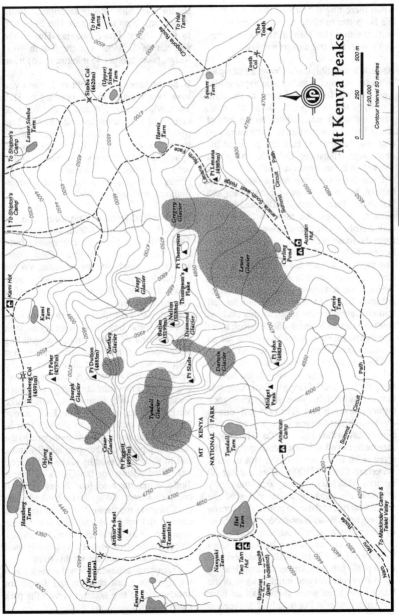

Mt Kenya Peaks

Scale 1:20,000

Contour Interval 50 metres

0   250   500 m

when there might be more chance of mist. It's far better to camp an extra night on the way, at either Hut Tarn or American Camp, and spread this stage over two days.

Ascent From Shipton's Camp a faint path leads steeply up the valley side to the south-west, aiming for a ridge crest to the right (north) of the main peaks. Go up this path, passing a few hundred metres to the right of Kami Tarn. From the tarn the path climbs up a yellow scree slope to a low point on the next ridge, Hausberg Col (4591m), about 1½ to two hours from Shipton's.

Drop down the scree on the other side of the col, heading towards Oblong Tarn and Hausberg Tarn, reached after another 30 minutes. Beyond the tarns, a large ridge called Arthur's Seat extends westwards out from the main peaks and ends abruptly at a large cliff-face called the Western Terminal. The main path leads between the two tarns then climbs up scree to a col in between the Western Terminal and the highest point of Arthur's Seat. (Avoid tending too far left immediately after the tarns, as this leads to another faint path which climbs much more steeply over serious scree to reach a col on the east side of Arthur's Seat summit.)

The path drops down the other side of the col and crosses large boulders at the base of steep cliffs to reach Nanyuki Tarn. Keep this tarn on your right, then go up over rock terraces to reach Hut Tarn (4490m), one to 1½ hours from Oblong Tarn. You can camp here or stay in the small Two Tarn Hut (which may be removed in future), or drop down the scree slope to the south of the tarn to reach American Camp (4300m) after another 30 minutes. This is a flat grassy area with plenty of room for tents, and fine views of the south-west side of the main peaks. There are no facilities here. Water is available from the near-by stream, so far unpolluted. Keep it that way.

From American Camp a path aims south to the head of the Teleki Valley and meets the main path from Mackinder's Camp leading up to Austrian Hut and Point Lenana, at the foot of the large scree slope, half an hour from Mackinder's. For details of this section

see the Naro Moru Route description. From American Camp to Austrian Hut takes two to four hours. From Austrian Hut to the summit of Lenana, via the South-West Ridge, takes another 45 minutes to one hour.

Descent From the summit of Lenana you have two choices for descending to Hall Tarns: via Austrian Hut and Tooth Col (three hours), or via Harris Tarn and Simba Tarn (two hours), as described in Descent Options from Lenana to Hall Tarns. The second option should not be taken in bad visibility, or if snow obscures the route, as the path zigzags between steep cliffs and a route-finding error could be fatal.

Stage 4: Hall Tarns to Chogoria Gate
14km, 4½-6½ hours, 1280m descent
This is the usual way of descending from Hall Tarns to the Chogoria Park Gate, although a tough alternative route, via the Gorges Valley, can be followed by experienced trekkers with energy remaining after the summit ascent.

From Hall Tarns the path aims eastwards, through some bowl-like depressions then past an area of eroded rocks resembling mushrooms, to follow a broad ridge crest with the main Gorges Valley down to the right (south). On clear days you get spectacular views down into the valley, past huge rock towers and pinnacles, with Lake Michaelson and the Vivienne Falls below. Looking the other way, to the left (north-east), you can see across the moorland to the subsidiary peaks of Ithanguni and Rutundu, and to their right (south) to the flat-topped hill called Kilingo or the Giants' Billiards Table. After three to four hours the path crosses a stream. Go up the far bank to reach the Chogoria roadhead (the top of the track coming up from Chogoria). You could camp here (there's a toilet block and water is available from the stream), but it's normally used only by trekkers coming up this route.

From the roadhead, follow the track down through the giant heather and forest for another 1½ to two hours, to reach the park gate (3017m).

Alternatively, from the roadhead you can follow the path that leads through heather and bush to the south of the track. This path is overgrown in places and crossed by animal trails, so a compass is essential. This is also a favourite area for buffalo, so make a lot of noise as you walk. After an hour you'll reach the edge of the forest and Urumandi Hut. The hut is in bad condition, but there's plenty of room for camping in the pleasant glade (more useful if you're coming up this route). Just before the hut the path crosses a stream on a high natural bridge; water is available from the stream, reached by a steep path that goes down the gorge on the east side of the bridge. (Urumandi means 'the place where water flows underground'.) From Urumandi Hut a track leads in an easterly direction through the forest (keep making anti-buffalo noises) to reach the gate after 1½ hours.

Just before the park gate, on the right side of the track, is the Parklands camp site. You can also camp at the gate itself (with permission from the rangers). Accommodation is also available at the Meru Mt Kenya Bandas, a group of simple log cabins about 500m from the gate. Beds with sheets and blankets, log fires, hot showers, and a shop selling beer and chocolate tempt many a hardened camper after a long Mt Kenya trek! (For more details see the Places to Stay section.)

Note that the Chogoria Park Gate may be moved to a position lower down the mountain in the future.

Stage 5: Chogoria Park Gate to Chogoria Town
29km, 6-8 hours, 1500m descent

From the park gate a dirt road winds down through the forest for 23km to the forest gate. The track is sometimes impassable for cars after rain, but you'll have no problem getting through on foot. The walk is not hard, but it can seem very long after several days on the mountain. There are no junctions to worry about, but unfortunately no views either, as the route passes through thick bamboo and forest; although the forest is beautiful, after a while you switch to automatic pilot and just keep plodding down.

From the Forest Station gate at the end of the track, it's still about 6km through fields and villages to Chogoria town. If the first 23km is enough for one day, you can ask to camp at the Forest Station here. Supplies are available from nearby *dukas*.

If you don't want to walk, you might be lucky and find a lift going down some of the way. Vehicles from Chogoria town often bring trekkers up to this point and go down empty. You'll still need to negotiate a fair fee, though. The drivers will look to see how tired you seem and raise the price accordingly! You can sometimes also arrange a lift in the Land Rover from the bandas. The starting price is around US$40 for the vehicle (but don't expect to have it all to yourself).

The Chogoria-Sirimon Traverse

Area Mt Kenya National Park
Distance 71km or 77km
Duration 5 days minimum
Start Chogoria Town
Highest Point Point Lenana (4985m)
Overall Altitude Gain 3485m
Finish Sirimon Park Gate
Nearest large towns Embu, Nanyuki
Accommodation Bunkhouses or camping
Access Bus & walk/hitch, organised trek
Summary Combines two routes less frequently used than the Naro Moru ascent and provides much better trekking, especially good for independent trekkers without a car, planning to camp all the way, as access is easy and there are several good camp sites. Bunkhouses also available, but one night's camping essential. Note: a slower ascent than the Naro Moru route means altitude sickness is less of a problem on this route, but still not uncommon. All trekkers are advised to take at least one extra day on the ascent.

The Sirimon-Chogoria Traverse already described can also be done in reverse. Much of the information required is in that description, but a few things are important to know if you're going in this direction, so the route is described briefly here.

Stage 1: Chogoria Town to Chogoria Park Gate

29km, 7-10 hours, 1500m ascent

This is a long stage, along a dirt road through the forest, although conditions underfoot are not too strenuous and route-finding is no problem. To reduce this walk you can camp at the bottom forest gate, near the Forest Station 6km from the town, and only have 23km to walk the next day. This stage can also be broken in two by camping at Bairunyi Clearing, about two-thirds of the way up, but water supplies here are not reliable, so you'll have to carry all you need for a night's stop, which makes the walk even harder. It's better to make an early start and go for it in one day.

Alternatively, arrange a lift up to the park gate at one of the hotels in Chogoria town mentioned in the Places to Stay section. The hire of a battered old Land Rover will cost about US$50 for the vehicle (more if the track is wet). Note that the dirt road is sometimes impassable to vehicles after rain, especially the last 7km, which are very steep. To cut costs you might be able to arrange a lift as far as Bairunyi Clearing or the bottom of the steep section, and walk the rest of the way.

Note that the Chogoria Park Gate may be moved to a position lower down the mountain in the future.

Sidetrack: Lake Ellis, Mugi Hill & Kilingo Hill

12km circuit from roadhead, 6-8 hours

If you do get a lift up to Chogoria Gate, it's worth spending two days here or at the Chogoria roadhead, to help acclimatisation. On the day in between you can sidetrack to Mugi Hill, Lake Ellis and Kilingo Hill (also called the Giants' Billiards Table). To reach these, take the branch that heads right off the track about 1km below the roadhead. A small track descends to a stream. Just before the stream a faint path leads uphill with the stream on the left. Continue this way for 1½ to two hours to reach the lake. About halfway up this path you can cross the stream

and walk through light bush to reach the summit of Mugi Hill. There is no path.

From the summit of Mugi Hill, you can make out the easiest way to the top of the flat-topped Kilingo Hill. Again there is no path. The best way is to aim north-east from Mugi Hill, down across the Mutonga stream and then up Kilingo on its north-western side.

Stage 2: Chogoria Park Gate to Hall Tarns

14km, 6-9 hours, 1280m ascent

From the park gate follow the track up to the Chogoria roadhead (two to three hours). Camping is possible here. There are toilets, and water is available from the stream, but there are no other facilities.

From the roadhead, the path drops to cross a stream then follows the broad ridge to the east of the Gorges Valley to reach Hall Tarns (4297m), about four to six hours from the roadhead.

Stage 3A: Hall Tarns to Point Lenana (via Harris Tarn); plus descent to Shipton's Camp

4½-7 hours, 685m ascent;
plus 2-4 hours, 755m descent

From Hall Tarns the path aims westwards towards the main peaks and divides after about an hour, above a flat green area at the head of the valley known as Temple Fields. (The left path aims south-west steeply up to Square Tarn and Tooth Col.) Go straight on, then keep left to avoid steep cliffs, to reach (Upper) Simba Tarn, and from there follow a path up steep scree to Harris Tarn (reached after another two to three hours). For details of the route from Harris Tarn to Point Lenana by the north face see Stage 3A of the Sirimon-Chogoria Traverse description.

The north face is a serious route and can be blocked by snow. If it is blocked, Lenana can still be reached if you go to Square Tarn and through Tooth Col to reach Austrian Hut. If it is misty, the section between Tooth Col and Austrian Hut can be tricky, and several trekkers have become seriously lost here. The important thing is not to drop down into the Hobley Valley. The path contours around the head of the valley and rises slightly to reach Austrian Hut. Green posts mark the route. From Austrian Hut, approach the summit of Lenana by the South-West Ridge (for details see Stage 3 of the Naro Moru Route description).

From the summit of Lenana you have two choices. If the section up the north face from Harris Tarn is passable, you can retrace this way, back to Harris Tarn, and from there down the scree to Shipton's Camp (two to three hours). If the north face is blocked by snow, do not attempt to descend this way. The other way is down the South-West Ridge to Austrian Hut, then east, round the head of the Hobley Valley, through Tooth Col, past Square Tarn and Simba Col, and down to Shipton's (three to four hours).

Stage 3B: Hall Tarns to Point Lenana, plus descent to Shipton's Camp via American Camp

4½-7 hours, 685m ascent;
plus 4-5½ hours, 755m descent
This is a long route which can be done in a day if you're fit and well acclimatised, but it is much better split into two with a night at either American Camp or Hut Tarn.

Follow the same directions from Hall Tarns to Lenana as described in Stage 3A, ascending either via Harris Tarn or via Tooth Col and Austrian Hut. From Lenana, descend to Austrian Hut, then head west, keeping south of the main peaks, to American Camp (1½ to two hours from Lenana) and round the Summit Circuit Path, via Oblong Tarn

and Kami Tarn, as described in Stage 3C of the Sirimon-Chogoria Traverse, to Shipton's (four to 5½ hours from American Camp).

Stage 4: Shipton's Camp to Judmaier Camp

13km, 3-4 hours, 890m descent
From Shipton's, the path aims north-west down the Mackinder Valley. About an hour from Shipton's Camp, the path divides: fork left, closer to the river, for the direct route. (Right is the longer route – via Liki North Hut.) Continue down the valley, over the ridge at the end, across the Liki North River, to descend to Old Moses Bunkhouse and Judmaier Camp.

Stage 5: Judmaier Camp to Sirimon Park Gate

9km, 2-3 hours, 690m descent
The dirt road down to the park gate is easy to follow. From there to the main road is another 9km, gently downhill.

The Timau Route

This is a rarely used route on the northern side of Mt Kenya. It meets the Chogoria Route at Hall Tarns, to the east of the main peaks. It follows a good dirt road on the lower slopes, but this deteriorates gradually into a track then a path about halfway up the mountain. For the final section of the route, there's not even a path and you walk through open country, relying totally on your map

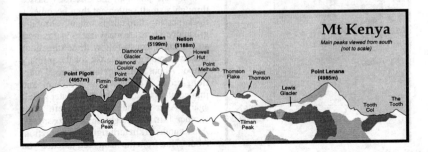

and compass for navigation. There are no facilities of any kind, although there are several good places to camp, making this is an excellent route for experienced, self-sufficient trekkers.

From the start of the route to Hall Tarns usually takes three days (two nights, with the third night at Hall Tarns). The long first stage can be driven, which cuts the walking by one day, although if you do this you should camp two nights on the ascent to help acclimatisation. If you're walking, this stage can be split into two sections, and the second section can be joined to Stage 2.

From Hall Tarns you can reach Point Lenana by various ways in anything from a few hours to a few days, depending on your route (see the Chogoria-Sirimon Traverse for details). After Lenana, you can descend on the Sirimon, the Chogoria or the Naro Moru route, with one or two more nights, to reach the foot of the mountain.

There is no park gate on this route, so before starting out you have to pay park fees at either the Sirimon Gate (which is nearer) or the Naro Moru Gate. For safety reasons, all trekkers on the mountain have to sign out at a park gate after their trek. If you come

down the Timau, you'll have to go to the Naro Moru or Sirimon Gate again afterwards.

It may be tempting to go up this route without paying park fees. Don't try it. The national park warden patrols the whole mountain by plane, and there are armed park rangers protecting the forest and moorland from poachers. If you're caught without tickets you could be arrested and fined.

Access

This route starts near Timau village, which is 20km north-east of Nanyuki, on the main tar road that circles the mountain. The first stage of this route follows drivable dirt roads for 29km to the West Marania roadhead at about 3300m, so if you have a car you can cut the first day's walking. It is also possible to arrange a lift to the roadhead at either Mountain Rock Hotel or Naro Moru River Lodge. (Naro Moru vehicles do not use the tracks described here but pass through the lodge's own farm to the west of this route.) But transport is by no means essential: the walk is not unpleasant or difficult, and also helps acclimatisation. The first stage can also be split into two sections.

Stage 1: Timau Track Junction to West Marania Roadhead
29km, 8-10 hours, 860m ascent

About 6km east of Timau village, the Timau dirt road turns off the main tar road, signposted to 'District Officer Timau', and 'CCM Nkiria Primary School'. If you're on public transport, get off at this junction. If you're driving from Nanyuki, turn right here.

From the junction, the dirt road passes through a small settlement then becomes a track passing through farmland, climbing gradually. There are many tracks in this area, so it's important to follow these directions closely. If you get lost, ask for the primary school. About 3km from the main road junction, cross a bridge over a stream and immediately fork left, and 100m later go left again. After another 1km, turn left. After another 1km go straight on at a crossroads. After another 1km turn right at a T-junction. About 7km from the main road junction you

KENYA

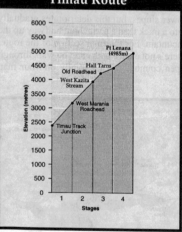

Timau Route

Elevation (metres)

6000
5500
5000 — Pt Lenana (4985m)
4500 — Hall Tarns
4000 — Old Roadhead
       West Kazita Stream
3500
3000 — West Marania Roadhead
2500 — Timau Track Junction
2000
1500
1000
500
0

1 2 3 4
Stages

enter a forested area and reach another T-junction, where you go left and ignore the right fork immediately afterwards. The track fords a stream and after another 1km leaves the forest and re-enters farmland. About 14km from the main road junction you reach the CCM Primary School. After this there are fewer forks and the track is easier to follow, although driving conditions get a lot worse.

Continue uphill from the school. Leave the farmland and enter low heath. About 2km from the school, a firetower is visible on the top of a conical hill straight ahead. About 5km from the school you pass a concrete water tank and some buildings. The track appears to stop at a gate, but actually turns right about 100m before this gate. This area, 19km from the main road, is a good place to camp if you want to split this section. The next section (10km) could be done on its own, or joined to Stage 2.

As you continue up the track, you can see a radio mast on top of a hill to your right. About 2km from the gate, the track swings sharply right and heads directly for the mast. After 2km the track turns sharp left up the hillside opposite the mast.

After another 1km you emerge suddenly onto the edge of Mbaru Crater, the remains of a small volcano. To your left (south-east) you can see across the open moorland to the huge dome of Ithanguni, a subsidiary peak of Mt Kenya, with the smaller dome of Rutundu to its left (north).

Follow the spectacular crest of the crater ridge for 2km to meet a larger track (coming from Embari Farm), and pass two upright posts (which once had a sign attached). About 1km beyond the posts (or 4km from the first view of Mbaru Crater) the track reaches a steep rock-step. This is the West Marania roadhead (3300m).

Vehicles should be left at the roadhead as the track beyond is badly eroded in places. (If you drive to this point, it is recommended that you walk from here to help acclimatisation.) To your left is the West Marania stream. Camping is possible here amongst the heather.

Stage 2: West Marania Roadhead to West Kazita Stream
14km, 4-5 hours, 550m ascent

From the West Marania roadhead follow the old track away from the stream and gradually uphill. Ten minutes from the roadhead, the track becomes a path and swings round to the left. You head towards a prominent peak to the south-west with an obvious rock-band. Behind you, to the north, the views open out. On a clear day, you can see across the dusty plains around Isiolo, beyond the Ewaso Nyiro River, to the red block of Ololokwe Peak.

Continue to gain altitude gradually. About 1½ hours from the roadhead, a large bowl-shaped valley lies down to the left. The path meets an old dry stream bed and undulates slightly. Keep the stream on your left and continue, to reach a fairly flat section of the West Marania Valley in between two hills. About three to four hours from the roadhead you can see through a broad col on your left (east) towards the dome of Ithanguni.

Soon after this, the valley of the Sirimon River (not the Sirimon Route) is clearly visible below and to the right (north-west). The path goes left and up to a col at the end of a ridge between the Sirimon and the Kazita valleys, reached after another hour. (Several sections of the path are faint or non-existent in this area, so great care should be taken. Check frequently with your compass against the map.)

Go through the col, and drop down, keeping right (south-east), to cross two streams. By the second stream (20 minutes from the col) is an excellent camping spot (3850m).

Stage 3: West Kazita Stream to Hall Tarns
9km, 5½-7 hours, 450m ascent

From the camping spot by the second stream, the path climbs to a spur on the east side of the valley, then turns sharply right south to follow the crest of the ridge between the West and East Kazita Valleys. Continue up the ridge for two to 2½ hours to reach a patch of boulders where the path seems to disappear. Keep right for a short distance, then up, rejoining the crest after a few minutes, to find the path again. After another 20 minutes the path stops abruptly. This is the old roadhead. You can see the remains of a turning circle (4150m).

From the old roadhead you can see a flat spot in the ridge on the opposite (south) side of the East Kazita Valley. There is no path, so either drop down to cross the stream and go up to this flat spot, or contour round the valley sides. Next to the stream is another good area for camping if you want to break the trek here.

You'll reach the flat spot, which is marked by some small cairns, about one to 1½ hours from the old roadhead. There is no path but very little vegetation, so the going underfoot is not too hard. Pass through the flat spot and drop steeply down to cross the Nithi North River, then steeply up the other side of the valley on scree and tussock grass to reach another col about two to three hours from the old roadhead.

Through the col is a steep, bouldery scree slope. Go up this for about 30 minutes, tending slightly right, to reach the crest of the ridge running eastwards from the peak called The Hat, in between the Nithi and Gorges valleys. The Hall Tarns area is directly below, reached after another half hour.

For full details on the camp site at Hall Tarns, and nearby Minto's Hut, see the Sirimon-Chogoria Traverse description, noting especially the advice about water. The hut may be removed in the future, but this will not worry trekkers on the Timau route, who have to be completely self-sufficient anyway.

Other Routes on Mt Kenya

On old maps of Mt Kenya, you may notice several other routes from the foothills up to the main peak area of the mountain. No paths of any sort exist on these routes and the going is generally very hard. They are rarely, if ever, used and should not be attempted unless you are a very experienced trekker

and have skilled local guides to accompany you. These include the following.

THE KAMWETI ROUTE

On the south side of the massif, this route involves several days of hacking through the forest zone where it is at its most dense and impenetrable, followed by a long stretch across empty moorland on the upper slopes. The route runs from the old Castle Forest Resthouse, north of Kianyaga village, and leads north towards the main peaks area. Trekkers attempting to follow this route as a descent, from the section of the Summit Circuit Path between Austrian Hut and Tooth Col, have become hopelessly lost. Some lucky ones were able to return to Austrian hut. Others disappeared without trace.

THE OLD MOSES ROUTE

On the west side of the mountain, in between the Naro Moru Route and the Burguret Route, the lower section of this route passes through a large section of dense forest. It is very rarely used and there is no path. Conditions in the forest are more serious than on the Burguret Route (see that route description for more details). The upper section of the route can be followed, and is described in the Burguret Route section.

THE KAZITA ROUTE

On the north-east side of the mountain, the lower section of this route is also called the Meru Route. It starts near the village of Katheri, near Meru town, and leads past Rutundu Hill, before crossing a very wide area of open, pathless moorland to finally link with the Timau Route north of Hall Tarns.

The Loroghi Hills

The Loroghi Hills rise from the plains around the town of Maralal, to the north of Kenya's Central Highlands. These plains and hills are the homeland of the Samburu people, a group of cattle-herding pastoralists closely related to the Maasai, with whom they share many cultural traditions including a taste for beads, ochre and bright red blankets.

The hills are composed of grassy ridges and lightly forested valleys, and generally enjoy pleasant weather conditions – ideal for trekking. However, the hills are seldom visited, and the only way most travellers see them is from the back of a fast-moving safari truck, as the main dirt road from Nairobi to Lake Turkana passes this way.

A trek in the Loroghi Hills is a good way to see the Samburu people, and an ideal way to explore a little-visited part of Kenya, without the expense of the national parks, and avoiding the logistical worries normally connected with visiting some of the more remote areas.

GEOGRAPHY

The Loroghi Hills (also spelt Lerogi or Lorochi) are a relatively small highland area, about 30km across and 20km long above 2000m, some 160km north of the Central Highlands, and bounded on the west by the Great Rift Valley. Their highest section is a broad ridge, dotted with several rounded peaks, running east-west across the northern part of the hills, with its highest point, a peak called Poror (2580m), roughly in the centre.

To the north of this ridge the ground falls sharply to the dry and dusty Marti Plains. To the west the drop is even steeper and more spectacular where the hills end abruptly at the sheer Lesiolo escarpment which overlooks the floor of the Rift Valley almost 600m below. To the south and east of the main ridge the incline is more gradual, and the hills are dissected by a series of parallel forested valleys running between broad grassy ridges.

TREKKING INFORMATION

There are no set trekking routes in the Loroghi Hills, as in the higher mountains more geared to tourism. However, across the ridges and through the forests there's a network of tracks and paths used by local people for driving cattle to water, or simply for getting from one *manyatta* to the next. The trek described here, which we've called the Loroghi Hills Circuit, is only one of many that are possible in this area.

If you've got the time you can combine trekking in the Loroghi Hills with a camel safari in the area south of Maralal around Barsalinga, using the Yare Club & Campsite as a base (see Places to Stay, Maralal). The cool, forested highlands contrast sharply with the semi-desert scrubland, and this is an ideal way to get a broader impression of the fascinating Samburu landscape and lifestyle.

Costs

Costs for trekking in this area are minimal. You pay only for your guide (details below), plus of course your food and supplies.

Route Standard & Days Required

The route described here goes from Maralal up to Poror, crossing several ridges and valleys, then to the edge of the Rift Valley escarpment at Lesiolo, returning to Maralal along a large broad ridge that runs through the centre of the hills. The route follows paths and tracks all the way, through several different sorts of landscape, and the going is generally easy. There's one major sidetrack – a long loop where you can go right down the Lesiolo escarpment wall onto the floor of the Rift, which is highly recommended, although conditions are more demanding.

The trek can be done in three days, or five if you do the Lesiolo Loop sidetrack. The five-day trek involves three long days interspersed with two short days, making the trek less strenuous overall – although, if you're feeling fit, some stages can be combined. It

KENYA

is also possible to shorten this trek by cutting the first and last stages, and travelling between Maralal and Poror by matatu or hitching.

Guides

It is not absolutely essential to have a guide, but taking one does have several advantages. With a guide you'll feel less of a stranger when you meet people along the way, and the guide can help you communicate with the locals, so you'll be able to get to know them as real people rather than as just part of the landscape. This is a close-knit community and your guide will probably do a bit of family visiting along the way, so you might be invited into a manyatta. Courtesy and manners are important features of Samburu culture, and it's customary to ask permission before walking though peoples' land. If your Swahili isn't up to much your guide can help

you with the formalities. And, of course, being with a local guide, you can ask questions and learn from him much more about all aspects of Samburu life and the landscape you're passing through.

A guide is also useful when your route passes through the forested valleys where buffalo and even lion are sometimes encountered. This is not a major problem and, if you make enough noise when you pass through these forested areas, you'll scare most animals off long before you even know they were there, but having a guide with a spear, and a general 'feel' for the bush, is a lot more comforting.

The best place to get guides is the Yare Club & Campsite in Maralal (see Places to Stay). You can book ahead at Yare's Nairobi office (see Yare Safaris under Organised Treks & Tours in this chapter), or just turn up

---

The Samburu

The Samburu people number about 75,000. Their territory is in the shape of a triangle with its base between the towns of Rumuruti and Archer's Post and the apex near the southern tip of Lake Turkana. Their name is thought to mean 'butterfly' in the Maa language (which they share with the Maasai), presumably a reference to their bright and colourful clothing, but this derivation may be erroneous.

Brightest of them all are the *morans* (warriors), young men aged between about 15 and 30, who traditionally protect the people and their cattle from wild animals and human enemies. They keep their hair long and plaited, coloured orange with thick ochre, with beads at the back and sometimes a peak-like 'comb' at the front. Headbands of beads and buttons and earrings made from bone are *de rigueur*, and a thin chain around the ears and across the chin seems to be an essential part of the get-up. Armbands, wristbands and waistbands, all made from beads and strips of leather, are also important. Clothes are minimal: a loin cloth and a blanket worn as a robe (or two if it's cold) and a pair of sandals complete the outfit. Vital accessories are a long thin spear, a broad-bladed knife tied round the waist, and a *runga*, or fighting stick, often with a lump of sharp metal attached to ensure maximum damage to enemies in times of emergency.

The Samburu migrated to this part of northern Kenya about 300 years ago from the drier regions west of Lake Turkana. The hills provided good water and grazing for their cattle when the plains were hot and dry. Much later, in the early 1900s, the colonial government of Kenya also recognised the area's potential for farming, but the hills were never settled by Europeans in a big way and the land has stayed safely in the hands of the Samburu. ∎

DAVID ELSE

and arrange things on the spot. Guides arranged at Yare are English-speaking *moran* (warriors); they can accompany you for as long as you want, whether on a day-walk or longer trek. The charge for a guide is US$15 per day, payable to the club, which then pays the guide. If you are happy with the guide's service, a tip of around an extra day's pay for every three to five days is appropriate.

When arranging a long trek, spending some nights out in the bush, you need a tent, sleeping bag, stove, food, and so on. The moran will provide for himself. It's important to make sure he understands the number of days involved and the route you want to take, and that he carries enough food, or knows where to get some along the way. It's a matter of pride for a moran to be able to walk for days on end with no food or water, but it can be difficult when you stop for lunch and the guide just sits and watches you eating.

Porters are generally not used in this area, but if you're planning a really long trek you can arrange to hire a camel from Yare Club to carry your gear. (One camel can carry gear for three people.) Starting and ending at Maralal this costs from US$35 per day and needs to be arranged at least a few days in advance.

Your other option in this area is the Plastic Boys – a youth cooperative based in a curio shop near Maralal market. The group consists of blacksmiths and leatherworkers making things to sell in the shop, motor and tyre mechanics ready to help passing motorists, and local guides. The guides can show you round Maralal, accompany you on short walks in the immediate area, or arrange longer safaris (using donkeys to carry the gear) through the Loroghi Hills, or further afield to Mt Nyiro and the Suguta Valley (see the separate section on this area later in this chapter). Some travellers have described the Plastic Boys as a 'bit of a rough bunch', while others have found them friendly and helpful. If you're thinking of a long trek, it's worth arranging a day-walk first to make sure you and your guide get on OK. For more information visit the Plastic Boys at their curio shop, although the chances are they'll find you first – as soon as you get off the bus!

Park Fees & Regulations

Maralal is at the centre of a National Sanctuary wildlife reserve, where hunting is forbidden and grazing restricted, but there are no regulations concerning trekkers. The route passes through the reserve but fees are not required.

Maps & Guidebooks

The Loroghi Hills and the area around Maralal are covered by the Survey of Kenya 1:50,000 map sheet number 78/3 *(Maralal)*, but see general note on Maps in the Planning section of this chapter.

For day walks, *Mountains of Kenya* (see Guidebooks, in the Facts for the Trekker section in this chapter) has sections on the area around Maralal.

Supplies

Maralal has several shops where you can buy all you need for a trek as long as your tastes aren't too elaborate: items such as bread, tins of margarine and jam, tinned meat and fish, packet soups, biscuits, chocolate, tea, coffee and dried milk. There's a market for fruit and vegetables. Anything more specialised should be brought from Nairobi or one of the bigger towns.

PLACES TO STAY
Maralal

Maralal is a regional administrative centre, and the Samburu capital. With its dusty streets and crooked lines of clapperboard shops and bars, complete with verandas and swinging signs, the place has a frontier feel about it, and more than one writer has drawn obvious Wild West analogies. On the main street is *Buffalo Lodge*, the biggest bar in town, usually with a group of local cowboys lurking on the front step, and reasonable single/double rooms out the back for US$4/6 per person, although it gets noisy at night. A better deal is the *Jamaru Hotel* where basic but clean rooms are US$4/7 (US$6/11 en suite). Couples can share a single. The restaurant is the best in town, with breakfast at US$1.20, snacks from US$0.30 to US$1, and full meals US$1 to US$2. The manager

---

The Maralal International Camel Derby

The Maralal International Camel Derby is held in October every year, and it's worth tying in your trip to northern Kenya with this unique race if you can. Similar camel derbies are held in Tanzania, Tunisia, South Africa, Egypt and Dubai, but Kenya's version is noted as being the hardest, longest and most spectacular, following a cross-country route rather than being held on a race track. There are four main classes of rider: Professional, Semi-Pro, Amateur and Novice. The race is open to Kenyans and non-citizens, and the Novice class means tourists who may never even have seen a camel before, let alone raced one, can enter. There's also a Junior class for younger bravehearts. Prize money totals several thousand US dollars. The entry fee for novices and amateurs is US$30 and all money raised goes to local charities. The 1996 race attracted a large field of entrants from Kenya, Tanzania, the UK, the USA and Japan. If you fancy having a go, camels can be hired for US$125 (including saddle and handler). The main organisers of the event are Yare Safaris – you can get more information at their Nairobi office (listed in the Getting Around section of this chapter) or from Yare Club in Maralal. ∎

---

is a quiet guy called Patrick; he knows all the local guides and can advise on any onward travel plans you may have. If you're on a tight budget, down the street from the Jamaru are a few cheap lodging houses, with rooms starting at US$1, but don't expect much privacy.

The most popular place for travellers is *Yare Club & Campsite* (☎ (0368) 2295), in a pleasant patch of countryside about 3km south of Maralal town. Self-contained bandas (bungalows) cost US$14/17/19 for one/two/three people. Breakfast is US$2 and other meals are available. A half-board double is US$29. Camping costs US$4 per person. There's a bar and restaurant for reasonably priced meals or snacks. The club is run by Yare Safaris who also operate camel-trekking safaris in the area south-east of Maralal, along the Ewaso Nyiro River. A transfer service ties in with these safaris, going from Nairobi to Maralal every Saturday, returning every Friday. If you're on the safari, transport is free. You can get more information or make bookings at the Yare Safaris office in Nairobi (listed under Organised Treks & Tours).

On the west side of town, about 3km from the centre is *Maralal Safari Lodge* (☎ (0368) 2060), under new management since 1996. Rooms in very comfortable wooden chalets, with log fires and views over the surrounding wildlife reserve, cost US$100/140 per single/double full board. In the low season this drops to US$60 per person. The staff are

friendly and the food is excellent, and there's also a bar open to non-residents. Even if you're not staying here, the lodge is a good place to come for a celebratory meal or a beer in luxurious surroundings after your trek. Taken separately, lunch is US$15 and dinner US$18. There's also a swimming pool. The lodge also organises game walks accompanied by a ranger in the surrounding National Sanctuary, and other day walks with or without camels in the area. They can also advise on longer safaris, using donkeys as pack animals, in the semi-desert areas of northern Kenya. You can get more details or make reservations from the Lodge's agent in Nairobi, Let's Go Travel (listed under Organised Treks & Tours).

On the Hills

This area is not used to tourists (even, or especially, those on foot), so there are no huts or lodgings. You need a tent and a full set of camping gear.

GETTING THERE & AWAY

The nearest town to the Loroghi Hills is Maralal, about 250km directly north of Nairobi, or about 300km by road.

To get here from Nairobi take a bus or shared taxi to Nakuru or Nyahururu. From there minibuses run about five times a day to Maralal. The fare from Nyahururu is US$4. If you're staying at Yare Club (see Places to Stay), get the minibus to drop you off before you reach town.

If you're heading to/from Nanyuki (for Mt Kenya), a useful service might be the daily bus between Isiolo and Maralal, via Wamba (US$7).

If you're doing a Turkana truck trip that passes through Maralal after seeing the lake, you could get dropped off here and make your own way back to Nairobi after your trek.

For independent travel further north, battered Land Rovers carry passengers most days from Maralal to Poror (US$2), Marti (US$4) and Baragoi (US$8) on a go-when-full basis. If these don't fit in with your plans you can hire a small pick-up (with driver) from the dusty car park near Buffalo Lodge. From Maralal to Poror is about US$20, to Losiolo US$40, including petrol (all rates negotiable).

Loroghi Hills Circuit

Area Maralal National Sanctury
Distance 68km or 78km
Duration 3 to 5 days minimum
Start/Finish Maralal Town
Highest Point Poror Peak (2580m), but viewpoints at Lesiolo and Lepedera (2476m) are more impressive
Nearest large towns Maralal
Accommodation Camping
Access Bus, car
Summary Non-strenuous walking through grassy hills and forested valleys in a rarely visited area. Homeland of Samburu people.
Note: employment of guides to provide introductions and interpret trekkers and local people, as much as to show the way.

Access

The route described here starts in Maralal town. To get there from Yare Club & Campsite, you can follow the main dirt road, but it's much more pleasant on the footpath which runs behind the hostel and continues for 3km, roughly parallel to the road, straight into the main street on the southern side of

town. From the roundabout by the Shell petrol station, go past the market, then 0.5km to the next roundabout and the road out of town. If you're staying at Maralal Safari Lodge you can join the route near the showground (see Stage 1 below).

Stage 1: Maralal to Poror
25km, 6-8 hours

From Maralal head south-west along the main dirt road that leads to Poror, Baragoi and Lake Turkana. Go straight on at a roundabout (the right turn leads up to Kenyatta House, where Jomo Kenyatta was imprisoned before Kenya's independence; the building is now a national monument), and just after another road on the right (which you ignore), take a path that leads round the edge of the showground and down to the Yamo River. Cross this river onto the west bank and follow the path northwards, keeping the river on your right, to meet a track coming in from the left. Keep on this for about half an hour, passing a large house (the Provincial Commissioner's official residence) up to your left, until a path branches off on the left just before the track crosses the river. Follow the path up the valley side through the edge of the forest, keeping the river down to your right. At a fork, take the left path and keep on going up, more steeply through dense bush. The path then levels out, following the crest of a broad ridge until it meets the main dirt road (about 1½ hours from the Commissioner's house).

Turn right and follow the dirt road for about three km to the scattered village of Il Bartuk (about two to three hours from Maralal). Take the small track branching off left towards Seketet Ridge (the locals just call this area Seketet), then aim north-west on small paths through Il Bartuk, passing between the church (up to your right) and the *duka* (down to your left). Drop gradually into a forested valley to meet the upper reaches of the Nundoto River. Cross the Nundoto and go up the valley side onto the northern end of Seketet Ridge.

There are many paths through the forest and over the ridges in this area. Depending on the way your guide takes you, you'll either continue north on Seketet Ridge, or head north-west to cross another river, the Ntotoi, and come up onto another ridge called Loiting. Both ridges have a track running along their crest, climbing gradually, passing occasional huts. These ridges blend into the main east-west ridge that runs across the centre of the Loroghi Hills, and the tracks pass through wheat fields. (The farm is managed by a European farmer on land he leases from the local Samburu people. You may see tractors or combine harvesters, looking slightly incongruous in this pocket of cultivation surrounded by manyattas and natural forest.) Some of the tracks around the wheat farm may be changed each year but at least one will lead to Poror village (four to five hours from Il Bartuk).

There are no lodgings in Poror, but one of the shopkeepers may let you pitch a tent on the grass behind the shops. You can also ask for permission to camp at the primary school or the police station. Your guide may be able to sleep with friends or family near the village (although you'll need to check this before you leave Maralal). Camping is also possible at the Forest Guard Post, about 2km from Poror just on the other side of the main Baragoi-Maralal road. The rangers are friendly and seem happy to have company, although if their head ranger is due to visit then camping may not be allowed. A small tip for their help is appropriate.

Stage 2: Poror to Lesiolo
10km, 2-3 hours

If you're going for the five-day trek, this is an easy stage. If you're not taking the Lesiolo Loop, and want to do a three-day trek, you can combine this stage with Stage 4 and get back to Poror on the same day.

From Poror follow the track through the wheat fields, aiming south-west then west, keeping to the crest of the broad ridge. Keep right at all forks, to reach the end of the track, at a grassy patch on the very edge of the Rift Valley escarpment (two to three hours from Poror).

The Samburu name for this area is Lesiolo, and the viewpoint itself is often called World's View. From here you can see down onto the valley floor and across to the Tiati Hills and the faint outline of the Cherangani Hills, some 120km away on the other side of the Rift.

Camping at World's View In the manyatta near World's View lives a Samburu man called Lele. His job is to see that nobody camps on the actual viewpoint, but it's OK if you put your tent up near his hut for which he charges around US$4. Some other locals had established a rival camp site when we passed through, but there was no-one around to take money. The situation seems fluid so be prepared for changes when you arrive here.

If you haven't brought a guide from Maralal, a local guide can be arranged here, for the sidetrack to Lependera or the Losiolo Loop described below. He will also show you where to find water, from a spring in a clump of trees on the edge of the escarpment. Local boys will offer to bring you firewood. (Although you perhaps shouldn't encourage this as the boys are likely to tear down live branches in their enthusiasm.) If you leave your tent you should also hire an *askari* (watchman) for while you're away.

Sidetrack to Lependera
2 hours return

To the left (south-west) of World's View a spur juts out westwards perpendicular to the main escarpment. On the end of this spur you can see the peak of Lependera (although it's marked on some maps as Lesiolo). To reach this peak, follow the path that runs south from World's View, parallel to the main escarpment. It drops down into a forested valley and climbs up the other side over a grassy hill, then drops into another valley before climbing again through bushes to reach the summit (2476m) about one hour from World's View.

The spur sticks out just far enough so that from the summit of Lependera you can see south down the valley all the way to Lake

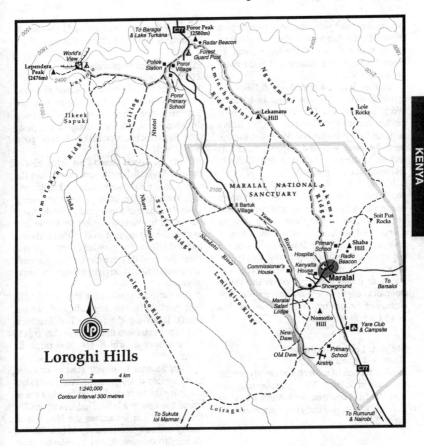

Loroghi Hills

0   2   4 km

1:240,000
Contour Interval 300 metres

Baringo, straight across (west) to the Cheranganis, and north up the Rift, towards the blistering heat of the Suguta Valley. When it's cold and misty on the edge of the escarpment, it's hard to imagine that you're only just over 150km away from one of the hottest places on earth (see the Suguta Valley section).

Retrace your steps to World's View.

Stage 3: The Lesiolo Loop
12km, 8-10 hours

From Lesiolo you can drop down the spectacular escarpment onto the floor of the Rift Valley, and then come back up on another path to the north which brings you to Lesiolo again. You are strongly recommended to take a guide for this section. Before you leave Maralal ensure he knows this area; this is serious territory, and no place to start getting lost.

From World's View you follow the path described in the Lependera sidetrack, then keep going down the small path which follows the sharp ridge down towards the valley floor. You then tend right (northwards) across the flat section of the floor visible from the summit, along the foot of the escarpment until you cut across another path about 5km further north, which climbs up a valley between two of the large spurs, to reach the top of the escarpment to the north of World's View.

Another way up and down follows the forested valley that you cross in between World's View and Lependera, but this is harder, especially after rain. (After heavy rain, all the paths up and down the escarpment become wet and slippery, and this section of the route becomes very difficult, and dangerous in places.)

If you leave World's View at sunrise, you'll be on Lependera by 8 am, and down on the valley floor after another two to three hours. It takes two to three hours to work round the base of the escarpment, then at least another two to follow the winding escarpment path back up to the top. Allow eight hours, minimum. Carry plenty of water, as it can get very hot on the valley floor and supplies there are not reliable. This section of the trek requires commitment, but is well worth the effort.

Stage 4: Lesiolo to Poror
10km, 2-3 hours
For this section of the trek you simply retrace the route of Stage 2. This is a short stage so, if you're fit, it could be done after the Lesiolo Loop (if you started early), or combined with Stage 5.

Sidetrack: Poror Peak
1 hour return
If you're a peak bagger, you might want to reach the summit of Poror (2580m), the highest point of the Loroghi Hills. This is no north face of the Eiger; a small dirt road leads all the way to the top, servicing the radar station. Walk up the track, but make sure it's OK with the guards for you to be there. Photos are not a good idea. North of Poror is another peak, easily reached by leaving the dirt road on its last bend before the radar station, and walking a few hundred metres through the grassland. From here you get very good views northwards over the plains

around Marti and east towards the Ndoto Mountains and the Mathews Range.

Stage 5: Poror to Maralal
21km, 6-7 hours
This route follows an old disused dirt road that runs down the Lminchoominyi and Sakumai ridges, some 5km east of the main dirt road. Since it fell into disuse it's impassable for vehicles, but makes a very good path.

From the Forest Guard Post to the east of Poror village, follow a path down into the valley on the left (north) side of the rangers' hut, then up the other side, contouring around the base of Poror peak, with the radar station on the summit visible up to the left, to meet the old disused road. Turn right onto this and follow it as it swings south-east and keeps going in this direction, along the crest of a broad ridge, through light bush and areas of grass.

After an hour you reach a fork. Keep right (left goes down into the valley of Ngurumaut), following the ridge. The Samburu word for the bushes that grow in this area is Lminchoominyi, which give the ridge its name.

After another hour you start to descend more steeply through dense bush, although it's still easy to pass, then go in a big curve round the side of a hill called Lekamaru. To the left you can see across the Ngurumaut Valley to the exposed outcrop of Lole Rocks, directly to the east. About 45 minutes from Lekamaru you reach an indistinct fork, which is easy to miss. Take the left track up through trees, keeping Lole Rocks in view (the right goes downhill towards Il Bartuk).

The route becomes more distinct as you continue descending towards Maralal. About four to five hours from Poror are the first outlying huts. Down on the left is the Loikas Valley, with huts and shambas spreading up the hillside. Another hour and you'll reach Maralal town, passing the hospital on your right, to reach the roundabout by the Shell station in the town centre. Time for a celebratory beer in the nearby Buffalo Lodge before returning to your accommodation.

The Suguta Valley

The Suguta Valley is a large section of the Great Rift Valley, between Lake Baringo and Lake Turkana, in the far north of Kenya. At its northern end, the valley floor is only a few hundred metres above sea level, making it one of the lowest parts of the Rift Valley system. It's also one of the hottest parts of Kenya: a harsh and inhospitable region of desert, salt lakes, volcanic cones and jagged lava fields. Not the most obvious place to go for a walk.

But despite the unrelenting heat and the rugged landscape (or perhaps because of it), the northern Suguta offers some exciting wilderness treks and a fascinating contrast to the alpine moorlands and snowy peaks of the mountains further south.

Very few visitors come to this area. Due to the harsh nature of the terrain and climate, the logistics of an independent trek can be complicated and time-consuming, although organised treks are available. But if you've got the time, and fortitude in great store, the trekking here is undeniably worth it.

HISTORY

For many centuries, the Suguta area has been a meeting point for the territories of the Samburu and Turkana people. The Samburu (described more fully in the Loroghi Hills section earlier in this Kenya chapter) are cattle-herders, travelling vast distances across the plains in search of grazing. The Turkana live in remote settlements; they are also traditionally herders, but in recent times many have lost their cattle (due to droughts and restrictions on migration routes) and switched to farming or catching fish from the lake.

The first Europeans to reach the area were the Austro-Hungarian Count Samuel Teleki and Ludwig von Hohnel, in 1888. Their journey, sometimes called the last of the great East African expeditions, had also taken them past Kilimanjaro and Mt Kenya, before they reached the southern shore of Lake Turkana. They named this vast inland sea Lake Rudolph, after the prince of Austria, and the title stuck until the 1970s, when it was named after the people who inhabit its shores.

GEOGRAPHY

The whole section of the Rift, from just north of Lake Baringo to the southern tip of Lake Turkana, is the Suguta Valley, but the area crossed by the routes described here is its far northern section, between Mt Nyiro in the east and the Loriyu Plateau in the west.

Mt Nyiro (also spelt Ngiro or Ngiru) stands to the east of the Suguta. Even though it is surrounded by desert, its higher slopes are covered in forest, and small springs emerge lower down to feed the villages of Tum and South Horr, and several other small settlements in the foothills.

From the top of Nyiro to the bottom of the

> **Warning**
> The information in this section mostly dates from 1993, when we trekked here as part of the research for the first edition of this book. When we returned in late 1996 for the second edition, the area was closed to visitors. Drought had created intense competition amongst local peoples (Samburu, Turkana, Pokot, Rendile and Somali) for cattle water holes and grazing land. Cheap guns, brought into Kenya from conflicts in neighbouring Uganda, Sudan and Somalia meant that every dispute turned into a war, with hundreds of lives lost. Although tourists might not be directly targeted, the area is definitely not safe.
>
> On top of this, local bandits called *Ng'oroko* were taking advantage of the general unrest, stealing from villages and vehicles. Several European aid workers were shot at while driving in the area, and at least one group of tourists was attacked by Ng'oroko while trekking across the Suguta. This dangerous situation may continue for many years, or it may be over by the time you read this book. The introductory information has been updated, and route descriptions have been retained, but it is very important to familiarise yourself with the local security situation before starting any trek in the Suguta area. ■

KENYA

KENYA

Suguta, the land drops over 2500m in less than 20km. This area is sliced through by deep ravines, called *luggas*, which are usually dry but become awash with sudden flash floods after rain.

North of the Suguta, several volcanoes have erupted from the Rift Valley floor to create a gigantic natural dam, called The Barrier, which holds back the waters of Lake Turkana. These volcanoes are still active – even since Teleki's time there have been small eruptions – but there are no definite peaks. The highest point is Kakorinya, and nearby are the remains of Teleki's Volcano, although it's unlikely that he actually went to this exact spot.

South of The Barrier, the seasonal Suguta River flows into Lake Logipi Namakat. The water cannot flow out and evaporation is high, so the lake is saline and the shores encrusted with vast deposits of 'soda'. The name of the lake means, not surprisingly, 'salt water' in the local Turkana language.

An obvious feature of Logipi is a large outcrop of yellow rock, rising out of the lake like an island, called Naperito, or Cathedral Rock. The other main feature is the large flock of flamingos which feed on algae in the shallows at the lake's edge. Although not as pink as their cousins in the lakes further south, these birds are still a fascinating sight.

Lake Turkana is the largest of Kenya's Rift Valley lakes, and one of the largest desert lakes in the world. The lake is often, rather romantically, called the Jade Sea, and in certain light conditions it does have a muddy green tinge. More noticeable are the white-capped waves which often skip across its surface, kicked up by the strong winds that blow in from the desert to the east. Sometimes these winds get up to hurricane force, transforming the lake into a stormy sea.

TREKKING INFORMATION

The treks described in this section start at the small town of Baragoi, on the main dirt road between Maralal and Lake Turkana, and end at Loyangalani, (also spelt Loiengalani and Loiyangelani), a village on the south-east shore of Lake Turkana.

Costs

Your costs for trekking in this area will be for your guide and pack donkeys (more details below). Other costs are your food and supplies, plus transport to the start of the trek and away at the end.

Route Standard & Days Required

This section describes two routes (imaginatively called the Long Route and the Shorter Route). By their nature, routes do not always follow a set path. It cannot be emphasised enough that conditions in the Suguta Valley are very very tough; by far the most demanding trekking described in this book.

To do either of these treks independently you're looking at eight or nine days for the Long Route and six or seven for the Shorter Route, plus another one or two if you do the sidetrack up Mt Nyiro.

Guides & Porters

Guides are essential, as are donkeys to carry gear and water supplies. You can ask around for a guide in Baragoi, but it's more likely that one will find you, soon after you step off the matatu. It is very important to choose your guide carefully. Most are reliable, although even the good ones generally know only the Shorter Route, from Parkati straight to the lake. Very few guides know the Long Route past Lake Logipi and over The Barrier to the west of Kakorinya.

Once you've arranged your guide, he can help you sort out donkeys and handlers. If you're doing the Shorter Route, and happy to rough it, you can get by with one or two donkeys per trekker. On the Long Route you'll need two or three each. After Tum, you should allow for at least 7L of water per person per day, although this can be reduced to about five on some days if you cook with the saline water from the springs or from Lake Turkana. Check whether the guides and handlers will be drinking spring water or relying on the supply being carried. A litre of water weighs a kilogram, and donkeys can carry about 40kg each in these conditions. You can carry your own food and kit, but it makes the walking much easier if you get a donkey for this as well.

Daily rates for a guide are between US$3 and US$5 per day. A donkey costs about the same depending on how many you need, and the fee normally includes the handler. (The guide may offer to be the handler as well, but it's better to have somebody extra to look after the donkeys.)

Another option, if you're coming through Maralal, is to contact the Plastic Boys – a youth cooperative which offers guiding services (see the Loroghi Hills section for more details). We've heard from travellers who have arranged treks with them. Rates seem very negotiable: a six-day trip, including transport from Maralal, accommodation in Baragoi, donkeys and food costs between US$150 and US$250 each for two people, or US$100 to US$200 each for four people.

If the logistics of organising your own trek in the Suguta put you off, Kenya Hiking & Cycling (listed under Organised Treks & Tours in this chapter) are the only company running good quality treks here, as part of their longer Lake Turkana safari. They go from Tum via Parkati and the west side of The Barrier. After Nabuyatom, the long slog to Loyangalani is avoided by using a boat. If you were thinking of going to Turkana anyway, this might be an option to consider.

Maps

The Suguta area is on Survey of Kenya 1:250,000 sheets NA-37-5 *(South Horr)* and NA-37-9 *(Maralal)*, although the Maralal map only covers Stage 1. More detail on the stages between Parkati and Nabuyatom is shown on the 1:100,000 sheet 53 *(Ng'iro)*, but see the general note on Maps in the Planning section of this chapter.

Supplies

In Baragoi the shops are surprisingly well stocked with food, although there's not much in the way of fresh fruit and veg. There's more choice, and a better market, in Maralal.

Whichever route you take, it's most important to consider your water supply. After Tum there are no reliable sources of

good water until you reach Loyangalani. Parkati has salty but drinkable spring water. There is one small spring on Lake Logipi's north-east corner, called Maji Moto, with warm, very salty water which local people and their goats can survive on, but you'd really be pushing yourself to the limit to rely on this. Lake Turkana is also quite saline; you can live by drinking it, but it never quenches your thirst.

Unless you've had some experience of desert survival techniques, it's strongly recommended that you carry most of your water requirements for the trek. Plastic jerry cans are not usually available in Baragoi. You can sometimes hire some with your donkeys, but not always. Even old ones left behind by other trekkers tend to be split, or are badly patched and not reliable. It's better to buy your own, either from Maralal, or from Nairobi, where they're cheaper.

Dangers

A dangerous feature of Lake Turkana is its population of Nile crocodiles. Many thousands of years ago the lake was larger, filling much of the Suguta Valley and emptying into the River Nile. When the lake shrank, the crocs got cut off; there's now more crocs in Lake Turkana than in the Nile itself. They're supposed to be fairly timid, but you should still be very careful about going for a swim!

By far the most dangerous feature of a trek in this area (apart from the bandits mentioned in the warning at the start of this section) is the heat. The Suguta Valley is certainly the hottest place in Kenya (and probably one of the hottest places on earth), with daytime temperatures often above 50°C. There's very little shade anywhere on the whole route, and the heat is intensified by the black lava.

PLACES TO STAY
Baragoi

Along the main street are a couple of basic lodging houses where a bed costs US$2 to US$3, and a smarter place charging US$7. About 3km north of town is a camp site used mainly by Turkana safari trucks; independent campers pay US$4 per night.

KENYA

The Baragoi Balkan Link

As you pass through Baragoi, look out for a bar called Bosnia Wines & Spirits. It's on the village's main (and only) road, unofficially dubbed Yugoslavia Street. Strange names to find in Samburuland – a long way from the Balkans – but there is a reason.

In the early 1990s, regiments from Kenya's army served as part of the peace-keeping forces in the former Yugoslavia. The UN paid well, and Kenyan soldiers found themselves earning ten times their usual wage. The Samburu (together with their Maasai cousins) are regarded as natural warriors, and make up a significant proportion of Kenya's army (the chief of staff is Samburu). After their tour of duty, soldiers returning to the Baragoi area were rich men. Several invested their pay by building shops and bars – hence Bosnia Wines & Spirits.

But the money was not earned easily. In a report in the British newspaper the *Independent* by Mary Anne Fitzgerald (author of *Nomad* – see Books section) she notes: 'Although the ferocity of the fighting they witnessed left the Samburu unfazed, the atrocities they saw shocked them deeply. Says one: "The Serbs and Croats are not soldiers like we are. They slaughter women and children like dogs. Real soldiers only fight men"'. ∎

Loyangalani

Loyangalani is a frequently windy village, the area's main settlement and the Turkana safari truck terminus.

Just north of the centre are two camp sites, *Sunset Strip* and *El Molo Lodge*, where you can pitch a tent for US$2; both are about the same standard. El Molo also has some concrete bungalows, which get incredibly hot, for about US$40, plus a pool, bar and restaurant.

The Oasis Lodge caters for exclusive fly-in visitors, but you can rent a self-contained bungalow for US$100 per person full board. There's a bar, restaurant and swimming pool open to non-residents for US$12 per day.

On the Treks

There is no accommodation along the routes described. A tent is not essential, as rain is very unlikely, but a mosquito net is useful to keep out sand-flies. A sleeping bag is worth taking for the few hours each night, usually just before sunrise, when it gets cool.

GETTING THERE & AWAY

The treks described start at Baragoi, about 450km north of Nairobi. The only public transport is via Maralal (see Getting There & Away in the Loroghi Hills section). The treks end at Loyangalani. There is no public transport and your only way in or out is by hitching (or private air charter). Most vehicles you'll see are Turkana safari trucks, usually full of people who have paid for the whole trip and they don't stop to pick up hitchers! You'll also be competing for that valuable space with local people, who have probably been waiting longer than you.

The Suguta Valley Long Route

Area Great Rift Valley, northern Kenya
Distance 179km
Duration 8 days
Start Baragoi
Finish Loyangalani
Highest Point The Barrier (approx 1000m), between Lake Logipi and Lake Turkana
Nearest large town Maralal
Accommodation Camping
Access Bus/hitch, car, organised trek
Summary Long, hard and very serious trek through a harsh and inhospitable region, with complex logistics and few escape routes, yet immensely rewarding with stunning scenery. Homelands of Samburu and Turkana people.
Note: unrelenting heat, severe walking conditions and rugged landscape make this by far the most serious trek described in this book. Approach with caution.

Stage 1: Baragoi to Kowop

32km, 7-10 hours

This is a long walk, but straightforward and not too bad if you get an early start. From Baragoi follow the dirt road north towards Lake Turkana, with Mt Kowop, an outlier of Mt Nyiro, to your north. About 18km from Baragoi take a small dirt road on the left, heading north-west between Mt Kowop and Mt Nyiro, to reach the small settlement of

Kowop. Alternatively, your guide should know shortcut paths that lead more directly to Kowop, but can be harder underfoot.

Stage 2: Kowop to Tum
22km, 5-6 hours

Continue northwards on the small dirt road. Up to your right, the densely forested slopes of Mt Nyiro contrast sharply with the dry, dusty landscape you're walking through. There are a few faint junctions, but keep straight on to reach Tum, a one-street village surrounded by Turkana and Samburu huts. If you're doing the sidetrack up Mt Nyiro, you can camp at the Forest Station, about one to 1½ hours above the village. (A small fee is expected.)

Sidetrack: Tum Forest Station to Mt Nyiro Summit & return
15km, 5-6½ hours, 1300m ascent;
plus 15km, 4-5 hours descent

This diversion takes you up to cool, forested high ground – a pleasant change to the heat of the semi-desert. With an early start you can do this sidetrack in a day. If your guide is not sure of the way, arrange for somebody in Tum or at the Forest Station to show you.

From the Forest Station, a clear path climbs steeply up to a low point on the main Nyiro ridge, reached after two to three hours. Turn left (north) and follow faint paths through the forest, keeping to the ridge and rising gradually. You'll reach the summit, called Mowongo Sowan ('Buffalo Horns'; 2830m) after three to 3½ hours. Just beyond the summit is another outcrop with spectacular views down to Cathedral Rock and the Suguta and across The Barrier to Lake Turkana, with Nabuyatom and South Island clearly visible.

From Mowongo Sowan, return to Tum by the same route.

Stage 3A: Tum to Parkati
22km, 6-7 hours

This section of the trek is the only way loaded donkeys can go. From Tum, take the rough track aiming north. It follows the crest of a broad ridge, winding gradually downhill, to reach the small settlement of Parkati.

Stage 3B: Tum to Parkati (via Lemun Lugga)
20km, 7-9 hours

If you've got a good guide and donkey handlers you can walk this stage, while the donkeys go the easier way (Stage 3A). From Tum, aim north-east, crossing bare rocks, to reach the edge of the escarpment from where you can see down into the Suguta. A steep path zigzags down into Laraguti Lugga then follows it northwards to meet the larger Lemun Lugga coming in from the right. At the end of the lugga, tend right across rocky mounds to reach the track which comes down the ridge to the east. Keeping Nyiro on your right shoulder, follow this track to reach Parkati.

Stage 4: Parkati to Lake Logipi
20km, 6-8 hours

From Parkati aim west, over a stony plain, crossing an old airstrip, aiming for a very distinctive yellow mountain visible over the near skyline. This is Namurinyang, which means (not surprisingly) 'yellow mountain'. Cross the right (northern) shoulder of Namurinyang, then drop steeply down towards Lake Logipi. Aim for some trees visible on the edge of a ridge in between Namurinyang and the lake. This is a good place to wait for several hours to avoid the intense midday heat.

From the trees, continue dropping over ridges of black lava to finally reach the edge of Lake Logipi. Pass Maji Moto, the saline spring, and continue heading west with Lake Logipi to your left and The Barrier up to the right. At the end of the lake, several sandy luggas flow down from a dark mountain called Kalolenyang. Follow the largest of these luggas up away from the lake to reach a clump of stunted palm trees and a good place to camp. There is absolutely no water here.

Stage 5: Lake Logipi to Lake Turkana (South Shore)
18km, 5-7 hours

Walk northwards out of the lugga, up towards the top of The Barrier. As you gain height, there are some excellent views back

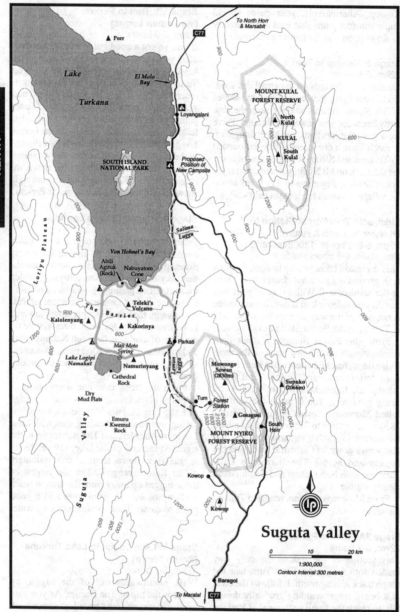

Suguta Valley

0   10   20 km

1:900,000
Contour Interval 300 metres

KENYA

down to Lake Logipi and, if you're lucky, the hint of a breeze. When you reach the crest of The Barrier, the vista of Lake Turkana opens out before you, with South Island clearly visible in Von Hohnel's Bay.

From the crest, descend over gravelly hills towards the lake. There's a clump of large trees growing by the side of a wide lugga, about 500m back from the shore, where a tent can be pitched. Nearby are a few huts used by Turkana as a temporary fishing camp.

Stage 6: Across Lake Turkana South Shore (to Nabuyatom)
17km, 5-7 hours

Keeping the lake on your left, aim towards the large yellow outcrop of Abili Agituk. Watch out for crocodiles as you walk along this section. Go south of Abili Agituk, and back down to the lake shore, where there's a perfectly circular pool of green water, used as a hatchery and nursery by the local crocs. Step extra carefully here!

The second half of this stage is over a recent lava field, where the setting magma has broken up into huge angular slabs, which makes for slow going. Keep the lake to your left as you work round the bay towards Nabuyatom Cone. Pass to the right (south) of Nabuyatom, to reach a small beach, with a couple of stunted thorn trees growing at one end. These provide shade, but it's better to camp higher up the beach where it's flatter.

Nearby are the remains of a crashed aircraft, used several years ago to bring in rich tourists looking for an exciting place to do a spot of angling. There's also a pattern of stones on the beach placed by a group of young British explorers to mark the centenary of Teleki's arrival at the lake.

Sidetrack: Up Nabuyatom Cone
1 hour return

From the beach it's possible to walk up to the top of Nabuyatom Cone. The sides of the cone are smooth and very steep, but provide good traction for shoes. Before you go too far up, try coming down again; it's no good finding you can't do it when you're at the top! Just as you'd expect from an old volcano, the top

dips steeply inwards to form a crater. Views from the rim, across the eastern end of The Barrier, with Mt Nyiro in the background, and along the eastern shore of the lake out to South Island, are worth the scramble.

Stages 7 & 8: Nabuyatom to Loyangalani (via Salima Lugga)
50km approx, 2-3 days

From the beach below Nabuyatom, keep the lake to your left, and aim northwards. Don't follow the edge of the lake too closely, so that you can cut across peninsulas between the many bays, and avoid the crocodiles. Salima Lugga is a large gorge. Keep near the lake edge here to avoid the steep walls.

Continue north on the other side of the gorge to meet the end of a rough track used by a truck carrying fish to the factory in Loyangalani. You may be amazingly lucky and meet the truck, and get a lift. Otherwise camp the night here, or continue to meet the dirt road from Baragoi as it comes down the lake escarpment. From here to Loyangalani is another 20km along the dirt road.

It might take you three days to do these last two stages, if you camp at Salima and somewhere else between there and Loyangalani. There's a new camp site planned 10km south of Loyangalani, which, if it's finished, would be an obvious place to break the journey.

The Suguta Valley Shorter Route

Stages 1 to 3: Baragoi to Parkati
As described in the Long Route.

Stage 4: Parkati to Nabuyatom (direct)
25km, 10-12 hours

This is a long day, but there's no ideal place to break the stage. It's best to start at first light, which also means you can do some of the steep section while it's still cool.

From Parkati, a path leads up a lugga aiming north through scrubby bush. There are several faint paths, which can be confusing, but keep going north to reach the crest of The Barrier. After you cross the crest of The Barrier another path aims north towards Salima. Ignore it, and tend left (north-west) towards Nabuyatom Cone. The going is hard, across jagged rocks and lava. You'll eventually reach the beach east of Nabuyatom, as described in Stage 6 of the Long Route.

Stages 5 & 6: Nabuyatom to Loyangalani (via Salima Lugga)

Follow the directions in Stages 7 and 8 of the Long Route.

Alternative Shorter Route

We heard from Australians Tracey Wilson and Ian Smith who arranged a trek with the Maralal Plastic Boys in 1996. After following the usual route from Baragoi to Tum, they went direct from Tum to the Salima Lugga, without dropping down to Nabuyatom. They walked from Tum up into the hills east of the valley and camped at a place called Lororok Lasamis. From there they descended to reach the banks of Lake Turkana at Salima, where they camped and paid off their donkey handler who returned to Baragoi. Their final day was a real long one: from Salima all the way to Loyangalani. They left before dawn and arrived after midnight, but their fortitude paid off as they managed to hitch a ride back to Nairobi on a plane that had been chartered by a film crew. All it cost was a cup of coffee for the pilot!

Other Trekking Areas in Kenya

Mt Elgon

Mt Elgon is an extinct volcano in the far west of Kenya, straddling the border with Uganda. The mountain is shaped like a broad dome, with a large crater surrounded by several peaks at its highest point. The lower parts of the mountain are covered in dense forest, but on the upper slopes there is a large area of open moorland, which is excellent trekking country. Unfortunately, access to the moorland and peaks from the Kenyan side is difficult (but not impossible) for independent trekkers without a vehicle, so a relatively small number of people come here for walking and trekking. For those that do make the effort, this emptiness is of course a major attraction.

Since the mid-1990s, Mt Elgon park has made great efforts to attract more visitors, and walkers and trekkers are seen as a market yet to be fully tapped. A tourism officer has been appointed. Some short nature trails which can be followed on foot through forest on the lower slopes have been established and day walks on the high moorland are also possible for those with cars, but provisions for trekkers looking for multi-day trips are still being established. The situation is likely to improve, however, so a visit to Mt Elgon is well worth considering.

Logistics for trekkers are a lot simpler on the Uganda side of Mt Elgon. For details on this, plus general information on the local history and geography of Mt Elgon, see the Uganda chapter.

Park Fees & Regulations

The main route up Mt Elgon is in Mt Elgon National Park. All visitors entering the park must pay fees, these are:

Entrance	US$15	per day
Children	US$5	
Vehicles	US$4	per day
Camping	US$2	per night
Armed ranger	US$10	per day

A lower entrance rate for trekkers (as on Mt Kenya) may be introduced.

On either side of the park are Forest Reserves. Plans to incorporate these reserves into the park have been shelved. There is a degree of cooperation between Kenya Wildlife Services (in charge of the park) and the Department of Forestry, but not enough to allow tourists to pass between the two areas.

Tourist access to the Forest Reserve was temporarily suspended when we were researching this book. When the reserves re-open to the public, trekking will once again be possible here, so information on the main trekking route in the reserves is carried over from the last edition of this book, with a few small updates.

Warning

Any walk or trek on the high moorland of Mt Elgon can be serious. Routes are often indistinct and the weather can be a lot worse than on Mt Kenya. The mountain is often covered in mist, and hail or driving rain is not uncommon, even in the dry season. Temperatures drop below freezing most nights. You should be properly equipped and competent with a map and compass.

Altitude sickness can also be a problem on the higher parts of Mt Elgon. It is advisable not to drive straight up to one of the roadheads and start walking immediately, as this does not give you time to acclimatise. ∎

Maps & Guidebooks

The national park produces a small leaflet covering the vegetation, geology and wildlife, plus background on the caves and descriptions of nature trails. The only map readily available is *Mt Elgon Map & Guide* by Andrew Wielochowski, available from specialist maps shops in Britain, and possibly from bookshops in Nairobi.

Access

Mt Elgon is about 400km west of Nairobi. The nearest large town is Kitale, linked to Nairobi by tar roads and regular bus services (express buses charge US$8 for the eight hour trip). From Kitale, it's another 29km to Chorlim Gate, the only entrance to Mt Elgon National Park. If you're driving, take the road west towards Suam; after 14km branch left (signposted) onto dirt roads which pass through farmland for another 15km. On public transport, matatus run from Kitale to Enderbess and Suam; ask to be dropped at the 'park junction' 14km from Kitale – from there you'll have to walk or hitch to the park gate.

Places to Stay

In Kitale there are several cheap lodging houses. Better than most is the *Bongo Hotel* with singles/doubles at US$6/10 (US$2 extra for en suite) including breakfast. Better again is the friendly new *Alakara Hotel* with rooms at US$8/12 (US$12/18 en suite) including breakfast. Another option to consider if you're driving is *Sirikwa Safaris Guest House*, about 25km north of Kitale (covered in the Cherangani Hills section).

About 28km from Kitale, near Chorlim Gate, is *Mt Elgon Lodge*, a grand old colonial farmhouse, now a seldom-used and slightly faded hotel with single/double rooms for US$94/120 full board. Visitors can usually negotiate resident rates (US$55/85) and further discounts are available if you don't take lunch and dinner.

In the national park itself, *Kapkuro Campsite* is just 1km from the gate, in a beautiful forest clearing frequented by bushbuck, monkeys and birds, with water and a basic toilet. There are also some other sites deeper in the forest with no facilities. Elsewhere on the mountain there are no huts – trekkers need to be self-sufficient with tents and camping gear. If you want to save money you can camp outside the park gate, while arranging your ranger and other aspects of the trek. Mt Elgon Lodge may also allow camping.

If the Kimilili Route through the forest reserve re-opens, Kimilili town has a few lodging houses plus the slightly smarter *New Crest Hotel*. Camping is usually allowed at the Kaberua Forest Station, near the start of the route.

Trekking Routes

There are at least three routes from the forested foothills to the crater and main peaks

KENYA

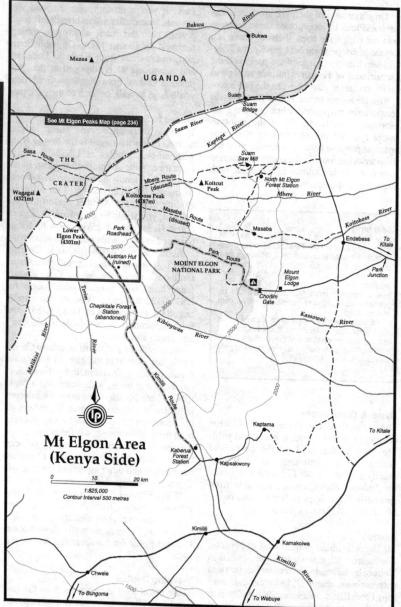

Mt Elgon Area (Kenya Side)

0   10   20 km

1:825,000
Contour Interval 500 metres

UGANDA

Muzoa ▲

Bukwa
● Bukwa

River

Suam
Suam
Bridge

Suam River

Kaptega River

Sasa Route

THE
CRATER

Wagagai ▲
(4321m)

See Mt Elgon Peaks Map (page 234)

Mbere Route
(disused)

▲ Koitoboss Peak
(4187m)

▲ Koitcut
Peak

Suam
Saw Mill

● North Mt Elgon
Forest Station

Mbere   River

Masaba Route
(disused)

● Masaba

Koitoboss River

Lower
Elgon Peak
(4301m)

4000

Park
Roadhead

3500

Austrian Hut
(ruined)

Endebess

To Kitale

Park
Route

MOUNT ELGON
NATIONAL PARK

Mount
Elgon
Lodge

Park
Junction

Terim

Malikisi River

River

Chepkitale Forest
Station
(abandoned)

3000

Kibioywan
River

Chorlim
Gate

Kassowai   River

2500

Kimilili Route

2000

Kaptama

To Kitale

Kaberua
Forest
Station

Kapsakwony

Kimilili

Kamakoiwa

Kimilili River

Chwele

To Bungoma

1500

To Webuye

on the Kenyan side of Mt Elgon, although those seldom used quickly become overgrown and very difficult to follow. The only route open to tourists in 1997 was the Park Route, an up-and-down route through the national park. When the Kimilili Route reopens it will make a long traverse theoretically feasible, although this may still be complicated by the rules forbidding tourists to cross from the reserve into the park and vice versa. However, it is likely that the situation will be further relaxed in future, so both routes are outlined briefly here.

The Park Route Most visitors to Mt Elgon National Park come with a car. It's usual to camp overnight at one of the sites near the park gate, then early next morning drive up through the forest to the park roadhead (about 32km, two hours), then walk through the moorland up to the crater rim (about 2½ to three hours).

From the rim, you can reach the summit of Koitoboss Peak, the highest point on this side of the mountain. Follow a faint path leading up the southern shoulder of the peak, then along the base of cliffs on its western side, to scramble up a steep, densely vegetated gully to reach the flat top, and a large cairn that marks the summit (4187m). From the rim to the summit it's one to 1½ hours.

The descent from the summit to the roadhead takes about three hours, which gives you time to drive back down to the camp site in the same day. This is an excellent day walk and gives you a good taste of the mountain, but don't be fooled into thinking it's a doddle, just because it's shorter than other routes described in this book.

Walkers have to be accompanied by an armed park ranger, so you'll need a spare seat in the car for him.

Another option, which makes things less of a rush, is to camp at the park roadhead. Then, from the crater rim you can reach the Lookout Block and the Hot Springs (another two to three hours each way). This option needs to be discussed in advance with the tourism officer at the park gate, as the ranger

needs to be equipped with tent and sleeping bag. You may have to provide food.

If you don't have a car, you might be able to hire a park vehicle to transport you and your ranger to the park roadhead. Alternatively, the Park Route can be trekked in its entirety, but from the gate to the roadhead in a day with a full pack is really pushing it. Another option might be to get a lift about halfway and walk the rest. Whatever, you need to discuss your plans at least a day in advance with the tourism officer, so that tents, equipment and food can be arranged for the armed ranger who will accompany you. For groups of more than two, or if you want to descend into the crater, two rangers may be obligatory.

The Kimilili Route This route goes through the forest reserve on the southern side of the mountain to Chepkitale Forest Station, but since this was abandoned in the 1980s, the drivable track has become badly eroded and overgrown in places. This route was closed to tourists in the mid-1990s due to an outbreak of cross-border cattle smuggling in the area, but is likely to re-open in the future.

Access is via the small town of Kimilili, the village of Kapsakwany and the forest station at Kaberua. You should report here before going up the mountain, to ensure that the security situation is OK.

From Kaberua the route leads through forest to reach the ruined Chepkitale Forest Station after about 20km (with two points on the way where the track crosses streams where camping is possible). Then it's another 7km through heath to the end of the once-drivable track; nearby is a flat spot good for camping and a ruined hut (once known as 'Austrian Hut' as some Austrian volunteers made repairs here in the 1980s).

From the ruined hut it's about three to four hours along a faint (often non-existent) path across the moorland to reach Lower Elgon Tarn. Camping is possible here. From the tarn you can scramble up the gully in the cliffs to reach the summit of Lower Elgon Peak.

Overall, you need two days to reach the hut, another day or two to explore the peaks

KENYA

KENYA

Mt Elgon Peaks (Kenya Side)

0   1   2 km

1:130,000
Contour Interval 100m

and crater area, plus at least one more day to descend.

An Elgon Traverse If you came up the Park Route, from the crater rim near Koitoboss you could attempt a complete traverse of the mountain by circling the rim and descending on the Kimilili Route (if it reopens). This is a very demanding trek, taking at least four days and requiring good navigation, but it's also spectacular and very satisfying, and worth considering if you're properly equipped and supplied.

From Koitoboss Col, aim generally south-west, inside the crater rim, contouring and keeping high to avoid dropping down into the deep valleys to your right (west), but keeping below the crest of the rim to avoid rocky outcrops. There is no path, and the going is hard, through groundsels and low bush. After about three hours, you'll reach a large dome-topped buttress at the north-eastern end of Lower Elgon Peak. Pass to the right of this, then contour right (do not go steeply up) through a col in the crater rim to the west of Lower Elgon Peak. Keep contouring left and then down over a series of flat terraces to reach Lower Elgon Tarn.

From the tarn, aim south, keeping to the right of Sudek – the huge separate buttress standing to the south of the main peak. Cross the southern shoulder of this buttress and continue south down the crest of a broad grassy ridge, finally to reach the abandoned 'Austrian Hut', about 3½ hours from Lower Elgon Tarn.

From here it's about 27km, mainly downhill, along the track, past the abandoned Chepkitale Forest Station, to reach Kaberua Forest Station.

Future Possibilities There have been proposals to enlarge Mt Elgon National Park to include the area of forest around the Kimilili Route, and to reopen Chepkitale Forest Station. If this happens, the track will be improved, making vehicle access possible and day walks to Lower Elgon Peak easier.

As part of the changes, the Kimilili track may be extended north-eastwards to join the existing national park track near its current roadhead. If this happens, it will be possible to do a 'car-assisted' walk in a long day from the Kimilili roadhead up to Lower Elgon Peak, then round the crater rim to Koitoboss, and back down to the national park roadhead, to be met by a vehicle there.

The Cherangani Hills

The Cheranganis are about 300km northwest of Nairobi. Although usually referred to as 'Hills' there are several summits here above 3000m, and the highest peak, Nakugen or Kamalagon, is at 3529m, which makes the Cheranganis the fourth-highest range in Kenya.

Unlike the other major mountains of Kenya, the Cheranganis are not volcanic in origin. They were created by localised uplift and the erosion of the surrounding landscape. Steep escarpment walls surround the range on three sides, separating the fertile farmland and forest on the high ground from the semi-desert scrubland at their base.

The Cheranganis also differ from most other large mountain ranges in Kenya in that they are populated. The people grow crops and keep sheep and cattle. The lower areas on the southern and eastern parts of the range are quite densely inhabited, with farms and extended villages. The best trekking is in the higher northern areas, but even here there are small scattered villages; the whole mountain range is crisscrossed by a network of paths and tracks, which makes it ideal trekking country.

Maps

The northern section of the Cheranganis is covered by Survey of Kenya 1:50,000 map sheets 75/2 *(Sigor)*, 76/1 *(Chesegon)*, 75/4 *(Cherangani)* and 76/3 *(Tot)*, and the whole range is covered by the 1:250,000 sheet NA-36-12 *(Kapenguria)*, but see the general note on Maps in the Planning section of this chapter.

Access

Access is fairly straightforward: the main sealed road north from Kitale towards Lodwar on the west side of Lake Turkana passes along the west side of the range. Public transport runs along this road. There are also several smaller roads which can be used if you've got your own car.

In colonial times the Cheranganis were a restricted area, but during the 1970s and 1980s the region was opened up and several local farm development schemes were introduced. Although access to the higher parts of the range was made considerably easier, the Cheranganis remained rarely visited. Some enterprising walkers did make it this far, and several good car-assisted day walks are now established as 'regulars'.

The number of outside visitors is slowly increasing, and we've heard from several intrepid parties who have trekked for several days in this area. Conditions are usually less serious than on the other high mountains, such as Mt Elgon and Mt Kenya, and the Cherangani Hills offers enormous potential for further exploration.

KENYA

Trekking Routes

Walking conditions are generally not strenuous, and most paths and tracks pass through rolling grassy hills, farmland or patches of forest. Weather in the dry season can be pleasant, but days of rain, mist and very cold winds are not at all unknown, so you should be well equipped with proper clothes, and self-contained with tent and camping gear. There are some small shops in the larger villages, but you should plan to be fairly self-sufficient with food. Water is generally available, except on the higher ridges.

There are no set routes, so you'll just have to follow local paths, using your compass and asking directions as you go (some basic Swahili or a guide is almost essential).

A popular four-day trek on the northern side of the range starts at the village of Sigor, and goes up Mt Koh then down to Tamkal before going round the head of the Weiwei Valley, and returning along the Sondhang Ridge to Ortum or dropping off the ridge to reach Parua and the main road at Ortum. Also on the northern side of the range, a three-day trek is possible on the Cheranganis' main outlier, a massif called Sekerr, taking you to Mtelo (the highest point) for fantastic views of the main range to the south and east, the semi-desert Lake Turkana Basin to the north and the mountains of Uganda to the west.

A longer trek of five to six days starts in Parua, on the eastern side of the range, follows the Sondhang Ridge southwards to reach another peak called Kalelaigelat, and then follows the edge of the huge Tangasia Valley to the village of Sina. From here it drops off the escarpment to cross the Moruny River at Kachemogon and goes through dry bush country to meet the main road north of Chepareria.

Another popular route (involving three to five days trekking) on the eastern side involves getting public transport along the dirt 'Cherangani Highway' to the village of Kabichbich, and then following small dirt roads, tracks and paths to Kalelaigelat and on to the tiny settlements of Kamelei and Chepkotel. from here you can head east to finally reach the summit of Kamalagon (shown on some maps as Nakugen), the highest peak in the Cheranganis, with splendid views overlooking the Weiwei Valley. You can then either continue north to reach Sigor or return south via Tangul.

Places to Stay

At the foot of the hills are two excellent places for accommodation, where you can also get more route information, hire local guides, and make inquiries about other possible routes and destinations.

The first of these is *Sirikwa Safaris Guest House*, a beautiful old colonial settler farmhouse in lush gardens on the eastern side of the hills, run by the friendly team of Julia and Jane Barnley. Camping on the grassy site, with fire pits, clean showers and toilets, costs US$6 per person. Accommodation in large walk-in tents costs US$18 per person. Bed and breakfast in comfortable rooms (complete with hot water bottles!) costs US$36/54 for singles/doubles. Evening meals and lunches are also available. Full board is US$90 per double. Apart from camping, government taxes of 30% have to be added to accommodation rates.

Jane and Julia don't get up into the hills much these days, but they have a team of guides who know the area very well and can help you plan a trip of anything between three hours and a week. Frequently recommended by visitors is a guide called Salim, but the others are all good. The charge is US$6 to US$12 per day, depending on where you want to go. The guides also know about market days, water points, camping spots and local matatus which run along the dirt roads through the hills, from where the highest peaks can be reached. Trekking with one of these guys is an absolute delight and highly recommended. Jane's husband, Tim Barnley, was a well-known ornithologist and several Sirikwa Safaris guides are also skilful birders, so if this is your scene it's an extra bonus.

The guesthouse has no phone, but you can try booking ahead by writing to Sirikwa Safaris at PO Box 332, Kitale, but a deposit is normally required to reserve a room. Most independent travellers simply turn up; if there's space you're made very welcome. The guesthouse is signposted about 25km north of Kitale just off the main road towards Lodwar. Minibuses running between Kitale and Mukatano (near Kapenguria) will drop you at the signpost – from there it's about a 400m walk. The fare is US$0.75.

The other place to stay in the Cherangani area is *Marich Pass Field Studies Centre*. This contrasts sharply with Sirikwa Safaris; although only 75km further north, the climate and setting here is very different. Instead of a colonial farmhouse in lush grounds, the Field Studies Centre is a group of African-style huts on the edge of the semi-desert, in a shady patch of trees overlooking the large River Moruny, which flows out of the Cheranganis at this point. The centre was founded by David Roden with the full backing of the local community, primarily for school groups from Kenya and overseas, but also to attract visitors to this seldom-reached area. Dorm beds cost US$5, single/double/triple bungalows cost US$10/15/20 and camping is US$4. Hot and cold drinks, snacks and meals are sold at reasonable prices. Supplies are available from the nearby village. The staff at the centre are friendly and knowledgeable and can arrange short walks to local villages, longer hikes in the surrounding hills or multi-day treks across the Cheranganis. Guides cost US$4 per half day, US$6 per full day (8 hours) or US$12 per 24 hours for longer treks (this includes food and equipment for the guide). Porters can also be hired at about half this rate. Also available are vehicle trips to the remote South Turkana National Reserve, the Turkwell Gorge or local Pokot markets. Other options include bird-watching and even gold-panning.

The Field Studies Centre has no phone. Reservations are not usually required, but if you need to arrange something in advance you can write to PO Box 564, Kapenguria. The Centre is 100km north of Kitale, on the road towards Lodwar. A few km beyond Marich Pass (where the main road cuts through a narrow gap in the hills) there's a

junction on the right (east) to Sigor. Ignore this and continue for 2.5km to see a sign indicating the Field Studies Centre on the right from where it's another 1km down a sandy road. If you're on public transport, drop at Marich village, from where there's a short cut to the Centre. A matatu from Kitale to Mukatano (where you change) is US$1, Mukatano to Marich is US$2.

The Aberdare Range

The Aberdare Range, between Mt Kenya and the Great Rift Valley, was named after Lord Aberdare, president of the Royal Geographical Society, by the explorer Joseph Thomson in 1883. The local Kikuyu people, who farmed the range's well-watered slopes, called it Nyandarua, which means 'drying hide'; the mountains' shape resembled an animal skin pegged out to dry, with sticks under the spinal ridge to keep it clear of the ground.

To the west of the range, the Maasai herders on the Rift Valley plains called the highest peak Oldoinyo Lesatima, 'the mountain of the bull-calf'. Today this name is usually shortened to the more manageable Satima. The summit is just over 4000m (13,120 ft), which makes the Aberdares the third-highest range in Kenya.

Most of the range falls within the boundaries of the Aberdare National Park (also called Aberdare Ranges National Park), which encloses the high mountains plus a large area of lower forest called the Salient where most of the park's big game is found. Above the forest are areas of bush and open grassy moorland – an ideal place for wilderness trekking. But the Salient gets the limelight and the high moorlands remain little-visited – an attraction, of course, for trekkers.

For independent low-budget trekkers, access is a problem. You're not allowed to walk *into* the park (although you can walk when you're *in* the park), and there's no public transport. Many visitors to the high moorland come by car and use it to reach

KENYA

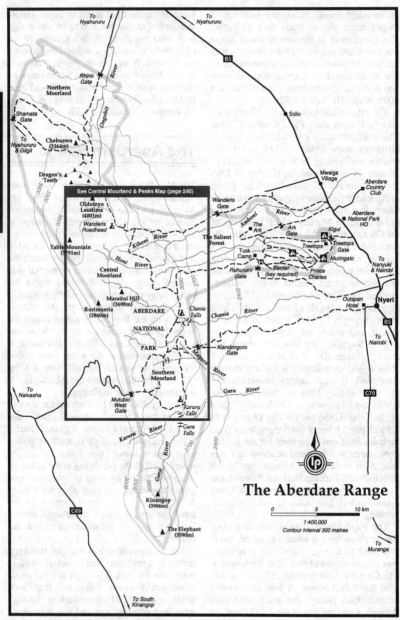

See Central Moorland & Peaks Map (page 240)

The Aberdare Range

0	5		10 km

1:400,000
Contour Interval 300 metres

different areas for walks of one or two days. Or they use the vehicle to carry tents and gear from one camp site to the next, with one person driving while the others walk. Another option is to join an organised trek. Several of the specialist operators (listed in Organised Treks & Tours in this chapter) run trips here. Using their vehicles, staff, equipment and local knowledge of course costs money, but compared with car hire rates and the time you'd spend arranging things, prices are not unreasonable.

Geography

The Aberdare Range is a long, narrow massif, stretching north-south for about 70km, with its southern end about 80km north of Nairobi. Along the centre of the range are the main peaks: Chebuswa (3364m), Satima (4001m) and Table Mountain (3791m) are in the Northern Moorland; Rurimueria (3860m) and Maratini (3698m) are in the Central Moorland; and Kinangop (3906m) and The Elephant (3590m) are in the Southern Moorland.

Maps

The Survey of Kenya (SK) produces a *Tourist Map of the Aberdare National Park* which should be available from bookshops. This is fine for the Salient, but not much good for moorland walking. If you need more detail, use SK 1:50,000 sheets 120/1 *(Ndaragwa)*, 120/3 *(Kipipiri)* and 134/1 *(Kinangop)*, but see the general note on Maps in the Planning section of this chapter.

Trekking Information

Altitude Most of the trekking is in moorland above 3000m, and the Aberdares' highest point is Satima (4001m). If you're not acclimatised, you'll certainly feel the effects of altitude, but you're unlikely to have any serious symptoms. If you do start to suffer, the advice is the same as on any other mountain – go down.

Costs Vehicle rental and organised treks are covered in the Getting Around section earlier in this chapter. Other costs are park and ranger fees, detailed below.

Route Standard There are no set trekking routes in the Aberdares. The lower slopes of the range are covered in thick forest, cut through only where small dirt roads lead to the park gates. On the upper slopes, the forest is not so dense, but no footpaths exist. So trekkers usually follow the small drivable tracks. This part of the park sees very few vehicles so you're unlikely to be disturbed.

With your ranger (details below), it is also possible to leave the park tracks, and make your own way across open grassland or follow animal trails through forest, bamboo and dense bush, although the going is hard and a few hours' bushbashing each day is usually enough for most people. It also gets the adrenaline going when there are fresh buffalo or elephant droppings on the ground and you can never see more than a few metres in front. In the Hagenia zone (see the illustrated Flora & Fauna section for more details), the trees are widely spaced, making a parkland landscape which is very pleasant for walking.

Guides Animals such as lion, elephant and buffalo sometimes come up from the Salient onto the high forest and moorland. Although you're unlikely to see any large wildlife while walking here, all trekkers must be accompanied by an armed park ranger, and he's definitely not there for decoration.

Rangers have to be collected from the park headquarters at Mweiga, 7km north of Nyeri. Although it may be possible to organise a ranger within 24 hours, it's better if you phone or write in advance to the Assistant Warden (☎ (0171) 55024), Aberdare National Park, PO Box 22, Nyeri, saying that you need a ranger for trekking. Even then, you may have to wait for a few hours, or go to a park gate to collect the ranger allocated. The fee is US$10 per day. This goes to the national park; an extra tip for the ranger is appropriate if the service has been good.

The ranger will provide his own sleeping bag and waterproof jacket. You must provide

KENYA

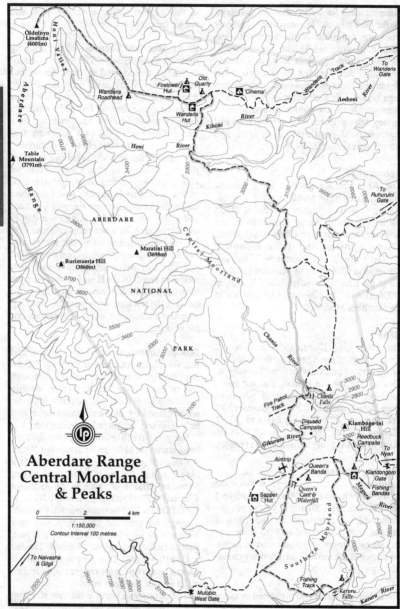

Aberdare Range Central Moorland & Peaks

0   2   4 km

1:150,000
Contour Interval 100 metres

him with food and a place to sleep. If tent space is limited, there are some huts where the ranger may sleep.

Park Fees & Regulations Entry to the park costs US$27 per person per day (US$10 for children). Camping costs US$8 per night. ('Special' private camp sites cost US$15, plus a US$100 booking fee, and are mostly used by safari groups.) There are plans to reduce the park fees for trekkers on the high moorland areas (possibly on a par with the Mt Kenya 'climbers rates'), while high-rollers going to the Salient will still pay full fees.

Places to Stay
The nearest large town to the Aberdares is Nyeri, about 150km by road from Nairobi, on the east side of the range, with hotels of various standards. In the Salient section of the park are two famous and expensive hotels; *Treetops* and *The Ark*. Other places to stay in the park include *Tusk Camp*, about 1km up the park track from the Ruhuruini Gate, 23km from Nyeri, giving good access to the Salient and excellent views of Mt Kenya. The camp consists of three wooden bandas, sleeping a total of eight people, with fireplaces, verandas, bedrooms, beds with mattresses, kitchen with wood burning stove, plus a washroom with flush loo and hot water. The whole place is looked after by a caretaker, and there's a separate hut for rangers. Luxury, and a bargain at US$100 per night for the whole camp, if there's four or more in your group. Another option is the smaller and more basic *Sapper Hut* on the Magura River, which costs US$40 per night. Bookings for both places can be made through Let's Go Travel in Nairobi (see Organised Treks & Tours in this chapter).

For trekkers on the high moorland the only public camp site is *Reedbuck Campsite*, a few km from Kiandongoro Gate. Nearby are the *Fishing Bandas*, a set of wooden cabins, which cost US$10 per person per night.

Suggested Routes
The following suggested routes take in several of the Aberdares' highlights. You can follow some of them, or combine them into a three or four-day trek, designing your own variations according to time and inclination.

A good start is Karuru Falls, where the Karuru River plunges over 300m into the valley below. Viewing platforms overlook the falls and the forest below, and on the other side of the valley are the equally impressive Gura Falls. Views are best in the morning. There's a place for camping nearby, but if there's no tent space for your ranger, then camp at Reedbuck Campsite (where he can sleep in the caretaker's hut) and come to the falls the next day, either doing the whole circuit on foot, or using the car to get here early, then walking back to Reedbuck for a second night.

From Karuru Falls you can walk to Chania Falls. This is 15km to 20km (four to eight hours) depending on whether your route sticks to the park tracks or goes through the bush. Go via Queen's Cave, a large cave with a picturesque waterfall flowing over its entrance, and a pool where you can swim – a good place for a lunch break. If you're tempted to stay longer, there's an area for camping next to Queen's Banda (built in 1952 for Princess Elizabeth, who became Queen during her visit to the Aberdares, as her father George VI died while she was staying at Treetops.

From Queen's Cave there are several different ways to reach Chania Falls. Allow 1½ hours if you keep to the tracks and anything up to four hours if you're bush-bashing. You can camp at Chania Falls, but take heed of the 'Beware Lions' notice. (If you have no tent space for your ranger you'll need to return to Reedbuck Campsite.)

From Chania Falls go through the rolling hills of the Central Moorland to reach the Wanderis Track. This 16km takes four to five hours (500m ascent), but there are also some routes through the bush which will add a bit of distance and a lot of time. Camping places along the Wanderis Track include the Old Quarry and a place called Cinema or Gorillas (given this name by rangers because the *Gorillas in the Mist* film crew camped here), although the latter is a 'special' site (see Park

Walking Safaris

The Swahili word *safari* simply means 'journey', and the original safaris in East Africa – Arab slave raids, European explorations or early colonial hunting trips – were of course journeys on foot. Only later did the term come to mean tourists looking at animals.

Today, the term 'walking safari' refers to organised tours in wildlife areas which include, to a greater or lesser degree, travel on foot. Many visitors to East Africa like to combine a trek with a safari, and walking safaris are very popular. (Most people think: 'We've come all this way to climb a mountain. It would be good to see some animals too, but we don't want to sit in a car all day'.)

At one end of the spectrum, a walking safari can involve one or two days in a lodge or camp, going out each day to explore the surroundings on foot. Longer safaris may include some days of walking combined with the more conventional form of vehicle-based game viewing. At the other end of the spectrum, it might be an 'old style' safari where you walk from one camp to the next with teams of porters or pack animals carrying the gear. Sometimes the pack animals (usually camels or donkeys) are part of the attraction. On some 'mobile walking safaris' a vehicle is used to transport gear between camps, but it travels a separate route to avoid disturbing the walkers.

Generally, the object of a walking safari is not to 'conquer' high peaks or cover long distances,

DAVID ELSE

as it might be for trekking on the mountains. Rather the aim is to see animals (small mammals, birds and insects) in their natural surroundings, or simply to enjoy the wilderness undisturbed and unenclosed by a vehicle. (For safety reasons, it is not usual to stalk large animals such as lion or buffalo; for viewing these a vehicle is used.) Thus walking safaris are generally not for people who simply want to tick off the 'Big Five' every morning. They are more for aficionados who appreciate Africa's more subtle aspects.

Another factor to consider is that walking safaris are not always cheap. Most are 'fully serviced' luxury affairs where guests are treated like royalty, with comfortable tents, plus good food and wine each evening. Just because you're sweating, don't expect a discount! Usually the logistics required and the small groups involved make them more expensive than standard vehicle safaris, although there are some good low and mid-budget exceptions.

Fees & Regulations). Nearby is the semi-ruined Wanderis Hut. Or continue up to Firetower Hut, which can be used by the ranger and has a place for camping nearby. None of these camping places have a water supply; bring all you need from the Kihoni River.

About 1.5km up from Firetower Hut is the Wanderis roadhead, from where a path leads to the summit of Satima (7km, 4-5 hours, 400m ascent, plus 4-5 hours descent). If you stay at any of the Wanderis camp sites, this can be done in a day. Most people go out-and-back, keeping east and north of the Honi River valley.

When approaching Satima from the east, the mountain looks like a broad table dipped slightly in the middle. Aim directly towards the north peak (which appears higher) and scramble up some rocky ledges to its top, which is marked by a small cairn. From there, cross the dip to the south peak, the true summit of Satima (4001m), marked by a

KENYA

National Parks & Reserves In Kenya, walking safaris are not allowed in most national parks. Exceptions to this rule include of course the main mountains covered in this chapter – Mt Kenya, Mt Elgon and the moorlands of the Aberdares – and some other smaller parks where wildlife is not a danger (eg Hells' Gate and Siawa Swamp). Generally, walking safaris take place in national reserves, forest reserves or other conservation areas, or in areas of wilderness which have no official protection. They may also be conducted in areas which have a light human population, for example the Loroghi Hills around Maralal, homeland of the Samburu people (covered in this chapter), or the Loita Hills in Maasai territory. Other areas of Kenya where walking safaris are operated include the Mathews Range, South Turkana, Mt Suswa and the Kedong Valley, Mt Longonot and Hell's Gate, the Rift Valley around lakes Bogoria and Baringo, the Chyulu Hills and the Taita Hills. Other places, declared conservation areas in the mid-1990s with the support of local inhabitants, include Shaba, the Northern Mara and Magadi. Another new place is Kimana Wildlife Sanctuary, a unique community-based conservation project with a range of habitats, and fascinating animal and human inhabitants.

The Masai Mara Area One of the most popular and most interesting areas for walking safaris is around Kenya's most celebrated wildlife area – the Masai Mara National Reserve. Walking in the reserve itself is not allowed, but it is permitted in surrounding areas (there's no boundary fence and the scenery is similar). This includes the Loita Hills – an area of rolling grassland and forested valleys to the east of the main reserve – and the new Northern Mara Conservation Area.

Most of the companies arranging walking safaris (or game viewing safaris including walking) have their own camps and lodges around the edge of the main Masai Mara Reserve. These range from the straightforward to the totally luxurious. Companies specialising in walking safaris here (as well as in other areas) include Bushbuck, Bike Treks, Kenya Hiking & Cycling and EWP (all listed under Organised Treks & Tours in the Getting Around section this chapter).

On the western side of the reserve, the local Maasai people have established *Olperr-Elong Sekenani Public Campsite*, where camping is US$5 per person. You can hire a tent for another US$5, and guides for walking safaris can be hired for US$5 per three hours. More information is available from Bike Treks or Let's Go Travel in Nairobi (see Organised Treks & Tours in this chapter).

Inside the reserve itself, a top-end lodge called *Mara Intrepids Club* offers walking safaris as an optional extra for guests. Intrepids is in an ideal setting; it's hard to reach by road, so the surrounding savanna remains in good condition and relatively free of vehicles, with very good wildlife-viewing opportunities. But it's also near the edge of the reserve so that walking safaris are easy to arrange. Walkers are accompanied by a ranger, armed with a gun, and a Maasai *moran* (warrior), armed with a spear. A short stay combining traditional game viewing by vehicle with a day's walking safari has been highly recommended. Rates are not cheap, but staying here can be an ideal way to enjoy the savanna landscapes often missed by trekkers, to see some of Kenya's magnificent wildlife and to unwind after your trek. High season prices start from US$220/300 (half this in the low season), which includes accommodation in large luxury ensuite tents and all meals in the topnotch restaurant, plus an extra US$25 for the walking safari. Access is by air; flights between Nairobi and the Masai Mara on Eagle Aviation cost US$158 return. Intrepids is represented by Let's Go Travel (listed under Organised Treks & Tours); it often has special all-inclusive flight and lodge deals that work out less than a self-drive option, and save you a day each way of bone-crunching agony on the road between Nairobi and the Mara. ∎

---

larger cairn. (Alternatively, you can miss the scramble up to north peak by aiming straight for the lowest point of the dip.) From the summit of Satima, the large Honi Valley is clearly visible to the south. To the east, Mt Kenya can sometimes be seen, while to the west the land falls away towards the Great Rift Valley.

From the summit there is a more satisfying (although harder) circuit option which brings you back down a ridge to the west of the Honi Valley, to a point opposite the roadhead. You then descend into the valley, cross the river and slog up through the tussock grass on the other side to reach the roadhead itself. Paths are faint on the east side and non-existent on the west side, so your ranger/guide is essential here.

Other Walks in the Aberdares Area
We've heard from trekkers who have camped at *Wajee Camp*, a low-key locally run

place at the small village of Mahuti, about 6km by road south of Karatina, off the main road between Marang'a and Nyeri, on the lower eastern slopes of the Aberdare Range. This is not a base for wilderness trekking – it's in the heart of Kikuyu farmland – but is an interesting place to stay. Hikes through the local villages can be arranged, and a nature trail has been set up.

The Loita Hills

Long walks are feasible in the Loita Hills, to the south-west of Nairobi in Maasai land. This is a fascinating area, with good walking through areas of bush and grassland where there's a chance of seeing wildlife and the possibility of meeting local Maasai people. Possible routes include a three or four-day north-south traverse of the range from the village of Maji Moto down towards Osubuko (or Supugo, and various other spellings), the highest point in the hills at about 2680m. There are also several other possibilities in the plains to the west of the hills nearer the Masai Mara National Reserve. Unfortunately, the Loitas are very difficult to reach without your own car, and you need to be completely self-sufficient with food and gear when you get there. Guides, usually Maasai morans, are also essential to help find water and to smooth any encounters with other warriors. By far the easiest way of walking here for several days is to join an organised trek (see Organised Treks & Tours in this chapter).

The North

Further afield, the semi-deserts of northern Kenya have several remote mountain areas including the Mathews Range (also called the Lengyio or Lenkiyio Range), the Ndoto Mountains and Mt Kulal, to the east of Lake Turkana. Local conditions usually limit walks to a day or two, and reaching these

mountains usually takes much longer than the walking itself, although there are some longer possibilities if you've got time, money and full vehicle support. Organised treks, with camels to carry gear and water, are available in the Ndotos area and camel treks operate in the Mathews Range (see Organised Treks & Tours in this chapter for more details).

Hills & Smaller Mountains

Kenya has several excellent smaller mountains which can be covered in short walks of a day or two, but they are beyond the scope of this book. These include the Ngong Hills, near Nairobi, and the volcanoes of Suswa and Longonot in the Great Rift Valley, still within easy reach of the capital. Not as high, but just as dramatic, is the walk through the gorge in Hell's Gate National Park, also in the Rift Valley near Lake Naivasha. The Mau Escarpment, to the west of the Rift, is mainly farmland with no dramatic peaks; it is very rarely reached by visitors. Short walks in some of the hills and smaller mountains are covered in *Mountains of Kenya* (for more details see under Guidebooks in the Facts for the Trekker section of this chapter).

Forest Walks

Two parts of Kenya, both off the usual tourist routes, are excellent for walking and well worth a visit if you're in the area. These are Kakamega Forest, in western Kenya, about 50km south-east of Mt Elgon, and Arabuko Sokoke Forest, on the coast. Trekking (ie multi-day walks) is not really possible here, although you could base yourself in either place and go out on various day walks. Kenya Wildlife Services have produced some beautiful little guidebooks to both forests, with information on vegetation, wildlife and walking routes.

Kakamega Forest is a remnant of the vast

forests that once extended from West Africa into Uganda and Kenya. It's now a national reserve, covering 240 sq km, with a good network of walking tracks, and a wide range of animals and plants, some closely linked to West African species and not found elsewhere in Kenya. Seven primate species occur and the birdlife is particularly fascinating. We've heard from several travellers who combined some easy walking here with harder treks on the main mountains.

The nearest large town is Kakamega, which is easily reached by car or public transport from Nairobi. Places to stay include the charming *Forest Resthouse* at Isecheno, east of the village of Shinyalu, where a bed costs US$2 and camping US$1. At *Udo's Bandas* at Buyangu, in the northern part of the reserve, a bed is US$5 and camping is also available. Knowledgeable local guides can be arranged at both places. If you need specialist flora and fauna guiding, Sirikwa Safaris (listed in the Cherangani Hills section) and a Mr Ingati in Nairobi (☎ 811404) have been recommended.

Arabuko Sokoke is the largest section of indigenous forest on the coast of East Africa. Nearby are the mangroves of Mida Creek. Once again, there's a good range of vegetation and natural habitats. A small population of elephant remains here, but these are rarely seen. Rare mammal species include Ader's duiker and the golden-rumped elephant shrew. The forest is also noted for its birds and butterflies. You can get maps and information at the visitor centre near Gede village, on the main road 15km south-east from Malindi (which has several places to stay). Some short walking paths start near here. There's also a network of drivable tracks which can be explored by foot, or even by bike (for hire in Malindi).

KENYA

Uganda

During the dark days of Idi Amin and the various civil wars that followed his rule, Uganda was essentially off-limits for trekkers and travellers. But the long years of terror ended in the late 1980s, and Uganda once again opened up to visitors.

For trekkers, Uganda's main attraction is the Rwenzori Range, the fabled Mountains of the Moon, a vast area of highland wilderness, which includes the third-highest peak on the continent. Less well known is Mt Elgon, in the far east of the country on the border with Kenya, another East African giant, which has recently been made a national park and is positively welcoming trekkers.

Facts about the Country

HISTORY
The early history of Uganda up to the end of the 19th century is covered briefly in the Facts about the Region chapter.

The Colonial Period
When the European colonial powers divided up East Africa at the end of the 1880s, the large African kingdoms of Buganda and Bunyoro, plus some other smaller ones, were combined to form a British protectorate. Its name was changed to Uganda in the early 1900s after the British government agreed to recognise the *kabaka* (king) as ruler of the Buganda people, and the kabaka agreed to recognise the authority of the protectorate.

DAVID ELSE

Uganda – Trekking Highlights
Intrepid trekkers can head for the wild and vast **Rwenzori Range**, the fabled Mountains of the Moon. Less well known is **Mt Elgon**, until recently a forgotten giant, with good access and excellent trekking opportunities.

In the 1930s the railway line from Mombasa to Lake Victoria was extended to Kampala, the capital of Uganda. Plantations were established and the local people were encouraged to grow cotton and coffee as cash crops, but European settlement was minimal compared with the neighbouring colony of Kenya.

Transition & Independence
Moves towards independence gained ground in the late 1950s, and the colony became independent in 1962. The kabaka became president and head of state, while Milton Obote, who had been active in the nationalist movements of the 1950s, became prime minister.

After this relatively smooth transition, things began to go downhill. In 1966 Obote

Warning
At the time this book went to press, parts of northern and western Uganda were politically volatile, and *may* be unsafe for travel by the time you arrive. Please read the Dangers & Annoyances section on page 252 for more information. ∎

ordered his army commander, one General Idi Amin, to attack the kabaka's palace. The king escaped to the UK and Obote declared himself president. In 1971, when Obote was abroad at a conference, Amin pulled a similar trick and, with the backing of the army, took control of the country. The terrors of the period that followed are well recorded elsewhere. Thousands of Ugandan peasants were killed, merely for being members of the wrong tribe, or even for being Christian (Amin was a Muslim). Educated people in the towns were also seen as a threat and many were murdered openly by army death squads. All Asians living in Uganda, mainly involved in business and commerce, were expelled and their property confiscated. Factories and plantations were nationalised, then mismanaged and virtually destroyed. Hundreds of millions of dollars disappeared into the overseas bank accounts of Amin and his supporters while the country fell apart.

During this time the western powers condemned Amin's actions, but continued to support his regime by buying coffee (Uganda's economic mainstay). In 1978 sanctions were finally imposed by the UK and the USA. To create a diversion for his increasingly dissatisfied generals, later the same year Amin ordered an invasion of northern Tanzania, supposedly to punish president Julius Nyerere for assisting Ugandan exiles. The Tanzanian army later repulsed the Ugandan forces and went on to 'liberate' Kampala. Amin escaped to Libya.

If anything, the period that followed was even more anarchic than the Amin years. Ugandan and Tanzanian soldiers turned into bandits and highwaymen. Death and chaos were still very much the order of the day. Two new presidents were appointed but they had little authority.

Elections were finally held in 1980 and Milton Obote came to power for the second time, but tribal mass killings and the murder of suspected opponents continued. In fact, more people were killed during Obote's rule than during Amin's. Meanwhile, a guerrilla group called the National Resistance Army (NRA) led by Yoweri Museveni was established

in western Uganda. In 1985, before the NRA was in a position to take control, Obote was deposed in a military coup led by Tito Okello, an officer from Obote's own troops.

Modern Times

Peace talks between the new Okello government and the NRA rebels failed, setting the stage for civil war and yet another period of terror and suffering for the Ugandan people. In 1986, after gradually pushing across the country, the NRA finally took Kampala and the forces of Okello were chased across the border into Sudan.

The NRA became the National Resistance Movement (NRM) – Uganda's new government. Museveni firmly believed in good governance and his army remained disciplined; both became increasingly popular as the country returned towards normality with increasing momentum and confidence.

Through the early 1990s many of Kampala's main buildings were renovated and roads from the capital to the east and west of the country completely rebuilt. Financial controls were lifted, factories started making goods and there was food in the shops for the first time in decades. Many Asians were invited back by Museveni to pick up the commercial activities they'd been forced to abandon 20 years earlier.

In 1993 the Bugandan monarchy was restored (although with no political power) and a new draft constitution introduced a system of 'no-party' politics for at least another five years, extending the NRM's mandate. A Constituent Assembly was formed, and elections in 1994 showed overwhelming support for the NRM government (except in the north of the country).

Democratic 'no-party elections' were held in May 1996, although the main bodies contesting the election *were* essentially parties, with Museveni's NRM opposed by former foreign affairs minister Dr Paulo Ssemogerere and supported by the Democratic Party (DP) in alliance with former president Obote's Ugandan Peoples Congress (UPC). Museveni won a resounding victory, capturing almost 75% of the vote. The only area

UGANDA

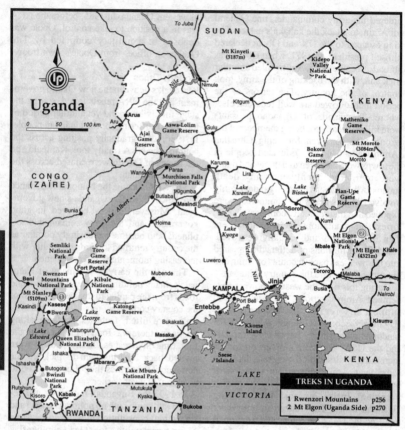

TREKS IN UGANDA

| 1 Rwenzori Mountains | p256 |
| 2 Mt Elgon (Uganda Side) | p270 |

where Ssemogerere had any real support was the anti-NRM north. Despite Museveni's election success and the economic boom in southern and eastern Uganda, through the rest of 1996 and into 1997 security became an increasing problem in the northern areas and, to a lesser extent, in the west of the country.

Various anti-government factions gained in strength, most notably the bizarre Lords Resistance Army (LRA), led by Joseph Kony and supported by Sudan in retaliation for Uganda's suspected support for the rebel Sudanese Peoples Liberation Army. By mid-1997 the LRA controlled parts of northern Uganda. Other rebel factions were active in western Uganda and added to the general unrest, while bandits took advantage of the poor security situation. Museveni and the army promised a crackdown and the restoration of law and order, but it is uncertain how effective this will be, and so these areas may not be safe for tourists. Despite these doubts, overall the future looks bright for Uganda. Tourism and other industries are set to grow, while the government remains relatively accountable and popular in a region beset by increasing political intolerance.

GEOGRAPHY

Uganda measures about 500km north to south and 450km east to west, at its widest points, with an area of around 236,000 sq km. On the western edge of the African High Plateau, much of the country is undulating plain, averaging 1500m above sea level in the south, sloping gradually to about 1000m in the north.

Uganda is a country dominated by lakes: in the south is Lake Victoria, in the west Lake Albert and Lake Edward (once, briefly, Lake Idi Amin), and in the centre is Lake Kyoga, linked to Lake Victoria by the River Nile.

The western branch of the Great Rift Valley forms Uganda's natural and political western boundary. The Rwenzori Mountains rise above the plains beyond the Rift in the south-west corner of the country. Mount Elgon, Uganda's other major peak, is on the east side of the country straddling the border with Kenya.

CLIMATE

The dominant feature of Uganda's climate pattern is the band of rain which moves across the region, creating two wet seasons and two dry seasons each year. The dry seasons are from the end of May until early October and from late November to early March. In the far north there is only one rainy season, from April to September.

In the southern and central parts of the country, maximum daytime temperatures during the May to October dry season are around 25°C. In the November to March season they can rise to about 27 or 28°C. On the mountains, the higher you go the colder it gets. Like all African equatorial mountains, although the daily maximum temperatures vary only slightly throughout the year, there are great differences between day and night-time temperatures. On the lower slopes of Mt Elgon or the Rwenzoris, maximum daytime temperatures are usually around 15 to 20°C, falling to 10 to 15°C in moorland zones, where night-time temperatures often drop to near freezing. Above 4000m on the Rwenzoris, maximum daytime temperatures are around 5°C and always below freezing at night. Daytime temperatures on the high slopes of Elgon are similar and frosts at night are not uncommon.

ECONOMY

Uganda's economy is predominantly agricultural and through the first half of the 1990s it was one of the fastest growing in Africa. The main export is coffee, forming over 90% of total exports, although around two-thirds of Uganda's foreign earnings are used to pay off debts to western banks. Most rural people are employed on large plantations or farm small plots for their own needs. *Matoke* (green banana or plantain) is the staple food crop. Further economic diversification is being encouraged, particularly in tourism. Most former state-run hotels and national parks lodges have been privatised and massively improved.

POPULATION & PEOPLE

Uganda's population was estimated at about 21 million in 1996, growing at a rate of around 3% per year. Around Lake Victoria, and in the west and south of the country, the people are of Bantu origin (including the predominant Buganda and the Bakonjo people of the Rwenzori). Also in the west are groups of pre-Bantu (Pygmy) people. North of Lake Kyoga and in the north-east of the country, the people belong to the Nilotic group (including the Lango, Acholi and Karamajong).

RELIGION

Most people are Christians, while the remainder, to a greater or lesser degree, follow traditional beliefs. There are also small groups of Muslims.

LANGUAGE

All the main groups have their own languages and dialects. English is the official language and very widely spoken throughout the country. Swahili is used as a trading language and is spoken mainly in the east, although people can usually speak a few words wherever you go.

Facts for the Trekker

PLANNING
When to Trek
The best time for trekking on the mountains of Uganda is during the dry seasons, from the end of May early October, when it's dry and cool, and from late November to early March, when it's warmer (see the Climate section for more details). At the end of the dry season, haze and smoke from the burning of old crops can reduce visibility.

Having said that, the Rwenzoris are notoriously wet, even in the dry season, when it can (and does) rain at any time, with snow and hail at higher altitudes. However, after rain the air is clear and you may get better views.

Mount Elgon also has an unpredictable weather pattern, with the local climate influenced by air movements over Lake Victoria. It can rain at any time, although generally you can count on there being more in the wet season! Hail and snow are not uncommon at any time of year.

Maps
Maps of East Africa are covered in the Regional Facts for the Trekker chapter. For general travel around the country, the best is the *Uganda Traveller's Map* published by Macmillan. This shows all but the smallest roads, all the national parks (including those gazetted in the last few years) and has contour shading. On the back are detailed maps of Kampala and the Murchison Falls, Queen Elizabeth and Rwenzori Mountains national parks. A fancy looking map (US$7) produced by the Uganda Tourist Board is available from its office in Kampala (see Tourist Office below) and hotels around the country, but it glibly reproduces some very out of date information and should be treated with caution.

For more details, most parts of the country are also covered by the Uganda Survey Department maps, originally drawn by the British Directorate of Overseas Surveys. These maps may be available from the Map Sales Office in the Department of Land Surveys & Mapping, near the post office in Entebbe (off the road towards the airport), although stocks are unreliable.

For the mountains and trekking areas covered in this chapter, some detailed maps and guidebooks are available (see the individual trekking sections).

TOURIST OFFICE
The Uganda Tourist Board (☎ 242196/7; fax 242188; email utb@starcom.com.ug) has an office on Parliament Ave in Kampala. Uganda is making a determined effort to attract visitors and the office staff are very helpful.

VISAS
Uganda has liberal entry regulations, and visas are not needed by citizens of most countries including the European Union, several other European and Scandinavian countries, plus Israel, Japan, the USA, Australia, New Zealand, Canada and most Commonwealth countries. If your own country is not on this list, one to three-month tourist visas cost about US$25. As always, entry regulations are liable to change, so check the latest requirements with your nearest embassy, high commission or tourist office.

At Kampala airport, officials are hot on yellow fever vaccination certificates: make sure yours is in order, otherwise you'll be sent to the very suspect medical room for a jab.

EMBASSIES
Ugandan Embassies Abroad
Ugandan embassies, consulates and high commissions abroad include:

Belgium
    Ave de Tervuren 317, 450 Brussels
    (☎ (02) 762 5825; fax 763 0438)
Canada
    231 Cobourg St, Ottawa, Ontario KIN 8J2
    (☎ (613) 233 7797; fax 232 6689)
Denmark
    Sofievej 15, DK 2900, Hellerup (☎ 3962 0966)
France
    13 Ave Raymond Poincare, 75116 Paris
    (☎ 01 47 27 46 80; fax 01 47 55 12 21)

Germany
    Duerenstrasse 44, 5300 Bonn 2
    (☎ (0228) 355027; fax 351692)
Italy
    Via Ennio Quirino Visconti 8, 00193 Rome
    (☎/fax (06) 322 5220)
Japan
    39-15 Oyama-chi, Shibuya-ku, Tokyo 151
    (☎ (03) 3465 4552; fax 3465 4970)
Kenya
    Uganda House, Baring Arcade, 4th floor, Kenyatta Ave, Nairobi (☎ (02) 330801; fax 330970)
South Africa
    Trafalgar Court, Aprt 35B, 634 Park St, Arcadia 0083, Pretoria (☎ (012) 344 4100; fax 343 2809)
Tanzania
    Extelecoms Building, 7th floor, Samora Ave, Dar es Salaam (☎ (051) 31004; fax 46256)
UK
    Uganda House, 58/59 Trafalgar Sq, London WC2N 5DX (☎ (0171) 839 5783; fax 839 8925)
USA
    5909 16th St NW, Washington DC 20011-2896 (☎ (202) 726 0416; fax 726 1727)

Foreign Embassies in Uganda
Countries which maintain diplomatic missions in Uganda include the following (all in Kampala). Some are open in the afternoon, but the best time to visit is between 9 am and noon. The telephone area code for Kampala is ☎ 041.

France
    9 Parliament Ave (☎ 242120; fax 241252)
Italy
    11 Lourdel Rd, Nakasero
    (☎ 241786; fax 250448)
Kenya
    Nakasero Rd (☎ 258235; fax 267369)
Netherlands
    Kisozi Complex, Nakasero Lane (☎ 231859)
South Africa
    Plot 9, Malcolm X Ave, Kololo (☎/fax 259156)
Tanzania
    6 Kagera Rd (☎ 256272)
UK
    10 Parliament Ave (☎ 257301)
USA
    Rear of UK High Commission Building, 10 Parliament Ave (☎ 259791)

MONEY
The section covers money in Uganda. Outlines of costs and other general money aspects are given in the Regional Facts for the Trekker chapter.

Currency Exchange
The unit of currency is the Ugandan shilling (USh). There are no hard currency restrictions, but you are not allowed to import or export more than USh 5000. Currency declaration forms are no longer used, although there's always a possibility of them being reintroduced.

Since the relaxation of currency laws the black market demand for money has disappeared and inflation has steadied, but is still unpredictable. Therefore we have quoted the prices of most things in US dollars (US$) throughout this chapter. Many items (such as rooms in large hotels, national park entrance fees and some organised safaris) have to be paid for in US$ or another hard currency. Although the actual exchange rate may have altered by the time you reach Uganda, the cost of things in US$ (or any other hard currency) will not have increased much. The approximate exchange rates in 1997 were:

| US$1 | = | USh 1100 |
| UK£1 | = | USh 1600 |

Changing Money
Money can be changed in foreign exchange (forex) bureaus, which offer a better rate than the banks, although many banks also have forex desks (ensure you go to the right desk). Most towns have a bank and forex bureau.

Smart Money
Uganda's largest note is USh 10,000, so if you change more than a few hundred dollars you'll be lumbered with a large wad of local currency. To avoid this problem, the International Credit Bank issues 'Smart Money' debit cards. You pay the bank the amount you anticipate using, and they 'load' it onto the card, which is accepted in major tourist hotels. Some hotels will also allow you to draw cash using the card. At the end of your trip any money still 'in' the card is repaid to you. ■

UGANDA

BOOKS

Books covering all or part of East Africa are listed in the Regional Facts for the Trekker chapter. Guidebooks on individual mountain areas are covered in the relevant sections.

Guidebooks

For independent travel around the country, your best option is Lonely Planet's *East Africa*, which has a good chapter on Uganda and also covers several other countries in the region. The *Guide to Uganda* by Philip Briggs has more detailed coverage of the country, with keen observations and an emphasis on natural history.

PUBLIC HOLIDAYS

As well as Christmas Day, Boxing Day, New Year's Day, and Easter Friday and Monday, public holidays include:

26 January	NRM Government Day
8 March	Women's Day
1 May	Labour Day
3 June	Martyrs' Day
9 June	Heroes Day
9 October	Independence Day

DANGERS & ANNOYANCES

Compared with Nairobi and Dar es Salaam, you are pretty safe walking the streets of Kampala. However, there's a lot of poverty in the city so common sense must be applied at all times: avoid carrying obvious symbols of wealth (eg cameras); avoid back alleys, especially at night; and avoid looking like a lost tourist!

Of far more concern in 1997 were the activities of anti-government rebel forces in the north and west of the country. While tourists are unlikely to be deliberately targeted by the army or the rebels, you may find yourself caught up in the unrest, while bandits taking advantage of the poor security also pose a real danger. This situation may continue into 1998 and beyond, or things may be brought quickly under control and the whole country may be peaceful by the time you arrive. Before travelling in northern and western Uganda you should check the latest security situation.

PLACES TO STAY IN KAMPALA

If you arrive by air, or come overland from Nairobi, you'll probably spend a night or two in Kampala, arranging return transport or stocking up on supplies in between treks. There's something for most budgets, although nothing like the choice you get in Nairobi. More details on places to stay in or near the trekking areas are given in the relevant sections.

Places to Stay – bottom end

The cheapest place in town is the *YMCA* at the far end of Buganda Rd, about 2km outside the city centre. For US$2 you can sleep on the floor, and might even find a mattress if you get there early. This place is a school so you have to be up before 8 am, but you can hang around or eat in the canteen during the day. Camping in the grounds is allowed, but it still costs US$2 and is probably not safe.

A welcome addition to this range, popular with independent travellers and overland trucks, is the Aussie-run *Natete Backpackers* (☎ 258469; fax 272012; e-mail ptcu@star com.co.ug), west of the centre on the road towards Masaka. Camping costs US$2 per person, dorm beds are US$4 and double rooms US$11. Meals are available and there are some local restaurants nearby. The management can provide up to date information on security and general conditions on the Rwenzoris, Mt Elgon and other national parks. To get there, take a Natete minibus-taxi from the new taxi park (US$0.30) and ask the driver to drop you at Backpackers.

Budget hotels include *Mukwano Guest House* (☎ 232248) on Nakivubo Place, near the taxi parks, with friendly staff and clean singles at US$11, doubles at US$7 and quads at US$6. Nearby is *Kadepro Guest House* with dorm beds at US$3 and singles/doubles at US$12/16, *Samalien Guest House* charging US$15/18 and *3 Steps Inn* with similar prices.

Places to Stay – middle & top end

Outside the city centre, on Natete Rd (next to the Namirembe Cathedral), the quiet and relaxed *Namirembe Guest House* (☎ 272071) has singles/doubles from US$14/18 (US$16/20 en suite). Meals are available. Slightly nearer to town, the *Rena Hotel* (☎ 272336) on Namirembe Rd has good value rooms at US$17/25 (US$25/35 en suite), including breakfast, and its own bar and restaurant. If you want to be more central, the *New Gloria Hotel* (☎ 257790) on William St has good en suite rooms for US$25/45.

Very popular in the middle range is the *Speke Hotel* (☎ 259221; fax 235345) on Nile Ave, with en suite rooms good value at US$50/70, including breakfast. The terrace bar is a local meeting place. Up in style from this, the central *Hotel Equatoria* (☎ 250780; fax 250146) has good rooms at US$79/89 (US$89/94 with air-con) including breakfast. There's also a restaurant and pool. South of the centre, the friendly *Diplomate Hotel* (☎ 267625; fax 267690) also has quality rooms with views of the city, which are good value at US$66/78, including breakfast. In the same league, the *Fairway Hotel* (☎ 259471; fax 234160; email fairway@starcom.co.ug) at the bottom of Sezibwa Rd has singles/doubles for US$75/95, including breakfast, and an excellent restaurant.

At the top of town, and the top of the price range, is the *Sheraton Hotel* (☎ 244590; fax 256696), with most of the features you'd expect, and prices too, with singles/doubles from US$220/250, including breakfast.

Getting There & Away

Getting to Uganda from Europe or further afield is covered in the Getting There & Away chapter. The following section assumes you're already in Uganda and need to go elsewhere; it covers travel *from* Uganda *to* Kenya, Malawi and Tanzania using air, road or rail transport. For going the other way (eg from Kenya to Uganda), see the relevant country chapters.

How you travel depends on how much time you've got, and the amount of travelling (as opposed to trekking) you want to do. In this section it's presumed you want to take fairly direct routes between the trekking areas in the various countries.

The international airport is at Entebbe, about 30km from Kampala.

KENYA
Air
There are international flights between Kampala (Entebbe) and Nairobi; usually about five or six flights a week in each direction. The one-way fare is about US$100.

Road
The main border crossing between the two countries is at Malaba, linked to Kampala and Nairobi by tar roads.

The main bus company running direct between Kampala and Nairobi is Akamba. Its Kampala office is in De Winton Rd, and the fare is about US$18 one way (for more information see the Getting There & Away section of the Kenya chapter). If you're doing the journey in stages, minibuses go from Kampala bus station to the border for about US$4. You can walk across the border – it's only a few hundred metres between the two border posts. On the Kenya side there are regular buses and matatus between the border and Bungoma, Eldoret or Nairobi (see the Kenya chapter for details).

Train
There is a direct train from Kampala to Nairobi every Wednesday (Nairobi-Kampala every Tuesday). This service may be increased. For more details see the Kenya chapter.

TANZANIA
Air
International flights between Kampala (Entebbe) and Dar es Salaam go about three times a week in each direction, and cost around US$200 one way. In Tanzania there are regular flights (at least once per day) between Dar and Kilimanjaro international

airport (KIA) which is nearer the main trekking areas. There are no direct flights between Kampala and KIA. For travelling quickly between Uganda and northern Tanzania you're better off flying between Kampala and Nairobi, and going by road between Nairobi and Arusha or Moshi (see the Getting There & Away section of the Kenya and Tanzania chapters).

Road

The easiest way to get between the trekking areas of Uganda and those in Tanzania by road is through Kenya, via Nairobi (see the Getting There & Away section of the Kenya chapter).

MALAWI
Air

Flights between Kampala and Lilongwe go about twice a week and cost about US$400 one way. They usually go via Nairobi and/or Dar es Salaam.

Road

Uganda and Malawi do not share a common border, so the easiest way to travel overland between these two countries is through Kenya and Tanzania (see the Getting There & Away and Getting Around sections of the Kenya and Tanzania chapters).

Getting Around

The usual way of getting around Uganda is by road, although you could also use a train. There are no scheduled domestic flights of use to trekkers, but if your time is short and pocket deep you can charter a plane; contact the tourist office or one of the companies listed in the Organised Treks & Tours section.

ROAD

The main routes through Uganda, from Kampala to Malaba, Mbarara, Kasese and Fort Portal are in very good condition. Many other roads around the country have also been repaired in recent years.

Bus & Minibus

On all the main routes there are buses, which tend to be rather slow, and minibuses (locally called 'minibus-taxis' or simply taxis), which are faster and gradually replacing buses on the main routes. In Kampala all public transport leaves from the main minibus/bus stations ('taxi parks'), next to each other in the downtown area; transport heading east goes from the old taxi park; transport heading west goes from the new taxi park. It can be hard to find the right bus or minibus, but just ask around and you'll soon be shown to the transport you want. In other towns there's either a small bus station, or vehicles leave from the market.

Most vehicles leave when full (really full), but others seem to keep to some kind of a departure timetable and leave half empty, picking up people along the way. Some sample minibus fares are: Kampala to Malaba US$3; Kampala to Mbale US$6; and Kampala to Kasese US$10. Buses are about half this price.

Local Transport

Taxis ('private taxis' or 'special hire taxis') in Kampala are hard to recognise, often indistinguishable from private cars (usually because they *are* private cars, moonlighting). A trip across town will cost US$2 to US$3, and from town to the airport at Entebbe (about 30km) US$20. If you're flying into Kampala and the bank is closed at the airport, taxi drivers will take you into town for US$25 (payable in any hard currency).

In Kampala and several other towns you'll see bicycle taxis or motorbike taxis where the passenger sits on a large cushion on the rack behind the saddle. This is the nearest Africa gets to a rickshaw! Short bike rides of 1km or so cost US$0.30 (about double for a motorbike). Heavy rucksacks cost extra.

TRAIN

From Kampala, the main railway line goes east to Tororo and Malaba, and on to Nairobi (see Getting There & Away). This is in good condition. There's a weekly international train to Nairobi (see Getting There & Away in this chapter) and local services to Tororo, but these are very slow and uncomfortable (3rd class only).

There's also a line heading west to Kasese. At the time of writing this was in very bad condition, with very frequent delays and cancellations. Derailments are common, but not usually serious as the train goes so slowly. There are plans for a major renovation but in the meantime you're better off going by road.

ORGANISED TREKS & TOURS

If you're short of time you can use the services of a tour company to organise your trekking (and other aspects of your trip, such as transport or hotel reservations), although it's generally much cheaper to arrange things yourself. Uganda's tourist business is small compared with those in Kenya or Tanzania, but there are several companies operating tours and wildlife safaris (although none arrange only trekking, as the market is so small). For the same reason, not many companies in Uganda cater for 'walk-in' clients (ie independent travellers who prefer to arrange things on the spot), although if this is the only choice most can easily set things up within a couple of days. Most deal with advance bookings. If you want something specialised, or prefer things pre-arranged, it's best to contact them from your home country to set up things before you arrive. Almost without exception, tour companies running treks use guides and porters from Rwenzori Mountaineering Services (covered more fully in the Rwenzori Mountains section) and from the Mt Elgon Guides & Porters Association (see Mt Elgon section).

A selection of companies is listed here. The area code for Kampala is ☎ 041. Omit the 0 if you're phoning or faxing from outside East Africa. Uganda's country code is ☎ 256.

Hot Ice
PO Box 22464, Kampala (☎ 266597/8; fax 267441; email hotice@starcom.co.ug). An experienced and long-established company doing luxury and standard wildlife safaris in most of Uganda's national parks, several of which include watching gorillas, chimps and other primates. Very good quality all-inclusive treks on the Rwenzoris (with technical ascents of the peaks if required) are also available; a 10-day trip from Kampala with six nights trekking, plus three nights in Queen Elizabeth National Park costs from US$1500 per person for groups of four.

Let's Go Travel
UDC Building (Plot 9/11), Parliament Avenue, PO Box 22851, Kampala (☎ 346667/8/9; fax 346666; website http//:www.kenya-direct .com/letsgo). This long-standing and experienced Kenya-based travel agent opened a Kampala office in 1997 and now offers flights between Kampala and any other part of East Africa (or the rest of the world), plus Rwenzori treks, tours to lowland national parks and walking safaris in the various primate sanctuaries.

Nile Safaris
Farmers House, Parliamentary Ave PO Box 12135, Kampala (☎/fax 345092). This reliable company organises a range of safaris, with all-inclusive treks on Mt Elgon and the Rwenzoris (including transport to/from Kampala and hotel accommodation before/after the trek. A seven-day Mt Elgon trek is US$600 per person, a nine-day Rwenzori trek is US$960. Gorilla and chimpanzee viewing treks are also arranged. Nile Safaris have a UK office: 5 St Albans Mansions, Kensington Court Place, London W8 5QH (☎/fax (0171) 938 4066).

African Pearl Safaris
Embassy House, Kampala (☎ 233566; fax 235770). A mainstream operator with a few trekking and walking safari options, including four-day gorilla-tracking safaris to Bwindi National Park, staying at their very comfortable Buhoma Homestead, right at the park headquarters, for US$662 or more.

Gametrackers
Raja Chambers, Parliament Ave, PO Box 7703, Kampala (☎ 258993; fax 244575). Part of the well known Kenyan company (listed in Kenya chapter) running a range of good-value trips, some with walking, including four-day Bwindi gorilla-tracking trips for US$610, or into eastern Congo (Zaïre) for US$570, and six-day wildlife safaris for US$900 per person in groups of four, with discounts for larger groups.

Several specialist trekking and mountaineering outfits doing Rwenzori trips are based in Nairobi. These include Natural Action and EWP (listed under Organised Treks & Tours in the Getting Around section of the Kenya chapter).

UGANDA

The Rwenzori Mountains

The Rwenzoris, often called the Mountains of the Moon, lie on the border of Uganda and Congo (Zaïre) and mark the frontier between the high savanna plains of East Africa and the low dense forests of the west. Unlike the other major mountains in this region, the Rwenzoris are not volcanic in origin; they were formed by uplift associated with the formation of the western branch of the Great Rift Valley, which runs just to the west of the range.

Unlike the other major African mountains, which rise as single peaks, the Rwenzoris are a true mountain range covering a wide area. There are six main massifs, each with several peaks, most with glaciers and coverings of permanent snow. The highest point in the Rwenzoris is Margherita Peak on Mt Stanley. At 5109m (16,763 ft), this is the third-highest point in Africa. Many of the other peaks are above, or just under, 5000m. Perhaps not surprisingly, the Rwenzoris are also known as the Alps of Africa.

One of the last mountain ranges to be 'discovered' by European explorers, today the Rwenzoris remain comparatively unknown and rarely visited, still with an air of mystery and remoteness. The paths are narrow and trekkers often have to push through dense bush and bamboo forest, wade though deep bogs, or simply follow a vague line of cairns across bare rock slabs. The Rwenzoris are a true African mountain wilderness and a trek here, although demanding, can be a very satisfying experience.

HISTORY

Although the local Bakonjo people had been hunting in the forested foothills of the Rwenzoris for centuries, the early European explorers knew nothing of the range, as it was usually hidden by mist and clouds of rain. It is this almost constant rain that creates the snow and ice on the main peaks, and feeds the streams and rivers lower down which eventually become headwaters of the White Nile.

The explorer Henry Stanley was probably the first European to see the Rwenzoris, when he explored the region around Lake Victoria in the 1870s. On a return expedition in 1888, Stanley named the range Mt Gordon Bennet, after the owner of the New York Times who funded his trip, but fortunately the name never stuck (see boxed text for more details). It wasn't until 1906, after all the other great East African mountains had been explored and climbed, that Prince Luigi di Savoia, better known as the Duke of Abruzzi, led a huge expedition into the Rwenzoris to properly map the central part of the range for the first time, and reached the top of all the major peaks.

GEOGRAPHY

The Rwenzori Range is roughly oval in shape, about 100km long and 40km wide at the 1500m contour, where the mountains rise steeply from the surrounding plains. In the centre of the range are the main massifs. These are (with their highest points): Mt Stanley (Margherita, 5109m), Mt Speke (Vittorio Emanuele, 4890m), Mt Baker (Edward, 4843m), Emin (Umberto, 4798m), Gessi (Iolanda, 4715m) and Mt Luigi di Savoia (Sella, 4627m). Each massif also has several other peaks; the most notable are

Rwenzori Names

Rwenzori is also spelt Ruwenzori, but both are corruptions of one of the mountains' many local names. These include Rwenjura and Rwenzururu, both meaning 'hills of rain' in the language of the Bakonjo and Batoro people. According to Osmaston & Pasteur's classic *Guide to the Ruwenzori*, other names for the range include *Gambalagala* (the place which strains the eye), *Gamalaga gafumba biri* (the great leaf in which the clouds are boiled), *Balitume mpunga* (send an eagle up there) or simply *Virika* (snow). ■

Rwenzori Vegetation & Weather

One of the most notable features of the Rwenzoris is the vegetation. Although similar to that found on other high East African mountains, the lower forests are particularly dense. Above about 3500m, the forest gives way to more open zones, where the giant lobelias and groundsels are even bigger than on the other major East African mountains. The soil in the Rwenzoris is very thin, and easily eroded when the fragile vegetation cover is disturbed. This has been a problem on the upper slopes, where trekkers trying to avoid boggy sections have gradually increased the width of the paths.

But the most important feature of the Rwenzoris is the weather. The range is notoriously wet: even in the dry season, rain and thick mist are not uncommon. Apart from the highest sections of the route, thick mud is very much the order of the day, and many trekkers do the entire route in rubber boots (wellies or gumboots). I've seen people in fishing waders, and even in toe-to-thigh leggings made out of wet-suit material. On the steep slopes, where you'd expect the water to run off, the path can still be a thick morass, and the only thing likely to be flowing downhill is you! One writer has pointed out that Mt Kenya's infamous Vertical Bog is like a gently sloping damp patch compared with some parts of the Rwenzoris. ∎

Alexandra (5091m) and Albert (5087m), both on Mt Stanley.

The border between Uganda and Congo (Zaïre) passes through the highest part of the Rwenzoris, but because the western side is much steeper, only about a fifth of the range is in Congo (Zaïre) territory. All the main peaks are on the Ugandan side. The Rwenzoris were declared a World Heritage Site by UNESCO in 1994.

TREKKING INFORMATION

On many Rwenzori maps dotted lines indicate several routes from the foothills up onto the higher peaks. In reality, all but two of these routes are completely overgrown and very rarely used. The two main routes that do exist follow the Bujuku and Mubuku rivers, on the eastern side of the mountains, and can be combined to make a satisfying circular trek through the very heart of the range.

To get to the summit of the three main peaks involves walking across steep snow and ice, for which you need ice axe, rope and crampons, plus the technical mountaineering knowledge to use them. The highest point normally reached by trekkers is Elena Hut (4540m), at the snout (lower end) of the Elena Glacier, where the technical routes up Mt Stanley begin. It is also possible for trekkers to cross two major cols, the Scott-Elliot

Pass (4370m) and the Freshfield Pass (4280m), and these are included in the trek described in this section.

Costs

Costs for Rwenzori trekking break down into two distinct categories: guide and porter fees, and national park entry fees. Other aspects to consider are food and supplies for the trek and equipment hire if required, plus the costs of getting there and away. These points are all covered in detail in this section.

Route Standard & Days Required

The Bujuku-Mubuku Circuit can be very tough. The paths are often boggy and you may have to wade through knee-deep mud on several occasions. In the forest the vegetation is dense and you'll also have to clamber over fallen branches and exposed roots. On the boglands you often have to leap from tussock to tussock in an attempt (often vain) to keep out of the mud. This is not a route for the faint-hearted. But for many trekkers, the tough conditions, combined with the weird vegetation and spectacular views of the main massifs and their glaciers, occasionally glimpsed through the cloud, are all part of the attraction. The Rwenzori range is a splendid example of African mountain wilderness, but if you want your wilderness easy this is not the place to be.

UGANDA

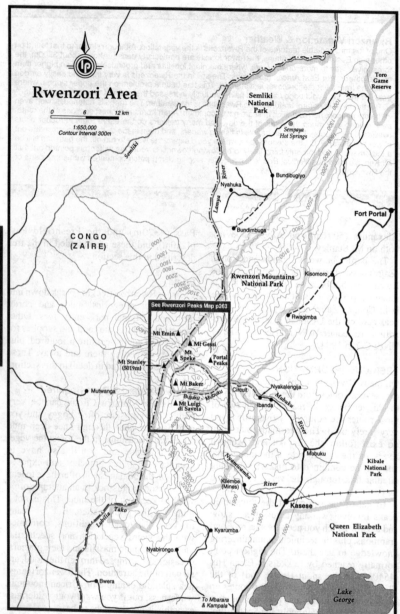

Rwenzori Area

0   6   12 km

1:650,000
Contour Interval 300m

Toro
Game
Reserve

Semliki
National
Park

Sempaya
Hot Springs

Nyahuka

Bundibugiyo

Lamya River

Semliki

Bundimbuga

CONGO
(ZAÏRE)

Fort Portal

Rwenzori Mountains
National Park

Kisomoro

Rwagimba

See Rwenzori Peaks Map p263

▲ Mt Emin

▲ Mt Gessi

Mt
Speke ▲

Portal
Peaks

Mt Stanley
(5019m)

▲ Mt Baker

Bujuku

Circuit

Nyakalengija

Mubuku

▲ Mt Luigi
di Savoia

Mutwanga

Ibanda

Mubuku

Kibale
National
Park

Nyamwamba River

Kilembe
(Mines)

Kasese

Tako

Labilia

Kyarumba

Queen Elizabeth
National Park

Nyabirongo

Bwera

To Mbarara
& Kampala

Lake
George

UGANDA

The Bujuku-Mubuku Circuit takes a minimum of seven days six nights, and extra nights can be spent at higher huts, if you're going to sidetrack to any of the other valleys and passes in the main peak area.

Although the range is not as high as Kilimanjaro or Mt Kenya, acclimatisation is still important. The gradual ascent forced by the position of the huts and the route itself should help, but if you do feel bad effects from the altitude, the advice is the same as anywhere else: go down. (See Altitude Sickness in the Health, Safety & First Aid chapter.)

Guides & Porters

You can trek in the Rwenzoris without using guides and porters; for short treks (say, up to three days) this is OK for experienced trekkers, although even then it is unwise to go without at least one other companion. For treks of four days or longer (you need seven days to do the Bujuku-Mubuku Circuit), most trekkers take local guides and porters. Guides are highly recommended as the paths are not always clear, and misty conditions often make route-finding difficult. Porters are optional but make the trekking much easier.

Guides and porters are arranged through Rwenzori Mountaineering Services (RMS), a local cooperative supported by the American development organisation USAID. Money raised goes into local community projects. So far, a school and a dispensary have been built. RMS also control the huts on the Bujuku-Mubuku Circuit.

The RMS headquarters is at Nyakalengija, near Ibanda, at the start of the route, and they also have an office in Kasese, at 33 Alexandra Street, a few blocks up from the Saad Hotel see Places to Stay in Kasese). Guides and porters can be reserved in advance by writing to RMS at PO Box 33, Kasese, but in practice this doesn't speed up the process very much. If you arrive in Kasese in the afternoon, you can still arrange a trek to start the next day.

RMS fees are as follows (all per person, and rounded to the nearest US$5). They are payable in USh or any hard currency at the current rates of exchange.

One-day hike (no overnight)	US$30
Two-day hike (with overnight at first hut)	US$65
Three-day trek (two nights)	US$150
Five-day trek (four nights)	US$200
Seven-day (six nights) circuit trek	US$250

These fees include transport both ways between Kasese and Nyakalengija/Ibanda (the start of the trek), wages and food for guide and porters, charcoal, and a service fee to cover the use of the mountain huts and for organising the trek. The service fee works out at US$10 per person per day and is liable for tax at 17%. The charcoal is for trekkers, guides and porters to cook with (to prevent deforestation open fires are not allowed). If you are taking your own stove and fuel, you might be able to negotiate a small 'charcoal discount'.

The fee includes the porters'/guides' daily wage of US$4/5 per day. Without exception, the RMS guides and porters are trustworthy, hard-working and among the nicest people you could meet anywhere in Africa. We have never heard any complaints, either from them or about them. A tip at the end of the trek is usually appropriate and this should normally be around an extra day's pay for every three or four days.

You need to provide your own food and cooking gear, sleeping bag and mat, plus of course trekking clothes and any personal items, although some stuff can be hired from RMS.

Park Fees & Regulations

Most of the range and all of the trek described in this section are inside the Rwenzori Mountains National Park (RMNP). (The RMNP should not be confused with Ruwenzori National Park, still shown on some maps, on the lowlands between Lakes Edward and George, which has reverted to its original name of Queen Elizabeth National Park.) The RMNP headquarters are in Nyakalengija, near Ibanda. At present, entrance fees are included in the fees paid to RMS.

The main park regulation concerning trekkers is that open fires are not allowed.

Mountaineering If you want to go all the way to the summit of Mt Stanley (or some of the Rwenzoris' other peaks requiring technical ascents) RMS can provide skilled guides, for which you pay US$20 on top of the standard trek rates. You also have to provide climbing gear (rope, crampons, ice axe, snow goggles, gloves and boots) for you and the guide.

Equipment Hire RMS rent out the following (with charge per day): sleeping bag (US$10), waterproof jacket (US$5), gaiters US$2.50, gumboots (US$5), walking boots (US$5), crampons (US$5), rope US$10, ice axe (US$5) and snow goggles (US$2.50).

Guidebooks

The best, and only, dedicated guidebook to the range is *Guide to the Ruwenzori* by H Osmaston & D Pasteur. Originally published in 1972, much of the information it contains is of course out of date, but some details on walking and climbing routes are still relevant, and the copious background material on the history, vegetation and geology of the range is fascinating. This beautiful book is now a minor classic and hard to find these days.

The *East Africa International Mountain Guide* (see Books, in the Regional Facts for the Trekker chapter) has a small Rwenzori chapter with brief details on trekking and climbing routes.

Maps

Detailed maps of the mountain range include RMS/USAID *Rwenzori Tourist Routes*, which shows only essential features on the Bujuku-Mubuku Circuit and has no contours, and the Uganda Surveys *Central Rwenzori* map (1:25,000), with sufficient detail for a trek and re-issued in the early 1990s with colour shading.

The easiest map to find and to use is *Ruwenzori*, published by Andrew Wielochowski, although older editions of this map do not show the two new huts (Guy Yeoman and John Matte) on the Bujuku-Mubuku Circuit.

Rwenzori Trek Administration

Although the Rwenzoris are relatively rarely visited, it is still possible to find some of the huts very crowded if your visit coincides with a large group. You can avoid this by checking the situation with Rwenzori Mountaineering Services (RMS), and delaying your start if necessary until the route is clear. However, this plan falls down if a group decides to spend more than one night at any of the huts.

The official line at RMS is that they keep a tight control of numbers entering the park, and if any of the huts are likely to be full, they will prevent more people from going up. This plan is hard to implement, however, as RMS takes bookings at both its Ibanda and Kasese offices, and communication between the two isn't always efficient. If the number of trekkers continues to increase, this problem will have to be tackled more seriously. One of the stumbling blocks is that RMS and the Rwenzori Mountains National Park (RMNP) authorities do not always agree on how trekking and trekkers' facilities in the Rwenzoris should be administered.

Before the park was created, RMS effectively controlled all visits to the mountains and now there is resentment that the park administrators are taking over some of its affairs. However, there may be advantages: it had been suggested that some local businessmen had a more than healthy interest in the organisation's finances.

There has also been some disagreement between RMS and its USAID backers on one side and some conservationist bodies on the other about the future siting of huts, the building of boardwalks across bogs, provisions for porters and guides, and so on.

Over the last few years RMS and the RMNP have established their respective responsibilities and, hopefully, now work together for the benefit of the mountain environment and the local people who depend on it. However, visitors should always be prepared for changes in the way Rwenzori trekking is organised. ■

There's a lot of useful information on the back of the map. Copies are available from RMS or the Saad Hotel (see Places to Stay) in Kasese, in Kampala and Nairobi, and from specialist map shops overseas.

The Uganda Surveys 1:50,000 sheet number 65/2 (*Margherita*) is hard to find, although it may be re-issued. In the meantime an enlargement of 65/2 entitled *Ruwenzori Mountains* (now at a scale of 1:25,000) is published by Uganda Lands & Survey Department.

Supplies
To provide for a trek in the Rwenzoris, you can buy what you need in Kasese, which has a few shops with reasonable stocks and a good market, although you get a lot more choice in Kampala. In Kasese market you can also buy rubber gumboots. Nyakalengija has a small shop, but don't rely on it for anything more than biscuits and soft drinks. There is nothing inside the park.

PLACES TO STAY
Kasese
Most trekkers stay at the friendly *Saad Hotel* in the centre of town. It's basic, although these days you get water and electricity most of the time. En suite singles/doubles are US$17/27 and dorm beds are US$5. There's a good-value restaurant (meals around US$4) and the hotel will store extra gear while you're trekking.

If you're counting every shilling, there are some cheapie lodging houses in the area between the Saad and the market, with beds for around US$3. In the same area are some local restaurants and bars.

Top of the range is the *Hotel Margherita*, about 5km outside town, which underwent a massive refit during 1996 in expectation of a large influx of expat engineers for the nearby Kilembe cobalt mines. A pool and camp site are also planned. Smart en suite singles/doubles cost US$36/55, with full breakfast. (A taxi between town and the hotel costs US$5, and the hotel has a car which will pick up and drop off guests.)

Nyakalengija
Nyakalengija is at the end of the dirt road from Ibanda and is the start of the main trekking route into the Rwenzoris. At the *RMS bunkhouse* beds cost US$5 and a basic evening meal US$2. Camping is free.

On the Mountains
The main trekking route through the Rwenzoris has huts built along it, spaced a day's walk apart. Some huts are new and in good condition, others are old and dilapidated. Each hut (sometimes called 'tourist camp') has another hut nearby for the use of guides and porters. Rock shelters are no longer used on this route.

There are no facilities at any of the huts, apart from wooden sleeping platforms and tables, and possibly some old saucepans. You will need sleeping bags, mats and cooking equipment. One of the most popular huts, Bujuku, is also one of the smallest, and it can get crowded if a couple of groups turn up at the same time. Although a tent is not essential, if you've got one, you might as well take it in case any of the huts are busy.

GETTING THERE & AWAY
The nearest town to the Rwenzori Range is Kasese, about 300km directly west of Kampala (almost 500km by road via Mbarara).

Road
Buses and minibuses run between Kampala and Kasese every day, via Masaka and Mbarara. Direct buses leave early in the morning; later in the day you may have to do the journey in stages. The direct bus between Kampala and Kasese costs about US$6, minibuses about US$10.

Train
The train between Kampala and Kasese runs about twice a week in each direction, supposedly overnight but it sometimes takes more than two days. See Getting Around in this chapter for more details.

UGANDA

The Bujuku-Mubuku Circuit

Area Rwenzori Mountains National Park
Distance 59km or 62km
Duration 7 days minimum
Start/Finish Nyakalengija, near Ibanda
Highest Point Elena Hut (4540m)
Overall Altitude Gain 2900m
Nearest large town Kasese
Accommodation Huts or camping
Access Bus & walk/hitch or organised trek
Summary Tough trekking through true African highland wilderness, with frequent mists and boggy paths. For afficionados only, but a very satisfying experience.
Note: distances appear short, but the demanding conditions make for slow and tiring progress.

Access

This trek starts at the small village of Nyakalengija, a few km up the dirt road from the slightly larger village of Ibanda. In reality, Nyakalengija is a 'suburb' of Ibanda and the two names seem to be used interchangeably.

If you've arranged a trek through RMS, your fee includes transport between Kasese and Nyakalengija/Ibanda. If you're going alone, from the roundabout between the Saad Hotel and the train station in Kasese, take the main road towards Fort Portal. After about 12km, a dirt road branches off on the left. Ibanda and the RMS headquarters are signposted. Buses and minibuses run between Kasese and Fort Portal, and can drop you at this junction. From there you'll have to walk, or hitch a ride with a tractor or pick-up. From the junction to Nyakalengija is another 12km.

Before starting your trek, you have to pay park fees at the Nyakalengija park HQ. The receipts will be checked at the park gate about 2km beyond the HQ, and if they're not in order you'll be sent back.

Stage 1: Nyakalengija to Nyabitaba Hut
10km, 4-5 hours, 1000m ascent
From the park HQ continue up the track, around a pond and over a brick bridge, and through a grassy area near the school. Continue past huts and through fields, and through patches of bamboo and high elephant grass (there are several forks and junctions, but the main path is usually the most well trodden) to reach the park gate, about 45 minutes from Nyakalengija.

The path continues through the forest with the large Mubuku River on your right. You cross a couple of smaller streams flowing into the main river. The bush is dense: it'll rip your legs, if you're wearing shorts, and anything tied to the outside of your rucksack.

About 1½ hours from the start of the park the bush thins slightly and the path climbs steeply up a ridge with forested valleys on either side. Follow this ridge for another 1½ to two hours, to reach Nyabitaba Hut (2650m).

Nyabitaba is in poor condition, with sleeping platforms for about 20 people. There's a toilet and water from a tap about 50m further up the path towards a more basic hut used as a shelter by porters.

Across the valley from the hut (mist permitting), you can see the steep walls of Rutara, the nearest of the Portal Peaks. (In this route description, every time we mention the view that can be seen from a col, peak or valley bottom, this is always presuming that the weather is clear. Most often it isn't, but it gets a bit repetitive putting 'mist permitting' every time!)

Stage 2: Nyabitaba Hut to John Matte Hut
7km, 5-6 hours, 700m ascent
From Nyabitaba Hut continue along the path to a fork. Take the path to the right and drop to the Kurt Shafer Bridge (see boxed text), just below the confluence of the Bujuku and Mubuku rivers (half an hour from the hut).

From the bridge continue steeply through mud and dense vegetation, and over rocks and roots. After an hour, you reach the base of some large mossy cliffs on your right, while down to the left the valley side drops steeply to the river. After another two hours you reach Nyamuleju Hut, which is now in very bad condition and not normally used.

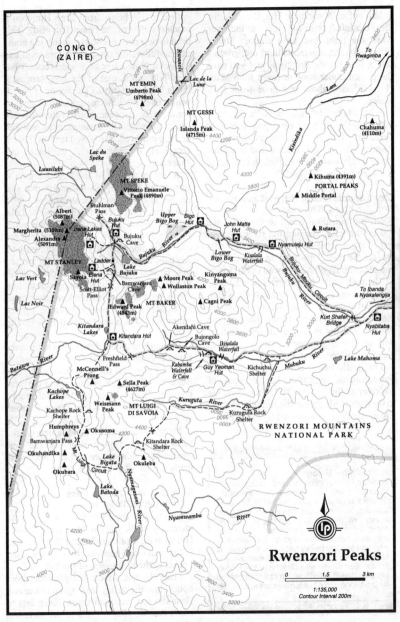

Rwenzori Peaks

0   1.5   3 km

1:135,000
Contour Interval 200m

Just before Nyamuleju Hut, the path divides: the left fork keeps closer to the river, while the right fork stays slightly higher. Either way, the vegetation thins out, groundsels appear for the first time, and you enter the giant heather zone to reach John Matte Hut (3350m), about one hour from Nyamuleju.

John Matte Hut was built in the early 1990s and is in good condition. From the veranda you get great views down the Bujuku Valley, with Rutara and the other Portal Peaks on the left and the steep sides of Kinyangoma on the right.

Stage 3: John Matte Hut to Bujuku Hut
6km, 5-6 hours, 630m ascent

From the hut, drop down to the river and follow the path, keeping the river on your left. Fifteen minutes from the hut the path crosses the river. Upstream, to the west, you can see the bulk of the east wall of Mt Speke.

The path skirts the left-hand (south) edge of the Lower Bigo Bog to reach Bigo Hut. This hut is small, basic and not used very much. There is plenty of room for camping though, and it's in a pleasant open setting, with good views of the surrounding peaks. Nearby is a cave for porters.

The path turns south-west, passing through dense vegetation, keeping south of the river as the Bujuku Valley narrows. Up to the right is Mt Speke; the summit, Vittorio Emanuele Peak, is obscured by lower peaks.

Kurt Shafer Bridge
The Kurt Shafer Bridge crosses the Bujuku and Mubuku rivers just below their confluence. Before this large suspension bridge was built, crossing the rivers here was a risky enterprise which involved boulder-hopping on slippery rocks, often resulting in unplanned dips in the icy water. It was particularly hard for the porters who had to carry heavy gear as well. Previous bridges were smaller and got washed away in floods. Kurt Shafer was director of the USAID programme in Uganda, which provided finance for the bridge and other facilities in the park. ■

One to 1½ hours from Bigo Hut, you'll reach the edge of the Upper Bigo Bog. This used to be a major obstacle, involving hours of painfully slow progress across mud and tussocks. Now a line of wooden boards has been laid across part of the bog, turning it into a 15 minute stroll. (The laying of boardwalks like this has created a great deal of controversy between conservationists and 'developers', and the boards may be replaced or even removed. See boxed text on 'Rwenzori Trek Administration', earlier in this chapter.)

At the other end of the bog, the path is steeper but over slightly easier ground, as it crosses and re-crosses the stream for almost two hours before reaching the edge of Lake Bujuku. When the lake is low, the water flowing from it runs underground and you can walk along the dry stony stream bed. Keep the lake to your left. Up to your left you may be able to see the summit peaks of Mt Stanley. On your right is a large rock shelter; this is Bujuku Cave (marked on some maps as Cooking Pot Cave). Continue up the valley for 20 minutes to reach Bujuku Hut (3977m).

Bujuku Hut is one of the oldest huts on the Bujuku-Mubuku Circuit. It is also the smallest and, being near the main peaks of Speke, Baker and Stanley, it is also one of the most popular. There's room for 10 comfortably, but be prepared for a squeeze if a group arrives.

Margherita, the summit of Stanley, cannot be seen from Bujuku Hut. For the best chance of a view, return to Lake Bujuku in the late evening or early morning.

Sidetrack 1: Stuhlman Pass
2 hours return, 180m ascent

If you've got the time and energy for an afternoon stroll, you can walk from Bujuku Hut up to the Stuhlman Pass (4160m), which is the main col between Mts Stanley and Speke, to the north-west of the hut.

From the hut, follow the path that goes uphill, into the valley leading up to the col. Near the top, the path forks. Keep left to reach the col. (Right leads to the technical route up Mt Speke.) This col marks the watershed of the Rwenzoris, but all streams to the east and west flow into Lake Albert and eventually into the Nile.

The watershed is also the traditional boundary between Uganda and Congo (Zaïre), although the actual border is a straight line from Margherita Peak to a point between the summits of Mts Emin and Gessi, passing about 1km to the west of the watershed.

Views from the pass are worth the walk up. Looking back over the hut, the dark walls of Mt Baker can be seen on the other side of the valley. Up to the right are the flanks of Mt Stanley, while to the left are the peaks of Mt Speke.

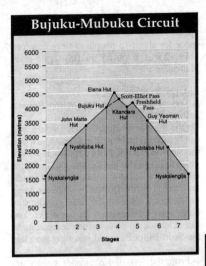

Bujuku-Mubuku Circuit

Sidetrack 2: Stuhlman Pass & Lac du Speke
4-5 hours return, 270m ascent

If you spend two nights at Bujuku Hut, you can walk to Lac du Speke on the day in between. Like many of the features on the west side of the Rwenzoris, it has a French name, as Congo (Zaïre) is a former Belgian colony.

The first part of the route, up to the Stuhlman Pass is as described in Sidetrack 1. From the pass, you need to tend right, below the west side of Mt Speke, gaining height slightly to avoid passing below the lake. Allow about 1½ hours from the pass to the lake, and then another two to get back to the hut. A guide is recommended for this route, which should not be attempted in bad weather.

Stage 4: Bujuku Hut to Kitandara Hut
4km, 5-6 hours, 390m ascent;
plus 340m descent

From the hut follow the path downhill to Bujuku (Cooking Pot) Cave, then aim south, across the boggy valley floor, to start going up the valley side, with the main peaks of Mt Stanley on your right. If it's clear you'll be able to see Margherita and the surrounding glaciers on the summit. After an hour of steep uphill climbing through groundsels, the path enters a gully with a steel ladder leading up to level ground and a fork in the paths. The

right fork leads up to Elena Hut and the snout of the Elena Glacier (see the Elena Hut sidetrack description).

Keep straight on and continue up as the groundsels thin out and it gets rockier, to reach the Scott-Elliot Pass (4370m), the main col between Mts Stanley and Baker, 2½ to three hours from Bujuku Hut. Just before the pass, there's a fork where the path down from Elena Hut comes in from the right. Keep left here. Up to the left, on top of a rock buttress, is a large pole, used as a marker when deep snow hides the path.

Cross the col and continue downhill, passing another large marker pole. Up to the right, the main glaciers are visible, with Elena Hut at their base. Straight ahead, down in the valley bottom, you can see the Kitandara Lakes with Mt Luigi di Savoia behind them. Continue, mainly downhill, to reach a viewpoint overlooking the upper Kitandara Lake. Pass to the left of the lake, to reach the porters' hut, then down for another five minutes to reach Kitandara Hut (4027m) and the lower lake, about two hours from the Scott-Elliot Pass.

Kitandara Hut is in poor condition, but the setting is one of the best in the Rwenzori,

UGANDA

right next to the lake with great views back up the valley to the main peaks. There's space for about 15 people to sleep comfortably (25 at a push) on the triple-level platforms.

Sidetrack: Elena Hut
2-3 hours return, 170m ascent from Stage 4 path

On the route from Bujuku to Kitandara, you can branch off at the fork in the path, just past the steel ladder (described in Stage 4), and go up to Elena Hut and the snout of the Elena Glacier. The hut is small but in good condition, and is normally used by climbers doing the technical routes on Mt Stanley, who stay here to get an early start for the peaks. You can sidetrack up here, before descending to the Scott-Elliot Pass and rejoining the main route.

From the fork, the path goes steeply up, winding and zigzagging, past occasional cairns. After an hour, you pass Bamwanjara Rock Shelter on your left. Continue up, with the cliffs on your left. The vegetation thins out and you cross lichen-covered rocks. Twenty minutes from the rock shelter the path changes direction sharply, turning back on itself. The cliffs are now on your right. After 50m you reach some marker posts and more cairns. The path coming up from the Scott-Elliot Pass joins from the left. Con-

tinue across bare rock, which is slippery, especially after rain. There is no path and only occasional cairns, so care should be taken. Head for the snout of the glacier, due west. You reach Elena Hut (4540m) about 1½ to two hours from the fork above the ladder.

Elena Hut is a wild place, far above the vegetation line, perched on bare rock, with spectacular views up to the huge white bulk of the glacier looming overhead, and down into the Kitandara Valley.

From Elena Hut, retrace the route to the point where the path coming up from Scott-Elliot Pass forks right (about 20 minutes from the hut). Take this path, steeply down over scree, slabs and boulders, to meet the main Bujuku-Kitandara path about one hour from Elena Hut. Turn right, and go up for a few metres to reach the crest of the Scott-Elliot Pass. From here resume Stage 4.

Stage 5: Kitandara Hut to Guy Yeoman Hut
5km, 5-6 hours, 250m ascent;
plus 830m descent

From Kitandara, the path climbs very steeply over boulders and through dense groundsels. As you get higher, you can see westwards into the Butawu Valley, with its river flowing down towards Congo (Zaïre). On the right side of this valley, the southern shoulder of

Elena Hut
If you want to extend your trek and stay at Elena your gear needs to be up to scratch, as it gets very cold here. There's no firewood, and water has to be melted from snow or collected from pools, although some of these are not very clean. It's better to bring some clean water with you from Bujuku. Porters do not normally stay at Elena Hut as it's too cold and there's not enough room in the hut. They will carry stuff up here, then return to Bujuku, coming up to collect you again the next day (or after however long you want to stay). Guides will stay at Elena but must be provided with extra blankets and paid a bonus (see Porters & Guides in Trekking Information). ■

DAVID ELSE

UGANDA

Mt Stanley leads up to Luigi di Savoia Peak, with the tongue of the Savoia Glacier to its right. Even higher up this path, the Edward Glacier on the top of Mt Baker also comes into view.

An hour from Kitandara, the path reaches more level ground. Looking back now towards Mt Stanley you can see the Elena Glacier and the tiny dot of Elena Hut. Even the ridge that extends east from Margherita can be seen although the peak itself is obscured by Savoia. From this point, the tilted block formation of the whole range is clearly evident. It plays games with your perspective and even makes the horizon appear to slope.

Where the path levels out, there's a fork. (Left leads up to the summit of Mt Baker, another route for mountaineers.) Keep straight on, through undulating moorland. To the right are the peaks of Sella and Weismann on Mt Luigi di Savoia (called 'Rigi' by local guides), with the rock pillar of McConnell's Prong on the western end of the ridge.

After half an hour the path crosses the Freshfield Pass (4280m), the main col between Mts Baker and Luigi di Savoia. You get your last views of Mt Stanley, and a whole new vista opens up in front. This is the Mubuku Valley, crossed by hills of jagged slanting strata, with Lake Mahoma at its end, and the distant plains just visible beyond.

From the pass, go steeply down through mud and boulders to cross a stream after about an hour. From here, slog through bog and tussocks, gradually downhill. After half an hour, up a small valley to the left, you can see Moore Glacier, with the Moore and Wollaston Peaks to its right. The Mubuku River flows in from the left in the valley down below, as you follow a muddy ledge to reach the large Akendahi Cave. Sound from the river below echoes off the back wall of the cave as if water is flowing behind it.

Continue to reach another large cave called Bujongolo (two to three hours from the Freshfield Pass). This was where the Duke of Abruzzi's expedition camped during the 1906 expedition. Carved on the wall of the cave are several European and African names. Some guides point out the names of

their older relatives who carried gear on this original Rwenzori trek.

From Bujongolo the path enters giant heather. Through a gap you can see a long grassy clearing on the valley floor below, with Guy Yeoman Hut just visible at its end. Continue down, beside the Mubuku River. About an hour from Bujongolo, you cross a small stream flowing into the river from the right. Up to the right is the picturesque Kabamba Waterfall, flowing down from a cliff and cascading off a large boulder. You enter a long grassy clearing and half an hour from the waterfall reach Guy Yeoman Hut (3540m).

Guy Yeoman Hut is in good condition, with room for about 20 people. From the hut veranda, you can look straight across the valley to Cagni Peak. At the far end of the valley, the snow and ice-covered main peaks of Mt Baker can also be seen.

Stage 6: Guy Yeoman Hut to Nyabitaba Hut

6km, 4-5 hours, 800m descent

From the hut, the path continues down the Mubuku Valley, through dense vegetation. Down to the left you can see the Ikisalala Waterfall. Just over half an hour from the hut, cross to the north side of the Mubuku River, and shortly after that start descending very steeply beside a stream bed of bare rock, which you cross and re-cross several times. This section requires a fair bit of concentration: one slip in the wrong place and you could go a long way down. Take extra care in the wet. (When the river is in flood, the section is virtually impassable. Some maps show a new route around this tricky section, but it is rarely used and is very overgrown.) At the foot of this steep section is Kichuchu Rock Shelter, two to three hours from Guy Yeoman Hut. There's room for a couple of tents here, but the rock shelter does not provide much protection for porters.

From Kichuchu, cross the stream again, then pass through thick vegetation and thicker bog for about an hour to reach the main Mubuku River, which you cross on a wide rocky ford to its south bank. (Again, take great care if the river is in flood. In 1992 somebody got swept away here and drowned.) There are more flowers and birds here, after the relatively barren sections further up. You may even see monkeys.

The path follows a narrow ridge, with steep drops to the Mubuku River to the left, through bogs, crossing and re-crossing a small stream. After an hour the path becomes drier and the path in from Lake Mahoma joins from the right. Fifteen minutes further and the path from the Kurt Shafer Bridge joins from the left. Another five minutes further down the valley is Nyabitaba Hut (see Stage 1).

You can stay here or continue down to Nyakalengija. If you do these two stages in one go, guides and porters should be paid for two days.

Stage 7: Nyabitaba Hut to Nyakalengija
10km, 2-3 hours, 1000m descent
Retracing the route of Stage 1, drop down the steep ridge to meet the Mubuku River, leave the park, and pass through the fields to Nyakalengija.

Other Routes on the Rwenzori Mountains

The Bujuku-Mubuku Circuit is the only trekking route in the Rwenzoris that is relatively easy to use, although steep gradients, deep bogs and dense vegetation means trekking conditions are often hard. Apart from this circuit, other routes marked on maps are very difficult to use. It is very important to realise that these paths are not just overgrown – they simply do not exist at all.

If you lust for adventure and want to attempt one of the other routes, you have to cut your own path for some of the way. This requires a team of porters, hired specially for path-cutting, plus another team to carry their blankets and food, plus a team to carry your own gear. Even with good cutters and porters you could expect to cover only a few km a

day in this way. If you are not properly equipped and supplied the chances of getting seriously, even fatally, lost are high.

Obviously, for anything off the main route, a very experienced guide is also essential. You may have to wait a day or two while RMS summon a guide who knows the particular area you want to visit. Of course you have to be completely self-sufficient with tent and gear. When deciding on a route, you must plan to spend each night at a large rock shelter for the porters.

If all this hasn't put you off, the following route is a feasible proposition, if you really want to experience Rwenzori wilderness at its wildest.

MT LUIGI CIRCUIT
This route branches off the usual Bujuku-Mubuku Circuit at Kitandara Hut and rejoins the route at Kichuchu Shelter between Guy Yeoman and Nyabitaba huts, circling the western, southern and eastern sides of Mt Luigi di Savoia. Despite the route being indicated on maps (including the one on this book) the path is non-existent, the vegetation is very dense, and the going is absolutely exhausting. This route takes at least four long days (seven to nine hours of walking to cover 4km to 5km), although you'll probably want to stop for a rest day about halfway. This is added onto the five or six days it takes you to do the rest of the usual circuit.

Two people will need at least 10 porters for the whole trek, although there will be difficulties finding big enough rock shelters. The best thing is to arrange to be re-supplied at Kitandara by some extra porters coming up the Mubuku Valley. In this way you can do the Mt Luigi Circuit with just seven or eight porters and a guide.

Stage 1: Kitandara Hut to Kachope Rock Shelter
From Kitandara Hut, go south along the southern lake and the Butawu stream, then steeply up and down while crossing ridges on the west side of the mountain for several hours. From a viewpoint you can see the lower Kachope Lakes, as you go up to the higher

lake and walk along its northern and eastern shore. The going is hard, across piles of rocks with dense vegetation. Between the rocks are deep holes, some of them big enough to fall into. There is no rock shelter by the lake so continue uphill, south from the lake for about an hour, to reach the large shelter and a place to camp.

Stage 2: Kachope to Kitandara Rock Shelter

Note: Kitandara Rock Shelter lies directly to the north of Okuleba Peak, not to be confused with the hut of the same name that you left yesterday. From the Kachope Rock Shelter, continue southwards to pass between the peaks of Humphreys and Okusoma at the Bamwunjara Pass (4450m). There are good views from the pass: north to the Kitandara Valley, south down to Lake Batoda. Continue downhill, tending east around the southern slope of Mt Okusoma to reach Lake Bigata, where there is a very small rock shelter. From here aim north-east, over the northern shoulder of Mt Okuleba to reach the Kitandara Rock Shelter and a place to camp.

Stage 3: Kitandara to Kuruguta Rock Shelter

From Kitandara Rock Shelter continue north-east, uphill past a small lake. Continue up, over very loose ground, through a col at about 4400m, across a bog, and descend very steeply down, into the densely vegetated Kuruguta Valley. Go eastwards down the valley, where a lot of cutting is needed, to reach Kuruguta Shelter, and a space for camping. (This stage is probably the hardest, and you might consider staying here two nights, to rest and soak up the atmosphere.)

Stage 4: Kuruguta to Kichuchu Rock Shelter

Continue east down the valley (the easiest thing to do is actually walk in the stream), then tend left as the valley swings north. The vegetation gets increasingly dense, with strenuous panga-wielding called for, until you reach Kichuchu Shelter. It takes about six hours to cover the 2km from Kuruguta.

You are now back on the main path. You can camp here, although the cave for the porters is small, or continue downhill to reach Nyabitaba Hut after another two hours.

SMUGGLERS' PATHS

The only other routes in the Rwenzoris that might be possible to follow are the smugglers' paths that are still occasionally used. At certain times, there's a lot of illicit trade in coffee, millet, even gold and guns, going across the mountains between Congo (Zaïre) and Uganda. Ask your guide for more information, although you'll need to use a certain amount of diplomacy here.

FUTURE POSSIBILITIES

The park authorities plan to reduce pressure on the main circuit route by opening up new trekking routes. Even if the routes have been opened by the time you get here, new huts are unlikely, so you'll need to be self-sufficient and spend each night by a rock shelter for porters. Planned new routes include:

North From Bundibugiyo and the villages of Nyahuka and Bundimbuga, using the ridge to the east of the Lamya River, crossing between Mt Gessi and the Portal Peaks to meet the main circuit at Bigo Hut.

East From Rwagimba, following the Rwimi Valley west to meet the route from Bundibugiyo just north of Portal Peaks and another route south from this, passing to the east of Portal Peaks to reach the Mubuku River opposite Nyabitaba Hut.

South From Kilembe Mines, near Kasese, going up Nyamwamba Valley to meet the Mt Luigi Circuit route at Kitandara Rock Shelter, and then continuing via Bamwunjara Pass to Kitandara Hut on the main route.

There are also very long-term plans for routes from Kyarumba up the ridge west of Nyamagasani River, and from Bwera, via Ruata Peak area, past Lake Batoda and through the Bamwunjara Pass to Kitandara Hut.

Congo (Zaïre) Route

There is another trekking route on the Congo (Zaïre) side of the Rwenzoris, starting from Mutwanga and leading through the Virunga

UGANDA

National Park to Moraine Hut on the west side of Mt Stanley. There are no regularly used paths linking this route to the Bujuku-Mubuku Circuit, and a traverse is not possible anyway, due to border restrictions.

For descriptions of this route (which may be very dated) have a look at *Guide to the Ruwenzori* and the *East Africa International Mountain Guide* (see Guidebooks in this section earlier under Trekking Information).

Mt Elgon

Mount Elgon is the second-highest mountain in Uganda, in the far east of the country, straddling the border with Kenya. It is also the fifth-highest mountain in East Africa, offering high-quality wilderness trekking, although despite these attractions it is frequently overlooked by visitors.

Like many of the other major East African mountains, Mt Elgon is volcanic in origin. It has a very broad base, which leads geologists to believe that at one time Elgon may have been higher than Kilimanjaro or Mt Kenya. At the top of the mountain is a large crater, surrounded by a ring of peaks. You can easily trek to the highest part of the mountain and descend onto the crater floor without technical climbing.

The western half of the mountain was made a national park in 1993, and the authorities are making positive steps to encourage hiking and trekking. Over the next few years the number of visitors is likely to increase but for now the Ugandan side of Mt Elgon remains one of the great undiscovered secrets of East Africa

HISTORY

The mountain's title is a corruption of its local name, Oldoinyo Ilgoon, meaning 'Breast Mountain' in the Maasai language. The people who lived in caves on the forested eastern slopes of the mountain until the middle of this century were called Elgony or Il-Kony (there are several spelling variations), related to the Maasai who now inhabit the plains of Kenya and Tanzania. On the western side of the mountain the people are predominantly Bagusu (or Gusi), of Bantu

origin. They originally named the two main peaks Wagagai and Bamasaba, meaning Father and Mother. Bamasaba appears highest from this view and the name seems to have been transferred to the whole mountain. The explorer Henry Stanley referred to a mountain called Masaba which he saw when travelling through this area in 1878. The geographer CW Hobley, writing in 1897 after a complete circumnavigation of Mt Elgon, called it Masawa.

During early colonial times, the whole mountain was called Elgon and the name Wagagai returned to the highest peak. Bamasaba was renamed Jackson's Summit after one F Jackson, a colonial official and later governor of the Uganda protectorate, who, in 1890, was probably the first European to reach the crater rim.

Through the 1970s and 1980s, the Ugandan side of Mt Elgon was very seldom (if ever) visited by tourists. Several rebel groups were active in the area, there was a lot of poaching, and the whole Uganda-Kenya border zone was notorious bandit country. Due to the general anarchy, and a complete breakdown of local government, many people moved into the supposedly protected areas of forest reserve on Elgon's western slopes and cleared the vegetation for planting crops.

The civil war ended in 1986 and by the early 1990s Uganda was receiving a lot of overseas aid money for development and conservation schemes. One of these included a project on Mt Elgon and in 1993 the forest reserve was turned into a national park, giving considerably more protection. The park boundary was re-established to prevent further encroachment (while still allowing the local people to harvest wood and bamboo at a sustainable level). The authorities started to encourage visitors to come for hiking and trekking, realising this could provide revenue and employment for local people, thereby greatly increasing the park's chance of survival in an area where the already high demand for land for cultivation is increasing. This is good news for local people and for trekkers. The Ugandan Government should be congratulated for its support of this new project.

GEOGRAPHY

The Mt Elgon massif is roughly circular in shape, slightly elongated north to south, measuring about 110km by 90km where the main bulk of the mountain rises from the surrounding plains. The base of the mountain is actually broader than Kilimanjaro's, and Elgon is described as 'encompassing the largest surface area of any extinct volcano in the world'.

Although Mt Elgon was probably higher than Kilimanjaro once, it has since been eroded to its present broad dome. The top of the dome dips inwards to form a crater (technically a caldera), now a large basin some 7km across, with an area of around 40 sq km, making it the second largest caldera in the world after Tanzania's Ngorongoro Crater.

The crater rim is dotted with several peaks, forming a ring. There are several cols or passes between the peaks, and the rim is broken completely in one place by the Suam Gorge. The crater is a large catchment for the Suam River which flows down the gorge, forming the border between Kenya and Uganda at this point.

The northern, eastern and southern sides of Mt Elgon slope gradually down to the plains, but the western side of the mountain is steeper. The highest peak on the whole massif is Wagagai, at 4321m (14,172 ft), on the western rim of the crater and easily reached by the main route on this side. Just to the north of this is Jackson's Peak (4160m), also easy to reach. To the south-

east another peak has been named Wagagai (4298m) which seems to be the result of an early cartographic error. In an attempt to avoid confusion the smaller peak is called Little Wagagai in this book.

Other major peaks on Mt Elgon include Mubiyi, Cepkwango, Kapkwammesawe and Kabiyagut, which together form a long ridge, mainly above 4000m, on the north side of the crater rim. There is also Koitoboss (4187m), an impressive, steep-sided peak on the eastern (Kenyan) side, and Lower Elgon Peak (4301m) on the south-eastern side, which is split by the Kenya-Uganda border.

TREKKING INFORMATION

Mount Elgon is a spectacular mountain area, which receives relatively few visitors. It's not as high or as demanding as the Rwenzoris, but for trekkers in Uganda that may be an advantage. Elgon is a close second in terms of wilderness and scenery, with less mud, and a much better chance of clear skies and good views.

The trekking routes and facilities (camp sites, latrines etc) have been improved by the park authorities with assistance from various aid organisations including the US Peace Corps. This is still ongoing so you may find some changes to the descriptions here by the time you arrive.

Costs

Costs for trekking on Mt Elgon break down into guide and porter fees, national park entry fees and costs associated with food, supplies and getting there and away. All points are covered separately below.

Route Standard & Days Required

The main approach to the crater and peaks on the Ugandan side of the mountain is the Sasa Route, which starts at the village of Budadiri, the site of the national park office (where you pay entrance fees and arrange guides and porters).

Mount Elgon is a seldom-visited area, so paths are narrow and faint in places. Some parts of the Sasa Route ascent are steep, but the daily distances on the main route are not

UGANDA

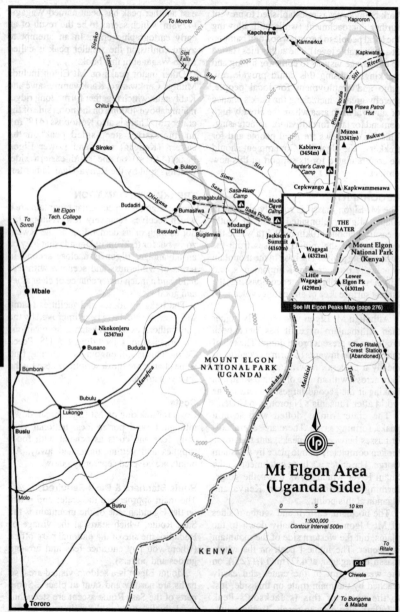

Mt Elgon Area
(Uganda Side)

0   5   10 km

1:500,000
Contour Interval 500m

long. One particularly steep section, through mud and dense bush, gives you a taste of Rwenzori conditions, but for the rest of the route the going underfoot is generally good through forest and open moorland.

The trek described in this section takes five days (four nights), although this includes two out-and-back days for the ascent of Wagagai and the stage across the crater floor to the Hot Springs, so it could be done in three days if these were omitted.

Another option is a complete traverse of the massif by going up the Sasa Route and descending the Piswa Route on the northern side of the mountain, down to the village of Kamnerkut. This can be done in five days, but inclusion of the Wagagai and Hot Springs sidetracks brings it up to six or seven days.

Although altitude should not be a big problem if you ascend sensibly, you will feel the effects if you are not acclimatised, so an extra day can also be spent on the ascent to prevent this.

Guides & Porters

Guides are not obligatory but are strongly recommended, especially if you are going to the peaks. Porters are also useful, and hiring them also means you put some money into the local economy. Guides and porters can be arranged at the park office in Budadiri. They are not park employees and so have formed a cooperative called the Mt Elgon Guides & Porters Association. Guides have been trained by park rangers and are quite knowledgeable about flora, fauna and other aspects of the park.

Guides are paid US$8 per 'stage' – this is normally a day's walk, the distance between two camps. Porters are paid US$7 per stage. If you combine two stages in one day, they get double wages. This fee also covers their food and park entrance fees. Porters carry a maximum of 18kg. About US$2 is payable in advance so they can buy food; the rest is payable on satisfactory completion of the trek. The guides and porters are all reliable. A tip for good service might be an extra day's pay for every three to four days of work.

Park Fees & Regulations

The national park headquarters is in Mbale near the Mt Elgon Hotel. There's also an information centre here, but for porters and guides it's better to arrange things at the park office in Budadiri (which is also an information centre and small museum), where you also pay park fees. For non-citizens the Mt Elgon park fees are:

Entrance (one day)	US$15
Entrance (two to five days)	US$30
Entrance (for every day over five days)	US$5
Camping (per night)	US$10
Ranger escort (one day, per ranger)	US$7
Ranger escort (two to five days, per ranger)	US$15
Ranger escort (each day over five days, per ranger)	US$2

Park regulations require you to be escorted by a ranger (who is armed) if you plan to go to the Hot Springs or anywhere else in the crater. This is because cattle theft is a problem in this area, and Mt Elgon crater is a handy route for moving contraband cows between Uganda and Kenya. If you happen to run into any rustlers during your trek they are unlikely to be friendly. You pick up the ranger at Sasa Patrol Hut about halfway between Sasa River Camp and Mude Cave Camp. If you're keeping to the peaks around the rim a ranger is not necessary.

Guidebooks

There are no guidebooks specifically on the Ugandan side of Mt Elgon, although the national park has produced a small leaflet. *Mountains of Kenya* (see the Guidebooks section in the Kenya chapter) covers the crater area, and several of the main peaks, which will be particularly useful if trekkers coming from Uganda are allowed access to the Kenyan side of the mountain in future (see Other Routes on Mt Elgon).

Maps

The trekking routes on the Ugandan side of Mt Elgon, as described in this section, are covered by the Uganda Survey 1:50,000 sheets 54/4 *(Budadiri)*, 55/3 *(Elgony)*, and 55/1 *(Kaproron)*. (The Elgony sheet is numbered

UGANDA

74/3 by the Survey of Kenya.) The whole mountain is also covered by a 1:250,000 tourist map with additional information and altitude tinting, but this was published in the 1960s and may be hard to find these days.

The main peaks and crater, plus the Kenyan side of the mountain, are shown in detail in the *Mt Elgon Map & Guide* published by Andrew Wielochowski. This map also shows the roads around the whole Mt Elgon area. It is available in Nairobi.

Supplies

In Mbale you can buy a good range of foods in tins and packets, mainly imported from Kenya, and there is also a good market for fruit and veg. In Budadiri there is also a market selling vegetables and a few small shops with basic tinned foods. Buy what you can locally as it all helps the local economy.

PLACES TO STAY
Mbale

One of the cheapest places is *St Andrew's Hostel*, basic but clean and safe, and the best value for budget travellers, with singles/doubles for US$5/8 and dorm beds for US$3. The *Mukwano Hotel*, opposite the main bus station, has reasonable rooms for US$10/15 and a busy local restaurant with good food. Much better value is the *Mount Elgon View Hotel*, a block away from the bus station; it's clean, safe and friendly with doubles at US$12 and a nice roof-top terrace where you

---

Warning

Mount Elgon is a big, wild mountain. Even the established routes are sometimes hard to follow, especially on the higher slopes and peak areas, where rain and thick mists are not uncommon. Guides may not be familiar with every part of the mountain, so if you're going off the established routes you should know how to use your compass, have good gear and at least one day's extra food. If you leave your tent and go out for a day walk, take adequate clothing. This might sound a bit over the top, but Mt Elgon is exhilarating precisely because it can be serious, and you can only enjoy it fully if you're properly equipped. ∎

---

can get breakfast and other meals. Top of the range, on the outskirts of town, is the *Mount Elgon Hotel* (☎ (045) 33454), with pleasant gardens and en suite doubles for US$35 including breakfast.

About 5km outside Mbale, near the junction to Budadiri, an aid organisation called the Salem Brotherhood have a small *guesthouse*, charging about US$20 per person. Good meals are available. The management also have vehicles and outdoor equipment for hire, and can organise treks on Mt Elgon or trips to other parts of western Uganda.

Budadiri

Budadiri is a large village near the start of the Sasa Route. The park office is here. The only place to stay is *Wagagai Lodge*, which has no sign and when we passed through seemed to have been turned into a nursing home. They have a few spartan rooms (about US$2.50 per person) for tourists, and the manager is very friendly. Camping is permitted in the grounds. Vehicles can be parked here, and guards arranged if required. There's also a small basic *camp site* at the village of Busolani, further up the road near Bumasifwa.

On the Mountain

There are long-term plans for Rwenzori-style huts for trekkers, but until these are built trekkers must camp at one of the established camp sites. You need to be fully self-sufficient with tent and camping equipment.

GETTING THERE & AWAY

The nearest large town to Mt Elgon is Mbale, about 250km by road east of Kampala. This is the third-largest town in Uganda, with shops, banks, hotels and a big market, plus a Mt Elgon National Park information centre.

Bus

Buses and minibuses run regularly between Kampala and Mbale every day, generally leaving in the morning. Buses take most of the day and cost US$2. Minibuses are quicker and cost US$5.

Mbale can also be very easily reached from Kenya, by crossing the border at Malaba (see the Uganda Getting There & Away section in the Kenya chapter). From the border to Mbale by minibus is US$2.

In Mbale, transport for Kampala and the Kenya border leaves from the main bus station in the centre of town.

Train

You can also go from Kampala to Tororo on the train, and get a minibus from there to Mbale (US$2). If you're coming from Kenya, the direct service which leaves Nairobi on Tuesday passes through Tororo on Wednesday morning on its way to Kampala (for more details see the Uganda Getting There & Away section in the Kenya chapter).

The Sasa Route

> **Area** Mt Elgon National Park
> **Distance** 38km to 86km
> **Duration** 3 to 5 days
> **Start/Finish** Budadiri
> **Highest Point** Wagagai summit (4321m)
> **Overall Altitude Gain** 3270m
> **Nearest large town** Mbale
> **Accommodation** camping
> **Access** Bus or car
> **Summary** Frequently overlooked mountain with excellent trekking opportunities and straightforward access. A reader's comment: 'Rwenzori without rain, Kilimanjaro without crowds'.

Access

To reach this route, you need to get to Budadiri, about 30km from Mbale. There are several minibuses each day to Budadiri from the bus station about 1km from the centre of Mbale on Kumi Rd, which leads north out of town towards Soroti. The fare is about US$1.30.

If you're driving or hitching, leave Mbale on the main road towards Soroti, turn right after 6km (signposted Siroko). Continue for 5km, to reach a dirt road on the right, marked by several signposts including one to the national park. Continue up the dirt road through several villages to reach Budadiri.

Stage 1: Budadiri to Sasa River Camp
13km, 6-8 hours, 1800m ascent

From the park office in Budadiri, continue up the dirt road through the village of Bumasifwa (which means 'the place of the beer-pot dregs'!) to reach the smaller villages of Bumagabula and Bumasola (two hours walk from Budadiri). The drivable road ends here. (Some minibuses go this far, but only if the road is dry.)

Follow the main path beyond the villages uphill through fields. The path forks in several places. Even if you're not taking a guide up to the top, one is certainly useful for this section. Continue for another two to three hours, gaining height all the time, to reach the park boundary, marked by a signpost.

As you leave the cultivated area and enter the park, the path gets steeper. After 20 minutes you reach Mudangi Cliffs, sheer rock slabs ascended by precarious wooden ladders. It may feel a bit wobbly, but when you see a young boy climbing in bare feet with a huge bundle of bamboo on his head, you'll feel you shouldn't make such a big deal of it.

Above Mudangi, the path is not so steep and enters the forest proper. At a fork, after about 45 minutes, keep left. The forest begins to thin out and you enter the bamboo zone. Continue, gaining height all the time, to reach the Sasa River, about two hours from Mudangi. Cross the stream and go up the far bank to reach Sasa River Camp (2850m). This is an area of flat grass, good for camping, and there's a shelter nearby for guides and porters.

Stage 2: Sasa River Camp to Mude Cave Camp
6km, 3-3½ hours, 700m ascent

From Sasa River Camp, continue up the path through the bamboo then dense bush. The path is steep and boggy, crossing roots and boulders. About two hours from Sasa River, you come out of the bush and into heathland. The site of the old Sasa Hut is down to your right; it's completely rotted away now, but a new patrol hut for the rangers has been built in this area (in case of emergency they are in radio contact with the park HQ at Mbale). A

UGANDA

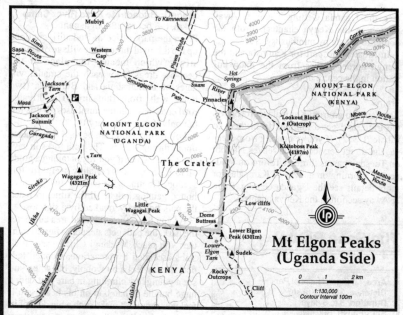

Mt Elgon Peaks (Uganda Side)

0   1   2 km

1:130,000
Contour Interval 100m

short distance beyond here the path tops a small rise and you can see the domed peak of Jackson's Summit on the skyline. To its left are the more angular peaks of Mubiyi. Wagagai is hidden from view.

After another one to 1½ hours you reach a camp site and porters' shelter at Mude Cave Camp (3460m).

Sidetrack: Jackson's Summit
4km, 2½-3 hours, 660m ascent;
plus 4km, 1½ hours descent
As Stage 2 is only a half-day walk, Jackson's Summit is an ideal point to aim for during the afternoon.

About 45 minutes from Mude Cave Camp you reach a fork. Keep right at this fork and continue up as the heath gives way to grassy moorland. Cross a few streams and keep aiming directly for the peak of Jackson's Summit, to reach Jackson's Tarn (a small pool) on your left, about one hour from the fork.

The dome of Jackson's Summit is clearly visible from the tarn. Take a faint path due south, aiming directly for the summit. Continue, rising gently, for 45 minutes, to reach the base of a steep section of angular boulders. Scramble up these to reach Jackson's Summit (4160m). A small cairn marks the highest point.

(On a nearby rock, when I was there, were some coins and even some notes held down by stones. My guide laughed when I asked about offerings to Mother Masaba, but left the money where it was.)

Return to Mude Cave Camp by the same route.

Stage 3: Mude Cave Camp to Wagagai Peak & return
8km, 3½-4½ hours, 820m ascent;
plus 8km, 2-3 hours descent
This outing from Mude Cave Camp is best done with an early start to get a better chance of views from the top. Follow the directions

in the Sidetrack above to reach Jackson's Tarn. Keeping the tarn to your left, go round its eastern side, then tend right and up again to see Jackson's Caves, a series of overhangs below cliffs, on your right.

Keep heading roughly east, uphill, on a faint path through the grass. Jackson's Summit is to your right (south) obscured at first, but then coming into view. Half an hour from the caves, the path curves round the head of a small hanging valley which drops away to the right, then goes up the next ridge diagonally (left to right) to reach the crater rim (about 2-2½ hours from Mude Cave), and your first chance to see down into the crater itself.

The crater is about 7km across, surrounded by a circular rim, with several peaks rising above the rim. Directly opposite your viewpoint, due east, you can see a large gap in the crater wall. This is the Suam Gorge, where all the water collected in the huge bowl of the crater flows out towards the east. The River Suam, which flows down the gorge, forms the Uganda-Kenya border. To the right (south) of the gorge, a ridge of minor peaks rises towards the prominent rock tower of Koitoboss (4187m). Further round (south-west), the next major peak is Lower Elgon (4301m), with a distinct dome-topped buttress on its left (northern) end. Due south from your viewpoint, at the end of the ridge, is the flat-topped peak of Wagagai, looking deceptively close.

Continue along the crest of the broad ridge, following a small path that runs due south, between the crater on your left (east) and the head of the Guragado Valley on your right (west), aiming straight for Wagagai. After half an hour, you reach a fork. Keep right (left drops down into the crater), to cross a large area of flat bare rock. Down to the left, in the crater, is a small tarn.

From here, the path gets steeper as it goes up through groundsels and over rocks towards the main summit. You reach the summit of Wagagai (4321m) about 1½ to two hours from the viewpoint where you reached the rim. A large cairn marks the top.

From the summit, to the north and east,

you can see the whole expanse of the crater, with its ring of peaks, while to the south and west the broad valleys on the outer slopes of the crater drop away towards the forest and the farmland far below.

Return by the same route.

Stage 4: Mude Cave Camp to Hot Springs & Return
24km, 8-10 hours

This long stage can be omitted, although if you do have the time you'll find it worth the effort. It takes you through the gap between Mubiyi and Jackson's Summit, and then across the floor of the crater to the Hot Springs at the head of the Suam Gorge. If you do this walk after you've been up to Wagagai, the views from the crater rim will help your orientation on the crater floor. Alternatively, as the crater floor is lower, it can help you acclimatise for the stage to Wagagai. Whichever way you do it, it's easiest to base yourself at Mude Cave Camp for at least three nights, doing the walks on the days in between. Of course, if the walk to the Hot Springs is too far, you can simply do part of this stage, up to the Western Gap or a short way into the crater, before turning back.

From Mude Cave Camp follow the path to the junction where a right turn leads to Jackson's Summit. Keep left, up the valley; this is now the Smugglers' Path (see boxed text on page 278). Keep aiming east towards the col in the crater rim, called Uganda Pass or the Western Gap, reached about two hours from Mude Cave Camp.

From the Western Gap, the path is fairly clear as it drops gradually and crosses two tributaries of the Suam River, then continues to head south-east, keeping between 0.5km and 1km south of the river. The entrance to the gorge lies due east. About 1½ to two hours from the Western Gap you reach a junction of two paths. Keep straight on, aiming towards a group of large pinnacles and rock towers on the valley side to the south of the gorge entrance. Below these pinnacles, swing left (north), keeping to fairly level ground. Ignore the main path

UGANDA

which leads steeply uphill to the right (south) of the pinnacles (this continues into Kenyan territory), and keep aiming north to cross the stream again onto the north bank. (Be careful after rain, as the Suam River can rise very quickly and become too fast to cross safely.)

Almost immediately after crossing the river, at the base of the steep valley side are several small pools of hot water. These are the Hot Springs (about two to three hours from the Western Gap). Don't expect steaming geysers here. Even the depth of the pools seems to alter; sometimes they're deep enough to bathe in, but at other times they're no more than warm puddles. The walk across the crater floor is much more interesting.

After a dip in the springs, return to Mude Cave Camp by the same route.

Sidetrack: Mude Cave Camp to Lower Elgon Peak & Tarn
2 days return

Lower Elgon Peak lies to the south-east of Wagagai, about a fifth of the way round the crater rim. The walk between these two peaks is spectacular, but long and hard, requiring good navigation. It goes through low bush and tussock grass for much of the way, although you do run across faint poachers' paths and game trails. Do not attempt it if

---

The Smugglers' Path
The Smugglers' Path leads from Mude Cave Camp to the low point in the crater rim, between Jackson's Summit and Mubiyi, which is called Uganda Pass or the Western Gap. This path goes into the crater itself, aiming towards the east side of the crater and Kenya. It descends on the Kenyan side of the mountain towards the village of Suam.

During Uganda's various civil wars, when trade with Kenya came to a virtual standstill, this route was used by local people smuggling coffee into Kenya and coming back with maize or other things they couldn't buy in Uganda. The name is still used by some guides, but note that the paths described here may get increasingly faint, as there's no need for Ugandans to smuggle coffee into Kenya any more. ∎

---

you're not fit, well acclimatised and competent with map and compass. You cross into Kenyan territory briefly near Lower Elgon Peak, but this is unlikely to be a problem.

From Mude Cave Camp to Wagagai takes about four hours up and 2½ down. From the summit of Wagagai to Lower Elgon Peak takes 3½ to five hours each way. This makes it a two-day walk, requiring an overnight camp at Lower Elgon Tarn.

In between Wagagai and Lower Elgon Peak are three other peaks. The middle of these is Little Wagagai. From the summit of Wagagai and from the crater floor, these separate peaks cannot be easily distinguished. Little Wagagai and the peak to its east appear to be one long peak when seen from the north.

From Wagagai summit, drop down by a series of rocky ledges, to the ridge that extends roughly south-east from the summit. Follow this to its end, then descend steeply again, down the side of a rock buttress. With great care, keep aiming east and then south-east, contouring round the inner wall of the crater. You might cut across a faint path that leads from the small tarn to the north of Wagagai towards a low point on the crater rim to the east of Little Wagagai. Keep contouring where possible north of Little Wagagai and the peak to its east, to reach a col between that peak and Lower Elgon Peak. Cross through this col onto the south (outside) of the crater rim (and into Kenyan territory). Tend left and keep contouring, dropping gradually over a series of flat rocky ledges to reach Lower Elgon Tarn.

From the tarn, you can see a steep gully to the left of the highest cliffs directly to your north-east. Scramble up this gully to the flat top of the peak, then turn left (north-west) to reach a large cairn marking the summit of Lower Elgon Peak (4301m).

Return to Mude Cave Camp by the same route.

Stage 5: Mude Cave Camp to Budadiri
19km, 7-8 hours descent

If you're returning by the same route, you simply retrace Stage 2 and Stage 1 back to

Budadiri. (If you're taking the traverse option, brief details on the Piswa Route are included below.)

Other Routes On Mt Elgon

THE PISWA ROUTE

You can combine an ascent of the Sasa Route with a descent on the Piswa Route to make an excellent traverse of the Ugandan side of Mt Elgon. On the descent, it's usual to camp at a point called Hunters' Cave, near the col between the peaks of Chepwango and Kapkwammesawe on the north side of the crater, and at Piswa Patrol Hut, about 5km inside the park boundary at around 2800m. The best option is to follow the Sasa Route as described above, and then on Stage 4 go from Mude Cave Camp to the Hot Springs, then straight to the Hunters' Cave. Stage 5 then goes from Hunters' Cave down to Piswa Patrol Hut, and Stage 6 goes from Piswa Patrol Hut down to the villages of Kamnerkut and Kapchorwa.

There are a few local places to eat and sleep at Kapchorwa (the *Paradise* has been recommended at US$5 per person) and fairly regular transport to/from Mbale (US$3). Trekkers we've heard from who have done this full traverse rate it very highly – 'a real high African wilderness experience' said one; 'missing only the rain of the Rwenzori and the crowds of Kilimanjaro' said another.

It's also possible to ascend the Piswa Route. It mostly follows ridges, keeping to the east side of the Siti River beyond Piswa Patrol Hut, then up a valley between the peaks of Kabiswa (also called Piswa) and Muzoa, crossing the broad col (just over 4000m) between the peaks of Chepwango and Kapkwammesawe, to the east of Mubiyi, to enter the crater. It then goes in a southerly direction, crosses the Suam River, and meets the main Smugglers' Path that goes between the Western Gap (Uganda Pass) and the Hot Springs.

A park office and information centre is planned for Kapchorwa. Porters and guides are also available. You could ascend the Piswa and descend the Sasa or do an out-and-back route on the north side, still reaching the crater and Hot Springs. Another option is to return via the new route which leads down to the village of Kapkwata, west of Kapchorwa.

Between Mbale and Kapchorwa is the small village of Sipi; **Sipi Falls** is an impressive waterfall plunging over the mouth of a huge cave. A minibus between Mbale and Sipi is US$2.50. There is an old colonial-style resthouse, now called *Sipi Falls Resort*, which is set in a nice garden overlooking the falls. Rooms are US$5 per person and camping is US$3. If you're not staying, entry to their grounds (the best viewpoint) costs US$1. Various day walks are possible in the area, and several trekkers have stayed here for a few days to 'limber up' before a major trek on Mt Elgon. No food is available, but the nearby village has a few shops selling basics. Your other option is the new *Elgon Masai Lodge*, passed on the left as you come from Mbale. A sign says 'Stop: No Accommodation Beyond This Point', which is an outright lie as Sipi Falls Resort is about half a km up the road!

THE CRATER CIRCUIT

In the future, the Ugandan and Kenyan national park authorities may begin to work more closely and allow trekkers from the Ugandan side into Kenyan territory. This was originally proposed in the early 1990s but shelved for various security reasons. It now stands more chance of being implemented as the authorities on both sides are getting a grip on the local cattle rustling and smuggling, and also because border restrictions between Uganda and Kenya are being relaxed as the old East African Community is gradually rebuilt.

If trekkers are allowed to cross into Kenya it will make a three-quarter circuit (or even a full circuit) of the crater rim a viable option. From Wagagai you could continue to Lower Elgon Peak, as described above, then continue round the inside of the rim to Koitoboss

Col and Koitoboss Peak, and from there to the Lookout Block and the Hot Springs, as outlined in the Kenya Mt Elgon section. From the Hot Springs you can complete the three-quarter circuit by following the Smugglers' Path westwards across the crater, back to the Western Gap. This circuit could also be done the opposite way, but the direction outlined here (anticlockwise) is easier.

The circuit would take three days, and would be a serious undertaking. You would have to be well kitted out, and completely self-sufficient with good camping gear and food for three days (plus extra for emergencies). A guide is recommended, but as he may not actually know this route you would have to know how to use a map and compass; much of the route does not follow paths at all and would rely on good cross-country navigation. Water is available with certainty at only two points, and these would make obvious places for overnight camps.

From Mude Cave Camp, you should allow one day to go via Wagagai to Lower Elgon Peak, where you could camp near the tarn. On the next day you could reach Koitoboss Col by following faint paths or simply making your own way through tussock grass and low bush around the inner edge of the crater, and then circle round to camp by the Hot Springs (with an optional sidetrack up to the summit of Koitoboss if you had the time and energy). On the last day you'd return to Mude Cave Camp by the Smugglers' Path, or go the harder (longer) way via the northern ridge and the peaks of Kapkwammesawe, Chepwango and Mubiyi.

This complete walk around the crater rim has been recorded only once in recent years, done by two hardy stalwarts from the Mountain Club of Kenya. As access continues to improve on the Ugandan side of the mountain, the route may soon be successfully followed by lesser mortals.

Malawi

The tourist brochures bill Malawi as 'the warm heart of Africa' and, for once, the hype is true; Malawi really is a most beautiful country and (although we hate to generalise) Malawians do seem to be among the friendliest people you could meet anywhere.

For most visitors, the country's main attraction is Lake Malawi, one of the Great Rift Valley lakes, stretching some 500km down the eastern border. Most of Malawi's high-profile wildlife reserves are near the lake, and a number of large hotels and resorts have been built along the southern shore.

The main attractions for trekkers are the highland wilderness areas of Mt Mulanje and the Nyika Plateau. There are no snowcapped summits in Malawi, but there are high mountains, with deep valleys, sheer escarpments and dramatic peaks, and some of the most enjoyable hill-walking routes in Africa.

Facts about the Country

HISTORY
The pre-colonial history of Malawi is linked to the history of East Africa as a whole, which is covered in more detail in the Facts about the Region chapter.

The Slave Trade
In the early 19th century Swahili and Arab slave-traders were beginning to move inland from the coast. Some settled around the north of Lake Malawi, founding several towns including Karonga and Nkhotakota. The slave-traders had considerable influence in the area: large boats on the lake are still built in the Arab dhow design, and many of the people in the northern lake-shore regions are Muslim.

The horrors of the slave trade were witnessed by the missionary-explorer David Livingstone, the first European to travel in the area (in the mid-19th century). His descriptions later inspired more missionaries to

DAVID ELSE

Malawi – Trekking Highlights
The wilderness areas of **Mt Mulanje** and the **Nyika Plateau** offer high mountains, with deep valleys, sheer escarpments and dramatic peaks, and some of the most enjoyable hill-walking routes in Africa.

come to Malawi with the intention of halting the slave trade and spreading Christianity among the local people.

The Missionaries
The first missionaries in Malawi suffered terribly from malaria and other illnesses, and were forced to return to the coast. But Livingstone's death in 1873 rekindled missionary zeal in Britain and support for missions in this part of Africa. In 1875 a group of missionaries from the Free Church of Scotland arrived at Lake Malawi and built a new mission at Cape Maclear, which they named Livingstonia, after the great man himself. Their early mission sites on the lake shore were malarial, so in 1894 the Livingstonia Mission was moved to an area of high

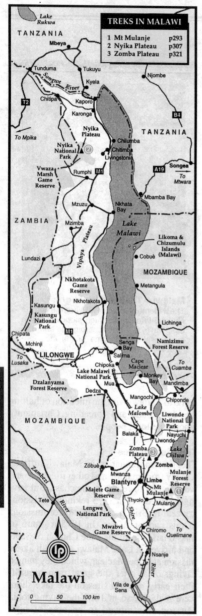

TREKS IN MALAWI

1	Mt Mulanje	p293
2	Nyika Plateau	p307
3	Zomba Plateau	p321

Malawi

ground in between the eastern escarpment of the Nyika Plateau and Lake Malawi. This site was successful; the mission flourished and is still there today.

Meanwhile, in 1876, another group of missionaries from the Established Church of Scotland built a mission in the Shire Highlands which they called Blantyre, after Livingstone's birthplace. Blantyre is now Malawi's commercial capital and the mission is still an important centre with a church, hospital and school.

The Colonial Period
The early missionaries were followed by pioneer traders, and behind them came the first settlers from Europe. By 1878 the African Lakes Company, later to become the Mandala Trading Company, had built a trading centre in Blantyre. By 1883 it even had its own bank. Settlers continued to arrive and at the end of 1889 the area to the west of the lake and south into the Shire Highlands was declared a British protectorate, called Nyasaland. In 1891 the borders were officially defined and Blantyre became the centre of the colonial government. But it wasn't all a smooth ride: in the mid and late 1890s there were several confrontations between the colonial forces and local chiefs engaged in the slave trade, which was still flourishing.

More opposition to the colonial government came in the early 1900s from John Chilembwe, a local priest who had studied at mission colleges in Britain and America. He protested about forced labour schemes used in the new plantations that were being established by the settlers, but he was largely ignored. At the outbreak of WWI, Chilembwe continued to speak out against the conscription of African men into the colonial army. He organised several attacks on plantations and government buildings around the country, but his rebellion was short-lived and swiftly crushed.

Transition & Independence
After WWI the British began to introduce ways for the African population to become involved in the administration of the country.

Things happened slowly, however, and it wasn't until the 1950s that Africans were actually allowed to enter the government.

In 1953 Nyasaland was joined to the Federation of Northern and Southern Rhodesia (today's Zambia and Zimbabwe), but this move was opposed by the newly formed anti-colonial Nyasaland African Congress Party (NACP). The leading figure of the NACP was Dr Hastings Banda, who had studied and worked in Britain and Ghana before returning to Malawi in 1958.

By the end of the 1950s the British Empire was on the wane. In 1963 Nyasaland left the Federation and in 1964 became the independent country of Malawi. Banda was the first prime minister and became president two years later. The NACP changed its name to the Malawi Congress Party (MCP), and Malawi became a one-party state.

The Banda Years

President Banda continued to consolidate his position in the government and in 1971 he was declared president for life. By 1977 he was also Minister for Foreign Affairs, Commander in Chief of the Armed Forces, Chancellor of the University, and Chairman of the MCP (still the only legal party in the country).

Through the 1980s and into the early 1990s, President Banda continued to rule Malawi in his rigid and rather unconventional style, but all over the country there was increasing opposition. In 1992, the Catholic bishops of Malawi issued a pastoral letter which condemned the regime and called for change. This was a brave action, for even bishops were not immune from Banda's iron grip. Demonstrations, both peaceful and violent, added their weight to the bishops' move. As a final blow, donor countries restricted aid until Banda agreed to relinquish total control.

In June 1993 a referendum allowed the people of Malawi to choose between a multi-party political system and Banda's autocratic rule. Over 80% of eligible voters took part: the vote for a new system more than doubled the vote for the status quo. Banda accepted

the result, and the main political parties to emerge were the United Democratic Front (UDF), led by businessman (and former MCP Secretary-General) Bakili Muluzi, and Alliance for Democracy (AFORD), led by trade unionist Chakufwa Chihana. Banda's Malawian Congress Party (MCP) also remained prominent.

Malawi's first full multi-party election was on 17 May 1994; it was essentially a three-horse race between the MCP, the UDF and AFORD. All the parties' election promises were equally optimistic, and voting was largely along ethnic and regional grounds: the MCP held in the centre of the country, and AFORD dominated the north, but support in the more heavily populated south of the country gave the UDF victory, although not an overall majority.

Modern Times

Bakili Muluzi became Malawi's second president, quickly introducing several changes: the political prisons were closed, freedom of speech and a free press was permitted, and free primary school education was to be provided for all Malawian children. The unofficial night curfew which had existed during Banda's time was lifted. For tourists, the most tangible change was the repeal of Banda's notorious dress code which forbade women to wear trousers and men to have long hair.

The Muluzi government also made several economic reforms with the help of the World Bank and the IMF; this included the withdrawal of state subsidies and the liberalisation of foreign exchange laws. Further measures led to the closure of many state-owned businesses. The downside of this was a consequent rise in unemployment. A rationalisation of the civil service was also planned, which added to the job losses.

By 1996 the UDF's honeymoon period was well and truly over. Running the country was proving a tough job. Civil servants had gone on strike in mid-1995, following pay and job cuts. A scandal involving ministerial funds surfaced briefly, but was weathered.

The post-election economic reforms were

MALAWI

hitting the average Malawian citizen very hard. Food prices soared as subsidies were reduced or withdrawn. The price of bread doubled, and the price of maize flour (the country's staple food) rose eight-fold between mid-1994 and mid-1996. Unemployment was officially recorded at 50%, but may have been higher. There were reports of increased malnutrition, especially among the young. Crime, particularly robbery, often at night, increased in urban areas. The slow resumption of aid made matters worse.

Although many of the problems Malawi faces today have been inherited by the Muluzi government from Banda's time, there is a growing dissatisfaction around the country. After 30 years of totalitarianism, the country is now in a state of bewilderment. Many Malawian people we spoke to during our research for this book ruefully admitted that the new freedom of speech was marvellous, but then politely pointed out that they now have no money and no food. When well fed politicians are frequently seen in large cars and helicopters, or reported to be voting themselves increased salaries, this does little to alleviate resentment.

It hasn't escaped the attention of the newspapers that many of today's leading government figures are ex-MCP politicians. Charges of corruption and mismanagement of funds are frequently reported. The general feeling seems to be that little has changed since the old days. If anything, for the average Malawian, things have got worse. This comes at a time when the economy is under strain from weak commodity prices and poor rural people (ie the vast majority of Malawi's population) feel the pinch even more.

As so often happens in Africa (and elsewhere), the improvements promised by new politicians have simply not materialised. Many people are already starting to hanker after the old days, and say they'd be happy if the MCP took control again. Thirty years of enforced allegiance to Banda is taking time to wear off, and there's still considerable respect for the 'old statesman'.

On the economic front there are some improvements after what's been seen as a slow period. International aid is flowing back into the country once again. The challenge now for President Muluzi's government is to satisfy the heightened expectations of the Malawian people.

GEOGRAPHY

Malawi is a small country, long and narrow, wedged between Zambia, Tanzania and Mozambique, with no direct access to the sea. The country is roughly 900km long, and between 80km and 150km wide, with an area of about 120,000 sq km. The country's most obvious geographical feature is Lake Malawi, the third-largest lake in Africa, covering almost a fifth of Malawi's total area.

The Great Rift Valley passes through Malawi, and the lake lies in a trough formed by the valley. The lake shore is sandy in many places, with natural beaches, particularly round the southern part of the lake, where several hotels and resorts have been built.

Beyond the beaches, a narrow strip of low ground runs along the west side of the lake, then the land rises steeply in a series of escarpments to a high rolling plain that covers much of the northern part of the country. This area is lightly populated. In the south and centre of the country the land is lower, densely populated and intensively cultivated, with farms and plantations.

Malawi's main highland areas are the Nyika and Viphya plateaus in the north, and Mt Mulanje in the south. There are also several isolated hills and small mountains dotted around the country. The largest is the Zomba Plateau, near the town of the same name.

With the vast majority of the population living in rural areas, Malawi has very few urban centres. There are four cities: Lilongwe, the administrative capital, in the centre of the country; Blantyre, the commercial capital, with its sister city, Limbe, in the south; Zomba, the political capital, between Lilongwe and Blantyre; and Mzuzu, the main town in the north. There are some other towns, mainly along the lake shore. Fewer than a million people live in towns and cities;

the rest of the population live in scattered villages and individual homesteads.

CLIMATE

Malawi has a single wet season, from October to April, and a dry season from May to September. During the wet season, daytime temperatures are warm and conditions humid in lowland areas. The dry season is cooler, with July being the coolest month. During September, at the end of the dry season, it can become hot and humid at midday, especially in lowland areas.

Daily temperatures in the lower areas do not fluctuate much, averaging about 26°C in January and 21°C in July. In the highland areas, daytime temperatures in July are usually between 10 and 15°C, while in September they get up to 20°C and above. Night-time temperatures on the highlands are low, sometimes dropping below freezing on clear nights in July.

ECONOMY

Malawi's economy is dominated by agriculture. About 85% of the population are subsistence farmers or plantation workers. The main exports are tea, tobacco and sugar, usually grown on large plantations but also on smaller farms cultivated by a single family. Most people cultivate their own plot of land, to provide food for their needs. Any surplus is sold in markets or to the government-run agricultural cooperatives. Maize and rice are staple food crops. Until recently Malawi was self-sufficient in food crops, but some food now has to be imported.

POPULATION & PEOPLE

Estimates in 1996 put Malawi's total population at around 11 million. The population is growing by about 4% a year, one of the fastest rates in Africa. All the African people are of Bantu origin: the main groups are Chewa in the central region, Yao in the south and Tumbuka in the north.

There are small populations of Asian and European people, living mainly in the cities, who are involved in commerce, plantations, aid and development, or the diplomatic service.

RELIGION

Most people in Malawi are Christian, usually members of one of the Protestant churches originally founded by the missionaries who came to Malawi in the late 19th century. There are large groups of Muslims in the north. Along with the established religions many Malawians also hold traditional beliefs, such as the intercedence of ancestors.

LANGUAGE

All the main groups in Malawi have their own language or dialect. The Chewa are the dominant group; their language, called Chichewa, is the national language and widely used throughout the country as a common tongue. English is the official language and very widely spoken, particularly in the main towns.

Facts for the Trekker

PLANNING
When to Trek

The best time for trekking in Malawi is during the dry season. As outlined in the Climate section this is from May to September; it's cooler in the first months (July is the coolest time), then increasingly warm towards September. On Mulanje during the early months of the dry season, mist called a *chiperone* (pronounced chiperoni) can settle, sometimes for up to five days at a go, making route-finding difficult and conditions potentially dangerous.

August is a busy period, because the weather is good, and it's school holiday time. The more popular huts on Mulanje are likely to be full, especially at weekends, although if you're trekking in the remoter parts of this massif or on the Nyika Plateau, you're unlikely to see many other people.

In the month before the rains, the views from both Mulanje and Nyika can sometimes be obscured by haze and smoke from grass burning on the lower plains.

In recent years, the weather patterns in Malawi have become less predictable. The

MALAWI

rain has been arriving later (so October can also be dry), and the chiperones seem to be occurring less frequently. On the high mountain areas, though, you should always be prepared for rain and thick, wet mist, even in the dry season.

Maps

Maps of Malawi, suitable for general travelling, are not widely available outside the country, but you can easily buy them in bookshops in Malawi. These include *Malawi* (1:1,000,000) showing shaded relief features and most roads, and *Malawi Road & Tourist Map* (at the same scale) showing all main roads and some minor roads, and national parks (but no relief) plus street maps of the main towns.

For more detail, government survey maps (at 1:50,000 and 1:250,000) are available from the Department of Surveys Public Map Sales Offices; in Blantyre, it's on the corner of Victoria Ave and Independence Drive; in Lilongwe, it's about 500m south of the roundabout where Glyn Jones Rd meets Kamuzu Procession Rd.

The staff are helpful, there are no formalities, and maps cost about US$2. Maps of popular areas, such as Mulanje, occasionally go out of stock.

Specific maps on individual trekking areas are covered in the relevant sections.

TOURIST OFFICES

Outside the country, most Malawian embassies and high commissions have a Tourism Department which can help with inquires and send out general information leaflets. Inside Malawi there are tourist offices in Blantyre (on Victoria Ave) and Lilongwe (on Kamuzu Procession Rd, near Huts Restaurant). In both places, the people are friendly but information is limited, especially on trekking and hiking matters. For details of tours, flights and hotels you're better off at a travel agency; see the Organised Treks & Tours section in Getting Around.

In Lilongwe, the Department of National Parks and Wildlife (☎ 730853) in Murray Rd can assist with reservations for government-run accommodation in national parks, and may be able to answer straightforward questions about trekking on Nyika. The nearby Department of Forestry office may be able to assist with information on Mulanje and other forest reserves.

VISAS

Visas are not required by citizens of Commonwealth countries, Belgium, Denmark, Finland, Germany, Iceland, Ireland, Luxembourg, the Netherlands, Norway, Portugal, South Africa, Sweden and the USA. If you do need a visa, they are available from embassies. You can get visa extensions at the immigration office in Blantyre or Lilongwe. The process is straightforward and free.

All entry regulations are liable to change, so contact your nearest Malawian embassy, high commission or tourist office for up to date information.

Malawian immigration officials are always polite and friendly, but they play strictly by the rules. If everything is in order you'll have no problems.

EMBASSIES
Malawian Embassies Abroad

Malawian embassies, consulates and high commissions abroad include:

Kenya
    Malawi High Commission, Waiyaki Way, Westlands, PO Box 30453, Nairobi (☎ 440569; fax 440568
Tanzania
    Malawi High Commission, 6th Floor, NIC Building, Samora Ave, Dar es Salaam (☎ 46673)

There are also Malawian embassies or consulates in Canada (Ottawa), France (Paris), Mozambique (Maputo), South Africa (Johannesburg), the UK (London), the USA (Washington), Zambia (Lusaka) and Zimbabwe (Harare).

Foreign Embassies in Malawi

Countries which maintain diplomatic missions in Malawi include those listed below (all in Lilongwe, unless otherwise stated). Some are open in the afternoon, but the best time to visit is between 9 am and noon. There are no telephone area codes in Malawi.

Germany
    Convention Drive, Capital City, Lilongwe (☎ 782555)
Mozambique
    Commercial Bank Building, African Unity Ave, Capital City, Lilongwe (☎ 784100);
    and Kamuzu Highway, Limbe (☎ 643189)
South Africa
    Impco Building (in Capital City Shopping Centre), Capital City, Lilongwe (☎ 783722)
UK
    Kenyatta Rd, Capital City, Lilongwe (☎ 782400)
USA
    Kenyatta Rd, Capital City, Lilongwe (☎ 783166)
Zambia
    Convention Drive, Capital City, Lilongwe (☎ 782100/635)
Zimbabwe
    Near Development House, off Independence Drive, Capital City, Lilongwe (☎ 784988)

Tanzania Be warned that there is no Tanzanian high commission in Malawi so if you need a visa it must be obtained elsewhere. If you're coming from the south, Lusaka and Harare are the closest places. (If you do need a visa and you're flying in, you can get it on arrival at the airport.)

MONEY

This section covers money in Malawi. Outlines of costs and other general money aspects are given in the Regional Facts for the Trekker chapter.

Currency Exchange

Malawi's unit of currency is the kwacha (MK), divided into 100 tambala (t). The largest note is MK 200. Others are MK 100, MK 50, MK 20, MK 10 and MK 5. Coins include MK 1, 50 t, 20 t, 10 t, 5 t and 1 t.

There are no customs restrictions on the amount of foreign currency you can bring in or out, but you are not allowed to import or export more than MK 200. Inflation has steadied, but is still unpredictable. Therefore we have quoted the prices of most things in US dollars (US$) throughout this chapter. Although the actual exchange rate may have changed by the time you reach Malawi, the cost of things in US$ (or any other hard currency) will not have altered much. You can pay for most things in Malawi in hard currency or kwacha. As a guide, here are some exchange rates from mid-1997:

US$1	=	MK 17
UK£1	=	MK 28

Changing Money

You can change cash and travellers cheques at branches of the National Bank of Malawi and the Commercial Bank of Malawi. Banks in small towns open only a few mornings per week. The bank at Lilongwe airport usually opens to coincide with international flights.

You can also get cash advances with a Visa card at the Commercial Bank of Malawi in Blantyre and Lilongwe, but the process sometimes takes more than a day.

Recent deregulation has allowed foreign exchange (forex) bureaus to open in the cities and large towns. These usually offer a slightly better rate than the banks, and have lower charges (or none at all), so are worth checking. If you've got time, shop around, as rates and commissions can vary.

There's no real black market. You might get one or two kwacha more for your dollar on the street, but the chances of robberies or con-men (plus fake US$100 and US$50 bills) make this not worth the risk. Alternatively, shops which sell imported items sometimes need dollars and buy at around 5% to 10% more than the bank or bureau rate.

BOOKS

The bookshops in Malawi's main towns are well stocked with imported and locally produced general guidebooks, field guides and histories, including those listed below. Specific guidebooks on individual national parks and trekking areas are covered in the relevant sections.

Lonely Planet

Lonely Planet's *Malawi, Mozambique & Zambia* covers Malawi in great detail, with large sections on neighbouring Mozambique

MALAWI

and Zambia, and has information for visitors of all budgets. For further travels, Lonely Planet's *Africa – The South* covers nine countries in the region, from Malawi to the Cape.

Guidebooks

The *Visitors' Guide to Malawi* by Martine Maurel covers the whole country, although it's aimed mainly at car drivers. Much better is *Guide to Malawi* by Philip Briggs with good public transport information and a knowledgeable bias towards natural history.

More specific for trekkers and outdoor fans is *Malawi: Wildlife, Parks & Reserves* by Judy Carter – a beautiful combination of coffee table book and field guide with good quality wildlife and landscape shots, plus comprehensive background information. Easier to find and carry around is *Malawi's National Parks & Game Reserves* published by the Wildlife Society of Malawi. If you're in the country for longer than a few weeks, the Wildlife Society also publishes *Day Outings from Blantyre* and *Day Outings from Lilongwe*; these are aimed at local car owners, but cover several areas with good walking.

A good selection of specific field guides devoted to aspects such as the fish, orchids, snakes, trees and so on are available in local bookshops or from the Wildlife Society (see Useful Organisations).

General

Books of interest to trekkers in Malawi include *Venture to the Interior* by Laurens van der Post which describes the author's 'exploration' of Mt Mulanje and the Nyika Plateau in the 1940s, although in reality this was hardly trail-blazing stuff.

USEFUL ORGANISATIONS

The Mountain Club of Malawi is a disparate organisation mainly for Malawians and foreign residents. Occasional club nights and walking meets are arranged, but they don't normally cater for tourists. However, visitors, especially members of other walking and climbing organisations, are welcome to join club activities although it is not always possible to help with transport, equipment and so on. A newsletter is produced every two months and is available from the Tourist Office in Blantyre, or direct from the club, PO Box 240, Blantyre.

The Wildlife Society of Malawi (☎ 643 428), PO Box 1429, Blantyre, is an active conservation organisation, formerly called the National Fauna Preservation Society. It publishes several field guides to different parts of Malawi, and has close links with the Department of National Parks and Wildlife. Contact the society direct for more information and a list of publications, or visit the shop at the Heritage Centre next to the Shire Highlands Hotel in Limbe.

PUBLIC HOLIDAYS

As well as Christmas Day, Boxing Day, New Year's Day, and Easter Friday and Monday, public holidays include:

16 Jan	John Chilembwe Day
3 March	Martyrs' Day
1 May	Labour Day
14 June	Freedom Day
6 July	Republic Day
2nd Monday in October	Mother's Day
2nd Monday in December	National Tree Planting Day

When one of the above dates falls on a weekend, normally the following Monday is a public holiday. In northern Malawi and along the lake, many people are Muslim and observe Islamic holidays.

PLACES TO STAY IN LILONGWE

Lilongwe is Malawi's government capital, while Blantyre is the commercial capital. If you are flying into Malawi, you will arrive at Lilongwe (unless you taking a connecting flight to Blantyre). If you're travelling by land, you'll probably pass through one or both of these cities while travelling between the mountain areas. The listings here will give you an idea of what accommodation is available in Lilongwe. Blantyre is listed under the Mulanje section. More details about

Top: Jackson's Summit (4160m) near the top of the Sasa Route, Mt Elgon, Uganda
Left: A ladder up part of the Mudangi Cliffs, Mt Elgon, Uganda
Right: The spectacular Sipi Falls, in the western foothills of Mt Elgon, Uganda
Bottom: Giant groundsels in the Bujuku Valley, Rwenzori Mountains, Uganda

DAVID ELSE

CORINNE ELSE

DAVID ELSE

DAVID ELSE

DAVID ELSE

DAVID ELSE

DAVID ELSE

The Mulanje massif rises out of fields of tea in Malawi's south (top left). Sombani Hut (top right), is one of six huts on the mountain. The most distinctive features of the Mulanje area are the high rock cliff faces and the mists which often envelop them (bottom). Peaks jutting above the mists have earnt the mountain it's local name, 'The Island in the Sky'.

other places to stay in or near the trekking areas are given in the relevant sections.

Lilongwe is a small but sprawling city, divided into two sections: the new part is called City Centre, with government offices, embassies and some smarter shops and travel agents; Old Town has the bus station, the market, a good range of shops and most of the hotels.

Places to Stay – bottom end

If you're on public transport and short of cash, there are several cheap options around the bus station. Nearest is the *Council Rest-house*, where basic rooms are US$4 to US$6. Much better is *Annie's Coffee House* which has a small dorm for US$3 per person, and *The Gap*, a South African-run backpackers' lodge, in the suburbs of Old Town where dorm beds are US$3, camping US$1.50, breakfast US$1 and meals around US$3.

For campers, *Lilongwe Golf Club* has been popular for a long time, although its prices have shot up in the last few years. However, for US$7 per person you get a clean, safe site with hot showers. Included in the fee is day membership of the club, so you can use the bar, restaurant, swimming pool and some of the sporting facilities.

In the same part of town is *St Peter's Guesthouse*: quiet, clean and safe, but unfortunately nearly always full. A bed in doubles or triples is US$4, and a private double costs US$7. Breakfast costs US$1. If you do get in here, remember it's a church place and behave accordingly.

Top of this range, and good value, is the *Golden Peacock Hotel* (☎ 742638), still known affectionately as the Golden Cockroach, although these days it is very clean and safe, with standard doubles/triples for US$10/12, and en suite doubles for US$17. It's on the corner of Johnstone Rd and Lister Ave, in Old Town.

Places to Stay – middle & top end

All rooms in this category are en suite and include breakfast in the price, unless otherwise stated.

Cheapest place in this bracket is *Annie's*

Lodge (☎ 721590) a house in Area 47, just off Kamuzu Procession Rd, north of Old Town, where self-contained singles/doubles are US$30/35. On Chilambula Rd, is the *Lingadzi Inn* (☎ 720644), which is clean and friendly but a little frayed around the edges, with a nice large garden, an incredibly small restaurant, and rooms for US$50/65. Both places are best reached by taxi.

In the heart of Old Town on Kamuzu Procession Rd is the *Lilongwe Hotel* (☎ 740 488; fax 740505; central reservations ☎ 620071) with a collection of accommodation wings set around small areas of garden. Single/double en suite rooms are US$120/145. Facilities include a travel desk and swimming pool. Staff are efficient and friendly, and the hotel has a comfortable atmosphere.

Top of the range in Lilongwe is the *Capital Hotel* (☎ 783388; fax 781273; central reservations ☎ 620071) used mainly by high-rolling tourists, business travellers and diplomats, with rooms at US$150/195 although as a full international-class hotel it is rather lacking in character. There's a giftshop, bookshop, pharmacy, business centre (which also handles Coachline bookings), swimming pool, several airline offices, plus car hire and travel desks.

Both the Lilongwe and the Capital hotels were due for refurbishment in 1997, so there may be some changes by the time you arrive.

Getting There & Away

Getting to Malawi from Europe or further afield is covered in the Getting There & Away chapter earlier in this book. This section assumes you're already in Malawi and need to go elsewhere; it covers travel *from* Malawi *to* the neighbouring East African countries of Kenya, Tanzania and Uganda using air, road or rail transport. For going the other way (eg from Tanzania to Malawi), see the relevant country chapters.

How you travel depends on how much time you've got, and the amount of travelling (as opposed to trekking) you want to do. In this section it's presumed you want to take fairly direct routes between the trekking areas in the various countries.

TANZANIA
Air
International fights between Lilongwe and Dar es Salaam go twice a week, and cost around US$200 one way. Kilimanjaro international airport (KIA) is much nearer Tanzania's main trekking areas so, if you're going to fly from Lilongwe, you might as well go all the way to KIA, which means taking one of the daily Dar-KIA flights (see the Getting Around and Getting There & Away sections in the Tanzania chapter).

Road
The only land crossing between Malawi and Tanzania is at the Songwe River bridge north of Kaporo. The road is tar all the way between Karonga (Malawi) and Mbeya (Tanzania). (A new bridge is planned further upstream, but it's likely that the current border crossing point will remain the most heavily used, with the best transport options.)

If you want to go the whole way between Lilongwe and Dar in one go, there's a weekly (sometimes twice-weekly) bus operated by Metro Coach Company. In Lilongwe, its office is at the Council Resthouse, opposite the bus station. There is also supposed to be a direct bus service between Mzuzu and Dar (via Karonga and Mbeya), but days and times are vague, so inquire at the bus station in Mzuzu.

Most people go from Malawi to Tanzania in stages. There are three buses per day from Mzuzu to Karonga. Between Karonga and Songwe Bridge is a twice-daily bus (the fare is US$0.50), and occasional minibuses (US$1). It's a few hundred metres (an easy walk) across the bridge to the Tanzanian border post on the other side.

From here there's no public transport, so you'll have to walk or hitch about 7km to the junction with the road between Kyela and Mbeya. Alternatively, enterprising youths on

bicycles will pedal you there for US$1. You can also change money with them. From the junction you can find a bus (there's two or three each day) or a lift to Mbeya, where you can pick up a bus or train to Dar es Salaam. If you're heading north, there's no need to go into Kyela along this route as the town is 5km south-east of the junction and in the wrong direction for Mbeya.

We've received reports of a new bus service running directly between the Songwe River Bridge border and Dar es Salaam, via Kyela and Mbeya. It leaves the border in the evening (around 4.30 pm) and goes to Kyela, where you can sleep on the bus until 4 am, when it departs for Dar, arriving late in the afternoon. The fare is around US$15.

There are plans to tar the road between Karonga and Mpulungu (Zambia) via Chitipa and Nakonde. From Nakonde, the Tanzanian town of Tunduma is just across the border. In the next few years, if the road is completed, this will probably be an easier way to go between Malawi and Tanzania.

KENYA
Air
Flights between Lilongwe and Nairobi go four times a week, and a one-way flight costs between US$200 and US$300.

Road
Malawi and Kenya do not share a common border, so all road journeys between these two countries have to go through Tanzania. For details see the Getting Around and Getting There & Away sections in the Kenya and Tanzania chapters.

UGANDA
Air
Flights between Lilongwe and Kampala go about twice a week and cost about US$400 one way. (See the Getting There & Away section in the Uganda chapter for more details.)

Road
Malawi and Uganda do not share a common border, so the easiest way to travel overland

between these two countries is through Tanzania and Kenya. For details see the Getting There & Away and Getting Around sections in the Kenya and Tanzania chapters.

Getting Around

Malawi has good public road and air transport systems making travel between the trekking areas fairly hassle-free. Your other options are boat (slow but good fun) and train (just slow).

AIR

Air Malawi's domestic flights are reasonably priced and reliable. There are at least two flights a day between Lilongwe and Blantyre, for US$55 one way, and three flights a week between Lilongwe and Mzuzu for US$55 one way. Other flights are unlikely to be useful for trekkers.

From the city centre to the airport by taxi, in Blantyre is US$10 and in Lilongwe US$17.

ROAD

Most of the main roads in Malawi are tarred. Secondary roads are usually graded dirt, and normally in fairly good condition. Other routes are not so good, and after heavy rain they are often impassable, sometimes for weeks.

The main route through Malawi runs from the north of the country down to Mzuzu, then through the centre of the country to Lilongwe and on to Blantyre in the south; it's good quality tar all the way.

Bus & Minibus

Most buses around Malawi are operated by a private company called Stagecoach and come in several different types. Top of the range is Coachline, a daily luxury service that runs non-stop between Blantyre and Lilongwe (US$17) and between Lilongwe and Mzuzu (US$19) with air-conditioning, toilet, free newspapers, in-flight food, steward service and top-quality drivers.

Next comes Express, fast buses between the main towns with limited stops and no standing passengers allowed, and Intercity, similar to express buses but with more stops. As a rule of thumb, Express buses charge between US$2 and US$2.50 per 100km, and Intercity buses slightly less. Stagecoach also run local services which cover the quieter rural routes and tend to be slow and crowded, but are often the only public transport available.

As well as the above, a few smaller outfits compete with Stagecoach: these include Yanu Yanu and Nyika Express. There are also local minibus services around towns and to outlying villages, or along the roads which the big buses can't manage. Prices are about the same as Stagecoach, or slightly more, depending on the severity of the route.

Reservations For luxury Coachline and Express buses you can buy tickets in advance and have a reserved seat. The day before is usually sufficient for Express, but on the Coachline a week's notice is sometimes required, particularly for Friday and Sunday services.

Bus Stations All towns have a main bus station where long-distance and local buses arrive and leave. Note that in Blantyre the Coachline service goes to/from the Mount Soche Hotel. In Lilongwe, it goes to/from the Capital Hotel and the Stagecoach depot on Kamuzu Procession Rd.

Taxi

Taxis operate in the main towns only. You can find them outside bus stations, airports or large hotels. There are no meters, so rates are negotiable, particularly on airport runs. Check the price at the start of the journey.

Car Rental

For trekking in Malawi a car is not essential, as most areas can be reached by public transport. A car can be useful, though, if time is short, or you want to combine trekking with some wildlife viewing or general travelling around Malawi.

There are several car-hire companies in Blantyre and Lilongwe. Whoever you hire from, be prepared for a car not up to international standards. Check the tyres and as much else as you can. If anything is worn or broken, demand a repair or a discount.

Self-drive rates for a small car start at US$25 to US$35 per day, plus around US$0.30 per km. Unlimited mileage (minimum seven days) costs US$50 to US$55. Larger cars are around US$45 to US$65 a day, plus around US$0.50 per km. To this add 20% government tax, plus another US$5 to US$7 a day for insurance.

Car rental companies in Malawi include the following. Contact them direct or go through an agent (see Organised Treks & Tours).

Avis, PO Box 460, Blantyre, (☎ 624533). Avis has offices at Lilongwe and Blantyre airports, and reservations can be made in advance at any Avis office in the world, although their rates tend to be higher than those of local companies.

Car Hire Limited, PO Box 51059, Haile Selassie Rd, Blantyre (☎ 623792); PO Box 695, off Chilambula Rd, Lilongwe (☎ 723812)

SS Rent-a-car, PO Box 997, Kamuzu Procession Rd, Lilongwe (☎ 721179); PO Box 2282, Glyn Jones Rd, Blantyre (☎ 636836)

These companies also have offices at Lilongwe and Blantyre airports and in some of the large hotels.

TRAIN

The main railway line goes between Blantyre and Mchinji, via Salima on the lake shore, which isn't very useful if you're trying to get to the trekking areas. Trains are very slow and crowded, and only 3rd class is cheaper than the bus.

BOAT

A passenger boat called the *Ilala* steams up and down Lake Malawi, between Monkey Bay in the south and Chilumba or Kaporo in the north, stopping at several lakeside villages. Local people use it as public transport, but many visitors take a cruise just for the experience. For trekkers it can be an interesting way to do part of the journey between Mulanje in the south and Nyika in the north. The whole trip, from one end of the lake to the other, takes about three days and the boat does one round trip per week.

The *Ilala* has three classes: Cabins, which were once luxurious and are still in reasonable condition; First Class Deck, which is generally quite spacious, with seats, a small area of sun-shade and a bar; and Economy – the entire lower deck – which is dark and crowded, with engine fumes permeating from below.

Fares are reasonable, for example: Monkey Bay to Nkhata Bay, the most popular section, costs US$66/50/10.

Another boat, called *Mtendere*, is due to be re-launched and will have a timetable that fits in with the *Ilala's*.

ORGANISED TREKS & TOURS

There are no specialised trekking operators in Malawi. However, there are some safari companies, listed below, who can arrange tours including sections of walking or trekking. The international telephone code for Malawi is 265 and there are no area codes.

Central African Wilderness Safaris, PO Box 489, Lilongwe (☎ 781393 or 781153; fax 781397; email wildsaf@eo.wn.apc.org)

Heart of Africa Safaris (& Nyika Horse Safaris), PO Box 8, Lilongwe (☎/fax 740848)

Land & Lake Safaris, PO Box 2140, Lilongwe (☎/fax 744408)

Malawi's safari scene is much smaller than Kenya's and Tanzania's, so you can't just go into an office and expect to join a trip next day. Most tours are aimed at the middle and top end of the market. Central African Wilderness Safaris operate regular departures (one or two per month, starting at US$100 per day); the others operate on demand. All do tailor-made trips, and prefer to take bookings in advance (most of their clients come from agents and operators overseas). Contact the companies direct for more information. If you're in Malawi and fancy joining a trip, it's always worth giving them a ring to see what they've got going.

Mt Mulanje

Mt Mulanje rises steeply and suddenly from an undulating plain in the extreme south of Malawi. It is often misty in this region and Mulanje's high peaks sometimes jut out above the cloud. Appropriately, one of the mountain's local names is 'Island in the Sky'. The stunning scenery, plus easy access, clearly marked paths and a series of well maintained huts make Mulanje one of the finest hill-walking areas in Africa.

HISTORY

Mulanje has been popular with walkers for many years. At the end of the last century, soldiers based at a nearby fort explored much of the area, and in the 1920s, tea-planters working in the plains around Mulanje established an Indian-style 'hill station' on the south-western corner of the massif.

Before the Europeans arrived in Malawi it seems that Mulanje was not inhabited by large numbers of people. Although several archaeological sites have been discovered, research indicates that conditions on the massif were not conducive to settlement. The plains around Mt Mulanje are still used mainly for tea plantations and farmland. The region is densely populated, with great pressure on the land. The massif has been gazetted as a forest reserve, but pine plantations have been established on some of the upper plateaus. However, the plantations cover only a small part of the massif and you can enjoy most of your trekking through untampered natural surroundings.

The Department of Forestry, the Ministry of Natural Resources, and the government of Malawi should be congratulated for maintaining the paths and huts on Mt Mulanje. By preserving this place of beauty and ecological importance, its benefits can be enjoyed by visitors and the people of Malawi.

GEOGRAPHY

Mt Mulanje is roughly square, measuring about 30km west to east and 25km north to south, with an area of at least 600 sq km. On its north-east corner is the outlier, Mchese Mountain (also spelt Michese), separated from the main massif by the Fort Lister Gap.

Mulanje is sometimes called a plateau, implying that it's flat on the top. It isn't. The massif is composed of several separate plateaus and broad river basins, all separated by a series of rocky peaks and ridges. The highest peak on Mulanje is Sapitwa, at just over 3000m (9840 ft), the highest point in Malawi and all of Central Africa.

Mulanje's most obvious features are the steep, almost vertical, cliffs of bare rock which surround the massif, rising abruptly from the flat plain, many over 1000m high. The cliffs are dissected by vegetated valleys, where rivers drop in spectacular waterfalls. Most of the paths up onto the top of the massif follow these valleys.

TREKKING INFORMATION

There are several peaks on Mt Mulanje above 2500m, and you can reach most of the

Mulanje Pine

The pine plantations on Mulanje were first established by the colonial government in the early 1950s, mainly around Chambe and, to a lesser extent, Sombani. The sides of the massif are too steep for a road, so all the timber is sawn by hand and then carried down on a cableway (called the Skyline) or on the heads of forest labourers. As you're going up the Chambe Plateau Path you'll see these guys, sometimes running down, with huge planks of wood balanced on their heads.

The plantations provide employment for local people and wood for the whole of southern Malawi. A bad side effect, apart from plantations being ugly, is the tendency of pine trees to spread slowly across the natural grassland as seeds are blown by the wind. These introduced trees disturb the established balance. The Wildlife Society of Malawi recommends pulling up any young pine trees that you see growing outside the plantation areas. ■

MALAWI

summits without technical climbing (although sections of steep scrambling are sometimes involved). If you prefer a less demanding trek, Mulanje's basins and valleys provide fine open walking through undisturbed country, while the peaks themselves create a dramatic backdrop.

Costs

Costs for trekking on Mulanje break down into hut fees, guide and porter fees (optional) and the cost of your own supplies. The cost of getting there and away is also an important point to consider. All are detailed separately in the relevant sections below.

Route Standard & Days Required

There are at least 10 routes from the plains up onto the higher parts of Mulanje. Some of these are steep, and the rest are even steeper. Many are also badly overgrown or particularly slippery, and the only way up is to haul yourself from tree to tree. This leaves five or six ascent routes that you might consider using. Of these, three start at Likabula Forest Station, where all trekkers have to register and pay for huts or camping. Unless you've got your own transport, Likabula is the easiest place to start, so the two routes described in this section both begin here. Once you're on top of the massif, there's a whole network of paths linking the various huts and peaks, and many different permutations are possible. The main routes are described in detail, and some other trekking possibilities are outlined later in this section.

The number of days given for each route is the usual amount. It normally takes about three to six hours to walk between one hut and the next, which means you can walk in the morning, dump your kit, then go out to explore a nearby peak or valley in the afternoon. You can spend two or more nights at one hut if you want, and go out in a different direction each day, or just sit in the sun and take it easy. Similarly, if you're feeling fit, you can do either of these treks in a day less, although because of the way the huts are spaced, it normally means combining two stages into one, rather than doing an extra bit on each day.

Briefly, the main routes described in this section are as follows.

A Mulanje Traverse This is only one of many ways of traversing Mulanje. It's a good one though, crossing the heart of the massif, passing through plantation, natural forest and open grassland, with plenty of opportunities for sidetracking to bag a few peaks or ridges or explore small valleys. The first section of the route, up onto the top of the massif, is steep but steps have been cut for much of the way, which makes things easier. The main paths between the huts are all clear and generally in good condition, mainly undulating with a few short, steep sections. Routes from the huts up to the peaks vary: some are clear, although still strenuous, others are overgrown and in bad condition, making route-finding difficult. A trek on this route takes five days and four nights, although you can add an extra stop about halfway through for a rest day.

The Chambe-Lichenya Loop This is a shorter trek, which keeps to the western side of the massif, passing through two of Mulanje's largest basins, with some spectacular views from the edge of the western escarpment, and the chance to bag two impressive peaks. Conditions are as described for the Mulanje Traverse. A trek on this route takes three days and two nights.

Guides & Porters

It is not essential for trekkers on Mulanje to use guides and porters, but they are available if you need them. As on any mountain, porters make the trekking easier, especially for the first day's steep walk from Likabula. it is not usual to hire a specific guide, as most Mulanje porters will also act as guides if required. They can show you the routes between huts, although these are generally clearly visible. This service is usually included in the daily fee.

Some of the routes up to the peaks are not clear, and not all porters are knowledgable enough to show you the way, especially in more obscure areas, in which case you will need to verify your porter/guide's skills at Likabula Forest Station before agreeing to hire his services. If the guiding is 'specialised' (ie beyond the main routes) you'll need to check if an extra fee is expected. Forestry workers, or men and older boys from the nearby village, can be hired as porters. Don't worry about finding them: as you arrive in Likabula you'll be besieged by hopeful locals looking for work. Some are school-boys (although because of the way the Malawian education system works, they can be up to 25 years old) working in holiday periods to raise money for school fees. You may also be approached by porters looking for work in Mulanje town or at Chitikali (Likabula junction), but you should arrange things only at Likabula.

The Likabula Forest Station keeps a list of registered porters, who are known to be reliable. Always check your porter is on the list. Some schoolboys are not on the list but are known by the Forestry staff. Most speak good English, and are generally honest and hard working. They will stay with you while you're trekking, or go ahead with the bags and wait at the hut, whatever you prefer. Porters also act as guides, if required, although not all of them know the lesser-used routes up to the peaks.

The Forestry Department, with the agreement of the porters, has set a standard rate of US$4 per day, per porter (not per hiker) payable in kwacha. The maximum weight carried is 18kg. The daily rate is payable however long or short the day, or however hard or easy the walking. If your porter is also to act as guide up the peaks, an extra fee may be payable. Before agreeing to anything though, check with the Forestry Station that your guide is familiar with the routes you want to do. To avoid misunderstandings, the total fee for the whole trip should be agreed before departure, and written down, then paid at the end of the trip. From this money the porter will provide his own food while on trek, so some of it (say 25%) may be required in advance. Make sure your porter

brings everything he needs, and tell him that no other food can be provided. Even if you do this, you'll still feel guilty when you stop for lunch, while the porters sit and watch you, so take a few extra packets of biscuits for them.

You may want to tip your porter/s if the service has been good. A rule of thumb is to pay something like an extra day's wage for every three to five days.

Porters can usually be arranged within an hour, but if you want to leave straight away, your porter will carry your load to Chambe Hut, then return to his house to collect his food and blanket, and then return to the hut in time for the next morning's departure. An extra day's fee is payable for this but it might save a lot of hanging around.

Park Fees & Regulations

Mt Mulanje is gazetted as a forest reserve and all visitors must register at Likabula Forest Station (☎ 465218) before going up onto the massif. No charge is made to enter the forest reserve, but you must pay your hut or camping fees here. The office is open from 7 am to noon and from 1 to 5 pm every day, including weekends and most holidays. The Tourist Attendant at Likabula is a very friendly lady called Dorothy. She makes sure the porters you take are registered, and will answer any questions about huts and facilities.

Camping is permitted only near huts, and nowhere else on the massif. Open fires, even by the huts, are not allowed. This is especially important during the latter part of the dry season, from August to October, when there is a serious fire risk. Also forbidden is the picking or collecting of plants and animals.

Maps

Mt Mulanje is covered by the government survey 1:50,000 map sheet number 1535 D3 (Mulanje), which shows most paths, and all the huts, except Minunu Hut, which is at approximate grid reference 826377. The 1:30,000 Tourist Map of Mulanje covers a similar area, overprinted with extra information for walkers.

MALAWI

The Forestry Department produces a small leaflet with information for visitors; this also contains a map of the Mulanje area.

Guidebook

The *Guide to the Mulanje Massif* by Frank Eastwood (available in Malawi and South Africa) has information on ascent routes and main peaks, but nothing on the routes between the huts. It also includes a large section on Mulanje's rock-climbing routes, and information on geology and wildlife.

Supplies

There are no shops on the massif, and only a very small local store at Likabula. Mulanje town has a small supermarket (near the Likabula junction), with enough to provide for a trek, and a market selling fruit and veg. For the best choice of food, Blantyre and Limbe have large, well-stocked supermarkets.

PLACES TO STAY
Blantyre

Blantyre is more compact and livelier than Lilongwe, with most facilities within walking distance of the city centre.

Places to Stay – bottom end If you've come by public transport, head for *Wayfarers Lodge* (formerly Doogles), a dedicated backpackers' place where camping is US$2 and a bed in the dorm US$4. There's good security, and the friendly staff know a lot about travel in Malawi. Some budget tour outfits run excursions from here.

The *Grace Bandawe Conference Centre* (☎ 634267) is a small church hostel on Chileka Rd, about 2km from the city centre, with clean en suite singles/doubles for US$10/14. Breakfast is US$2 and other meals US$3.50.

Places to Stay – middle & top end All places include breakfast. Cheapest in this range is *Nyambadwe Cottage* (☎ 633561) in the quiet suburb of Nyambadwe, off Chileka Rd, with straightforward singles/doubles at US$17/22 (US$4 extra for en suite). Camping costs US$3.

In the centre, the *Hotel & Catering School* (☎ 621866), Chilembwe Rd, has clean en suite rooms for US$35/55 (no twin rooms), and good four-course meals for US$7 (book in advance).

Blantyre's best is the *Mount Soche Hotel* (☎ 620588), part of the South African-run Protea chain (Malawi central reservations ☎ 620071), where international-standard en suite single/doubles with air-con and TV cost US$150/195. This place is favoured by business travellers, UN workers and visiting

---

Warning

Although Mt Mulanje is small compared with Mt Kenya and Kilimanjaro, it is still a serious mountain, and not to be taken lightly. The main problem for trekkers is unpredictable weather. In the wet season, or after periods of heavy rain at any time of year, beware of streams suddenly becoming swollen and impassable. Do not try to cross them. Wait until the flood subsides, sometimes after a few hours, or adjust your route to cross in safety further upstream.

Even during dry periods, it's not uncommon to get rain, cold winds and thick mists which can occur very suddenly. It is easy to get lost. Even on the main paths you can miss a junction, or mistake a firebreak for a path. This isn't too much of a problem as long as you've got some warm, waterproof gear. If you haven't, you risk suffering from severe exposure. It's not unknown for trekkers to get lost and die up here. In conditions of poor visibility you should keep to the main paths, and take extra care.

Acclimatisation on Mulanje is not usually a problem, unless you've flown in virtually from sea level and start trying to do Sapitwa on your second day. But even then, you'll only feel slightly out of breath and be forced to go slower. Altitude sickness of any sort is unlikely.

The massif is crisscrossed with firebreaks, some of which are followed by paths. Most firebreaks are composed of three parallel cut-lines about 50m apart, but as these can become overgrown and re-cut you should be prepared for 'extra' or 'missing' firebreaks in the route descriptions. Some footpath junctions are signposted, but you shouldn't rely on this, as signs may be destroyed by fire or simply go missing. ■

diplomats. A major refurbishment was due in 1997. Some visitors have recommended the smaller *Ryall's Hotel*, with standard rooms costing US$85/100 and superior rooms at US$100/115.

Mulanje Town

Just downhill from the bus station is the straightforward *Mulanje Motel*, with basic rooms for US$2. Next door is the *Mulanje View Motel*, with a better choice of rooms; bed and breakfast costs from US$3.50 for singles to US$8 for en suite doubles. There's a bar and good-value food in the restaurant. Camping is possible at *Mulanje Golf Club*, on the eastern outskirts of town. The cost is US$2.50, which includes day membership, so you can use the showers, bar and swimming pool, and enjoy the fabulous views of the massif from the terrace.

Likabula

Just uphill from the Forest Station, there's the very good *Forestry Resthouse*, spotlessly clean, with a kitchen, comfortable lounge and several twin bedrooms. The charge is US$3 per person per night. This includes the services of a cook, who will prepare your food, wash up etc. You can camp in the grounds of the forest station for US$0.35 per tent, or outside the resthouse for US$1.25 and use the kitchen facilities.

The *Likabula CCAP Mission Guest House*, next to the forest station, has self-contained chalets for US$2.25 per person (or US$5 for the whole chalet which sleeps four), or you can sleep in the dormitory for US$1.50. Camping is US$0.75 per tent. Meals are available. There are usually school or church groups staying at the mission.

On Mt Mulanje

On Mulanje are six *forestry huts*, run by the Forestry Department. There used to be seven, but Lichenya Hut burnt down in 1995, and there are no immediate plans to rebuild it. Each hut is equipped with benches, tables, and open fires with plenty of wood available. Some have sleeping platforms (no mattresses); in others you just sleep on the floor.

Rescue Procedure

Until recently, each hut had a log book where trekkers wrote details of their destination, intended route and expected arrival time. In the last few years it seems log books have gone missing, or have been filled up and not replaced. If there is a log book in your hut, fill in your details, and be as clear as possible.

If you do have an accident, a rescue will be arranged from Likabula Forest Station, so you would need to send a message for help there. The alarm can be raised at Chambe Forest Station, Lujeri Estate and Phalombe Police Station, all of which are linked by telephone to Likabula. Full details of rescue procedures are posted at the forest station and each hut. ∎

You provide your own food, cooking gear, candles, sleeping bag and stove (although you can cook on the fire). Each hut has a caretaker who chops wood, lights fires and brings water, for which a small tip should be paid. The huts are (from west to east): Chambe (with room for 16 people); Thuchila (pronounced 'Chuchila'; 16); Chinzama (12); Minunu (also spelt Mununu or Mnunu; 4); Madzeka (12); and Sombani (8).

Reservations and payments for huts can be made at Likabula Forest Station on arrival, or in advance by writing to the Forest Officer, PO Box 50, Mulanje. The huts cost US$1 per person per night (an absolute bargain), although this may rise in the future. Space is usually available, but some huts may be full at weekends and during holidays. If any hut is full on a particular night, you can normally adjust your trek and go to another. As the Forestry Department's reservation system does not require a deposit, some local residents reserve space and then don't turn up. It's worth checking the reservation book to see if this has happened.

Some old maps may show other huts, but these have fallen into disuse. The only other place to stay on the massif is the *CCAP Cottage*, on the Lichenya Plateau, run by Likabula CCAP Mission. This hut is quite near the site of the Lichenya forestry hut which burnt down, which means there is still a place to stay in this part of the massif. The hut is similar to the forestry huts, but there are utensils in the kitchen, and mattresses and blankets in the bedrooms. For this extra luxury you pay US$1.25 per night. You can reserve and pay for the cottage at the mission in Likabula.

There is a small mud and thatch shelter at Chisepo, at the start of the route up Sapitwa Peak, but this is normally only used in emergencies, or for hardy walkers aiming to bag the summit by sunrise.

Camping is permitted outside the huts (US$0.60 per person), but not allowed anywhere else on the massif. You can use the huts for cooking and eating in.

GETTING THERE & AWAY

The nearest city to Mt Mulanje is Blantyre, which can be reached by air and road (see the Getting Around section for details).

At the foot of the mountain is Mulanje town, linked to Blantyre by a tarred road. There are regular local buses and minibuses between Blantyre and Mulanje town. The twice-daily express bus takes around two hours and costs US$2.

From Mulanje town, you have to get to Likabula Forest Station (also spelt Likhabula and Likhubula), about 12km from Mulanje town. The dirt road to Likabula turns off the main tarred Blantyre-Mulanje road about 2km before (west of) Mulanje town, at a place called Chitikali ('Likabula junction'), and is signposted to Likabula Pool and Phalombe. There is one bus a day from Blantyre to Phalombe, leaving in the early morning, and going through Likabula. If you're coming from Blantyre on any other bus, or hitching, ask to be dropped at the Likabula junction. From there, you can wait for the irregular minibus which runs between Mulanje and Phalombe (via Likabula), which costs US$0.20. Alternatively, you can hitch; a ride in a pick-up is US$0.30.

Or you can walk (10km, two to three hours). It's a pleasant hike along the dirt road through tea estates, with good views of the south-west face of Mulanje beyond the tea on your right.

A Mulanje Traverse

Area Mulanje Mountain Forest Reserve
Distance 44km to 49km
Duration 4 or 5 days
Start Likabula Forest Station
Finish Lujeri Estate or Fort Lister Gap
Highest Point Sapitwa summit (3001m)
Nearest large town Blantyre
Accommodation Huts
Access Bus or car
Summary One of many ways of traversing Mulanje. A fine route, crossing the heart of the massif, through plantation, natural forest and open grassland, with plenty of opportunities for sidetracking, to bag a few peaks and ridges or explore small valleys.
Note: the stage from Madzeka to Lujeri may be impassable. If so, take the alternative descent route to Fort Lister Gap.

This route is one of many traverses that can be made across Mt Mulanje. It begins at Likabula and ends at Lujeri, on the southern side of the massif; both are easy to reach with or without your own transport. The route described here can be done in five days and four nights, but there are several variations which can shorten or extend this period.

The route down to Lujeri may not be passable in some conditions, in which case a descent to the Fort Lister Gap on the north side of the massif makes a good alternative. This alternative route is also described, and can be used to reduce the trek by a day.

Stage 1: Likabula Forest Station to Chambe Hut

7km, 2-4 hours, 1000m ascent
From the forest station follow the signposted Chambe Plateau Path up through the compound. After 10 minutes you'll reach a junction. Fork left, signposted 'Chambe Plateau'. The right track, signposted 'Chapaluka Path, Bottom Skyline Station', also leads to Chambe Hut – this route takes longer (3½ to 5 hours), but it's less steep and more scenic, and is preferred by some walkers.

The main path climbs very steeply, up steps in places, parallel to the Skyline (see the boxed text on 'Mulanje Pine'). After 1½ to three hours (depending on your rate of ascent) the path nears the edge of the Chambe Plateau and aims towards the top skyline station (150m to the right). Take a small steep path up to the left for 100m to reach a track on level ground. There's a shelter here, sometimes used by people preparing food for the forest workers. Go straight across the track and follow a path down through pine forest to cross a stream on a log bridge. (If the water is high, go upstream about 200m where there's a larger bridge.) When you reach another track, turn right and continue through pine plantation. Ignore the tracks forking off left. The Chapaluka Path joins from the right. Half an hour from the food shelter, you reach a junction by a bridge. Turn right, cross the bridge, and then turn immediately left. Keep on the track, turning right onto a footpath to reach Chambe Forest Station, one hour from the top skyline station.

Follow the track through the compound, then down to the right to reach Chambe Hut, standing apart from the other buildings, overlooking an area of short grass next to a stream. There are good views of the south-east face of Chambe Peak from the hut veranda.

Sidetrack: Chambe Hut to Chambe Peak Summit

3-4 hours, 700m ascent;
plus 2-3 hours descent

From the hut, follow the track back towards the forestry compound. Cross an area of open ground, and go down a grassy bank to meet another track. Turn right and follow this track, across two wooden bridges. Fifteen minutes from the compound, take a path on the right up through plantation and tend right in front of a huge grey rock wall (the eastern end of the south-west face of Chambe), to reach a large boulder on the left. Scramble up this, with the help of steps cut in a log, and then up bare rock to reach easier ground. To the right is a small stream in a narrow wooded gully; this is the last water point.

About one hour from the hut, the path reaches a col. Turn left here and go up the crest of the ridge, following cairns, and avoiding false trails which contour off to the right. The path levels, dips slightly, then climbs again to reach a small cliff (5m high) at the top of a bare rock slope. Turn right along the base of the cliff, then go up again to reach a large cairn on a broad level part of the ridge at the foot of the main face (two to 2½ hours from the hut).

You might be happy with reaching this point, which offers excellent views over the Chambe Basin to the escarpment edge and the plains far below. The next stage of the route requires some steep scrambling – which can be intimidating – and should definitely be avoided after rain.

From the cairn, a grassy slope is visible on the lower right side of the main face. To the right of this is a thin strip of bare rock. The path follows this strip to reach the foot of a shallow gully running down a steep cliff. The route goes straight up the gully. This is the most difficult section of the route and great care should be taken. Near the top of the gully, you reach a steep cliff, sloping down left to right. Keep right here, out of the gully, and follow cairns over to the right side of the ridge. Continue upwards, just to the right of the crest of the ridge, towards the apparent summit (the highest point visible). The path crosses boulders, then bare flat rock, to reach the foot of a bulging cliff with a boulder gully at its right side. Scramble up this gully and continue following cairns, keeping to the right of the ridge. Aim first towards the apparent summit, visible ahead, then towards the foot of a high (25m) rounded buttress at the left (north-east) end of the summit ridge. At the foot of the buttress turn left and up, then tend right, keeping the main cliff to your right.

Where the cliff becomes less steep, turn right to scramble up several grooves in the rock to reach the ridge crest. Turn left (south-west) to follow the ridge across easier ground to the summit (2557m), marked by a large concrete and metal beacon which is not visible until you're almost on it.

MALAWI

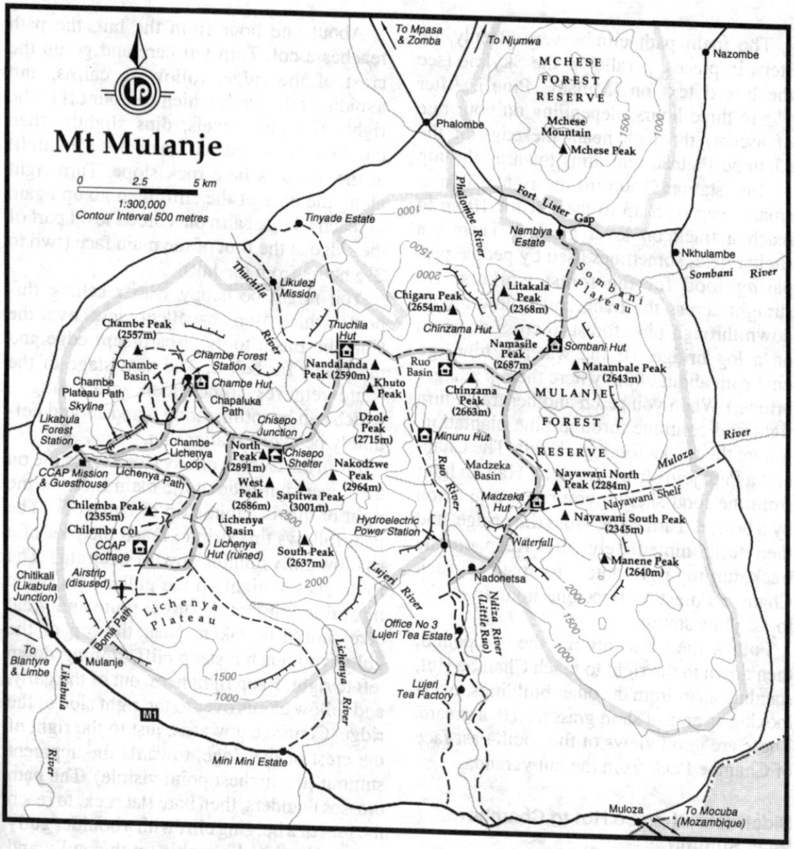
Mt Mulanje
0
2.5
5 km
1:300,000
Contour Interval 500 metres
To Mpasa & Zomba
To Njumwa
Nazombe
MCHESE FOREST RESERVE
Phalombe
Mchese Mountain
Mchese Peak
Fort Lister Gap
Nambiya Estate
Nkhulambe
Sombani River
Phalombe River
Tinyade Estate
Sombani Plateau
Thuchila River
Likulezi Mission
Chigaru Peak (2654m)
Litakala Peak (2368m)
Chinzama Hut
Thuchila Hut
Namasile Peak (2687m)
Sombani Hut
Chambe Peak (2557m)
Chambe Forest Station
Nandalanda Peak (2590m)
Ruo Basin
Matambale Peak (2643m)
Chambe Basin
Chambe Hut
Khuto Peak
Chinzama Peak (2663m)
MULANJE FOREST RESERVE
Chambe Plateau Path
Chapaluka Path
Skyline
Dzole Peak (2715m)
Likabula Forest Station
Chisepo Junction
Minunu Hut
River
Chambe-Lichenya Loop
North Peak (2891m)
Chisepo Shelter
Nakodzwe Peak (2964m)
Madzeka Basin
Muloza
CCAP Mission & Guesthouse
Lichenya Path
West Peak (2686m)
Sapitwa Peak (3001m)
Nayawani North Peak (2284m)
Nayawani Shelf
Madzeka Hut
Ruo River
Chilemba Peak (2355m)
Lichenya Basin
Chilemba Col
Hydroelectric Power Station
Nayawani South Peak (2345m)
CCAP Cottage
Lichenya Hut (ruined)
South Peak (2637m)
Waterfall
Manene Peak (2640m)
Chitikali (Likabula Junction)
Airstrip (disused)
Lujeri River
Nadonetsa
Lichenya Plateau
Boma Path
Office No 3 Lujeri Tea Estate
Ndiza River (Little Ruo)
To Blantyre & Limbe
Mulanje
Likabula River
Lichenya River
Lujeri Tea Factory
M1
Mini Mini Estate
Muloza
To Mocuba (Mozambique)

The views from the summit of Chambe Peak in clear weather are superb; you can see most of Mulanje's main peaks, and much of the western side of the massif. Long stretches of the escarpment that surrounds the massif can also be seen, and below this the plains stretch out towards the Zomba Plateau in the north and the mountains of Mozambique in the south. It is often possible to see the waters of Lake Chilwa to the north-east and on very clear days Lake Malombe, at the southern tip of Lake Malawi, can also be seen.

To get back to Chambe Hut, retrace the route. Go slowly on the way down; it's easy to go off route, and just as easy to slip and fall on some of the steeper sections.

Stage 2: Chambe Hut to Thuchila Hut

12km, 4-5 hours

The path towards Thuchila starts at Chambe Forest Station, passes about 50m to the south-west of Chambe Hut, and leads uphill, along the edge of pine plantation, following a wide firebreak. It can be complicated to find as there are other paths all over the place, so if you haven't got a porter ask the hut caretaker to show you the first half km or so. After 10 minutes, fork left as the path climbs steeply up through boulders. At a second fork, after another 10 minutes, take the right path through plantation and indigenous woodland before rejoining the firebreak. The path tends up and left across bare rock, then drops to cross a stream. Follow the path up to a small col and then along the left side of a steep valley. Drop to a large col, where the Chambe Basin is joined to the main massif, and contour around the side of a small hill, passing through woodland to reach a junction (about one to 1½ hours from the hut).

From the junction, keep straight on, up a steep path. (The path to the right leads to the old Lichenya Hut.) To the left are fine views down into the Thuchila Valley. The path reaches its highest point and begins to drop through the grassland of the Thuchila Plateau. About two hours from Chambe hut, you reach Chisepo Junction. The path on the right leads up to the summit of Sapitwa Peak (see Sidetrack in this stage).

Keep straight on, following the clear path, across several streams (some with large pools) to meet a firebreak, and tend left round the head of a large valley. Continue down the side of the valley to cross more streams and rivers, either by wooden bridges or by paddling. These are all the headwaters of the Thuchila River. At a fork, the right path leads to forestry workers' houses; keep straight on for 200m to a crossroads and turn right to Thuchila Hut.

If you sidetracked up Sapitwa, you will probably be pleased to spend the night here. If you didn't, you could carry on to Chinzama Hut.

Sidetrack: Chisepo Junction to Sapitwa Peak Summit

3-5 hours, 800m ascent;
plus 2-4 hours descent

The summit of Sapitwa is the highest point on the massif, at 3001m (some maps have 3002m). You can walk to the top, but it's a toughie, and the upper section involves some scrambling and tricky walking among large boulders and dense vegetation. ('Sapitwa' in the local language means 'don't go there'.)

If you're feeling fit, you could divert from the route between Chambe and Thuchila huts and go up to Sapitwa summit and back. Large rucksacks could be hidden in the bushes and collected again afterwards. Alternatively, spend two nights at either Chambe or Thuchila Hut and do Sapitwa on the day in between. However, Chisepo Junction, the start of the route, is about halfway between the two huts, so this doesn't save much time: it's still going to be a long day. If you're doing Sapitwa from either Chambe or Thuchila, add another four to five hours onto the times for doing the peak itself. If you do run out of time, the small Chisepo Shelter, near the junction, provides some basic protection. (Some hardy hikers bivvy here.)

From the junction, pass the shelter and cross a stream. Turn left and follow the broad ridge that aims roughly towards the summit. The route is clearly shown, for most of the way, by red marks painted on the rocks, so step-by-step directions are unnecessary. The paint spoils the image of untouched wilderness, but it stops a lot of people from getting lost – and there are a few marks missing, just to keep you on your toes! As you get near the summit you can see the top, but the route winds tortuously through an area of huge boulders and dense vegetation.

The views from the top, when you do finally make it, are worth the slog. On a clear day, you get a panoramic vista of the whole plateau, the other nearby peaks, the edge of the escarpment and the plains far below.

Stage 3: Thuchila Hut to Sombani Hut, via Chinzama Hut

12km, 4-5 hours

From Thuchila Hut, retrace to the main path and turn right to reach a bridge and junction. Turn right (straight on leads to Lukulezi, also called Tinyade), and follow the path as it climbs over bare rock and through bush to reach a col and junction. Take the left path (the right path leads to Minunu Hut) and drop down into a valley, keeping left to contour round the valley side. Cross several firebreaks, but avoid dropping towards the valley bottom until the hut is visible on the opposite side of the valley. At a clear junction, about

MALAWI

two hours from Thuchila Hut, turn right to drop down into the valley, cross two streams and climb steeply up to reach Chinzama Hut, after another 10 minutes.

From Chinzama Hut aim eastwards until the path climbs a small rise with a firebreak on the left and a narrow path forking off to the right. A signpost points back to Chinzama Hut. Take the narrow path as it heads right and climbs up the valley side, through grass and bush and across patches of rocks, to reach a small col. Cross into the next valley, and drop through rolling grassland, crossed by several firebreaks, to reach a junction. Take the left path (the right path leads to Madzeka Hut) and go through grassland to cross a wooden bridge and some small streams (no water during the dry season). The firebreak swings left; take the narrow path straight on, through woodland and plantation, to cross another small stream and reach a fork. The left path leads outside the plantation; the right path climbs through the trees to reach Sombani Hut, about two hours from Chinzama Hut.

Sidetrack: Sombani Hut to Namasile Peak Summit

2½-3 hours, 600m ascent; plus 1½-2½ hours descent

Namasile Peak is the large mountain that dominates the view across the Sombani River valley, directly opposite Sombani Hut. From the hut, the south-east face of Namasile is clearly visible, appearing almost vertical. The path to the summit, steep in places but not technically difficult, spirals round the north side of the mountain and approaches the summit from the west (the 'back' of the mountain when viewed from Sombani Hut).

From the hut aim north down a clear path to cross the stream in the valley bottom on a wooden bridge. On the opposite bank is a fork. Keep straight on (right leads towards the Fort Lister Gap), up a firebreak to its end. To the right is a small pool (sometimes dry). Head left, for 50m, to reach a large sloping rock slab to the right of the path. Go up the slab and follow the path, marked by cairns but indistinct in places, aiming towards a low

point in the ridge ahead. To the left is a small stream in a valley. The path tends towards this stream, and crosses it between two groups of waterfalls, about half an hour from the hut. This is the last reliable water point.

After crossing the stream, pass to the right of a very large boulder, and then aim west-north-west up towards a low point on the ridge (actually a false ridge), immediately to the right of the main cliffs of the mountain. A very large undercut boulder lies at the centre of this apparent low point. Pass to the left of this to reach the top of the false ridge. Now aim for a low point in the next ridge directly to the right of the main cliffs. You'll reach the foot of the main cliffs about 1½ to two hours from the hut.

Continue up through grass and bush, keeping the base of the main cliffs on your immediate left, to enter a broad gully, covered with vegetation, separating the main cliffs of Namasile from a minor peak lying to the north. Go up the broad gully towards a small col but, before reaching the col, head steeply left and up towards the main summit. The summit beacon is visible at the highest point.

You'll think you're nearly there, but now comes the hard bit! The path crosses bare rock and enters an area of large boulders and dense vegetation. The path is marked by cairns, but care should be taken not to get lost on this section. Beyond the boulders the summit beacon is again visible, although the path does not aim directly for it, but zigzags up over boulders and grassy slopes below the beacon to curve round the summit area and approach it from the north-east. Scramble over large rocks to reach the summit beacon (2687m), about three hours from the hut.

Views from the summit of Namasile Peak are excellent: over the north-eastern side of Mt Mulanje across the Ruo and Madzeka basins and the upper part of the Sombani River valley. To the north-east the escarpment drops to the Fort Lister Gap, with the separate peak of Mchese beyond.

Return to Sombani Hut by the same route. Take care on the way down; it's easy to miss cairns and go off route. Allow 1½ to 2½ hours for the total descent.

MALAWI

Stage 4: Sombani Hut to Madzeka Hut
9km, 3-4 hours

From Sombani Hut retrace Stage 3 back to the junction. Keep straight on (right goes to Chinzama and Thuchila), then drop steeply to cross a stream in a narrow valley by a 'danger' sign. The path climbs out of the valley then passes through undulating grassland, across a wooden bridge in bad condition, then up to cross two small cols separated by a swampy basin. The path drops towards the valley, following a firebreak.

About two hours from Sombani Hut you'll reach a fork, marked by a stone pole, where the firebreak aims straight on. Take the left path. Ten minutes on, a path to the left goes towards Nayawani. Keep straight on, down the clear path, across several small bridges, to reach Madzeka Hut after another hour.

Sidetrack 1: Madzeka Hut to Nayawani North Peak Summit
1½-2 hours, 440m ascent;
plus 1-1½ hours, descent

There are no major peaks that can be easily reached from Madzeka Hut, but Nayawani North is a pleasant little summit. This stroll can be turned into a longer circular walk, taking in the dramatic northern ridge of the mountain (see Sidetrack 2).

From Madzeka Hut, cross the stream that runs past the hut and follow the firebreak (zigzagging steeply in the final section) to a col between the peaks of Nayawani North and South. (From the col the path drops to reach Nayawani Shelf, a rounded terrace covered in natural woodland, on the north-east slope of Nayawani South.)

From the col, turn left (north) to follow a firebreak. Cross a section of steep rock slabs (slippery after rain, avoidable by scrambling up the boggy tussock grass to the side) to reach Nayawani North Peak (2285m), which offers an excellent panoramic view of the south-eastern part of Mt Mulanje.

Descend by the same route.

Sidetrack 2: Nayawani Ridge Circuit
8km, 3½-5 hours, 440m ascent

This is an excellent route, with fine views from the ridge, but it follows firebreaks for much of the way, and these are steep and rocky, or overgrown and indistinct, in places, and can be quite strenuous, especially if you have already done a long walk to reach Madzeka Hut.

From Madzeka Hut follow the description given in Sidetrack 1 to reach the summit of Nayawani North after 1½ to two hours. Continue to follow the firebreak along the crest of the ridge, which is steep and narrow in places. There are excellent views down into the Muloza Valley on the right (east) and to the Madzeka Basin on the left (west).

About two to 2½ hours from the hut, the path/firebreak descends to a distinct col, crossed at right angles by a firebreak running down into the valleys on either side. Turn left (west), to follow the right side of the valley down towards the floor of the Madzeka Basin. The going is tough when the grass is high. Keep right, to avoid losing too much height, then meet another firebreak that contours along the side of the main ridge. Turn right onto this firebreak and follow it up the valley (north then north-west), crossing several other firebreaks, to reach a large stream that flows along a wide (10m to 15m) strip of exposed rock down the centre of the Madzeka Basin, about 45 minutes to one hour from the col.

Cross the stream (which may be impassable after heavy rain) and follow the firebreak uphill until it meets the main path running from Sombani and Chinzama to Madzeka Hut. Turn left onto this path and follow it down the valley to reach Madzeka Hut, about 1½ to two hours after crossing the large stream.

Stage 5: Madzeka Hut to Lujeri Estate
9km, 3-5 hours, 1100m descent

This section may be impassable. See the warning above, and take one of the alternative routes suggested if necessary.

From Madzeka Hut follow the path that heads south-west, across a stream, and down into the large Ndiza Valley (also called the Little Ruo Valley). You'll pass through dense woodland in steep-sided tributary valleys,

MALAWI

and over open grassland on the dividing spurs. The path crosses bare rock slabs on the edge of the escarpment and then begins to drop very steeply down almost vertical cliffs. Ladders and staircases have been positioned on the steepest sections. To the left (east) of the path the Ndiza (Little Ruo) River plunges off the escarpment in a spectacular waterfall. Far below, the smooth green fields of the Lujeri tea plantations can be seen.

Continue going down. Your progress will probably be slow: the path is very steep in places, and some of the ladders are rotten, but the views are spectacular. (Great care should be taken when descending in wet conditions.) Three to four hours from Madzeka Hut, the path finally begins to level out and enter conifer plantation, then the outskirts of Nadonetsa, a scattered village. To get through the village, follow the path, fork right, and cross a small stream. A path joins from the right; keep left at the next junction, enter small fields of tea, pass down the village main street, fork right and cross a small bridge. A path joins from the right. Continue straight on, pass more huts, fork right, and pass some large white huts on the right, to cross the (Big) Ruo River on a large steel and concrete footbridge. (There's a fair chance of getting lost here; if in doubt ask for directions to the big bridge. Local kids will be happy to guide you here, or all the way to Office No 3, so keep some change handy for small tips.)

From the bridge, the path runs parallel and to the right (west) of the river and then heads right, through tea, to meet a dirt road. Turn left onto this, keeping straight on at all junctions to reach Office No 3, a collection of low white buildings on the left side of the road, about half an hour from the large bridge.

Lujeri Estate to the Main Road From Office No 3 it's still 13km to the main road that goes back to Mulanje town and Blantyre. You may be lucky and find somebody in the office with a car or a tractor who can help you with a lift. If you're out of luck, you'll have to start walking. From the office, follow the dirt road through the tea plantation, aiming generally south, away from the massif. After 3km, turn sharp right at a junction towards the large buildings of the tea factory, then right again, keeping the factory on the left, over a large river bridge. Turn left at a junction, and follow this road for about 9km to reach the main tarred road. It'll take you three to four hours to do this walk, depending on the state of your knees after the descent from Madzeka.

When you reach the main road, Mulanje town and Blantyre are to the right (west). Wait here for a bus (several each day) or hitch.

Alternative Descent: Sombani Hut to Fort Lister Gap
5km, 2-3 hours
This is an alternative descent to take if the route described above is not possible due to the ladders on Stage 5 being damaged.

From Sombani hut aim north down a clear path to cross the stream in the valley bottom on a wooden bridge. On the opposite bank is a fork. Go right (straight on leads towards Namasile Peak), through plantation and grassland, over another bridge, left at two

---

Warning
The path described in Stage 5 includes ladders for sections of steep descent. Some of these have been damaged and may not have been replaced by the time you visit Mulanje. Without the ladders, sections of this route involve technical climbing and are treacherous in wet conditions; they should therefore be avoided. Check at the forest station before departure. If the Madzeka to Lujeri stage is impassable, you should descend from Sombani Hut to Fort Lister Gap and Phalombe. This is described as an alternative descent at the end of this section.
    Alternatively, stay your last night at Minunu Hut (see Stage 3 of the route description), and descend to Lujeri through the (Big) Ruo Gorge. From the hut to the hydroelectric power station takes about three to four hours. From there to Office No 3 is 10km on a good dirt road (allow another three hours). ∎

forks and then down towards the gap itself. The path leads through some patches of indigenous forest, with great views over the surrounding plains, and keeps descending, although it is not as steep as the Chambe path coming up, and nowhere near as precipitous as the route from Madzeka down to Lujeri. There's a lot of forks, so a porter is useful to show you the way. If you're hiking alone though, the rule of thumb at every fork is 'keep going down'. For the last section you follow a dirt track. Camping is possible at Fort Lister Forest Station (US$0.35).

Fort Lister Gap to Phalombe From Fort Lister Gap to Phalombe village is another 8km along the dirt road. It is in bad condition and there's very little traffic, so you'll have to walk (about two hours), but it's pleasant enough – through a couple of small villages. Most porters include this section in the fee you pay for the final day.

From Phalombe you can get a bus or pick-up back to Likabula or Mulanje. One bus a day goes direct to Limbe and Blantyre (US$3), on the 'old road' (to the north of the main road through Thyolo). There's also transport to Zomba.

The Chambe-Lichenya Loop

> **Area** Mulanje Mountain Forest Reserve
> **Distance** 27km
> **Duration** 3 days
> **Start/Finish** Likabula Forest Station
> **Highest Point** Chambe Peak (2557m)
> **Nearest large town** Blantyre
> **Accommodation** Huts
> **Access** Bus or car
> **Summary** A neat accessible trek, providing a good taste of Mulanje's delights, with spectacular views and the chance to bag two impressive peaks.

This is a short route, good if you want to get a taste of Mulanje but haven't got time for a complete traverse of the whole massif. It starts and finishes at Likabula Forest Station, so access and exit before and after the trek are no problem. The route can be done in either direction.

Stage 1: Likabula Forest Station to Chambe Hut
7km, 2-4 hours, 1000m ascent
This section of the route is the same as Stage 1 of the Mulanje Traverse.

Sidetrack: Chambe Hut to Chambe Peak Summit
This route is also described in the Mulanje Traverse section.

Stage 2: Chambe Hut to Lichenya CCAP Cottage
12km, 4-5 hours
The path towards Lichenya starts at Chambe Forest Station, passes about 50m to the south-west of Chambe Hut, and leads uphill, through pine plantation, following a wide firebreak. After 10 minutes, fork left as the path climbs steeply up through boulders. At a second fork after another 10 minutes, take the right path through plantation and indigenous woodland before rejoining the firebreak.

The path heads up and left across bare rock, then drops to cross a stream. Follow the path up to a small col and then along the left side of a steep valley. Drop to a large col, where the Chambe Basin is joined to the main massif, and contour round the side of a small hill, passing through woodland to reach a junction (about one to 1½ hours from Chambe Hut).

Turn right at this junction (straight on leads to Thuchila), and descend through natural forest. The path levels out and crosses several small streams, the headwaters of the Likabula River. Down to the right is the Likabula Valley, while up to the left are North Peak and West Peak, outliers of Sapitwa.

About 1½ hours from the junction, you'll enter a confusing section, where several firebreaks meet and cross the path. Keep straight

MALAWI

on. After a few minutes, the firebreak goes straight on and the path forks off right at a small cairn. Ten minutes later another firebreak comes in from the right. Turn left here, and you'll almost immediately reach another junction. Ignore the path on the right, which goes back towards Likabula and Lichenya CCAP Cottage, and keep straight on down into the Lichenya Basin. Continue for half an hour to reach the site of Lichenya Hut (destroyed by fire in 1995).

Follow the path in a south-westerly direction, going straight on at a junction five minutes from the hut. Continue on the path as it follows wide firebreaks to reach a crossroads. Straight on goes nowhere, left goes to the disused airstrip. Turn right to reach Lichenya CCAP Cottage, about one hour from the site of Lichenya Hut.

Sidetracks from Lichenya Hut site

You can head south past the old airstrip to the top of the frighteningly steep Boma Path that goes down to Mulanje town, for good views over the escarpment. It's also possible to go up to Chilemba Peak from Lichenya Hut (see Stage 3 description) instead of sidetracking off Stage 3.

Stage 3: Lichenya CCAP Cottage to Likabula, via Chilemba Col

8km, 3-4 hours, 360m ascent;
plus 1400m descent

From the CCAP cottage, two parallel firebreaks lead up towards an obvious col in the ridge, north-east of the cottage. Follow the left-hand firebreak to start with, then cross over to the one on the right when the left gets steep. The col is half an hour from the cottage. Chilemba Peak lies to the left of the col (see Sidetrack in this stage).

From the col, drop to a junction. Go left (right goes back towards Lichenya Hut and the Chambe-Thuchila path), downhill through forest and across sections of bare rock. About one hour from the col you reach another junction; keep straight on downhill to cross a stream and get on a good-quality path which has actually been paved in some places. The going is steep but easy now, with

the path crossing streams and gullies on well-built bridges and causeways. About 1½ hours from the col the path crosses a wide riverbed of flat rock, then continues down to enter light forest. Firebreaks come in from the left. (If you're coming up this route, it's important not to follow these firebreaks, as they go directly to the foot of the main cliffs of Lichenya. Keep left, on the main path, and keep the cliffs some 800m away on your right shoulder.)

Continue down on the wide path through the forest, keeping right at the main fork, to reach the Likabula River. Before this main fork, smaller paths branch off on the right to the river.

Wade through the river, or jump from rock to rock, and go up the far bank to reach the dirt track between the Mulanje-Phalombe road and Likabula Forest Station. Turn right then left to reach the forest station.

Sidetrack: Chilemba Col to Chilemba Peak

1-1½ hours, 150m ascent;
plus 1 hour descent

From the left (west) firebreak, on the crest of the col, a faint path leads up the ridge towards the summit. The path is indistinct in places; keep to the crest of the broad ridge if you lose it. Towards the top, the going gets less steep. Pass through boulders and grass to reach a minor summit, marked by a tall cairn. Drop down to cross a small saddle then scramble up over bare rock to the main summit, marked by a concrete beacon and another tall cairn.

From the summit, to the north you can look across the Likabula River and see the Chambe Basin looking like, well, a basin full of trees. Beyond this is the main south-east face of Chambe Peak. To the left of the Chambe escarpment you can see the flat-topped dome of Chiradzulu Mountain on the horizon. In the other direction you can look back over the Lichenya Plateau, to the sharp edge of the escarpment, and the hazy mountains of Mozambique in the distance.

Retrace the route back to Chilemba Col.

MALAWI

Other Routes on Mt Mulanje

There are several ascent routes from the plains up to the top of Mt Mulanje, and many paths linking the huts and peaks, giving you an almost endless set of combinations.

LIKULEZI MISSION TO THUCHILA HUT

This is a recommended ascent route, on the north side of the massif. A guide is useful, as the route is not always clear. This route can also be used as a descent after, say, a two or three-day trip taking in Chambe Hut and Chambe Peak, Sapitwa Peak and Thuchila Hut. From Likulezi (the area is also called Tinyade) you can catch the daily bus that leaves Phalombe around midday back to Likabula, Mulanje town or Blantyre.

BOMA PATH

If you're feeling brave, a possible descent route is the incredibly steep Boma Path from the Lichenya Plateau down to Mulanje town. If you go up from Likabula, coming down this way means you can still do a circuit and be back in Mulanje town without having to worry about transport. This path is very, very steep and precipitous, overgrown in places, slippery in dry conditions and impassable after rain – it's only for very experienced trekkers.

If that hasn't put you off, from the disused airstrip, follow the path that aims in a south then south-westerly direction, forking left and then right at two junctions. At the plateau edge, an old signpost marks the start of the route down. There are some patches of red paint marking the way, but you'll probably have to bushbash in some places as you lurch from tree to tree. Below the woodland you enter a grassy area and a maze of woodcutters' paths. Keep going down to the edge of the forest reserve. Paths lead to the tea factory, visible on the right side of Mulanje town, or straight to Mulanje town itself. As you get lower, you'll find plenty of people about, so you can ask directions.

The Nyika Plateau

The Nyika Plateau is in the north of Malawi, overlapping the border with Zambia, and is completely different to Mt Mulanje in both size and character. Although called a plateau, Nyika is by no means flat: it consists mainly of rolling grassy hills, split by forested valleys, and surrounded by steep escarpments and several peaks, making it an excellent area for trekking.

The wild open nature of the Nyika Plateau also attracts visitors who come to view the birds and animals, study the flowers, or simply sit in the sun and absorb the scenery.

In 1996 plans were announced that are likely to change the nature of the Nyika Plateau considerably. See the boxed text 'Future Changes on Nyika' for more details.

HISTORY

This wide expanse of wilderness has probably existed in its current form for many centuries, and a small population of hunter-gatherers is believed to have inhabited the Nyika more than 3000 years ago. Ancient rock paintings have been found at Fingira Cave, at the southern end of the plateau. For the peoples living on the plains below Nyika, the plateau was a place to hunt and smelt iron, but it was never settled in a big way.

The first Europeans to see Nyika were Scottish missionaries, inspired by the explorer David Livingstone, who reached this area in 1894. The mission station they built, between the plateau's eastern edge and Lake Malawi, was named Livingstonia, and is still a thriving centre today.

Scientists and naturalists who visited Nyika in the early 20th century recognised the biological importance of the plateau. In 1933 measures were taken to protect the juniper forests on the southern part of the plateau from bushfires, and in 1948 this section was made into a forest reserve, and pine plantations were established around Chelinda.

In 1965 the whole of the upper plateau was made a national park, and in 1976 this area was extended further to include the lower slopes of the plateau, which are an important water catchment area. This most recent boundary extension included several small settlements, and the people living here were relocated to areas outside the park. When they moved they took the names of their villages with them and now, in the area bordering the park, there are several settlements which share names with valleys and other features inside the park itself.

GEOGRAPHY

The Nyika Plateau is roughly oval in shape, about 80km long and almost 50km across, at its widest points, covering some 3000 sq km, plus the area in Zambian territory. Most of the plateau top is at about 2000m, but there are several peaks on its edge which rise above this height, and overlook the steep escarpments that surround the plateau on its western, northern and eastern sides.

The highest point on Nyika is Nganda Peak (2607m, 8553 ft), which overlooks the northern section of the plateau; from here you can see the plains of Zambia in one direction and the distant mountains of Tanzania in the other, as well as the waters of Lake Malawi shining in the distance.

TREKKING INFORMATION

Nyika may not have the high drama of the snowcapped massifs further north but, without a doubt, it is a uniquely beautiful place, quite unlike any other trekking area described in this book.

Costs

Costs for trekking on Nyika break down into three major areas: park and national park entrance fees, the costs of hiring a scout (park ranger) as guide (obligatory) or porters (optional), and the cost of your own supplies. The cost of getting there is also an important point to consider. All these points are detailed separately below.

Route Standard & Days Required

A series of walking routes have been set by the national park authorities, varying in length from one day to over a week. These are called wilderness trails, and are based on the South African concept: trails are not way-marked, and often do not even follow a path or track, so that on some sections you simply find your own way through forest, or across open grassland, using a compass, a sense of direction, and the local knowledge of your guide.

There are many variations to each trail, particularly the longer ones, and the actual route you take may depend on the time of year, where you're likely to see wildlife, the skill of the guide, or just how you're feeling on the day.

Future Changes on Nyika

In 1996 plans were announced that are likely to change the nature of the Nyika Plateau considerably. Following several years of neglect, during which poaching became a major problem, the national park authorities will be provided with funds (from the German government) so that the area can be completely rehabilitated. The main changes to affect visitors will be: moving the park headquarters from Chelinda Camp to Thazima Gate; a new all-weather access road from Rumphi to Chelinda Camp via Thazima; new improved tracks and roads around the park; renovation of existing park accommodation; construction of a new lodge; and possibly more. It is not clear how long it will take for these various plans to come to fruition. Of course, the landscape itself will remain the same, and the quality of the wildlife viewing will probably improve, thanks to increased anti-poaching measures, staff training and better all-round management. Whatever, some of the descriptions in this book are likely to be out of date by the time you arrive, so be prepared for changes. ∎

MALAWI

Some of the wilderness trails are out-and-back routes, whereas others start and finish at different points. The best areas for trekking are the escarpments on the plateau edge, so most of the trails are in these areas, and you need to allow at least another day at either end of the trail to walk from, and back to, Chelinda Camp. If you have a car, these first stages can usually be covered by vehicle. Park vehicles are not available for hire, although you may be able to arrange a ride if a vehicle is making an official journey.

But you don't have to keep to these wilderness trails. They are provided only as suggestions by the park authorities. Basically, you can go anywhere you like for as long as you like. All you need is a guide to go with you, and enough equipment and food to keep going. In this section, several other trekking possibilities are outlined. The routes mentioned briefly here are described in more detail later in this section.

For all trekking on the Nyika, you must provide all the equipment and food you need. Guides have their own sleeping bags, tents, cooking pots and food. Camp sites are not fixed, although in practice the better sites are used more frequently. No facilities of any kind exist at the sites.

On all the routes described in this section, the landscape is undulating, but there are no long (ie all day) ascents and descents as on the larger mountains of Kenya and Tanzania. Consequently, total height gains/losses are very small and not indicated in the descriptions.

As well as an outline of the wilderness trails, the main routes described in this section are:

The Nyika Highlights Route This is not an official wilderness trail, like the ones set by the park, as it follows paths and tracks for much of the way, rather than going through open country. The title is not official either; we've used this name because it takes in many of Nyika's main attractions.

The daily distances are quite long, but there are no major gradients to contend with. On the sections of the routes which follow

Flora & Fauna on Nyika

The vegetation on Nyika is unique in Malawi (and unusual in Africa) and so worthy of special attention. Above 1800m, most of Nyika is covered in rolling hills of montane grassland. The land below this altitude, in valleys and on the escarpment edges, is covered in light open miombo (or *Brachystegia*) woodland and in between the two vegetation zones you can often see areas of large protea bush. Other areas are covered in dense evergreen forest, which are thought to be remnants of the extensive forest that once grew all over Malawi, as well as southern Tanzania, northern Zambia and Mozambique. The plateau also contains small areas of damp grassy bog.

This range of vegetation attracts a variety of wildlife, and a major feature of a visit to Nyika is the number of birds and animals you are likely to see. Because of the general lack of trees and bushes, spotting wildlife is easy too. (In fact, many animals seem to deliberately pose on the skyline for that classic wildlife shot.) Most common are the large roan antelope and the smaller reedbuck which move about through the grassland in herds. From a car or on foot, you'll also see zebra, wart hog and eland (although, because they are a favourite target for poachers, these are very shy). Walking quietly, and crossing hilltops slowly, you might also see klipspringer, duiker, hartebeest and jackal. You might even catch a glimpse of hyena and leopard, but you'll be more likely to see their footprints and droppings. In the woodland areas, you may see blue monkey. More than 250 species of bird have been recorded in the park.

Nyika is also famous for its wildflowers. The best time to see them is during the rains (mid-October to April), but conditions are also good in August and September, when the grassland is covered in colour and small outcrops turn into veritable rock gardens. Over 120 species of orchid alone grow on the plateau. ∎

DAVID ELSE

MALAWI

park tracks and pass through areas of short grass, the going is easy, but in some areas the grass is long and tussocky, which can be very tiring. Some of the park tracks are drivable, but are very rarely used by vehicles, so you're unlikely to be disturbed. This circular route takes four days, although you could do it in three. The route can be done in either direction.

The Livingstonia Route This route follows tracks and paths for its entire length, and drops dramatically down the wooded escarpment on the eastern edge of the plateau to leave the park and reach the mission centre of Livingstonia, from where you can get to Lake Malawi. Daily distances are not long, and most of the route is downhill.

The route takes three days, with the possibility of a fourth if you can't find a lift out of Livingstonia. If you're short of time, and feeling fit, the first two stages can be done in one day, but it's long and hard. This route cannot be done in reverse.

Guides & Porters

All trekkers have to be accompanied by a park ranger, called a scout, who will act as a guide. Other scouts are available for hire as porters if you need them. Scouts cost US$10 per day. If you're booking chalets (see Places to Stay) in advance, scouts can also be arranged then. Alternatively, they can be hired at Chelinda with a day's notice. The park authorities are trying to promote more trekking on the Nyika, as it's a useful way of providing extra patrols and keeping a check on poaching. It has been known for scouts to see groups of poachers while guiding trekkers and go off to give chase. This is unlikely, but don't complain if it happens, as it's part of the deal.

All the scouts speak English, and are generally very pleasant, knowledgeable about the birds and wildlife, and good company on a long trek. They receive no extra money from the park for this work, so a tip (of around US$2 to US$3 per day) at the end of your trek is appropriate if the service has been good.

If your trek finishes outside the park, you must pay for your scout's public transport back to Chelinda, and an 'allowance' if he stays out another night. For Livingstonia, a single fee of US$10 seems to cover transport, accommodation and other incidentals.

Even though you've got a guide it's still important to be familiar with the route, conditions, likely times and so on, as the scouts are very fit, and their ideas about daily distances may be different to yours! Let your scout know how long you want to walk for each day, and whether you are 'strong' or 'not so strong'.

Park Fees & Regulations

The Nyika Plateau is a national park and fees are payable. For non-citizens there is an entrance fee of US$15 per person per day, and a car fee of US$15 per day.

These fees are payable at the gate where you enter the park (for most people this is Thazima). if you decide to extend your stay, extra days can be paid for at Chelinda. You are not allowed to enter the park unless you are in a vehicle. Once in the park, however, you can leave your car, at your own risk, to walk short distances to visit viewpoints, areas of forest, or other places of interest. For longer walks, all visitors must be accompanied by a scout.

Some of the park tracks are for management use only and not open to public vehicles. However, it is OK to walk on them.

Maps

The entire Nyika Plateau is covered by the government survey 1:250,000 map sheet 2, but many of the park tracks are not shown, and the scale is too limiting for trekkers. The national park produces a simple map which shows the tracks and main peaks but has no topographical detail. The plateau is covered by twelve 1:50,000 maps: 1033 B1 to B4, 1033 D1 to D4, 1034 A1 and A3, 1034 C1 and C3. These have excellent topographical detail, but do not show all the park tracks. Chelinda Camp area is covered by 1033 D2.

Guidebooks

The national park produces a small booklet with good background information on the wildlife and vegetation found on the plateau. There are also leaflets and displays in the excellent information centre at Chelinda Camp. For more details, see one of the guidebooks to the national parks, mentioned in the Malawi Guidebooks section.

Supplies

The best place for supplies is Mzuzu, which has a couple of large supermarkets and a very good market for fruit and vegetables. There is also a market and several shops in Rumphi.

PLACES TO STAY

Mzuzu

The nearest large town to Nyika is Mzuzu – 'the Capital of the North' – which has grown considerably in the last decade or so, changing from a sleepy frontier town to a fairly large administrative centre, with banks, shops, post office, supermarket, pharmacy, museum, petrol stations and other facilities.

Most budget travellers head for the *CCAP Resthouse*, just off Boardman Rd, about 500m north-east of the bus station, where beds cost US$3 per person, in safe, clean rooms with two, three or four beds. Also near the bus station is *Flame Tree Guesthouse*, where a friendly Malawian lady called Mrs Phipps does bed and breakfast in the English tradition for US$6 per person, or US$4 if you don't want breakfast. This place is a real little gem (there are only three bedrooms, with two beds each, and you share the rest of the house with the family) so unfortunately it's often full, although always worth trying.

If you're really short of cash, try the *Jambo Resthouse* on M'Membelwa Rd. Basic rooms here cost US$1 per person. Smarter double rooms out back are US$2.50. The bathrooms are bearable, but what you'd expect in this price range.

Up the scale from here is the *Chenda Hotel*, just to the east of the bus station and connected to the Chenda Entertainment Centre, which is basically a huge bar, with music or discos some evenings. In the hotel,

> **Warning**
> During dry periods, sectors of the park are burnt to prevent larger fires later in the season. Before setting off on a trek, inquire at the park office about where burning is taking place, and avoid the area. ■

clean en suite single/doubles are US$10/15 with breakfast.

Top of the range is the *Mzuzu Hotel* (☎ 332622; central reservations ☎ 620071), on the east side of town, overlooking the golf course. This hotel is run by the South African Protea group, so facilities are of a relatively high standard. En suite rooms with air-con and phone cost US$104/135, with full buffet breakfast.

Rumphi

Rumphi (pronounced Rumpy) is a small town about 70km north of Mzuzu, east of the main road between Mzuzu and Karonga, on the road to the Nyika Plateau. Cheap places to stay include the *Yagontha Hideout Resthouse*, with simple but OK rooms for US$2 per person. On the edge of town, as you come in from Mzuzu, is the friendly and good value *Simphakawa Inn*, where clean en suite rooms with hot showers cost US$3.50 (for one or two people).

On the Nyika Plateau

As outlined in the boxed text near the start of this section, big changes are planned for Nyika. More than anything else, the accommodation setup is likely to alter drastically in the next few years, as the chalets and camp site are improved and a new lodge is built. The exact time-scale for these changes is not known, but you should be prepared for some of the following information to be out of date by the time you arrive.

Nyika National Park's main accommodation centre is *Chelinda Camp*. There are self-contained chalets, with two bedrooms (each with two beds), a bathroom, kitchen and dining area, costing US$20 for the whole chalet or US$10 per room. There are also

MALAWI

blocks of double bedrooms, with shared bathrooms and common room, for US$10. All have fireplaces, firewood, electricity and hot water. A fully equipped central kitchen (with staff to assist with cooking) and lounge area is open to all visitors.

The camp site, about 2km north of the park office, costs US$3 per night if you use your own tent. Large tents, with beds inside, are also available for US$8. The youth hostel is mainly for school groups but can be used if the chalets and bedrooms are full (US$5 per person).

Near the Juniper Forest (in the southern part of the park, about 30km from Chelinda by winding park track) is a small cabin with one room containing four beds and basic furniture (US$4 per person), but this may be removed as part of the rehabilitation plan. A caretaker lives nearby.

Accommodation is also available at the *Zambian Resthouse*, in Zambian territory, to the left of the track from Thazima Gate to Chelinda, about 45km from the gate. There are no border formalities. The resthouse is well maintained, with bedrooms (sleeping about 10 people in total), a lounge, and a well equipped kitchen. A caretaker and cook are on duty all the time, and a notice board has good information on short walking routes in the area. To hire the whole resthouse costs US$100 per night; otherwise it costs US$15 per person. Camping may also be allowed. You may also have to pay Zambian national park fees, which are US$5 per person. You can turn up on spec; if nobody else has reserved the resthouse, you can stay. If you would like to make a reservation, in Malawi contact Central African Wilderness Safaris (listed under Organised Treks & Tours).

GETTING THERE & AWAY

The nearest large town to Nyika is Mzuzu, about 400km north of Lilongwe. From Mzuzu, you need to get to Rumphi, then to the main park entrance at Thazima Gate (pronounced Tazima, and often spelt this way). From the gate to Chelinda Camp it is another 55km through the park.

The other park entrance is Kaperekezi Gate, on the west side of the park, passed if you're travelling to/from Chitipa and Nthalire, but rarely used by visitors. You cannot reach Chelinda by road from Livingstonia or any other town on the east side of the plateau, despite a road being indicated on some old maps.

Bus

There's a daily bus in each direction between Mzuzu and Chitipa, via Rumphi and the park gates at Thazima and Kaperekezi, with a loop up to Chelinda. If the bus doesn't go to Chelinda, ask the driver to drop you at the Zambian Resthouse Junction, from where you can walk or hitch the 12km to Chelinda. This is against park regulations, as no entry to the park is allowed unless you are in a vehicle, although local staff do it all the time and nobody seems to mind. This bus only runs in the dry season when the road is in good condition, and even then, it can still be a problem getting on at Rumphi as it's often full by the time it reaches here. It's best to get on it in Mzuzu. When the road to Chelinda is improved (as planned) the bus will run all year.

If you miss the Chelinda bus, from Rumphi there's a bus most days for Katumbi, passing Nyika Junction (44km from Rumphi), from where it's a 10km walk or hitch to Thazima Gate. You can wait at the gate for a lift to Chelinda or Zambian Resthouse Junction (from where you can walk or hitch the rest of the way to Chelinda).

It is also possible to reach Chelinda by bus from the north, from Chitipa via Nthalire and Kaperekezi Gate and Zambian Resthouse Junction, from where you follow the directions given earlier.

The Wilderness Trails

An outline of each trail is included here. Due to the nature of the trails on Nyika (see Route Standard & Days Required), detailed route descriptions are not possible. They are also unnecessary, as you will be accompanied at all times by a scout. The number of days required are counted from, and back to, the trail head, usually a point on one of the park tracks towards the outer edge of the park. If you're walking from Chelinda Camp to the trail head, and back again after the trek, add at least one extra day either side. The park has numbered each trail.

Trail 1: Mwanda Peak
1 day

On the south-western edge of the park, Mwanda Mountain sits astride the Malawi-Zambia border. The route starts on the main drivable track between Chelinda Camp and Thazima Gate, next to a signpost marking the park boundary. The route crosses grassland then follows the northern ridge of the mountain to reach the summit (2148m). The faint trail along the ridge is crossed by several clear trails used by local villagers and poachers walking between Zambia and Malawi. From the summit you get some good views to the south over towards Vwaza Marsh and northwards to the Viphama Hills in Zambia. Return by the same route. Allow six to eight hours for the round trip.

Trail 2: Nthakati Peak
2-3 days

Nthakati Peak (2501m) is one of the highest peaks in the park, overlooking the eastern edge of the Nyika Plateau. The trail starts at an area called Ndenbera on the drivable track between Chelinda Peak and Kasaramba Peak and follows the edge of the escarpment to camp beside the Phata Stream below Nthakati Peak. On the second day you go up Nthakati Peak. From there you either head back towards the Chelinda-Kasaramba track, or continue north-west down to the Dembo Valley, camping another night there, before heading back to Chelinda.

Trail 3: Nkonjera Peak
1-3 days

Nkonjera is a large, flat-topped mountain on the southern boundary of the park (also spelt Nkhonjera and Nkonjela). The route starts at the end of the drivable track that heads

directly south from Chelinda, where another track branches off right to Fingira Rock. From here, you pass the Ulera Patrol Hut and continue to Nkonjera Peak (2208m), which takes about five to six hours. You can do this in one day with an early start, although it's better to take two days, camping on the mountain. You can make it into a good three-day trip by diverting to Fingira Rock, a large conical peak rising some 60m above the surrounding woodland. At its base is a shallow cave containing some very faint paintings, presumed to be pre-Bantu.

Trail 4: Fishing Trail

As the name implies, this trail is not designed for trekkers. It follows the upper stretches of the North Rumphi River for a fairly short distance, and does not take in any peaks. It can be added on to Trail 2, as the Dembo River flows into the North Rumphi.

Trail 5: Jalawe Peak & Nganda Peak
4-5 days

This is a long trek in the northern part of the park, mainly through wooded hills below the main plateau. The route starts near Jalawe Peak, at the end of the most northerly drivable track in the park, and descends to the Chipome Valley, the first night's camp. A second day is spent exploring the valley, returning to the same camp, although you can keep going if you prefer. On the third and fourth days you follow the Chipome and the Lower Mondwe rivers upstream, back up towards the plateau. You reach the summit of Nganda Peak, the highest point on Nyika, on the last day.

Trail 6: Jalawe, Kawozia and Mpanda Peaks
5-6 days

This route is the most strenuous but most rewarding of all the wilderness trails on Nyika and should be attempted only by fit and experienced trekkers. It is possible only in the dry season as it involves crossing several rivers which are too deep to ford during the rains. The route starts near Jalawe Peak, in the northern part of the park, then

MALAWI

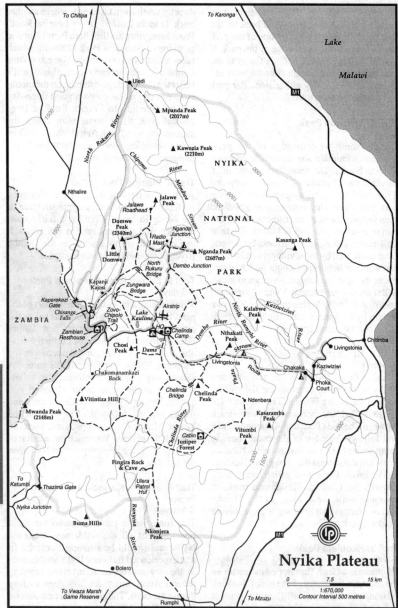

Nyika Plateau

0   7.5   15 km

1:1,670,000
Contour Interval 500 metres

drops into the Chipome Valley, where you camp for one or two nights, before rising to the summit of Kawozia Peak (2210m). From here you follow a spectacular broad ridge, dropping to camp beside one of the small streams that flow off either side, to reach the twin summits of Mpanda Peak (2017m). This mountain offers one of the most impressive views in Malawi. From here you can see east to Lake Malawi, north to the mountains of Tanzania and west to Zambia, while the broad mass of the Nyika Plateau lies to the south. Near Mpanda are the ruins of Bleak House, originally built as an outstation by the missionaries of Livingstonia in the early 1900s. From Mpanda, most trekkers drop to the small village of Uledi, just outside the northernmost corner of the park, and return to Chelinda or Thazima by road via Nthalire. You could walk back the way you came, but this, of course, would double the length of the trek.

The Nyika Highlights Route

Area Nyika National Park (Nyika Plateau)
Distance 88km
Duration 4 days
Start/Finish Chelinda Camp (park HQ)
Highest Point Nganda Peak (2607m)
Nearest large town Mzuzu
Accommodation Camping
Access Bus or car
Summary A fine trek through open grassland, taking in many of Nyika's main attractions. The daily distances are quite long, but there are no major gradients to contend with.

This is not a wilderness trail, like the ones set by the park, as it follows paths and drivable tracks for much of the way, rather than cutting through open country. But a trek on this route takes in some of the main attractions and features of the Nyika Plateau including Lake Kaulime, Zovo-Chipolo Forest, Chisanga Falls, Domwe Peak, the western escarpment and Nganda Peak, the highest point on the plateau. This trek starts and finishes at Chelinda Camp. It can be done in four days, but it could be cut to three by combining Stages 2 and 3 to make a very long middle day, but the other stages are quite long anyway.

Stage 1: Chelinda Camp to Chisanga Falls
29km, 7-8 hours
From Chelinda Camp, follow the drivable tracks uphill, to the left of the main plantation, to reach Lake Kaulime (see boxed text) after 1½ hours. From Kaulime, follow the track towards Thazima Gate. After an hour or so, there's a shortcut on the right, which drops down into a valley and then up the other side, cutting off a big loop in the track. Local people carrying maize and other goods between Chelinda and the villages in Zambia use this path. You meet the track again and after another 1km reach a junction, about three hours from Chelinda. This is the Zambian Resthouse Junction (see Places to Stay).

Turn right, following the track towards Kaperekezi Gate. This road was improved by a regiment of the British Army in the mid-1970s; a stone plinth near the junction has the faint picture of an ant on it, a symbol of the regiment's hard work. Ten minutes from the junction on the right, a small path leads to Zovo-Chipolo Forest, where a small circular trail has been established to show examples of the three main types of vegetation on the plateau: montane grassland, evergreen forest and bog. It takes about half an hour to walk round the trail. A booklet about the trail is sometimes available from Thazima Gate or the office at Chelinda. The word *zovo* means 'elephant' in the local Tumbuka language. One was killed in the forest by a man called Chipolo. Before the lower slopes of the plateau were heavily populated, elephants were more common in these patches of woodland.

The drivable track here is the border between Malawi and Zambia. Almost opposite the path to Zovo-Chipolo, another path

MALAWI

Lake Kaulime

Lake Kaulime is the only natural lake on the Nyika Plateau and the subject of many local stories and beliefs. In the days before Nyika was a park, local people came here to pray for rain or to throw white beads in the lake as a sign of respect for their ancestors. If you listen hard you're supposed to be able to hear the sound of doves calling, or women pounding maize. The lake was thought to be bottomless, and on a misty day it does have a certain air of mystery about it. But it's actually not that deep: you can often see roan antelope wading through it, eating reed shoots. ■

leads to the Zambian Resthouse. Follow this, through Zambian territory, past the resthouse to meet the track again, and follow it for about an hour (your scout will know short-cuts across loops in the main track) until you reach a path on the right going down towards Chisanga Falls. From here are excellent views northwards down the North Rukuru Valley, running along the foot of the western escarpment. Domwe Peak is visible in the distance.

The clear descent path drops steeply through the grassland, through protea bush and into woodland, leading to the top of Chisanga Falls. On the right, next to the river, are a few places where you can pitch a tent. It's another 20 minutes down the path to the viewpoints overlooking the falls.

Stage 2: Chisanga Falls to Domwe Peak
17km, 6-7 hours

From Chisanga Falls go back upstream to meet a small drivable track which you follow north. A bridge is planned across the river here; if it hasn't been built yet, you'll have to wade, or use a temporary log bridge built by local honey-gatherers. Follow the track through an area called Zungwara, the name of a village that used to be here, to reach a big rock called Kapanji Kajosi – a natural viewpoint on the edge of the escarpment, 2½ hours from the falls. (Kapanji Kajosi means 'cave of smoke'; local people used to live in a cave below the rock, but now it's

used only by poachers.) From here, you get some spectacular views over the North Rukuru Valley and across to the hills of Zambia, and along the escarpment edge to the summit of Domwe Peak.

Follow the track parallel to the edge of the escarpment for another hour, then branch off left to follow a faint path that used to be the park boundary before the 1976 extension. You cross two streams, and pass a hill called Little Domwe to your left, to reach the summit of Domwe Peak, 2½ hours from Kapanji Kajosi. This is the highest point on the western escarpment (2340m).

The best place to camp is in the valley to the north of Domwe Peak near an old patrol post. It's hard to find, so check that your scout knows where it is before you leave.

Stage 3: Domwe Peak to Lower Mondwe Stream
17km, 5-6 hours;
plus 2-3 hours for Nganda Peak

From Domwe Peak follow the drivable track in an easterly direction. The radio mast by Nganda Junction can be seen on the horizon. You can cut off a big loop in the track by crossing one of the North Rukuru headwaters. When you meet the track again, continue towards the radio mast. Near the mast (about three hours from Domwe), before going straight for Nganda, you can find a place to camp and go up the peak without carrying your gear (although it may be misty, in which case pitch camp anyway and go up next morning). There's a place to camp down on the right, just before you reach the junction, but the water isn't very clean. It's better to continue, past the mast and along the track towards Nganda Peak. Down on the left are some patches of woodland, next to the source of the Lower Mondwe Stream, where you can pitch a tent. Some patches are a bit boggy, but they get drier as you go downstream.

From your camp site, regain the drivable track which runs along the ridge between the radio mast and Nganda Peak. The track turns into a path by two wooden posts, and from there it's about 45 minutes to the summit. Nganda Peak (2607m) is the highest point on the Nyika Plateau. From the summit, the rolling expanse of the plateau spreads towards the south, and to the north-east you can often see the glistening waters of Lake Malawi.

Sidetrack: Jalawe Peak

Instead of going straight from Domwe Peak to Nganda, you can follow tracks to Jalawe Peak, which overlooks the steep escarpment of the Chipome Valley, separating the main part of the plateau from its northerly outliers.

When you reach the Jalawe roadhead, about two hours walk from Domwe, follow the path that drops down to cross a flat area of grass before rising again up the side of Jalawe Peak. From the summit the path continues to a rocky outcrop overlooking the floor of the Chipome Valley, some 1000m below. With the help of binoculars, you used to be able to spot elephant down here, but in several visits over the last seven years we've never seen any. (It's always worth a try though, and if poaching is controlled as part of the new park rehabilitation scheme, you may have more luck than us.)

Beyond the valley, the land rises steeply again to the peak of Kawozia, and beyond to the twin peaks of Mpanda, the northernmost summit in the park. From Jalawe Peak retrace to the track and continue to Nganda Junction, another three hours.

This sidetrack adds five hours to Stage 3, so if you're going to include it, save the ascent of Nganda Peak until the morning of Stage 4.

From Jalawe it's also possible to descend into the Chipome Valley and follow the Mondwe River or elephant trails around the base of the escarpment to the foot of Nganda Peak and go up to the summit from there. This is a tough walk, taking about five to seven hours, and you have to be determined – once you've started there are no shortcuts!

Stage 4: Lower Mondwe Stream to Chelinda Camp

25km, 8-10 hours, via Nganda Peak; or 20km, 6-7 hours, direct

If you're doing Nganda this morning, follow the directions at the end of Stage 3. Alternatively, if you're going straight back to Chelinda

Camp, from your camp site retrace to the ridge and then cut across the top of the North Rumphi Valley to meet the drivable track aiming south. Follow this all the way back to the airfield on the north side of the Chelinda plantation, (five to six hours from the Lower Mondwe Stream camp site). Go across the grassy airstrip and through the plantation back to Chelinda Camp (another hour).

The Livingstonia Route

> **Area** Nyika National Park (Nyika Plateau)
> **Distance** 46km or 71km
> **Duration** 3 or 4 days
> **Start** Chelinda Camp (park HQ)
> **Finish** Livingstonia
> **Nearest large town** Mzuzu
> **Accommodation** Camping (Resthouse at Livingstonia)
> **Access** Bus or car
> **Summary** An excellent trek, following tracks and paths across grassland, then dropping dramatically through wooded escarpments, to leave the park and reach the mission centre of Livingstonia, near Lake Malawi. Daily distances are not long and most of the route is downhill.

This route is not a wilderness trail, as it follows tracks and paths all the way, but it goes through some of the most beautiful grassland areas on Nyika and drops dramatically down the wooded escarpment on the eastern edge of the plateau. Only half of the trek is inside the park boundary; the second section passes through villages and fields, but this provides an interesting contrast to the untouched landscape of the park.

The trek goes from Chelinda Camp to the mission town of Livingstonia, via the villages of Chakaka and Phoka Court, and takes three days, with the possibility of a fourth from Livingstonia down to the main road between Karonga and Mzuzu that runs beside the lake. If you're short of time, and feeling fit, the first two stages can be done in one day, but it's long and hard.

MALAWI

If you do this route you have to pay your scout and porters extra to cover the costs of transport and accommodation on their way back to the park (see the Guides & Porters section). Even if they decide to keep the money and walk back, it's fair enough: going back up onto the plateau is one hell of a trek! An alternative if you want to save expense is to hire a guide for the first part of this route, to the top of the escarpment, then go alone for the second part.

This route cannot be done in reverse. You are not allowed to enter the park on foot unless accompanied by a scout, which can only be arranged at Chelinda.

Stage 1: Chelinda Camp to Phata Stream
18km, 6-7 hours
From Chelinda Camp, go to the east side of the Chelinda River and follow the track eastward, then south towards Chelinda Peak. There's a shortcut footpath that keeps nearer the river. To your right you can see the Chelinda dams. You meet a drivable track, follow it briefly, then take another path on its north side. About four hours from Chelinda you cross the track to Nthakati Peak a few times, then drop to cross a tributary of the Phata (pronounced Pata) Stream, reached after another 1½ hours. From there, go over a rise, then down to reach the main Phata Stream, crossed by a very basic log bridge. There's a good place for camping next to the river, with the main peak of Nthakati to the north-west overlooking the site.

Stage 2: Phata Stream to Chakaka
12km, 5-6 hours
From Phata Stream follow the path up the east side of the valley for about 1½ hours to reach the crest of a large broad ridge. For the first time on this trek you can see the edge of the escarpment, with Livingstonia on top of its own small plateau in the middle distance, and the blue haze of Lake Malawi beyond. The path runs along the crest of the ridge, roughly south-east, following the line of the park boundary before the 1976 expansion.

Turn off the main ridge onto the secondary ridge. Far below in the valley you can see a patchwork of fields, stopping at the edge of the forest which marks the park boundary today. Continue following the ridge down, through forest, bush and long grass, as the ridge turns to a narrow spur with the steep Mpondo and Thithi valleys on either side. You leave the park, and pass huts and small fields. This is the outskirts of Chakaka. Continue down steeply, to finally reach a bridge near the junction of the Mpondo and Thithi rivers. On the other side of the bridge is a small coffee-drying compound. The manager is friendly and will let you camp here.

Stage 3: Chakaka to Livingstonia
16km, 5-6 hours
Follow the small dirt road which leaves the coffee compound and goes down the valley. To your left is the large North Rumphi River. Keep going for about two to three hours to reach the main dirt road between Livingstonia and Rumphi, at a small village called Phoka Court.

This used to be the main road through the north of Malawi between Mzuzu and Karonga. It's not used much now, as the new lake shore road runs on the other side of Livingstonia. Phoka is the name of the people in this area, and there was a local chief's court here in colonial times. Today there's a small resthouse, a market and a few shops. A bus from Rumphi arrives in Phoka Court most afternoons, 'sleeps' there, and returns to Rumphi early next morning. In dry weather it continues to Livingstonia, but in the rainy season the bus doesn't even reach Phoka Court.

From Phoka Court, follow the main dirt road uphill, across the North Rumphi River then the Kaziwiziwi River, and past the old road to the coal mine to reach some steep switchbacks. (The mine is now linked to the new main road.) You can follow the road all the way to Livingstonia, although your scout will probably know some shortcuts through fields and across one last valley to reach the edge of the town near the secondary school. Follow the neat dirt road past the school and church to reach the Stone House, a museum and small guesthouse. You can buy tea here, and this is where you'll pay off your scout.

Places to Stay in Livingstonia There are two places to stay: the *Stone House*, built in 1903 and used by Dr Laws, the leading missionary, for 25 years, where comfortable bedrooms, complete with Victorian furniture, cost US$2.50 per person; and the *Resthouse*, where things are a little more spartan, for US$2. At both places you can camp for US$1.50. Straightforward but filling meals are available at the Stone House and the Resthouse for around US$2, or you can use the kitchen to prepare your own food at both places. Views are good from the Stone House, but better from the Resthouse; you can see down to Lake Malawi, and the beautiful curved spit of land on the north side of the bay that appears in the picture in the church window.

Some enterprising locals have plans to open private resthouses near the mission area. Nothing was finished (or even started) when we passed through, but it might be

worth asking around when you're there to see if anything has materialised. There are also a couple of camp sites on the road down the escarpment towards the lake shore road. One of the nicest is at *Falls Grocery*, on the road opposite the path to Manchewe Falls, where the friendly shopkeeper, Mr Edwin, lets you pitch a tent for US$0.60. There is a tumbledown toilet and water comes from the stream nearby. The shop however is very well stocked with food and drink (including beer).

If you need to re-supply after your trek, in Livingstonia town there are a few shops selling a fairly good range of basic groceries. There's also a market on the road between the Resthouse and the hospital.

Stage 4: Livingstonia to Chitimba
25km, or 20km with shortcuts, 4-5 hours
From the crossroads near the Resthouse at the end of the main street, continue downhill

---

Livingstonia
The history of Livingstonia is described briefly in the introductory section of this chapter. It's a fascinating place; like a small Scottish town teleported into the heart of Africa, complete with red-brick shops, post office, church and clock tower. You might want to spend two nights here after your trek from Nyika, before continuing towards the lake.

Even if you want to push on the next day, it's well worth spending a few hours wandering around the town. The **museum** at the Stone House has a good collection of exhibits telling the story of early European exploration and missionary work in Malawi. Many items that once belonged to Dr David Livingstone and his fellow missionaries are still here, including an amazing collection of magic lantern slides.

There's a **secondary school**, with a facade just like any other Victorian English grammar school, and an impressive **church**, built in Scottish style with a beautiful stained glass window of David Livingstone and his two companions Juma and Guze (sometimes spelt Suzi), with his sextant and medicine chest, and Lake Malawi in the background.

Other places of interest include the **old post office** and **clock tower** (now a small bookshop), the nearby **industrial block**, built in the early 1900s as a training centre, now a technical college, and a huge **bell** on a pedestal that is now a memorial to the Laws family. Down the road from here is the **David Gordon Memorial Hospital**, once the biggest hospital in Central Africa, and the **stone cairn** that marks the place where Dr Laws, the founder of Livingstonia, and his African companion Uriah Chirwa camped in 1894 when they reached this area and decided to build the mission. Also nearby is **House Number 1**, the original home of Dr Laws before he moved into the Stone House.

Your final call might be Khondowe Craft Shop, which sells carvings and clothing made by local people. (Khondowe was the original name of this area, before it was changed to Livingstonia.)

You can also visit the Manchewe Falls, about 5km from the town. This is a spectacular waterfall, about 50m high, with a cave behind it where local people used to hide from slave-traders. There are several paths leading to the falls and several young boys hanging around the Resthouse who will show you the way for a few kwacha. Allow an hour going down and 1½ hours back up. Alternatively, if you're walking to Chitimba, you can go via the falls on the way down. ■

> **Warning**
> Take care on the descent to Chitimba: we heard from a traveller who unfortunately was mugged walking down this road. This may have been an isolated incident – probably hundreds of visitors walk up and down every year – but it may be worth checking the latest situation before you set off, or taking a local guide. ∎

then turn right to meet a larger dirt road that comes from the other side of the town. Then you just keep going down and down and down. This is the notorious Livingstonia Escarpment road. The road goes round some pretty sharp bends, and the last 20 are real hairpins. You know there are 20, because each one is numbered. From Livingstonia town down to the start of the steep section, there are some shortcuts through the fields: the easiest thing to do is to ask one of the local boys to show you the way, and pay him a small fee. Paths cut across some of the lower bends too, but many of these are so steep they're hardly any quicker than the road and a lot harder on the legs. From the bottom of the escarpment it's less than 1km to the village of Chitimba and the junction with the main (tar) lake shore road running between Karonga and Mzuzu.

Transport from Livingstonia If you don't want to walk down the escarpment, you have a couple of options. In the dry season, there's a bus most days to Rumphi, running along the old road through Phoka Court. If it's not running all the way to Livingstonia, you might have to walk to Phoka Court and catch it from there. Otherwise you can look for transport going down the escarpment towards the lake. There's no bus, but local shop owners often go to Mzuzu for supplies and will give lifts. Ask one of the young boys lurking near the Resthouse or the Stone House to look around for you – they normally know what's going on. A lift in a pick-up costs about US$1. If there's nothing going when you want it, a private hire to the foot of the escarpment will cost about US$10.

Chitimba At Chitimba, you can stay at the *Florence Bay Resthouse* or the *Nyabweka Restaurant & Resthouse*, both basic and friendly, charging US$0.50 per night. Or head for *Des's Chitimba Beach Campsite*, popular with overland trucks and independent travellers, a few hundred metres east of the main road, about 1km north of the Livingstonia turn-off. There are chalets for US$3, camping for US$1.50, and a lively bar right on the beach. Meals cost around US$3.

If you want to keep moving, the bus stop is at the junction. There are three buses a day each way between Karonga and Mzuzu.

Other Routes on Nyika

Due to the nature of the trekking on Nyika, there's an almost endless selection of routes that you can plan yourself, using the map, the knowledge of the game scouts, and a sense of adventure. The national park authorities are keen to promote walking and trekking in the park. You can discuss your ideas with the chief game scout, Manfred Kmwenda; he's been working here for many years and is very knowledgeable about trails and other walking options around the park. He may be available to guide you himself, but if he's not free he will arrange another scout suitable for the type of route you want to do. Below are a few more routes that have been suggested by the park staff and other trekkers.

CHAKOMANAMKAZI ROCK TO FINGIRA ROCK

This route traverses the lower wooded hills of the south-western part of the park. Starting from Chakomanamkazi Rock, to the south of the Zambian Resthouse, follow a track south-westerly, then aim south to Vitintiza Hill and follow the Runyina River southwards, camping on its eastern bank, before crossing a major ridge and tributary of the Runyina to reach the huge rocky cone of Fingira Rock. Allow three days for this section. To reach Chakomanamkazi from Chelinda, take the drivable tracks via Lake

DAVID ELSE

DAVID ELSE

DAVID ELSE

Top: Strolling across the Nyika Plateau's trackless rolling grassland
Left: On the shores of Lake Malawi at Cape Maclear
Right: Pleasant walking below Mwanda Peak on the Nyika Plateau, Malawi

DAVID ELSE

DAVID ELSE

Spectacular scenery in the Simien Mountains, Ethiopia. Overlooking the surrounding plains and peaks from the northern escarpment near Imet Gogo (top) and the sheer drops and stunning views at the Geech Abyss (bottom).

Kaulime and the Zambian Resthouse Junction, as described in the Nyika Highlights Route (one day), or cut straight across from Kaulime, via Chosi Peak (one long day). From Fingira back to Chelinda by track is almost 30km, another long day.

FINGIRA ROCK TO THAZIMA GATE

Starting from Fingira Rock, you can follow the last section of the route described in the previous paragraph in reverse to reach the Runyina River, then continue westwards to meet the main drivable track just north of Thazima Gate. Allow one to two days.

NKONJERA PEAK TO RUMPHI TOWN

If you do Wilderness Trail 3, described earlier, after reaching Nkonjera Peak, instead of going back north towards Chelinda, you can continue heading south from the summit

and follow old hunters' paths to Rumphi town. This is another day's walk, and it takes you outside the park boundary. This route cannot legally be done in reverse, as you are not allowed to walk into the park without a game scout.

CHELINDA CAMP TO JUNIPER FOREST

From Chelinda Camp follow the Chelinda River southwards, keeping to the valley sides to avoid boggy sections. You meet the park track which crosses the Chelinda River by Chelinda Bridge, below a small mountain called, strangely enough, Chelinda Peak. It's worth going up to the top: this is one of the few peaks in the centre of the plateau with exposed rock at its summit. From there you can continue down to the Juniper Forest. Allow one long day for this, or two shorter days.

Other Trekking Areas in Malawi

The Zomba Plateau

The steep-sided Zomba Plateau, with sheer escarpments rising more than 1000m above the plain, overlooks the town of Zomba, the former capital of Malawi and still the site of the country's parliament and main university. The Zomba Plateau cannot be called a wilderness in the same way as Mulanje and Nyika can, but it does have several narrow ridges along the edge of the escarpment with dramatic views over the plains below, plus a network of paths and tracks in the centre of the plateau through silent pine forests and patches of indigenous woodland, passing waterfalls and small lakes. You could easily spend three or four days doing some fairly easy hiking here, between more strenuous treks on Mulanje and Nyika.

As well as being smaller, Zomba differs from Mulanje in other ways: Mulanje is made up of several separate basins, whereas

Zomba is composed of only two, divided by the Domasi Valley; you can't go up Mulanje by car (which keeps it remote and untouched); but Zomba has roads to the top, and much of the southern section of the plateau has been planted with pines. Zomba also has a hotel, a camp site and several picnic places to cater for visitors (mainly local residents who come up at the weekend), plus a permanent population of forestry workers. Several large houses, set in private grounds, have also been built along the south-eastern edge of the plateau.

You can walk on Zomba at any time, but the best weather is during the dry period from May to October. After the rains, in May and June, the wild undergrowth is difficult to pass through and paths can be indistinct. As the grass and bushes dry out, and the risk of fire becomes more serious, firebreaks on the plateau are cleared, and the paths, which often follow the firebreaks, are easier to find.

The Zomba Plateau is a forest reserve. A lot of the southern part of the plateau has

MALAWI

been planted with pine, but the northern part (north of the Domasi Valley) has been set aside as a wilderness area. There are no tracks or paths in this area and visitors are not encouraged to walk here.

On the southern part of the plateau, the walking routes follow paths and tracks. Some visitors drive around the plateau, but you're unlikely to see more than a few cars, especially on weekdays. All the track junctions on Zomba are numbered. These numbers are indicated on signboards at each junction, and are referred to in this section by the prefix J.

Maps & Guidebooks
The Zomba Plateau is covered by the government survey 1:50,000 map sheet 1535/A4 *(Zomba)*, which shows most paths and drivable tracks on the plateau, although some new tracks have been constructed since the map was published. Much more useful is *A Guide to Zomba Plateau*, a single sheet map with information on the back, including several suggested hiking routes, produced by the Wildlife Society in 1990, available in Blantyre and at the Ku Chawe Inn (see Places to Stay on the Zomba Plateau), for around US$1.50.

A small pamphlet called *Zomba Mountain, A Walkers' Guide* may be available for sale in the reception of the Ku Chawe Inn. This was written in 1975, and much has changed since then, but it contains many route descriptions, plus some useful background information.

Supplies
Zomba town has several supermarkets and a big, well-stocked market. There is no shop or market on the plateau. Drinks, snacks and meals are available at the hotel (see Places to Stay on the Zomba Plateau). Local children sell fruit, vegetables, breadcakes, and some other basic foods, on the roadside between the hotel and the camp site.

Places to Stay
Zomba Town Cheapest is the *Council Resthouse* opposite the bus station; the rooms are

clean but the toilet block is disgusting. Singles/doubles cost US$2/3 (or US$5 for en suite) and there may be some dorm beds for US$0.50. There's a noisy bar and good restaurant, with several other cheap eating houses nearby. The manager will store gear if you want to travel light up to the plateau.

Much better is the nearby *Ndindeye Motel*, down a dirt road past the brightly painted Zomba Tavern. Large clean rooms cost US$3/6 or US$7/13 for en suite with breakfast. The restaurant does meals from US$2.

Up the price scale, the *Government Hostel* is a fairly smart hotel dating from colonial times, which is used by ministers when parliament is in session and open to the public the rest of the time. En suite rooms cost US$50/60 with breakfast and satellite TV. Main dishes in the restaurant are around US$3 to US$5, and the set menu is US$10.

On the Zomba Plateau Most trekkers head for the pleasant *Forest Campsite*, set among large pine trees, just beyond the top of the road up the plateau. Camping costs US$1 and there are toilets and wood-fired hot showers.

Your other main option is the *Ku Chawe Inn* (☎ 522342; fax 522509), a top-quality hotel built on the edge of the escarpment with excellent views over the surrounding plains. The old hotel unfortunately burnt down a few years ago, and the new place re-opened in 1996. Very smart singles/doubles cost US$104/171. There's a good restaurant and bar, where they keep a fire going on cold nights, and the terraced gardens are particularly pleasant. This hotel is part of the Protea group, so you can book a room through their central reservations if required (☎ 620071).

Alternatively, about 2km from the hotel, accommodation is also available at the home of Lt-Col Burgess (☎ 522143): a comfortable, fully equipped and serviced cottage with two double bedrooms costs US$120 per night.

Access
At the foot of the southern slopes of the Zomba Plateau is the large town of Zomba,

linked to Blantyre and Lilongwe by good tar roads. From Zomba town a tar road leads through the outskirts, past the State House and then steeply up the escarpment to the top of the plateau (about 10km). After the last junction, the road is one-way only, and called the Up Road. The Down Road descends further to the east.

There's no bus up to the plateau, so you'll have to take a taxi for US$10.

Alternatively, you can walk up the Up Road, which has excellent views (often missed by drivers, who have to concentrate on the narrow turns), or you can try hitching.

The best way is to walk up the Potato Path, which goes straight up the escarpment.

The Potato Path This is a footpath linking the Domasi Valley to Zomba town, running straight over the southern half of the Zomba Plateau. The Domasi Valley has fertile soil and a reliable water supply ideal for growing vegetables, which the local people carry to the big market in Zomba town along this path, making it well worn and easy to follow.

The start of the path is signposted at a sharp left-hand bend on the Up Road about 2km from Zomba town. The path climbs steeply, through woodland, crossing a forestry track and the Down Road, to reach the top of the plateau near the hotel. Allow two to three hours for the ascent.

Routes on the Plateau

Once you've reached the top of the plateau, you can base yourself at the hotel or the camp site for a couple of nights and explore the area on the days in between. You can go where you like anywhere south of the Domasi Valley. There's a maze of paths and tracks, but with a compass and a map, you're unlikely to get hopelessly lost. For help with orientation, there's even a model of the plateau in the hut by the hotel.

Williams Falls & Ngondola Village From the hotel or camp site follow drivable tracks to the crossroads at junction three (J3), over a bridge, past a track on the left to the trout farm, past a track on the right (J4) towards

Mandala Falls, and past a track on the left (J5) to the forestry houses. The small but picturesque Williams Falls are down to your left after about an hour. The track curves round to the right, but take the path straight on, over the stream. This is the Potato Path. You'll probably see local people walking along it.

Follow the path up through plantation to meet a track at a junction (J21). The path follows the track again until a left curve, where the path goes straight on, over a small bridge, and meets another track. Turn left onto this track and follow it until, at a right bend, the path forks off left and up over a small hill to rejoin the track on the other side. This track meets the Outer Circular Drive (OCD) at a junction (J10) near several small huts. This is Ngondola village. (Allow about three hours from the camp site.)

At the junction (J10) avoid the small path leading straight on between the huts. Turn right onto the OCD, then fork immediately left to follow a track down through trees to the edge of the Domasi Valley. Here you get a good view of the northern half of the Zomba Plateau (also called the Malosa Plateau). The rolling open grassland of the north contrasts sharply with the pine forests of the south, showing how the whole plateau would have appeared before the plantations were established.

From Ngondola village you can retrace the route to the hotel and camp site or make your own way back by other paths and tracks. The following description is only one of many ways.

From J10 continue east on the OCD. A track from Ngondola village joins from the left. Turn right off the OCD onto a minor track, dropping down through plantation, to meet another track at a junction (not numbered). Turn left onto this track (effectively straight on) and continue downhill to J20 where a track joins from the right. Keep straight on, crossing a small bridge. A track joins from the left, but this is not obvious. Keep straight on, crossing the main Mlunguzi River, to meet the OCD again (J6). Turn right, and follow the OCD past the track on

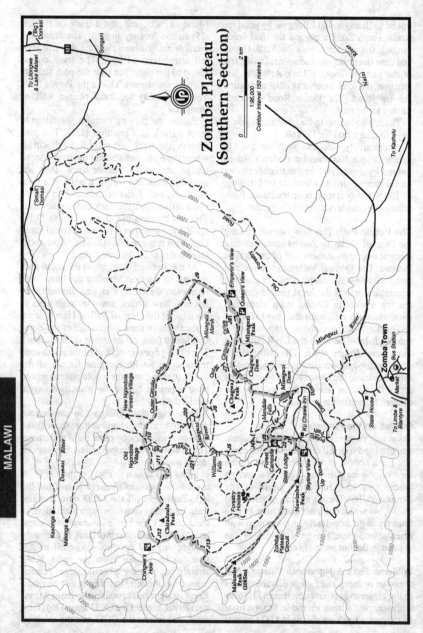

Zomba Plateau
(Southern Section)

2 km

1:95,000

Contour Interval 150 metres

the left that goes up to the summit of Chagwa Peak (an interesting diversion, with excellent views from the top, which takes an extra one to 1½ hours), to reach the Williams Falls on the right. From here retrace the route described earlier from the falls back to the camp site and hotel.

The Zomba Plateau Circuit The Zomba Plateau south of the Domasi Valley takes the form of a large basin, surrounded by a rim of higher peaks and ridges. This basin is the catchment area for the Mlunguzi River, which begins as a marsh on the eastern side of the plateau then flows in an arc across its centre, finally leaving the basin at the lowest point in the rim to drop down the Mlunguzi Gorge to Zomba town.

This route follows the outer rim of the basin, using a combination of paths and tracks, and passes many of Zomba's highlights, including Malumbe Peak (the highest point on Zomba), Chingwe's Hole, Queen's View and the Mlunguzi Dam.

Start near the hut (by the hotel) that has the model of the plateau. Fork immediately left, towards State Lodge, and follow the tar road up to Skyline View (a viewpoint and site of the cableway which used to link the plantations on the plateau with the sawmill outside Zomba town). From Skyline View the ridge up towards Nawimbe Peak, with a firetower near the summit, can be clearly seen. Aim towards this, along a track, passing between huts, to follow a firebreak along the ridge crest. Another firebreak runs to the right of the one on the ridge. Take the firebreak which is easiest to follow, to reach the firetower and the beacon on the summit of Nawimbe Peak. From the firetower you get an excellent view to the north-east over the Zomba Plateau, and to the south down to Zomba town and the surrounding plains, with Mt Mulanje often visible in the distance.

From Nawimbe summit, follow the firebreak along the ridge crest, rocky and overgrown in places, to reach the radio masts on the summit of Malumbe Peak (2085m).

From the summit of Malumbe a track leads down the north-western side of the

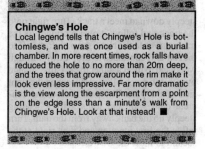

Chingwe's Hole
Local legend tells that Chingwe's Hole is bottomless, and was once used as a burial chamber. In more recent times, rock falls have reduced the hole to no more than 20m deep, and the trees that grow around the rim make it look even less impressive. Far more dramatic is the view along the escarpment from a point on the edge less than a minute's walk from Chingwe's Hole. Look at that instead! ∎

ridge to meet the OCD at J13. (Just before this junction a footpath on the left cuts off a large loop in the track.) Follow the OCD, turning left onto a small track (J12), to reach Chingwe's Hole, about three to four hours from the camp site.

From Chingwe's Hole you leave the dramatic outer edge of the Zomba Plateau and follow the OCD along a low ridge that separates the northern rim of the Mlunguzi Basin from the Domasi Valley. Keep on the track, past J11 to reach J10, where the Potato Path crosses the OCD.

Continue on the OCD, past several minor tracks on the left and right, to reach J9 (two to three hours from Chingwe's Hole), where a track turns off left towards Songani. Keep on the OCD, and take the next track on the left to reach Queen's View (named after Queen Elizabeth, wife of King George VI, who visited Zomba in 1957) and Emperor's View (after Emperor Haile Selassie of Ethiopia, who visited here in 1964) where you get excellent views over Zomba town and the plains on the south-eastern side of the plateau.

From Queen's View follow the track that runs along the escarpment edge, then tends right, away from the edge and into woodland. A track joins from the right, and another branches off to the left (leading to the summit of Mlunguzi Peak). Keep straight on, to reach Chagwa Dam on your right. As the track curves right to cross the dam wall, take the path straight on into a grassy area, heading right and down to cross a stream and enter woodland. A path joins from the right.

Continue through bush and woodland, steeply down to meet a track. Turn right onto the track and follow it over a bridge. As the track curves to the right, the path forks off to the left and continues to drop down through woodland to meet another track. Cross straight over this to reach Mlunguzi Dam on the right side of the path. The path crosses the concrete dam wall and joins a track leading steeply up the bank away from the dam. Turn left at the first junction and then right at the second to meet the Down Road.

Turn right onto the Down Road (ie heading up), and follow it, past a track on the right to Mandala Falls – a few hundred metres off the route, and worth a diversion. (There are plans to enlarge the Mlunguzi Dam, which will push the body of water back upstream almost to the foot of Mandala Falls.) Retrace to the Down Road, continue uphill, to fork left at the next junction, past the school on the left to reach the camp site (two to three hours from Queen's View).

Leaving the Plateau There are several ways off the plateau. You can retrace the Potato Path, or follow the Down Road, where you might get a lift with a car or logging truck.

Alternatively, from J9 on the OCD, take the track towards Songani, and follow old logging tracks and paths all the way down (steeply) to Songani village (about 15km from the OCD) on the main tar road about 15km north-east of Zomba town. From here

---

Lake Malawi

We had a long and fascinating letter from David Wise (UK), who wrote to Lonely Planet about his epic 685km trek along the shore of Lake Malawi. The journey took a total of 41 days (27 days of walking, with time out for rests and a bout of malaria), heading north to south, and was divided into four main sections. Here are some extracts from his journal.

Karonga to Chitimba (110km, 4 days) After crossing the border from Tanzania, I changed money in the bank at Karonga, walked five minutes down the road to the beach, turned south and started my walk. This section was flat and shady and a good way to get started. The people I met were not used to seeing a European on foot, and I was treated with a mixture of curiosity and incredible generosity. On one occasion, a guy in ragged clothing asked why I was walking along the beach. I replied 'Because I want to'. He shook his head and said 'I know you are too proud to tell me, but I think it is because you have no money for the bus. Here, take this and return it when you come back this way'. He offered me a wad of money. He had very little in the material sense yet he was willing to give a lot of money to a stranger with no promise of its return. Of course, I declined. I have never experienced this level of kindness anywhere else in Africa. The atmosphere amongst locals was great until I neared a camp site at Chitimba owned by an ex-overland truck driver, when it became slightly tense. I was told by the locals that they were not allowed on the beach in front of the camp site. I stayed at another place, a few km further along the beach.

Chitimba to Nkhata Bay (120km, 6 days) This section was simply stunning. Imagine scenery that surpasses the Otter Trail in South Africa or the Big Sur in California. Add hospitable local people and no other trekkers and it's a walkers' paradise. If you only have a week to spare, this is the section to do. I spent 18 months trekking in Africa, and I experienced more genuine African culture in this bit of Malawi than in any other place I reached. At Kondowe the main lake shore road goes up the escarpment, but a dirt road continues southwards next to the lake. This soon turns into a narrow path which is the main 'highway' between numerous villages. Their only other contact with the outside world are visits from the lake steamers, but this does mean the shops are relatively well stocked. The route is very hilly in parts and the path is sometimes difficult, winding over steep outcrops and along sheer rock faces, sometimes with wooden ladders to help you cross the vertical bits. There are plenty of little sandy bays and streams entering the lake which are good places to rest. Every summit gives you a view to die for. If the going gets too tough, local boats carry passengers to Usisya and Nkhata Bay. If you don't have time to do this whole section, you could get a boat from Nkhata Bay to Usisya and walk back in three or four days.

you can get public transport back to Zomba town. It may also be possible to branch off right on the way down, to follow some of the old forest tracks that run (more gradually) down the eastern escarpment straight to the northern end of Zomba town.

It is also possible to drop off the northern escarpment into the Domasi Valley. This is the northern section of the Potato Path. From Ngondola village the path aims downhill and divides in several places, leading either to Malonga, the small settlement at the head of the valley, or to any of the others spread along on the valley floor. A large path leads eastwards along the valley floor, and meets a track running close to the river, which reaches the small village of Domasi. The track continues down to Songani village on the main tarred road, about 15km north-east of Zomba town. (Do not confuse 'small' Domasi with 'big' Domasi, a larger village on the east side of the main road.)

Cape Maclear

Cape Maclear has become a travellers' byword for sun, sand, rest and recreation – the closest thing you'll find to an Indian Ocean beach in inland Africa (though the 'ocean' here is a freshwater lake) – and most people passing through Malawi stay here at one time or another. It's a great place to relax after a trek,

Nkhata Bay to Senga Bay (335km, 12 days) This long section is not terribly exciting, and for the first part I kept to the road, as there are swamps along the lake shore. There are several lodges and camps along the shore near Chintheche, all good places to stay. I passed one called Kande Beach, full of overland trucks and people who think they can change the state of third world education by throwing pens and sweets at children. As I walked through the nearby village, when I wouldn't give the kids any money I was pelted with stones and mangoes. The locals I'd met in the remote areas further up the lake wouldn't dream of acting in this way. Is this a coincidence? (I know, I'm a travel snob!)

For the next 50km or so, all the way to Dwangwa, there are a few more hotels. One is Heidi's Hide-away, where I spent six days, recovering from malaria; they have good chalets and do a wicked fry-up breakfast. Between Dwangwa and Nkhotakota, sleeping out is less advisable as there are lots of hippo. The section from here to Senga Bay cannot be recommended – the scenery is uninspiring and I was subjected to endless shouts of 'Give me pen/sweets/money'. One village near Senga Bay called Kaphatenga has a particularly nasty reputation, and some local guys insisted on walking with me until I was clear of the place, so they must have been genuinely concerned for my safety.

Senga Bay to Cape Maclear (120km, 5 days) This final section was really interesting, mainly because the main road is far from the lake shore so the people are extremely friendly. The terrain (impassable in the wet season) is flat: first sand and then dried mud covered in potholes which are in fact hippo prints. There are also several rivers to wade across, some with crocodiles. I went via Chipoka and Melembo and reached Cape Maclear, after skirting inland from the mountains on the main peninsula.

Some general points Don't expect privacy: people will offer to guide you, you'll be surrounded by curious kids, and everyone will want to know where you're going. I never carried any food, as every few hours I found a small village store selling biscuits and soft drinks, or a tea room selling basic meals. Outside the main towns I slept on the beach after obtaining permission from local people. I was often invited to sleep in huts or share meals, for which I gave small gifts. In the dry season tents are totally unnecessary and will only serve to isolate you from surrounding communities. I believe this is one of the few places in Africa where such an adventure can be had, due to the general lack of harmful animals and dishonest people, and the abundance of hospitality. Essential items for this trek are lots of small gifts and a massive sense of fun!

David Wise also wrote to tell us about his other intrepid hikes in Tanzania and northern Kenya. We wish him well in his future travels. Any trekkers keen to follow his footsteps along Lake Malawi should read the lines on Cultural Responsibility in the Kipengere Range section at the end of the Tanzania chapter. ■

and as it's about halfway down the country, many travellers stop off here in between visits to Nyika and Mt Mulanje.

Much of the lake shore and peninsula around Cape Maclear, the lake itself and several offshore islands are part of Lake Malawi National Park, one of the few freshwater aquatic parks in Africa. Local boys arrange boat trips, and several of the lodges and resthouses arrange windsurfing, water-skiing, diving and snorkelling.

For walkers, there's a good range of hikes in the hills that form a horseshoe around the plain behind the village (technically called Chembe but usually called Cape Maclear) and beach. You can go alone or arrange a guide, either from the village or at the national park HQ: the park rate is US$10 for a full-day trip. The main path starts by the missionary graves, near the entrance to Golden Sands Holiday Resort (see Places to Stay & Eat). From here the path leads up through woodland, through a small valley to a col formed between a small spur and the main peak of Nkhunguni, the highest and westernmost peak on the Nankumba Peninsula. The col offers great views over the Cape Maclear plain, the lake and surrounding islands. If you go for the summit it's three hours walking up and about the same coming down.

Another interesting place to visit on foot is Mwala Wa Mphini ('the rock of the tribal face scars'), which is just off the main dirt road into Cape Maclear, about 5km from the park HQ. This huge boulder is a national monument. It is covered in lines and patterns which seem to have been gouged out by long-forgotten artists, but are in fact a natural geological formation.

If you want a longer walk, a small lakeside path leads south-west from Otter Point, through woodland above the shore, for about 4km to a small fishing village called Msaka (which has a small bar/shop serving cold drinks). From here a track leads inland (west) to meet the main dirt road between Cape Maclear and Monkey Bay. Turn left and head back towards Cape Maclear, passing Mwala Wa Mphini on the way. The whole circuit is about 16km and takes four to five hours.

Places to Stay & Eat

The long-running *Stevens' Resthouse* used to one of *the* places to stay on the backpackers' Cape to Cairo route, but there's stiff competition these days and it's lost some of its once legendary atmosphere. Clean singles/doubles are US$1/2 (US$3 for en suite). Breakfast is US$0.50, and other meals US$1.50 to US$2. The bar on the beach is popular with travellers, especially at sunset.

Other places include the *Top Quiet Resthouse*, with simple clean rooms around US$1 per person and meals for US$2 to US$3. Further along the beach is *The Ritz*, with camping for US$0.60. Next is *The Gap*, where camping is US$0.60 and simple rooms are US$1. Snacks start at US$1, and meals are US$2 to US$3.

In the village, you can get cold drinks, bread, tinned foods and groceries at *Mr Banda's Store*. Nearby is *Chip's Bar* which serves, naturally, deep-fried potato pieces plus other takeaway snacks at budget prices.

At the southern end of the beach *Golden Sands Holiday Camp* has camping and basic chalets for US$3 per person and en suite rondavels for US$5 per person. This is also the national park HQ, so you have to pay park fees to stay here, but the beach is cleaner and the atmosphere quieter than at some other places in Cape Maclear. Watch out for the monkeys – they'll run off with anything edible! At the other end of Cape Maclear beach is *Chembe Lodge*, up a few grades in quality and style, with permanent walk-in tents under thatch shelters, set in beautiful gardens, from US$22/25 for singles/doubles, including breakfast. Other meals cost US$3.50 to US$5, and there's a very nice bar.

Getting There & Away

When the dirt road between Monkey Bay and Cape Maclear is in good condition there's a Stagecoach bus, once a day in each direction, between Cape Maclear and Blantyre (via Mangochi). The fare is US$5. The Monkey Bay to Cape Maclear section is US$0.50. Alternatively the Stevens' truck (see Places to Stay & Eat) does the run a couple of times a day for US$1 per person.

Ethiopia

This section was mostly written by James Grey and Richard Bendy, with additional contributions from Peter Bennett and Miles Roddis.

Ethiopia is sometimes known as 'Africa's largest mountain range'. A vast plateau called simply the Ethiopian Highlands covers most of the country, stretching 1500km north to south and 700km west to east. Much of the land is at an altitude of over 2000m, with several significant parts over 3000m, while at 4543m Ras Deshen is the country's highest peak and the fifth-highest summit in Africa after Kilimanjaro, Mt Kenya, the Rwenzoris and Mt Meru. (The height of Ras Deshen is usually given as 4543m and Mt Meru as 4566m but as the measurements on both peaks could be several metres out, Deshen's sometime claim to be the fourth-highest peak is a matter for hot debate.)

Much of the Ethiopian Highlands remains unexplored and seldom visited by tourists. There is very little in the way of established trekking routes; however, Ras Deshen and the surrounding Simien Mountains in northern Ethiopia can be easily reached and this is an excellent trekking area. Other areas where walking is possible include the Bale Mountains, south-east of Addis Ababa.

Although Ethiopia is generally regarded as being outside East Africa, we have included a Simien Mountains section in this book because it is a fascinating area and there is little information available elsewhere. The material on Ethiopia itself is necessarily brief in this book, so you may need another guide for wider travels, but the details here will be enough to get you to (and through) the trek.

Facts about the Country

GEOGRAPHY

Ethiopia is a country dominated by mountains. Over thousands of years, the highland

DAVID ELSE

Ethiopia – Trekking Highlights
The vast Ethiopian Highlands cover much of this fascinating country, only recently reopened to visitors after decades of civil strife. The region remains largely unexplored and is seldom reached by trekkers. The main goal of those who do come here is a trek to **Ras Deshen** – Africa's fifth-highest summit – through the spectacular **Simien Mountains**.

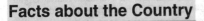

plateau has been cut by numerous rivers to form valleys, gorges, escarpments and mountains. Today the rivers are still flowing, so another of Ethiopia's evocative titles is the 'Water Tower of Eastern Africa'. The most notable of these rivers is the Blue Nile which flows from Lake Tana in the north-west into Sudan and eventually Egypt. In the south, the River Omo flows into Kenya's Lake Turkana.

Below the mountains, landscapes include moorland, savanna, forest and desert. Ethiopia also has the lowest point on the earth's surface: the Danakil Depression, a sub-sea-level point in the Great Rift Valley (for a fuller description of the Great Rift Valley see the Geography section in the Facts about the Region chapter at the beginning of this book) where it cuts a dramatic north-south line through the heart of the country, forming a chain of lakes between Addis Ababa and the Kenyan border.

CLIMATE

As with other countries in this part of Africa, most of Ethiopia has a climate dominated by wet and dry seasons. The main rainy period is June to September, although rainfall is heaviest in July and August. The dry season is October to May, although rain can fall sporadically until March.

In the far south of the country, there are two rainy seasons – March to mid-April and October to November – more in line with the pattern of northern Kenya (see that chapter for more details). In north-eastern parts of the country the rainy season follows the pattern of the rest of the country but rainfall is less reliable and the area is often prone to drought. The infamous famines of the 1980s, brought to world attention by (among others) Kenyan cameraman Mohamed Amin and Irish rock star Bob Geldof, were the results of such droughts, although the scale of the tragedy was exacerbated by the military tactics of the ongoing civil war.

Within these main wet and dry seasons, Ethiopia's climate is as varied as its geography. Snow and hailstorms are not uncommon on the Bale and Simien peaks while maximum daytime temperatures top 50°C in the Danakil. In between these two extremes, the Rift Valley has average maximum daytime temperatures of 25 to 30°C, while it's usually 15 to 20°C in the highlands around 3000m. This makes the climate in the Simien Mountains ideal for trekking: you may be walking in shorts and T-shirt, often with pleasant cooling winds, although you're also likely to need a raincoat and thermals at any time of year. The temperature drops to around 3°C at night most of the year, and usually dips below freezing point (even down to -5°C) during the October to January 'winter' period.

Facts for the Trekker

PLANNING
When to Trek

As outlined in the Climate section above, the best time to visit Ethiopia and trek in the Simien Mountains is during the dry season: October to May. Even in the wet season, however, rain tends to fall in short sharp downpours, leaving several hours of clear, dry conditions for walking.

Maps & Books

Maps of the country include *Ethiopia* (at a scale of 1:2,000,000) produced by the Ethiopian Tourism Commission, available in tourist shops in Addis Ababa, and possibly from good quality map shops overseas. It's perfectly adequate for getting around. Maps of the Simien Mountains are discussed later in this chapter.

Lonely Planet's forthcoming *Ethiopia, Eritrea & Djibouti*, a comprehensive guide for all tastes and budgets, is being researched as this book goes to print, while *Africa on a shoestring* is the all-time classic low-budget guide to the whole continent.

Guide to Ethiopia by Philip Briggs has down-to-earth practical information on cities, towns, historical sites and wildlife areas.

TOURIST OFFICES

Around the world, most Ethiopian embassies have tourist information desks. In some countries tourist information is handled by the Ethiopian Airlines office. In either case, information is usually limited to mainstream material, but some decent (though dated) glossy brochures on national parks and historical sites are sometimes available.

In Ethiopia, the National Tourist Organisation (NTO) has offices in Addis Ababa and some other large towns (including Gonder), where you can also pick up the same glossy brochures, buy souvenirs, postcards and books, and possibly make general inquiries about hotels and public transport.

ETHIOPIA

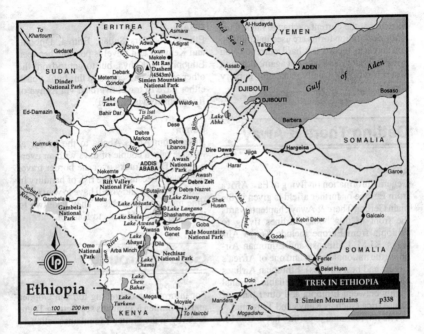

Ethiopia

| 0 | 100 | 200 km |

TREK IN ETHIOPIA

| 1 Simien Mountains | p338 |

VISAS

Everyone except Kenyan nationals needs a visa. You may be asked to produce an onward air ticket or visa for the next country on your itinerary plus proof that you have sufficient funds. Visas are single entry only and cost US$63 each.

Yellow fever and cholera inoculations are mandatory if you arrive from an infected area.

Visa Extensions

Visa extensions (US$20) aren't always readily granted to travellers. They are available from the Immigration Office on Churchill Ave in Addis Ababa. Exit visas are only required for stays of over 30 days.

EMBASSIES
Ethiopian Embassies Abroad

Ethiopia has embassies in the following countries: Djibouti, Egypt, Eritrea, France, Germany, Italy, Kenya, the UK and the USA. There is a consulate in Australia.

Foreign Embassies in Ethiopia

Embassies in Addis Ababa include:

France
    Omedia St (☎ 550066)
Germany
    Afewerk St (☎ 550433)
Kenya
    Fikre Maryam Aba Techan St (☎ 610033)
UK
    Fikre Maryam Aba Techan St (☎ 612354)
USA
    Entoto Ave (☎ 550066)

MONEY

The currency in Ethiopia is the birr. In 1997 the approximate exchange rate was:

| US$1 | = | 7 birr |
| UK£1 | = | 10 birr |

In common with the other chapters in this book, all prices have been quoted in US dollars even though they are payable in local currency at the current exchange rates. Currency declaration forms are used in Ethiopia; you have to record the hard currency you bring in, change and take out again, although customs officials usually make only cursory checks.

Getting There & Away

AIR

General information on flying to East Africa from Europe or further afield is given in the main Getting There & Away chapter towards the front of this book. Airlines flying to Ethiopia from Europe include Kenya Airways, KLM, Lufthansa and Ethiopian Airlines (the national carrier and one of Africa's largest and best airlines). Ethiopian Airlines also operates regular and reliable regional flights between Ethiopia and other parts of East Africa (such as Kenya and Tanzania).

The international departure tax is US$10.

ROAD

Ethiopia borders Sudan, Eritrea, Djibouti and Kenya. Land travel is possible between Ethiopia and Kenya, but to get to/from the other countries described in this book you'll either have to travel overland via Kenya or fly (probably via Nairobi).

Kenya

Buses from Addis Ababa to the border at Moyale take a couple of days with an overnight in Dila. Trucks over the border travel in convoys because of the risk of banditry in northern Kenya and you'll have to wait some time until one assembles. They take two to three days from Moyale to Nairobi.

Getting Around

For information on getting to/from Gonder and the Simien Mountains see Getting There & Away in the Simien Mountains section.

The Simien Mountains

Trekking in the Simien Mountains is a wonderful and unique experience. They are quite unlike any other mountain region in East Africa, with the ever-present contrast between lowland and highland, and numerous examples of indigenous flora and fauna. They also lack the intensive tourism sometimes found elsewhere in East Africa.

GEOGRAPHY

The Simien Mountains (also spelt Simyen, Simen and Semien) are on the north-western edge of the Ethiopian Highlands. This area consists of a plateau-like massif, tilted to the south with an enormous escarpment over 60km long marking its northern edge. The high rainfall feeds strong-flowing rivers which have eroded gullies and ravines into the escarpment, most notably at the Geech Abyss, passed on the trek described in this

section. Beyond the escarpment, the land has been carved into towers, spires, mesas and statue-like formations, creating some of the most impressive views in Africa.

A large section of the Simien Mountains has been incorporated into the Simien National Park, covering 179 sq km at an elevation of 3,300m. The highest point in the range is Ras Deshen (4543m), although this lies outside the park's eastern boundary. The Simien Escarpment is often compared to Colorado's Grand Canyon (well, one side of it) and the park has been declared a World Heritage Site by UNESCO.

Unlike the national parks in Tanzania, Kenya, the Simien range is inhabited. These are Amhara, traditional subsistence farmers, most of whom are Christian (with a Muslim minority) You'll pass several of villages and churches on the trek described in this section.

Simien Flora & Fauna

The Simien range is noted for its unusual species of plants and animals. As on other East African mountains the most fascinating plants are the giant lobelia that grow to extraordinary proportions. Some lobelia reach over 4m high.

Endemic animals (ie those found only in Ethiopia) are: the walia ibex – a large member of the goat family with impressive curved horns; the Simien red fox – similar in appearance to a European fox, but with longer legs and less bushy tail, now correctly named the Ethiopian wolf; and the gelada baboon – quite different to its olive baboon cousins in Kenya and elsewhere, with long golden fur and an exposed patch of red flesh on its chest. Other larger mammals occasionally seen include klipspringer and bushbuck.

Although Ethiopia is a noted bird area, the Simiens do not offer the keen birder a great selection, although trekkers will often see augur buzzard and Verraux's eagle. Most impressive is the huge lammergeier. Kestrels and falcons also soar on the mountain thermals, while swifts and martins are found on the escarpment edge. ■

The impressive lammergeier, with a wing-span of 3m, is noted for its habit of dropping large bones from scavenged carrion onto stony ground, splitting the bone to retrieve the marrow

TREKKING INFORMATION

The Simien landscape consists of a rolling massif cut by several valleys. A trek here can be either short or long, and as arduous as you plan to make it. The availability of mules to ride and carry gear is another factor to consider.

It is important to realise that a trek here is not a true wilderness experience; the mountains are high, the scenery is stunning and the views go on for ever, but the Simiens are home to the local Amhara and you'll inevitably meet people along the way. Some of the overnight camps are near small villages. The trekking routes described in this section often follow paths through the mountains that have been used by local people for centuries to get from their highland homes to the towns and markets on the plains. Meeting the people is another feature which makes a trek here so rewarding.

Costs

Your costs comprise three main parts: national park fees (entrance and obligatory ranger – called a 'scout' locally), guide and mule hire, and your own supplies. All these are detailed separately below.

Route Standard & Days Required

There are several trekking options from a couple of days to a week or more. Wherever you go, walking conditions are straightforward on paths, tracks or small dirt roads, although some days are quite long. Gradients are not too severe but there are a few steep sections, often cunningly built in just when you think the day's walk is over.

The most popular trekking route in the Simiens stays within the national park, on the western side of the massif, taking in the most impressive sections of escarpment with overnights at the national park camps of Sankaber, Chenek and Geech. It's common to stay at Chenek or Geech for two nights, to explore the surrounding area on the day in between, and most trekkers stay at Sankaber on the way up and on the way down, which makes a total of five or six days (four or five nights). A shorter option goes from Sankaber

ETHIOPIA

straight to Chenek and back to Sankaber, involving only four days (three nights).

To reach Ras Deshen you have to continue eastwards and trek outside the park. From Chenek to Ras Deshen and back normally adds another two or three days onto the total. The Ras Deshen section of the trek is harder underfoot, with rough paths and some very steep and long gradients, although doing this part of the trek gives you a better feel of the whole Simien range, plus of course you get to bag the highest peak in Ethiopia.

The number of days on the trek can also be adjusted by using a vehicle to cover the first and last stages, to and from Sankaber. The former mule-track has been widened and is now drivable (although trekkers can avoid this dirt road by following paths near the escarpment edge – which they should do anyway, because the views are much better).

As this book goes to print, local work gangs continue to toil away, slowly pushing the dirt road beyond Sankaber through the highlands towards Chenek. This development is a double-edged sword: on the positive side, it will be a beneficial link for local people in remote villages, and will enable more (non-walking) visitors to reach the park, thereby helping to ensure its survival. Additionally, the road will allow trekkers to reach the remote areas in a shorter time, although fast ascents hinder proper acclimatisation. On the down side, the increased number of visitors and the very presence of a road through the park will make the area less attractive to trekkers, although several parts of the range will always be beyond the reach of vehicles.

Guides & Mules

It is compulsory for trekkers to be accompanied by a guide. These are not park employees, but freelancers based in Gonder and Debark (jumping-off points for the Simiens), who will no doubt approach you at your hotel or as soon as you get off the bus. Guides speak good English, and will organise and oversee the other crew members if you decide to take mules. They will also act as interpreter between you and local people you meet along the way. Guides cost US$7 per day, which includes their park fees. This is set by the park and not negotiable.

It is important to get a good guide. Most of the guys touting for work are friendly, helpful and knowledgeable, and understand what westerners want from a trekking trip. Others are complete wasters, and only want to get you from camp to camp as quickly as possible. The best recommendations always come from other travellers, so it might be worth trying to meet a returning group and hearing their advice. Failing that, check with the staff at the park HQ that the guide you have is genuine. Good guides will have letters and testimonials from previous clients. Those recommended by previous travellers include Jetenet and Victor. In Gonder try Fasil Mesfin or Mulat.

If you are in a large group or just want to take things easy, you can hire a cook (known locally as a 'cooker') in Gonder or Debark for US$3 per day. Once again, recommendations from previous clients are advised.

Porters are not used in the Simiens, but mules are available to carry your gear and to ride if you want. They can be hired at the park HQ in Debark and come with a handler to take care of loading, feeding etc. It's important to make sure your mules are good. You don't have to be a horse expert: ask the handler to sit on the mule (in place of a load) then walk it up and down – if there's a hint of a limp, forget it. Lift up the saddle and blanket – if there are sores or wounds on the mule's back, once again forget it. There are plenty of good mules in Debark, so don't believe anyone who says only bad mules are available. Mules cost between US$1.50 and US$4 per day, and handlers are also US$1.50 to US$4 per day. All fees for mules, guides and other staff can be paid in birr.

You are not expected to provide food or provisions for your guides, scouts, mules or handlers, but their own stuff inevitably runs out part way through the trip and they will, in the most polite way, look to you for sustenance. Make it very clear right from the start that they should bring enough for their own needs, and check that they do.

Be aware that at the end of the trek all your staff will expect a tip. As with anywhere in Africa these are not automatic, but depend on good service. Having said that, you are very unlikely to get bad service. A rule of thumb for tipping is an extra day's pay for every three days of work.

Park Fees & Regulations

To enter the Simien National Park costs foreigners US$10 per person per 48 hours, which compares well with fees for other parks in Africa. Fees are payable at the national park HQ in Debark, and can be paid for in birr.

Park regulations make it obligatory for trekkers to take a scout (park ranger), due to the unlikely event of hostile encounters with wild animals or humans. He will guard you with his trusty old AK47 and ensure all goes well. Scouts will accompany you for your entire trek, even if you go outside the park boundary (eg to Ras Deshen). More often than not scouts do not speak English, but what they lack in conversation they make up for as willing helpers and crew members.

> ### Warning
> As the highland regions are at an average altitude of 3500m, trekkers should not underestimate the effects of altitude (for more details see the Health, Safety & First Aid chapter). Although the Simien camps are well placed to aid acclimatisation, the combination of altitude, fatigue and extremes of temperature can take their toll. Do not try to rush a trek here, and pack your kit as for any big mountain, putting in warm clothes and sleeping bags and plenty of UV protection sunblock. ■

The charge for a scout is US$3 per day.

Fires are permitted only at camp sites. As in other East African national parks an effort should be made by trekkers to avoid using local wood as deforestation is a problem here. Cheap kerosene stoves and plastic cans to carry fuel can be bought in Gonder or Addis. Encouraging guides and scouts to do the same is hard as they have used fires for generations and have no money for fancy stoves or fuel.

No public vehicles are allowed along the dirt road beyond Sankaber.

Ecology & Environment
The face of the Simiens is changing rapidly, unfortunately for the worse, as the local people cut down what trees there are for firewood, plough up montane grassland for planting crops and graze their ever-increasing herds of cattle (which are more profitable than crops). Soil erosion and the destruction of natural habitat are major problems.

Visitors can help preserve the rugged beauty of the Simiens for as long as possible by limiting the use of firewood. All cooking should be done on stoves – it's easier than cooking on wood anyway. If you want a fire to sit around at night, the mule-drivers may be happy to share their fire, or you can make your own small fire by buying wood from local villagers. It is important to buy only dead wood.

Clear up and take all your rubbish out of the park. No one wants the Simiens to develop the toilet paper trails found on some other East African mountains. ■

DAVID ELSE

ETHIOPIA

Maps

The best (and only) map available is the *Simen* (sic) *Mountains Trekking Map*, at a scale of 1:100,000, compiled by the Institute of Geography at the University of Berne in Switzerland and available by mail order direct from them. Availability is random in Ethiopia (it has been seen for sale at the park HQ) but good quality map shops overseas (eg Stanfords in London) sometimes have stock. Another option is the Tactical Pilotage Chart (TPC) – air map – of the Simien region, also available from good map shops.

Supplies

There are no shops inside the trekking area described in this book, although local people will sell eggs, chickens, sheep or goats if required (your guide will negotiate prices, and mule handlers will gladly kill, skin and roast a sheep if they get to share the meal with you). Apart from these items, it's best to bring food with you.

Debark has little to offer the trekker in the way of supplies, though you can buy a limited selection of vegetables and tinned goods in the market. Fresh bread is also available. Gonder has some well-stocked shops and a large market selling most things you're likely to need including pasta, tins of fish, bread, fruit, sugar, tea and coffee. Also available are stoves, lanterns, kerosene (paraffin) and bottles of very reasonable local red wine. Anything 'specialised', such as cheese, packet soups, porridge oats and imported tinned food, should be bought in Addis Ababa (where prices are cheaper).

PLACES TO STAY & EAT

Gonder

Gonder is the nearest large town to the Simien Mountains and the provincial capital, with reasonable facilities including post and telephone office, bank, cinema, fuel station, and a pleasant piazza (a remnant of Ethiopia's brief Italian occupation) with some good pavement cafés serving coffee, pastries and fruit juice cocktails.

Most bottom-end hotels are near the piazza. The *Ethiopia Hotel* and the *Yaiew*

Aker Kassie Hotel have very basic rooms (and communal bucket showers) for about US$1.50 per person. Uphill from the piazza, near the NTO office, are some slightly better places, with fairly clean rooms but still with communal bucket showers, including the *Kassegn Atem Ayhn* charging US$3.50 per room, and the *Yimam* or the *Metasebia* both charging around US$7. Another worth trying is the modern but bland *Misrak Pension* next to the Fogera (see below) with clean pleasant en suite rooms in a garden for US$7/10. Water is unreliable in all budget hotels – hence the bucket showers.

In the mid-range, there are three government hotels. The one with most style is the *Fogera Hotel*, built in the 1930s as the Italian governor's villa, which still has wonderful gardens. Cool, spacious and reasonably clean en suite rooms in the main building or smaller rustic bungalows in the garden cost US$15/20 per single/double (although this can be reduced to about US$10/15 with some friendly bargaining).

More central is the *Qara Hotel* on the piazza with simple rooms at US$12/15 (en suite US$15/18) and good, if basic, meals for around US$4. Another to try is the new *Nile Hotel*, on the piazza, with rooms at US$15/23. In all mid-range places water is sporadic but it is reported to be better at the Nile, which has its own well.

By far the best place to stay in Gonder is the *Goha Hotel* on the hill overlooking the city, a few km from the centre, with wonderful views from the terrace where you can enjoy a basic but good meal or drink – even if you're not staying. Clean, pleasantly decorated en suite rooms cost US$36/48. There's usually water, and the staff are friendly and efficient.

Debark

Debark (also spelt Debarek and Debarq) is a small town, 100km by road north of Gonder. The park HQ is here, where all treks start from. It's also where you arrange scouts, guides and mules.

The place most trekkers stay is the *Simen Hotel*, a block back from the main street, a short walk from the bus stop and market. Basic rooms cost US$3, there's a single bucket shower, and the yard fills with truck drivers (and their trucks) at night. However, the food is good, the bar lively and the staff friendly. Along the main street are several other local eating houses.

Another place has recently opened in Debark, called the *Simien Park Hotel*, on the right as you come in from Gonder, past the park HQ. Prices are about the same, but this place is reported to be cleaner.

On the Mountains
The national park has camps at Sankaber, Geech and Chenek, but the good stone huts were damaged in the war and are nothing more than ruined shells. They may be repaired in the future to provide tourist accommodation. Some have already been repaired, but are used by park rangers who live here with their families. Either way, for now you have to camp, so you need to be fully self-sufficient with tent, sleeping bag and cooking gear. It's usual to put up tents at the national park camps, as there is flat ground, water supplies and some simple shelters used by guides, scouts and mule handlers (although they may retire to a nearby village and stay with friends or family). Trekkers without tents may also arrange to sleep in local huts. Discuss this with your guide beforehand, but you should still bring a groundsheet and sleeping bag, and be prepared to share floor space with children, goats, mice and fleas!

GETTING THERE & AWAY
The nearest large town to the Simien Mountains is Gonder, about 400km directly northwest of Addis Ababa but around 550km by road. From Gonder you must reach Debark, 100km by road north of Gonder, which is the starting point for all Simien treks.

Air
The easiest way to get from Addis to Gonder is by air. Ethiopian Airlines runs a daily direct service between Addis and Gonder costing about US$50/100 single/return.

There's also a service via Bahir Dar. Total flying time is 1½ hours, plus another hour or so at Bahir Dar. Gonder airport is 25km from the city centre over very bumpy roads. A taxi will cost US$15 to US$20 depending on your negotiating skills.

Another option is to fly from Addis to Bahir Dar, from where you can visit the spectacular Blue Nile Falls, also called Tis Isat Falls, then continue by bus to Gonder. This takes about five hours, but the views of Lake Tana and the mountains are well worth the extra time.

Road
Buses go from Addis Ababa direct to Gonder at about 6 am daily and take about two days, depending on how often they break down. Once in Gonder, there are buses to Debark twice daily, theoretically at about 6 am and 11 am. The journey takes four to five hours along the main dirt road. The fare is US$4. Be sure to book your ticket the afternoon before for the 6 am bus, which is faster. Arrive at the bus station in good time to load your luggage on the roof.

Your other option, especially worth considering if you're in a group, is to hire a local taxi to drive you up to Debark. Taxis can be found around the piazza in Gonder, but some of these are very old. It's well worth choosing a car that looks like it will do 100km uphill on dirt. Check the tyres and make sure it's got a spare wheel, jack and wheel brace. The trips costs around US$90 for the car (and includes the 'empty' return journey, even if the driver finds passengers).

Alternatively, you can hire a more comfortable 4WD vehicle through the Goha Hotel (see Places to Stay in Gonder) for around US$150 from Gonder to Debark. On to Sankaber will cost another US$70 (although by doing this you miss the gentle transformation from lowland to plateau and also miss out on some worthwhile acclimatisation).

For the return journey, you can arrange for your taxi to collect you on a certain day, or simply take the bus back to Gonder. There are two each day – both slow and crowded.

ETHIOPIA

The Simien Traverse

Area Simien National Park
Distance 130km
Duration 8 days
Start/Finish Debark village (park HQ)
Highest Point Ras Deshen (4543m)
Overall Altitude Gain 1650m
Nearest large town Gonder
Accommodation Camping
Access Bus or car
Summary The mountains are high, the scenery is stunning and the views go on for ever. This route is just one of several options available. Gradients are not too severe, and the walking conditions are straightforward, although some days are quite long. Meeting the local Amhara people is another rewarding aspect of this trek.

Access & Preliminaries

All Simien treks start at Debark. If you come by the early bus from Gonder, you'll probably arrive about 11 am. The bus overshoots the park HQ by about 1.5km, but you'll be met at the bus stand by several local men who will offer their services as guide. If you don't have a recommended guide in mind, it might be best to retire to a hotel or restaurant for a cup of tea to check you like the guy and to discuss terms. If you come by taxi it can drop you at the park HQ, but guides are not always available here, so you might have to go to one of the hotels anyway.

When you've hired your guide he will organise mules and drivers, and while they are loading your equipment he will walk back to the park HQ with you, so you can pay park fees and arrange a scout. You'll also pay your team's wages for the full period you intend to be in the park; these will be given to the guide who will then pay his team. While you are doing this the rest of your party have an excellent opportunity to sample the local fare at a very hospitable family-run restaurant, right by the bus stop.

If you're in a rush, you could hire a guide, pay park fees and arrange your scout, mules and handlers in about two hours minimum, but this would be pushing it, especially if you want to be sure your guide, crew and mules are reliable. To do things in a more relaxed manner you could sort things out in the afternoon, stay overnight in Debark, and leave the next day. If you do this, your crew and mules will come to your hotel in the morning and you can load up there.

Stage 1: Debark to Chinkwanit
12km, 4-5 hours

This first day's walk can be long and tiring, especially if you need to acclimatise, or if you're leaving on the same day you arrive, as this means walking in the hottest part of the day. Most trekkers aim for Sankaber, but we suggest staying overnight at Chinkwanit, as this reduces the distance.

From Debark's main street, follow a dirt road eastwards through the market and the town outskirts to a point where open grassland stretches out to the left. Take the path forking left off the dirt road, which is likely to be busy with local people on their way to or from market. Drop down from the road into the grassland area, heading east on a very bumpy path which undulates with height differentials of up to 200m and passes several local villages. After about 5km you reach the Lamma River (marked on maps as Lamma Wenz – *wenz* is Amharic for river), which is a good water stop for the mules and a rest stop for trekkers. Cross this river, and

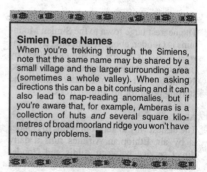

Simien Place Names
When you're trekking through the Simiens, note that the same name may be shared by a small village and the larger surrounding area (sometimes a whole valley). When asking directions this can be a bit confusing and it can also lead to map-reading anomalies, but if you're aware that, for example, Amberas is a collection of huts *and* several square kilometres of broad moorland ridge you won't have too many problems. ■

ETHIOPIA

ascend very steeply for 40 minutes onto the plateau.

At the top you will rejoin the dirt road from Debark. Turn left (north-east) onto this and follow it for about 2km to a point where a path breaks off to the right, skirting the side of a hill, passing through a village and then eventually meeting the road again. Follow this down the hill to reach a sharp bend to the right. To your left is an area called Chinkwanit. Although it's usual to aim for Sankaber (another 5km and two hours further), this is a good place to camp, with reasonable water supplies from a stream which runs under the dirt road nearby. About 100m to the north, and hidden by a slight incline, is the top of the main Simien Escarpment with the most spectacular view of the lowlands, especially at sunset. If you come here early in the morning you may see klipspringer leaping over the crags below you.

Stage 2: Chinkwanit to Geech Camp via Sankaber
15km, 7-8 hours
This is quite a long day, and you're likely to spend a lot of time admiring the views, so an early start is recommended. The dirt road leads straight to Sankaber, but the best way to get there is to follow the narrow path that keeps close to the escarpment edge. This was the scene of fierce fighting during the civil war in the early 90s, and you may see spent cartridges lying around. Towards Sankaber, the escarpment narrows to a ridge with awesome views on both sides, and it is here that you are likely to catch sight of your first troop of gelada baboons. Chinkwanit to Sankaber takes about two hours, or three if you stop to look at the views – which you will.

At Sankaber Camp some original buildings have been repaired and more new huts have been built. There are plans to move the park HQ here to provide accommodation and other facilities for tourists. But until these are finished, if you overnight here, you'll have to camp. Water is available from a rather vegetated well. Fill up here, as there's no more water available for several hours. From Sankaber, you can either follow the escarp-

ment edge again or keep to the dirt road, before descending into a valley called Michotis, along the floor of which is the often dry bed of the Wazla River (this is called the Koba River on some maps). Keep following the dirt road steeply up the other side. At the top you will see to the north-east the waterfalls of the Jinbar River (also called the Jin Bahir River) plummeting into the spectacular Geech Abyss, a vast canyon cut into the main wall of the escarpment. Also noteworthy in this area are the large quantities of red-hot poker plants (*Kniphofia*). Keep following the dirt road for about 1.5km, then take a path which branches to the left and begins gently descending to the Jinbar River. Cross the river and take the steep path to Geech village and the camp beyond.

From Sankaber to Geech is about four to five hours walking. Geech Camp has several broken buildings, which are slowly being restored for use by trekkers and park staff. For now, you have to camp: there's a good flat site and a long-drop toilet. There's also a hut, usually used for cooking, and a convenient nearby waterfall for washing and soothing tired limbs.

Stage 3: Geech to Chenek via Imet Gogo
20km, 7-9 hours
Geech to Chenek direct takes about five to six hours, but a very worthwhile diversion from Geech heads north-east for about 5km (1½ to 2 hours each way) following the path to the promontory of Imet Gogo. At 3926m it gives spectacular views over the lowlands with their rock spires and mesas. You can also see where you have come from and where you are going to. Some trekkers take all day to reach Imet Gogo, reaching another viewpoint called Saha, and staying another night at Geech. Others push on to Chenek on the same day. If you take this second option, while you are walking to and from Imet Gogo, your mules and crew will go straight to Chenek to set up camp.

From Imet Gogo you have two choices: the first is to return to Geech by your outward route, then head directly south, back across the Jinbar River and up to an area called

Ambaras where you meet the dirt road and follow it all the way to Chenek; the second is to follow the escarpment edge south by way of another promontory viewpoint called Gedadere. Whichever way you go, just before arrival at Chenek you will pass a place called Kebrat Metia which appears to be a solid wall of rock, but unexpectedly a gap appears revealing imposing views of the lowlands below and the escarpment edge to the west. The same views can be seen from the camp and are particularly beautiful at sunset. There is also a good chance of seeing a graceful lammergeier wheeling and soaring in the lift generated by the escarpment.

Chenek Camp consists of a group of huts. Most have been repaired, and were supposedly intended for trekkers' accommodation, although they have instead been occupied by park staff and their families. This is fair enough, as it seems no accommodation was provided for park staff, but the huts unfortu-nately impair the view from the camp site. More huts for tourists may be provided in the future. There is a fast-running stream about five minutes walk to the south of the camp.

Sidetrack: Chenek to Bwahit
6km, 3 hours

If you've still got energy to spare, from Chenek you could divert up to the summit of Bwahit (4430m) to the south-east of the camp. Go down to cross the stream, and pick up a path aiming towards the peak. At a junction, go left and keep heading up for the highest point. As you go up, the landscape changes from coarse moorland to barren scree slopes. At the summit you have com-manding views of the whole area. Return by the same route.

Another option is to do the ascent in the morning before starting Stage 4. After reach-ing the summit, descend northwards down the ridge (or close to it) to the viewpoint on

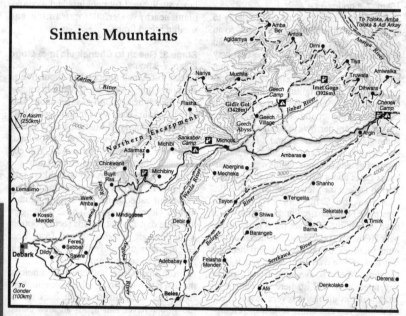

the main track up from Chenek (see Stage 4). Either way, this adds another three hours onto your day.

Stage 4: Chenek to Ambikwa
11km, 8-9 hours

From Chenek a track leads easterly then south-easterly up towards a viewpoint on the eastern escarpment, to the north of Bwahit. This is a fine viewpoint: to the east, across the vast valley of the Mesheha River, you can see the bulk of Ras Deshen, although it's hard to pick out among the other peaks and cliffs.

From the viewpoint north of Bwahit, the path drops steeply. You descend approximately 1000m and pass through the little village of Chiro Leba, then follow a stream bed through a rocky gorge to finally reach the large Mesheha River, about five to six hours from Chenek. Wade across the river and take the path which climbs sharply up the east side of the valley to reach the village

of Ambikwa. There's a place for camping near the village and a good river nearby.

Stage 5: Ambikwa to Ras Deshen and return
17km, 8-10 hours

It's usual to stay two nights at Ambikwa and go up to the summit of Ras Deshen on the day in between. An early start is also usual; leaving at first light is best. The path climbs steeply, through a cluster of huts called Mizma to reach a ridge crest about 1½ to two hours from Ambikwa. The clear path then aims south-east climbing gently along a valley side, aiming directly for the imposing grey cliffs and peaks of Ras Deshen. After a further two hours, at a pass, you meet another path heading roughly north-south; turn right (south) and follow this for a short distance then leave it to aim east again, swinging round to the north, to enter a huge semicircular basin of rocky peaks and buttresses. This is Ras Deshen. There are three distinct

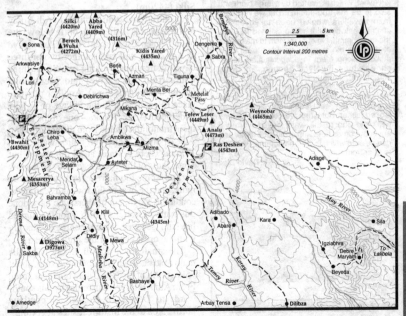

ETHIOPIA

points, and most people head for the one on the left. Some go for the one in the middle (see boxed text). Whichever peak you go for, the total walk from Ambikwa to reach one summit is about five to six hours. Add two or three hours to reach the other, optional, summits. Return by the same route (about three to four hours).

Stages 6-8: Ambikwa to Debark
55km, 3 days

Most trekkers return from Ambikwa to Debark via Chenek and Sankaber. The return route generally follows the track and dirt road, although there are opportunities to re-visit the escarpment for more view-gazing. De-

The Ras Deshen Horseshoe

Ras Deshen has two major summits, with a third minor peak to the east. When you're standing at their base it's difficult to see which is the highest. On two previous treks here, our guide has always taken us up the one on the left (west) which is marked by a large cairn and said to be the true summit. But we've heard from travellers who've been taken up the central peak by guides who claimed *this* was the true summit. On our last visit, to make sure of reaching the summit, we went to all three peaks, linking them in a spectacular horseshoe, which involved sections of tricky scrambling, although this could always be avoided by descending onto lower ground. It made a long but very satisfying day out. On the summit of the west peak, the central peak looked higher. But when we got to the central peak the one to the west looked higher! If anybody comes here with an altitude meter and can be sure which is the true summit, we'd like to hear from them.

David Else

DAVID ELSE

pending on the time of year there's usually plenty of activity in the fields and villages along the way. Return times are generally shorter than on the outward journey as the route is more direct and more downhill. There are, however, a number of other options which take you through some of the more remote and interesting villages of the southern Simiens. Your guide will be able to suggest routes depending on your timetable.

Alternative Return Route: Ambikwa to Adi Arkay
65km (approx), 3-5 days

One very different alternative for the return route would be to trek from Ambikwa to Arkwasiye, to the north-east of Chenek, where you can camp on the edge of the village, which is positioned on a broad saddle at 3000m with excellent views of the surrounding area. You could stay two nights here and on the day in between trek up the nearby peak of Beroch Wuha (4272m) and even continue from there to the summit of Silki (4420m).

On the next day you continue to Adi Arkay in the lowlands to the north of (ie below) the main Simien Escarpment. From Arkwasiye to Adi Arkay will take another two or three days of strenuous walking, via Sona (three hours from Arkwasiye) and Mekarebya (seven hours from Sona). Another possible place to camp is near the village of Toloka underneath Amba Toloka – one of the prominent monoliths visible from the escarpment. Adi Arkay is then four hours walk from Toloka. There is water at all the camps but Sona. Parts of this route lead through narrow ravines, some too narrow for a fully packed mule, and the heat of the lowlands can make conditions tough, but trekkers who have done this route reckon it's worth it for the rugged lowland scenery which contrasts sharply with the open vistas of the high plateau.

The small town of Adi Arkay is on the main road between Gonder and Axum, about 75km north of Debark. There is a local hotel. From Adi Arkay you can return by bus southwards to Debark or Gonder, or continue northwards to the historical sites at Axum.

Alternative Connecting Route: Ras Deshen to Arkwasiye

Mountain aficionados with a head for heights and taste for adventure may like to consider another option which avoids the return route from Ras Deshen back to Ambikwa and Chenek. We heard from British mountaineer Jon Rigby, who added extra interest to a trek by going round the east and north sides of the Mesheha River, well away from the usual trekking route.

From Ras Deshen summit, his party continued northwards over the peaks of Analu and Tefew Leser, which involved some sections of scrambling on loose rock, then descended north-west to Metelal Pass, where they camped the night. The whole route from Ambikwa to Metelal took eight hours. Meanwhile their mules had gone directly from Ambikwa to Metelal, via the village of Menta Ber to collect water, as there is none at the pass. From Metelal Pass they followed a major ridge via the big peaks of Kidis Yared (4453m) and Abba Yared (4409m) and several smaller summits.

They finished off with ascents of Silki (4420m) and Beroch Wuha (4272m) to make a complete horseshoe before descending to Arkwasiye. This excellent high-level ridge walk took seven hours. The going was mostly good, although some careful route-finding was needed among the cliffs and buttresses coming down from Abba Yared. There is no water source between Mizma (the small village just up the valley from Ambikwa, where it's also possible to camp) and Arkwasiye.

If all this sounds a bit daunting for lone trekkers, UK-based tour company Gane & Marshall International (listed in the main Getting There & Away chapter at the front of this book) are now offering 'the Rigby Route' as an option on their organised Simien treks.

Intrepid Trekking in the Simiens

If you get a copy of the Simien map produced by the University of Berne you'll notice that walking times to villages and towns just off the map are given in the margin: Adi Arkay – two hours; Deresge – three hours; Lalibela – eight days. We heard from Steve and Emlyn Thomas (UK) who were inspired by this annotation and walked south-east beyond Ras Deshen aiming for Lalibela, site of Ethiopia's most famous rock-hewn churches.

They hired a guide to accompany them, although he had never done the whole walk, and found their way simply by asking directions from local people as they travelled. As Lalibela is an important religious centre the route was well trodden and not difficult to follow. However, walking conditions were very hard: hot, dry and dusty, with a lot of up and down and very little water in some places. After three days they crossed the Tekeze (Takazze) River (a major river rising in the highlands, eventually flowing west into Sudan), and after six days they reached Sekota, about 80km directly north of Lalibela. The track south to Lalibela, indicated on some maps, proved impossible to locate, so they hitched a ride on a truck that went to Lalibela via Korem and Kobo. They later found out that for walking all the way to Lalibela they should have followed the Tekeze (Takazze) River southwards to a point about 20km west of Lalibela, from where another track leads to the town itself.

There's always next time! ■

Glossary

askari – security guard

banda – cabin, hut or bungalow
Bantu – one of four main groups of people (based on language) in East Africa
boda-boda – bicycle-taxi
boma – compound, homestead

cairn – pile of stones for waymarking
chiperone – heavy mist, sometimes lasting for 4-5 days at a time (Malawi)
col – pass between two hills or mountains
crampons – set of metal spikes, strapped to boots, for climbing or walking on ice or snow
crevasse – deep fissure, especially in the ice of a glacier
Cushitic – one of four main groups of people (based on language) in East Africa

dala dala – public transport minibus (southern Tanzania)
drift – dry river bed
duka – small shop

fundi – expert, repair-man; eg *fundi ya gari* (car mechanic), *fundi ya dawa* (doctor)

gendarme – pinnacle

hakuna matata – no problem
hoteli – small tea shop or basic restaurant (not for sleeping)

inselberg – isolated rocky hill rising from a plain

kabaka – king (Uganda)
Khoisan – one of four main groups of people (based on language) in East Africa
Kiswahili – Swahili for Swahili (the language)

kop – *see* inselberg

lodgings – small basic hotel (for sleeping)
lugga – dry river bed (northern Kenya)

mandazi, ndazi – deep-fried dough ball
manyatta – Maasai or Samburu homestead (technically an enclosure for warriors, but also used more generally)
matatu – minibus
moran – warrior (Maasai or Samburu)
mzee – old man
murram – dirt used for road building

Nilotic – one of four main groups of people (based on language) in East Africa
nival – high-altitude desert
nsima – stiff 'porridge' made from maize meal (Malawi)

panga – broad, heavy knife used as a tool or weapon (machete)

runga – fighting stick
runnel – small stream

sambusa – samosa
scree – accumulation of loose stones, usually on slopes below cliffs
shamba – small farm, plot of land
snout – lower end of a glacier
soda – fizzy drink
soda lake – saline lake

tarn – small mountain lake or pool
turaco – brightly coloured species of bird

ugali – maize meal ('nsima' in Malawi)
uniport – tin hut (used on Kilimanjaro and Mt Kenya, mostly in bad condition)

Index

TEXT

Map references are in **bold** type.

Aberdare Range (Ken) 237-42,
    236, 240
    geography 239
    places to stay 241
acclimatisation 119
accommodation 73
Adi Arkay (Eth) 342
air travel
    departure taxes 95
    from Ethiopia 332
    from Kenya 177
    from Malawi 290
    from Tanzania 106-8
    from Uganda 253
    to/from East Africa 90
    within East Africa 96
    within Ethiopia 337
    within Kenya 179
    within Malawi 291
    within Tanzania 108
altitude sickness 80, 119, 193
Ambikwa (Eth) 341
Arabs 16

Arabuko Sokoke Forest (Ken) 244
Arkwasiye (Eth) 343
Arusha (Tan) 143

Bantu people 15, 27
Baragoi (Ken) 225
bicycle travel *see* overland travel
birds 41
Blantyre (Mal) 296
boat travel
    within Malawi 292
books 63
    Ethiopia 330
    health 77
    Kenya 174
    Malawi 287
    Tanzania 105
    Uganda 252
Budadiri (Uga) 274
bus travel *see* overland travel
Bwahit (Eth) 340

Cape Maclear (Mal) 327
    getting there & away 328
    places to stay & eat 328

car travel *see* overland travel
Chenek (Eth) 339
Cherangani Hills (Ken) 235-7
    places to stay 236
Chinkwanit (Eth) 338
Chitimba (Mal) 319, 326
Chogoria (Ken) 192
Chwezi kingdom 15
cinema 64
climate 22
    Ethiopia 330
    Kenya 171
    Malawi 285
    Tanzania 101
    Uganda 249
Congo 93
conservation 25
Crater Highlands (Tan) 150-8,
    155
    getting there & away 153
    places to stay 153
Cushitic people 15, 27

Dar es Salaam (Tan) 105
Debark (Eth) 336

TREKS

PLANET TALK

Lonely Planet's FREE quarterly newsletter

We love hearing from you and think you'd like to hear from us.

When...is the right time to see reindeer in Finland?
Where...can you hear the best palm-wine music in Ghana?
How...do you get from Asunción to Areguá by steam train?
What...is the best way to see India?

For the answer to these and many other questions read PLANET TALK.

Every issue is packed with up-to-date travel news and advice including:

- a letter from Lonely Planet co-founders Tony and Maureen Wheeler
- go behind the scenes on the road with a Lonely Planet author
- feature article on an important and topical travel issue
- a selection of recent letters from travellers
- details on forthcoming Lonely Planet promotions
- complete list of Lonely Planet products

To join our mailing list contact any Lonely Planet office.

Also available: Lonely Planet T-shirts. 100% heavyweight cotton.

LONELY PLANET ONLINE

Get the latest travel information before you leave or while you're on the road

Whether you've just begun planning your next trip, or you're chasing down specific info on currency regulations or visa requirements, check out Lonely Planet Online for up-to-the minute travel information.

As well as travel profiles of your favourite destinations (including maps and photos), you'll find current reports from our researchers and other travellers, updates on health and visas, travel advisories, and discussion of the ecological and political issues you need to be aware of as you travel.

There's also an online travellers' forum where you can share your experience of life on the road, meet travel companions and ask other travellers for their recommendations and advice. We also have plenty of links to other online sites useful to independent travellers.

And of course we have a complete and up-to-date list of all Lonely Planet travel products including guides, phrasebooks, atlases, Journeys and videos and a simple online ordering facility if you can't find the book you want elsewhere.

www.lonelyplanet.com
or
AOL keyword: lp

LONELY PLANET PRODUCTS

Lonely Planet is known worldwide for publishing practical, reliable and no-nonsense travel information in our guides and on our web site. The Lonely Planet list covers just about every accessible part of the world. Currently there are eight series: *travel guides*, *shoestring guides*, *walking guides*, *city guides*, *phrasebooks*, *audio packs*, *travel atlases* and *Journeys* – a unique collection of travel writing.

EUROPE

Amsterdam • Austria • Baltic States phrasebook • Britain • Central Europe on a shoestring • Central Europe phrasebook • Czech & Slovak Republics • Denmark • Dublin • Eastern Europe on a shoestring • Eastern Europe phrasebook • Estonia, Latvia & Lithuania • Finland • France • French phrasebook • German phrasebook • Greece • Greek phrasebook • Hungary • Iceland, Greenland & the Faroe Islands • Ireland • Italian phrasebook • Italy • Mediterranean Europe on a shoestring • Mediterranean Europe phrasebook • Paris • Poland • Portugal • Portugal travel atlas • Prague • Russia, Ukraine & Belarus • Russian phrasebook • Scandinavian & Baltic Europe on a shoestring • Scandinavian Europe phrasebook • Slovenia • Spain • Spanish phrasebook • St Petersburg • Switzerland • Trekking in Greece • Trekking in Spain • Ukrainian phrasebook • Vienna • Walking in Britain • Walking in Switzerland • Western Europe on a shoestring • Western Europe phrasebook

Travel Literature: The Olive Grove: Travels in Greece

NORTH AMERICA

Alaska • Backpacking in Alaska • Baja California • California & Nevada • Canada • Florida • Hawaii • Honolulu • Los Angeles • Mexico • Miami • New England • New Orleans • New York City • New York, New Jersey & Pennsylvania • Pacific Northwest USA • Rocky Mountain States • San Francisco • Southwest USA • USA phrasebook • Washington, DC & the Capital Region

CENTRAL AMERICA & THE CARIBBEAN

Bermuda • Central America on a shoestring • Costa Rica • Cuba • Eastern Caribbean • Guatemala, Belize & Yucatán: La Ruta Maya • Jamaica

SOUTH AMERICA

Argentina, Uruguay & Paraguay • Bolivia • Brazil • Brazilian phrasebook • Buenos Aires • Chile & Easter Island • Chile & Easter Island travel atlas • Colombia • Ecuador & the Galápagos Islands • Latin American Spanish phrasebook • Peru • Quechua phrasebook • Rio de Janeiro • South America on a shoestring • Trekking in the Patagonian Andes • Venezuela

Travel Literature: Full Circle: A South American Journey

ANTARCTICA

Antarctica

ISLANDS OF THE INDIAN OCEAN

Madagascar & Comoros • Maldives• Mauritius, Réunion & Seychelles

AFRICA

Africa - the South • Africa on a shoestring • Arabic (Moroccan) phrasebook • Cape Town • Central Africa • East Africa • Egypt • Egypt travel atlas• Ethiopian (Amharic) phrasebook • Kenya • Kenya travel atlas • Malawi, Mozambique & Zambia • Morocco • North Africa • South Africa, Lesotho & Swaziland • South Africa, Lesotho & Swaziland travel atlas • Swahili phrasebook • Trekking in East Africa • West Africa • Zimbabwe, Botswana & Namibia • Zimbabwe, Botswana & Namibia travel atlas

Travel Literature: The Rainbird: A Central African Journey • Songs to an African Sunset: A Zimbabwean Story

MAIL ORDER

Lonely Planet products are distributed worldwide. They are also available by mail order from Lonely Planet, so if you have difficulty finding a title please write to us. North American and South American residents should write to Embarcadero West, 155 Filbert St, Suite 251, Oakland CA 94607, USA; European and African residents should write to 10 Barley Mow Passage, Chiswick, London W4 4PH; and residents of other countries to PO Box 617, Hawthorn, Victoria 3122, Australia.

NORTH-EAST ASIA

Beijing • Cantonese phrasebook • China • Hong Kong • Hong Kong, Macau & Guangzhou • Japan • Japanese phrasebook • Japanese audio pack • Korea • Korean phrasebook • Mandarin phrasebook • Mongolia • Mongolian phrasebook • North-East Asia on a shoestring • Seoul • Taiwan • Tibet • Tibet phrasebook • Tokyo

Travel Literature: Lost Japan

MIDDLE EAST & CENTRAL ASIA

Arab Gulf States • Arabic (Egyptian) phrasebook • Central Asia • Iran • Israel & the Palestinian Territories • Israel & the Palestinian Territories travel atlas • Istanbul • Jerusalem • Jordan & Syria • Jordan, Syria & Lebanon travel atlas • Middle East • Turkey • Turkish phrasebook • Turkey travel atlas • Yemen

Travel Literature: The Gates of Damascus • Kingdom of the Film Stars: Journey into Jordan

ALSO AVAILABLE:

Travel with Children • Traveller's Tales

INDIAN SUBCONTINENT

Bangladesh • Bengali phrasebook • Delhi • Hindi/Urdu phrasebook • India • India & Bangladesh travel atlas • Indian Himalaya • Karakoram Highway • Nepal • Nepali phrasebook • Pakistan • Rajasthan • Sri Lanka • Sri Lanka phrasebook • Trekking in the Indian Himalaya • Trekking in the Karakoram & Hindukush • Trekking in the Nepal Himalaya

Travel Literature: In Rajasthan • Shopping for Buddhas

SOUTH-EAST ASIA

Bali & Lombok • Bangkok • Burmese phrasebook • Cambodia • Ho Chi Minh City • Indonesia • Indonesian phrasebook • Indonesian audio pack • Jakarta • Java • Laos • Lao phrasebook • Laos travel atlas • Malay phrasebook • Malaysia, Singapore & Brunei • Myanmar (Burma) • Philippines • Pilipino phrasebook • Singapore • South-East Asia on a shoestring • South-East Asia phrasebook • Thailand • Thailand's Islands & Beaches • Thailand travel atlas • Thai phrasebook • Thai audio pack • Thai Hill Tribes phrasebook • Vietnam • Vietnamese phrasebook • Vietnam travel atlas

AUSTRALIA & THE PACIFIC

Australia • Australian phrasebook • Bushwalking in Australia • Bushwalking in Papua New Guinea • Fiji • Fijian phrasebook • Islands of Australia's Great Barrier Reef • Melbourne • Micronesia • New Caledonia • New South Wales & the ACT • New Zealand • Northern Territory • Outback Australia • Papua New Guinea • Papua New Guinea phrasebook • Queensland • Rarotonga & the Cook Islands • Samoa • Solomon Islands • South Australia • Sydney • Tahiti & French Polynesia • Tasmania • Tonga • Tramping in New Zealand • Vanuatu • Victoria • Western Australia

Travel Literature: Islands in the Clouds • Sean & David's Long Drive

THE LONELY PLANET STORY

Lonely Planet published its first book in 1973 in response to the numerous 'How did you do it?' questions Maureen and Tony Wheeler were asked after driving, bussing, hitching, sailing and railing their way from England to Australia.

Written at a kitchen table and hand collated, trimmed and stapled, *Across Asia on the Cheap* became an instant local bestseller, inspiring thoughts of another book.

Eighteen months in South-East Asia resulted in their second guide, *South-East Asia on a shoestring*, which they put together in a backstreet Chinese hotel in Singapore in 1975. The 'yellow bible', as it quickly became known to backpackers around the world, soon became *the* guide to the region. It has sold well over half a million copies and is now in its 9th edition, still retaining its familiar yellow cover.

Today there are over 240 titles, including travel guides, walking guides, language kits & phrasebooks, travel atlases and travel literature. The company is the largest independent travel publisher in the world. Although Lonely Planet initially specialised in guides to Asia, today there are few corners of the globe that have not been covered.

The emphasis continues to be on travel for independent travellers. Tony and Maureen still travel for several months of each year and play an active part in the writing, updating and quality control of Lonely Planet's guides.

They have been joined by over 70 authors and 170 staff at our offices in Melbourne (Australia), Oakland (USA), London (UK) and Paris (France). Travellers themselves also make a valuable contribution to the guides through the feedback we receive in thousands of letters each year and on our web site.

The people at Lonely Planet strongly believe that travellers can make a positive contribution to the countries they visit, both through their appreciation of the countries' culture, wildlife and natural features, and through the money they spend. In addition, the company makes a direct contribution to the countries and regions it covers. Since 1986 a percentage of the income from each book has been donated to ventures such as famine relief in Africa; aid projects in India; agricultural projects in Central America; Greenpeace's efforts to halt French nuclear testing in the Pacific; and Amnesty International.

'I hope we send people out with the right attitude about travel. You realise when you travel that there are so many different perspectives about the world, so we hope these books will make people more interested in what they see. Guidebooks can't really guide people. All you can do is point them in the right direction.'

– Tony Wheeler

lonely planet

LONELY PLANET PUBLICATIONS

Australia
PO Box 617, Hawthorn 3122, Victoria
tel: (03) 9819 1877 fax: (03) 9819 6459
e-mail: talk2us@lonelyplanet.com.au

USA
Embarcadero West, 155 Filbert St, Suite 251,
Oakland, CA 94607
tel: (510) 893 8555 TOLL FREE: 800 275-8555
fax: (510) 893 8563
e-mail: info@lonelyplanet.com

UK
10 Barley Mow Passage, Chiswick,
London W4 4PH
tel: (0181) 742 3161 fax: (0181) 742 2772
e-mail: lonelyplanetuk@compuserve.com

France:
71 bis rue du Cardinal Lemoine, 75005 Paris
tel: 1 44 32 06 20 fax: 1 46 34 72 55
e-mail: 100560.415@compuserve.com

World Wide Web: http://www.lonelyplanet.com
or AOL keyword: lp